Lecture Notes in Computer Science　　11445

Commenced Publication in 1973
Founding and Former Series Editors:
Gerhard Goos, Juris Hartmanis, and Jan van Leeuwen

More information about this series at http://www.springer.com/series/7410

Claude Carlet · Sylvain Guilley ·
Abderrahmane Nitaj · El Mamoun Souidi (Eds.)

Codes, Cryptology and Information Security

Third International Conference, C2SI 2019
Rabat, Morocco, April 22–24, 2019, Proceedings
In Honor of Said El Hajji

 Springer

Editors
Claude Carlet
Université Paris 8
Saint-Denis, France

Sylvain Guilley (ID)
Institut MINES-TELECOM
Paris, France

Abderrahmane Nitaj
Université de Caen
Caen, France

El Mamoun Souidi
Mohammed V University
Rabat, Morocco

ISSN 0302-9743   ISSN 1611-3349 (electronic)
Lecture Notes in Computer Science
ISBN 978-3-030-16457-7   ISBN 978-3-030-16458-4 (eBook)
https://doi.org/10.1007/978-3-030-16458-4

Library of Congress Control Number: 2019935476

LNCS Sublibrary: SL4 – Security and Cryptology

This Springer imprint is published by the registered company Springer Nature Switzerland AG
The registered company address is: Gewerbestrasse 11, 6330 Cham, Switzerland

Preface

The Third International Conference on the Theory and Applications of Cryptographic Techniques, Coding Theory, and Information Security was held at the Faculty of Sciences at the University of Mohammed V in Rabat, Morocco during April 22–24, 2019. This volume contains the papers accepted for presentation at C2SI-El Hajji 2019, in honor of Professor Said El Hajji, from this university.

One aim of C2SI-El Hajji 2019 was to pay homage to Professor Said El Hajji for his valuable contribution to research, teaching, and disseminating knowledge in numerical analysis, modeling, and information security in Morocco, Africa, and worldwide. We are deeply grateful to him for his great services in contributing to the establishment of a successful research group in coding theory, cryptography, and information security at Mohammed V University in Rabat, organizing a master's course in this field and many other academic activities.

The other aim of the conference is to provide an international forum for researchers from academia and practitioners from industry from all over the world to discuss all forms of cryptology, coding theory, and information security.

The organization of C2SI-El Hajji 2019 was initiated by the Moroccan Laboratory of Mathematics, Computing Sciences, Applications, and Information Security (LabMIA-SI), and performed by an active team of researchers from Morocco and France. The conference was organized in cooperation with the International Association for Cryptologic Research (IACR), and the proceedings are published in Springer's *Lecture Notes in Computer Science* series.

C2SI-El Hajji 2019 was the third of the C2SI series. The first conference of the C2SI series was held at the University Mohammed V in Rabat during May 26–28, 2015, in honor of Professor Thierry Berger from Limoges University, and the second conference of the series was held at the same university during April 10–12, 2017, in honor of Professor Claude Carlet, from Paris 8 University. The proceedings of both conferences were published in Springer's *Lecture Notes in Computer Science*.

The C2SI-El Hajji 2019 Program Committee consisted of 46 members. There were 90 papers submitted to the conference. Each paper was assigned to three members of the Program Committee on average and reviewed anonymously. The review process was challenging and the Program Committee, aided by reports from 38 external reviewers, produced a total of 240 reviews in all. After this period, 19 papers were accepted on January 20, 2019. Authors then had the opportunity to update their papers until February 15, 2019. The present proceedings include all the revised papers. We are indebted to the members of the Program Committee and the external reviewers for their diligent work.

The conference was honored by the presence of the invited speakers Abdelmalek Azizi from Mohammed First University in Oujda, Morocco, Thomas Johansson from Lund University, Sweden, Grigory Kabatiansky from Skolkovo Institute of Science and Technology (Skoltech), Sihem Mesnager from University of Paris 8, France, and

Amr Youssef from Concordia University, Canada. They gave talks on various topics in cryptography, coding theory, and information security and contributed to the success of the conference, and will contribute to the success of these proceedings. We are grateful to them.

The conference hosted a co-located one-day Workshop on Side-Channel Analysis (SCA). This workshop was held on April 21, 2019. It introduced the audience to the non-invasive test methodology compliant with international standard ISO/IEC 17825, through practice exercises on vulnerability analysis of hardware and software AES implementation, software RSA implementation, and classic and post-quantum cryptography implementation. Then, it featured three talks on recent research issues concerning the field of side-channel analysis SCA, namely, Boolean-level SCA, cache-timing attacks on a software cryptographic library, and side-channel attack on multiplications. The three papers related to the workshop are printed in the "Side-Channel Analysis" part of the proceedings. Please note that these papers went through a separate selection process.

We had the privilege to chair the Program Committee. We would like to thank all committee members for their work on the submissions, as well as all external reviewers for their support. We thank the authors of all submissions and all the speakers as well as the participants. They all contributed to the success of the conference.

We also would like to thank Professor Said Amzazi, Minister of National Education, Vocational Training, Higher Education and Scientific Research, for his support in teaching and research in the field of cryptology and information security when he was professor, and Dean of Faculty of Sciences, and president of Mohammed V University in Rabat. Similarly, we would like to thank Professor Mohamed El Ghachi, President of Mohammed V University in Rabat for his unwavering support to research and teaching in the areas of cryptography, coding theory, and information security. We also want to thank Professor Mourad El Belkacemi, Dean of the Faculty of Sciences in Rabat.

Along with these individuals, we wish to thank all our local colleagues and students who contributed greatly to the organization and success of the conference.

Finally, we heartily thank all the local Organizing Committee members, all the sponsors, and everyone who contributed to the success of this conference. We are also thankful to the staff at Springer for their help with producing the proceedings and to the staff of EasyChair for the use of their conference management system.

April 2019

Claude Carlet
Sylvain Guilley
Abderrahmane Nitaj
El Mamoun Souidi

Organization

C2SI-El Hajji 2019 was organized by the Moroccan Laboratory of Mathematics, Computing Sciences, Applications, and Information Security (LabMIA-SI) at the Faculty of Sciences of the Mohammed V University in Rabat.

Honorary Chair

Said El Hajji   University Mohammed V, Rabat, Morocco

General Chair

El Mamoun Souidi   Mohammed V University in Rabat, Morocco

Program Chairs

Claude Carlet   LAGA, University of Paris 8, France and University
                                   of Bergen, Norway
Sylvain Guilley   Secure-IC and Télécom-ParisTech, Paris, France
Abderrahmane Nitaj   University of Caen Normandie, France
El Mamoun Souidi   Mohammed V University in Rabat, Morocco

Invited Speakers

Abdelmalek Azizi   University Mohammed the First, Oujda, Morocco
Said El Hajji   Mohammed V University in Rabat, Morocco
Thomas Johansson   Lund University, Sweden
Grigory Kabatiansky   Skolkovo Institute of Science and Technology,
                                   Russia
Sihem Mesnager   University of Paris 8, France
Amr Youssef   Concordia University, Canada

Organizing Committee

El Mamoun Souidi (Chair)   Mohammed V University in Rabat, Morocco
Ghizlane Orhanou (Co-chair)   Mohammed V University in Rabat, Morocco
Souad El Bernoussi (Co-chair)   Mohammed V University in Rabat, Morocco
Abderrahim Benazzouz   ENS, LabMIA-SI, Rabat, Morocco
Hafida Benazza   FSR, LabMIA-SI, Rabat, Morocco
Hicham Bensaid   INPT, Morocco
Youssef Bentaleb   ENSA, Kenitra, Morocco
Mohammed Boulmalf   UIR, Rabat, Morocco

Azzouz Cherrabi	FSR, LabMIA-SI, Rabat, Morocco
Sidi Mohamed Douiri	FSR, LabMIA-SI, Rabat, Morocco
Abderrahim El Abdllaoui	FSR, LabMIA-SI, Rabat, Morocco
Said El Hajji	FSR, LabMIA-SI, Rabat, Morocco
Mustapha Esghir	FSR, LabMIA-SI, Rabat, Morocco
Hassan Essanouni	FSR, LabMIA-SI, Rabat, Morocco
Touria Ghemires	FSR, LabMIA-SI, Rabat, Morocco
Ahmed Hajji	FSR, LabMIA-SI, Rabat, Morocco
Samir Hakam	FSR, LabMIA-SI, Rabat, Morocco
Aiz Hilali	INPT, Morocco
El Mostafa Jabbouri	FSR, LabMIA-SI, Rabat, Morocco
Abderrahim Messaoudi	ENS, Rabat, LabMIA-SI, Rabat, Morocco
Hassan Mharzi	ENSA de Kenitra (CMRPI), Morocco
Jilali Mikram	FSR, LabMIA-SI, Rabat, Morocco
Mounia Mikram	ESI, Rabat, Morocco
Ali Ouadfel	FSR, LabMIA-SI, Rabat, Morocco
Bouchta Rhanizar	ENS, Rabat, LabMIA-SI, Rabat, Morocco
Rachid Sadaka	ENS, Rabat, LabMIA-SI, Rabat, Morocco
Aoutif Sayah	FSR, LabMIA-SI, Rabat, Morocco
Fouad Zinoun	FSR, LabMIA-SI, Rabat, Morocco
Karim Zkik	UIR, Rabat, Morocco

Program Committee

Elena Andreeva	Katholieke Universiteit Leuven, Belgium
François Arnault	University of Limoges, France
Emanuele Bellini	Darkmatter LLC, Abu Dhabi, UAE
Thierry Berger	XLIM, University of Limoges, France
Lilya Budaghyan	University of Bergen, Norway
Claude Carlet	University of Paris 8, France
Miguel Carriegos	RIASC, Spain
Chen-Mou Cheng	Osaka University, Japan
Alain Couvreur	LIX, Ecole Polytechnique, France
Pierre Dusart	XLIM UMRS 7252, University of Limoges, France
Said El Hajji	Mohammed V University in Rabat, Morocco
Nadia El Mrabet	SAS, CGCP, EMSE, Saint-Etienne, France
Caroline Fontaine	CNRS, France
Maria Isabel Garcia Planas	Universitat Politecnica de Catalunya, Spain
Sanaa Ghouzali	King Saud University, Saudi Arabia
Kenza Guenda	UVIC/USTHB, Algiers, Algeria
Cheikh Thiecoumba Gueye	Universite Cheikh Anta Diop, Dakar, Senegal
Sylvain Guilley	Secure-IC S.A.S. and Télécom-ParisTech, Paris, France
Abdelkrim Haqiq	FST, Hassan 1st University, Settat, Morocco
Tor Helleseth	University of Bergen, Norway
Shoichi Hirose	University of Fukui, Japan

Tetsu Iwata	Nagoya University, Japan
Thomas Johansson	Lund University, Sweden
Grigory Kabatyansky	Skolkovo Institute of Science and Technology (Skoltech) Moscow, Russia
Muhammad Rezal Kamel Ariffin	Institute for Mathematical Research, UPM, Malaysia
Ahmed Khoumsi	University of Sherbrooke, Canada
Juliane Krämer	TU Darmstadt, Germany
Jalal Laassiri	Ibn Tofail University, Morocco
Jean-Louis Lanet	Inria-RBA, France
Juan Lopez-Ramos	University of Almeria, Spain
Sihem Mesnager	University of Paris 8 and LAGA, France
Marine Minier	University of Nancy, France
Tarik Moataz	Brown University, USA
Abderrahmane Nitaj	LMNO, University of Caen, France
Ghizlane Orhanou	Mohammed V University in Rabat, Morocco
Emmanuel Prouff	ANSSI, France
Palash Sarkar	Indian Statistical Institute, India
El Mamoun Souidi	Mohammed V University in Rabat, Morocco
Pantelimon Stanica	Naval Postgraduate School, Monterey, USA
Noah Stephens-Davidowitz	New York University, USA
Joseph Tonien	University of Wollongong, Australia
Alev Topuzoglu	Sabanci University, Istanbul, Turkey
Amr Youssef	Concordia University, Montreal, Canada
Yongjun Zhao	The Chinese University of Hong Kong, SAR China

Additional Reviewers

Maryem Ait El Hadj	Hisham Galal	Baslam Mohamed
Nurdagül Anbar	Aurore Guillevic	Lina Mortajine
Meryeme Ayache	Cem Güneiri	Ousmane Ndiaye
Sébastien Bardin	Vincent Herbert	Ferruh Özbudak
Nina Bindel	Hind Idrissi	Buket Ozkaya
Olivier Blazy	Nikolay Kaleyski	Enes Pasalic
Delphine Boucher	Karim Khalfallah	Simon Pontié
Pierre-Louis Cayrel	Jean Belo Klamti	Olivier Potin
Ayca Cesmelioglu	Adrien Koutsos	Olivier Ruatta
Ilaria Chillotti	Chunlei Li	Essaid Sabir
Abderrahman Daif	Nian Li	Patrick Struck
Ahmed El Kiram	Pierrick Méaux	Karim Zkik
Thomas Fuhr	Wilfried Meidl	

Sponsoring Institutions

Ministère de l'Education Nationale, de la Formation Professionnelle, de l'Enseignement Supérieur et de la Recherche Scientifique, Kingdom of Morocco
Ministère de l'Industrie, du Commerce de l'Investissement, et de l'Economie Numérique, Kingdom of Morocco
Université Mohammed V de Rabat, Morocco
Faculté des Sciences de Rabat, Morocco
L'Académie Hassan II des Sciences et Techniques, Morocco
Islamic Educational, Scientific and Cultural Organization – ISESCO
Centre National pour la Recherche Scientifique et Technique – CNRST, Morocco
Le Centre Marocain de Recherches Polytechniques et d'Innovation (CMRPI), Morocco
Le Groupement d'Assurance des enseignants du Supérieur – GASUP, Morocco
Centre de Mathématique de Rabat, Morocco

Origin of Submissions

Algeria
Belgium
Cameroon
Canada
China
Colombia
Finland
France
Germany
Honduras
Hong Kong
India
Italy
Japan
Lebanon
Luxembourg
Mexico

Morocco
Poland
Qatar
Romania
Russia
Senegal
Singapore
Slovenia
South Africa
Spain
Sweden
Tunisia
Turkey
United Arab Emirates
USA
Venezuela

Biography of Said El Hajji

Professor Said El Hajji graduated from Pierre and Marie Curie University (Paris VI, France) and received his PhD from Laval University in Quebec (Canada). He subsequently became senior lecturer (Maître Assistant) at "Ecole Normale Supérieure" of Rabat and then associate professor (Maître de Conférences) at the same institute. Until 2018, he was professor at the Faculty of Sciences, Mohammed V University in Rabat, Morocco.

His research interests include modeling and numerical simulation, numerical analysis, operating systems and network security, information security, management of information security.

He has (co-)written more than 100 papers in scientific journals and proceedings and has been chapter (co-)author or (co-)editor of seven books. He has also been a member of more than 20 Program Committees (seven as (co-)chair).

Professor Said El Hajji has been at the Faculty of Sciences in Rabat the head of the Research and Teaching Unit (UFR) DESA CS&ANO, of "DESA Analyse Numérique et Optimisation," of "DESA Mathématiques, Informatique et Applications," of the master's course "Codes, Cryptographie et Sécurité de l'Information," and finally, from 2015 to 2018, the head of the master's course "Cryptographie et Sécurité de l'Information."

He was also the head of "Groupe d'Analyse Numérique et Optimisation" and finally the head of the "Laboratoire de Mathématiques, Informatique et Applications—Sécurité de l'Information", (LabMiA-SI), formerly called LabMiA, from 2005 to 2018.

Professor Said El Hajji has supervised more than 21 theses and is currently supervising five others. He has been plenary invited speaker in four international conferences and invited speaker in ten other conferences and workshops. He has organised four Summer Schools and seven international conferences in relation with his research and teaching interests and he was the initiator and one of the organizers of the C2SI conference series.

Invited Papers and Talks

Privacy Preserving Auctions
on Top of Ethereum
(Abstract for Invited Talk)

Amr M. Youssef

Concordia Institute for Information Systems Engineering,
Concordia University, Montréal, QC, Canada

Abstract. Blockchain is an evolving technology with the potential to reshape a variety of industries by allowing mutually distrusting parties to interact with each other without relying on a trusted centralized party. Informally, a blockchain is an immutable append-only distributed ledger that records transactions in a way that greatly increases reliability and removes the need for trust. Nevertheless, many organizations are reluctant to fully adopt this technology owing to several issues such as scalability and privacy. The current transaction throughput in blockchains pales in comparison to the throughput needed to run mainstream payment systems or financial markets. Furthermore, organizations and users are particularly not keen on having all of their transaction information published on a public ledger that can be arbitrarily read without any restrictions by anyone.

In this talk, my focus will be on the privacy issue in blockchains particularly on Ethereum. There are various cryptographic techniques that can realize privacy-preserving applications on top of blockchains. As part of my work, I will show how the privacy requirements of building sealed-bid auctions on top of Ethereum can be addressed. Specifically, I will present three different constructions [1–3] that utilize cryptographic protocols and primitives including zero-knowledge proofs, commitment schemes, and trusted hardware environments such as Intel SGX. Finally, I will show the pros and cons of each construction and draw out conclusions based on the presented schemes.

References

1. Galal, H.S., Youssef, A.M.: Succinctly verifiable sealed-bid auction smart contract. In: Data Privacy Management, Cryptocurrencies and Blockchain Technology - ESORICS 2018 International Workshops, DPM 2018 and CBT 2018, Barcelona, Spain, 6–7 September 2018, Proceedings, pp. 3–19 (2018)
2. Galal, H.S., Youssef, A.M.: Verifiable Sealed-Bid Auction on the Ethereum Blockchain. In: Zohar, A. et al. (eds.) Financial Cryptography and Data Security. FC 2018. LNCS, vol. 10958. Springer, Heidelberg (2019)
3. Galal, H.S., Youssef, A.M.: Trustee: full privacy preserving vickrey auction on top of ethereum. In: International Conference on Financial Cryptography and Data Security, Trusted Smart Contracts Workshop. Springer (2019)

Contents

Applied Cryptography

Security

Side-Channel Analysis

Virtual Security Evaluation

An Operational Methodology for Side-Channel Leakage Detection at Source-Code Level

Youssef Souissi[1], Adrien Facon[1,2], and Sylvain Guilley[1,2,3]([envelope])

[1] Secure-IC S.A.S., 15 Rue Claude Chappe, Bât. B, 35 510 Cesson-Sévigné, France
sylvain.guilley@secure-ic.com
[2] École Normale Supérieure, Département d'informatique, 75 005 Paris, France
[3] LTCI, Télécom ParisTech, Institut Polytechnique de Paris, 75 013 Paris, France

Abstract. "An ounce of prevention is worth a pound of cure". This paper presents a methodology to detect side-channel leakage at source-code level. It leverages simple tests performed on noise-less traces of execution, and returns to the developer accurate information about the security issues. The feedback is in terms of location (where in code, when in time), in terms of security severity (amount and duration of leakage), and most importantly, in terms of possible reason for the leakage. After the source code (and subsequently the compiled code) has been sanitized, attack attempts complement the methodology to test the implementation against realistic exploitations. This last steps allows to validate whether the tolerated leakages during the sanitizing stage are indeed benign.

Keywords: Virtual evaluation methodology · Pre-silicon analysis · Source code vulnerability · Exploitability checking

1 Introduction

It is known since more than twenty years (recall the seminal paper of Kocher about timing attacks [12] in 1996) that some non-functional aspects of computation can be exploited to extract information from sensitive computations. Such key recovery attacks are referred to as side-channel analyses. They are very popular since they have allowed to break many real-world products in the past. Their threat was so scaring that side-channel analyses have been formalized in evaluation and test methodology, such as Common Criteria (ISO/IEC 15408), FIPS 140 and its international extension (ISO/IEC 19790), etc.

Today, side-channel analyses are well understood. It is clear how their success probability is related to the cipher architecture (e.g., through confusion coefficients [8]) and to the measurement conditions (e.g., the signal-to-noise ratio [16, Sect. 4.3.2, p. 73]). Countermeasures, such as hiding [16, Chap. 7], masking [16, Chap. 9], shuffling [23], resilience [13], etc. have been proposed and widely studied.

© Springer Nature Switzerland AG 2019
C. Carlet et al. (Eds.): C2SI 2019, LNCS 11445, pp. 3–12, 2019.
https://doi.org/10.1007/978-3-030-16458-4_1

Alongside with side-channel analysis becoming more mature, the validation of protections on real (i.e., complex) systems has emerged as a new topic of interest [11]. The first step has been to set up some evaluation frameworks [19,20, 24]. They were complemented by tests to assess for leakage presence: this practice is called leakage detection. The leakage is characterized by differences [10], T-tests [9], or variance tests [2]. Such tests allow to detect vulnerabilities, but still, they apply only on the final product.

Checking whether attacks would be successful on source code is already a known technique [21]. In this paper, we highlight a novel methodology to detect leakages directly on the source code. The motivation is to allow for a fast feedback to the developer about vulnerabilities present in the source code. It is known that curing security issues in advance allows very quickly to converge to a side-channel-clean design, whereas chasing leakages late in the product development phase is costly and slow.

The rest of this paper consists in a explanation of the methodology (Sect. 2). The key messages are then gathered in a conclusion (Sect. 3), which also opens some perspectives for still better high-level detection techniques.

2   The Presented Methodology

We illustrate a situation where the design to be evaluated is a cryptographic application, which has the requirement to keep the secret key confidential. Moreover, we focus on a hardware implementation, since the security of hardware (in comparison with that of software) is the less easy to control. In particular, hardware consists in sequential ressources (which are clocked and are responsible to keep the state of the design) and in combinational ressources (which evaluate as soon as inputs change). The difference between the two ressources is illustrated in Fig. 1. The workflow to have the design be validated as correctly protecting the key is depicted in Fig. 2. It presents the methodology implemented in Secure-IC Virtualyzr^{TM} tool.

This figure shows that the path to obtain a secure design is iterative. First of all, the developer writes source code of its security application. Second, he provides a testbench. It can be written specifically for the application, or generated by the automated maintenance system. For instance, the testbench can be reused from a functional verification tool for security validation. The source code together with the testbench enable a simulator tool (e.g., Secure-IC Virtualyzr^{TM} supports Cadence ncsim^{TM}, Synopsys vcs^{TM}, Mentor Graphics modelsim^{TM} or veloce^{TM}, etc.) to generate traces. As a next step, traces are analyzed with respect to leakage. For this purpose, the Virtualyzr shall be aware of the name of the assets to protect. Hence the indication of secrets as a user input in Fig. 2. Security analysis will reveal multiple information:

- for every bit in the system, at each clock cycle,
- how much and when is there a non-negligible dependency?

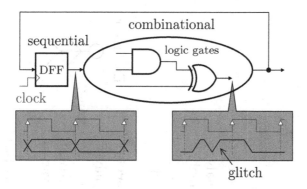

Fig. 1. Illustration of hardware as a Moore state machine, where sequential ressources sample at clock rising edge whereas combinational ressources evaluate each time an input changes, hence glitches at their output. Exemplar chronograms are displayed in the grey boxes

At bit level and without noise, all statistical tools to analyse dependency collapse to the same distinguisher, namely the Pearson correlation. Notice that this analysis is exhaustive. However, it is feasible since estimation of dependency can be achieved with little amount of traces. For example, for an accuracy of 1%, only $(1/0.01)^2 = 10,000$ traces are needed. The outcome of the analysis is a table containing those pieces of information:

- list of events (i.e., signal-time pairs),
- amount of correlation,
- duration of leakage. For sequential signals (registers), the duration is irrelevant, since those signals vary only exactly once per clock period. However, for combinational signals (output of Boolean or arithmetic gates), the duration is important when the code is not simulated at Register Transfer Level (RTL). Indeed, at RTL, combinational gates are evaluated without delay. But at later stages of refinement (RTL synthesized to logic gates), the combinational signals feature delays. The duration of correlation therefore indicates how transient the vulnerability is showing up. In particular, it is relevant to make a difference between *steady* versus *glitching* leakage [15]. A steady leakage basically means that some gates take on a value which can be exploited. This situation is more critical than glitch leakage where the leakage is transient: the dependency does not last until the end of the clock cycle, but shows up surreptitiously only at the favor of input signals uncoordinated arrival times.

In theory, all vulnerabilities should be fixed, which is the purpose of the feedback loop to the original design (cf. Fig. 2). The tool must be fast and automated to make this iterative sanitation process as smooth as possible. Now, in practice, some vulnerabilities might be identified as tolerable. This is the intent of the security policy. Examples are as follows:

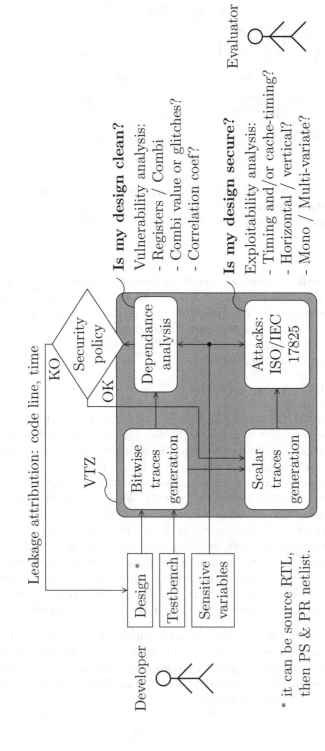

Fig. 2. Usage of Virtualyzr^{TM} (VTZ^{TM}) tool to validate for errors at source-code level

- Key scheduling logic is certainly dependent on the key, however, exploitability requires a *template attack* [5], since the key cannot (in general) be manipulated by the user (i.e., the attacker);
- Leakage within cryptographic primitives might be computationally hard to exploit. Refer for example to the exploitation of HMAC: all executions of the hash primitive depend on the key, however only the head and tail ones are really affected in a realistic manner by the leakage of the HMAC key; exploiting others would require for the attacker the ability to inverse hash functions. If this was feasible, side-channel attacks would not be the easiest attack paths.

Apart from these exceptions, all vulnerabilities on RTL source are expected to be fixed, since they make up structural weaknesses. After this step, the design is refined into a netlist, either post-synthesis (delays are added in the gates) or post place-and-route (delays are added in the interconnection between the gates as well). Therefore, more avenues for leakage occur: indeed, the combinational gates evaluate as soon as one input changes (contrary to sequential gates). In addition, after synthesis, some restructurations or even optimizations are carried out. They include:

- gate factorization,
- gates reordering,
- simplification.

Due to these modifications, the architectural structure and the signal names are altered. Thus one aspect is to keep track of RTL resource names with netlist resource names. The vulnerability analysis now might evolve. The differences can be classified in two categories:

1. regressions (such as countermeasure alteration),
2. refinement (such as providing more details for a primitive, which induces more complex timing behavior).

Regressions must be addressed, because they highlight problems arising from the use of EDA tools. For instance, the first-order masked AND gate (computing $c = a \wedge b$, where each Boolean variable x is randomly split in two, as per perfect masking [3], that is $x = x' \oplus x''$) represented in Fig. 3(a)) will leak with:

- correlation 1 (because the sensitive signal c appears in the clear) with simplification of Fig. 3(b), and
- correlation $1/2$ (because $a' \wedge b' \oplus a' \wedge b'' = a' \wedge b$, which is equal to b if $a' = 0$ and to 0 otherwise, hence a match with clear value b half of the time—a' is a random mask, i.e., $\mathbb{P}(a' = 0) = \mathbb{P}(a' = 1) = 1/2$) with simplification of Fig. 3(c).

Both netlists (b) and (c) are functionally correct. They are even improved in terms of critical path (for equal gate-count), as compared with (a). Nonetheless, their rearrangement induced a side-channel leakage. Interestingly, the amount of leakage (e.g., correlation 1 versus $1/2$) reveals a precious hint to the designer. It helps him understand if the problem is structural (case of correlation = 1) or due to some unbalance in the masking scheme (case of correlation = $1/2$, refer for instance to [18]).

The correction can be some actions either on the compilation side (typically by placing *constraints* in scripts), or on the design-side (typically by adopting a *robust coding style*, which resists optimizations).

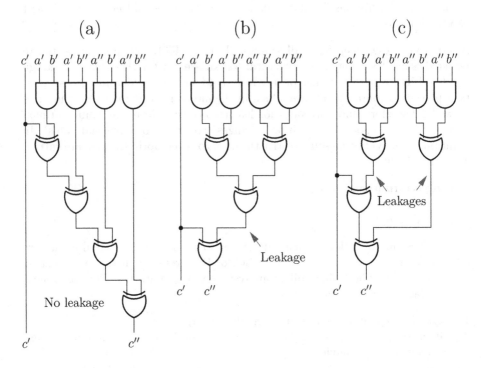

Fig. 3. Example of simplifications on masked $c = a \wedge b$ which induce side-channel leakage of sensitive information. In this figure $x \in \{a, b, c\}$ is randomly split as (x', x'') such that $x = x' \oplus x''$.

Refinements might highlight transient leakages due to glitches [17]. Here, the security policy decides whether those glitches are tolerable or not. Indeed, it might be time-consuming to remove all glitches which carry (thence leak) sensitive information. Typically, if the glitch lasts 10 ps and that the attacker makes use of a sampling device which allows only to measure at a bandwidth of 1 GHz, then the glitch will be smoothed by the measurement system and its energy will be spread over 100 time samples, thereby making its exploitability 100 times more difficult. In these conditions, a decision to live with such glitch can be made. An exemplar security policy is exposed in Table 1. It makes a difference between the type of incriminated resource, either seq(uential) or combi(national).

As mentioned, leakage of sequential ressources is to be considered more seriously than combinational ressources, because the leakage is synchronized, hence the signal-to-noise ratio measured by an attacker is high. Also, sequential elements (typically flip-flops or memories) consume/radiate much more than combinational gates, and their leakage model is simple (Hamming weight and/or Hamming distance [4, Sect. 2]).

Table 1. Exemplar security policy

Type	Duration	Correlation	Origin	Policy
Seq.	One clock period	$=1$	Structural	Fatal design bug or simplification upon synthesis optimization
Seq.	One clock period	<1	Unbalanced mask, causing first-order leakage	Critical countermeasure issue
Combi.	Steady	$=1$	Structural	Critical design bug
Combi.	Steady	<1	Unbalanced mask, causing first-order leakage	Serious countermeasure issue
Combi.	Transient	<1	Timing race	Can be tolerated—typically requires 100,000+ traces

Finally, attacks are tested on aggregated traces. The methodology applied to virtual traces is that of ISO/IEC 17825 [6]. It is a classical approach, where:

- *timing* and *cache-timing* analyses are experienced first,
- second *single trace* leakage is assessed, and
- finally, *vertical attacks* are tested.

We refer the reader to papers such as [22] for in-depth discussions about the use of simulation for exploitability analysis.

3   Conclusion and Perspectives

We have presented a fast methodology based on simulation to identify precisely and with little number of test vectors the presence of leakage. We show that some basic characterizations allow to narrow down the root cause of the leakage, which allows to accompany the developer in researching for leakage reduction or cancelling techniques (based on coding style or compilation options). This approach is innovative and can be implemented in a tool (we illustrate the case of Secure-IC Virtualyzr).

As a perspective, we notice that formal methods could complement the presented methodology. Formal methods ensure 100% coverage and are typically faster to yield their conclusions than dynamic methods. It is also to be noticed that formal methods (as of today, such as [7]) cannot discriminate between serious and tiny leakages. Moreover, formal methods are more comfortable at high-level since they need to approximate the design; therefore, they do not allow a traceability after compilation stages. Still, the synergy between static (i.e., formal) and dynamic leakage evaluation is foreseen as a winning combination for side-channel eradication from secure designs.

Eventually, we underline that the methodology presented in this paper could apply as well to software evaluation, where the most threaten leakage arises from cache-timing problems. A parallel between hardware and software is sketched in Table 2. Recall that:

- Hardware of secret key applications is computing in constant time, but features exploitable *vertical* leakage [14];
- Software is mostly vulnerable regarding *horizontal* leakage. Indeed, software development practices today is at a less advanced stage, security-wise, than that of dedicated cryptographic hardware.

Table 2. Comparison between security issues in hardware vs software

Programme nature	Cause of information leakage		
	Structural leakage	Optimization upon code generation	Dynamic leakage
Hardware	Unmasked or unbalanced signals	Simplification (recall Fig. 3)	Glitches
Software	Conditional control flow and/or table lookups	Seldom, since unpredictability hurts performances	Cache hit/miss, speculation, out-of-order execution

References

1. 3rd IEEE International Verification and Security Workshop, IVSW 2018, Costa Brava, Spain, July 2–4, 2018. IEEE (2018)
2. Bhasin, S., Danger, J.L., Guilley, S., Najm, Z.: NICV: normalized inter-class variance for detection of side-channel leakage. In: IEEE International Symposium on Electromagnetic Compatibility (EMC 2014/Tokyo), May 12–16 2014. Session OS09: EM Information Leakage. Hitotsubashi Hall (National Center of Sciences), Chiyoda, Tokyo, Japan (2014)
3. Blömer, J., Guajardo, J., Krummel, V.: Provably secure masking of AES. In: Handschuh, H., Hasan, M.A. (eds.) SAC 2004. LNCS, vol. 3357, pp. 69–83. Springer, Heidelberg (2004). https://doi.org/10.1007/978-3-540-30564-4_5
4. Brier, E., Clavier, C., Olivier, F.: Correlation power analysis with a leakage model. In: Joye, M., Quisquater, J.-J. (eds.) CHES 2004. LNCS, vol. 3156, pp. 16–29. Springer, Heidelberg (2004). https://doi.org/10.1007/978-3-540-28632-5_2
5. Chari, S., Rao, J.R., Rohatgi, P.: Template attacks. In: Kaliski, B.S., Koç, K., Paar, C. (eds.) CHES 2002. LNCS, vol. 2523, pp. 13–28. Springer, Heidelberg (2003). https://doi.org/10.1007/3-540-36400-5_3

6. Easter, R.J., Quemard, J.-P., Kondo, J.: Text for ISO/IEC 1st CD 17825 - Information technology - Security techniques - Non-invasive attack mitigation test metrics for cryptographic modules, March 22 2014. Prepared within ISO/IEC JTC 1/SC 27/WG 3 (2014)

7. Facon, A., Guilley, S., Lec'hvien, M., Schaub, A., Souissi, Y.: Detecting cache-timing vulnerabilities in post-quantum cryptography algorithms. In: 3rd IEEE International Verification and Security Workshop, IVSW 2018, Costa Brava, Spain, July 2–4, 2018 [1], pp. 7–12 (2018)

8. Fei, Y., Luo, Q., Ding, A.A.: A statistical model for DPA with novel algorithmic confusion analysis. In: Prouff, E., Schaumont, P. (eds.) CHES 2012. LNCS, vol. 7428, pp. 233–250. Springer, Heidelberg (2012). https://doi.org/10.1007/978-3-642-33027-8_14

9. Gilbert Goodwill, B.J., Jaffe, J., Rohatgi, P.: A testing methodology for side-channel resistance validation, September 2011. In: NIST Non-Invasive Attack Testing Workshop (2011). http://csrc.nist.gov/news_events/non-invasive-attack-testing-workshop/papers/08_Goodwill.pdf

10. Jaffe, J., Rohatgi, P., Witteman, M.F.: Efficient side-channel testing for public key algorithms: RSA case study, September 2011. In: NIST Non-Invasive Attack Testing Workshop (2011). http://csrc.nist.gov/news_events/non-invasive-attack-testing-workshop/papers/09_Jaffe.pdf

11. Kocher, P.: Complexity and the challenges of securing SoCs. In: Stok, L., Dutt, N.D., Hassoun, S. (eds) Proceedings of the 48th Design Automation Conference, DAC 2011, San Diego, California, USA, June 5–10, 2011, pp. 328–331. ACM (2011)

12. Kocher, P.C.: Timing attacks on implementations of Diffie-Hellman, RSA, DSS, and other systems. In: Koblitz, N. (ed.) CRYPTO 1996. LNCS, vol. 1109, pp. 104–113. Springer, Heidelberg (1996). https://doi.org/10.1007/3-540-68697-5_9

13. Kocher, P.C.: Leak-resistant cryptographic indexed key update, March 25 2003. United States Patent 6,539,092 filed on July 2nd, 1999 at San Francisco, CA, USA (2003)

14. Kocher, P., Jaffe, J., Jun, B.: Differential power analysis. In: Wiener, M. (ed.) CRYPTO 1999. LNCS, vol. 1666, pp. 388–397. Springer, Heidelberg (1999). https://doi.org/10.1007/3-540-48405-1_25

15. Liu, H., Qian, G., Tsunoo, Y., Goto, S.: The switching glitch power leakage model. JSW **6**(9), 1787–1794 (2011)

16. Mangard, S., Oswald, E., Popp, T.: Power Analysis Attacks: Revealing the Secrets of Smart Cards. Springer, New York (2006). ISBN 0-387-30857-1. http://www.dpabook.org/

17. Mangard, S., Schramm, K.: Pinpointing the side-channel leakage of masked AES Hardware implementations. In: Goubin, L., Matsui, M. (eds.) CHES 2006. LNCS, vol. 4249, pp. 76–90. Springer, Heidelberg (2006). https://doi.org/10.1007/11894063_7

18. Moradi, A., Guilley, S., Heuser, A.: Detecting hidden leakages. In: Boureanu, I., Owesarski, P., Vaudenay, S. (eds.) ACNS 2014. LNCS, vol. 8479, pp. 324–342. Springer, Cham (2014). https://doi.org/10.1007/978-3-319-07536-5_20

19. Souissi, Y., Danger, J.-L., Guilley, S., Bhasin, S., Nassar, M.: Common framework to evaluate modern embedded systems against side-channel attacks. In: IEEE International Conference on Technologies for Homeland Security (HST), pp. 86–91, November 15–17 2011. Westin Hotel, Waltham, MA, USA (2011). https://doi.org/10.1109/THS.2011.6107852

20. Standaert, F.-X., Malkin, T.G., Yung, M.: A unified framework for the analysis of side-channel key recovery attacks. In: Joux, A. (ed.) EUROCRYPT 2009. LNCS, vol. 5479, pp. 443–461. Springer, Heidelberg (2009). https://doi.org/10.1007/978-3-642-01001-9_26

21. Takarabt, S., et al.: Pre-silicon embedded system evaluation as new EDA tool for security verification. In: 3rd IEEE International Verification and Security Workshop, IVSW 2018, Costa Brava, Spain, July 2–4, 2018 [1], pp. 74–79 (2018)

22. Veshchikov, N., Guilley, S.: Use of simulators for side-channel analysis. In: 2017 IEEE European Symposium on Security and Privacy, EuroS&P 2017, Paris, France, April 26–28, 2017, pp. 51–59. IEEE (2017)

23. Veyrat-Charvillon, N., Medwed, M., Kerckhof, S., Standaert, F.-X.: Shuffling against side-channel attacks: a comprehensive study with cautionary note. In: Wang, X., Sako, K. (eds.) ASIACRYPT 2012. LNCS, vol. 7658, pp. 740–757. Springer, Heidelberg (2012). https://doi.org/10.1007/978-3-642-34961-4_44

24. Whitnall, C., Oswald, E.: A fair evaluation framework for comparing side-channel distinguishers. J. Crypt. Eng. 1(2), 145–160 (2011)

Cache-Timing Attacks Still Threaten IoT Devices

Sofiane Takarabt[1,2], Alexander Schaub[2], Adrien Facon[1,3],
Sylvain Guilley[1,2,3(✉)], Laurent Sauvage[2,1], Youssef Souissi[1],
and Yves Mathieu[2]

[1] Secure-IC S.A.S., 15 Rue Claude Chappe, Bât. B, 35 510 Cesson-Sévigné, France
`sylvain.guilley@secure-ic.com`
[2] LTCI, Télécom ParisTech, Institut Polytechnique de Paris, 75 013 Paris, France
[3] École Normale Supérieure, Département d'informatique, 75 005 Paris, France

Abstract. Deployed widely and embedding sensitive data, The security of IoT devices depend on the reliability of cryptographic libraries to protect user information. However when implemented on real systems, cryptographic algorithms are vulnerable to side-channel attacks based on their execution behavior, which can be revealed by measurements of physical quantities such as timing or power consumption. Some countermeasures can be implemented in order to prevent those attacks. However those countermeasures are generally designed at high level description, and when implemented, some residual leakage may persist. In this article we propose a methodology to assess the robustness of the MbedTLS library against timing and cache-timing attacks. This comprehensive study of side-channel security allows us to identify the most frequent weaknesses in software cryptographic code and how those might be fixed. This methodology checks the whole source code, from the top level routines to low level primitives, that are used for the final application. We retrieve hundreds of lines of code that leak sensitive information.

1 Introduction

Formerly known as PolarSSL, MbedTLS library provides many cryptographic implementations and primitives that can be easily used by developers to design or implement new applications for embedded systems. However side-channel attacks are known to be an efficient way to break many of those applications. They exploit physical measurements like power consumption, electromagnetic emanation and even timing characteristics to retrieve the secret key. Using different techniques based on statistical tools, an attacker is able to extract a secret key using only one (or very few) measure(s) for unprotected implementations. The timing attack is the first side-channel attack presented by Kocher [14] in order to retrieve the exponent bits of RSA. More perfected versions of timing attack have been derived to break more secured implementations like Square-and-Multiply Always and Montgomery Ladder. Combined with power acquisition, a key can be extracted with less than one thousand traces [10].

© Springer Nature Switzerland AG 2019
C. Carlet et al. (Eds.): C2SI 2019, LNCS 11445, pp. 13–30, 2019.
https://doi.org/10.1007/978-3-030-16458-4_2

Securing implementation against some attacks becomes more and more challenging for designers and developers. They should take care about all attacks that use timing properties, inputs dependency [6,15,16] and different other parameters. However some developers still use different (already) available libraries to implement their cryptographic applications. So, even if they design a (secure) software from the top level description (loop iterating over the scalar, like Montgomery Ladder, Atomic Multiply Always, etc.) based on some primitive functions, they usually do not check whether or not those primitives actually respect the constant-time coding constraints. In the following we present our results based on MbedTLS cryptographic library.

2   Previous Works

2.1   Timing Attacks and Cache-Timing Attacks

Timing attacks exploit the timing variations induced by different inputs. For example, in asymmetric cryptography, operations like modular multiplication or division can cause timing variations in the execution time, which might be exploited to retrieve secret keys. We mention also the cache-based timing attack [7,11,18–20] that exploit difference between the access time of slow main memory, or RAM, and the much faster processor cache. If the value to be accessed depends on secret values, the number of cache hits and misses can be correlated to the secret values. This can eventually lead to a full retrieve. This kind of attack was first presented by Bernstein in [3], where he targets the OpenSSL tabulated AES implementation that was supposed to be constant-time. This attack is a profiled template attack, which exploits the fact that looking up the same data twice is faster than looking up at two different addresses.

Considering the cache-timing attack, one can distinguish between two kinds of attacks:

- **Passive:** Only the inputs can be controlled and no additional process needs to be run on the targeted device. The timing variations are only caused by the cache miss and hit of the tabulated computation.
- **Active:** This attack needs an additional process, that is able to "erase" the cache contents, which forces the victim process to reload the data (or instructions) from the main memory (for instance, FLUSH+RELOAD [20] attack).

Many cache-timing attacks have been published in 2018. They all exploit timing differences in either the control flow or the data access patterns. See a reasoned presentation of cache-timing attacks (as of December 2018) in Fig. 1. We focus on such attacks in this paper.

In Algorithm 1 we give the high level description of a naive implementation of Elliptic Curve Scalar Multiplication (ECSM). The bits of k are scanned from left to right, and a conditional point addition is performed in order to deal with bit values at 1. If an attacker is able to probe the cache memory, she can retrieve the bits of k by measuring the access time of an instruction during the addition

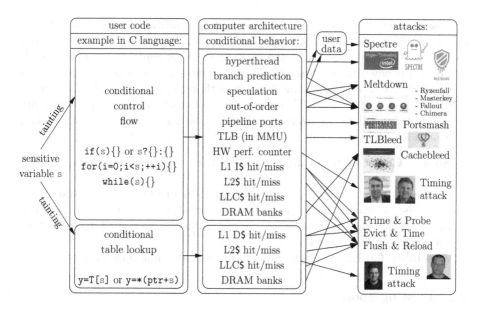

Fig. 1. Genealogy of cache-timing attacks

Algorithm 1. ECSM fast implementation: Double-and-Add—*Prone to cache-timing attacks*

---

1 // **Input** :
  – P: base point
  – $k = (k_0 \ldots k_{n-1})_2$: scalar

Output: $[k]P$

---

2 $Q \leftarrow O$; O is the point at infinity
3 $i = n - 1$
4 **while** $i > -1$ **do**
5 $\quad Q \leftarrow [2]Q$; Point Doubling
6 $\quad$ **if** $k_i = 1$ **then**
7 $\quad\quad Q \leftarrow Q + P$; Point Addition
8 $\quad$ **end**
9 $\quad i = i - 1$
10 **end**
11 **return** Q

---

function which was initially flushed from the cache. If the access is long, then the victim code has not called the point addition. Otherwise, it has. When the ECSM is used to perform a signature generation or any other private operation, the secret key will be recovered.

Cache vulnerabilities are not only caused by conditional operations. As the size of the cache memory is limited to few thousand of bytes, the content needs to be erased and reloaded from the main memory. A concrete example of such a situation is when the processor deals with relatively big tables. As mentioned in the Sect. 2.1, the cause of the leakage is that the tables of AES cannot be fully loaded into the cache. Therefore, when different indexes of the array are accessed, data needs to be reloaded, which causes non-constant time execution.

Cache timing attacks can be prevented at various levels:

- **Source Code:** by balancing the control flow, by fetching all values from a table, etc.
- **Compilation Time:** by alignment constraints of tables to minimize cache effect (since cache lines are nowadays quite large); refer for instance to the following declaration of aligned table T: `unsigned char T[256] __attribute__((aligned))`;
- **Assembly Code:** with `cmov` and `setcc` constant-time operations.

2.2 Existing Tools

Our goal is to identify the lines of code which can produce timing leakages when executed on a processor. Those leakages can be caused by a conditional operation, non-constant time operations and also cache accesses.

Some debugger tools were recently used for side-channel analysis, like gdb and Valgrind [4,5]. Some of the identified vulnerabilities depend on the target device, but others are actually present in the source code. In the first case, the code should be fixed at low level (assembly instructions). In the second case, this can be done at high-level source code (e.g., C).

3   Our Methodology

3.1   Leakage Types

The cache vulnerabilities are exploited by timing measurements. These variations are caused when the data requested by the processor is present or not in the cache memory. This data can be simple variables, arrays or even functions. The last two are the most vulnerable cases. In fact, if the array is relatively large, accessing different indexes will cause time variation. If those indexes can be controlled in some way, an attacker can correlate it with the sensitive data. In the case of functions, the same method can be applied, by guessing which functions have been executed, and correlating the observed timing measurements with the sensitive data.

3.2   Principle of the Tool

Evaluation of a source code against timing and cache-timing attacks should track the sensitive variables over all sub-routines, and check if any time variation can be caused by conditional branching or array access. The static analysis tool is based on four main steps:

1. **Input preparation.** To analyze a source code, we need to specify the sensitive variable involved in computation.
2. **Dependency and vulnerability.**
   (a) **Dependency analysis.** The specified variable will be tracked over all sub-functions and if any dependency is detected, it will be logged.
   (b) **Vulnerability identification.** All the dependency of the code with the sensitive data is built and analyzed. The instructions are filtered by keeping only some patterns that cause time variation (conditional branch), or array access (cache vulnerabilities).
3. **Vulnerability analysis.** A post-processing is then applied on the reported leakages to classify them, remove the potential false positives (see Sect. 3.3) and produce a report readable by the designer.

The global work flow is illustrated in Fig. 2.

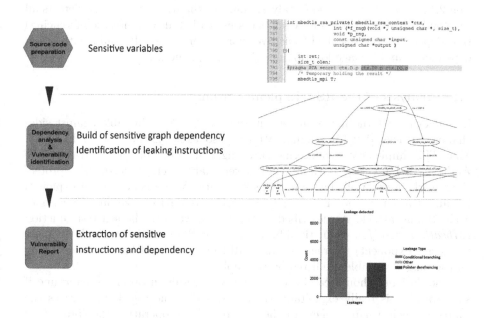

Fig. 2. Static analysis tool principle

3.3 False Positives

The tool can report false positives in those cases:

- The incriminated line of code is not called in the execution context.
- The vulnerability leaks too little:

- either too little times;
- or the leakage is too local, e.g., a table access where the table is so small it fits in a line of cache;
- At the opposite, the leakages are too frequent in time, thereby making it challenging, if not impossible, to catch them all and/or to synchronize with them.

- Leakages sometimes happily disappear at compilation, e.g., when a structure such as if(s){y=a;}, which is compiled with a *conditional move* (cmov) instruction.
- Leakages which occur in exploitable places, e.g., in the middle of a hash function (which clearly cannot been related simply to the sensitive variable due to difficulty of preimage finding problem).

4 Evaluating MbedTLS Source Code

In this section we present our results on the main cryptography implementations: RSA, ECDSA, AES, DES and other block ciphers, from MbedTLS version 2.14.1. Our tool, named Catalyzr, analyzes the whole source and detects all the conditional branches and array accesses (called also pointer dereferencing) that depend on the specified (sensitive) parameters. The full results with graph dependency and leakage location are given in Appendix A.

4.1 Analysis of the RSA Implementation

It is known that the naive implementation of RSA is vulnerable against side-channel attacks [1,2,17]. Similar attacks also exist in the case of ECC [9]. MbedTLS implements countermeasures against some of these attacks, like Address-Bit DPA [12,13], timing and power analysis, etc. Indeed, those protections work pretty well, but some sensitive parts of the code can be exploited by an attacker in order to easily disturb the device, like in the case of cache-timing attack. As described in the Fig. 2, we take the self test function (*Mbedtls_rsa_self_test*) in the library and tag the sensitive variable (namely the secret exponent) to track (*rsa.D*). All the conditional branches depending on the tagged variable are listed by the tool.

The designer should carefully analyze each result in order to determine if such warning is really exploitable in his use case. The Fig. 3 summarizes the source of such a dependency. In the case of private operation the (protected) *Mbedtls_mpi_exp_mod* function performs modular exponentiation based on sliding window, Montgomery Multiplication and Montgomery Reduction.

The Montgomery Reduction performs fake subtraction to prevent timing attacks (see Fig. 4), when the result is lesser than the modulus N.

The Fig. 5 shows the vulnerable line code in the *mpi_sub_help* function. This kind of vulnerabilities can be exploited by an attacker by chosen inputs, which may induce time variation induced by the carry propagation.

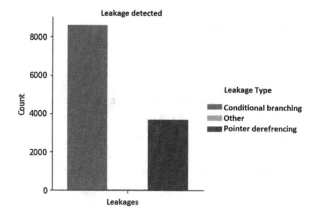

Fig. 3. Source of vulnerabilities detected on RSA signature

```
1593    if( mbedtls_mpi_cmp_abs( A, N ) >= 0 )
1594        mpi_sub_hlp( n, N->p, A->p );
1595    else
1596        /* prevent timing attacks */
1597        mpi_sub_hlp( n, A->p, T->p );
```

Fig. 4. Extra reduction in the Montgomery Modular Multiplication-*bignum.c* file

```
965
966    while( c != 0 )
967    {
968        z = ( *d < c ); *d -= c;
969        c = z; d++;
970    }
```

Fig. 5. Carry leakage for ECDSA and RSA

4.2   Analysis of ECDSA Implementation

In the case of ECDSA signature, we have analyzed the *Mbedtls_ecdsa_sign* function. We tagged the scalar r used to sign the message. As in the previous section, we note that these leakages are found in the primitives that implement the arithmetic field operation using big integers.

The Fig. 6 shows a vulnerable code line that breaks out of the loop when the number of limbs has been determined. Such an optimization induces also a time variation (non-constant time implementation), which is susceptible to a timing attack.

```
999         X->s = 1;
1000
1001        ret = 0;
1002
1003        for( n = B->n; n > 0; n-- )
1004            if( B->p[n - 1] != 0 )
1005                break;
1006
1007        mpi_sub_hlp( n, B->p, X->p );
1008
```

Fig. 6. Vulnerable code location for ECDSA and RSA

As we can see, the variable n is then passed to the *mpi_sub_help* function which performs subtraction using only the n first limbs. The loop is therefore flagged as potential timing vulnerability, as shown in Fig. 7. This function is used in both RSA and ECDSA signatures, and this vulnerability is common for both. The more interesting leakage is the manner how we deal with the carry in the subtraction function.

In fact, we have tested the *Mbedtls_mpi_exp_mod* function with real data, to simulate actual algorithm execution times. The first identified leakage (Fig. 6) may not be significant as the size of inputs remains the same, and no variation is observed. However the total time to perform the subtraction is different due to the second vulnerability (Fig. 5). The feasibility of a timing attack depends on the ability of an attacker to measure the time of a decryption with high accuracy, which is the case in most of embedded platforms.

```
955    static void mpi_sub_hlp( size_t n, mbedtls_mpi_uint *s, mbedtls_mpi_uint *d )
956    {
957        size_t i;
958        mbedtls_mpi_uint c, z;
959
960        for( i = c = 0; i < n; i++, s++, d++ )
961        {
962            z = ( *d < c );      *d -= c;
963            c = ( *d < *s ) + z; *d -= *s;
964        }
```

Fig. 7. Vulnerable code location and annotation for ECDSA and RSA: subtraction function

4.3 Analysis of AES Implementation

In the MbedTLS AES implementation, the SubBytes operation is performed using a table of 256 bytes (*Sbox*). If the size of the cache is large enough, the whole table Sbox can be fully loaded. Regarding the cache vulnerabilities, no time variation should occur in this case. However, in the case of active attack, an attacker can probe the cache contents, and gain knowledge about the lines and banks accessed during the Sbox computation.

The tool has also listed some vulnerabilities in the key-scheduling step (*mbedtls_aes_setkey_enc*), where the Sbox accesses depend directly on the key value.

```
578          RK[4] = RK[0] ^ RCON[i] ^
579          ( (uint32_t) FSb[ ( RK[3] >> 8 ) & 0xFF ]       ) ^
580          ( (uint32_t) FSb[ ( RK[3] >> 16 ) & 0xFF ] << 8 ) ^
581          ( (uint32_t) FSb[ ( RK[3] >> 24 ) & 0xFF ] << 16 ) ^
582          ( (uint32_t) FSb[ ( RK[3]       ) & 0xFF ] << 24 );
```

Fig. 8. Vulnerable code location and annotation for AES

In Fig. 8, all the lines from 595 to 598 are listed as vulnerable. The exploitation of this vulnerability depends on the ability of an attacker to probe the cache content [18,20]. More leaking code was found in the encryption and decryption functions, *mbedtls_internal_aes_encrypt* and *mbedtls_internal_aes_decrypt* respectively, as the cache behaviour depends on a controllable parameter (plaintext or ciphertext).

The Fig. 9 shows the inter-procedural graph that gives all the leakages. The bubble-shape gives the function name, and the tables list the leaking code with the line number (first column). The corresponding file is shown in the arrow title. At the top figure, we have the *mbedtls_aes_crypt_ecb* function that calls either

- *mbedtls_internal_aes_encrypt* (line 918), or
- *mbedtls_internal_aes_decrypt* (at line 916)

in the *aes.c* file. The lowest tables show the leaking lines (first column), that depend on the input. In this case, the attack is less difficult, because we need to probe only one Sbox at each encryption, and by repeating at most 256 time the same (or wisely chosen) message, we can deduce the key value. If Sbox table cannot be fully loaded into cache memory, time variation can be observed. With chosen inputs, this variation can be controlled and leads to high correlation between those inputs and encryption time. This is equivalent to the attack described in [3].

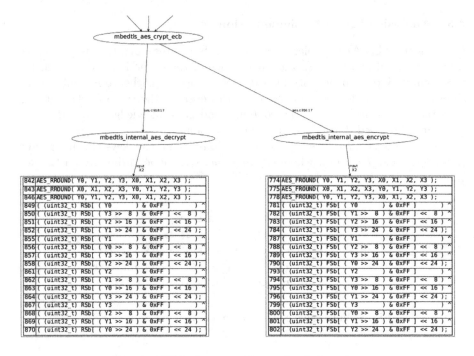

Fig. 9. AES leakage tracking and code location

4.4 Analysis of DES Implementation

The MbedTLS DES implementation uses eight tables for SubBytes operation, each has 16 × 4 half-bytes. In order to analyze this algorithm we have tagged the *des3_test_keys* in the file *des.c*.

The Fig. 10 shows all the vulnerabilities listed by the tool. In the left side we have the two encryption functions based on simple DES and triple DES. In this case we have the *DES_ROUND* macro that perform the SubBytes operation, which depends on the secret data *ctx.sk* and *SK*. In the right side the lines 437 to 440, and 442 to 444 show the vulnerable part in the key-schedule function. The first leakage is related to the encryption datapath and as explained in the previous section, it is less difficult to exploit. The second one is present only at the key schedule step, which make it very difficult to exploit.

4.5 Analysis of Blowfish Implementation

Blowfish is a symmetric algorithm also based on Sbox-tables to perform the SubBytes operation. Four tables of 256 32-bits word are used to perform this operation. This leads to 4 kB of data. Loading the whole table in cache memory may not be possible on constrained devices. This function is called *F*, and it is

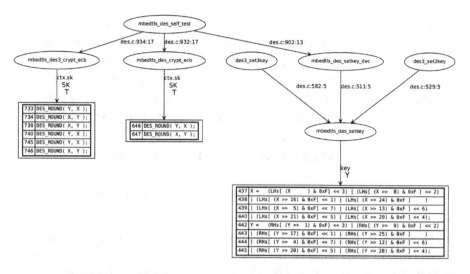

Fig. 10. DES graph with leakage dependency: *mbedtls_des_self_test* function

```
89        y = ctx->S[0][a] + ctx->S[1][b];
90        y = y ^ ctx->S[2][c];
91        y = y + ctx->S[3][d];
```

Fig. 11. Vulnerable code location and annotation for Blowfish

called from the *blowfish_enc* function that encrypts a plaintext x using a secret key. We tagged the key ($ctx.P$) as a sensitive variable to track, and the tool has pointed four vulnerabilities in the F function.

The Fig. 11 shows the first leaking code line, which contains two array accesses. The tool has pointed two times the line 89, and one time line 90 and 89. The variables a, b, c, and d, depend on the input x of the function F, which are actually xored with the secret key in the *blowfish_enc* function. Regarding the cache-timing attacks, it is difficult to exploit such vulnerabilities. For example, to identify the value of a (b, c or d), the attacker need to probe cache line to see which word is loaded, and hence deduce the value of the key if the input (or the output) is known.

4.6   Analysis of Camellia Implementation

For the Camellia algorithm, we have tagged variable *camellia_test_ecb_key* that is used as a secret key. Similar to the previously presented algorithm, Camellia resorts to a table for the SubBytes operation. Four different tables of size 256 bytes are used for this purpose, which leads to 1 kB memory.

```
304        I0 = ((uint32_t) SBOX1((I0 >> 24) & 0xFF) << 24) |
305             ((uint32_t) SBOX2((I0 >> 16) & 0xFF) << 16) |
306             ((uint32_t) SBOX3((I0 >> 8) & 0xFF) << 8) |
307             ((uint32_t) SBOX4((I0    ) & 0xFF)      );
308        I1 = ((uint32_t) SBOX2((I1 >> 24) & 0xFF) << 24) |
309             ((uint32_t) SBOX3((I1 >> 16) & 0xFF) << 16) |
310             ((uint32_t) SBOX4((I1 >> 8) & 0xFF) << 8) |
311             ((uint32_t) SBOX1((I1    ) & 0xFF)      );
```

Fig. 12. Vulnerable code location and annotation for Camellia

The tool has underlined the array access in *camellia_feistel* function as shown in Fig. 12. Depending on the cache size, the time to access those tables may differs from one message to another. We note also that, for each byte position, a different Sbox table is used, which leads to high probability of cache miss events.

5   Discussion

In Sects. 4.1, 4.2, we present some of our results that we hope will be taken into account in future release of the library. Those vulnerabilities are not necessarily known by developers, as they implement new applications based on already existing software for low-level primitives. We designed Catalyzr in order to help such developers to check their implementations, as an end-to-end workflow integration check. We see that in most cases, the top level functions are well protected against the cited attacks. However, leakages are detected at the low level primitives, that are not updated in order to respect the specified constraints. We have seen that some of those leakages can be exploited by a simple timing analysis.

In the case of symmetric implementations, most leakages are related to array accesses. In fact, those vulnerabilities are target dependent. They should be analyzed by considering the cache specification. Since caches might be shared by different applications, cache vulnerabilities can arise even when the SBoxes might fit into cache, because less memory is available for each application. This can lead to the vulnerabilities mentioned in Sects. 4.3, 4.5, 4.6. In all cases, we have identified all the array accesses that depend on the sensitive parameter. The most interesting parts are those depending also on the encryption datapath, like Sbox access, in the encryption functions. The vulnerabilities which depend only on the key are very difficult to exploit (case of key-schedule), because the attacker would need to repeat many times the cache probing to have only some information about the line accessed and then the value that was processed. Besides, in most of the optimized implementations this step is performed once, which makes the attack almost impractical.

Table 1. Summary of leakage reported

Function	# Leakage	# Functions	# Lines
mbedtls_rsa_self_test	11131	40	147
mbedtls_ecdsa_sign	12588	34	124
mbedtls_aes_self_test	95	4	59
mbedtls_des_self_test	85	3	16
blowfish_enc	4	1	3
mbedtls_camellia_self_test	83	2	13

In Table 1 we summarize the details about the leakages reported for each function (named in the first column). The second column gives the total number of reported leakages. Those are all of the possible paths through the control flow graph (this estimation is optimistic, since not all paths are exercised—more precisely, the paths can be taken, but may not depend on the inputs). The third one shows the number of leaking functions (that induce the leakage). And the last one corresponds to the number of leaking code lines. This information can be deduced from the inter-procedural graph given in Appendix A.

6   Conclusion and Perspectives

In this paper we have presented some (automated) static analysis on MbedTLS library. The reported leakages are either related to a non-constant time implementation (as it was supposed to be), or to a potential cache vulnerability. In the first case, we have seen that a simple timing attack is possible, not only for the analyzed algorithms, but also for the future applications that will be based on the same routines. Exploiting the sensitive parts by a cache-active attack may be very difficult or impracticable in some cases. This depends on the ability of an attacker (in terms of speed, regularity, etc.) to probe the cache. However in some conditions, equivalent time variation could occur and reveal information about the processed data. This is the case when the cache size is limited, or when the machine is so loaded that it is shared with other threads.

As a perspective, we intend to attribute each identified leakage to existing attacks, such as exploitation of "extra-reductions" in RSA/ECC Montgomery Modular Multiplication [10] or the exploitation of the correlation between the computation duration and the length of the nonce in ECDSA signature generation algorithm [8].

Acknowledgments. The authors are grateful to Matthieu Lec'hvien for having initiated this work (under the guidance of Alexander Schaub). This work has benefited from a funding via TEAMPLAY (https://teamplay-h2020.eu/), a project from European Union's Horizon2020 research and innovation programme, under grand agreement No. 779882. Besides, this work has been partly financed by NSFC grant No. 61632020, and French PIA (Projet d'Investissment d'Avenir) grant P141580, of acronym RISQ (Regroupement de l'Industrie pour la Sécurité post-Quantique).

A   Appendix

Here we give all the inter-procedural graphs that show the dependency and the leakage location for each algorithm (Figs. 13, 14, 15, 16, 17, and 18).

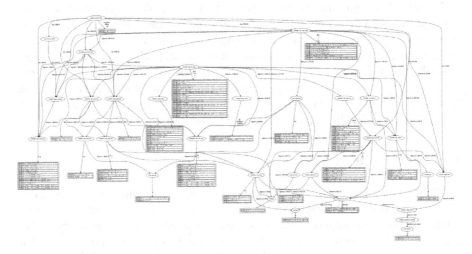

Fig. 13. Full RSA graph with leakage dependency for *mbedtls_rsa_private* function

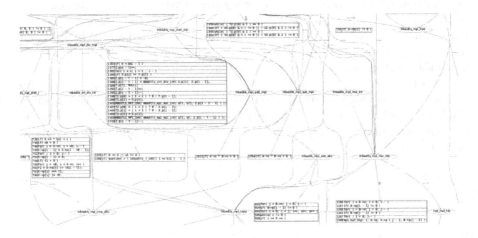

Fig. 14. Part of ECDSA graph with leakage dependency for *mbedtls_ecdsa_sign* function

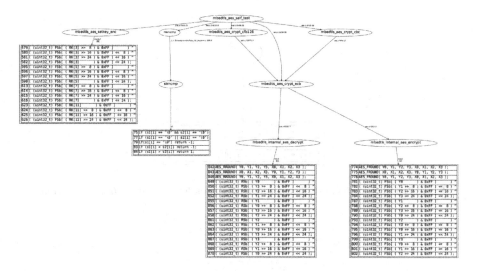

Fig. 15. Full AES graph with leakage dependency: *mbedtls_aes_self_test*

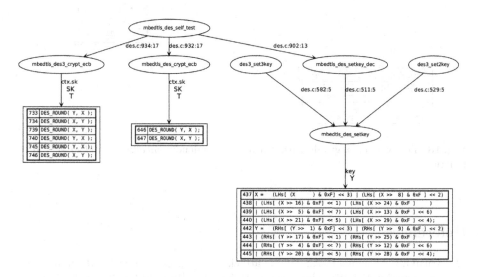

Fig. 16. Full DES graph with leakage dependency: *mbedtls_des_self_test* function

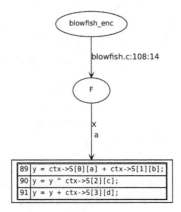

Fig. 17. Full Blowfish graph with leakage dependency: *blowfish_enc* function

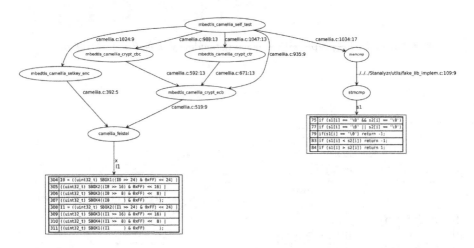

Fig. 18. Full Camellia graph with leakage dependency: *mbedtls_camellia_self_test* function

References

1. Arnaud, C., Fouque, P.-A.: Timing attack against protected RSA-CRT implementation used in PolarSSL. In: Dawson, E. (ed.) CT-RSA 2013. LNCS, vol. 7779, pp. 18–33. Springer, Heidelberg (2013). https://doi.org/10.1007/978-3-642-36095-4_2
2. Bauer, A., Jaulmes, E., Lomné, V., Prouff, E., Roche, T.: Side-channel attack against RSA key generation algorithms. In: Batina, L., Robshaw, M. (eds.) CHES 2014. LNCS, vol. 8731, pp. 223–241. Springer, Heidelberg (2014). https://doi.org/10.1007/978-3-662-44709-3_13

3. Bernstein, D.J.: Cache-timing attacks on AES (2005)
4. Bos, J.W., Hubain, C., Michiels, W., Teuwen, P.: Differential computation analysis: hiding your white-box designs is not enough. In: Gierlichs, B., Poschmann, A.Y. (eds.) CHES 2016. LNCS, vol. 9813, pp. 215–236. Springer, Heidelberg (2016). https://doi.org/10.1007/978-3-662-53140-2_11
5. Bouvet, A., Bruneau, N., Facon, A., Guilley, S., Marion, D.: Give me your binary, I'll tell you if it leaks, pp. 1–4 (2018)
6. Brier, E., Clavier, C., Olivier, F.: Correlation power analysis with a leakage model. In: Joye, M., Quisquater, J.-J. (eds.) CHES 2004. LNCS, vol. 3156, pp. 16–29. Springer, Heidelberg (2004). https://doi.org/10.1007/978-3-540-28632-5_2
7. Groot Bruinderink, L., Hülsing, A., Lange, T., Yarom, Y.: Flush, gauss, and reload – a cache attack on the BLISS lattice-based signature scheme. In: Gierlichs, B., Poschmann, A.Y. (eds.) CHES 2016. LNCS, vol. 9813, pp. 323–345. Springer, Heidelberg (2016). https://doi.org/10.1007/978-3-662-53140-2_16
8. Brumley, B.B., Tuveri, N.: Remote timing attacks are still practical. In: Atluri, V., Diaz, C. (eds.) ESORICS 2011. LNCS, vol. 6879, pp. 355–371. Springer, Heidelberg (2011). https://doi.org/10.1007/978-3-642-23822-2_20
9. Coron, J.-S.: Resistance against differential power analysis for elliptic curve cryptosystems. In: Koç, Ç.K., Paar, C. (eds.) CHES 1999. LNCS, vol. 1717, pp. 292–302. Springer, Heidelberg (1999). https://doi.org/10.1007/3-540-48059-5_25
10. Dugardin, M., Guilley, S., Danger, J.-L., Najm, Z., Rioul, O.: Correlated extra-reductions defeat blinded regular exponentiation. In: Gierlichs, B., Poschmann, A.Y. (eds.) CHES 2016. LNCS, vol. 9813, pp. 3–22. Springer, Heidelberg (2016). https://doi.org/10.1007/978-3-662-53140-2_1
11. Facon, A., Guilley, S., Lec'hvien, M., Schaub, A., Souissi, Y.: Detecting cache-timing vulnerabilities in post-quantum cryptography algorithms. In: 2018 IEEE 3rd International Verification and Security Workshop (IVSW), pp. 7–12. IEEE (2018)
12. Itoh, K., Izu, T., Takenaka, M.: Address-bit differential power analysis of cryptographic schemes OK-ECDH and OK-ECDSA. In: Kaliski, B.S., Koç, K., Paar, C. (eds.) CHES 2002. LNCS, vol. 2523, pp. 129–143. Springer, Heidelberg (2003). https://doi.org/10.1007/3-540-36400-5_11
13. Itoh, K., Izu, T., Takenaka, M.: A practical countermeasure against address-bit differential power analysis. In: Walter, C.D., Koç, Ç.K., Paar, C. (eds.) CHES 2003. LNCS, vol. 2779, pp. 382–396. Springer, Heidelberg (2003). https://doi.org/10.1007/978-3-540-45238-6_30
14. Kocher, P.C.: Timing attacks on implementations of Diffie-Hellman, RSA, DSS, and other systems. In: Koblitz, N. (ed.) CRYPTO 1996. LNCS, vol. 1109, pp. 104–113. Springer, Heidelberg (1996). https://doi.org/10.1007/3-540-68697-5_9
15. Kocher, P., Jaffe, J., Jun, B.: Differential power analysis. In: Wiener, M. (ed.) CRYPTO 1999. LNCS, vol. 1666, pp. 388–397. Springer, Heidelberg (1999). https://doi.org/10.1007/3-540-48405-1_25
16. Le, T.-H., Canovas, C., Clédiere, J.: An overview of side-channel analysis attacks. In: Proceedings of the 2008 ACM Symposium on Information, Computer and Communications Security, pp. 33–43. ACM (2008)
17. Nakano, Y., et al.: A pre-processing composition for secret key recovery on android smartphone. In: Naccache, D., Sauveron, D. (eds.) WISTP 2014. LNCS, vol. 8501, pp. 76–91. Springer, Heidelberg (2014). https://doi.org/10.1007/978-3-662-43826-8_6

18. Osvik, D.A., Shamir, A., Tromer, E.: Cache attacks and countermeasures: the case of AES. In: Pointcheval, D. (ed.) CT-RSA 2006. LNCS, vol. 3860, pp. 1–20. Springer, Heidelberg (2006). https://doi.org/10.1007/11605805_1
19. Yarom, Y., Benger, N.: Recovering OpenSSL ECDSA nonces using the FLUSH+RELOAD cache side-channel attack. In: IACR Cryptology ePrint Archive, 2014:140 (2014)
20. Yarom, Y., Falkner, K.: FLUSH+RELOAD: a high resolution, low noise, L3 cache side-channel attack. In: USENIX Security Symposium, pp. 719–732 (2014)

Speed-up of SCA Attacks on 32-bit Multiplications

Robert Nguyen[1], Adrien Facon[1,3], Sylvain Guilley[1,2,3(✉)], Guillaume Gautier[4], and Safwan El Assad[5]

[1] Secure-IC S.A.S. - Think Ahead Business Line, 35 510 Cesson-Sévigné, France
{sylvain.guilley,robert.nguyen}@secure-ic.com
[2] LTCI, Telecom ParisTech, COMELEC Department, 75 013 Paris, France
[3] École Normale Supérieure Département d'Informatique, 75 005 Paris, France
[4] Univ Rennes, INSA Rennes, CNRS, IETR - UMR 6164, 35 000 Rennes, France
[5] IETR Laboratory, UMR CNRS 6164; VAADER Team, Nantes, France
safwan.elassad@univ-nantes.fr

Abstract. Many crypto-algorithms, Deep-Learning, DSP compute on words larger than 8-bit. SCA attacks can easily be done on Boolean operations like XOR, AND, OR, and substitution operations like s-box, p-box or q-box, as 8-bit hypothesis or less are enough to forge attacks. However, attacking larger hypothesis word increases exponentially required resources: memory and computation power. Considering multiplication, 32-bit operation implies 2^{32} hypotheses. Then a direct SCA attack cannot be efficiently performed. We propose to perform instead 4 small 8-bit SCA attacks. 32-bit attack complexity is reduced to 8-bit only complexity.

Keywords: SCA · Arithmetic multiplication · 32-bit ·
Divide and conquer · 8-bit · Reduce partition size · Fault model ·
Neural network · Deep learning · Signal processing · PID ·
Automotive · Avionic · LFSR · PUF ·
Chaotic pseudo-random generator

1 Introduction

Following the low cost of 32-bit microcontrollers that substitute to 8-bit and 16-bit microcontrollers in embedded product, more and more algorithms use 32-bit operators. IoT firmware may then embed technical secret values of processing, meaning then key-knowledge of the product. SCARE approach (SCA+RE) is a way to retrieve such secret. It uses Side Channel Analysis (SCA) [1] to extract statistical information from product behavior (consumption and/or EM radiation) to perform Reverse Engineering (RE) and the retrieve secret.

Initial work has been done on a Vernam-like cipher using a PRNG based on Chaotic cell [2–5]. The purpose of work was to retrieve 15 words of 32-bit from the secret keys of the PRNG. 12 words are used in a sum of products for a linear

© Springer Nature Switzerland AG 2019
C. Carlet et al. (Eds.): C2SI 2019, LNCS 11445, pp. 31–39, 2019.
https://doi.org/10.1007/978-3-030-16458-4_3

feedback. This article describes a side-channel attack on 32-bit multiplication, alone multiply operation or multiply-and-add operation. The attack has been performed on "ma" instruction of ARM-v2 which computes a multiply-and-add operation.

This 32-bit multiplication vulnerability can be applied on multiple other targets and for a large spectrum of applications. One can consider targets using neuronal network for deep learning [6,7] (see example in Fig. 1). Also coefficients of FIR-IIR filter for signal processing are sensitive goods (e.g. FIR parameter used for preprocessing by a SCA attack at [8] could be retrieved by SCA counterattack) (see example in Fig. 2). Also coefficients of PID for control loop in avionic or automotive actuators [9] are goods for advanced fonctionalities (see example in Fig. 3). Last examples of applications deal with cryptographic functions in TPM may also include such 32-bit operations for Linear Return Function (LRF) in LFSR (pseudo-random generator), for HASH function or for PUF [10] (post-processing of PUF measurements) (see example in Fig. 4).

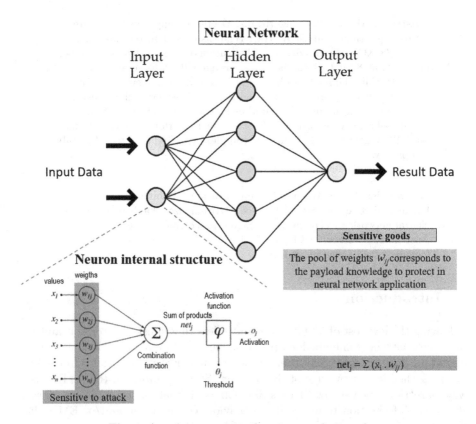

Fig. 1. Attack on sensitive data in neural network

2   Complexity of Attacking 32-bit Multiplication

The targeted operation to attack is an arithmetic multiplication of two 32-bit values. The result is truncated at 32 bits, a modulus 2^{32}. This 32-bit multiplication vulnerability against SCA has been identified on multiple targets. As the whole 32-bit word is needed for computation, following [11] statistical SCA attacks with a leakage model should need 2^{32} partitions to discriminate the secret multiplicand value. This implies a large memory resource to store 4 billion independent traces and associated computing power to calculate intermediate results for CPA or DPA at each new measurement of a multiplication activity.

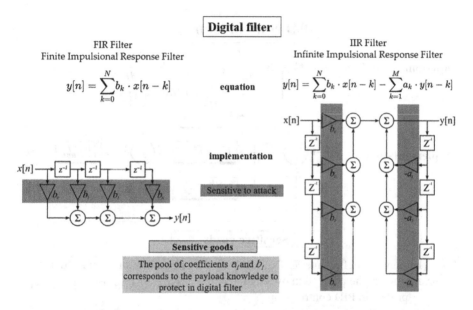

Fig. 2. Attack on sensitive coefficients of FIR-IIR Filter

Actually, current available computer resource can be enough for such partition and computation power. But it is still a waste of resources (memories and computation time). For example, attacking with 1k-points traces, makes $2^{32} = $ 4G partitions of 1k-points of 4 (or 8) bytes each. This imply to manage 16 TB of memory to store intermediate differential traces. When 10k-traces are enough to discriminate 8-bit hypothesis, 40k-traces will be needed at least for 32-bit hypothesis.

This will imply to manage $16 \times 10^{12} \times 40 \times 10^3 = 640 \times 10^{15}$ Bytes, meaning more than 10^{18} operations (31 years of computation on 1 GHz computer).

3   Split the Attack

Instead of attacking the whole word, we propose a different approach based on divide and conquer. The single attack with 2^{32} partitions is substituted by 4 small and sequential attacks on 2^8 partitions.

You can note this strategy to attack 32-bit word can be extended to larger word, $(N \times 8)$ bits word can be attacked through N successive attacks on 8-bit value.

The proposed approach will split this single attack into 4 small attacks on 8 bits of secret key but computation still use 32-bit multiplication.

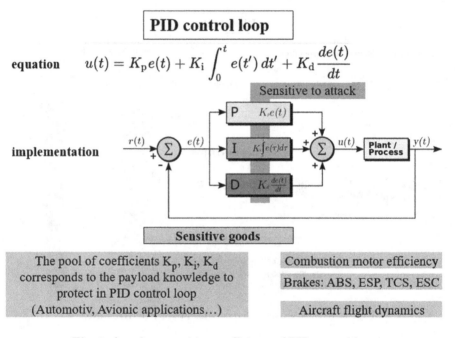

Fig. 3. Attack on sensitive coefficients of PID control loop

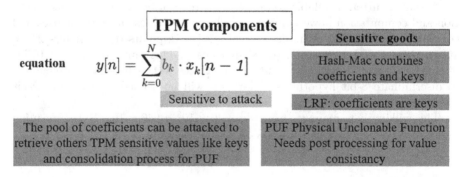

Fig. 4. Attack on sensitive goods inside a TPM

First of all is to describe the operands and elementary operations of the multiplication.

Each 32-bit word can be assumed as a vector of four 8-bit bytes:

- $Y = [Y3, Y2, Y1, Y0]$: result $Y = K \times X$
- $K = [K3, K2, K1, K0]$: secret key which is the multiplier constant
- $X = [X3, X2, X1, X0]$: data to multiply

Note: "$\ll$" operator corresponds to a bit-shifter operator, $c = a \ll b$ sets c to a value left shifted from b bits. The operation of "left shift from 1 bit" is equivalent to "multiply by 2". Using the "$\ll$" operator, Y can be rewrite in byte sub-operation as the following:

$$
\begin{aligned}
Y = &(K3.X0) \ll 24 + (K3.X1) \ll 32 + (K3.X2) \ll 40 + (K3.X3) \ll 48 \\
&+ (K2.X0) \ll 16 + (K2.X1) \ll 24 + (K2.X2) \ll 32 + (K2.X3) \ll 40 \\
&+ (K1.X0) \ll 8 \ + (K1.X1) \ll 16 + (K1.X2) \ll 24 + (K1.X3) \ll 32 \\
&+ (K0.X0) \ll 0 \ + (K0.X1) \ll 8 \ + (K0.X2) \ll 16 + (K0.X3) \ll 24
\end{aligned}
$$

As result of multiplication is truncated to 32-bit, "Y" expression can be simplified as:

$$
\begin{aligned}
Y = &(K3.X0) \ll 24 \\
&+ (K2.X0) \ll 16 + (K2.X1) \ll 24 \\
&+ (K1.X0) \ll 8 \ + (K1.X1) \ll 16 + (K1.X2) \ll 24 \\
&+ (K0.X0) \ll 0 \ + (K0.X1) \ll 8 \ + (K0.X2) \ll 16 + (K0.X3) \ll 24
\end{aligned}
$$

Amongst 16 initial intermediate multiplications, only 10 multiplications are really needed. This triangle representation reveals that part of the key can be selected in operation only by selecting Xi values.

4 Attack Steps

4.1 Step 1 - Retrieve K0

If X0, X1 and X2 can be forced to zero (0), then
$Y = ((K0.X3) \ll 24)$ & 0xFF000000.
A SCA attack with variation on X3 enables to retrieve K0 with only 256 partitions and up-to 256 traces. The leakage model is (only 8 low weight bits):
$\mathcal{L}(K0) : HW(Y) = HW((K0.X3)$ & 0xFF$)$
$HW(Y)$ takes value in $[0:8]$
In case of noisy measurements, multiple traces can be acquired and average for each X3 value to reduced noise impact.

4.2 Step 2 - Retrieve K1

The attack strategy is the same but with different Xi forced to zero. If X0, X1 and X3 can be forced to zero (0), then
$Y = (K1.X2) \ll 24 + (K0.X2) \ll 16$.
A SCA attack with variation on X2 enables to retrieve K1 with only 256 partitions and up-to 256 traces. This attack needs to know the value of $K0$.

   The leakage model is:
$\mathcal{L}(K1) : HW(Y) = HW(((K1.X2) \ \& \ \text{0xFF}) \ll 8 + (K0.X2))$
$\mathcal{L}(K1) : HW(Y) = HW(((K1 \ll 8 + K0).X2) \ \& \ \text{0x0000FFFF})$
$HW(Y)$ takes value in $[0:16]$
In case of noisy measurements, multiple traces can be acquired and average for each X2 value to reduced noise impact.

4.3 Step 3 - Retrieve K2

The attack strategy is the same but with different Xi forced to zero. If X0, X2 and X3 can be forced to zero (0), then
$Y = (K2.X1) \ll 24 + (K1.X1) \ll 16 + (K0.X1) \ll 8$.
A SCA attack with variation on X1 enables to retrieve K2 with only 256 partitions and up-to 256 traces. This attack needs to know the value of $K0$ and $K1$.
The leakage model is:
$\mathcal{L}(K2) : HW(Y) = HW(((K2.X1) \ \& \ \text{0xFF}) \ll 16 + (K1.X1) \ll 8 + (K0.X1))$
$\mathcal{L}(K2) : HW(Y) = HW(((K2 \ll 16 + K1 \ll 8 + K0).X1) \ \& \ \text{0x00FFFFFF})$

   $HW(Y)$ takes value in $[0:24]$
In case of noisy measurements, multiple traces can be acquired and average for each X1 value to reduced noise impact.

4.4 Step 4 - Retrieve K3

The attack strategy is the same but with different Xi forced to zero. If X1, X2 and X3 can be forced to zero (0), then
$Y = (K3.X0) \ll 24 + (K2.X0) \ll 16 + (K1.X0) \ll 8 + (K0.X0) \ll 0$.
A SCA attack with variation on X0 enables to retrieve K3 with only 256 partitions and up-to 256 traces. This attack needs to know the value of $K0$, $K1$ and $K2$.
The leakage model is:
$\mathcal{L}(K3) : HW(Y) = HW(((K3.X0) \ \& \ \text{0xFF}) \ll 24 + (K2.X0) \ll 16 + (K1.X0) \ll 8 + (K0.X0))$
$\mathcal{L}(K3) : HW(Y) = HW(((K3 \ll 24 + K2 \ll 16 + K1 \ll 8 + K0).X0) \ \& \ \text{0xFFFFFFFF})$
$HW(Y)$ takes value in $[0:32]$
In case of noisy measurements, multiple traces can be acquired and average for each X0 value to reduced noise impact.

4.5   Conclusion

The complex attack on K (32-bit) is replaced by 4 small attacks on 8-bit word: $K = [K3, K2, K1, K0]$. The order of the sequence of attacks remains as the last constraint to know few sub-keys K_i before attacking next sub-key K_j.

5   Benchmark

5.1   SCA Attack on 8-bit Multiplication

Each of 8-bit SCA attack presented in the previous chapter is based on the same attack scenario.

The 8-bit attack, used by the previous attacks, is a classical statistical SCA. CPA is chosen as distinguisher as it can converge quickly, even in noisy condition.

5.2   Performance on Software Implementation

A single 8-bit attack on 1k-points traces requires $256 \times 1024 \times 8 = 2$ M-bytes of memory and for computational resources $32 \times 1024 \times 256 = 8M$ multiplications and $256 \times 1024 \times 256 = 32M$ additions.

For the whole attack, this corresponds to 2M-bytes of memory, 32M-multiplications and 128M-Additions.

In comparison, a direct 32-bit attack needs 16 TB (16 Million of MB) of memory and 10^{18} operations ($10^{12} \times$ 1M operations).

6   Conclusion

By splitting big-word variables into an array of bytes, the complex attack of a N-Bytes word multiplication can be substituted by N small attacks on 8-bit words. The attack complexity $O(2^{32})$ is replaced by $4 \times O(2^8)$. The gain of memory is over 10 million and the gain of computation is 1 billion. Then the new method allows to compute the attack in 1 s on embedded computer (1 GHz mono-core, 4 MB of memory) instead of 31 years with 16 TB of memory.

7   Glossary

Chaotic Cell	Compute a value x(n+1) with $x(n + 1) = f(x(n))$ that makes a prediction of x(n+p) very complex if p>1.
CPA	Correlation Power Analysis.
CEMA	Correlation Electro-Magnetic Analysis.
Double	an extended floating-point value on 64-bit (8 bytes), IEEE defined.
EM	ElectroMagnetic.

FIR	Finite Impulse Response, a filter defined by:
	$Y(n) = \sum_{i=1}^{N}[X(n-i)*a(i)]$
Float	a floating-point value on 32-bit, IEEE defined.
GB	Giga-Bytes $= 10^9$ Bytes (Billion).
HASH	Data transformation to produce a compressed signature. This signature is used to test data integrity.
HD	Hamming Distance, HW of the transition of a register value when update: $HD(reg(n)) = HW(reg(n)XORreg(n-1))$.
HW	Hamming Weight, number of "1" in binary representation of a number.
IRR	Infinite Impulse Response, a filter defined by
	$Y(n) = \sum_{i=1}^{N}[X(n-i)*a(i)] - \sum_{j=1}^{M}[Y(n-j)*b(j)]$
LFSR	Linear-Feedback Shift Register.
LRF	Linear Return Function.
MAC	Multiply-and-Accumulate, same as Multiply-and-Add.
MB	Mega-Bytes $= 10^6$ Bytes (Million).
Multiply-and-Add	Two operation executed by a single instruction $Y = a*X+b$.
Neural Network	In Artificial Intelligence (A.I.) context, set neurons organized and interconnected in layers to process and reduce number of values.
Neuron	Each neuron of a layer computes a value from sum of product of its inputs and propagate a post-processed value to upper layer of neurons.
PID	Proportional, Integral and Derivative; definite a three-term controller in a control loop feedback mechanism.
PRNG	Pseudo-RaNdom Generator, produce a predetermined sequence of value that simulate random, an initial seed give the beginning of the sequence.
PUF	Physical Unclonable Function. Use silicon intrinsic property to produce a unique ID, even from the same logical gate/transistor definition. Post-processing using multiplication can be used to forge better quality PUF.
RE	Reverse Engineering.
RNG	Random Number Generator, can be a TRNG or a PRNG.
SCARE	Side-Channel Analysis for Reverse Engineering.
SCA	Side-Channel Analysis.
TB	Tera-Bytes $= 10^{12}$ Bytes (Millions of million).
TPM	Trusted Platform Module.
TRNG	True Random Number Generator, use physical property to produce unpredictable random number (Eg. atomic desintegration).
XOR	eXclusive OR.

References

1. Kocher, P., Jaffe, J., Jun, B.: Differential power analysis. In: Wiener, M. (ed.) CRYPTO 1999. LNCS, vol. 1666, pp. 388–397. Springer, Heidelberg (1999). https://doi.org/10.1007/3-540-48405-1_25
2. Assad El, S., et al.: Chaos-based block ciphers: an overview. In: IEEE 10th International Conference on Communications, COMM-2014, pp. 23–26. Romania, May, Bucharest (2014)
3. El Assad, F.: A new chaos-based image encryption system. Signal Process. Image Commun. **41**, 144–157 (2016)
4. Gautier, G., El Assad, S.: Design and efficient implementations of a chaos-based stream cipher for securing Internet of Things (2017)
5. Gautier, G., El Assad, S.: A promising chaos-based stream cipher (2018)
6. Batina, L., Bhasin, S., Jap, D., Picek, S.: CSI neural network - using side-channels to recover your artificial neural network information. arXiv:1810.09076v1 [cs.CR], 22 October 2018
7. Moellic, P.-A.: The dark side of neural networks: an advocacy for security in machine learning. J1–05. CESAR (2018)
8. Oswald, D., Paar, C.: Improving side-channel analysis with optimal pre-processing, p. 16. CARDIS (2012)
9. Bansal, H.O., Sharma, R., Shreeraman, P.R.: PID controller tuning techniques - a review. J. Control Eng. Technol JCET. **2**(4), 168–176 (2012). www.vkingpub.com
10. Physically Unclonable Function - PUF, SR2I301. https://perso.telecom-paristech.fr/danger/SR2I301/PUF.pdf
11. Brier, E., Clavier, C., Olivier, F.: Correlation power analysis with a leakage model. In: Joye, M., Quisquater, J.-J. (eds.) CHES 2004. LNCS, vol. 3156, pp. 16–29. Springer, Heidelberg (2004). https://doi.org/10.1007/978-3-540-28632-5_2

Cryptography

Arabic Cryptography and Steganography in Morocco

Abdelmalek Azizi[(✉)]

Department of Mathematics, Faculty of Sciences,
Mohammed Premier University, Oujda, Morocco
abdelmalekazizi@yahoo.fr

Abstract. Moroccans have used Cryptography and Steganography since very distant times especially during the reign of the different dynasties in Morocco. They have used most of the methods of Arabic cryptography as methods of substitution and transposition. They had also used Al-Mo'tamid's method of steganography, which consists of using a correspondence between a set of letters of the Arabic alphabet and a set of the bird names, and manipulate the names of birds instead of letters to encrypt a message hidden in poetry. In addition, before the end of the 16th century Moroccans had invented methods of cryptography and steganography as the method of digital cryptography used by King Al Mansour and which was based on use of the hash function "hissab Al Jommal calculation" and the factorization of integers. They had used also a grid filled with verses of poetry in the form of a chess table to crypt a letter by three digits representing the position of the letter in the grid. The poetry is thus the secret key that two people choose to exchange secret messages.

Between the 16th and the 19th century, there was intense use of the hash function "Hissab al Jommal calculation" to crypt numbers by letters and to crypt words by numbers as in the case where a number had used for the digital signature in the 18th century (signature in El-Malhoun poems). Similarly, Moroccans had used cryptography and Steganography for the security of financial and legal acts as in inheritance or marriage certificates.

This is an overview of some ideas used by Moroccans that we developed using the new computer technologies; however, there are undoubtedly many other ideas, to be found, in the old manuscripts.

Keywords: Instance of Moroccan cryptography and steganography ·
Digital signature · Numerical cryptography

1 Introduction

The use of difficult or unconventional notions to establish cryptographic or steganography algorithms was a tradition among Arab Scholars. They used, among other things, poetry as transmission means and used, for example, grammatical mistakes to indicate the beginning and the end of the encrypted message

© Springer Nature Switzerland AG 2019
C. Carlet et al. (Eds.): C2SI 2019, LNCS 11445, pp. 43–54, 2019.
https://doi.org/10.1007/978-3-030-16458-4_4

hidden in a poem. They also used difficulties when writing some pieces of poetry verses according to a given model as the basis of cryptographic or steganography Algorithms. Thus, Arabic poetry was a means of edition and publication, transmission, steganography and cryptography.

Al Khalil (718–786) and Al Kindi (801–873) built the pillars of Arab Steganography and Arab Cryptography. Other Arab scholars had written important documents on Cryptography and Steganography, including Ibn Dunainir (1187–1229), Ibn Adlan (1187–1268), Ibn Ad-Duraihim (1312–1361) and Al-Qalqashandi (1355–1418), see [3,9].

The Moroccans, following the study of some linguistic, mathematical and astronomic questions, had developed several cryptographic or steganography methods for sending secret messages. Most of the methods used in Morocco were based on some numerical encoding of Arabic letters, the hash function h "Hissab Al-Jommal" and some arithmetical operations see [4–7].

2   Arab Numerical Coding in Morocco and "Hissab Al-Jommal"

Arab Numerical Coding in Morocco
The numerical values of the Arab letters (numerical coding) in Morocco are given in the following table (Table 1).

Table 1. Numerical coding of Arabic letters

10	9	8	7	6	5	4	3	2	1
ي	ط	ح	ز	و	ه	د	ج	ب	ا
200	100	90	80	70	60	50	40	30	20
ر	ق	ض	ف	ع	ص	ن	م	ل	ك
		1000	900	800	700	600	500	400	300
		ش	غ	ظ	ذ	خ	ث	ت	س

Arab Calculus "Hissab Al-Jommal"
The calculus "Hissab Al-Jommal" is an arithmetic function h that associates each word or sentence with an integer equal to the sum of the numerical values of the letters constituting the word or the sentence. This function was used to write certain dates (such as some important events) at the beginning, in the middle or at the end of some words or sentences. For example, we found that in the 8th century, a Moroccan scholar, who had invented the writing of Arabic numbers [9], inserted the sentence

وهدفي حساب

in text that represent by the function h the number 176 (see [11]). The last number is the year (Hegira calendar) of the invention of Arabic numbers calligraphy that was inspired by the shape of Arabic letters in Kufi calligraphy.

3   The Moroccan Cryptographic and Steganography Methods

In particular, the Moroccan scientist used the following methods:

i. **Methods of substitution and transposition:** among these, we find the method which consists of encoding the letters by using names of birds and after coding the letters, the coded text is put in a poem: Al Moetamid Steganography. Al Moetamid Ibn Abad was the King of Ichbilia, the city now called Seville, from 1069 to 1092. He was a poet who had chosen his ministers among poets, such as the famous poet Ibn Zaydoune and the poet Ibn Ammare.

   Al Moetamid and Ibn zaydoune had the idea of using the names of birds to send and receive secret messages; they proceeded as follows:
   - first of all, Al Moetamid and Ibn zaydoun made a correspondence between all the letters of the Arabic alphabet and a set of names of birds.
   - if one of them wants to send a message to the other, he transforms the set of the letters of the message into an ordered set of bird names. Then, he composes a poem where he quotes the names of birds obtained by the transformation of the message in the same order.

   Then he sends this poem to the recipient. The recipient of Al Moetamid was in particular Ibn Zaidoune, who knew how to perform the various steps of this method of steganography and thus to secure a secret line with King Al Moetamid. It is Ibn Zaidoune, who once sent Al Moetamid a secret message announcing to him that he was ready to attack his enemy and later he sent him another secret message saying, "Destroy your enemy and get away".

ii. **Using h function, "hissab Al Jommal", to encrypt short messages.** The original message is transformed by the function h; we obtain a number that is decomposed into a product of two numbers n and m. Then we look for sentences P_1 and P_2 such that $h(P_1) = n$ and $h(P_2) = m$ and the multiplication symbol is replaced by its equivalent in Arabic "في". We thus obtain a text that can constitute the encrypted text (Cryptography of gold invented by Sultan Ahmed El Mansour at the end of the 16th century, see [6–8] and [16]). The following two verses contain two parts that are ciphered by two different methods:

وصفوا اشتياقي للحبيب وسرهم **** قول الحبيب أنا أنا فيه

قلبي له حجر، فقلت مغالطا **** للعاذل المؤذي أنا فيه

the last two words of the first line are encrypted using "hissab Al Jomal" and the integer factorization in the product of two integers (Table 2) while the three first words of the second line are encrypted by transposing Arabic letters in one word.

أنا فيه is the encryption of حقك و هيماني

Table 2. h function transformation of the last words of the first line

أنا فيه	ه	في	أنا
260	5	X	52

In particular, the ciphered text says, "my heart is like a stone to him" where the clear text is "I swear I'm in love with him" which is contrary to ciphered text. Moroccans had used the decomposition of an integer into a product of two integers to encrypt a message, which is practically very difficult especially if the message contains more than two words. This requires a huge calculation that could be realized only if our ancestors had a computer of our time. This explains why this method did not follow. It should be noted that the RSA method is also based on the difficulty of the factorization of a large integer that is a part of the RSA key, but not on the factorization of the digital encoding of the message as in the El Mansour method.

iii. **The third method consists in using numerical coding by position.** We insert a text in a grid with n lines and m columns; a letter, which belongs to case ij, is represented by ijk where k is the rank of the letter in case ij. Then three digits that represent a position of the letter in the grid code this letter; we call this Code "Al Ghazal's Code". It is thought that this method was used to encrypt messages in the 18th century. There is no evidence, but we found poems that had been coded by this method in [2]. The idea of Al Ghazal's code is close to the idea of Rebecca code (1942) which is coding by a book used to write secret messages. We have developed in [6] a cryptosystem with public key based on the code of Al Ghazal. Our cryptosystem is poly-alphabetical system as Vegner's ciphering but it can be used as a private key system and as a public key system. The fact that the numerical code of a letter can be two different three integers is very useful because in this case we can encrypt the message with several ways; this can cause difficulties for a spy to break the cryptosystem. In addition, we don't use arithmetic operations which reduce the execution time of algorithms.

iv. **The secret Telegram writing.** The fourth method is the secret writing of Moroccan Telegram used in the late 19th century. It consisted in giving numerical values to the different letters of the alphabet and then transforming the clear (the plain) text by numerically encoding the letters and separating them by a point. The same numbers with a bar at the top codes the digits. In addition, numbers (see [10]), has coded some important names, words or sentences. The Moroccans had used this method at the end of the 19th century to write secret messages by telegram.

v. **Use of the function "Hissab Al Jommal" to sign, to leave a digital imprint or to encode the author's name.** Some poets especially in the poems of al-Malhoun used it. As an example, we found the Qasida of Al-Qadi (the poem of the Judge) "قصيدة القاضي" which is signed using Hissab Al-Jommal, by writing the number 254 at the end of the poem. The unique

possible solution from the names of Moroccan poets living at this time is
"Najjar" which satisfies equality $h(Najjar) = 254$.

دير نص التا وزيد معها خمس الكاف ** لأهل العقال الراجحين والغشما قلت حسابن

اسمى ما يخفى نظهره ما بين عشر الكاف ** ما بين عشر ضاد معزول فى الرمز أشكالنا

vi. **Use of signatures by steganography methods.** Steganography methods
was used to hide the letters of the author's name in a poem as the first letters
of verses of poetry or as the second letters of the words of a verse...The
example of the signature of Al Mahdi Ghazal is exactly the insertion of the
letters that compose his name within a verse of the poem. They were the
second letters of each word composing the verse. The verse is as follows:

واغفر إلاهي لمن له مدح **** فيه بغرب وزنه ذا الكرم

There exist other examples using this method in [5].

vii. **Use of special coding of numbers (Al Kalam al-Fassi).** This coding
was used by the judges and by the notaries for financial safeguarding or
inheritance acts against the possible forgeries (see Fig. 2. Fès Numbers). For
more information on his methods, see [4–7].

4   Encryption Using a Poetry

We use Al Khalil models of the Arabic poetry: there are 16 models; in each
model a verse of poetry is a composition of schemes which can divide the poetry
in 6 or 8 columns as in the next two model examples.

• فعولن مفاعيلن فعولن مفاعلن

فعولن مفاعيلن فعولن مفاعلن

• مستفعلن مستفعلن مفعولات

مستفعلن مستفعلن مفعولات

We note that in this step, by the phonetic transcription, some letters are
added (ن) and others are taken off (ا) (see [1]).

Binary Coding of Shemes. We agree to replace the consonants (المتحرك)
by 1 and the vowels (الساكن) by 0; so we have (Table 3)

In the model "Attaouil" the first one in the above two examples: each verse
has the next coding form

$$1010100 \quad 10100 \quad 1010100 \quad 10100$$
$$1010100 \quad 10100 \quad 1010100 \quad 10100$$

The poetry model is determined if the coding form of one verse is found
using the phonetic transcription. Using Al Ghazal coding on a poetry with ten
verses (distributed in grid with ten lines and eight or six column's); we can
transform every clear message to a sequence of integers (each letter is represented
by its code) which is an encryption of the message. The decryption is the inverse
operation. Precisely, using Al Khalil models, we code every letter by a three digit

Table 3. Binary coding of shemes

shemes	Binary codes	shemes	Binary codes
فعولن	10100	مستفعلن	1001010
فاعلن	10010	فاعلاتن	1010010
مفاعلتن	1000100	مفعولات	010101010
متفاعلن	1001000	فاع لاتن	1010010
مفاعيلن	1010100	مستفع لن	1001010

numbers ijk. The first digit number i from 0 to 9, is the line's number in the grid of the verse of the poem that contains the letter. The second digit number j, from 1 to 8, is the column's number in the grid of the scheme in the verse written in the form of schemes; whereas the third digit number k, from 0 to 6, is the rank of the letter in the scheme of the verse inserted in the grid's case ij. The encryption and the decryption are based on the poetry and the decryption: the poetry is the key of encryption and the key of the decryption. We construct a Data Base that contains a large number of poetries with ten verses and having a form of Al Khalil models; we index the poetries from 1 to $p - 1$, where p is a large prime number. We use Diffie-Hellman exchange method of keys based on the multiplicative group $(\mathbb{Z}/p\mathbb{Z})^*$ so Ali et Bachir can choose their secret key: it is an integer between 1 and $p - 1$.

- Ali Encrypt his message using Al Ghazal Coding defined by their secret key,
- Bachir decrypt his message using Al Ghazal Coding defined by their secret key,
- A letter can be coded with different codes and one can encrypt a message with different manners, so we cannot broke this cryptosystem using frequency analysis.
- Diffie-Hellman key-exchange protocol can be implemented with other cyclic groups in which the Diffie-Hellman protocol is difficult as an elliptic curve group.
- The complexity of the Diffie-Hellman key-exchange protocol is exponential.
- The drawback of this cryptosystem is that the cipher text is longer than the plaintext.

Depending on the model, a scheme in the grid's case ij, is a set of n letters, where $4 < n < 8$. If $n = 4$, then we can't have $ij5$, $ij6$ and $ij7$. The same think for the model where we have only six columns in the grid; we cannot have $i7k$ and $i8k$. So the model of the poetry that is the key determine the ijk that cannot be a code of a letter coded using the key and Al Ghazal coding algorithm. Then we can define a steganography method using this idea:

- We encrypt a message using our method using Al Ghazal Coding with Al Khalil poetry key,
- We insert a numbers in the form $ij5$, $ij6$ and $ij7$ or $i7k$ and $i8k$, if this forms exist,

- We send the message,
- The recipient, using his key can pick up all the numbers in the form $ij5$, $ij6$ and $ij7$ or $i7k$ and $i8k$. He can't doing this if he hasn't the key,
- After the last stipe, he can then decrypt the message using Al Ghazal Code.

Example

We shose the next poetry as Key with two line only for sinplicity

هوَ البين حتّى لاسلامٌ وَلا راذٌ = وَلانظرةٌ يُقضى بِها حقّه الوَجد

لقد تاعب الوَابور بالبين بينهِم = فساروا وَلازاموا جمالا وَلا شدّو

Then we give the Key rwinten in Al Khalil Models Table 4. The key written in Al Khalil Model "Attaouil"

Table 4. The key written in Al Khalil Model "Attaouil"

ه ولبي	ن حتتلا	س لامن	و لارادن	و لانظ	ر ةنيقضى	ب هاحق	ق هلوجدن
ل قدتا	ع بلوابو	ر بلبي	ن بينيهم	ف سارو	و لازامو	ج مالا	و لاشددو

Clair message

اضاعوني واي الفتيان اضاعوا

Encryption

052123120162060651520531241341131501321741341141230630531261201240650 32

Steganographical message with the hidden numbers in red

0520171230161202361623450651520535751241341131504361321741342361141 23
063536053126036120124236065032226

The receiver of the message, using the key, determines the model of the poetry and thus can remove all the triplets that cannot represent a letter with the key. Then he determines letters that are represented by the remaining triplets. The sender could use a permutation before sending the message; in this case the receiver will have to apply the inverse of the permutation before using the poetry. In this case, the key is poetry and permutation.

5   Conclusions

Moroccans had used the factorization of an integer in a product of two integers in cryptography or steganography algorithms; they had used various codes or different secret key methods. With the advent of the new computing technologies, these methods can be improved and can resist more attacks.

The method using factorization can take advantage of computers Calculus and become simpler to use while the method using "Al Ghazal Code" can withstand the machinery of quantum computers.

Annex: Examples of Moroccan Manuscripts

See Figs. 1, 3 and 4.

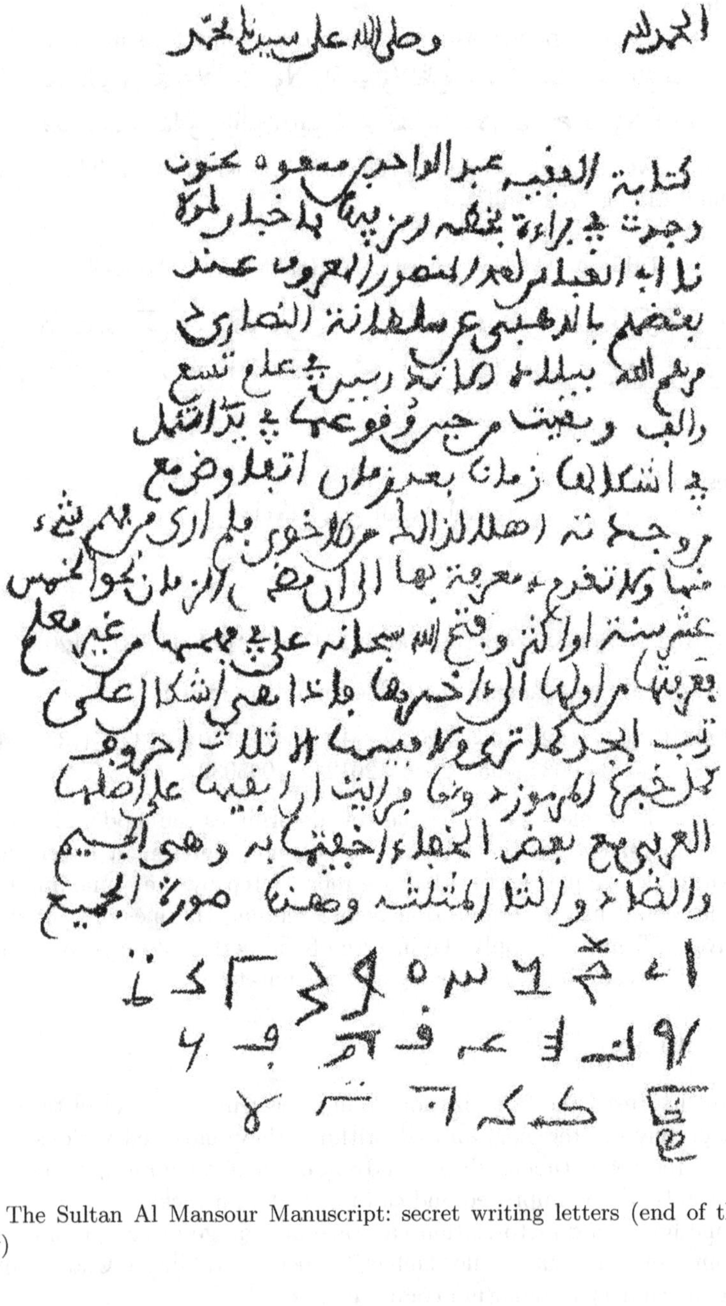

Fig. 1. The Sultan Al Mansour Manuscript: secret writing letters (end of the 16th century)

Fig. 2. Fès Numbers Manuscript

40مد 13مد هنـى 38مـا 1مد	51ل 44د نـقـى 63د 34د	46ز 46مـ زهـى 51مـ 48مـ	16ى 43ب بـرى 27ر 63ر		1ى 45ى ذكى 3ذ 52ى	38ر 7ر رضـى 28ض 32ر	27ى 1ع حفـى 4ح 19ع	49ر 42ر ولا...ى 29ر 6ر
64ل 49ل جلـى 1ل 47ل	2ل 50م صدوق 23م62ر	47ل 64د أديـب 6ل 2ل	15ع 56ب بحيـب 41ح33ب		39ع 62ب منيـب 39د 18ع	53ل 59ل أريـب 24ل 5ل	4ل 5ل لبيـب 59ل43ب	45ع32ى غنـى 33ع31ع
43ل 48ل أبـى 30ل 35ل	52ع 41د بديـع 64ب42ع	3ر 53ل وحيـد 3د 17ر	56مـ58مـ همـام 58ل 4مـ		18ل 4ل أميـر 26ل 29ل	14ل 37ل أغـرّ 40ر 20ل	57ر 25ر صفوح 53ر 7ر	41د 24مـ هـدى 18ى64مـ
44ل 31ل ملـى 31ل 16ع	19ل 14ل لبيـب 25ل 46ل	8ع 3د مَجيـد 2ع 28ع	21ر 20ر ود و د 17ر 23ر		29ل 17ل إمـام 34ل 8ل	28د 35د مُجيـد 7ع 44د	50ن22ن منيـف 32ع 30ع	7ى 27ر سـرى 35ر21ر
63ى33ر سنـى 61د 41د	11د 23د مفيـد 55د36ر	55ن34ى ظريـف 16ر 9ن	13ل 61ل أميـن 21ل 45ل		60ز 10ع أعـزّ 13ل 27ل	12د 26د نسيـب 15د 22د	23د11ب نجيـب 12د 11د	38د 16د نجـى 11ح50د
20ع 29ع مضى 42ى 60ع	31ر 8ر رشيـد 20ر15ر	37ب51ح حميـد 36ب24ح	6د 9د حسيـب 46د 39د		22ع 38ع بحيـر 19ع 10ع	61ح 60ع بحـاب 56ح 51ل	33ل 28ل أجـل 9ل 54ل	10ى18ى صفـى 8ى 56ى
24ى21ح حبى 62ذ37ح	30ع 52ب مصيـب 54مـ40مـ	26ع 55ح أخَيـد 45ل 59ل	17ر 2ع كريـم 22ر 14ك		62ع 54ع مهيـب 37ب53ع	35ع15ت مثيـب 47ع 26ع	34ح39ح حبيـب 14ر49ب	32مـ19مـ بـوى 50ب12ب
36د 12د نـدى 44د 58د	25د 36د نمـى 60ع 61د	9ر 40ع كمـى 57ع 38ع	54ع 6ع سمـى 49ك25ك		48ل 47ر رلـى 48ل 57ل	59ع 63ح علـى 10ل13ح	5ح 57ى سخـى 5ر 52ى	42ى30ح وعـى 43ر 55ح

(4) عرم بالأصل .

Fig. 3. Ahmad Al Ghazal(..-1777) Manuscript: coding using poetry in Morocco

Fig. 4. Secret writing Manuscript for Telegram (end of the 19 century)

References

1. Azakri, A.: Aerodah Programm determining Al Khalil Models for the Arabic Poetry. http://azahou45.free.fr/Accueil.htm
2. Al Iraki, A.: Ahmed El-Ghazal literary papers, رسائل أحمد الغزال الأدبية Imprimerie Info-Print, Fès Maroc (1999)
3. Al-Kadi, I.A.: Origins of cryptology: the Arab contributions. Cryptologia **16**(2), 97–126 (1992)
4. Azizi, A., Azizi, M.: Instance of Arabic cryptography in Morocco. Cryptologia **35**(1), 41–51 (2011)
5. Azizi, A., Azizi, M.: Instance of Arabic cryptography in Morocco II. Cryptologia **37**(4), 328–337 (2013)
6. Azizi, A.: Java cryptographical application based on Arabic poetry. In: 2012 IEEE International Conference on Computer Systems and Industrial Informatics, ICCSII 2012, 6454486 (2012)
7. Azizi, A.: Steganographical application based on Al Khalil Models of poetry. In: 2017 IEEE Joint International Conference on Information and Communication Technologies for Education and Training and International Conference on Computing in Arabic, ICCA-TICET 2017, 8095293 (2017)
8. Kahn, D.: The Codebreakers: The Story of Secret Writing. Macmillan, New York (1967)
9. Mrayati, M., Alam, M.Y., At-Tayyan, M.H.: Arabic Origins of Cryptology, vol. 1–5. Published by KFCRIS and KACST, Riyadh (2003)
10. Tazi, A.: Les Codes Secrets des correspondances Marocaines à travers l'histoire. Librairie Almaarif Aljadida, Rabat (1983)
11. Shakiry, A.S.: Arabic Numerals. T.C.P.H. Ltd. Publisher, London (2009). Registration N 1645411

An AEAD Variant of the Grain Stream Cipher

Martin Hell[1], Thomas Johansson[1(✉)], Willi Meier[2], Jonathan Sönnerup[1], and Hirotaka Yoshida[3]

[1] Department of Electrical and Information Technology, Lund University, Lund, Sweden
{martin.hell,thomas.johansson,jonathan.sonnerup}@eit.lth.se
[2] FHNW, Windisch, Switzerland
willi.meier@fhnw.ch
[3] Cyber Physical Security Research Center (CPSEC), National Institute of Advanced Industrial Science and Technology (AIST), Tokyo, Japan
hirotaka.yoshida@aist.go.jp

Abstract. A new Grain stream cipher, denoted Grain-128AEAD is presented, with support for authenticated encryption with associated data. The cipher takes a 128-bit key and a 96-bit IV and produces a pseudo random sequence that is used for encryption and authentication of messages. The design is based on Grain-128a but introduces a few changes in order to increase the security and protect against recent cryptanalysis results. The MAC is 64 bits, as specified by the NIST requirements in their lightweight security standardization process.

Keywords: Grain · Stream cipher · AEAD · NIST

1 Introduction

Due to widespread usage of Internet of Things (IoT) technology, the need of protection from security threats on resource-constrained devices has been continuously growing. Since 2003, the cryptography community has already recognized the importance of this need, and researchers and developers have focused on cryptography tailored to limited computation resources in hardware and software implementations. This has resulted in opening up a new subfield of cryptography, namely, lightweight cryptography, which led to the launch of the eSTREAM project. This project running from 2004 to 2008 can be viewed as the most important research activity in the area of lightweight stream ciphers. The eSTREAM portfolio contains four software-oriented ciphers and three hardware-oriented ciphers.

M. Hell, T. Johansson and J. Sönnerup—This work was in part financially supported by the Swedish Foundation for Strategic Research, grant RIT17-0032 and grant RIT17-0005.

© Springer Nature Switzerland AG 2019
C. Carlet et al. (Eds.): C2SI 2019, LNCS 11445, pp. 55–71, 2019.
https://doi.org/10.1007/978-3-030-16458-4_5

From an industrial point of view, it has been widely recognized that *maturity* is important regarding deployment of cryptographic mechanisms. In fact, the ISO/IEC 18033-1 [32] standard states this property as one criteria for inclusion of cryptographic mechanisms. The concept behind this it that, if cryptographic mechanisms are standardized, they should be in the public domain for many years. In this way, security and performance analysis of them can be performed by third parties, which would give the users a significant amount of confidence in security. The above mentioned eSTREAM project activity affected industry: one of the eSTREAM portfolio cipher, Trivium [14], is standardized in the lightweight stream cipher standard, ISO/IEC 29192-3 [31] together with Enocoro [48]. Grain-128a, which is based on the eSTREAM portfolio cipher Grain v1, is standardized in ISO/IEC 29167-13 [33] for the RFID application standard.

Despite of the above extensive academic and industry efforts, there is still an important gap to fill. There has been no authenticated encryption with associated data (AEAD) mechanism that meets very severe performance requirements in hardware and still offers 128-bit security, accompanied by serious evidence on cryptanalysis. In 2013, NIST initiated a lightweight cryptography project, followed by two workshops on the same subject. In 2017, NIST published a call for submissions for lightweight cryptographic mechanisms. One remarkable feature is that NIST requires each submission to implement the AEAD functionality. In [9], it was shown that lightweight stream ciphers are typically more suitable than lightweight block ciphers for energy optimization when encrypting longer messages, in particular when the speed can be increased at the expense of moderate extra hardware. Thus, a lightweight stream cipher seems to be a good starting point for a lightweight AEAD design.

This paper presents Grain-128AEAD, an authenticated encryption algorithm with support for associated data. The specification is in line with the requirements given by NIST and is based on the Grain stream cipher family. More specifically, it is closely based on Grain-128a, introduced in 2011, which has, already for several years, been analyzed in the literature. To benefit from the maturity of the Grain family, our strategy in the design of Grain-128AEAD is to have the changes made to Grain-128a as small as possible. Grain-128a is in turn based on Grain v1 and Grain-128, which have both been extensively analyzed, providing much insight into the security of the design approach. All Grain stream ciphers also allow the throughput to be increased by adding additional copies of the Boolean functions involved.

Industrial relevance of the Grain family can be explained as follows: Grain-128a receives a lot of attention from industry. ISO/IEC 29167-13:2015 specifying Grain-128a has been adopted in industrial applications. For instance, the passive IT70 RFID tag [30] that Honeywell has designed for automotive applications implements this security standard.

The outline of the paper is as follows. In Sect. 2 the specification of the new primitive is given. Then the overall design rationale, motivating the design choices, are given in Sect. 3. A security analysis, focusing on cryptanalysis of

Grain-128a is then given in Sect. 4. The hardware implementation is described in Sect. 5 and the paper is concluded in Sect. 6.

2   Design Details

Grain-128AEAD consists of two main building blocks. The first is a pre-output generator, which is constructed using a Linear Feedback Shift Register (LFSR), a Non-linear Feedback Shift Register (NFSR) and a pre-output function, while the second is an authenticator generator consisting of a shift register and an accumulator. The design is very similar to Grain-128a, but has been modified to allow for larger authenticators and to support AEAD. Moreover, the modes of usage have been updated.

2.1   Building Blocks and Functions

The pre-output generator generates a stream of pseudo-random bits, which are used for encryption and the authentication tag. It is depicted in Fig. 1. The content of the 128-bit LFSR is denoted $S_t = [s_0^t, s_1^t, \ldots, s_{127}^t]$ and the content of the 128-bit NFSR is similarly denoted $B_t = [b_0^t, b_1^t, \ldots, b_{127}^t]$. These two shift registers represent the 256-bit state of the pre-output generator.

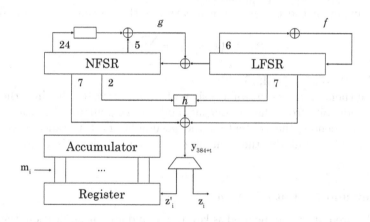

Fig. 1. An overview of the building blocks in Grain-128AEAD.

The primitive feedback polynomial of the LFSR, defined over GF(2) and denoted $f(x)$, is defined as

$$f(x) = 1 + x^{32} + x^{47} + x^{58} + x^{90} + x^{121} + x^{128}.$$

The corresponding update function of the LFSR is given by

$$s_{127}^{t+1} = s_0^t + s_7^t + s_{38}^t + s_{70}^t + s_{81}^t + s_{96}^t$$
$$= \mathcal{L}(S_t).$$

The nonlinear feedback polynomial of the NFSR, denoted $g(x)$ and also defined over $GF(2)$, is defined as

$$g(x) = 1 + x^{32} + x^{37} + x^{72} + x^{102} + x^{128} + x^{44}x^{60} + x^{61}x^{125}$$
$$+ x^{63}x^{67} + x^{69}x^{101} + x^{80}x^{88} + x^{110}x^{111} + x^{115}x^{117}$$
$$+ x^{46}x^{50}x^{58} + x^{103}x^{104}x^{106} + x^{33}x^{35}x^{36}x^{40}$$

and the corresponding update function is given by

$$b_{127}^{t+1} = s_0^t + b_0^t + b_{26}^t + b_{56}^t + b_{91}^t + b_{96}^t + b_3^t b_{67}^t + b_{11}^t b_{13}^t$$
$$+ b_{17}^t b_{18}^t + b_{27}^t b_{59}^t + b_{40}^t b_{48}^t + b_{61}^t b_{65}^t + b_{68}^t b_{84}^t$$
$$+ b_{22}^t b_{24}^t b_{25}^t + b_{70}^t b_{78}^t b_{82}^t + b_{88}^t b_{92}^t b_{93}^t b_{95}^t$$
$$= s_0^t + \mathcal{F}(B_t).$$

Nine state variables are taken as input to a Boolean function $h(x)$. Two of these bits are taken from the NFSR and seven are taken from the LFSR. The function is defined as

$$h(x) = x_0 x_1 + x_2 x_3 + x_4 x_5 + x_6 x_7 + x_0 x_4 x_8,$$

where the variables $x_0, \ldots, x_8$ correspond to, respectively, the state variables $b_{12}^t, s_8^t, s_{13}^t, s_{20}^t, b_{95}^t, s_{42}^t, s_{60}^t, s_{79}^t$ and s_{94}^t.

The output of the pre-output generator, is then given by the pre-output function

$$y_t = h(x) + s_{93}^t + \sum_{j \in \mathcal{A}} b_j^t,$$

where $\mathcal{A} = \{2, 15, 36, 45, 64, 73, 89\}$.

The authenticator generator consists of a shift register, holding the most recent 64 odd bits from the pre-output, and an accumulator. Both are of size 64 bits. We denote the content of the accumulator at instance i as $A_i = [a_0^i, a_1^i, \ldots, a_{63}^i]$. Similarly, the content of the shift register is denoted $R_i = [r_0^i, r_1^i, \ldots, r_{63}^i]$.

2.2   Key and IV Initialization

Before the pre-output can be used as keystream and for authentication, the internal state of the pre-output generator and the authenticator generator registers are initialized with a key and IV. Denote the key bits as k_i, $0 \le i \le 127$ and the IV bits as IV_i, $0 \le i \le 95$. Then the state is initialized as follows. The 128 NFSR bits are loaded with the bits of the key $b_i^0 = k_i$, $0 \le i \le 127$ and the first 96 LFSR elements are loaded with the IV bits, $s_i^0 = IV_i$, $0 \le i \le 95$. The last 32 bits of the LFSR are filled with 31 ones and a zero, $s_i^0 = 1, 96 \le i \le 126$, $s_{127}^0 = 0$. Then, the cipher is clocked 256 times, feeding back the pre-output function and XORing it with the input to both the LFSR and the NFSR, i.e.,

$$s_{127}^{t+1} = \mathcal{L}(S_t) + y_t, \quad 0 \le t \le 255,$$
$$b_{127}^{t+1} = s_0^t + \mathcal{F}(B_t) + y_t, \quad 0 \le t \le 255.$$

Once the pre-output generator has been initialized, the authenticator generator is initialized by loading the register and the accumulator with the pre-output keystream as

$$a_j^0 = y_{256+j}, \qquad 0 \le j \le 63,$$
$$r_j^0 = y_{320+j}, \qquad 0 \le j \le 63.$$

When the register and the accumulator are initialized, the key is simultaneously shifted into the LFSR,

$$s_{127}^{t+1} = \mathcal{L}(S_t) + k_{t-256}, \quad 256 \le t \le 383,$$

while the NFSR is updated as

$$b_{127}^{t+1} = s_0^t + \mathcal{F}(B_t), \quad 256 \le t \le 383.$$

Thus, when the cipher has been fully initialized the LFSR and the NFSR states are given by S_{384} and B_{384}, respectively, and the register and accumulator are given by R_0 and A_0, respectively. The initialization procedure is summarized in Fig. 2.

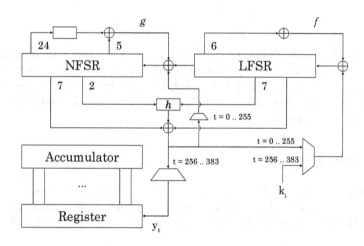

Fig. 2. An overview of the initialization in Grain-128AEAD. Note that, in hardware, the accumulator initialization is realized by first loading 64 pre-output bits into the register, followed by moving them to the accumulator.

2.3   Operating Mode

For a message $\boldsymbol{m}$ of length L, denoted $m_0, m_1, \ldots, m_{L-1}$, set $m_L = 1$ as padding in order to ensure that $\boldsymbol{m}$ and $\boldsymbol{m}\|0$ have different tags.

After initializing the pre-output generator, the pre-output is used to generate keystream bits z_i for encryption and authentication bits z_i' to update the register in the accumulator generator. The keystream is generated as

$$z_i = y_{384+2i},$$

i.e., every even bit (counting from 0) from the pre-output generator is taken as a keystream bit. The authentication bits are generated as

$$z_i' = y_{384+2i+1},$$

i.e., every odd bit from the pre-output generator is taken as an authentication bit. The message is encrypted as

$$c_i = m_i \oplus z_i, \quad 0 \le i < L.$$

The accumulator is updated as

$$a_j^{i+1} = a_j^i + m_i r_j^i, \quad 0 \le j \le 63, \quad 0 \le i \le L,$$

and the shift register is updated as

$$r_{63}^{i+1} = z_i',$$
$$r_j^{i+1} = r_{j+1}^i, \quad 0 \le j \le 62.$$

An AEAD scheme allows for data that is authenticated, but unencrypted. Grain-128AEAD achieves this simply by explicitly setting $y_{384+2i} = 0$ for bits that should not be encrypted, but should still be authenticated. This means that it is possible to control the associated data on bit level, and this data can appear anywhere in the message.

3   Design Rationale

This section presents a short overview of the Grain stream ciphers and how the design has evolved through the different versions. It also enumerates and discusses the differences between Grain-128a and the proposed Grain-128AEAD.

3.1   A Short History of the Grain Family of Stream Ciphers

The Grain family of stream ciphers are based on the idea behind the nonlinear filter generator. In a nonlinear filter, an LFSR is used to provide a sequence with large period, and a nonlinear function, taking parts of the LFSR sequence as input, is used to add nonlinearity to the keystream sequence. Much work has been put into analyzing the nonlinear filter generator and it is clear that it is very difficult to design a secure nonlinear filter generator with a reasonable hardware footprint [13]. In particular algebraic attacks have been shown to be very strong against this design, see e.g., [17,41].

In order to better withstand algebraic attacks, and to make the relation between state/key and keystream more complex, Grain adds an NFSR to the nonlinear combiner. The initial submission to the ECRYPT eSTREAM project was analyzed in [10,37], showing that the nonlinear functions required higher resiliency and nonlinearity. The modified design was subsequently published as Grain v1 [28] and was later selected for the final portfolio in eSTREAM. Grain v1 uses an 80-bit key, and a 128-bit key variant was proposed in [27]. Based on previous results on the Grain construction, Grain-128 was more aggressively designed, making the nonlinear NFSR feedback function of degree 2, but with high nonlinearity and resiliency. The relatively small functions compensated for the fact that the shift registers were increased to 128 bits each, which increased the hardware footprint. The low degree functions were exploited in [3,44] in order to cryptanalyze a significant number of initializations rounds. These results suggested that the nonlinear functions needed a higher security margin. Grain-128a was proposed in [50], and in addition to increasing the degree of the nonlinear feedback function, an optional authentication mode was added. Work on Grain-128 were subsequently improved [19–21,35], emphasizing the need for more complex Boolean functions, and Grain-128 is considered broken and should not be used. The design proposed in this paper, Grain-128AEAD, is closely based on Grain-128a, using the same feedback and output functions. However, slight modifications have been made in order to add security and make it resistant to the attack proposed in [46].

3.2 Differences Between Grain-128AEAD and Grain-128a

Grain-128AEAD takes Grain-128a as starting point, but introduces a number of slight modifications. The modifications are primarily motivated by the NIST Lightweight Cryptography Standardization Process, but inspiration also comes from recent results in [25,46].

Larger MACs. The register and the authenticator has been increased to 64 bits (instead of 32 bits) in order to allow for authentication tags (MACs) of size 64 bits.

No Encryption-Only Mode. Grain-128a allowed for an operation mode with only encryption, where the authentication was removed. This mode resulted in smaller hardware footprint since the two additional registers, and their associated logic, could be left out from an implementation. The encryption-only mode was also more efficient since the initialization process does not include initializing the register and the accumulator, and every pre-output bit was used as keystream. The proposed Grain-128AEAD is a pure authenticated encryption algorithm, and authentication of data is always supported. Thus, there is only one mode of operation.

Initialization Hardening. Based on the ideas in [25] and used in Lizard [26], Grain-128AEAD re-introduces the key into the internal state during the initialization clock cycles. More specifically, it is serially shifted into the LFSR in parallel to the initialization of the register and the accumulator. Several variants can be considered here, including where and when to add the key. The LFSR is chosen due to the fact that if the LFSR is recovered (e.g., in a fast correlation attack as in [46]), it is comparably easy to recover the NFSR state. Moreover, since the LFSR output is XORed with the NFSR input, the key bits will continue to affect also the NFSR during pre-output generation. As for when, we choose to re-introduce it during the last 128 clocks of the initialization. This provides maximum separation between its first introduction in the key loading part, where the key is loaded into the NFSR, and when it is re-introduced. Relations between keys are e.g., more difficult to exploit if the key is properly mixed into the state before the key is re-introduced.

By introducing the key as the last part of the initialization, we achieve the attractive effect that a state recovery attack does not immediately imply key recovery, as was the case for previous versions of Grain. While a state recovery would still render the cipher to be considered broken, the practical effect to deployed devices is highly limited. Recovering the state will only compromise the security of the current message, and not all messages using the same key.

Keystream Limitation. Grain stream ciphers have been designed to allow for encrypting large chunks of data using the same key/IV pair. Previously, the Grain ciphers have not had any explicit limitation on the keystream length. However, to rule out attacks that use very large keystream sequences, Grain-128AEAD restricts the number of keystream bits for each key/IV to 2^{80}. We believe that this is well above what will be needed in the foreseeable future. Restricting the number of keystream bits will also make attacks that use linear approximations more difficult, e.g., [46].

4 Security Analysis

The security of the Grain family of stream ciphers has been investigated by a large number of third party analysts, publishing various analysis results on the different variants of Grain. Since its first introduction in 2005, much have been learned about the construction and the design approach. There have also been several published ciphers inspired by the design, e.g., Sprout [2] and its successor Plantlet [42]. Also Fruit [23] and Fruit-80 [1] are based on the same design idea. These ciphers have in common that they attempt to realize extremely resource constrained encryption. To minimize the hardware footprint, the key is assumed to be stored in non-volatile memory (NVM) on a device, and this memory is made part of the cryptographic algorithm. Since the key needs to be stored on a device anyway, using the key directly from NVM in the algorithm does not impose additional hardware to the construction. This is not the case for Grain, as we allow the key to be updated in the device, and the key storage is not a part of the cipher. Still, the fact that the above mentioned ciphers use the Grain design idea shows that the design seems to be very suitable for lightweight cryptography.

4.1 General Security Analysis

A main class of attacks on stream ciphers is the Time/Memory/Data tradeoff (TMD-TO) attack, an efficient method of finding either the key or the state of ciphers by balancing between time, memory and keystream data. This can sometimes be much more efficient and more practically applicable than a simple exhaustive key search attack. Some stream ciphers are vulnerable to TMD-TO attacks and their effective key lengths could then be reduced. This typically happens if the state size is too small. A famous practical TMD-TO attack on A5/1 was given in [12].

A TMD-TO attack consists of two parts. The first is a preprocessing phase, during which a table is constructed. The mapping of different keys or internal states to some keystream segment is computed and stored in the table. It is sorted on keystream segments and this process is assumed to use time complexity P and memory M. In the second (real-time) phase, the attacker has intercepted D keystream segments and search for a collision with the table with time complexity T. A collision will recover the corresponding input. By a tradeoff between parameters P, D, M, and T, attackers can devise attacks according to available time, memory and data. Examples of tradeoffs are Babbage-Golic (BG) [4,24] and Biryukov-Shamir (BS) [11] with curves $TM = N$, $P = M$ with $T \leq D$; and $MT^2D^2 = N^2$, $P = N/D$ with $T \geq D^2$, where N is the input space, respectively.

For Grain-128AEAD, attackers have no direct way to reconstruct the internal state, since the cipher has an internal state of size 256 bits (128-bit LFSR + 128-bit NFSR), i.e. $N = 2^{256}$. The best attack complexity achieved under BG tradeoff is with $T = M = D = N^{1/2} = 2^{128}$, which is not favourable compared to exhaustive key search. Also the BS tradeoff does not give complexity parameters of particular interest. Some improvements to TMD-TO attacks can be achieved through so called BSW sampling [12] and the performance of such an approach is characterized by the sampling resistance of the stream cipher. Various generalizations of the concept of sampling resistance can be considered, e.g. [34], but it seems unlikely that this will lead to an attack with better performance than a standard Hellman-type time-memory tradeoff attack on the keyspace, a generic attack applicable to any cipher. Also, our limit on the length of keystreams affects such attacks.

Another class of general attacks are algebraic attacks, where the attacker derives a system of nonlinear equations in unknown key bits or unknown state bits and then solves the system. In general, solving a system of nonlinear equations is not known to be solvable in polynomial time, but there might be special cases that can be solved efficiently [16]. Due to the NFSR, the degree of the equations will gradually increase and it does not look promising to try to derive a system of nonlinear equations due to this property as well as the algebraic degree of the h function.

A general cryptanalytic technique is a guess-and-determine attack, where one guesses parts of the state and then from the keystream tries to determine other parts of the state. The goal is to guess as few positions as possible and determine as many as possible from equations involving the keystream. Again, since the dependence between a keystream symbol and the state includes many different positions in the state and some of them in nonlinear expressions, one has to guess a large portion of state variables in order to use an equation to determine a single state variable.

Being a binary additive stream cipher, Grain-128AEAD does not allow reuse of a key/IV pair since this will leak information about the corresponding plaintexts. Moreover, since Grain-128AEAD closely resembles Grain-128a, a key/IV pair used in one cipher may also not be reused in the other. Such cross-cipher key/IV reuse in a related cipher model is outside the security model of Grain-128AEAD.

In the subsequent subsections, we now describe the attacks that we consider as the main threat against lightweight stream ciphers in general and Grain-128AEAD in particular.

4.2   Correlation Attacks

Grain-128a was designed to resist conventional (fast) correlation attacks that exploit correlations between the state of the LFSR and the corresponding key stream. There has been devised a fast correlation attack on small state Grain-like stream ciphers in [49]. Due a much bigger state, this attack does not apply to Grain-128a. On the other hand, a recent paper [46] reveals that there are multiple linear approximations in Grain-128a that together with a viewpoint based on a finite field allow a fast correlation attack on the raw encryption mode of Grain-128a (and on the other members of the Grain family), where every keystream bit is assumed to be accessible by an opponent. This attack recovers the state of Grain-128a with data and time complexity of about 2^{114}. The data needs to come from the same secret key and the same IV.

It should be noted that this fast correlation attack does not apply to Grain-128a in authentication mode, as then only every second key stream bit may be accessible to an opponent. Thus, it does not apply to Grain-128AEAD.

4.3   Chosen IV Attacks

A variety of chosen IV attacks on Grain have been proposed, in both fixed key scenario as well as in the related key setting, and either for distinguishing purpose or for key recovery. In a fixed key scenario, chosen IV attacks have been devised on reduced-round versions using conditional differentials and using cube attacks, or combinations of both [22,38–40]. On Grain-128, a dynamic cube attack has been developed that succeeds in finding the secret key for the full 256-round initialization for a fraction of keys, [19]. Dynamic cube attacks have not been successful on Grain-128a thus far. Most of these results are experimental in nature, and do work only if the computational effort is practically feasible.

More recently, division property has been developed to improve cube attacks. Division property is an iterated technique for integral distinguishers introduced by Todo, in [45] and was applied initially to block ciphers. It turned out that it also applies to the initialization of stream ciphers, not only for distinguishers but also for key recovery. As opposed to conventional cube attacks, it can provide theoretical results. The latest result on Grain-128a in this direction is a key recovery on 184 initialization rounds, [47]. The data complexity is 2^{95}, and the computational complexity corresponds to about 2^{110} operations.

An attack that reaches the largest number of initialization rounds of Grain-128a in a fixed key scenario thus far is a conditional differential distinguishing attack and reaches 195 initialization rounds, but it works only for a fraction of all keys, [40].

The relevance of related key cryptanalysis of stream ciphers has been a subject of debate. A related key attack on Grain-128a in [18] recovers the secret key with a computational complexity 2^{96}, requiring 2^{96} chosen IVs and about 2^{104} keystream bits. It requires only 2 related keys. Another related key attack in [8] recovers the secret key using 2^{64} chosen IVs and 2^{32} related keys, where these figures need to be multiplied by some factor (about 2^{8}). Due to the modified initialization procedure, related key attacks on Grain-128AEAD are expected to be less efficient than those against Grain-128a.

4.4 Fault Attacks

In the scenario of fault attacks on stream ciphers, the attacker is allowed to inject faults into the internal state, which means either flipping a binary value in memory or assigning a value to zero. By analyzing the difference in keystreams for the faulty and the fault-free case, one attempts to deduce the complete or some partial information about the internal state or the secret key. Fault attacks on stream ciphers have recently received some attention, starting with the work of Hoch and Shamir [29]. The most common methods of injecting faults is by using laser or through clock glitches. Fault attacks usually rely on assumptions that is beyond the model of cryptanalysis and for this reason one can often find rather efficient fault attacks on most ciphers. In some scenarios they are, however, not unrealistic and the exact complexity and the related requirements are of interest to study.

Fault attacks on the Grain family of stream ciphers were studied in [15] and [36]. More recently, there was a number of papers providing improved attacks, [5–7,43]. In [43] the model is the most realistic one as it considers that the cipher has to be re-initialized only a few times and faults are injected to any random location and at any random clock cycle. No further assumptions are needed over location and timing for injections. In the attack one constructs algebraic equations based on the description of the cipher by introducing new variables so that the degrees of the equations do not increase. Following algebraic cryptanalysis, such equations based on both fault-free and faulty key-stream bits are collected. Then a solving phase using the SAT Solver recovers the state of any Grain member in minutes, For Grain v1, Grain-128 and Grain-128a, it uses only 10, 4 and 10 injected faults, respectively.

We stress that we are not claiming resistance against fault attacks for Grain-128AEAD. Rather, when fault attacks is a realistic threat, one has to implement protection mechanisms against fault injection.

5   Implementation

Lightweight ciphers are important in constrained devices. A minimal design is desirable, e.g., minimum area and very low power consumption since they often must operate for an extended period of time, without a battery change. In some cases, devices run without its own power supply, something that is often the case with RFID tags.

Table 1. The gate count for different functions.

Function	Gate count
NAND2	1.0
NAND3	1.5
NAND4	2.0
XOR2	2.5
XOR3	6.5
Flip flop	8.0

Grain-128AEAD can be constructed using primitive hardware building blocks, such as NAND gates, XOR gates and flip flops. In order to get an idea of the hardware footprint related to an implementation of the cipher, we implement the stream cipher using 65 nm library from ST Microelectronics, stm065v536. For synthesis and power simulation, the Synopsys Design Compiler 2013.12 is used. It can be noted that the result is highly dependent on what kind of gates are available and how the tool utilizes the standard cells. We define a 2-input NAND gate to have a gate count of 1 and other gate counts are given in relation to this NAND gate. An excerpt from the standard-cell library documentation is given in Table 1.

We synthesize the design and extract the gate count for each building block. A summary of the gate count for each building block, and for different parallelization levels, is given in Table 2. The control logic and accumulator logic is extra circuitry and state machines for controlling the stream cipher, i.e., loading key and IV, multiplexing data, etc.

The gate count remains constant during synthesis, but the physical area, power and speed changes based on the optimization techniques employed. First,

Table 2. Gate count for the different building blocks, for different levels of parallelization, s.

Building block	Gate count		
	$s = 1$	$s = 2$	$s = 32$
LFSR	1024	1024	1024
NFSR	1024	1024	1024
f	19	38	608
g	62.5	125	2000
h	41.5	83	1328
Control logic	219.5	475.5	942.5
Accumulator	512	512	512
Register	512	512	512
Accumulator logic	224	224	4160
Total	3638.5	4017.5	12110.5

Table 3. Implementation results running at 100 kHz, for different levels of parallelization.

Parallelization	Area	Power	Throughput
1	$4934\,\mu m^2$	313 nW	50 kbit/s
2	$5336\,\mu m^2$	368 nW	100 kbit/s
32	$16853\,\mu m^2$	574 nW	1600 kbit/s

we synthesize the design at clock frequency 100 kHz. The design is synthesized for three levels of parallelization; 1, 2, and 32 times. The result is given in Table 3.

We also synthesize for the maximum possible speed, to achieve maximum throughput, without constraints on area. The results are given in Table 4.

Table 4. Implementation results running at maximum possible speed, for different levels of parallelization.

Parallelization	Speed	Area	Power	Throughput
1	1.12 GHz	$5258\,\mu m^2$	3.6 mW	560 Mbit/s
2	1.18 GHz	$5629\,\mu m^2$	4.3 mW	1.18 Gbit/s
32	662 MHz	$17632\,\mu m^2$	4.0 mW	10.59 Gbit/s

6   Conclusions

We have presented Grain-128AEAD, a new cipher in the Grain family. It is closely based on Grain-128a and takes advantage of the well-analyzed design principle behind the Grain stream ciphers. By making slight modifications to Grain-128a, the cipher meets the requirements in the NIST lightweight standardization process, providing 64-bit MAC, 128-bit key and 96-bit IV. The hardware footprint makes the cipher well suited for constrained environments, but the design is flexible enough to allow for also very high speed requirements at the expense of additional hardware.

A   Test Vectors

Here, we give some test vectors for different keys, IVs, and messages. The test vectors are given in hexadecimal, e.g., the key

$$0x01234FFFFFFFFFFFFFFFFFFFFFFFFFFFFF$$

corresponds to

$$(k_0, ..., k_{127}) = (0,0,0,0,0,0,0,1,0,0,1,0,0,0,1,1,0,1,0,0,1,...,1).$$

The message stream is given with the padding included. A padding bit of 1 equals a padding byte of 0x80. Note that for an empty message, the message stream is just the padding.

```
Key:        0x00000000000000000000000000000000
IV:         0x000000000000000000000000
Keystream:  0xc800a52f948b89b85cee6cfd8571f90f
Message:    0x80
Tag:        0xaab555c073e67664

Key:        0x0123456789abcdef123456789abcdef0
IV:         0x0123456789abcdef12345678
Keystream:  0xc2b918c6baf6dea0865200d46858a37b
Message:    0xFF80
Tag:        0x782f4c4a8907ba7f
```

References

1. Amin Ghafari, V., Hu, H.: Fruit-80: a secure ultra-lightweight stream cipher for constrained environments. Entropy **20**(3), 180 (2018)
2. Armknecht, F., Mikhalev, V.: On lightweight stream ciphers with shorter internal states. In: Leander, G. (ed.) FSE 2015. LNCS, vol. 9054, pp. 451–470. Springer, Heidelberg (2015). https://doi.org/10.1007/978-3-662-48116-5_22
3. Aumasson, J.P., Dinur, I., Henzen, L., Meier, W., Shamir, A.: Efficient FPGA implementations of high-dimensional cube testers on the stream cipher Grain-128. In: SHARCS 2009 Special-purpose Hardware for Attacking Cryptographic Systems, p. 147 (2009)
4. Babbage, S.: Improved "exhaustive search" attacks on stream ciphers. In: IET Conference Proceedings, pp. 161–166(5), January 1995

5. Banik, S., Maitra, S., Sarkar, S.: A differential fault attack on Grain-128a using MACs. In: Bogdanov, A., Sanadhya, S. (eds.) SPACE 2012. LNCS, pp. 111–125. Springer, Heidelberg (2012). https://doi.org/10.1007/978-3-642-34416-9_8

6. Banik, S., Maitra, S., Sarkar, S.: A differential fault attack on the grain family of stream ciphers. In: Prouff, E., Schaumont, P. (eds.) CHES 2012. LNCS, vol. 7428, pp. 122–139. Springer, Heidelberg (2012). https://doi.org/10.1007/978-3-642-33027-8_8

7. Banik, S., Maitra, S., Sarkar, S.: A differential fault attack on the grain family under reasonable assumptions. In: Galbraith, S., Nandi, M. (eds.) INDOCRYPT 2012. LNCS, vol. 7668, pp. 191–208. Springer, Heidelberg (2012). https://doi.org/10.1007/978-3-642-34931-7_12

8. Banik, S., Maitra, S., Sarkar, S., Meltem Sönmez, T.: A chosen IV related key attack on Grain-128a. In: Boyd, C., Simpson, L. (eds.) ACISP 2013. LNCS, vol. 7959, pp. 13–26. Springer, Heidelberg (2013). https://doi.org/10.1007/978-3-642-39059-3_2

9. Banik, S., et al.: Towards low energy stream ciphers. IACR Trans. Symmetric Cryptol. **2018**(2), 1–19 (2018)

10. Berbain, C., Gilbert, H., Maximov, A.: Cryptanalysis of grain. In: Robshaw, M. (ed.) FSE 2006. LNCS, vol. 4047, pp. 15–29. Springer, Heidelberg (2006). https://doi.org/10.1007/11799313_2

11. Biryukov, A., Shamir, A.: Cryptanalytic time/memory/data tradeoffs for stream ciphers. In: Okamoto, T. (ed.) ASIACRYPT 2000. LNCS, vol. 1976, pp. 1–13. Springer, Heidelberg (2000). https://doi.org/10.1007/3-540-44448-3_1

12. Biryukov, A., Shamir, A., Wagner, D.: Real time cryptanalysis of A5/1 on a PC. In: Goos, G., Hartmanis, J., van Leeuwen, J., Schneier, B. (eds.) FSE 2000. LNCS, vol. 1978, pp. 1–18. Springer, Heidelberg (2001). https://doi.org/10.1007/3-540-44706-7_1

13. Braeken, A., Lano, J.: On the (Im)possibility of practical and secure nonlinear filters and combiners. In: Preneel, B., Tavares, S. (eds.) SAC 2005. LNCS, vol. 3897, pp. 159–174. Springer, Heidelberg (2006). https://doi.org/10.1007/11693383_11

14. Cannière, C.D., Preneel, B.: Trivium. New Stream Cipher Designs - The eSTREAM Finalists, pp. 244–266 (2008)

15. Castagnos, G., et al.: Fault analysis of GRAIN-128. In: IEEE International Workshop on (HST) Hardware-Oriented Security and Trust, pp. 7–14 (2009)

16. Courtois, N., Klimov, A., Patarin, J., Shamir, A.: Efficient algorithms for solving overdefined systems of multivariate polynomial equations. In: Preneel, B. (ed.) EUROCRYPT 2000. LNCS, vol. 1807, pp. 392–407. Springer, Heidelberg (2000). https://doi.org/10.1007/3-540-45539-6_27

17. Courtois, N.T.: Fast algebraic attacks on stream ciphers with linear feedback. In: Boneh, D. (ed.) CRYPTO 2003. LNCS, vol. 2729, pp. 176–194. Springer, Heidelberg (2003). https://doi.org/10.1007/978-3-540-45146-4_11

18. Ding, L., Guan, J.: Related key chosen IV attack on Grain-128a stream cipher. IEEE Trans. Inf. Forensics Secur. **8**(5), 803–809 (2013)

19. Dinur, I., Güneysu, T., Paar, C., Shamir, A., Zimmermann, R.: An experimentally verified attack on full Grain-128 using dedicated reconfigurable hardware. In: Lee, D.H., Wang, X. (eds.) ASIACRYPT 2011. LNCS, vol. 7073, pp. 327–343. Springer, Heidelberg (2011). https://doi.org/10.1007/978-3-642-25385-0_18

20. Dinur, I., Shamir, A.: Breaking Grain-128 with dynamic cube attacks. In: Joux, A. (ed.) FSE 2011. LNCS, vol. 6733, pp. 167–187. Springer, Heidelberg (2011). https://doi.org/10.1007/978-3-642-21702-9_10

21. Fu, X., Wang, X., Chen, J., Stevens, M.: Determining the nonexistent terms of non-linear multivariate polynomials: how to break Grain-128 more efficiently. IACR Cryptol. ePrint Archive **2017**, 412 (2017)
22. Ghafari, V.A., Hu, H.: A new chosen IV statistical attack on Grain-128a cipher. In: 2017 International Conference on Cyber-Enabled Distributed Computing and Knowledge Discovery (CyberC), pp. 58–62. IEEE (2017)
23. Ghafari, V.A., Hu, H., Xie, C.: Fruit: ultra-lightweight stream cipher with shorter internal state. eSTREAM, ECRYPT Stream Cipher Project (2016)
24. Golić, J.D.: Cryptanalysis of alleged A5 stream cipher. In: Fumy, W. (ed.) EURO-CRYPT 1997. LNCS, vol. 1233, pp. 239–255. Springer, Heidelberg (1997). https://doi.org/10.1007/3-540-69053-0_17
25. Hamann, M., Krause, M.: On stream ciphers with provable beyond-the-birthday-bound security against time-memory-data tradeoff attacks. Cryptogr. Commun. **10**(5), 959–1012 (2018)
26. Hamann, M., Krause, M., Meier, W.: Lizard-a lightweight stream cipher for power-constrained devices. IACR Trans. Symmetric Cryptol. **2017**(1), 45–79 (2017)
27. Hell, M., Johansson, T., Maximov, A., Meier, W.: A stream cipher proposal: Grain-128. In: 2006 IEEE International Symposium on Information Theory, pp. 1614–1618. IEEE (2006)
28. Hell, M., Johansson, T., Meier, W.: Grain: a stream cipher for constrained environments. Int. J. Wirel. Mob. Comput. **2**(1), 86–93 (2007)
29. Hoch, J.J., Shamir, A.: Fault analysis of stream ciphers. In: Joye, M., Quisquater, J.-J. (eds.) CHES 2004. LNCS, vol. 3156, pp. 240–253. Springer, Heidelberg (2004). https://doi.org/10.1007/978-3-540-28632-5_18
30. Honeywell: IT70 Secure Passive RFID Tag. Technical Specifications (2017). https://www.honeywellaidc.com/products/rfid/tags-labels/it70
31. ISO/IEC 29192-3:2012 information technology - security techniques - lightweight cryptography - part 3: Stream ciphers (2012)
32. ISO/IEC 18033-1:2015 information technology - security techniques - encryption algorithms - part 1: General (2015)
33. ISO/IEC 29167-13:2015 information technology – automatic identification and data capture techniques – part 13: Crypto suite Grain-128A security services for air interface communications (2015)
34. Jiao, L., Zhang, B., Wang, M.: Two generic methods of analyzing stream ciphers. In: Lopez, J., Mitchell, C.J. (eds.) ISC 2015. LNCS, vol. 9290, pp. 379–396. Springer, Cham (2015). https://doi.org/10.1007/978-3-319-23318-5_21
35. Karlsson, L., Hell, M., Stankovski, P.: Not so greedy: enhanced subset exploration for nonrandomness detectors. In: Mori, P., Furnell, S., Camp, O. (eds.) ICISSP 2017. CCIS, vol. 867, pp. 273–294. Springer, Cham (2018). https://doi.org/10.1007/978-3-319-93354-2_13
36. Karmakar, S., Roy Chowdhury, D.: Fault analysis of Grain-128 by targeting NFSR. In: Nitaj, A., Pointcheval, D. (eds.) AFRICACRYPT 2011. LNCS, vol. 6737, pp. 298–315. Springer, Heidelberg (2011). https://doi.org/10.1007/978-3-642-21969-6_19
37. Khazaei, S., Hasanzadeh, M.M., Kiaei, M.S.: Linear sequential circuit approximation of Grain and Trivium stream ciphers. IACR Cryptol. ePrint Archive **2006**, 141 (2006)
38. Knellwolf, S., Meier, W., Naya-Plasencia, M.: Conditional differential cryptanalysis of NLFSR-based cryptosystems. In: Abe, M. (ed.) ASIACRYPT 2010. LNCS, vol. 6477, pp. 130–145. Springer, Heidelberg (2010). https://doi.org/10.1007/978-3-642-17373-8_8

39. Lehmann, M., Meier, W.: Conditional differential cryptanalysis of Grain-128a. In: Pieprzyk, J., Sadeghi, A.-R., Manulis, M. (eds.) CANS 2012. LNCS, vol. 7712, pp. 1–11. Springer, Heidelberg (2012). https://doi.org/10.1007/978-3-642-35404-5_1

40. Ma, Z., Tian, T., Qi, W.F.: Conditional differential attacks on Grain-128a stream cipher. IET Inf. Secur. **11**(3), 139–145 (2016)

41. Meier, W., Pasalic, E., Carlet, C.: Algebraic attacks and decomposition of Boolean functions. In: Cachin, C., Camenisch, J.L. (eds.) EUROCRYPT 2004. LNCS, vol. 3027, pp. 474–491. Springer, Heidelberg (2004). https://doi.org/10.1007/978-3-540-24676-3_28

42. Mikhalev, V., Armknecht, F., Müller, C.: On ciphers that continuously access the non-volatile key. IACR Transaction Symmetric Cryptology, pp. 52–79 (2016)

43. Sarkar, S., Banik, S., Maitra, S.: Differential fault attack against Grain family with very few faults and minimal assumptions. IEEE Trans. Comput. **64**(6), 1647–1657 (2015)

44. Stankovski, P.: Greedy distinguishers and nonrandomness detectors. In: Gong, G., Gupta, K.C. (eds.) INDOCRYPT 2010. LNCS, vol. 6498, pp. 210–226. Springer, Heidelberg (2010). https://doi.org/10.1007/978-3-642-17401-8_16

45. Todo, Y.: Structural evaluation by generalized integral property. In: Oswald, E., Fischlin, M. (eds.) EUROCRYPT 2015. LNCS, vol. 9056, pp. 287–314. Springer, Heidelberg (2015). https://doi.org/10.1007/978-3-662-46800-5_12

46. Todo, Y., Isobe, T., Meier, W., Aoki, K., Zhang, B.: Fast correlation attack revisited. In: Shacham, H., Boldyreva, A. (eds.) CRYPTO 2018. LNCS, vol. 10992, pp. 129–159. Springer, Cham (2018). https://doi.org/10.1007/978-3-319-96881-0_5

47. Wang, Q., Hao, Y., Todo, Y., Li, C., Isobe, T., Meier, W.: Improved division property based cube attacks exploiting algebraic properties of superpoly. In: Shacham, H., Boldyreva, A. (eds.) CRYPTO 2018. LNCS, vol. 10991, pp. 275–305. Springer, Cham (2018). https://doi.org/10.1007/978-3-319-96884-1_10

48. Watanabe, D., Owada, T., Okamoto, K., Igarashi, Y., Kaneko, T.: Update on Enocoro stream cipher. In: 2010 International Symposium on Information Theory its Applications, pp. 778–783, October 2010

49. Zhang, B., Gong, X., Meier, W.: Fast correlation attacks on Grain-like small state stream ciphers. IACR Trans. Symmetric Cryptol. **2017**(4), 58–81 (2017)

50. Ågren, M., Hell, M., Johansson, T., Meier, W.: Grain-128a: a new version of Grain-128 with optional authentication. Int. J. Wirel. Mob. Comput. **5**(1), 48–59 (2011)

Construction for a Nominative Signature Scheme from Lattice with Enhanced Security

Meenakshi Kansal$^{(\boxtimes)}$, Ratna Dutta, and Sourav Mukhopadhyay

Department of Mathematics, Indian Institute of Technology Kharagpur,
Kharagpur, India
{kansal,ratna,sourav}@maths.iitkgp.ernet.in

Abstract. The existing secure nominative signature schemes are all based on bilinear pairings and are secure only on classical machines. In this paper, we present the *first* lattice based nominative signature scheme. The security of our scheme relies on the hardness of short integer solution (SIS) and learning with error (LWE) problems for which no polynomial time quantum algorithms exist till now. Consequently, our scheme is the *first* nominative signature scheme that withstand quantum attacks. Furthermore, we propose *stronger* security models for unforgeability and invisibility and prove our construction achieve these enhanced security. Besides, our scheme exhibits impersonation and non-repudiation following standard security model. We emphasis that the security analysis against all the security attributes for our scheme are in standard model except the security against malicious nominator which uses random oracle.

Keywords: Lattice based cryptography · Nominative signature ·
Unforgeability · Invisibility · Non-repudiation

1 Introduction

A nominative signature scheme, introduced by Kim et al. [6], is an important cryptographic primitive which enables a nominator to select a nominee and produce a nominative signature corresponding to the nominee. Moreover, *only* the nominee can prove (convince) the validity of a nominative signature to a verifier. A nominative signature should satisfy the following security attributes − unforgeability, invisibility, non-impersonation and non-repudiation. Unforgeability ensures that a nominator or a nominee cannot produce a valid nominative signature alone while invisibility features that the verification of a nominative signature can be performed by nominee only. Non-impersonation guarantees that only the nominee can prove (convince) the validity of a nominative signature to a verifier. Non-repudiation holds certain control on the nominee. It ensures that inspite of having the ability of verification and checking validity of a nominative

© Springer Nature Switzerland AG 2019
C. Carlet et al. (Eds.): C2SI 2019, LNCS 11445, pp. 72–91, 2019.
https://doi.org/10.1007/978-3-030-16458-4_6

signature, the nominee cannot deceive a verifier by proving the validity of an invalid nominative signature or invalidity of a valid nominative signature.

Nominative signature has several practical applications in user identification system, banking, insurance, mobile communication etc. For instance, suppose a government body (nominator) certifies and issues signature on passport of a countryman (nominee) who requests for it. Nominative signature scheme can be an ideal cryptographic primitive to handle this situation by producing a mutual agreement (nominative signature) between the government body and the countryman. The government body cannot make false claims on the countryman and vice versa if the scheme is unforgeable. The invisibility property of the scheme permits only the countryman to verify whether the issued passport contains all the correct details or not. Impersonation allows only the countryman to prove (convince) to the airport authority (verifier) that the passport belongs to him/her. Moreover, if the countryman has a fake (or an original) passport then he should not be able to mislead the airport authority by proving the fake passport to be an original (or an original passport to be a fake) passport. This feature is ensured by non-repudiation.

Related Work: Nominative signature was introduced by Kim et al. [6] in 1996 based on Schnorr's signature and claimed to be secure under the hardness of discrete logarithm problem. However, the scheme is found flawed by Huang and Wang [5] in 2004. The concept of convertible nominative signature was introduced in [5]. They also proposed a construction for convertible nominative signature which is proven to be insecure in [15].

The formal definition and security model for a nominative signature was introduced by Liu et al. [10] in 2007 along with a nominative signature scheme. This construction is based on Chaum's undeniable signature and is secure under the hardness of computational Diffie-Hellman problem, decisional Diffie-Hellman problem and discrete logarithm problem. The scheme requires multi-round of communication between a nominator and a nominee for the signature generation. A more efficient design for nominative signature was proposed by Liu et al. [9] using ring signature with one round of communication between a nominator and a nominee. This construction is proven to be secure under the discrete logarithm assumption and computational Diffie-Hellman assumption. However, the schemes [9,10] exhibit the weak invisibility in the sense that the nominator does not take part in generating of some valid signatures.

Huang et al. [4] proposed a stronger security model by introducing stronger invisibility with an extra feature of considering nominator as an adversary. They designed a one-round nominative signature scheme which achieves security in this stronger security model. They proposed a security model stronger that of [4] by proposing a stronger unforgeability where adversary generates the challenge public nominee key. Together with the model of stronger unforgeability they have constructed a nominative signature scheme which is proven to be secure in this stronger security model.

The works of [4,14] are the only secure nominative signature schemes so far on the classical machine. Both these schemes use bilinear pairing. The scheme in [4] uses witness indistinguishable and is proven secure in the random oracle model under the hardness of weak discrete logarithm problem, weak Diffie-Hellman problem, bilinear Diffie-Hellman exponent problem, weak computational Diffie-Hellman (WCDH)-I problem and WCDH-II problem. It is an efficient scheme as it requires only one-round of communication between a nominator and a nominee to generate a nominative signature. The number of bilinear pairings used in the generation of the nominative signature is 3. The nominator's public-secret keys, nominee's public-secret keys all have size $|\mathbb{G}|$, nominative signature is of size $4|\mathbb{G}|$, communication cost is $|\mathbb{G}|$. On the other hand, the scheme in [14] uses zero knowledge proof of knowledge and is proven secure in the standard model under the hardness of discrete logarithm problem and discrete linear problem. It also requires only one-round of communication between a nominator and a nominee to generate a nominative signature and it uses 3 bilinear pairings in the generation of the nominative signature. The nominator's public-secret keys, nominee's public-secret keys are of size $(n+3)|\mathbb{G}|$, $|\mathbb{G}|$, $(n+6)|\mathbb{G}|$ and $(n+3)|\mathbb{G}|$ respectively, nominative signature is of size $4|\mathbb{G}|$, communication cost is $2|\mathbb{G}|$ where $|\mathbb{G}|$ is the bit size of an element of the group $\mathbb{G}$.

As there is a threat on the reality of quantum machine, a modern public key cryptosystem is required to withstand quantum attacks. Cryptosystems based on hash functions, lattices, codes, multivariate polynomials, isogenies etc are secure on the quantum machine. Lattice based cryptography is one of the most promising tools for the post quantum era as it offers security under worst-case intractability assumptions, efficient parallel computations and homomorphic computation in addition to the apparent resistance to quantum attacks. Although a number of cryptographic primitives have been designed using lattice, till now there are no lattice-based construction for nominative signature.

Our Contribution: In this paper, we propose a security model for the nominative signature scheme which is stronger than the models proposed in [4,14]. Further, we construct the *first lattice based* nominative signature scheme which achieves security in this stronger security model under the hardness of short integer solution (SIS) problem [1] and learning with error (LWE) problem [13]. More precisely, we note the following:

– At a high level, we design a nominative signature by employing the decomposition extension technique of Ling et al. [8] and integrate the non-interactive zero knowledge argument system of Libert et al. [7]. In our construction, the public key of a nominator or a nominee is a matrix $\mathbf{S} \in \mathbb{Z}_q^{n \times m}$ and the secret key $\mathsf{T}_\mathbf{S} \in \mathbb{Z}^{m \times m}$ is a short basis of the lattice $\Lambda_q^\perp(\mathbf{S}) = \{\mathbf{x} : \mathbf{Sx} = \mathbf{0} \bmod q\}$ where q, n, m are integers and $m = poly(n)$. The nominator can choose a nominee. The nominee, in turn, proves its identity to the nominator by issuing a signature Sig to the nominator which contains a non-interactive zero knowledge proof Π. The proof Π proves to the nominator that the nominee has the knowledge of a vector $\mathbf{y} \in \mathbb{Z}_q^m$ satisfying an equation of the form $\mathbf{Py} = \mathbf{v} \bmod q$. Here $\mathbf{P} \in \mathbb{Z}_q^{n \times m}$ and $\mathbf{v} \in \mathbb{Z}_q^n$ are suitably formed using the decomposition-extension technique and are publicly computable. After suitably verifying Sig, the nominator issues the nominative signature nsig which consists of a short solution $\mathbf{x}$ of an equation of the form $\mathbf{Ax} = \mathbf{b} \bmod q$ where $\mathbf{A}, \mathbf{b}$ are publicly available. The nominative signature nsig can be verified by the nominee and the validity (or invalidity) can be proven to the verifier only by the nominee using the confirmation protocol (or disavowal protocol).

- We propose a security model which is stronger than the security of [4,14] by exhibiting stronger unforgeability against malicious nominee, stronger unforgeability against malicious nominator together with stronger invisibility. Similar to [14], the security against impersonation in our model is included in the unforgeability against malicious nominator while non-repudiation follows the model of [4]. The unforgeability in our model is stronger in the following sense.

    (i) The forger is allowed to query for the signature on the forged tuple $(M^*, \mathsf{NE}, \mathsf{NR})$ only ones. Here M^* is the message on which the forged nominative signature nsig* is produced, NE is the malicious (or uncorrupted) nominee and NR is the uncorrupted (or malicious) nominator corresponding to nsig* for unforgeability against malicious nominee (or against malicious nominator). This query is not permitted in the security model of [4,14].

    (ii) Besides, the forger is provided the flexibility to choose the honest nominator NR (or the honest nominee NE) from all the uncorrupted nominators (or nominees) to achieve unforgeability against malicious nominees (or malicious nominators). In [4,14], honest nominee or honest nominator are chosen by the challenger.

    (iii) Additionally, the forger can corrupt nominator and nominees by querying their secret keys which is not permitted in the security model of [14].

    (iv) Furthermore, similar to [14], the forger is allowed to query for a proof for the validity or invalidity of the signature Sig (or nsig) issued by a honest nominee (or a honest nominator).

- Like [4,14] our scheme also offers non-transferability which ensures that the verifier cannot convince (or disavow) a third party that the verifier received a valid (or invalid) signature on a given message from the nominee. It follows from the combination of invisibility and zero knowledge argument system.

- We also achieve a stronger invisibility as our model gives the choice to the adversary to choose the honest nominee for the challenge query which is not permitted in [4,14].

- Our scheme is proven to be secure in this stronger security model. We achieve unforgeability against malicious nominee under the hardness of SIS search problem. The invisibility is obtained under the hardness of SIS decision problem and LWE problem. Non-repudiation follows from the completeness and soundness properties of the non-interactive zero knowledge argument system of [7]. Our security analysis is in the standard model without using any random oracles. However, we attain unforgeability against malicious nominator in the random oracle model under the hardness of SIS search problem. As mentioned earlier, we cover non-impersonation in the unforgeability against malicious nominator.

- In our scheme, the public key of a user (nominator or nominee) is a matrix $\mathbf{S} \in \mathbb{Z}_q^{n \times m}$ and the secret key $\mathsf{T}_{\mathbf{S}} \in \mathbb{Z}^{m \times m}$ is a short basis of the lattice $\Lambda_q^\perp(\mathbf{S}) = \{\mathbf{x} : \mathbf{Sx} = \mathbf{0} \bmod q\}$ where q, n, m are integers and $m = poly(n)$. Consequently, the size of user's public key and secret key is $\widetilde{\mathcal{O}}(n^2)$ each. On the other hand, the nominative signature in our scheme is $\mathsf{nsign_{NR}} = (\mathbf{z}, \mathbf{y}_1)$ where $\mathbf{z} \in \mathbb{Z}_q^m$ and $\mathbf{y}_1 \in \mathbb{Z}_q^n$. Therefore the size of the nominative signature is $\widetilde{\mathcal{O}}(n)$. The Sig issued by the nominee to prove his identity to the nominator is $\mathsf{Sig} = (\Pi, \mathbf{y}_1)$ where $\Pi = (\{\mathsf{COM}\}_{\gamma=1}^s, \mathsf{Ch}, \{\mathsf{RSP}\}_{\gamma=1}^s)$ is the proof of knowledge of a vector $\mathbf{y} \in \mathbb{Z}_q^m$ satisfying an equation of the form $\mathbf{Py} = \mathbf{v} \bmod q$. This implies that the communication cost for the non-interactive zero knowledge proof is $s \cdot |\mathsf{COM}| + s \cdot |\mathsf{RSP}| + s$. Here COM is the commitment function used by the nominee to produce a commitment about the knowledge of $\mathbf{y}$ to the nominator and RSP is the response on this commitment COM depending on the challenge Ch and $|\mathsf{RSP}| = \mathcal{O}(L)$, $L = 6(m+1)p$, $p = \lfloor \log_2 \beta \rfloor + 1$, $\beta = 2\sigma\sqrt{m}$ and σ is the standard deviation of the discrete Gaussian distribution.

2 Preliminaries

Notations. Here we define some basic terminology for our work. Throughout this paper, a vector $\mathbf{a} \in \mathbb{S}^n$ denotes a column vector of dimension $n \times 1$ with entries from the set $\mathbb{S}$. For $\mathbf{u} = (u_1, u_2, \ldots, u_n) \in \mathbb{R}^n$, $||\mathbf{u}||_\infty = \max_i |u_i|$ denotes the maximum norm and $||\mathbf{u}|| = \sqrt{u_1^2 + u_2^2 + \ldots + u_n^2}$ stands for the Euclidean norm. Let $\mathbf{A} = (\mathbf{a}_1, \mathbf{a}_2, \ldots, \mathbf{a}_m)$ be a matrix with m columns in $\mathbb{R}^n$ then $||\mathbf{A}|| = \max_{1 \le i \le m} ||\mathbf{a}_i||$. The notation $\mathbf{A} \hookleftarrow \Delta$ implies $\mathbf{A}$ is a matrix following the distribution Δ and $\mathbf{A}^t$ represents the transpose of the matrix $\mathbf{A}$. We refer $||$ for the concatenation of matrices and also for the concatenation of vectors. We say that a function f is negligible in λ if $f = \lambda^{-\omega(1)}$.

Definition 1 (Lattice). *For any $m \ge n$, let $\mathbf{B} = \{\mathbf{b}_1, \mathbf{b}_2, \cdots, \mathbf{b}_m\}$ be any linearly independent set of vectors in $\mathbb{R}^n$. A lattice generated by the set $\mathbf{B}$ is defined as $\Lambda(\mathbf{B}) = \{\sum_{b_i \in B} c_i \mathbf{b}_i : c_i \in \mathbb{Z}\}$ with basis $\mathbf{B}$.*
For $q \in \mathbb{N}$, matrix $\mathbf{A} \in \mathbb{Z}_q^{n \times m}$ and vector $\mathbf{u} \in \mathbb{Z}_q^n$, we define the following three q-ary lattices generated by $\mathbf{A}$: $\Lambda_q^\perp(\mathbf{A}) = \{\mathbf{x} \in \mathbb{Z}^m : \mathbf{Ax} = \mathbf{0} \bmod q\}$, $\Lambda_q^{\mathbf{u}}(\mathbf{A}) = \{\mathbf{x} \in \mathbb{Z}^m : \mathbf{Ax} = \mathbf{u} \bmod q\}$, $\Lambda_q(\mathbf{A}) = \{\mathbf{x} \in \mathbb{Z}^m : \mathbf{A}^t\mathbf{s} = \mathbf{x} \bmod q, \text{for some } \mathbf{s} \in \mathbb{Z}_q^n\}$, where m, n are integers with $m \ge n \ge 1$ and $\mathbf{0}$ is a zero vector of size $n \times 1$.

Definition 2 (Gaussian distribution over a lattice). *For a lattice Λ and a real number $\sigma > 0$, discrete Gaussian distribution over Λ centered at $\mathbf{0}$, denoted by $D_{\Lambda,\sigma}$, is defined as: $\forall \mathbf{y} \in \Lambda$, $D_{\Lambda,\sigma}[\mathbf{y}] \sim exp(-\pi||\mathbf{y}||^2/\sigma^2)$, i.e. $D_{\Lambda,\sigma}[\mathbf{y}]$ is proportional to $exp(-\pi||\mathbf{y}||^2/\sigma^2)$ where $D_{\Lambda,\sigma}[\mathbf{y}]$ means the vector $\mathbf{y} \hookleftarrow D_{\Lambda,\sigma}$. We say that $D_{\Lambda,\sigma}$ is a distribution with standard deviation σ.*

Lemma 1. *For any n-dimensional lattice Λ and for any real number $\sigma > 0$, we have the following results and probabilistic polynomial time (PPT) algorithms:*

(i) $Pr_{b \hookleftarrow D_{\Lambda,\sigma}}[\|\boldsymbol{b}\| \leq \sigma\sqrt{n}] \geq 1 - 2^{-\Omega(n)}$, *i.e. if $\boldsymbol{b} \hookleftarrow D_{\Lambda,\sigma}$ then $\|\boldsymbol{b}\| \leq \sigma\sqrt{n}$ with overwhelming probability.*

(ii) $\mathsf{TrapGen}(n, m, q) \longrightarrow (\boldsymbol{A}, \mathsf{T}_{\boldsymbol{A}})$ *[2]. This randomized algorithm outputs a matrix $\boldsymbol{A} \in \mathbb{Z}_q^{n \times m}$ and a short basis $\mathsf{T}_{\boldsymbol{A}} \in \mathbb{Z}^{m \times m}$ of $\Lambda_q^{\perp}(\boldsymbol{A})$ such that $\boldsymbol{A}$ is within the statistical distance $2^{-\Omega(n)}$ to $U(\mathbb{Z}_q^{n \times m})$ and $\|\widetilde{\mathsf{T}}_{\boldsymbol{A}}\| \leq \mathcal{O}(\sqrt{n \log q})$. Here $U(\mathbb{Z}_q^{n \times m})$ is the uniform distribution of integer matrices over $\mathbb{Z}_q$ of order $n \times m$ and $\widetilde{\mathsf{T}}_{\boldsymbol{A}}$ is the Gram-Schmidt orthogonalization of $\mathsf{T}_{\boldsymbol{A}}$.*

(iii) $\mathsf{SampleD}(\mathsf{T}_{\boldsymbol{A}}, \boldsymbol{A}, \boldsymbol{u}, \sigma) \longrightarrow (\boldsymbol{x})$ *[12]. Given a matrix $\boldsymbol{A} \in \mathbb{Z}_q^{n \times m}$ whose columns span $\mathbb{Z}_q^n$, a basis $\mathsf{T}_{\boldsymbol{A}} \in \mathbb{Z}^{m \times m}$ of $\Lambda_q^u(\boldsymbol{A})$, a vector $\boldsymbol{u} \in \mathbb{Z}_q^n$ and a real number σ, this randomized algorithm returns a vector $\boldsymbol{x} \in \mathbb{Z}^m$ from the distribution $D_{\mathbb{Z}^m, \sigma}$ (i.e., $\|\boldsymbol{x}\| \leq \sigma\sqrt{m}$ by (i)) satisfying $\boldsymbol{A} \cdot \boldsymbol{x} = \boldsymbol{u} \bmod q$.*

2.1 Computational and Decisional Problems

Definition 3 (Inhomogeneous short integer solution (ISIS) search problem) [1]. *Given an integer q, a real number β, a matrix $\boldsymbol{A} \in \mathbb{Z}_q^{n \times m}$ and a vector $\boldsymbol{u} \in \mathbb{Z}_q^n$, the ISIS problem is to find an integer vector $\boldsymbol{e} \in \mathbb{Z}^m$ such that $\boldsymbol{A}\boldsymbol{e} = \boldsymbol{u} \bmod q$ with $\|\boldsymbol{e}\| \leq \beta$ with non-negligible probability. If $\boldsymbol{u} = \boldsymbol{0} \in \mathbb{Z}_q^n$, then it is known as short integer solution (SIS) problem.*

Definition 4 (Short integer solution (SIS) decision problem) [11]. *Let χ be a distribution over $\mathbb{Z}_q$ having samples of the form $(\boldsymbol{A}, \boldsymbol{A}\boldsymbol{s}) \in \mathbb{Z}_q^{n \times m} \times \mathbb{Z}_q^{n \times 1}$ with standard deviation σ where $\boldsymbol{A} \in \mathbb{Z}_q^{n \times m}$ is a matrix and $\boldsymbol{s} \in \mathbb{Z}_q^{m \times 1}$ is a vector with $\|\boldsymbol{s}\| \leq \sigma\sqrt{m}$. The decisional SIS is to decide whether $(\boldsymbol{A}, \boldsymbol{A}\boldsymbol{s})$ follows χ distribution or uniform distribution $U(\mathbb{Z}_q^{n \times m} \times \mathbb{Z}_q^n)$ with non-negligible probability.*

Definition 5 (Learning with errors (LWE) problem) [13]. *Let $n \geq 1$ be any integer, $p \geq 2$ be any prime and χ be a distribution on $\mathbb{Z}$. For any fixed vector $\boldsymbol{s} \in \mathbb{Z}_p^n$, given arbitrarily many samples of the form $(\boldsymbol{a}, \langle \boldsymbol{a}, \boldsymbol{s} \rangle + e)$ with $\boldsymbol{a}$ uniform in $\mathbb{Z}_p^n$ and e sampled from χ, the problem of finding $\boldsymbol{s}$ is called the search LWE and the problem of distinguishing the distribution of $(\boldsymbol{a}, \langle \boldsymbol{a}, \boldsymbol{s} \rangle + e)$ from the uniform distribution $U(\mathbb{Z}_p^n \times \mathbb{Z}_p)$ is called the decisional LWE. Here $\langle \boldsymbol{a}, \boldsymbol{s} \rangle = \boldsymbol{a}^t \boldsymbol{s}$.*

2.2 Zero Knowledge Argument System [7]

This section deals with the zero knowledge argument system when the prover wants to prove the knowledge of the witness $\mathbf{x}$ satisfying the relation $\mathbf{P}\mathbf{x} = \mathbf{v}$ without giving $\mathbf{x}$ to the verifier. Here $\mathbf{P}$ is any matrix and $\mathbf{v}$ is a vector (or matrix), both publicly available and $\mathbf{x}$ is prover's secret vector (or matrix) with some conditions to be proven in zero knowledge to the verifier.

Let $q \geq 2$ be any integer and D, L be two positive integers. We consider a set $\mathsf{VALID} \subseteq \{-1, 0, 1\}^L$. Similar to Libert et al. [7], let S be any finite set of permutations such that for any $\pi \in S$, one can associate a permutation T_π of L elements satisfying

(i) $\mathbf{x} \in$ VALID $\Leftrightarrow T_\pi(\mathbf{x}) \in$ VALID.

(ii) If $\mathbf{x} \in$ VALID and π is uniform in S then $T_\pi(\mathbf{x})$ is uniform in VALID.

A zero knowledge argument of knowledge (ZKAoK) for the relation $\mathcal{R} = \{(\mathbf{P}, \mathbf{v}) \in \mathbb{Z}_q^{D \times L} \times \mathbb{Z}_q^D, \mathbf{x} \in$ VALID $: \mathbf{Px} = \mathbf{v} \bmod q\}$ written as $((\mathbf{P}, \mathbf{v}), \mathbf{x}) \in \mathcal{R}$ is a 3-round protocol ZKAoK = (Commitment, Challenge, Response, Verification) between a prover and a verifier, both having access to $\mathbf{P}$ and $\mathbf{v}$ where ZKAoK.Commitment, ZKAoK.Challenge, ZKAoK.Response are PPT algorithms and ZKAoK.Verification is a deterministic algorithm with the following requirements:

1. ZKAoK.Commitment$(\mathbf{P}, \mathbf{v}, \mathbf{x}) \longrightarrow (\text{COM} = (C_1, C_2, C_3))$. The prover does the following:
   (a) It samples randomness ρ_1, ρ_2, ρ_3 for generating commitments and selects $\mathbf{r} \hookleftarrow U(\mathbb{Z}_q^L), \pi \hookleftarrow U(S)$ where S is a finite set of permutation.
   (b) It computes the commitment COM $= (C_1, C_2, C_3)$ where $C_1 = \text{CMT}_1(\pi, \mathbf{Pr}; \rho_1)$, $C_2 = \text{CMT}_2(T_\pi(\mathbf{r}); \rho_2)$, $C_3 = \text{CMT}_3(T_\pi(\mathbf{x} + \mathbf{r}); \rho_3)$ are generated using randomness ρ_1, ρ_2, ρ_3 respectively and the permutation T_π corresponding to π. Here CMT_i, $i = 1, 2, 3$, is statistically hiding and computationally binding commitment scheme such that the hiding property holds even against all-powerful receivers while the binding property holds only for polynomially bounded senders.
   (c) Finally, the prover sends the commitment COM to the verifier.
2. ZKAoK.Challenge$(\mathbf{P}, \mathbf{v}) \longrightarrow (\text{Ch} \hookleftarrow U(\{1, 2, 3\}))$. The verifier sends a challenge Ch $\hookleftarrow U(\{1, 2, 3\})$ to the prover.
3. ZKAoK.Response$(\text{Ch}, \rho_1, \rho_2, \rho_3, \pi, \mathbf{r}, \mathbf{x}) \longrightarrow (\text{RSP})$. The prover sends a response RSP computed as follows:
   (a) If Ch $= 1$ then the prover sets $\mathbf{t_x} = T_\pi(\mathbf{x})$, $\mathbf{t_r} = T_\pi(\mathbf{r})$ and RSP $= (\mathbf{t_x}, \mathbf{t_r}, \rho_2, \rho_3)$ using T_π associated with π.
   (b) If Ch $= 2$ then the prover sets $\pi_2 = \pi$, $\mathbf{y} = \mathbf{x} + \mathbf{r}$ and RSP $= (\pi_2, \mathbf{y}, \rho_1, \rho_3)$.
   (c) If Ch $= 3$ then the prover sets $\pi_3 = \pi$, $\mathbf{r}_3 = \mathbf{r}$ and RSP $= (\pi_3, \mathbf{r}_3, \rho_1, \rho_2)$.
4. ZKAoK.Verification$(\mathbf{P}, \mathbf{v}, \text{RSP}, \text{Ch}, \text{COM}) \longrightarrow (\text{VRF})$. On receiving the response RSP from the prover, the verifier uses the commitment scheme CMT_i, $i = 1, 2, 3$ and proceeds as follows:
   (a) If Ch $= 1$ then the verifier checks whether $\mathbf{t_x} \in$ VALID and $C_2 = \text{CMT}_2(\mathbf{t_r}; \rho_2)$, $C_3 = \text{CMT}_3(\mathbf{t_x} + \mathbf{t_r}; \rho_3)$ using RSP $= (\mathbf{t_x}, \mathbf{t_r}, \rho_2, \rho_3)$ and extracting C_2, C_3 from COM.
   (b) If Ch $= 2$ then the verifier checks whether $C_1 = \text{CMT}_1(\pi_2, \mathbf{Py} - \mathbf{v}; \rho_1)$ and $C_3 = \text{CMT}_3(T_{\pi_2}(\mathbf{y}); \rho_3)$ extracting C_1, C_3 from COM and using RSP $= (\pi_2, \mathbf{y}, \rho_1, \rho_3)$ together with the permutation T_{π_2} associated with π_2.
   (c) If Ch $= 3$ then the verifier checks whether $C_1 = \text{CMT}_1(\pi_3, \mathbf{Pr}_3; \rho_1), C_2 = \text{CMT}_2(T_{\pi_3}(\mathbf{r}_3); \rho_2)$ using C_1, C_2 obtained from COM, RSP $= (\pi_3, \mathbf{r}_3, \rho_1, \rho_3)$ and permutation T_{π_3} corresponding to π_3.
   In each case, the verifier outputs VRF $= 1$ if the verification succeeds; otherwise VRF $= 0$.

The above zero knowledge argument protocol satisfies the following three properties [7]:

Let VRF $\leftarrow$ ZKAoK.Verification (**P**, **v**, RSP, COM), RSP $\leftarrow$ ZKAoK.Response (Ch, ρ_1, ρ_2, ρ_3, π, **r**, **x**), COM $\leftarrow$ ZKAoK.Commitment (**P**, **v**, **x**) and Ch $\leftarrow$ ZKAoK.Challenge (**P**, **v**) where ρ_1, ρ_2, ρ_3, **r**, π are as selected in algorithm ZKAoK.Commitment(**P**, **v**, **x**) by the prover.

Correctness: If $((\mathbf{P}, \mathbf{v}), \mathbf{x}) \in \mathcal{R}$ then $Pr[\text{VRF} = 1] = 1$.

Soundness: If $((\mathbf{P}, \mathbf{v}), \mathbf{x}) \notin \mathcal{R}$ then $Pr[\text{VRF} = 1] \leq \text{negl}(\lambda)$ where $\text{negl}(\lambda)$ is a negligible function in λ.

Zero Knowledge: If the statement proven by the prover is true then the cheating verifier learns only the fact that the statement is true.

Remark 1. The above protocol is repeated $s = \omega(\log n)$ times to achieve negligible soundness error and can be made non-interactive using Fiat-Shamir heuristic [3] as a triple $\Pi = (\{\text{COM}_\gamma\}_{\gamma=1}^s, \text{Ch}, \{\text{RSP}_\gamma\}_{\gamma=1}^s)$ where $\text{Ch} = H(M, \{\text{COM}_\gamma\}_{\gamma=1}^s, \text{aux}) \in \{1,2,3\}^s$, M is a message, aux is some auxiliary information and $H : \{0,1\}^* \rightarrow \{1,2,3\}^s$ is a cryptographically secure hash function. The prover sends s commitments COM_γ, $\gamma = 1, 2, \ldots, s$ to the verifier who in turn sends the challenge $\text{Ch} = H(M, \{\text{COM}_\gamma\}_{\gamma=1}^s, \text{aux}) \in \{1,2,3\}^s$ to the prover treating the hash function H as a random oracle. At the end, the prover outputs response RSP_γ generated by executing ZKAoK.Response($\text{Ch}[\gamma], \rho_1^{(\gamma)}, \rho_2^{(\gamma)}$, $\rho_3^{(\gamma)}, \pi^{(\gamma)}, \mathbf{r}^{(\gamma)}, \mathbf{x}$) where $\text{Ch}[\gamma]$ is the γ-th digit of $\text{Ch} \in \{1,2,3\}^s$ and $\rho_1^{(\gamma)}$, $\rho_2^{(\gamma)}, \rho_3^{(\gamma)}, \mathbf{r}^{(\gamma)}, \pi^{(\gamma)}$ are as selected by the prover in the γ-th run of the algorithm ZKAoK.Commitment(**P**, **v**, **x**) for $\gamma = 1, 2, \ldots, s$. For the verification, the response RSP_γ corresponding to the γ-th digit of $\text{Ch} \in \{1,2,3\}^s$ is verified following the algorithm ZKAoK.Verification(**P**, **v**, RSP_γ, $\text{Ch}[\gamma]$, COM_γ) that generates VRF_γ. If $\text{VRF}_\gamma = 1$ for all $\gamma = 1, 2, \ldots, s$ then this treats Π as a confirmation proof of the above zero knowledge argument system. On the other hand, $\text{VRF}_\gamma = 0$ for atleast one $\gamma = 1, 2, \ldots, s$ considers Π as a disavowal proof for the above zero knowledge argument system.

Theorem 1 [7]. *The protocol described above is a statistical* ZKAoK *for the relation $\mathcal{R}$ with soundness error 2/3 and perfect completeness having the communication cost $\mathcal{O}(L \log q)$.*

3   Our Nominative Signature Scheme

Communication Model: Informally speaking, our scheme involves a trusted authority together with nominees and nominators. The trusted authority generates the system parameters, public-secret key pairs of nominees and nominators. System parameters and public keys are made public and secret keys are sent secretly to the concerned parties by the trusted authority.

A nominee issues a signature Sig to the nominator. To generate Sig, the nominee firstly transforms the system of equations involving two equations into an equation of the form $\mathbf{D}_0\mathbf{x}_0 + \mathbf{D}_1\mathbf{x}_1 = \mathbf{v} \bmod q$. Then by using the decomposition-extension technique, the equation $\mathbf{D}_0\mathbf{x}_0 + \mathbf{D}_1\mathbf{x}_1 = \mathbf{v} \bmod q$ is transformed into an equation $\mathbf{Px} = \mathbf{v} \bmod q$. The decomposition-extension technique helps in converting $[\mathbf{x}_0||\mathbf{x}_1]$ to $\mathbf{x}$ such that $\mathbf{x} \in$ VALID. Further, the nominee proves to the nominator in zero-knowledge the possession of $\mathbf{x} \in$ VALID satisfying $\mathbf{Px} = \mathbf{v} \bmod q$.

After receiving the Sig from the nominee, the nominator verifies the validity of Sig and issues the nominative signature nsig. The verification of nsig can be done *only* by the nominee. Our scheme also involves a confirmation or disavowal protocol in which the nominee proves to the verifier in zero-knowledge the validity or the invalidity of the nominative signature nsig issued by the nominator.

Formally, our nominative signature NS = {Setup, KeygenNR, KeygenNE, SignNE, SignNR, Verify, ConfOrDisav = (TMnominee, TMverifier)} works as follows:

NS.Setup(λ) → param. Given a security parameter $\lambda > 0$, the key generation center (KGC) generates an integer n of size $\mathcal{O}(\lambda)$, a prime modulus q of size $\mathcal{O}(n^3)$ and an integer m such that $m = 2n + 8n\lceil \log q \rceil > n\lceil \log q \rceil$. The KGC also chooses a real number σ of size $\Omega(\sqrt{l \log q} \log n)$, an error bound $\beta = 2\sigma\sqrt{m}$ and two cryptographically secure hash functions $H_1 : \{0,1\}^* \to \mathbb{Z}_q^n$, $H : \{0,1\}^* \to \{1,2,3\}^s$ where s is of size $\omega(\log n)$. Observe that the size of β is $\sigma\omega(\log m)$. The KGC publishes the system parameters param $= (n, q, m, \sigma, \beta, H, H_1)$. We use σ for the standard deviation of the discrete Gaussian distribution.

NS.KeygenNR(param, u) → (PK$_u$, SK$_u$). To generate the public-secret key pair of a nominator u, the KGC invokes TrapGen(n, m, q) → ($\mathbf{A}_u$, $\mathsf{T}_{\mathbf{A}_u}$) described in Lemma 1 in Sect. 2 and sets the public and secret key

$$\mathsf{PK}_u = \mathbf{A}_u, \ \mathsf{SK}_u = \mathsf{T}_{\mathbf{A}_u}$$

for u where $\mathbf{A}_u \in \mathbb{Z}_q^{n \times m}$ and $\mathsf{T}_{\mathbf{A}_u} \in \mathbb{Z}^{m \times m}$. The public key PK$_u$ is made public while the secret key SK$_u$ is sent secretly by the KGC to u.

NS.KeygenNE(param, v) → (pk$_v$, sk$_v$). The KGC runs TrapGen(n, m, q) → ($\mathbf{B}_v$, $\mathsf{T}_{\mathbf{B}_v}$) (see Lemma 1 in Sect. 2) to produce the public-secret key pair of a nominee v. It sets the public key and secret key

$$\mathsf{pk}_v = \mathbf{B}_v, \ \mathsf{sk}_v = \mathsf{T}_{\mathbf{B}_v}$$

for v where $\mathbf{B}_v \in \mathbb{Z}_q^{n \times m}$ and $\mathsf{T}_{\mathbf{B}_v} \in \mathbb{Z}^{m \times m}$. The KGC makes pk$_v$ publicly available and sends sk$_v$ secretly to v.

NS.SignNE(param, sk$_{\mathsf{NE}}$, pk$_{\mathsf{NE}}$, PK$_{\mathsf{NR}}$, M) → (Sig$_{M,\mathsf{NE},\mathsf{NR}} = (\Pi, \mathbf{y}_1)$). Let M be a message to be signed. A nominee NE performs the following steps using param $= (n, q, m, \sigma, \beta, H, H_1)$, sk$_{\mathsf{NE}} = \mathsf{T}_{\mathbf{B}_{\mathsf{NE}}}$, pk$_{\mathsf{NE}} = \mathbf{B}_{\mathsf{NE}}$ and PK$_{\mathsf{NR}} = \mathbf{A}_{\mathsf{NR}}$ to generate the signature Sig$_{M,\mathsf{NE},\mathsf{NR}} = (\Pi, \mathbf{y}_1)$ on M.

(i) The nominee NE computes $\mathbf{y} = H_1(M||\mathbf{A}_{\mathsf{NR}}||\mathbf{B}_{\mathsf{NE}}) \in \mathbb{Z}_q^n$ and generates a short vector $\mathbf{v} \in \mathbb{Z}_q^m$ satisfying $\mathbf{B}_{\mathsf{NE}} \cdot \mathbf{v} = \mathbf{y} \bmod q$ with $||\mathbf{v}|| \leq \sigma\sqrt{m}$ by running the algorithm $\mathsf{SampleD}(\mathbf{T}_{\mathbf{B}_{NE}}, \mathbf{B}_{NE}, \mathbf{y}, \sigma) \rightarrow (\mathbf{v})$ using the short basis $\mathsf{sk}_{NE} = \mathbf{T}_{\mathbf{B}_{NE}}$ given in Lemma 1 in Sect. 2. Note that $||\mathbf{v}||_\infty \leq ||\mathbf{v}|| \leq \sigma\sqrt{m} \leq \beta$ as $\beta = 2\sigma\sqrt{m}$.

(ii) The nominee chooses a random number $r_1 \in [-\beta, \beta]$ and sets

$$\mathbf{y}_1 = \mathbf{B}_{NE}^t \cdot (r_1 \mathbf{y}) + \mathbf{v} \bmod q \tag{1}$$

where $\mathbf{B}_{NE}^t$ is the transpose of the matrix $\mathbf{B}_{NE}$. Note that, given the values of $(\mathbf{y}_1, \mathbf{B}_{NE}, \mathbf{y})$ then the problem to find $(r_1, \mathbf{v})$ from Eq. 1 is not feasible under the hardness of LWE.

(iii) The nominee rewrites the system of the equations

$$\mathbf{B}_{NE} \cdot \mathbf{v} = \mathbf{y} \bmod q,$$

$$\mathbf{y}_1 = \mathbf{B}_{NE}^t \cdot (r_1 \mathbf{y}) + \mathbf{v} \bmod q$$

into a single equation

$$\mathbf{D}_0 \cdot \mathbf{x}_0 + \mathbf{D}_1 \cdot \mathbf{x}_1 = \mathbf{b} \bmod q \tag{2}$$

with

$$\mathbf{D}_0 = \begin{bmatrix} (\mathbf{B}_{NE})_{n \times m} & \mathbf{0}_{n \times 1} \\ \mathbf{0}_{m \times m} & \mathbf{0}_{m \times 1} \end{bmatrix}, \mathbf{D}_1 = \begin{bmatrix} \mathbf{0}_{n \times 1} & \mathbf{0}_{n \times m} \\ (\mathbf{B}_{NE}^t \cdot \mathbf{y})_{m \times 1} & \mathbf{I}_{m \times m} \end{bmatrix},$$

$$\mathbf{x}_0 = \begin{bmatrix} \mathbf{v}_{m \times 1} \\ 0_{1 \times 1} \end{bmatrix}, \mathbf{x}_1 = \begin{bmatrix} (r_1)_{1 \times 1} \\ \mathbf{v}_{m \times 1} \end{bmatrix}, \mathbf{b} = \begin{bmatrix} \mathbf{y}_{n \times 1} \\ (\mathbf{y}_1)_{m \times 1} \end{bmatrix}$$

where $\mathbf{I}_{m \times m}$ is an identity matrix of size m.

(iv) Let $p = \lfloor \log_2 \beta \rfloor + 1$. We define the sets B_{mp}^3, S_{3mp} as:
$B_{mp}^3 = \{\mathbf{x} \in \{-1, 0, 1\}^{3mp} : \mathbf{x}$ has exactly mp co-ordinates equal to j for $j = -1, 0, 1\}$,
$S_{3mp} = \{\pi : \pi$ is a permutation on $3mp$ length vectors$\}$.
Then $\widehat{\mathbf{w}} \in B_{mp}^3 \Leftrightarrow \pi(\widehat{\mathbf{w}}) \in B_{mp}^3$ for any permutation $\pi \in S_{3mp}$.

(v) The Eq. 2 is then converted by the nominee into an equation of the form $\mathbf{Px} = \mathbf{b} \bmod q$ as follows using the algorithm $\mathsf{Dec\text{-}Ext}_{m,p}$ described in Fig. 1 which is the decomposition-extension technique of Ling et al. [8]. Note that $\mathbf{x}_0, \mathbf{x}_1 \in [-\beta, \beta]^{m+1}$. The nominee NE generates $\widehat{\mathbf{x}}_0 \in B_{(m+1)p}^3 \leftarrow \mathsf{Dec\text{-}Ext}(\mathbf{x}_0)$, $\widehat{\mathbf{x}}_1 \in B_{(m+1)p}^3 \leftarrow \mathsf{Dec\text{-}Ext}(\mathbf{x}_1)$ and sets
$\widehat{\mathbf{D}}_0 = \mathbf{D}_0 \cdot \widehat{\mathbf{K}}_{(m+1),\beta} \bmod q \in \mathbb{Z}_q^{(n+m) \times 3(m+1)p}$,
$\widehat{\mathbf{D}}_1 = \mathbf{D}_1 \cdot \widehat{\mathbf{K}}_{(m+1),\beta} \bmod q \in \mathbb{Z}_q^{(n+m) \times 3(m+1)p}$
where $\widehat{\mathbf{K}}_{m+1,\beta} = [\mathbf{K}_{m+1,\beta} || 0^{m+1 \times 2(m+1)p}] \in \mathbb{Z}^{(m+1) \times 3(m+1)p}$,
$\mathbf{K}_{m+1,\beta} = \mathbf{I}_{(m+1) \times (m+1)} \otimes [\beta_1, \beta_2, \ldots, \beta_p]$ and $\widehat{\mathbf{x}}_i \in B_{(m+1)p}^3$ satisfies

$$\widehat{\mathbf{K}}_{(m+1),\beta} \cdot \widehat{\mathbf{x}}_i = \mathbf{x}_i \tag{3}$$

for $i = 0, 1$ (see line 6 in Fig. 1). Next, the nominee sets $\mathbf{P} = [\widehat{\mathbf{D}}_0 || \widehat{\mathbf{D}}_1] \in \mathbb{Z}_q^{D \times L}$, $\mathbf{x} = [\widehat{\mathbf{x}}_0 || \widehat{\mathbf{x}}_1]^t \in \mathbb{Z}_q^L$ where $L = 6(m+1)p$ and $D = n + m$.

Input: $\mathbf{w} = (w_1, w_2, \ldots, w_m) \in [-\beta, \beta]^m$
Output: $\widehat{\mathbf{w}} \in B^3_{mp}$ where $p = \lfloor \log_2 \beta \rfloor + 1$

1. Define a super-decreasing sequence $\{\beta\}_{j=1}^p$ of integers by setting $\beta_1 = \lceil \frac{\beta}{2} \rceil$ and $\beta_j = \lceil \frac{\beta - (\beta_1 + \beta_2 + \cdots + \beta_{j-1})}{2} \rceil$ for $2 \leq j \leq p$.
2. **for**$(w_i \in [-\beta, \beta]$ and $i \leq m)$ **do**

   Compute $w_i^{(1)}, w_i^{(2)}, \ldots, w_i^{(p)} \in \{-1, 0, 1\}$ such that $\sum_{j=1}^p \beta_j w_i^{(j)} = w_i$.

   end do
3. Set $\mathbf{w}' = (w_1^{(1)}, \ldots, w_1^{(p)}, w_2^{(1)}, \ldots, w_2^{(p)}, \ldots, w_m^{(1)}, \ldots, w_m^{(p)}) \in \{-1, 0, 1\}^{mp}$. Then $\mathbf{w}'$ satisfies $\mathbf{K}_{m,\beta} \cdot \mathbf{w}' = \mathbf{w}$ where

$$\mathbf{K}_{m,\beta} = \mathbf{I}_{m \times m} \otimes (\beta_1, \beta_2, \ldots, \beta_p) = \begin{bmatrix} \beta_1 \, \beta_2 \ldots \beta_p & & & \\ & \beta_1 \, \beta_2 \ldots \beta_p & & \\ & & \cdots & \\ & & & \beta_1 \, \beta_2 \ldots \beta_p \end{bmatrix}.$$

4. Set $\widehat{\mathbf{K}}_{m,\beta} = [\mathbf{K}_{m,\beta} || 0^{m \times 2mp}] \in \mathbb{Z}^{m \times 3mp}$.
5. Select a random vector $\widetilde{\mathbf{w}} \in \{-1, 0, 1\}^{2mp}$ having exactly $(mp - \lambda_0)$ many 0's, $(mp - \lambda_1)$ many 1's and $(\lambda_0 + \lambda_1)$ many -1's where λ_0, λ_1 are respectively the number of 0's and 1's in $\mathbf{w}'$.
6. Set $\widehat{\mathbf{w}} = (\mathbf{w}' || \widetilde{\mathbf{w}}) \in B^3_{mp}$. Then $\widehat{\mathbf{K}}_{m,\beta} \cdot \widehat{\mathbf{w}} = \mathbf{K}_{m,\beta} \cdot \mathbf{w}' = \mathbf{w}$ and $\widehat{\mathbf{w}} \in B^3_{mp} \Leftrightarrow \pi(\widehat{\mathbf{w}}) \in B^3_{mp}$ for any permutation π on $3mp$ length vectors.
7. **return** $\mathbf{w} = (\mathbf{w}' || \widetilde{\mathbf{w}})$.

Fig. 1. Algorithm Dec-Ext$_{m,p}(\mathbf{w})$ where $p = \lfloor \log_2 \beta \rfloor + 1$ and $\mathbf{w} \in [-\beta, \beta]^m$.

As $\widehat{\mathbf{x}}_0, \widehat{\mathbf{x}}_1 \in \mathbb{Z}_q^{\frac{L}{2}}$, $\widehat{\mathbf{D}}_0, \widehat{\mathbf{D}}_1 \in \mathbb{Z}_q^{D \times \frac{L}{2}}$, we have

$$\begin{aligned} \mathbf{Px} &= \widehat{\mathbf{D}}_0 \cdot \widehat{\mathbf{x}}_0 + \widehat{\mathbf{D}}_1 \cdot \widehat{\mathbf{x}}_1 = \mathbf{D}_0 \cdot \widehat{\mathbf{K}}_{(m+1),\beta} \cdot \widehat{\mathbf{x}}_0 + \mathbf{D}_1 \cdot \widehat{\mathbf{K}}_{(m+1),\beta} \cdot \widehat{\mathbf{x}}_1 \\ &= \mathbf{D}_0 \cdot \mathbf{x}_0 + \mathbf{D}_1 \cdot \mathbf{x}_1 \quad \text{(by Eq. 3)} \\ &= \mathbf{b} \mod q \quad \text{(by Eq. 2)} \end{aligned}$$

(vi) Let VALID $= \{\mathbf{u} \in \{-1, 0, 1\}^L : \mathbf{u} = [\mathbf{u}_0 || \mathbf{u}_1]^t$ for some $\mathbf{u}_0, \mathbf{u}_1 \in B^3_{(m+1)p}\}$ and $\mathcal{S} = \mathcal{S}_{3(m+1)p} \times \mathcal{S}_{3(m+1)p}$. Then $\mathbf{x} = [\widehat{\mathbf{x}}_0 || \widehat{\mathbf{x}}_1]^t \in$ VALID as $\widehat{\mathbf{x}}_0 \in B^3_{(m+1)p}$, $\widehat{\mathbf{x}}_1 \in B^3_{(m+1)p}$. Also for any randomly selected permutation $\pi = (\pi_0, \pi_1) \in \mathcal{S}$ and vector $\mathbf{x} = [\widehat{\mathbf{x}}_0 || \widehat{\mathbf{x}}_1]^t \in$ VALID, the vector $T_\pi(\mathbf{x}) = (\pi_0(\widehat{\mathbf{x}}_0), \pi_1(\widehat{\mathbf{x}}_1)) \in$ VALID and $T_\pi(\mathbf{x})$ is uniform in VALID whenever $\mathbf{x} = [\widehat{\mathbf{x}}_0 || \widehat{\mathbf{x}}_1]^t$ is uniform in VALID.

(vii) The nominee NE invokes the algorithm ZKAoK described in Sect. 2.2 for the relation $\mathcal{R} = \{(\mathbf{P}, \mathbf{b}) \in \mathbb{Z}_q^{D \times L} \times \mathbb{Z}_q^D, \mathbf{x} \in \text{VALID} : \mathbf{Px} = \mathbf{b} \mod q\}$ to prove the knowledge of the witness $\mathbf{x}$ in statistical zero knowledge argument of knowledge and generates a proof

$$\Pi = (\{\text{COM}_\gamma\}_{\gamma=1}^s, \text{ Ch}, \{\text{RSP}_\gamma\}_{\gamma=1}^s)$$

where $\mathsf{COM}_\gamma \leftarrow \mathsf{ZKAoK.Commitment}(\mathbf{P}, \mathbf{b}, \mathbf{x})$, $\mathsf{Ch} = H(M, \{\mathsf{COM}_\gamma\}_{\gamma=1}^s,$ $\mathbf{y}_1) \in \{1, 2, 3\}^s$, $\mathsf{RSP}_\gamma \leftarrow \mathsf{ZKAoK.Response}(\mathsf{Ch}[\gamma], \rho_1^{(\gamma)}, \rho_2^{(\gamma)}, \rho_3^{(\gamma)}, \pi^{(\gamma)}, \mathbf{r}^{(\gamma)},$ $\mathbf{x})$ where $\mathsf{Ch}[\gamma]$ is the γ-th digit of $\mathsf{Ch} \in \{1, 2, 3\}^s$, $s = \omega(\log n)$ and $\rho_1^{(\gamma)},$ $\rho_2^{(\gamma)}, \rho_3^{(\gamma)}, \pi^{(\gamma)}, \mathbf{r}^{(\gamma)}$ are as selected by the nominee NE in the γ-th run of the algorithm $\mathsf{ZKAoK.Commitment}(\mathbf{P}, \mathbf{b}, \mathbf{x})$ for $\gamma = 1, 2, \ldots, s$.

(viii) Finally, the nominee NE sends the signature $\mathsf{Sig}_{M,\mathsf{NE},\mathsf{NR}} = (\Pi, \mathbf{y}_1)$ to the nominator NR over a public channel and stores $(r_1, \mathbf{v}, M, \mathsf{NR}, \mathbf{y}_1)$ in its current state $\mathsf{state}_{\mathsf{NE}}$ where $\mathbf{y}_1$ works as the session identity which is session specific.

NS.SignNR$(\mathsf{param}, \mathsf{SK}_{\mathsf{NR}}, \mathsf{PK}_{\mathsf{NR}}, \mathsf{pk}_{\mathsf{NE}}, M, \mathsf{Sig}_{M,\mathsf{NE},\mathsf{NR}}) \rightarrow (\mathsf{nsig}_{M,\mathsf{NE},\mathsf{NR}} = (\mathbf{z}, \mathbf{y}_1))$. On receiving the signature $\mathsf{Sig}_{M,\mathsf{NE},\mathsf{NR}} = (\Pi, \mathbf{y}_1)$ from the nominee NE, the nominator NR executes the following steps and issues a nominative signature $\mathsf{nsig}_{M,\mathsf{NE},\mathsf{NR}} = (\mathbf{z}, \mathbf{y}_1)$ using $\mathsf{SK}_{\mathsf{NR}} = \mathsf{T}_{\mathbf{A}_{\mathsf{NR}}}$, $\mathsf{PK}_{\mathsf{NR}} = \mathbf{A}_{\mathsf{NR}}$ and $\mathsf{pk}_{\mathsf{NE}} = \mathbf{B}_{\mathsf{NE}}$.

(i) The NR computes $\mathbf{y} = H_1(M \| \mathbf{A}_{\mathsf{NR}} \| \mathbf{B}_{\mathsf{NE}})$ and verifies the zero knowledge proof $\Pi = (\{\mathsf{COM}_\gamma\}_{\gamma=1}^s, \mathsf{Ch}, \{\mathsf{RSP}_\gamma\}_{\gamma=1}^s)$ for the equation $\mathbf{P}\mathbf{x} = \mathbf{b} \bmod q$ by computing $\mathsf{VRF}_\gamma \leftarrow \mathsf{ZKAoK.Verification}(\mathbf{P}, \mathbf{b}, \mathsf{RSP}_\gamma, \mathsf{Ch}[\gamma], \mathsf{COM}_\gamma)$ and verifying whether $\mathsf{VRF}_\gamma = 1$ for all $\gamma = 1, 2, \ldots, s$ where $\mathsf{RSP}_\gamma, \mathsf{Ch}[\gamma],$ COM_γ are as defined in step (vi) of the algorithm NS.SignNE(param, sk$_{\mathsf{NE}}$, pk$_{\mathsf{NE}}$, PK$_{\mathsf{NR}}$, M). Note that $\mathbf{P} = [\widehat{\mathbf{D}}_0 \| \widehat{\mathbf{D}}_1]$ and $\mathbf{b} = [\mathbf{y} \| \mathbf{y}_1]^t$ are publicly computable, $\mathbf{y}_1$ is extracted from $\mathsf{Sig}_{M,\mathsf{NE},\mathsf{NR}}$ and $\mathsf{pk}_{\mathsf{NE}} = \mathbf{B}_{\mathsf{NE}}$ where $\widehat{\mathbf{D}}_0 = \mathbf{D}_0 \cdot \widehat{\mathbf{K}}_{(m+1),\beta}$ and $\widehat{\mathbf{D}}_1 = \mathbf{D}_1 \cdot \widehat{\mathbf{K}}_{(m+1),\beta}$. The witness $\mathbf{x} = [\widehat{\mathbf{x}}_0 \| \widehat{\mathbf{x}}_1]^t$ is known only to the nominee NE.

(ii) If the verification fails, the nominator NR aborts; otherwise the nominator NR finds a short vector

$$\mathbf{z} \in \mathbb{Z}_q^m \text{ satisfying } \mathbf{A}_{\mathsf{NR}} \cdot \mathbf{z} = \mathbf{y}_1 \bmod q \text{ with } \|\mathbf{z}\| \leq \sigma\sqrt{m}$$

using the short basis $\mathsf{SK}_{\mathsf{NR}} = \mathsf{T}_{\mathbf{A}_{\mathsf{NR}}}$ following the algorithm $\mathsf{SampleD}(\mathsf{T}_{\mathbf{A}_{\mathsf{NR}}}, \mathbf{A}_{\mathsf{NR}}, \mathbf{y}_1, \sigma) \rightarrow \mathbf{z}$ as in Lemma 1 in Sect. 2 and issues the nominative signature $\mathsf{nsig}_{M,\mathsf{NE},\mathsf{NR}} = (\mathbf{z}, \mathbf{y}_1)$.

NS.Verify$(\mathsf{param}, \mathsf{state}_{\mathsf{NE}}, \mathsf{pk}_{\mathsf{NE}}, \mathsf{PK}_{\mathsf{NR}}, M, \mathsf{nsig}_{M,\mathsf{NE},\mathsf{NR}}) \in \{\mathsf{valid}, \mathsf{invalid}\}$. This algorithm is executed by the nominee NE with its current internal state $\mathsf{state}_{\mathsf{NE}}$ who on receiving $\mathsf{nsig}_{M,\mathsf{NE},\mathsf{NR}} = (\mathbf{z}, \mathbf{y}_1)$ uses $\mathsf{PK}_{\mathsf{NR}} = \mathbf{A}_{\mathsf{NR}}$ and $\mathsf{pk}_{\mathsf{NE}} = \mathbf{B}_{\mathsf{NE}}$ to compute $\mathbf{y} = H_1(M \| \mathbf{A}_{\mathsf{NR}} \| \mathbf{B}_{\mathsf{NE}})$ and verify whether

$$\mathbf{y}_1 = \mathbf{B}_{\mathsf{NE}}^t \cdot (r_1 \mathbf{y}) + \mathbf{v} \bmod q, \quad \mathbf{A}_{\mathsf{NR}} \cdot \mathbf{z} = \mathbf{y}_1 \bmod q \text{ and } \|\mathbf{z}\| \leq \sigma\sqrt{m}$$

where the nominee NE extracts $\mathbf{v}, r_1$ from its internal secret state $\mathsf{state}_{\mathsf{NE}}$ which contains $(r_1, \mathbf{v}, M, \mathsf{NR}, \mathbf{y}_1)$. If the verification succeeds, it outputs valid; otherwise it returns invalid.

NS.ConfOrDisav $=$ (TMnominee, TMverifier). This protocol satisfies the following requirements:

(i) TMnominee(param, state$_{NE}$, pk$_{NE}$, PK$_{NR}$, M, nsig$_{M,NE,NR}$) $\rightarrow$ (μ, $\Pi_{confORdisav}$). The nominee NE generates a proof

$$\Pi_{confORdisav} = (\{COM_\gamma\}_{\gamma=1}^s, Ch, \{RSP_\gamma\}_{\gamma=1}^s)$$

for the relations $\mathbf{B}_{NE} \cdot \mathbf{v} = \mathbf{y} \bmod q$, $\mathbf{B}_{NE}^t \cdot (r_1 \mathbf{y}) + \mathbf{v} = \mathbf{y}_1 \bmod q$ by converting this system of equations into an equation of the form $\mathbf{D}_0 \mathbf{x}_0 + \mathbf{D}_1 \mathbf{x}_1 = \mathbf{b} \bmod q$ which in turn is reduced to an equation of the form $\mathbf{Px} = \mathbf{b}$ as explained in steps (iii) and (iv) respectively of the algorithm $\mathcal{R}$.SignNE, and then invoking the algorithm ZKAoK for the relation $\mathcal{R} = \{(\mathbf{P}, \mathbf{b}) \in \mathbb{Z}_q^{D \times L} \times \mathbb{Z}_q^D, \mathbf{x} \in VALID : \mathbf{Px} = \mathbf{b} \bmod q\}$ as in step (vi) of the algorithm NS.SignNE. Note that $\mathbf{P} = [\widehat{\mathbf{D}}_0 || \widehat{\mathbf{D}}_1]$ and $\mathbf{b} = [\mathbf{y} || \mathbf{y}_1]^t$ are publicly computable from param, nsig$_{M,NE,NR}$ = ($\mathbf{z}$, $\mathbf{y}_1$) and pk$_{NE}$ = $\mathbf{B}_{NE}$. The witness $\mathbf{x} = [\mathbf{x}_0 || \mathbf{x}_1]^t$ is known only to the nominee NE which is stored in its current internal state state$_{NE}$. It runs NS.Verify(param, state$_{NE}$, pk$_{NE}$, PK$_{NR}$, M, nsig$_{M,NE,NR}$). If the output is valid then it returns ($\mu = 1$, $\Pi_{confORdisav}$) to the verifier VR. Otherwise, it sends ($\mu = 0$, $\Pi_{confORdisav}$) to the verifier VR.

(ii) TMverifier(param, pk$_{NE}$, PK$_{NR}$, M, nsig$_{M,NE,NR}$, μ, $\Pi_{confORdisav}$) $\rightarrow \beta$. On receiving a pair (μ, $\Pi_{confORdisav}$) from the nominee NE, the verifier VR checks the bit μ.

– If $\mu = 1$, then it verifies the following.
  (a) VRF$_\gamma$ = 1 for all γ where VRF$_\gamma$ $\leftarrow$ZKAoK.Verification($\mathbf{P}$, $\mathbf{b}$, RSP$_\gamma$, Ch[γ], COM$_\gamma$). Here $\mathbf{P}$, $\mathbf{b}$ are computed by the verifier using param, nsig$_{M,NE,NR}$ = ($\mathbf{z}$, $\mathbf{y}_1$) and PK$_{NE}$ = $\mathbf{B}_{NE}$. Note that the witness $\mathbf{x}$ is known only to the nominee NE.
  (b) $\mathbf{A}_{NR} \cdot \mathbf{z} = \mathbf{y}_1$ by extracting $\mathbf{z}$, $\mathbf{y}_1$ from nsig and using PK$_{NR}$ = $\mathbf{A}_{NR}$.
  If the verification succeeds, it outputs $\beta = 1$ indicating that the verifier VR agrees with the confirmation proof $\Pi_{confORdisav}$ and convinces in zero knowledge that the nominator is not a cheater. Otherwise it disagrees with the confirmation proof by returning $\beta = 0$. This means that the verifier VR is not satisfied with the confirmation proof $\Pi_{confORdisav}$.
– If the bit $\mu = 0$ then the verifier VR verifies whether any of the above mentioned conditions (a), (b) are violated, thereby agrees with the disavowal proof $\Pi_{confORdisav}$ and convinces in zero knowledge that the nominator NR is a cheater. Otherwise it disagrees with the disavowal proof and returns $\beta = 0$ indicating that the verifier VR is not convinced with the proof.

Correctness:

– $((n, q, m, \sigma, \beta, H, H_1) = $ param$) \leftarrow$ NS.Setup(λ),
– $(PK_{NR} = \mathbf{A}_{NR}, SK_{NR} = T_{\mathbf{A}_{NR}}) \leftarrow$ NS.KeygenNR($\mathcal{Y}$, NR),
– $(pk_{NE} = \mathbf{B}_{NR}, sk_{NE} = T_{\mathbf{B}_{NE}}) \leftarrow$ NS.KeygenNE($\mathcal{Y}$, NE),

- $(\text{Sig}_{M,\text{NE},\text{NR}} = (\Pi, \mathbf{y}_1)) \leftarrow \text{NS.SignNE}(\text{param}, \text{sk}_{\text{NE}}, \text{pk}_{\text{NE}}, \text{PK}_{\text{NR}}, M)$ where $\mathbf{y}_1 = \mathbf{B}_{\text{NE}}^t \cdot (r_1\mathbf{y}) + \mathbf{v} \bmod q$, $r_1 \in [-\beta, \beta]$, $\mathbf{v} \in \mathbb{Z}_q^m$ is a short vector satisfying $\mathbf{B}_{\text{NE}} \cdot \mathbf{v} = \mathbf{y} \bmod q$ with $||\mathbf{v}|| \leq \sigma\sqrt{m}$,
- $(\text{nsig}_{M,\text{NE},\text{NR}} = \mathbf{z}) \leftarrow \text{NS.SignNR}(\text{param}, \text{SK}_{\text{NR}}, \text{PK}_{\text{NR}}, \text{pk}_{\text{NE}}, M, \text{Sig}_{M,\text{NE},\text{NR}})$ where $\mathbf{z}$ satisfies the equation $\mathbf{A}_{\text{NR}} \cdot \mathbf{z} = \mathbf{y}_1 \bmod q$,
- $(\mu, \Pi_{\text{confORdisav}}) \leftarrow \text{TMnominee}(\text{param}, \text{state}_{\text{NE}}, \text{pk}_{\text{NE}}, \text{PK}_{\text{NR}}, M, \text{nsig}_{M,\text{NE},\text{NR}})$ where $\mu \in \{0, 1\}$ and $\Pi_{\text{confORdisav}} \leftarrow \text{NS.ConfOrDisav.TMnominee}$ is a zero knowledge proof for the relation $\mathcal{R} = \{(\mathbf{P}, \mathbf{b}) \in \mathbb{Z}_q^{D \times L} \times \mathbb{Z}_q^D, \mathbf{x} \in \text{VALID} : \mathbf{Px} = \mathbf{b} \bmod q\}$.

If the nominee NE, the nominator NR and the verifier VR are honest then we have the following.

(i) $\text{NS.Verify}(\text{param}, \text{state}_{\text{NE}}, \text{pk}_{\text{NE}}, \text{PK}_{\text{NR}}, M, \text{nsig}_{M,\text{NE},\text{NR}}) \rightarrow$ valid as $\mathbf{A}_{\text{NR}} \cdot \mathbf{z} = \mathbf{y}_1 \bmod q$.
(ii) $\text{NS.ConfOrDisav.TMverifier}(\text{param}, \text{pk}_{\text{NE}}, \text{PK}_{\text{NR}}, M, \text{nsig}_{M,\text{NE},\text{NR}}, \mu, \Pi_{\text{confORdisav}}) \rightarrow (\beta = 1)$

4 Security

Threat Model. Security attributes of a nominative signature can be broadly classified into four categories –

(*Unforgeability against malicious nominee*) The nominee NE alone cannot produce a valid nominative signature where the nominee NE and the message M both are chosen by the nominator NR.

(*Unforgeability against malicious nominator*) The nominator NR alone cannot produce a valid nominative signature and cannot convince a verifier about the validity or invalidity of a nominative signature.

(*Security against invisibility*) Only the nominee NE can verify the nominative signature nsig.

(*Security against repudiation*) If the nominative signature nsig is valid then the nominee NE cannot mislead a verifier VR and cannot prove the invalidity of nsig to the verifier VR and vice versa.

4.1 Oracles for Adversaries

An adversary $\mathcal{A}$ invokes the following oracles accessible in the attack games and interacts with a stateful interface I who runs NS.Setup to generate param and maintains seven private lists: LcreateNR, LcreateNE, LcorruptNR, LcorruptNE, LsignNR, LsignNE, LconfORdisav.

- CreateNR Query: When $\mathcal{A}$ invokes this oracle on a nominator u, the interface I returns PK_u to $\mathcal{A}$ by running $\text{NS.KeygenNR}(\text{param}, u) \rightarrow (\text{PK}_u, \text{SK}_u)$. The interface I stores $(\text{PK}_u, \text{SK}_u)$ in the list LcreateNR.
- CreateNE Query: In response to this query for a nominee v from $\mathcal{A}$, the interface I runs $\text{NS.KeygenNE}(\text{param}, v) \rightarrow (\text{pk}_v, \text{sk}_v)$ and passes pk_v to $\mathcal{A}$. The interface I stores the pair $(\text{pk}_v, \text{sk}_v)$ in the list LcreateNE.

- CorruptNR Query: On receiving this query on a nominator u from $\mathcal{A}$, the interface I checks whether $(PK_u, SK_u) \in$ LcreateNR. If not, it returns $\perp$. Otherwise, I sends SK_u to $\mathcal{A}$ and stores PK_u in the list LcorruptNR.
- CorruptNE Query: In response to this query on a nominee v from $\mathcal{A}$, the interface I checks whether $(pk_v, sk_v) \in$ LcreateNE. If not, it returns $\perp$. Otherwise, I returns $(sk_v, state_v)$ to $\mathcal{A}$ and stores pk_v in the list LcorruptNE. Here $state_v$ is the current internal secret state of the nominee v which is initially empty.
- SignNE Query: On querying this oracle on a tuple (v, u, M) by $\mathcal{A}$ where v is a nominee, u is a nominator and M is a message, the interface I checks whether $(pk_v, sk_v) \in$ LcreateNE and $(PK_u, SK_u) \in$ LcreateNR. If not, I returns $\perp$. Otherwise, I outputs the signature $\text{Sig}_{M,v,u} \leftarrow$ NS.SignNE(param, sk_v, pk_v, PK_u, M) of the nominee v on M and stores $(\text{Sig}_{M,v,u}, state_v)$ in the list LsignNE where $state_v$ is the current internal secret state of the nominee v.
- SignNR Query: In response to this query on $\text{Sig}_{M,v,u}$ from $\mathcal{A}$, the interface I verifies whether $(\text{Sig}_{M,v,u}, state_v) \in$ LSignNE. If so, the interface I returns the nominative signature $\text{nsig}_{M,v,u} \leftarrow$ NS.SignNR(param, SK_u, PK_u, pk_v, M, $\text{Sig}_{M,v,u}$) to $\mathcal{A}$ and stores $(\text{Sig}_{M,v,u}, \text{nsig}_{M,v,u})$ in the list LsignNR. Otherwise, I returns $\perp$.
- ConfOrDisav Query: The interface I responses on receiving this query on $\text{nsig}_{M,v,u}$ from $\mathcal{A}$ by checking if $(\text{Sig}_{M,v,u}, \text{nsig}_{M,v,u}) \in$ LsignNR. If not, I aborts. Otherwise, I extracts $state_v$ from $(\text{Sig}_{M,v,u}, state_v) \in$ LSignNE and returns $(\mu, \Pi_{\text{confORdisav}}) \leftarrow$ NS.ConfOrDisav.TMnominee(param, $state_v$, pk_v, PK_u, M, $\text{nsig}_{M,v,u}$) to $\mathcal{A}$. The interface I stores $(\text{nsig}_{M,v,u}, \mu, \Pi_{\text{confORdisav}})$ in the list LconfORdisav.

4.2 Security Model for Unforgeability Against Malicious Nominee

This is a security game $\text{Exp}_{\mathcal{F}}^{\text{unforg}}$ explained in Fig. 2 played between a forger $\mathcal{F}$ and a simulator $\mathcal{S}$.

Definition 6 (Unforgeability against malicious nominee). *We say that a nominative signature is secure under unforgeability against malicious nominee if*

$$\text{Adv}_{\mathcal{F}}^{\text{unforg}}(\lambda) = \text{Prob}[\text{Exp}_{\mathcal{F}}^{\text{unforg}}(\lambda) = 1] \le \text{negl}(\lambda)$$

for every PPT adversary $\mathcal{F}$ in the experiment $\text{Exp}_{\mathcal{F}}^{\text{unforg}}(\lambda)$ defined in Fig. 2 where $\text{negl}(\lambda)$ is a negligible function in λ i.e., $\text{negl}(\lambda) = \lambda^{-\omega(1)}$.

4.3 Security Model Under Unforgeability Against Malicious Nominator

Let $\mathcal{F}$ be a forger and $\mathcal{S}$ be a simulator. This security is modeled by the game $\text{Exp}_{\mathcal{F}}^{\text{unforgNR}}(\lambda)$ between $\mathcal{F}$ and $\mathcal{S}$ as provided in Fig. 3.

Definition 7 (Unforgeability against malicious nominator). *We say that a nominative signature is secure against malicious nominator if*

$$\text{Adv}_{\mathcal{F}}^{\text{unforgNR}}(\lambda) = \text{Prob}[\text{Exp}_{\mathcal{F}}^{\text{unforgNR}}(\lambda) = 1] \le \text{negl}(\lambda)$$

for every PPT adversary $\mathcal{F}$ in the experiment $\text{Exp}_{\mathcal{F}}^{\text{unforgNR}}(\lambda)$ defined in Fig. 3 and $\text{negl}(\lambda)$ is a negligible function of λ.

5 Security Model Against Invisibility

Let $\mathcal{D}$ be a distinguisher and $\mathcal{C}$ be the challenger. The invisibility game $\mathsf{Exp}_{\mathcal{D}}^{\mathsf{invis}}(\lambda, b)$ is described in Fig. 4.

Definition 8 (security against invisibility). *A nominative signature scheme is secure under invisibility*

$$\mathsf{Adv}_{\mathcal{D}}^{\mathsf{invis}}(\lambda) = |\mathsf{Prob}[\mathsf{Exp}_{\mathcal{D}}^{\mathsf{invis}}(\lambda, 0)] - \mathsf{Prob}[\mathsf{Exp}_{\mathcal{D}}^{\mathsf{invis}}(\lambda, 1)]| \leq \mathsf{negl}(\lambda)$$

---

1. The simulator $\mathcal{S}$ generates system parameters $\mathsf{param} \leftarrow \mathsf{NS.Setup}(\lambda)$ and sends it to the forger $\mathcal{F}$.
2. The forger $\mathcal{F}$ makes polynomially many, say α, queries to $\mathcal{S}$ for each of the oracles CreateNR, CreateNE, CorruptNR, CorruptNE, SignNR, SignNE, ConfOrDisav, thereby has the knowledge of VIEW where

$$\mathsf{VIEW} = \begin{cases} \mathsf{param}, \ \{\mathsf{PK}_u \mid (\mathsf{PK}_u, \mathsf{SK}_u) \in \mathsf{LcreateNR}\}, \ \{\mathsf{pk}_v \mid (\mathsf{pk}_v, \mathsf{sk}_v) \in \mathsf{LcreateNE}\}, \\ \{\mathsf{SK}_u \mid \mathsf{PK}_u \in \mathsf{LcorruptNR}\}, \ \{\mathsf{sk}_v \mid \mathsf{pk}_v \in \mathsf{LcorruptNE}\}, \\ \mathsf{LsignNE} = \{(\mathsf{Sig}_{M,v,u}, \mathsf{state}_v) \mid \mathsf{Sig}_{M,v,u} \leftarrow \mathsf{NS.SignNE}(\mathsf{param}, \mathsf{sk}_v, \mathsf{pk}_v, \mathsf{PK}_u, M)\}, \\ \mathsf{LsignNR} = \Big\{ (\mathsf{Sig}_{M,v,u}, \mathsf{nsig}_{M,v,u}) \mid (\mathsf{Sig}_{M,v,u}, \mathsf{state}_v) \in \mathsf{LsignNE} \ \text{and} \\ \qquad \mathsf{nsig}_{M,v,u} \leftarrow \mathsf{NS.SignNR}(\mathsf{param}, \mathsf{SK}_u, \mathsf{PK}_u, \mathsf{pk}_v, M, \mathsf{Sig}_{M,v,u}) \Big\}, \\ \mathsf{LconfORdisav} = \Big\{ (\mathsf{nsig}_{M,v,u}, \mu, \Pi_{\mathsf{confORdisav}}) \mid (\mathsf{Sig}_{M,v,u}, \mathsf{nsig}_{M,v,u}) \in \mathsf{LsignNR} \\ \qquad \text{and} \ (\mu, \Pi_{\mathsf{confORdisav}}) \leftarrow \mathsf{NS.ConfOrDisav.TMnominee}(\mathsf{param}, \\ \qquad\qquad\qquad\qquad \mathsf{state}_v, \mathsf{pk}_v, \mathsf{PK}_u, M, \mathsf{nsig}_{M,v,u}) \Big\} \\ \text{where each of } |\mathsf{LcreateNR}|, \ |\mathsf{LcreateNE}|, \ |\mathsf{LcorruptNR}|, \ |\mathsf{LcorruptNE}|, \\ |\mathsf{LsignNE}|, \ |\mathsf{LsignNR}|, \ |\mathsf{LconfORdisav}| \leq \alpha. \end{cases}$$

3. Finally, $\mathcal{F}$ outputs a forgery $(M^*, \mathsf{nsig}_{M^*,\mathsf{NE},\mathsf{NR}}^*)$ on a corrupted nominee NE and an uncorrupted nominator NR such that $(\mathsf{PK}_{\mathsf{NR}}, \mathsf{SK}_{\mathsf{NR}}) \in \mathsf{LcreateNR}$ and $\mathsf{pk}_{\mathsf{NE}} \in \mathsf{LcorruptNE}$.
4. The simulator $\mathcal{S}$ returns 1 if the following conditions hold:
   (a) $\mathsf{NS.Verify}(\mathsf{param}, \mathsf{state}_{\mathsf{NE}}, \mathsf{pk}_{\mathsf{NE}}, \mathsf{PK}_{\mathsf{NR}}, M^*, \mathsf{nsig}_{M^*,\mathsf{NE},\mathsf{NR}}^*) \rightarrow$ valid i.e., $\mathsf{nsig}_{M^*,\mathsf{NE},\mathsf{NR}}^*$ is a valid signature,
   (b) $\mathsf{PK}_{\mathsf{NR}} \notin \mathsf{LcorruptNR}$ i.e., nominator NR is not corrupted,
   (c) $(\mathsf{Sig}_{M^*,\mathsf{NE},\mathsf{NR}}', \mathsf{nsig}_{M^*,\mathsf{NE},\mathsf{NR}}^*) \notin \mathsf{LsignNR}$ where $(\mathsf{Sig}_{M^*,\mathsf{NE},\mathsf{NR}}', \mathsf{state}_{\mathsf{NE}}) \in \mathsf{LsignNE}$ i.e., $\mathsf{nsig}_{M^*,\mathsf{NE},\mathsf{NR}}' \neq \mathsf{nsig}_{M^*,\mathsf{NE},\mathsf{NR}}^*$ for the pair $(\mathsf{Sig}_{M^*,\mathsf{NE},\mathsf{NR}}', \mathsf{nsig}_{M^*,\mathsf{NE},\mathsf{NR}}') \in \mathsf{LsignNR}$, and SignNR query is made only ones on $\mathsf{Sig}_{M^*,\mathsf{NE},\mathsf{NR}}'$.
   (d) $(\mathsf{nsig}_{M^*,\mathsf{NE},\mathsf{NR}}', \mu, \Pi_{\mathsf{confORdisav}}) \notin \mathsf{LconfORdisav}$ i.e., $\mathsf{nsig}_{M^*,\mathsf{NE},\mathsf{NR}}^*$ has not been queried to the protocol $\mathsf{NS.ConfOrDisav}$ for the conformation or disavowal proof of the validity of the nominative signature $\mathsf{nsig}_{M^*,\mathsf{NE},\mathsf{NR}}^*$.
   Otherwise, $\mathcal{S}$ returns 0.
5. The forger $\mathcal{F}$ wins the game if $\mathcal{S}$ returns 1.

Fig. 2. Small Security game $\mathsf{Exp}_{\mathcal{F}}^{\mathsf{unforg}}(\lambda)$ under unforgeability against malicious nominee.

for every PPT adversary in the experiment $\mathsf{Exp}_{\mathcal{D}}^{\mathsf{invis}}(\lambda, b)$ *defined in Fig. 4 where* $b \in \{0, 1\}$ *and* $\mathsf{negl}(\lambda)$ *is a negligible function in* λ.

Remark 2. In the above security game (Fig. 2) if SignNR query is made more than ones on $\mathsf{Sig}'_{M^*,\mathsf{NE},\mathsf{NR}}$ then the adversary can compute a nominator's signature as follows:

Suppose an adversary queried SignNR on $\mathsf{Sig}'_{M^*,\mathsf{NE},\mathsf{NR}}$ two or more times then the adversary has $\mathbf{A}_{\mathsf{NR}} \cdot \mathbf{z}_1 = \mathbf{y}_1 \bmod q$ and $\mathbf{A}_{\mathsf{NR}} \cdot \mathbf{z}_2 = \mathbf{y}_1 \bmod q$. That gives to the adversary $\mathbf{A}_{\mathsf{NR}} \cdot (\mathbf{z}_1 + \mathbf{z}_2)/2 = \mathbf{y}_1 \bmod q$. As q is a prime, 2 is invertible in $\mathbb{Z}_q$. Thus the adversary has another signature $\mathsf{nsig}_{M^*,\mathsf{NE},\mathsf{NR}} = (\mathbf{z}_1 + \mathbf{z}_2)/2$.

---

1. The simulator $\mathcal{S}$ generates system parameters $\mathsf{param} \leftarrow \mathsf{NS.Setup}(\lambda)$ and sends it to the forger $\mathcal{F}$.
2. The forger $\mathcal{F}$ makes polynomially many, say α, queries to $\mathcal{S}$ for each of the oracles CreateNR, CreateNE, CorruptNR, CorruptNE, SignNR, SignNE, ConfOrDisav and has the same VIEW as given in Figure 2.
3. Finally, the forger $\mathcal{F}$ outputs a forgery $(M^*, \mathsf{Sig}_{M^*,\mathsf{NE},\mathsf{NR}}^*, \mathsf{nsig}_{M^*,\mathsf{NE},\mathsf{NR}}^*)$ on a corrupted nominator NR and an uncorrupted nominee NE such that $\mathsf{PK}_{\mathsf{NR}} \in \mathsf{LcorruptNR}$, $(\mathsf{pk}_{\mathsf{NE}}, \mathsf{sk}_{\mathsf{NE}}) \in \mathsf{LcreateNE}$.
4. The simulator $\mathcal{S}$ returns 1 if the following holds:
   (a) $\mathsf{NS.Verify}(\mathsf{param}, \mathsf{state}_{\mathsf{NE}}, \mathsf{pk}_{\mathsf{NE}}, \mathsf{PK}_{\mathsf{NR}}, M^*, \mathsf{nsig}_{M^*,\mathsf{NE},\mathsf{NR}}^*) \to$ valid.
   (b) $\mathsf{pk}_{\mathsf{NE}} \notin \mathsf{LcorruptNE}$.
   (c) $\mathsf{Sig}_{M^*,\mathsf{NE},\mathsf{NR}}^* \notin \mathsf{LsignNE}$ and $(M^*, \mathsf{NE}, \mathsf{NR})$ query is made only ones to the SignNE oracle.
   (d) $\mathsf{VRF}_\gamma = 1$ for all $\gamma = 1, 2, \ldots, s$ by computing $\mathsf{VRF}_\gamma \leftarrow \mathsf{ZKAoK.Verification}(\mathbf{P}, \mathbf{b}, \mathsf{RSP}_\gamma, \mathsf{Ch}[\gamma], \mathsf{COM}_\gamma)$ where $\mathsf{RSP}_\gamma, \mathsf{Ch}[\gamma], \mathsf{COM}_\gamma$ are as defined in step (vi) of the algorithm NS.SignNE.
   (e) $(\mathsf{nsig}_{M^*,\mathsf{NE},\mathsf{NR}}^*, \mu, \Pi_{M^*,\mathsf{NE},\mathsf{NR}}^*) \notin \mathsf{LcreateORdisav}$.
   Otherwise, $\mathcal{S}$ returns 0.
5. The forger $\mathcal{F}$ wins the game if $\mathcal{S}$ returns 1.

Fig. 3. Security game $\mathsf{Exp}_{\mathcal{F}}^{\mathsf{unforgNR}}(\lambda)$ under security against malicious nominator

5.1   Security Model for Non-repudiation

Let $\mathcal{A}$ be a cheating nominee and $\mathcal{C}$ be the challenger. Its security game $\mathsf{Exp}_{\mathcal{A}}^{\mathsf{rep}}(\lambda)$ is explained in Fig. 5.

Definition 9 (Non-repudiation). *A nominative signature scheme is secure against non-repudiation if*

$$\mathsf{Adv}_{\mathcal{A}}^{\mathsf{rep}}(\lambda) = |\mathsf{prob}[\mathsf{Exp}_{\mathcal{A}}^{\mathsf{rep}}(\lambda) = 1]| \leq \mathsf{negl}(\lambda)$$

for every PPT adversary in the experiment $\mathsf{Exp}_{\mathcal{A}}^{\mathsf{rep}}(\lambda)$ *defined in Fig. 5 and* $\mathsf{negl}(\lambda)$ *is a negligible function of* λ.

1. The challenger $\mathcal{C}$ generates system parameters param$\leftarrow$ NS.Setup(λ) and sends it to the distinguisher $\mathcal{D}$.
2. Next the distinguisher $\mathcal{D}$ makes polynomially many, say α queries to $\mathcal{S}$ for each of the oracles CreateNR, CreateNE, CorruptNR, CorruptNE, SignNR, SignNE, ConfOrDisav to get the knowledge of VIEW where VIEW is same as in Figure 2.
3. At any point of the game, $\mathcal{D}$ submits a tuple (M^*, NE, NR) where M^* is a message to be signed with NE as the nominee and NR as the nominator such that pk$_{NE}$, PK$_{NR}$ $\in$ VIEW but sk$_{NE}$ $\notin$ VIEW i.e., the nominee NE is not corrupted.
4. The challenger chooses a random bit $b \in \{0,1\}$. If $b = 1$, the challenger $\mathcal{C}$ generates Sig$_{M^*,NE,NR}$ $\leftarrow$NS.SignNE(param, sk$_{NE}$, pk$_{NE}$, PK$_{NR}$, M^*), nsig$_{M^*,NE,NR}$ $\leftarrow$ NS.SignNR(param, SK$_{NR}$, PK$_{NR}$, pk$_{NE}$, M^*, Sig$_{M^*,NE,NR}$) and sets K$_b$ = nsig$_{M^*,NE,NR}$. Else, K$_b$ is generated uniformly.
5. The distinguisher $\mathcal{D}$ observes K$_b$, outputs a guess b' and wins the game if
   (i) $b' = b$
   (ii) $\mathcal{D}$ does not corrupt sk$_{NE}$ i.e., pk$_{NE}$ $\notin$ LcorruptNE

Fig. 4. Security game Exp$_{\mathcal{D}}^{invis}(\lambda, b)$ against invisibility

1. The challenger $\mathcal{C}$ generates param$\leftarrow$ NS.Setup(λ) and sends it to the adversary $\mathcal{A}$.
2. The adversary $\mathcal{A}$ may make polynomially many, say α, queries to oracles CreateNR, CreateNE, CorruptNR, CorruptNE, SignNR, SignNE, ConfOrDisav. The adversary $\mathcal{A}$ has the same VIEW as in Figure 2.
3. The adversary $\mathcal{A}$ prepares a tuple (M^*, nsig$_{M^*,NE,NR}$, μ) where NE is any nominee with pk$_{NE}$ $\in$ LcorruptNE, NR is a nominator such that (PK$_{NR}$, SK$_{NR}$)$\in$ LcreateNR, nsig$_{M^*,NE,NR}$ is a signature on M^* and μ is a bit. If NS.Verify(param, state$_{M^*,NE,NR}$, pk$_{NE}$, PK$_{NR}$, M^*, nsig$_{M^*,NE,NR}$)$\rightarrow$ valid then $\mu = 1$. Else $\mu = 0$. Note that pk$_{NE}$ $\in$ LcorruptNE means $\mathcal{A}$ has the knowledge of (sk$_{NE}$, state$_{M,NE,NR}$).
4. To mislead, the adversary $\mathcal{A}$ runs the disavowal proof $\Pi_{confORdisav}$ if $\mu = 1$. Otherwise, $\mathcal{A}$ computes the confirmation proof $\Pi_{confORdisav}$. challenger $\mathcal{C}$ runs NS.ConfOrDisav.TMverifier(param, pk$_{NE}$, PK$_{NR}$, M^*, nsig$_{M^*,NE,NR}$, μ, $\Pi_{confORdisav}$)$\rightarrow$ β and returns β.
   The adversary $\mathcal{A}$ wins the game if $\beta = 1$.

Fig. 5. Security game Exp$_{\mathcal{A}}^{rep}(\lambda)$ under non-repudiation

Theorem 2. *Assuming the hardness of* SIS *search problem, the construction of our nominative signature scheme* NS $= \{$Setup, KeygenNR, KeygenNE, SignNE, SignNR, Verify, ConfOrDisav $=$ (TMnominee, TMverifier)$\}$ *described in Sect. 3 is secure under the unforgeability against malicious nominee as per the Definition 6 for the security game given in Fig. 2.*

Theorem 3. *Assuming the hardness of* SIS *search problem, the construction of our nominative signature scheme* NS $= \{$Setup, KeygenNR, KeygenNE, SignNE,

SignNR, Verify, ConfOrDisav = (TMnominee, TMverifier)} *described in Sect. 3 is secure in the random oracle model under the unforgeability against malicious nominator as per the Definition 7 for the security game given in Fig. 3.*

Theorem 4. *Assuming the hardness of* decisional SIS *and* LWE, *the construction of our nominative signature scheme* NS = {Setup, KeygenNR, KeygenNE, SignNE, SignNR, Verify, ConfOrDisav = (TMnominee, TMverifier)} *described in Sect. 3 is secure under invisibility as per the Definition 8 for the security game given in Fig. 4.*

Theorem 5. *Our nominative signature scheme is secure against repudiation by nominee if no PPT cheating nominee has a non negligible advantage in the security game given in Fig. 5.*

Proof. By the soundness property of a proof system, the verifier will accept a language $\mathbf{x} \notin$ VALID with probability atmost $\epsilon \in [0, 1/2)$ while for any language $\mathbf{x} \in$ VALID, the verifier will reject with probability $\epsilon \in [0, 1/2)$.

Proofs of all the above Theorems 2, 3 and 4 will be given in the full version of the paper.

References

1. Ajtai, M.: Generating hard instances of lattice problems. In: Proceedings of the Twenty-Eighth Annual ACM Symposium on Theory of Computing, pp. 99–108. ACM (1996)
2. Alwen, J., Peikert, C.: Generating shorter bases for hard random lattices. Theory Comput. Syst. **48**(3), 535–553 (2011)
3. Fiat, A., Shamir, A.: How to prove yourself: practical solutions to identification and signature problems. In: Odlyzko, A.M. (ed.) CRYPTO 1986. LNCS, vol. 263, pp. 186–194. Springer, Heidelberg (1987). https://doi.org/10.1007/3-540-47721-7_12
4. Huang, Q., Liu, D.Y., Wong, D.S.: An efficient one-move nominative signature scheme. Int. J. Appl. Cryptogr. **1**(2), 133–143 (2008)
5. Huang, Z., Wang, Y.: Convertible nominative signatures. In: Wang, H., Pieprzyk, J., Varadharajan, V. (eds.) ACISP 2004. LNCS, vol. 3108, pp. 348–357. Springer, Heidelberg (2004). https://doi.org/10.1007/978-3-540-27800-9_30
6. Kim, S.J., Park, S.J., Won, D.H.: Nominative signatures. In: ICEIC: International Conference on Electronics, Informations and Communications, pp. 68–71 (1995)
7. Libert, B., Ling, S., Mouhartem, F., Nguyen, K., Wang, H.: Signature schemes with efficient protocols and dynamic group signatures from lattice assumptions. In: Cheon, J.H., Takagi, T. (eds.) ASIACRYPT 2016. LNCS, vol. 10032, pp. 373–403. Springer, Heidelberg (2016). https://doi.org/10.1007/978-3-662-53890-6_13
8. Ling, S., Nguyen, K., Stehlé, D., Wang, H.: Improved zero-knowledge proofs of knowledge for the ISIS problem, and applications. In: Kurosawa, K., Hanaoka, G. (eds.) PKC 2013. LNCS, vol. 7778, pp. 107–124. Springer, Heidelberg (2013). https://doi.org/10.1007/978-3-642-36362-7_8
9. Liu, D.Y.W., Chang, S., Wong, D.S., Mu, Y.: Nominative signature from ring signature. In: Miyaji, A., Kikuchi, H., Rannenberg, K. (eds.) IWSEC 2007. LNCS, vol. 4752, pp. 396–411. Springer, Heidelberg (2007). https://doi.org/10.1007/978-3-540-75651-4_27

10. Liu, D.Y.W., et al.: Formal definition and construction of nominative signature. In: Qing, S., Imai, H., Wang, G. (eds.) ICICS 2007. LNCS, vol. 4861, pp. 57–68. Springer, Heidelberg (2007). https://doi.org/10.1007/978-3-540-77048-0_5

11. Lyubashevsky, V.: Lattice signatures without trapdoors. In: Pointcheval, D., Johansson, T. (eds.) EUROCRYPT 2012. LNCS, vol. 7237, pp. 738–755. Springer, Heidelberg (2012). https://doi.org/10.1007/978-3-642-29011-4_43

12. Micciancio, D., Peikert, C.: Trapdoors for lattices: simpler, tighter, faster, smaller. In: Pointcheval, D., Johansson, T. (eds.) EUROCRYPT 2012. LNCS, vol. 7237, pp. 700–718. Springer, Heidelberg (2012). https://doi.org/10.1007/978-3-642-29011-4_41

13. Regev, O.: On lattices, learning with errors, random linear codes, and cryptography. J. ACM (JACM) **56**(6), 34 (2009)

14. Schuldt, J.C.N., Hanaoka, G.: Non-transferable user certification secure against authority information leaks and impersonation attacks. In: Lopez, J., Tsudik, G. (eds.) ACNS 2011. LNCS, vol. 6715, pp. 413–430. Springer, Heidelberg (2011). https://doi.org/10.1007/978-3-642-21554-4_24

15. Susilo, W., Mu, Y.: On the security of nominative signatures. In: Boyd, C., González Nieto, J.M. (eds.) ACISP 2005. LNCS, vol. 3574, pp. 329–335. Springer, Heidelberg (2005). https://doi.org/10.1007/11506157_28

Reinterpreting and Improving the Cryptanalysis of the Flash Player PRNG

George Teşeleanu[1,2(✉)]

[1] Department of Computer Science, "Al.I.Cuza" University of Iaşi,
700506 Iaşi, Romania
george.teseleanu@info.uaic.ro
[2] Advanced Technologies Institute, 10 Dinu Vintilă, Bucharest, Romania
tgeorge@dcti.ro

Abstract. Constant blinding is an efficient countermeasure against just-in-time (JIT) spraying attacks. Unfortunately, this mitigation mechanism is not always implemented correctly. One such example is the constant blinding mechanism found in the Adobe Flash Player. Instead of choosing a strong mainstream pseudo-random number generator (PRNG), the Flash Player designers chose to implement a proprietary one. This led to the discovery of a vulnerability that can be exploited to recover the initial seed used by the PRNG and thus, to bypass the constant blinding mechanism. Using this vulnerability as a starting point, we show that no matter the parameters used by the previously mentioned PRNG it still remains a weak construction. A consequence of this study is an improvement of the seed recovering mechanism from previously known complexity of $\mathcal{O}(2^{21})$ to one of $\mathcal{O}(2^{11})$.

1 Introduction

JIT compilers (*e.g.* JavaScript and ActionScript) translate source code or byte-code into machine code at runtime for faster execution. Due to the fact that the purpose of JIT compilers is to produce executable data, they are normally exempt from data execution prevention (DEP[1]). Thus, a vulnerability in a JIT compiler might lead to an exploit undetectable by DEP. One such attack, called JIT spraying, was proposed in [7]. By coercing the ActionScript JIT engine, Blazakis shows how to write shellcode into the executable memory and thus, bypass DEP. The key insight is that the JIT compiler is predictable and must copy some constants to the executable page. Hence, these constants can encode small instructions and then control flow to the next constant's location.

To defend against JIT spraying attacks, Adobe employs a technique called *constant blinding*. This method prevents an attacker from loading his instructions

---

[1] The DEP mechanism performs additional checks on memory to help prevent malicious code from running on a system.

© Springer Nature Switzerland AG 2019
C. Carlet et al. (Eds.): C2SI 2019, LNCS 11445, pp. 92–104, 2019.
https://doi.org/10.1007/978-3-030-16458-4_7

into constants and thus, blocks the delivery of his malicious script. The idea behind constant blinding is to avoid storing constants in memory in their original form. Instead, they are first XORed with some randomly generated secret cookie and then stored inside the memory. If the secret cookie is generated by means of a weak PRNG[2], the attacker regains his ability to inject malicious instructions.

Instead of using an already proven secure PRNG, the Flash Player designers tried to implement their own PRNG. Unfortunately, in [1,9] it is shown that the design of the generator is flawed. In [1] a brute force attack is implemented, while in [9] a refined brute force attack is presented. These results have been reported to Adobe under the code CVE-2017-3000 [5] and the vulnerability has been patched in version 25.0.0.127.

In this paper, we refine the attack presented in [9] from a time complexity of $\mathcal{O}(2^{21})$ to one of $\mathcal{O}(2^{11})$. We also show that no matter the parameters used by the PRNG, the flaw remains. More precisely we show that for any parameters the worst brute force attack takes $\mathcal{O}(2^{21})$ operations. In [9] the authors do not present the full algorithm for reversing the PRNG, while in [1] we found the full algorithm, but it was not optimized. For completeness, in Appendix A we also present an optimized version of the full algorithm. Note that in this paper we only focus on the Flash Player PRNG. For more details about JIT spraying attacks and constant blinding we refer the reader to [6–9].

Structure of the Paper. Notations and definitions are presented in Sect. 2. The core of the paper consists of Sects. 3 and 4 and contains a series of algorithms for inverting a generalized version of the hash function used by the Flash Player. Experimental result are given in Sect. 5. We conclude in Sect. 6. Supplementary algorithms may be found in Appendix A.

2   Preliminaries

Notations. In this paper we use C language operators (*i.e.* |/& for bitwise or/and, $\ll$ for left shift and == for equality testing) as well as other widely adopted notations (*i.e.* $\oplus$ for the bitwise xor, $\leftarrow$ for assignment and $\gg_s$ for the right shift of a signed integer). Hexadecimal numbers will always contain the prefix 0x, while binary ones the prefix 0b. The subset $\{0, \ldots, q\} \in \mathbb{N}$ will be referred to as $[0, q]$.

By $0^\alpha 1^\beta 0^\gamma$ we will denote an $(\alpha+\beta+\gamma)$-bit word that has α bits of 0, followed by β bits of 1 and γ trailing zeros.

2.1   Constant Blinding in Flash Player

In this subsection we describe the implementation of the Flash Player PRNG, as presented in [3]. The generator has four components (described in Listing 1.1): a seed initialization function (*RandomFastInit*), a seed update function (*Random-FastInit*), a hash function (*RandomPureHasher*) and a cookie generation function

---

[2] *i.e.*, the seed used to generate the cookie can be recovered in reasonable time.

(*GenerateRandomNumber*). According to the source code, the hash function is adapted from [10]. Note that the variable uValue is initialized by a function found in the Windows API (*VMPI_getPerformanceCounter*).

The role of the hash function is to make attackers unable to retrieve the seed value (uValue) in reasonable time. Note that the default timeout in Flash Player is 15 s. Thus, an attacker must succeed in finding the seed, predicate the secret value into the next round and embed the desired value in the executable heap in 15 s.

```
1  #define  c3   15731L
2  #define  c2   789221L
3  #define  c1   1376312589L
4  #define  kRandomPureMax  0x7fffffffL
5
6  void  RandomFastInit(pTRandomFast pRandomFast){
7      int32_t  n = 31;
8      pRandomFast->uValue = (uint32_t)(
       VMPI_getPerformanceCounter());
9      pRandomFast->uSequenceLength = (1L << n) - 1L;
10     pRandomFast->uXorMask = 0x14000000L;
11 }
12 #define  RandomFastNext(_pRandomFast)\
13 (\
14     ((_pRandomFast)->uValue & 1L)\
15     ? ((_pRandomFast)->uValue = ((_pRandomFast)->uValue >> 1)
         ^ (_pRandomFast)->uXorMask)\
16     : ((_pRandomFast)->uValue = ((_pRandomFast)->uValue >> 1)
       )\
17 )
18 int32_t RandomPureHasher(int32_t iSeed){
19     int32_t   iResult;
20     iSeed = ((iSeed << 13) ^ iSeed) - (iSeed >> 21);
21     iResult = (iSeed*(iSeed*iSeed*c3 + c2) + c1) &
       kRandomPureMax;
22     iResult += iSeed;
23     iResult = ((iResult << 13) ^ iResult) - (iResult >> 21);
24     return iResult;
25 }
26 int32_t GenerateRandomNumber(pTRandomFast pRandomFast){
27     if (pRandomFast->uValue == 0) {
28         RandomFastInit(pRandomFast);
29     }
30     long aNum = RandomFastNext(pRandomFast);
31     aNum = RandomPureHasher(aNum * 71L);
32     return aNum & kRandomPureMax;
33 }
```

Listing 1.1. ActionScript PRNG implementation.

Algorithm 1. The algorithm for reversing f

Input: The value to reverse v.
Output: The set of possible solutions S.

1   $S \leftarrow \varnothing$;
2   **for** $low \in [0, \texttt{0x7ff}]$ **do**
3      $temp \leftarrow v \ \& \ \texttt{0x7ff}$;
4   **if** $temp > low$ **then**
5        $high = (1 \ll 11) + low - temp$;
6   **end**
7   **else**
8        $high = low - temp$;
9   **end**
10   **for** $mid \in [0, \texttt{0x3ff}]$ **do**
11        $s \leftarrow (high \ll 21) \ | \ (mid \ll 11) \ | \ low$;
12   **if** $f(s) == v$ **then**
13          $S \leftarrow S \cup s$;
14   **end**
15   **end**
16 **end**
17 **return** S;

2.2 Shifting Signed Integers

According to [2], if we left shift a signed integer (*e.g.* iSeed) the result is unpredictable and if we right shift a signed negative integer the result is implementation dependent. Thus, we will make a clear distinction between implementation independent or dependent attack strategies against the Flash Player PRNG. In some cases, the attacks devised for a particular implementation are faster than the corresponding implementation independent strategy (see Sect. 4).

For simplicity, when talking about targeted attacks we consider the behavior of shifts implemented in Microsoft Visual Studio [2] and GCC [4] on x86 and x64 architectures. Thus, left shifts are sign independent (*e.g.* 0b11000000 $\ll$ 1 = 0b10000000) and right shifts of signed integers use the sign bit to fill vacated bit positions (*e.g.* 0b11000000 $\gg_s$ 1 = 0b11100000 and 0b01000000 $\gg_s$ 1 = 0b00100000).

2.3 Previous Cryptanalysis Results

By abstracting the code described in Listing 1.1, we identify the three main components of the cookie generation function, *i.e.*:

$$f(x) = (x \ll 13) \oplus x - (x \gg_s 21),$$
$$g(x) = (c_3 \cdot x^3 + c_2 \cdot x + c_1) \ \& \ \texttt{0x7fffffff} + x,$$
$$h(x) = 71 \cdot x \bmod 2^{32}.$$

If these functions are reversed, then the PRNG is broken. In [9], the authors propose an algorithm for reversing f (Algorithm 1) and a backtracking algorithm for reversing g (the complete description is presented in Algorithm 7). For completeness, we provide in Appendix A the full algorithm (Algorithm 8) for reversing the PRNG (which includes the inverse of h). Note that Algorithm 1 has a time complexity of $\mathcal{O}(2^{21})$ and is implementation independent.

3   Reinterpreting

Let n be the word size in bits. As Algorithm 7 can be used to reverse any generic polynomial g and the linear function h can be easily reversed, we only focus on reversing the generic function

$$f(x) = (x \ll \ell) \oplus x - (x \gg_s r),$$

where $1 \leq \ell, r \leq n$ are integers. We further denote by v the output of $f(x)$.

Degenerate Cases. Let $ct = 10^{n-1} \gg_s n$. We consider the cases $\ell, r \in \{0, n\}$ as degenerate due to different inherent weakness induced by these choices. Thus, in our study we do not take in consideration degenerate cases. We further present the weakness associated with the degenerate cases:

- when $r = n$ and $0 < \ell \leq n$, the function $f(x) = x \oplus (x \ll \ell) + ct$ leaks ℓ bits of its seed;
- when $\ell = 0$ and $0 \leq r \leq n$, the function $f(x) = -(x \gg_s r)$ leaks $n - r$ bits of its seed and v has the rest of the bits constant;
- when $r = 0$ and $0 < \ell \leq n$, the function $f(x) = x \oplus (x \ll \ell) - x$ always outputs a v with ℓ trailing zeros;
- when $\ell = n$ and $0 < r \leq n$, the function $f(x) = x - (x \gg_s r)$ leaks r bits of its seed.

We further present a series of attacks that are implementation independent. In the case $n - r \leq \ell, n \leq 2r$ we generalized a different algorithm than Algorithm 1, due to a more direct adaptation to an implementation dependent version.

Lemma 1. *Let $c_{24} = \lfloor n/r \rfloor + 1$. For each (set of) condition(s) presented in Column 2 of Table 1 there exists an attack whose corresponding time complexity is presented in Column 3 of Table 1.*

Proof. When $n - r \leq \ell$, we can explicitly write the function f as shown in Fig. 1. Note that the bits used to fill vacated positions are represented as question marks. As we want a compiler independent attack we consider the ? bits as unknown and tailor our attacks accordingly.

In the first case, we first recover the most significant $n - r$ bits (*high*) and then extract the least significant $n - r$ bits (*low*) from $v + high$. For the rest of

Table 1. Attack parameters for Lemma 1

	Conditions	Time complexity
1	$n - r \leq \ell$ and $n \leq 2r$	$\mathcal{O}(2^r)$
2	$n - r \leq \ell$ and $n \geq 2r$	$\mathcal{O}(c_{24}2^r)$
3	$n - r \geq \ell$ and $n \leq 2r$	$\mathcal{O}(2^r)$
4	$n - r \geq \ell$ and $n \geq 2r$	$\mathcal{O}(c_{24}2^r)$

$$
\begin{array}{llllllll}
 & a_1 & \cdots & a_{n-\ell} & a_{n-\ell+1} & \cdots & a_r & a_{r+1} & \cdots & a_n \\
\oplus & a_{\ell+1} & \cdots & a_n & 0 & \cdots & 0 & 0 & \cdots & 0 \\
= & t_1 & \cdots & t_{n-\ell} & t_{n-\ell+1} & \cdots & t_r & t_{r+1} & \cdots & t_n \\
+ & ? & \cdots & ? & ? & \cdots & ? & a_1 & \cdots & a_{n-r}
\end{array}
$$

Fig. 1. Bit representation of $f(x)$

Algorithm 2. The algorithm for reversing f (Case 1)

Input: The value to reverse v.
Output: The set of possible solutions S.
1 $S \leftarrow \varnothing$;
2 **for** $high \in [0, 1^{n-r}]$ **do**
3 $\quad$ $temp \leftarrow v + high$;
4 $\quad$ $low \leftarrow temp \ \& \ 1^{n-r}$;
5 $\quad$ **for** $mid \in [0, 1^{2r-n}]$ **do**
6 $\quad\quad$ $s \leftarrow (high \ll r) \mid (mid \ll (n-r)) \mid low$;
7 $\quad\quad$ **if** $f(s) == v$ **then**
8 $\quad\quad\quad$ $S \leftarrow S \cup s$;
9 $\quad\quad$ **end**
10 $\quad$ **end**
11 **end**
12 **return** S;

$2r - n$ bits (mid) we do an exhaustive search. This leads to a time complexity of $\mathcal{O}(2^{n-r}2^{2r-n}) = \mathcal{O}(2^r)$.

In the second case, we can do better than simply using Algorithm 2. We first recover the least significant r bits (low) and then use low to gradually recover the rest of the bits (mid). This leads to the complexity $\mathcal{O}(2^r(q+1))$.

When $n - r \geq \ell$, we can explicitly write the function f as depicted in Fig. 2. Note that some of the bits resulted from the left shift overlap with some from the right shift. Thus, in the third case we recover the least significant $n - r$ bits (low), add the overlapping bits, and then recover the most significant $n - r$ bits ($high$) from v. For the rest of $2r - n$ bits (mid) we do an exhaustive search. So, similarly to the first case, we obtain a complexity of $\mathcal{O}(2^r)$.

In the last case, we slightly modify the algorithm used in the second case to take into account the overlapping bits. Thus, the resulting attack has the same complexity $\mathcal{O}(2^r(q+1))$.

Algorithm 3. The algorithm for reversing f (Case 2 and 4)

Input: The value to reverse v.
Output: The set of possible solutions S.

1 **Function** $Minus(temp_1, temp_2, size)$:
2   **if** $temp_2 > temp_1$ **then**
3 | $high = (1 \ll (size + 1)) + temp_1 - temp_2$;
4   **end**
5   **else**
6 | $high = temp_1 - temp_2$;
7   **end**
8   **return** $high$ & 1^{size};
9 **Function** $ComputeMid(low)$:
10     $q \leftarrow \lfloor (n - r)/r \rfloor$;
11     $m \leftarrow n - r \bmod r$;
12     $mid \leftarrow 0$;
13   **for** $i \in [1, q]$ **do**
14        $temp_1 \leftarrow (mid \ll r) \mid low$;
15        $temp_1 \leftarrow (temp_1 \oplus (temp_1 \ll \ell))$ & 1^{ir}; //only for Case 4
16        $temp_2 \leftarrow v$ & 1^{ir};
17        $mid \leftarrow Minus(temp_1, temp_2, ir)$;
18   **end**
19   **if** $m \neq 0$ **then**
20        $temp_1 \leftarrow (mid \ll r) \mid low$;
21        $temp_1 \leftarrow (temp_1 \oplus (temp_1 \ll \ell))$ & 1^{n-r}; //only for Case 4
22        $temp_2 \leftarrow v$ & 1^{n-r};
23        $mid \leftarrow Minus(temp_1, temp_2, n - r)$;
24   **end**
25   **return** mid
26 **Function** $Main(v)$:
27     $S \leftarrow \varnothing$;
28   **for** $low \in [0, 1^r]$ **do**
29        $mid \leftarrow ComputeMid(low)$;
30        $s \leftarrow (mid \ll r) \mid low$;
31   **if** $f(s) == v$ **then**
32 | $S \leftarrow S \cup s$;
33   **end**
34   **end**
35   **return** S;

$$
\begin{array}{ccccccccc}
 & a_1 & \cdots & a_r & a_{r+1} & \cdots & a_{n-\ell} & a_{n-\ell+1} & \cdots & a_n \\
\oplus & a_{\ell+1} & \cdots & a_{\ell+r} & a_{\ell+r+1} & \cdots & a_n & 0 & \cdots & 0 \\
= & t_1 & \cdots & t_r & t_{r+1} & \cdots & t_{n-\ell} & t_{n-\ell+1} & \cdots & t_n \\
+ & ? & \cdots & ? & a_1 & \cdots & a_{n-r-\ell} & a_{n-r-\ell+1} & \cdots & a_{n-r}
\end{array}
$$

Fig. 2. Bit representation of $f(x)$

Algorithm 4. The algorithm for reversing f (Case 3)

Input: The value to reverse v.
Output: The set of possible solutions S.

1 $S \leftarrow \varnothing$;
2 **for** $low \in [0, 1^{n-r}]$ **do**
3 $\quad temp_1 \leftarrow (low \oplus (low \ll \ell))$ & 1^{n-r};
4 $\quad temp_2 \leftarrow v$ & 1^{n-r};
5 $\quad high \leftarrow Minus(temp_1, temp_2, n - r)$;
6 $\quad$ **for** $mid \in [0, 1^{2r-n}]$ **do**
7 $\quad\quad s \leftarrow (high \ll r) \mid (mid \ll (n - r)) \mid low$;
8 $\quad\quad$ **if** $f(s) == v$ **then**
9 $\quad\quad\quad S \leftarrow S \cup s$;
10 $\quad\quad$ **end**
11 $\quad$ **end**
12 **end**
13 **return** S;

Corollary 1. *There exists an attack on the Flash Player PRNG with time complexity $\mathcal{O}(2^{21})$.*

4 Improving

In this section we consider implementation dependent attacks. For simplicity we assume the behavior of the Microsoft Visual Studio and GCC compilers on ×86 and ×64 architectures. Other compilers' behaviors can be modeled similarly (Table 2).

Lemma 2. *Let $c_{13} = \lfloor r/\ell \rfloor + 1$. For each (set of) condition(s) presented in Column 2 of Table 1 there exists an attack whose corresponding time complexity is presented in Column 3 of Table 1.*

Table 2. Attack parameters for Lemma 2

	Conditions	Time complexity
1	$n - r \leq \ell$ and $n \leq 2r$	$\mathcal{O}(c_{13}2^{n-r})$
3	$n - r \geq \ell$ and $n \leq 2r$	$\mathcal{O}(c_{13}2^{n-r})$

$$
\begin{array}{cccccccccc}
 & a_1 & \cdots & a_{n-\ell} & a_{n-\ell+1} & \cdots & a_r & a_{r+1} & \cdots & a_n \\
\oplus & a_{\ell+1} & \cdots & a_n & 0 & \cdots & 0 & 0 & \cdots & 0 \\
= & t_1 & \cdots & t_{n-\ell} & t_{n-\ell+1} & \cdots & t_r & t_{r+1} & \cdots & t_n \\
+ & a_1 & \cdots & a_1 & a_1 & \cdots & a_1 & a_1 & \cdots & a_{n-r}
\end{array}
$$

Fig. 3. Bit representation of $f(x)$

$$
\begin{array}{llllllll}
& a_1 & \dots & a_r & a_{r+1} & \dots & a_{n-\ell} & a_{n-\ell+1} & \dots & a_n \\
\oplus & a_{\ell+1} & \dots & a_{\ell+r} & a_{\ell+r+1} & \dots & a_n & 0 & \dots & 0 \\
= & t_1 & \dots & t_r & t_{r+1} & \dots & t_{n-\ell} & t_{n-\ell+1} & \dots & t_n \\
+ & a_1 & \dots & a_1 & a_1 & \dots & a_{n-r-\ell} & a_{n-r-\ell+1} & \dots & a_{n-r}
\end{array}
$$

Fig. 4. Bit representation of $f(x)$

Algorithm 5. The improved algorithm for reversing f (Case 1)

Input: The value to reverse v.

Output: The set of possible solutions S.

1 **Function** $Add(v, high)$:
2   **if** $high \in [0, 1^{n-r-1}]$ **then**
3 | $temp \leftarrow v + high$;
4   **end**
5   **else**
6 | $temp \leftarrow v + high \oplus 1^r 0^{n-r}$;
7   **end**
8   **return** $temp$;
9 **Function** $SpeedMid(low, temp, size, step)$:
10     $q \leftarrow \lfloor size/step \rfloor$;
11     $m \leftarrow size \bmod step$;
12     $temp_1 \leftarrow low$;
13   **for** $i \in [0, q-1]$ **do**
14 | $offset \leftarrow (i+1) \cdot step$;
15 | $temp_2 \leftarrow (temp_1 \oplus (temp \gg offset)) \ \& \ 1^{n-r}$;
16 | $mid \leftarrow mid \ | \ (temp_1 \ll (i \cdot step))$;
17 | $temp_1 \leftarrow temp_2$
18   **end**
19     $offset \leftarrow (q+1) \cdot step$;
20     $temp_2 \leftarrow (temp_1 \oplus (temp \gg offset)) \ \& \ 1^m$;
21     $mid \leftarrow mid \ | \ (temp_1 \ll (q \cdot step))$;
22   **return** mid;
23 **Function** $Main(v)$:
24     $S \leftarrow \varnothing$;
25   **for** $high \in [0, 1^{n-r}]$ **do**
26        $temp \leftarrow Add(v, high)$;
27        $low \leftarrow temp \ \& \ 1^\ell$;
28        $mid \leftarrow SpeedMid(low, temp, r-\ell, \ell)$;
29        $s \leftarrow (high \ll r) \ | \ (mid \ll \ell) \ | \ low$;
30   **if** $f(s) == v$ **then**
31 | $S \leftarrow S \cup s$;
32   **end**
33   **end**
34   **return** S;

Proof. When $n - r \leq \ell$, we can explicit the function f as shown in Fig. 3. Note that a_1 is the sign bit used to fill the gaps. With this in mind, we use the existing knowledge (low) to gradually recover the $2r - n$ bits (mid). Thus, we improve the exhaustive search of the mid part from Algorithm 2. This leads to a time complexity of $\mathcal{O}(2^r(q + 1))$.

When $n - r \geq \ell$, Fig. 2 becomes Fig. 4. In the third case, we adapt the algorithm used in Case 1 to take into account overlapping bits. Thus, we obtain the same time complexity.

Corollary 2. *There exist an attack on the Flash Player PRNG with time complexity $\mathcal{O}(2^{11})$.*

Corollary 3. *For any choice of ℓ and r there exists an attack whose time complexity is at most $\mathcal{O}(n2^{n/2})$.*

Proof. According to Lemma 1, Cases 2 and 4 there exists an attack with complexity $\mathcal{O}(2^r) \leq \mathcal{O}(2^{n/2})$. In Cases 1 and 3 we make use of the attacks presented in Lemma 2. Thus, there exists an attack with complexity $\mathcal{O}(c_{13}2^{n-r}) \leq \mathcal{O}(c_{13}2^{n/2}) \leq \mathcal{O}(n2^{n/2})$. As a result, in the general case we obtain our statement.

Corollary 4. *There exists an attack on the Flash Player PRNG with time complexity at most $\mathcal{O}(2^{21})$ independent of ℓ and r.*

Algorithm 6. The improved algorithm for reversing f (Case 3)

Input: The value to reverse v.
Output: The set of possible solutions S.
1   $S \leftarrow \varnothing; e \leftarrow n - r - \ell;$
2   **for** $low \in [0, 1^{n-r}]$ **do**
3      $temp_1 \leftarrow (low \oplus (low \ll \ell)) \& 1^{n-r};$
4      $temp_2 \leftarrow v \& 1^{n-r};$
5      $high \leftarrow Minus(temp_1, temp_2, n - r);$
6      $temp \leftarrow Add(v, high);$
7      $mid \leftarrow SpeedMid(low, temp, 2r - n + e, \ell);$
8      $mid \leftarrow mid \gg e;$
9      $s \leftarrow (high \ll r) \mid (mid \ll (n - r)) \mid low;$
10   **if** $f(s) == v$ **then**
11        $\mid \quad S \leftarrow S \cup s;$
12   **end**
13 **end**
14 **return** $S;$

---

5   Experimental Results

We implemented Algorithms 2, 3, 4, 5 and 6 and used 32 random seed values to test if our algorithms succeed in recovering the seed for all $1 \le r < 32$ and $1 \le l < 32$. The compilers we worked with are Microsoft Visual Studio 2017 version 15.7.5 with the C++14 extension activated and GCC version 5.4.0 with the C++11 extensions activated. The tests were a success.

In another experiment we run Algorithms 2, 3, 4, 5, 6 and 8 with 2000 random seed values and used the function $omp\_get\_wtime()$ to compute the running time necessary to invert the function f and the corresponding PRNG. The programs were run on a CPU Intel i7-4790 4.00 GHz and compiled with GCC with the O3 flag activated. The results for the 2000 iterations can be found in Tables 3 and 4. Note that the average time for brute forcing one value is 2.88861 s for f and 13.2578 s for PRNG.

Table 3. Running times for reversing the function f and the PRNG (Cases 1 and 2)

	Case 1 ($l = 13, r = 21$)			Case 2 ($l = 23, r = 11$)
	Algorithm 1	Algorithm 2	Algorithm 5	Algorithm 3
$f(x)$	2.16055 s	2.82102 s	0.00717478 s	0.00608366 s
PRNG	10.6442 s	13.8981 s	0.036917 s	0.0334592 s

Table 4. Running times for reversing the function f and the PRNG (Cases 3 and 4)

	Case 3 ($l = 9, r = 21$)		Case 4 ($l = 19, r = 11$)
	Algorithm 4	Algorithm 6	Algorithm 3
$f(x)$	2.77496 s	0.00708749 s	0.00809854 s
PRNG	14.6386 s	0.0432187 s	0.0437757 s

6   Conclusions

In this paper we improved the results from [9] and shown that no matter the parameters used by the Flash Player PRNG, there exists always a brute force attack with complexity at most $\mathcal{O}(n2^{n/2})$. As a consequence, we prove that the secret cookie used for constant blinding can always be recovered due to the weak design of the PRNG. Note that the results presented in this paper might be further improved if one uses other cryptanalytic methods, besides brute force. We leave this research direction as an open problem.

A   Additional Algorithms

In [9] the algorithm used to invert g is not presented in full. Based on the descriptions found in [1,9] we present the full algorithm in Algorithm 7. Note that the algorithm works for any generic polynomial g, not only for the one used in the Flash Player PRNG. Note that $\&S$ means that we pass S by reference.

Algorithm 7. Backtracking algorithm for reversing g

    Input: The value to reverse v
    Output: The set of possible solutions S

1 **Function** $Verify\_ith\_bit(v, i, sol)$:
2 | $b_1 \leftarrow g(sol) \ \& \ (1 \ll i)$;
3 | $b_2 \leftarrow v \ \& \ (1 \ll i)$;
4 | **return** $bit_1 == bit_2$;
5 **Function** $Add\_ith\_bit(v, i, sol, \&S, b)$:
6 | $sol \leftarrow sol \ | \ (b \ll i)$;
7 | **if** $Verify_ith_bit(v, i, sol) == $ **true then**
8 | $i \leftarrow i + 1$;
9 | $Reverse\_bit(v, i, sol, S)$;
10 | **end**
11 **Function** $Reverse\_bit(v, i, sol, \&S)$:
12 | **if** $i == n$ **then**
13 | $S \leftarrow S \cup sol$;
14 | **return;**
15 | **end**
16 | $add\_ith\_bit(v, i, sol, S, 0)$;
17 | $add\_ith\_bit(v, i, sol, S, 1)$;
18 **Function** $Reverse\_polynomial(v)$:
19 | $S \leftarrow \varnothing$; //the set of possible solutions
20 | $i \leftarrow 0$; //the target bit
21 | $sol \leftarrow 0$; //the current solution
22 | $reverse\_bit(v, i, sol, S)$;
23 | **return** S;

The only algorithm we found for reversing the Flash Player PRNG is described in [1]. We improve their attack in Algorithm 8. To reverse the bit manipulation function f and the polynomial g we use the abstract functions $Reverse\_bit\_manipulation$ and $Reverse\_polynomial$, respectively. Remark that Algorithm 8 works for any generic polynomial g and any generic function $h(x) = p \cdot x \bmod 2^n$ with p odd. In the Flash Player case we have $p^{-1} \equiv 3811027319 \bmod 2^{32}$.

Algorithm 8. The algorithm for reversing the PRNG

Input: The value to reverse v
Output: The set of possible solutions S

1 $v' \leftarrow v \mid (1 \ll (n-1))$;
2 $S_{bit} \leftarrow Reverse\_bit\_manipulation(v) \cup Reverse\_bit\_manipulation(v')$;
3 $S_{pol}, S_{hash}, S \leftarrow \varnothing$;
4 **for** $s_{bit} \in S_{bit}$ **do**
5   $\mid$ $S_{pol} \leftarrow S_{pol} \cup Reverse\_polynomial(s_{bit})$;
6 **end**
7 **for** $s_{pol} \in S_{pol}$ **do**
8   $\mid$ $S_{hash} \leftarrow S_{hash} \cup Reverse\_bit\_manipulation(s_{pol})$;
9 **end**
10 **for** $s_{hash} \in S_{hash}$ **do**
11 $\mid$ $s \leftarrow s_{hash} \cdot p^{-1} \bmod 2^n$;
12 $\mid$ $S \leftarrow S \cup s$;
13 **end**
14 **return** S;

References

1. A Full Exploit of CVE-2017-3000 on Flash Player Constant Blinding PRNG. https://github.com/dangokyo/CVE-2017-3000/blob/master/Exploiter.as
2. Left Shift and Right Shift Operators. https://docs.microsoft.com/en-us/cpp/cpp/left-shift-and-right-shift-operators-input-and-output?view=vs-2017
3. Source Code for the Actionscript Virtual Machine. https://github.com/adobe-flash/avmplus/tree/master/core/MathUtils.cpp
4. Using the GNU Compiler Collection. https://gcc.gnu.org/onlinedocs/gcc/Integers-implementation.html
5. Vulnerability Details: CVE-2017-3000. https://www.cvedetails.com/cve/CVE-2017-3000/
6. Athanasakis, M., Athanasopoulos, E., Polychronakis, M., Portokalidis, G., Ioannidis, S.: The devil is in the constants: bypassing defences in browser JIT engines. In: NDSS 2015. The Internet Society (2015)
7. Blazakis, D.: Interpreter exploitation. In: WOOT 2010. USENIX Association (2010)
8. Reshetova, E., Bonazzi, F., Asokan, N.: Randomization can't stop BPF JIT spray. In: Yan, Z., Molva, R., Mazurczyk, W., Kantola, R. (eds.) NSS 2017. LNCS, vol. 10394, pp. 233–247. Springer, Cham (2017). https://doi.org/10.1007/978-3-319-64701-2_17
9. Wang, C., Huang, T., Wu, H.: On the weakness of constant blinding PRNG in flash player. In: Naccache, D., et al. (eds.) ICICS 2018. LNCS, vol. 11149, pp. 107–123. Springer, Cham (2018). https://doi.org/10.1007/978-3-030-01950-1_7
10. Ward, G.: A recursive implementation of the perlin noise function. In: Graphics Gems II, pp. 396–401. Elsevier (1991)

A Key Exchange Based on the Short Integer Solution Problem and the Learning with Errors Problem

Jintai Ding, Kevin Schmitt, and Zheng Zhang$^{(\boxtimes)}$

Department of Mathematical Science, University of Cincinnati, Cincinnati, USA
zhang2zh@mail.uc.edu

Abstract. Short integer solution (SIS) and learning with errors (LWE) are two hard lattice problems. These two problems are believed having huge potential in application of cryptography. In 2012, Ding et al. [5] introduced the first provably secure key exchange based on LWE problem. On the other hand, we believe that it is very difficult to do key exchange on SIS problem only. In 2014, Wang et al. [6] did an attempt, but it was not successful. Mao et al. [7] broke the protocol by an attack based on CBi-SIS problem in 2016. However, their attack is not efficient. In this paper, we present a extremely straightforward and simple attack to Wang's key exchange and then we will construct a key exchange based on SIS and LWE problems.

Keywords: Key exchange · SIS · LWE · Attack · Lattice

1 Introduction

1.1 Background

Key exchange protocol makes it possible for two parties to exchange keys over untrusted channels. The first revolutionary key exchange protocol was presented by Diffie and Hellman [2], which is called Diffie-Hellman key exchange protocol. The security of Diffie-Hellman key exchange is based on a hard number theory problem called discrete logarithm problem. However, in 1994, Peter Shor [3] theoretically proved that these hard number theory problems can hardly resist the attack from a quantum computer. Therefore, a post-quantum key exchange is urgently needed. Key exchange based on hard lattice problems is considered to be one of the candidates of post-quantum key exchanges.

1.2 Key Exchange Based on SIS Problem

A well-know hard lattice problem is the SIS problem introduced by Ajtai [1]. Some efforts have been made to construct a key exchange based on SIS problem. Although there are other attempts of key exchange on SIS problem, the basic structure is the following.

© Springer Nature Switzerland AG 2019
C. Carlet et al. (Eds.): C2SI 2019, LNCS 11445, pp. 105–117, 2019.
https://doi.org/10.1007/978-3-030-16458-4_8

(1) Assume that Alice and Bob agree to do a key exchange. The system generates a random matrix $\mathbf{M} \in \mathbb{Z}_q^{n \times m}$.

(2) Alice chooses a secret key $\mathbf{s}_A \in \mathbf{Z}_q^m$ with norm $\|\mathbf{s}_A\| \leq \beta$. She computes $\mathbf{P}_A = \mathbf{M}\mathbf{s}_A$ and send $\mathbf{P}_A$ to Bob.

(3) Bob chooses a secret key $\mathbf{s}_B \in \mathbf{Z}_q^n$ with norm $\|\mathbf{s}_B\| \leq \beta$. He computes $\mathbf{P}_B = \mathbf{s}_B^T\mathbf{M}$, and sends $\mathbf{P}_B$ to Alice.

(4) Receiving $\mathbf{P}_B$, Alice computes $\mathbf{K}_A = \mathbf{s}_A^T\mathbf{P}_B^T = \mathbf{s}_A^T\mathbf{M}^T\mathbf{s}_B$.

(5) Receiving $\mathbf{P}_A$, Bob computes $\mathbf{K}_B = \mathbf{P}_A^T\mathbf{s}_B = \mathbf{s}_A^T\mathbf{M}^T\mathbf{s}_B$.

Note that in order to apply the SIS problem to ensure the security of Alice's secret key, we need the condition that $n \ll m$. On the other hand, we also need the condition that $m \gg n$ to apply the SIS problem to guarantee the security of Bob's secret key. Therefore both parties have to get much more numbers of variables than equations, which makes it impossible to do key exchange on SIS problem.

1.3 Key Exchange Based on LWE Problem

Another building block of lattice-based problem is the LWE problem introduced by Regev [4]. The LWE problem is attractive due to its security and efficiency. A lot of attempts have been made to build a key exchange on LWE problem, but not until 2012, the first provably secure key exchange based on LWE problem was published by Ding [5]. The scheme is very efficient in computation, and can be extended to Ring-LWE. A new invention in his protocol is to extract a shared secret from the two values which are very close by rounding with signal functions.

1.4 Our Contributions

We first present an attack to Wang's protocol [6] based on an elementary linear algebra problem: solving linear equations. We observe that any solution to the system of linear equations can be used to recover the shared key. Therefore we claim that SIS problem is irrelevant to Wang's key exchange and there is no need for Mao et al. [7] to solve any SIS related problem at all.

Next we present a key exchange based on both SIS problem and LWE problem. In other words, Alice will use LWE problem to ensure the security on what she sends to Bob and Bob will use SIS problem to ensure the security on what he sends to Alice. It is obvious that our system is not symmetric. After the switch, we can extract a shared key from the two values which are very close by signal function proposed by Ding [5] in key exchange based on LWE problem.

2 Attack to Wang's Protocol

2.1 Preliminary

Let us first recall the definition of SIS problem and its derivatives introduced in Wang et al.'s paper [6].

Definition 1 *(SIS problem). Given a random matrix* $\mathbf{A} \in \mathbb{Z}_q^{n \times m}$, *the goal of SIS problem is to find a nonzero vector* $\mathbf{z} \in \mathbb{Z}^m$ *that satisfies* $\mathbf{Az} = \mathbf{0}$ *with* $||\mathbf{z}|| \leq \beta$.

Note that a solution to the equation $\mathbf{Az} = \mathbf{0}$ is easy to obtain without the requirement on the length ($||\mathbf{z}|| \leq \beta$) by Gaussian elimination, however it is hard to find a solution of short length.

Next, Wang et al. extend this problem to Bi-ISIS* Problem.

Definition 2 *(Bi-ISIS* Problem). Given integers* n, m, q *(*$m > n \log q$*), a real* β *as in SIS, and a matrix* $\mathbf{A} \in \mathbb{Z}_q^{m \times m}$ *with rank* n, $\mathbf{e}_1$ *is linearly independent with column vectors of* $\mathbf{A}$, $\mathbf{e}_2$ *is linearly independent with row vectors of* $\mathbf{A}$, *given vectors* $\mathbf{b}_1 \in \{\mathbf{Az} + \mathbf{e}_1 : \mathbf{z} \in \mathbb{Z}^m, \langle \mathbf{e}_2, \mathbf{z} \rangle = 0 \mod q\}$, *and* $\mathbf{b}_2^t \in \{\mathbf{z}^t \mathbf{A} + \mathbf{e}_2^t : \mathbf{z} \in \mathbb{Z}^m, \langle \mathbf{e}_1, \mathbf{z} \rangle = 0 \mod q\}$, *the goal is to find a vector* $\mathbf{x} \in \mathbb{Z}^m$ *and a vector* $\mathbf{y} \in \mathbb{Z}^m$ *such that*

$$\begin{cases} \mathbf{Ax} + \mathbf{e}_1 = \mathbf{b}_1 \mod q \text{ and } ||x|| \leq \beta \\ \mathbf{y}^t \mathbf{A} + \mathbf{e}_2^t = \mathbf{b}_2^t \mod q \text{ and } ||y|| \leq \beta \end{cases} \tag{1}$$

Finally they define the CBi-ISIS problem.

Given the parameters n, m, q and $m > n \log q$ as in ISIS problem, a matrix $\mathbf{A} \in \mathbb{Z}_q^{m \times m}$ with rank equals to n. For any vectors $\mathbf{x} \in \mathbb{Z}$ with $||\mathbf{x}|| \leq \beta$, and $\mathbf{y} \in \mathbb{Z}$ with $||y|| \leq \beta$, there exists two vector sets $\{\mathbf{v}_1, ..., \mathbf{v}_n\}$ which is linear independent with rows vectors of $\mathbf{A}$, and $\{\mathbf{u}_1, ..., \mathbf{u}_n\}$ which is linear independent with column vectors of $\mathbf{A}$, such that $\langle \mathbf{v}_i, \mathbf{x} \rangle = 0 \mod q$ and $\langle \mathbf{u}_i, \mathbf{y} \rangle = 0 \mod q$. The CBi-ISIS problem is defined as follows:

Definition 3 *(CBi-ISIS problem). Given* $\mathbf{Ax} + \mathbf{e}_1$ *and* $\mathbf{y}^t \mathbf{A} + \mathbf{e}_2^t$, *the goal is to compute* $\mathbf{y}^t \mathbf{Ax} \mod q$, *where* $\mathbf{e}_1 = \sum_{i \in S} \mathbf{u}_i$. *and* $\mathbf{e}_2^t = \sum_{i \in S'} \mathbf{v}_i^t$. S *and* S' *are random subset of* $\{1, \cdots n\}$.

If there is an algorithm that solves the Bi-ISIS* problem, we can use this algorithm to solve CBi-ISIS problem.

Remark 1. *Given any poly-bounded* m, $\beta = poly(n)$, *as well as any prime* $q \geq \beta \sqrt{\omega(n \log n)}$, *the* $SIS_{q,m,\beta}$ *and* $ISIS_{q,m,\beta}$ *problems in the average case are as hard as approximating the problems* $SIVP_\gamma$ *and* $GapSVP_\gamma$ *in the worst case to within certain* $\gamma = \beta \cdot \tilde{O}(\sqrt{n})$ *factors.*

2.2 Notation

We will use the same notation in Wang et al.'s paper [6]: Let $\mathbb{Z}$ denote the ring of integers; $\mathbb{Z}_q$ is the finite field module q; $\mathbb{Z}_q^{m \times m}$ is the set of all $m \times m$ matrices with entries in $\mathbb{Z}_q$. We define the norm on $\mathbb{Z}^m$ to be the l_2 norm. We can view $\mathbb{Z}_q \subset \mathbb{Z}$ and use the l_2 norm on it. Furthermore, if t is a positive integer with $t \leq q$, we can view $\mathbb{Z}_t \subset \mathbb{Z}_q$.

Moreover, the operator $*$ is defined by $\mathbf{A} * \mathbf{x} = \mathbf{A} * \mathbf{x} = \mathbf{Ax} + \sum_{i \in S} \mathbf{u}_i \mod q$, in which S is a random subset of $\{1, .., n\}$. and $\mathbf{y}^t * \mathbf{A} = \mathbf{y}^t \mathbf{A} + \sum_{i \in S'} \mathbf{v}_i^t \mod q$, in which S' is a random subset of $\{1, .., n\}$.

2.3   Description of the Protocol

We now briefly describe the protocol [6].

1. Alice and Bob agree to use a random matrix $\mathbf{A} \in \mathbb{Z}_q{}^{m \times m}$ with rank n and a real number β.
2. Alice picks a random $\mathbf{x} \in \mathbb{Z}^m$ such that $\|\mathbf{x}\| \leq \beta$, then generates the set $\mathbf{V} = \{\mathbf{v}_1^t, \ldots, \mathbf{v}_n^t\}$, which is linear independent with row vectors of $\mathbf{A}$, and $\langle \mathbf{v}_i, \mathbf{x} \rangle = 0 \mod q$. Alice keeps $\mathbf{x}$ private and publishes $\mathbf{V}$. Now Bob picks a random vector $\mathbf{y} \in \mathbb{Z}^m$ such that $\|\mathbf{y}\| \leq \beta$, then generates $\mathbf{U} = \{\mathbf{u}_1 \ldots \mathbf{u}_n\}$ which is linear independent with column vectors of $\mathbf{A}$, and $\langle \mathbf{u}_i, \mathbf{y} \rangle = 0 \mod q$. Bob keeps $\mathbf{y}$ private and makes $\mathbf{U}$ public.
3. Alice uses $\mathbf{U}$ to compute $\mathbf{a} = \mathbf{A} * \mathbf{x} = \mathbf{A}\mathbf{x} + \sum_{i \in S} \mathbf{u}_i \mod q$, in which S is a random subset of $\{1, .., n\}$, and sends $\mathbf{a}$ to Bob.
4. Bob uses $\mathbf{V}$ to compute $\mathbf{b}^t = \mathbf{y}^t * \mathbf{A} = \mathbf{y}^t \mathbf{A} + \sum_{i \in S'} \mathbf{v}_i^t \mod q$, in which S' is a random subset of $\{1, .., n\}$, and sends $\mathbf{b}^t$ to Alice.
5. Alice computes $K_1 = \mathbf{b}^t \cdot \mathbf{x} = \mathbf{y}^t \mathbf{A}\mathbf{x} \mod q$.
6. Bob computes $K_2 = \mathbf{y}^t \cdot \mathbf{a} = \mathbf{y}^t \mathbf{A}\mathbf{x} \mod q$.

Therefore the shared secret key is $K = K_1 = K_2 = \mathbf{y}^t \mathbf{A}\mathbf{x} \mod q$.

2.4   Mao's Attack [7]

Mao et al. assume that the protocol was based on the Bi-ISIS* problem, their goal is to solve the CBi-ISIS problem. They try to keep the original $\mathbf{x}$ and $\mathbf{y}$ during the attack so that they will match the shared key. However, according to their experiments results [7], the decomposition of the matrix $\mathbf{A}$ and solving the matrix $\mathbf{T}_1$ such that $\mathbf{T}_1 \mathbf{A} = \mathbf{0}$ are very slow.

2.5   Our Attack

Our attack to this protocol is based on solving linear equations. An eavesdropper can obtain the information $\{\mathbf{a}, \mathbf{b}\}$. Since $\mathbf{A}$ and $\mathbf{U}$ are public, the eavesdropper has the linear equations

$$\begin{cases} \mathbf{A}\bar{\mathbf{x}} + \sum_{i \in \{1,..,n\}} \alpha_i \mathbf{u}_i = \mathbf{a} \mod q \\ \mathbf{v}_i^t \cdot \bar{\mathbf{x}} = 0 \mod q, \text{ for } i \in \{1, ..n\} \end{cases} \tag{2}$$

The linear independence of $\mathbf{U}$ with columns of $\mathbf{A}$ does not make any obstacle for the eavesdropper to solving the linear equations. Since $\mathbf{a}$ is of this form, the linear equations must contain at least one solution. Assume $\mathbf{A}$ has entires $[a_{ij}]$, in which

$1 \le i, j \le m$, $\mathbf{a} = (a_1, \cdots, a_m)^t$, $\mathbf{u}_i = (u_{i1}, \cdots, u_{im})^t$, and $\mathbf{v}_i = (v_{i1}, \cdots, v_{im})^t$. The equations have the following matrix form:

$$
\begin{bmatrix} a_1 \\ \vdots \\ a_m \\ 0 \\ \vdots \\ 0 \end{bmatrix}
=
\begin{bmatrix}
a_{11} & \cdots & a_{1m} & u_{11} & \cdots & u_{n1} \\
\vdots & \ddots & \vdots & \vdots & \ddots & \vdots \\
a_{m1} & \cdots & a_{mm} & u_{1m} & \cdots & u_{nm} \\
v_{11} & \cdots & v_{1m} & 0 & \cdots & 0 \\
\vdots & \ddots & \vdots & \vdots & \ddots & \vdots \\
v_{n1} & \cdots & v_{nm} & 0 & \cdots & 0
\end{bmatrix}
\begin{bmatrix} \bar{x}_1 \\ \vdots \\ \bar{x}_m \\ \alpha_1 \\ \vdots \\ \alpha_n \end{bmatrix}
\tag{3}
$$

The eavesdropper can solve the equations and get solutions $\bar{\mathbf{x}} = (\bar{x}_1, \cdots, \bar{x}_m)^t \in \mathbb{Z}_q^m$, and $\alpha_i \in \mathbb{Z}_q$. Although $\bar{\mathbf{x}}$ is not necessary equal to the original $\mathbf{x}$ and of course not necessarily short, the eavesdropper can still use it to recover the secret key. Once the eavesdropper obtains $\bar{\mathbf{x}}$, he computes

$$
\begin{aligned}
\mathbf{b}^t \cdot \bar{\mathbf{x}} &= \left(\mathbf{y}^t \mathbf{A} + \sum_{i \in S'} \mathbf{v}_i^t \right) \cdot \bar{\mathbf{x}} \mod q \\
&= \mathbf{y}^t \mathbf{A} \bar{\mathbf{x}} \mod q \\
&= \mathbf{y}^t \left(\mathbf{a} - \sum_{i \in \{1,..,n\}} \alpha_i \mathbf{u}_i \right) \mod q \\
&= \mathbf{y}^t \left(\mathbf{A}\mathbf{x} + \sum_{i \in S} \mathbf{u}_i - \sum_{i \in \{1,..,n\}} \alpha_i \mathbf{u}_i \right) \mod q \\
&= \mathbf{y}^t \mathbf{A} \mathbf{x} \mod q.
\end{aligned}
$$

Therefore, the eavesdropper successfully recovers the secret key. Similarly, one can do it on $\mathbf{b}^t = \mathbf{y}^t * \mathbf{A}$.

One can see that the process of our attack is very straightforward, which contains only two steps: (1) solve the linear equations. (2) compute the dot product $\mathbf{b}^t \cdot \bar{\mathbf{x}}$.

2.6 Experimental Results

We did the experiments with the same parameters in Mao et al.'s paper [7].

(q, m, n)	time_1	time_2
10007, 3854, 128	3.430 s	27842.89 s
6421, 3240, 80	2.250 s	8201.06 s
4099, 1536, 64	0.29 s	1638.64 s

Remark: time_1 is the time spent in our attack, and time_2 is the time Mao et al. spent in their attack [7]. We used the software of Magma student version on an Intel core i7 with CPU 3.2 GHz, 8 GB storage memory. Mao et al.'s plateform is an Intel Dual-Core2, CPU 2.6 Ghz, Windows 7 operating system with 4 G storage memory, they use the MATLAB version 7.9.

2.7   Toy Example

We show a toy example of our attack with parameters: $(q = 7, m = 5, n = 2, \beta = 3)$. We did this example on the software called Magma in our computer lab.

Alice and Bob agree on a random matrix $\mathbf{A}$ equal to

$$\begin{bmatrix} 1 & 3 & 6 & 4 & 1 \\ 3 & 5 & 1 & 1 & 3 \\ 6 & 2 & 3 & 1 & 6 \\ 3 & 4 & 2 & 0 & 3 \\ 2 & 6 & 5 & 1 & 2 \end{bmatrix}$$

Alice picks a random vector $\mathbf{x} = (1, 0, 2, 0, 1)^t$, then she generates the set $\mathbf{V}$ whose elements are:

$$\mathbf{v}_1 = (1, 3, 5, 6, 3)^t$$
$$\mathbf{v}_2 = (5, 6, 6, 6, 4)^t$$

Each $\mathbf{v}_i$ is orthogonal to $\mathbf{x}$, and neither of them is in the row space of $\mathbf{A}$. Alice keeps $\mathbf{x}$ as a secret and publishes the set $\mathbf{V}$.

Bob picks a random vector $\mathbf{y} = (1, 2, 3, 0, 0)^t$, then he generates the set $\mathbf{U}$ whose elements are:

$$\mathbf{u}_1 = (5, 2, 4, 2, 6)$$
$$\mathbf{u}_2 = (1, 1, 6, 6, 3)$$

Bob keeps $\mathbf{y}$ private and makes $\mathbf{U}$ public.
Alice now computes $\mathbf{a} = \mathbf{A} * \mathbf{x} = \mathbf{A}\mathbf{x} + \mathbf{u}_1 = (6, 1, 0, 2, 0)^t$.
Bob computes $\mathbf{b}^t = \mathbf{y}^t * \mathbf{A} = \mathbf{y}^t\mathbf{A} + \mathbf{v}_1^t + \mathbf{v}_2 = (3, 4, 2, 1, 1)$.
Alice computes $K_1 = \mathbf{b}^t \cdot \mathbf{x} = 1$. Bob computes $K_2 = \mathbf{y}^t \cdot \mathbf{a} = 1$. Hence the secret shared key is 1.

Now let Eve be the eavesdropper. He can get $\{\mathbf{a}, \mathbf{b}\}$. He now sets the equation of (3). In the matrix form:

$$\begin{bmatrix} 6 \\ 1 \\ 0 \\ 2 \\ 0 \\ 0 \\ 0 \end{bmatrix} = \begin{bmatrix} 1 & 3 & 6 & 4 & 1 & 1 & 5 \\ 3 & 5 & 1 & 1 & 3 & 3 & 6 \\ 6 & 2 & 3 & 1 & 6 & 5 & 6 \\ 3 & 4 & 2 & 0 & 3 & 6 & 6 \\ 2 & 6 & 5 & 1 & 2 & 3 & 4 \\ 5 & 2 & 4 & 2 & 6 & 0 & 0 \\ 1 & 1 & 6 & 6 & 3 & 0 & 0 \end{bmatrix} \begin{bmatrix} \bar{x}_1 \\ \bar{x}_2 \\ \bar{x}_3 \\ \bar{x}_4 \\ \bar{x}_5 \\ \alpha_1 \\ \alpha_2 \end{bmatrix} \qquad (4)$$

By solving the above linear equations, he can get the solution $(\bar{x}_1, \bar{x}_2, \bar{x}_3, \bar{x}_4,$ $\bar{x}_5, \alpha_1, \alpha_2,) = (2, 0, 6, 4, 0, 1, 0)^t$. It follows that $\bar{\mathbf{x}} = (2, 0, 6, 4, 0)^t$. Next he computes that $\mathbf{b}^t \cdot \bar{\mathbf{x}} = (3, 4, 2, 1, 1) \cdot (2, 0, 6, 4, 0)^t = 1 \mod 7$, which is exactly the secret shared key.

We see that even $\bar{\mathbf{x}}$ is not equal to the private key $\mathbf{x}$ that Alice keeps and has norm larger than β, $\bar{\mathbf{x}}$ still works to break the protocol.

3 Key Exchange on SIS and LWE

3.1 Preliminary

Now let us recall the learning with error (LWE) problem, the short integer solution problem, and the shortest independent vectors problem. For a finite set X, let $U(X)$ denote the uniform distribution on X.

Definition 4. *A function family is a probability distribution over a set of functions with common domain and range. For a function family $\mathcal{F}$ with a finite range and probability distribution χ over the common domain of $\mathcal{F}$, we say that $(\mathcal{F}, \chi)$ is pseudorandom if the distribution obtained from sampling $f \leftarrow \mathcal{F}$ and $x \leftarrow \chi$ and outputting $(f, f(x))$ and the distribution that samples $f \leftarrow \mathcal{F}$ and $y \leftarrow U(Y)$ and outputs (f, y) are indistinguishable. See [10] for more details.*

Definition 5. *The Learning With Errors (LWE) function family is the set of all functions $g_\mathbf{A}$ indexed by $\mathbf{A} \in \mathbb{Z}_q^{m \times n}$ with domain $\mathbb{Z}_q^n \times \mathbb{Z}_q^m$ and range $\mathbb{Z}_q^m$ defined by $g_A(s, e) = As + e$. The LWE function family is endowed with the uniform distribution over $\mathbb{Z}_q^{n \times m}$ to choose $g_\mathbf{A}$. For probability distributions χ on $\mathbb{Z}_q^n$ and Ψ on $\mathbb{Z}_q^m$, we denote by $LWE(m, n, q, \chi, \Psi)$ the distribution obtained by sampling a function $g_\mathbf{A}$ from the LWE function family, $s \leftarrow \chi$, $e \leftarrow \Psi$, and outputting $g_\mathbf{A}(s, e) = \mathbf{A}s + e$.*

Definition 6. *The Short Integer Solution (SIS) function family is the set of all functions $f_\mathbf{A}$ indexed by $\mathbf{A} \in \mathbb{Z}_q^{m \times n}$ with domain $\mathbb{Z}_q^n$ and range $\mathbb{Z}_q^m$ endowed with the uniform distribution over $\mathbb{Z}_q^{m \times n}$. For a probability distribution χ on $\mathbb{Z}_q^n$, we denote by $SIS(m, n, q, \chi)$ the distribution obtained by sampling a function $f_\mathbf{A}$ from the SIS function family and sampling $x \leftarrow \chi$ and outputting $f_\mathbf{A}(x) = \mathbf{A}x$.*

Proposition 1 [8]. *For any $n, m \geq n + \omega(\log n), q$, and distribution χ over $\mathbb{Z}^m$, the $LWE(m, n, q)$ function family is one-way (resp. pseudorandom, or uninvertible) with respect to input distribution $U(\mathbb{Z}_q^n) \times \chi$ if and only if the $SIS(m, m-n, q)$ function family is one-way (resp. pseudorandom, or uninvertible) with respect to the input distribution χ.*

Definition 7. *For $k \in \mathbb{N}$ and $\gamma > 0$, we denote by $SIVP(k, \gamma)$ the shortest independent vectors problem in dimension k with approximation factor γ.*

Definition 8. *For $x \in \mathbb{R}^n$ and $s > 0$, let $\rho_s(x) = exp(-\pi \|x/s\|^2)$. ρ_s can be normalized into a gaussian probability measure on $\mathbb{R}^n$, and is denoted by $D_s(x) = \rho_s(x)/s^n$. For a lattice $\Lambda \subset \mathbb{R}^n$, let $\mathcal{D}_{\Lambda,s}(x) = \rho_s(x)/\rho_s(\Lambda)$, where $\rho_s(\Lambda) = \sum_{y \in \Lambda} \rho_s(y)$. Then $\mathcal{D}_{\Lambda,s}$ is a probability distribution on Λ and is called the discrete Gaussian distribution on Λ.*

For n, m positive integers and $s > 0$, we denote by $\mathcal{D}_{\mathbb{Z}_q^{m \times n}, s}$ the distribution obtained by sampling from $\mathcal{D}_{\mathbb{Z}^m, s}$ n times and outputting $A \mod q \in \mathbb{Z}_q^{m \times n}$. We denote by $\mathcal{D}_{\mathbb{Z}_q^m, s}$ the distribution $\mathcal{D}_{\mathbb{Z}_q^{m \times 1}}$.

Lemma 2 [10]. *For any $s \geq \omega(\sqrt{\log n})$, then we have*

$$\mathbb{P}_{x \leftarrow \mathcal{D}_{\mathbb{Z}^n, s}}[\|x\| \geq s\sqrt{n}] \leq 2^{-n}.$$

Lemma 3 LWE Assumption [4]. *It has been shown that as long as $\alpha q > 2\sqrt{n}$, then $LWE(m, n, q, U(\mathbb{Z}_q^n), \mathcal{D}_{\mathbb{Z}_q^m, \alpha q})$ is pseudorandom. It has been shown that the LWE distribution remains pseudorandom when the input distribution on $\mathbb{Z}_q^n$ is given by $\mathcal{D}_{\mathbb{Z}_q^n, \alpha q}$, this is called the HNF-LWE assumption.*

Lemma 4 U-LWE Assumption [9]. *Let $n = 8k$ for some $k \in \mathbb{N}$, $0 \leq a \leq n^{O(1)}$, $m = 2n + a$, $t = \lceil (Cm)^{9/7 + (8a)/(7n)} \rceil$ for a large enough universal constant $C \geq 1$, and $16t^2 \leq q \leq n^{O(1)}$. Then $LWE(m, n, q, U(\mathbb{Z}_q^n), U(\mathbb{Z}_{t-1}^m))$ is pseudorandom under the assumption that $SIVP(k, \tilde{O}(\sqrt{k}q))$ is hard in the worst case. When k is assumed to be large enough so that $SIVP(k, \tilde{O}(\sqrt{k}q))$ is hard we call this the U-LWE assumption.*

Remark 2. *For $l \in \mathbb{N}$ and probability distributions χ over $\mathbb{Z}_q^{n \times l}$ and Ψ over $\mathbb{Z}_q^{m \times l}$, we can define the distribution $LWE(m, n, l, q, \chi, \Psi)$ to be given by sampling $A \leftarrow U(\mathbb{Z}_q^{m \times n})$, $\mathbf{s} \leftarrow \chi$, $\mathbf{e} \leftarrow \Psi$ and outputting $\mathbf{As} + \mathbf{e} \in \mathbb{Z}_q^{m \times l}$. We can also define $SIS(m, n, l, q, \chi)$ similarly. Notice that the LWE, HNF-LWE, and U-LWE assumptions hold with the added dimension l for these new distributions, i.e. they are pseudorandom under certain choices of distributions for $\mathbb{Z}_q^{n \times l}$ and $\mathbb{Z}_q^{m \times l}$.*

Remark 3. *Observe that we can also define the transpose function familys LWE^T and SIS^T which outputs $\mathbf{s}^T \mathbf{A}^T + \mathbf{e}^T$ and $\mathbf{x}^T \mathbf{A}^T$ respectively. We have that LWE^T is pseudorandom, and hence SIS^T is pseudorandom, under the LWE, HNF-LWE, or U-LWE assumptions respectively.*

Claim 1. *For n, m, k, and q positive integers, and matrices $\mathbf{A} \leftarrow U(\mathbb{Z}_q^{n \times m})$ and $\mathbf{B} \leftarrow U(\mathbb{Z}_q^{m \times k})$ we have that as nm k, and q are fixed, there exists an m computable in polynomial time such that AB is indistinguishable from uniform.*

One can see this claim by fixing q and taking a positive integer n. Then choosing $\mathbf{A}, \mathbf{B} \leftarrow U(\mathbb{Z}_q^{n \times n})$ and verifying that the distribution of $\mathbf{AB}$ approaches the uniform distribution on $\mathbb{Z}_q^{n \times n}$ for $n = \text{poly}(q)$. From this we can deduce the claim for non-square matrices.

3.2 Desciption of the Protocol

The diffie-Hellman key exchange is based on the fact that exponential map is commutative.

$$g^{ab} = (g^a)^b = (g^b)^a.$$

over some multiplicative group G with large order p. Ding's key exchange on LWE [5] uses the associativity of the bilinear form, namely

$$\mathbf{x}^T \mathbf{M} \mathbf{y} = \left(\mathbf{x}^T \mathbf{M}\right) \mathbf{y} = \mathbf{x}^T \left(\mathbf{M} \mathbf{y}\right).$$

for some vectors $\mathbf{x}$ and $\mathbf{y}$ in $\mathbb{Z}_q^n$ and a matrix $\mathbf{M} \in \mathbf{Z}_q^{n \times n}$. These two key exchange protocols are both symmetric. In other words, two parties do the same thing in the process of key exchange because the security that both parties rely on is from the same difficult problem. However, our key exchange protocol is different. It is not symmetric since one party will apply SIS and one party will apply LWE.

We give two similar key exchange protocols.

3.2.1   Normal Construction

Two parties Alice and Bob decide to do a key exchange over an open channel.

(1) The system first generates the public parameters q, n, m and α with $n \ll m$. Then generates the matrix $M \in \mathbb{Z}_q^{n \times m}$ uniformly at random. Let l and k be positive integers.

(2) Alice choose a secret matrix $s_A \leftarrow U(\mathbb{Z}_q^{l \times n})$ and an error matrix $e_A \leftarrow \mathcal{D}_{\mathbb{Z}_q^{l \times m}, \alpha q}$, then computes $\mathbf{P}_A = s_A \mathbf{M} + 2e_A$. She sends $\mathbf{P}_A$ to Bob.

(3) Upon receiving $\mathbf{P}_A$, Bob chooses a secret matrix $s_B \leftarrow \mathcal{D}_{\mathbb{Z}_q^{m \times k}, \alpha q}$ and computes $\mathbf{P}_B = M s_B$ and sends $\mathbf{P}_B$ to Alice. Next he computes

$$\mathbf{K}_B = \mathbf{P}_A s_B = \left(s_A \mathbf{M} + 2e_A\right) s_B = s_A \mathbf{M} s_B + 2e_A s_B.$$

(4) Upon receiving $\mathbf{P}_B$, Alice computes

$$\mathbf{K}_A = s_A \mathbf{P}_B = s_A \mathbf{M} s_B.$$

3.2.2   Uniform Construction

Two parties Alice and Bob decide to do a key exchange over an open channel.

(1) The system first generates the public parameters q, n, m, α, and t. Let $r \in \mathbb{N}$ and $m = 8r$, $0 \le a \le m^{O(1)}$, $n = 2m + a$, and $t = \lceil (Cn)^{9/7 + (8a)/(7m)} \rceil$ for a large enough constant C ([9] Lemma 4). We have the additional constraint on q that $16t^2 \le q \le m^{O(1)}$. The system then generates the matrix $M \in \mathbb{Z}_q^{n \times m}$ uniformly at random. Let k be a positive integer.

(2) Alice chooses a secret $s_A \leftarrow U(\mathbb{Z}_q^{n \times n})$, then she computes $\mathbf{P}_A = s_A \mathbf{M} + 2e_A$, where $e_A \leftarrow \mathcal{D}_{\mathbb{Z}^{n \times m}, \alpha q}$. She sends $\mathbf{P}_A$ to Bob.

(3) Receiving $\mathbf{P}_A$, Bob chooses a secret matrix $s_B \leftarrow U(\mathbb{Z}_{t-1}^{m \times k})$. He computes $\mathbf{P}_B = M s_B$. Bob sends $\mathbf{P}_B$ to Alice. Next, he computes

$$\mathbf{K}_B = \mathbf{P}_A s_B = \left(s_A \mathbf{M} + 2e_A\right) s_B = s_A \mathbf{M} s_B + 2e_A s_B.$$

(4) Receiving $\mathbf{P}_B$, Alice computes

$$\mathbf{K}_A = s_A \mathbf{P}_B = s_A \mathbf{M} s_B.$$

3.3   Remove the Approximation

We imitate the way to remove the approximation that Ding [5] presents in his key exchange on LWE. We need the help of a robust extractor which allows two parties to extract identical information from two close elements with signal functions.

3.3.1   Robust Extractor

An algorithm E is a robust extractor on $\mathbb{Z}_q$ with error tolerance δ with respect to a hint function S if the following holds:

(1) The deterministic algorithm E takes as input an $x \in \mathbb{Z}_q$ and a signal $\sigma \in \{0, 1\}$, outputs $k = E(x, \sigma) \in \{0, 1\}$.
(2) The hint algorithm S takes as input a $y \in \mathbb{Z}_q$ and outputs a signal $\sigma \leftarrow S(y) \in \{0, 1\}$.
(3) For any $x, y \in \mathbb{Z}_q$ such that $x - y$ is even and $|x - y| \leq \delta$, then it holds that $E(x, \sigma) = E(y, \sigma)$ where $\sigma \leftarrow S(y)$.

Signal function: For prime $q > 2$, we define $\sigma_0(x)$, $\sigma_1(x)$ from $\mathbb{Z}_q$ to $\{0, 1\}$ as follows.

$$\sigma_0 = \begin{cases} 0 \text{ if } x \in \left[-\left\lfloor \frac{q}{4} \right\rfloor, \left\lfloor \frac{q}{4} \right\rfloor\right] \\ 1 \text{ otherwise} \end{cases} \qquad \sigma_1 = \begin{cases} 0 \text{ if } x \in \left[-\left\lfloor \frac{q}{4} \right\rfloor + 1, \left\lfloor \frac{q}{4} \right\rfloor + 1\right] \\ 1 \text{ otherwise} \end{cases}$$

In our robust extractor, we define the hint algorithm S as: for any $y \in \mathbb{Z}_q$, $S(y) = \sigma_b(y)$, where $b \xleftarrow{\$} \{0, 1\}$. The robust extractor is defined as: $E(x, \sigma) = (x + \sigma \cdot \frac{q-1}{2} \mod q) \mod 2$.

By the construction of the robust extractor, Ding [5] proved that:

Lemma 5 [5]. *Let $q > 8$ be an odd integer, the function E defined above is a robust extractor with respect to S with error tolerance $\frac{q}{4} - 2$.*

Since our key exchange is of multiple bits, we need to extract the shared key from matrices. So we define a robust extractor over the space of matrices.

Definition 9. *Now for $i = 1, ..., l$ and $j = 1, ..., k$, given the robust extractor $E(x, \sigma_{i,j})$ on $\mathbb{Z}_q$ defined above, we define a robust extractor E' on $\mathbb{Z}_q^{l \times k}$:*

$$E'(\mathbf{A}, \sigma') = [E(a_{ij}, \sigma_{ij})] = \begin{bmatrix} a_{11} + \sigma_{11} \cdot \frac{q-1}{2} & \cdots & a_{1n} + \sigma_{1n} \cdot \frac{q-1}{2} \\ \vdots & \ddots & \vdots \\ a_{l1} + \sigma_{l1} \cdot \frac{q-1}{2} & \cdots & a_{ln} + \sigma_{l1} \cdot \frac{q-1}{2} \end{bmatrix} \mod q \mod 2.$$

where a_{ij} are the entires of $\mathbf{A}$ and σ' is a $l \times k$ matrix whose entries are σ_{ij}.

3.3.2 Extract the Shared Key

Alice has $\mathbf{s}_A$, Bob has $\mathbf{s}_B$.

Bob computes $\mathbf{P}_B$ as above and send it to Alice.

Receiving $\mathbf{P}_B$, Alice computes $\mathbf{K}_A$ as above and then she computes $\sigma' \leftarrow S(\mathbf{K}_A)$, then she obtains the shared key $\mathbf{SK}_A = E'(\mathbf{K}_A, \sigma')$. She also computes $\mathbf{P}_A$ as above and sends $(\mathbf{P}_A, \sigma')$ to Bob.

Bob receives $(\mathbf{P}_A, \sigma')$, and Bob computes $\mathbf{K}_B$ as above and computes $\mathbf{SK}_B = E'(\mathbf{K}_B, \sigma')$.

3.4 Correctness

We see that $\mathbf{K}_A - \mathbf{K}_B = -2\mathbf{e}_A\mathbf{s}_B$, and the entries of $\mathbf{K}_A - \mathbf{K}_B$ are even. We need to show that if each entry of the approximation $|2\mathbf{e}_A\mathbf{s}_B|$ is less than the error tolerance, then we obtain that $E'(\mathbf{K}_B, \sigma') = E'(\mathbf{K}_A, \sigma')$.

To complete the proof, we imitate a result from Ding's key exchange on LWE [5]:

Lemma 6. *If the uniform key exchange (Sect. 3.2.2) is run and $2\alpha q(t-1)\sqrt{n} \leq \frac{q}{4} - 2$, then $\mathbf{SK}_A = \mathbf{SK}_B$ with overwhelming probability. If the normal key exchange is run (Sect. 3.2.1) and $2(\alpha q)^2\sqrt{lm} \leq \frac{q}{4} - 2$, then $\mathbf{SK}_A = \mathbf{SK}_B$ with overwhelming probability.*

Proof. Let k_{ij} be an entry of $\mathbf{K}_A - \mathbf{K}_B$, so it can be expressed as $k_{ij} = -2\mathbf{v}_i^T\mathbf{u}_j$, where $\mathbf{v}_i$ is the i-th column vector of $\mathbf{e}_A^T$, $\mathbf{u}_j$ is the j-th column vector of $\mathbf{s}_B$. According to Lemma 2, if the Uniform key exchange is run, it is easy to see that

$$|k_{ij}| = |2\mathbf{v}_i^T\mathbf{u}_j| \leq 2\alpha q\sqrt{n}|u_j| \leq 2\alpha q(t-1)\sqrt{n}.$$

with overwhelming probability. According to Lemma 2 again, if the normal key exchange is run, it is easy to see that

$$|k_{ij}| = 2|\mathbf{v}_i^T\mathbf{u}_j| \leq 2\alpha^2 q^2\sqrt{lm}.$$

with overwhelming probability.

With such a choice of the parameters, we will have each entry of $|\mathbf{K}_A - \mathbf{K}_B|$ less than the error tolerance. By Lemma 5 and our definition of E', we have that

$$E'(\mathbf{K}_A, \sigma') = [E(x_{ij}, \sigma_{ij})] = [E(y_{ij}, \sigma_{ij})] = E'(\mathbf{K}_B, \sigma').$$

where x_{ij} is the entry of $\mathbf{K}_A$ and y_{ij} is the entry of $\mathbf{K}_B$.

Moreover we show that shared key is $E'(\mathbf{K}_A, \sigma') = E'(\mathbf{K}_B, \sigma') = \mathbf{s}_A\mathbf{M}\mathbf{s}_B + \frac{q-1}{2}\sigma' \mod q \mod 2$. It is clear that $\mathbf{s}_A\mathbf{M}\mathbf{s}_B + \frac{q-1}{2}\sigma' = \mathbf{K}_B + \frac{q-1}{2}\sigma'(\mathbf{K}_A) - 2\mathbf{e}_A\mathbf{s}_B$. Moreover we can observe that each entry of the matrix $|\mathbf{K}_B + \frac{q-1}{2}\sigma'(\mathbf{K}_A)|$ is less than $\frac{q}{4} + 1$. It follows that $\mathbf{s}_A\mathbf{M}\mathbf{s}_B + \frac{q-1}{2}\sigma' = \mathbf{K}_B + \frac{q-1}{2}\sigma'(\mathbf{K}_A) \mod q - 2\mathbf{e}_A\mathbf{s}_B$ because each entry of $|\mathbf{K}_B + \frac{q-1}{2}\sigma'(\mathbf{K}_A) \mod q - 2\mathbf{e}_A\mathbf{s}_B|$ is less than or equal to $\frac{q}{4} + 1 + \frac{q}{4} - 2 \leq \frac{q-1}{2}$. This implies that $\mathbf{SK}_B = E'(\mathbf{K}_B, \sigma') = \mathbf{s}_A\mathbf{M}\mathbf{s}_B + \frac{q-1}{2}\sigma'$. A similar proof shows that $\mathbf{SK}_A = E'(\mathbf{K}_A, \sigma') = \mathbf{s}_A\mathbf{M}\mathbf{s}_B + \frac{q-1}{2}\sigma'$. $\square$

3.5 Security

Theorem 7. *If either protocol described above is run honestly by both parties Alice and Bob and the LWE (and resp. U-LWE) assumption hold, then* $\mathbf{SK}_A$ *and* $\mathbf{SK}_B$ *are indistinguishable from uniformly chosen elements of* $\mathbb{Z}_q^{l \times k}$ *given* $\mathbf{M}$, $\mathbf{P}_B$, *and* $\mathbf{P}_A$. *Thus the protocol is secure against passive adverseries.*

Proof. We only prove the theorem for protocol Sect. 3.2.1, the proof is similar for Sect. 3.2.2. Assuming the protocol is run honestly, the distribution of $\mathbf{P}_A$ is computationally indistinguishable from the uniform distribution on $\mathbb{Z}_q^{l \times m}$ due to the LWE assumption that

$$\text{LWE}^T\left(m, n, l, q, U(\mathbb{Z}_q^{n \times l}), \mathcal{D}_{\mathbb{Z}_q^{m \times l}, \alpha q}\right) \text{ is pseudorandom.}$$

Now by the LWE assumption we have that

$$\text{LWE}(m, n, k, q, U(\mathbb{Z}_q^{n \times k}), \mathcal{D}_{\mathbb{Z}_q^{m \times k}, \alpha q}) \text{ is pseudorandom.}$$

Thus by Proposition 1 we conclude that $\text{SIS}(n, m, k, q, \mathcal{D}_{\mathbb{Z}_q^{m \times k}, \alpha q})$ is pseudorandom. Hence, as $\mathbf{P}_A$ is indistinguishable from uniform, it follows that $\mathbf{K}_B = \mathbf{P}_A s_B$ is computationally indistinguishable from the uniform distribution $\mathbb{Z}_q^{l \times k}$. Since $\mathbf{K}_B$ is indistinguishable from uniform, it follows that $\mathbf{SK}_B$ is indistinguishable from uniform by [4] (Lemma 3).

Now we focus on $\mathbf{SK}_A$. We have that $\mathbf{K}_A = s_A \mathbf{M} s_B$, where $\mathbf{M}$ and s_A are chosen uniformly at random. We invoke Claim 1, that for sufficiently large l and m, the distribution of $s_A \mathbf{M}$ is indistinguishable from the uniform distribution over $\mathbb{Z}_q^{l \times m}$. Again, by the LWE assumption, we have that

$$\text{LWE}(l, m, k, q, U(\mathbb{Z}_q^{l \times k}), \mathcal{D}_{\mathbb{Z}_q^{m \times k}, \alpha q}) \text{ is pseudorandom.}$$

Hence by Proposition 1 we deduce that $\text{SIS}(l, m, k, q, \mathcal{D}_{\mathbb{Z}_q^{m \times k}, \alpha q})$ is pseudorandom. Thus, as $s_A \mathbf{M}$ is indistinguishable from uniform and $s_B \leftarrow \mathcal{D}_{\mathbb{Z}_q^{m \times k}, \alpha q}$, we conclude that $K_A = (s_A \mathbf{M}) s_B$ is indistinguishable from the uniform distribution on $\mathbb{Z}_q^{l \times k}$. Therefore $\mathbf{SK}_B$ is indistinguishable from uniform on $\mathbb{Z}_q^{l \times k}$ by [4] (Lemma 3) and the proof is complete. □

Acknowledgement. This study is partially supported by U.S Air force.

References

1. Ajtai, M.: Generating hard instances of lattice problems. Quaderni di Matematica **13**, 1–32 (2004). Preliminary version in STOC (1996)
2. Diffie, W., Hellman, M.: New directions in cryptography. Inf. Theory **22**(6), 644–654 (1976)
3. Shor, P.: Polynomial-time algorithms for prime factorization and discrete logarithms on a quantum computer. SIAM Rev. **41**(2), 303–332 (1999)

4. Regev, O.: On lattices, learning with errors, random linear codes, and cryptography. In: STOC, pp. 84–93. ACM (2005)
5. Ding, J., Xiang, X., Lin, X.: A simple provably secure key exchange scheme based on the learning with errors problem. Cryptology ePrint Archive, Report 2012/688 (2012). https://eprint.iacr.org
6. Wang, S., Zhu, Y., Ma, D., Feng, R.: Lattice-based key exchange on small integer solution problem. Sci. China Inf. Sci. **57**(11), 1–12 (2014)
7. Mao, S., Zhang, P., Wang, H.: Cryptanalysis of a lattice based key exchange protocol. Sci. China Inf. Sci. **60**, 028101 (2016)
8. Micciancio, D., Peikert, C.: Hardness of SIS and LWE with small parameters. In: Canetti, R., Garay, J.A. (eds.) CRYPTO 2013. LNCS, vol. 8042, pp. 21–39. Springer, Heidelberg (2013). https://doi.org/10.1007/978-3-642-40041-4_2
9. Cabarcas, D., Florian, G., Patrick, W.: Provably secure LWE encryption with smallish uniform noise and secret. Cryptology ePrint Archive, Report 2013/164 (2013). https://eprint.iacr.org
10. Micciancio, D., Regev, O.: Worst-case to average-case reductions based on Gaussian measures. SIAM J. Comput. **37**(1), 267 (2007)

Non-interactive Zero Knowledge *Proofs* in the Random Oracle Model

Vincenzo Iovino[1]([⊠]) and Ivan Visconti[2]

[1] University of Luxembourg, Luxembourg City, Luxembourg
vinciovino@gmail.com
[2] DIEM, University of Salerno, Fisciano, Italy
visconti@unisa.it

Abstract. The Fiat-Shamir (FS) transform is a well known and widely used technique to convert any constant-round public-coin honest-verifier zero-knowledge (HVZK) proof or argument system $\mathsf{HVZK} = (\mathcal{P}, \mathcal{V})$ in a non-interactive zero-knowledge (NIZK) argument system $\mathsf{NIZK} = (\mathsf{NIZK.Prove}, \mathsf{NIZK.Verify})$. The FS transform is secure in the random oracle (RO) model and is extremely efficient: it adds an evaluation of the RO for every message played by $\mathcal{V}$.

While a major effort has been done to attack the soundness of the transform when the RO is instantiated with a "secure" hash function, here we focus on a different limitation of the FS transform that exists even when there is a secure instantiation of the random oracle: the soundness of NIZK holds against polynomial-time adversarial provers only. Therefore even when HVZK is a proof system, NIZK is only an argument system.

In this paper we propose a new transform from 3-round public-coin HVZK proof systems for several practical relations to NIZK *proof* systems in the RO model. Our transform outperforms the FS transform protecting the honest verifier from unbounded adversarial provers with no restriction on the number of RO queries. The protocols our transform can be applied to are the ones for proving membership to the range of a one-way group homomorphism as defined by [Maurer - Design, Codes and Cryptography 2015] except that we additionally require the function to be endowed with a trapdoor and other natural properties. For instance, we obtain new efficient instantiations of NIZK *proofs* for relations related to quadratic residuosity and the RSA function.

As a byproduct, with our transform we obtain essentially for free the first efficient non-interactive zap (i.e., 1-round non-interactive witness indistinguishable *proof* system) for several practical languages in the non-programmable RO model and in an ideal-PUF model.

Our approach to NIZK proofs can be seen as an abstraction of the celebrated work of [Feige, Lapidot and Shamir - FOCS 1990].

Keywords: FS transform · NIZK · Random oracle model

Electronic supplementary material The online version of this chapter (https://doi.org/10.1007/978-3-030-16458-4_9) contains supplementary material, which is available to authorized users.

1   Introduction

Non-Interactive Zero-Knowledge (NIZK) proof and argument systems have been studied for about 30 years [BFM88, FLS90, Gol01]. The concept of proving a statement in just one round without leaking any information has been intriguing for theoreticians and extremely useful as building block for designers of cryptographic protocols. The initial constructions for NIZK worked in the common reference string (CRS) model and because of various limitations (e.g., the need of NP reductions, the non-reusability of the CRS, the expensive computations) their impact was mainly in the theoretical foundations of cryptography.

Proofs vs Arguments. The gap between NIZK proof (NIZKP) systems and NIZK argument (NIZKA) systems consists in a different soundness requirement. The soundness property aims to prevent an adversarial prover from convincing the verifier about the veracity of a false statement. The powerful concept of a NIZK proof requires the soundness guarantee to be unconditional, therefore the adversarial prover can be unbounded. Instead, the notion of a NIZK argument has a significantly weaker soundness guarantee since it applies to PPT (corresponding to non-uniform polynomial-time algorithms) adversarial provers only.[1].

The difference seems subtle but may be fundamental in real-world applications. Consider an e-voting system that uses cryptographic proofs to ensure the election result claimed by the authorities to be authentic. If the system uses NIZK proofs, then there is a guarantee that the authorities cannot subvert the result of the election whatever computing power they have. If NIZK arguments are instead employed, then the guarantee is only *conditional* (it holds only if the authorities do not have enough computational power).

The Bridge Between Theory and Practice: the Fiat-Shamir (FS) Transform. The traditional power of the simulator in a NIZK proof/argument system consists in programming the common reference string (CRS). A popular alternative to the CRS model is the Random Oracle (RO) model [BR93]. The RO model assumes the availability of a perfect random function to all parties. One of the most successful applications of the RO model in cryptography is the FS transform that allows to obtain very efficient NIZK arguments [FS87]. The simulator of such a NIZK argument programs the RO (i.e., the simulator replaces at least in part the RO in answering to RO queries of the adversary).

In concrete implementations of this transform, prover and verifier replace the RO by some "secure" hash function.

Even if the RO methodology has been shown to be controversial already in [CGH98] and further negative results were published next [DNRS99, Bar01, GK03, BLV03, DRV12, GOSV14, KRR16], NIZK arguments via the FS transform

---

[1] In literature this difference is often overlooked. Despite this subtle difference, for simplicity we will call *proof* the string generated by the prover, irrespective of whether the prover be part of a proof or an argument system. We will however be precise on using the words "proof system" and "argument system".

are widely used in concrete cryptographic protocols (e.g., in e-voting). We remark that one could also consider an hybrid notion where the adversarial prover can be unbounded except that it can query the random oracle a polynomial number of times only. We stress that in this paper we consider a truly unbounded adversarial prover, and as such, a NIZK proof system does not impose any limitation on the number of RO queries. This difference can be crucial in applications.

1.1   Problem Statement

The FS transform induces a significant soundness loss. Indeed it receives as input a constant-round public-coin honest-verifier zero-knowledge (HVZK) *proof* system and outputs a NIZK *argument* system. This is a step back compared to the known NIZK *proofs* in the CRS model [BFM88, FLS90, GOS06b, GS08].

Of course if one is interested in a NIZK proof system in the RO model there is a trivial approach: just evaluate the RO on input the instance x to get a random string that can be used to compute a NIZK proof in the common reference string model (e.g., [FLS90]). However the trivial approach is very unsatisfying for the following two reasons: (1) it requires expensive computations (sometimes including an NP reduction) that make the NIZK proof completely impractical, and (2) it requires some complexity assumptions (e.g., trapdoor permutations in [FLS90]) therefore incurring a significant security loss in the zero-knowledge guarantee.

These limitations of the FS-transform and of the above trivial approach motivate the main question of this work.

Open question: *is there an alternative transform that outputs an efficient NIZK proof system (i.e., soundness is guaranteed also against unbounded adversarial provers) in the RO model for practical languages without introducing any additional unproven hypothesis?*

1.2   The FS Transform Internals

Formal definitions of NIZK proofs and arguments of knowledge in the RO model through the FS transform have been investigated in several papers [FKMV12, BPW12, BFW15] and are discussed in Appendix A.3. For simplicity here we will now discuss the specific case of a 3-round public-coin HVZK proof system $3\mathsf{HVZK} = (\mathcal{P}, \mathcal{V})$ where the decision of the verifier is deterministic. However our discussion can be generalized to any constant-round public-coin HVZK argument system.

P sends a first message a to V, also called the commitment. Then V sends back a random challenge c. Finally P outputs the final message z, the answer to c. The triple (a, c, z) is called the transcript of an execution of $3\mathsf{HVZK}$ for an instance x and V takes deterministically the decision of accepting or not the transcript.

The FS transform constructs $\mathsf{NIZK} = (\mathsf{NIZK.Prove}, \mathsf{NIZK.Verify})$ as follows. $\mathsf{NIZK.Prove}$ computes a precisely as P, but then the challenge c of V is replaced

by the output of the RO on input the statement x and a, i.e., $c = H(x,a)$.[2]
Finally NIZK.Prove computes z precisely as P would compute it.

NIZK is only computationally sound (i.e., it is an argument system) in the
random oracle model. Indeed one can easily see that computing with non-
negligible probability an accepting transcript for a false statement when the
adversarial prover runs in polynomial time, implies that the challenge is the output of one out of a polynomially bounded number of evaluations of the RO, and
this can be translated to proving with non-negligible probability a false statement to V. Soundness cannot be claimed when instead the adversarial prover is
unbounded and can therefore make an unbounded number of queries to the RO.

If 3HVZK is also HVZK (see Appendix A.1), then the resulting NIZK argument system is additionally a computational ZK argument system. Indeed the
ZK simulator can program the queries therefore being able to produce a simulated proof using the HVZK simulator that is computationally indistinguishable
from the a real proof.

If 3HVZK satisfies special soundness (i.e., there is a deterministic efficient
extractor that from 2 different accepting transcripts for the same statement with
the same first message outputs a witness), then the resulting NIZK argument
system additionally enjoys witness extraction but limited to PPT adversarial
provers. Known variations [Pas03,Fis05,FKMV12] of the FS transform produce
NIZK *argument* systems that suffer of the same limitation of witness extraction
with respect to PPT provers. We also stress that, to our knowledge, all previous variants of the FS transform (e.g., the ones of Pass [Pas03] and Fischlin
[Fis05]) only achieve *computational* soundness (i.e., there is no security guarantee against an unbounded adversarial prover that as such can have unlimited
access to the random oracle). In this paper we call NIZK proof of knowledge
(NIZKPoK) a NIZK *proof* (i.e., soundness unconditional) system that enjoys the
above extraction property (i.e., limited to PPT adversarial provers).

1.3   The Soundness Degradation of the FS Transform

Suppose that the underlying interactive protocol has the following properties.
The space of prover commitments has cardinality $\geq 2^{b(\lambda)}$, the verifier's challenges
have length $k(\lambda)$, the soundness error is $2^{-k(\lambda)}$, with $k(\lambda) \in \omega(\log(\lambda)), b(\lambda) \geq
\lambda + k(\lambda)$ where λ is the security parameter. Suppose further that the prover
computes the answer z deterministically based on (a,c) and suppose that for
each $x \notin L$ and each commitment a, there exists at least one challenge c such
that (a,c,z) is an accepted transcript (a natural Σ-protocol satisfying the above
requirements will be shown soon).

Fix an $x \notin L$ and consider the following unbounded prover NIZK.Prove*
that aims to compute an accepting proof for x. NIZK.Prove* searches over all
pairs of challenges and commitments (a_c, c) such that the above property holds

---

[2] When the challenge c is computed as $H(a)$, the FS transform offers weaker security
guarantees (see [BPW12,CPS+16]). In this work, we will consider the *strong* FS
transform.

(i.e., (a_c, c, z) is an accepting tuple, where z is the deterministic answer of the prover to (a_c, c)) *and* RO maps (x, a_c) into c; if NIZK.Prove* can find a pair (a_c, c) that verifies such conditions, it outputs (a_c, c, z) as its proof, otherwise outputs some error $\bot$.

For each challenge and commitment pair (a_c, c) the probability that the RO maps (x, a_c) into c such that (a_c, c, z) is an accepted transcript is $\geq 2^{-k(\lambda)}$ (by hypothesis on the soundness error). Thus, since there are $2^{b(\lambda)} \geq 2^{\lambda + k(\lambda)}$ commitments, NIZK.Prove* fails in proving the false statement x with probability $< (1 - \frac{1}{2^{k(\lambda)}})^{2^{\lambda + k(\lambda)}}$. Therefore, NIZK.Prove* succeeds with probability $\geq 1 - (1 - \frac{1}{2^{k(\lambda)}})^{2^{k(\lambda)} \cdot 2^\lambda} \approx 1 - (\frac{1}{e})^{2^\lambda}$.[3]

This example shows that an unbounded prover can break the soundness of the FS transform applied to some particular proof system satisfying the above requirements. This is not an artificial counter-example as such requirements are satisfied by very natural proof systems like the ones of [CP93, CDS94].

Example. Consider for instance the protocol of Chaum and Pedersen [CP93] for proving that a tuple (g, h, u, v) of 4 group elements, in a group of prime order q, is a Diffie-Hellman (DH, in short) tuple.[4]

The prover chooses a random $r \in \mathbb{Z}_q$, where q is the order of the group, and sends the commitment $a = g^r, b = h^r$. The verifier sends a random challenge $c \in \mathbb{Z}_q$. The prover sends back deterministically $z = r + cw \mod q$ and the verifier accepts iff $g^z = au^c$ and $h^z = bv^c$.

Let $k(\lambda) = \lambda$ with security parameter λ equals to the length of the group elements. Then, the challenges have length $k(\lambda)$, the commitments have length $2 \cdot k(\lambda)$ and $k(\lambda)$ is also the soundness parameter. By using the simulator (of the special HVZK), it is easy to see that for each false statement $x \notin L$ and for each challenge c, there exists (a, z) such that (a, c, z) is an accepted transcript for x. Thus, the Chaum and Pedersen's protocol satisfies the above requirements and the soundness can be broken in time $\approx 2^{k(\lambda)}$.

Ineffectiveness of Parallel Repetition. A natural approach to adjust the FS transform in order to circumventing the above attack would be to execute p instances of the protocol in parallel and computing each challenge c_i, for $i = 1, \ldots, p$, as $\mathcal{RO}(x||a_i||i)$. Unluckily, this strategy does not improve the situation. In fact, while the number of possible challenges increases (each challenge now consists of $k \cdot p$ bits) the number of possible commitments also increases. A simple analysis shows that an attack similar to the previous one can be applied to such variant of the FS transform as well. Observe also that the previous attack can be viewed as a special case for $p(\lambda) = 1$.

---

[3] This follows from the fact that $\lim_{\lambda \to \infty} 2^{k(\lambda)} = \infty$ and thus $\lim_{\lambda \to \infty} (1 - \frac{1}{2^{k(\lambda)}})^{-2^{k(\lambda)}} = e$..

[4] Our transform cannot be applied to Chaum and Pedersen's protocol. However there are examples of natural 3-round public-coin HVZK protocols that have a big ratio between space of commitments and space of challenges and can be made non-interactive through our transform (e.g., quadratic residuosity).

In fact, consider a false statement x and an unbounded prover NIZK.Prove* similar to before aiming at computing an accepting proof for x. By the previous analysis on the protocol without repetitions (that can be seen as a special case for $p(\lambda) = 1$) and since the $p(\lambda)$ executions are independent, NIZK.Prove* succeeds with probability $\left(1 - (\frac{1}{e})^{2^\lambda}\right)^{p(\lambda)}$ that is overwhelming in λ.

It is fundamental for the previous analysis to hold that the space of commitments is much bigger than the challenge space, as it is indeed the case in general for natural Σ-protocols for languages where deciding membership is non-trivial. In fact, if for instance the space of the challenges and commitments were of the same cardinality, the lower-bound on the winning probability of the previous prover would be only $\left(1 - \frac{1}{e}\right)^{p(\lambda)}$ that is a negligible function. As we will see next, our transform still uses parallel repetitions but in a more careful way achieving NIZK proof systems for several natural and practical languages.

2 Our Results

In the main result of this work we give a *positive* answer to the above open question: we show a transform that gives NIZK proof systems for practical languages.

We first (see Appendix A.3) provide formal definitions for NIZK proof/argument systems in the RO model following the lines of Faust *et al.* [FKMV12] and Bernhard *et al.* [BFW15] but taking into account unbounded adversarial provers, therefore considering statistical soundness. Then we propose a new transform from a specific class of 3-round public-coin HVZK proof systems for a given class of relations (see below) to NIZK *proof* systems in the RO model for the same class of relations.

The protocols and relations we support are a strengthening of the ones introduced by Maurer [Mau15]. Precisely, Maurer shows that most of the known practical sigma protocols can be viewed as special case of a sigma protocol for a group homomorphic one-way function (OWF). Sigma protocols are a special case of 3-round public-coin HVZK proof systems (see Appendix A.1). Similarly, our transform can be applied to sigma protocols for proving that an element y is in the range of a group homomorphic OWF but we also require additional properties on the function f. Namely, we require the following properties (this is only a sketch and the complete set of properties will be presented in Definition 11).

1. f is a *trapdoor* OWF with range $\subseteq \{0,1\}^{m(\lambda)}$ for some polynomial $m(\cdot)$. The witness for the relation includes the trapdoor, i.e., the prover needs the trapdoor to compute the proof. The trapdoor also allows to efficiently decide whether a string $y \in \{0,1\}^{m(\lambda)}$ is in the range of f or not.
2. The language of all strings $y \notin \mathsf{Range}(f), y \in \{0,1\}^{m(\lambda)}$ is in co-NP and using the trapdoor for f it is possible to compute a witness for the fact that $y \notin \mathsf{Range}(f)$. That is, there are: (a) an algorithm Prove_f that on input a string y and a trapdoor trap for f computes a proof π; (b) an algorithm Verify that on input y and a proof π accepts if and only if $y \notin \mathsf{Range}(f)$; (c) a PPT simulator Sim_f that, with input the security parameter, outputs a pair

(a, π) that is distributed identically to (a', π') where a' is selected at random in the space of strings $y \in \{0,1\}^{m(\lambda)}$, $y \notin \mathsf{Range}(f)$ and $\pi' \leftarrow \mathsf{Prove}_f(y, \mathsf{trap})$.

3. A random element in $\{0,1\}^{m(\lambda)}$ falls outside the range of f with probability $\leq \frac{1}{q}$ (up to a negligible factor) for some constant $q > 1$; this probability affects the length of the proof.

We call such a function a special one-way group homomorphic function (SOWGHF). To exemplify the requirements, consider the squaring function modulo a Blum integer N that acts on the group $\mathbb{Z}_N^\star$; sigma protocols for such f allow to prove whether a number is a quadratic-residue modulo N. The first condition requires the existence of a trapdoor that in this case is the factorization of N and the range of the function is $\mathbb{Z}_N$.

The second condition requires the existence of an efficient way for proving that a number is not a quadratic residue mod N. As N is a Blum integer, -1 is a quadratic non-residue and thus $-y$ is a quadratic residue mod N if and only if y is a quadratic non-residue mod N. Thus, there exists a witness for proving that a number y is not a quadratic residue. The simulator can simply pick a random number $r \leftarrow \mathbb{Z}_N$ and output $(-r^2 \mod N, r)$.

The third condition is also satisfied since a random number in $\mathbb{Z}_N^\star$ is a quadratic-residue modulo N with probability $\frac{1}{4}$ and only a negligible fraction of the integers in $\mathbb{Z}_N$ are not in $\mathbb{Z}_N^\star$.

The second and third conditions are trivially satisfied when f is a permutation, e.g., for the RSA permutation. In that case, it makes no sense to prove with our NIZKP that a string is in the range of the function because for permutations the soundness is trivially satisfied. Moreover, the knowledge extraction property is also guaranteed by the FS transform at a lower cost. Nevertheless, one might consider statements like $\exists x_1, x_2, x_3$ such that $((y_1 = f_1(x_1) \wedge y_2 = f_2(x_2)) \vee y_3 = f_3(x_3))$, where one or more of the functions f_1, f_2, f_3 are permutations and at least one is not a permutation and all the functions satisfy our requirements. Following Cramer et al. [CDS94], our transform can be likewise extended to support such compound statements.

One might be worried that the first condition is very restrictive in that we do not just require f to be a trapdoor OWF but in addition to feed the trapdoor as input to the prover. However, notice that for many practical statements this is the case, e.g., for a proof of correct decryption of a Goldwasser-Micali's ciphertext [GM84] we can assume that the prover is endowed with the factorization of N.

We defer the reader to Appendix A.2 for more details on what we call special one-way group homomorphic functions and special protocols. In Appendix B we show several examples of SOWGHFs that exemplify the usefulness and practicality of our notion. Combined with our transform, this gives efficient NIZK proof systems with statistical soundness for disparate relations of wide applicability.

Our transform preserves the same properties of the FS transform (except some efficiency loss) but maintains the unconditional soundness of the starting protocol (unlike the FS transform). Regarding knowledge extraction, if the starting protocol satisfies special soundness then NIZK will have the same guarantee of extractability (see Appendix E) of the FS transform (i.e., extraction is possible against a PPT adversarial prover). Our transform does not add any computational assumption and thus our NIZK proof will be secure in the RO model without any unproven hypothesis.

Therefore our work gives the first NIZK proof systems for a variety of useful languages in the RO model. See Theorems 10 and 12.

As noted and proved by Yung and Zhao [YZ06] (see also Ciampi *et al.* [CPSV16]), if the original 3-round public-coin HVZK proof system is witness indistinguishable (WI), then the FS-transformed argument is still WI, and the security proof for WI is RO-free. Since the same holds for our transform we get an efficient non-interactive WI *proof* system (also called non-interactive zap in previous work) [GOS06a, GS08, DN00] in the *non-programmable* RO model. The result is formally stated in Corollary G. In Sect. 5 we present applications of this result to hardware-assisted cryptography. In particular we achieve an unconditional NIWI proof system in an ideal-PUF model.

As shown earlier, if the starting interactive proof system has challenges of length λ (with λ security parameter) and space of commitments of cardinality 2^λ then the soundness guarantee of the FS transform is completely violated by adversaries running in $\Theta(2^\lambda)$ steps. Instead, the soundness of our transform is preserved with respect to adversaries running in $O(2^\lambda)$ steps, when the instantiation of the random oracle is resilient to adversaries running in time $O(2^\lambda)$ (e.g., idealized hash functions, PUFs). We formally state it in Conjecture 1.

3   Overview of Our Transform

We next describe our transform. Given an $x \notin L$, we denote by "space of bad commitments" S_x for x of a 3-round public-coin proof system the set of all commitments a such that there exist e, z such that $\mathcal{V}(x, a, e, z)$ is accepted by the verifier. With a slight abuse of notation, we say that the space of bad commitments S of 3HVZK has cardinality $\leq N$ if for all $x \notin L$, the cardinality of S_x is $\leq N$.

Let 3HVZK be a 3-round public-coin HVZK proof system 3HVZK $= (\mathcal{P}, \mathcal{V})$ with space of bad commitments of cardinality $\leq 2^{b(\lambda)}$, challenges of length $k(\lambda)$ and soundness error bounded by $s(\lambda)$. In Lemma 9 we prove that the FS transform applied to a such 3HVZK results into a NIZK proof system with statistical soundness that degrates "nicely" in relation to $s(\lambda)$ when the space of the bad commitments $2^{b(\lambda)}$ is not too "big" (see the Lemma and also Theorem 10 for a more precise statement).

As a consequence, the problem of transforming sigma protocols into NIZK proofs with statistical soundness can be reduced to the problem of transforming 3-round public-coin HVZK proof systems into ones having arbitrarily *small* ratio between soundness error and space of bad commitments. So, we first present a transform from interactive protocols (that do not use the RO) to interactive protocols in the RO model with shorter commitment space. Then, applying the FS transform to the latter protocol will result into a NIZK with statistical soundness.

Trapdoor One-Way Group Homomorphism and Special Protocols. Before presenting our transform, we define the class of relations supported by our protocols. As in Maurer [Mau15], the class of relations we consider are associated with an homomorphic OWF that in our case satisfies some additional requirements. We first recall the abstraction of Maurer [Mau15] and then we proceed to state the additional properties we require.

Consider two groups $(G, \cdot)$, $(H, *)$ and a one-way homomorphic function from G to H, that is a OWF with the property that $f(x_1 \cdot x_2) = f(x_1) * f(x_2)$. By abstracting several known protocols in the literature, Maurer presents a sigma protocol for proving that an element $y \in H$. In the Maurer's protocol, the prover knows x and the verifier knows $y = f(x)$. The prover selects a random element r in G and sends $a = f(k)$ to the verifier. The verifier sends back a number c selected at random in a challenge space that is a set of integers. The prover sends $z = k \cdot x^c$ to the verifier that accepts the transcript if and only if $f(z) = a * y^c$.

If a protocol is so defined and if in addition the function f satisfies the three conditions given in Sect. 2 we say that the protocol is *special*. We now show how to transform a special protocol (spec-prot henceforth) into one with shorter commitment space.

Reducing the Space of Commitments in Special Protocols. We construct a 3-round public-coin HVZK protocol 3HVZK = (3HVZK.Prove, 3HVZK.Verify) for proving that $y \in \mathsf{Range}(f)$ from a spec-prot SpecP = (SpecP.Prove, SpecP.Verify) for the same relation. We denote by Prove and Verify the efficient algorithms to prove and verify that a string $y \notin \mathsf{Range}(f)$ guaranteed by a spec-prot for f. We recall that in a spec-prot (see. Definition 13) the prover SpecP.Prove computes a commitment as $f(r)$ where r is a string drawn at random in the domain of f.

The idea behind the transform is to make the space of the commitments to be arbitrarily shorter than the space of the challenges. Specifically, we repeat the protocol a sufficient number of times p to increase the space of the challenges but at the same time we have to avoid that the space of the commitment increases with the same ratio. To that aim, we force the space of the commitment to be short by computing each commitment via the RO as $a_i = RO(y||i), i \in [p]$. In this way the space of the commitment is limited by $2^{|y|} \cdot p$ and thus, e.g, doubling p just double the space of the commitments while quadrupling the space of the challenges.

Under one of the assumptions for any spec-prot we can assume that with noticeable probability $a_i = f(r_i)$ for some r_i. If this is the case the prover, by means of the trapdoor, can invert a_i and get r_i. As mentioned above, the value r_i is meant to be the randomness used by SpecP.Prove to compute a commitment. Thus, using r_i 3HVZK.Prove can complete the protocol (i.e., computing the final answer to send to the verifier). Note that, by hypothesis, the trapdoor can be also employed to check whether $a_i \in \mathsf{Range}(f)$. On the other hand, if this is not the case, the prover can still use the trapdoor to show the verifier that $a_i \notin \mathsf{Range}(f)$. As in FS, the verifier has also to check that each commitment a_i received by the prover equals $\mathcal{RO}(y, i)$.

Overall Transform. We define our transform to be the result of applying the above transform to a spec-prot SpecP to obtain a protocol 3HVZK and then apply FS transform to 3HVZK to obtain a NIZK argument. It can be seen that our transform guarantees completeness if SpecP is perfectly complete. It can be seen that our transform guarantees computational ZK (see Appendix A.3) if SpecP is HVZK exactly as it is the case for the FS transform. It can be seen that our transform guarantees computational witness extraction (see Appendix E) if SpecP satisfies special soundness exactly as it is the case for the FS transform. More details will be given in Sect. 7.

The most important property of this new transform is that starting from a 3-round public-coin proof system that matches our requirements (i.e., what we call a spec-prot), our transform gives in output a non-interactive *proof* system, assuming a suitable choice of the parameters as we will specify later.

The parameter $p(\cdot)$ in our transform depends on the cardinality of the challenge space $k(\cdot)$ and the probability $q(\cdot)$ that a random element in the space of the commitments falls to be in the range of f. A more precise statement will be given in Sect. 7.

Connection to FLS. The reader may have noticed a connection to the work of Feige, Lapidot and Shamir (FLS) [FLS90]. A CRS-based NIZK like FLS can be easily converted to a NIZK in the RO model by setting the CRS to be the string $\mathcal{RO}(1^\lambda)$. In that case, the CRS in the FLS' NIZK can be seen as the first message in our protocol and then, by using a trapdoor, the prover in FLS is able to open the bits to the verifier in a selected way.

As we want to avoid expensive NP-reductions, in our case the trapdoor depends on the language. Moreover we have to handle the case when f is not a permutation.

4   Comparison

Comparison. Here we compare in more detail the NIZK proofs obtained through our transform with other NIZK arguments and proofs discussed before.

In Table 1 we present a comparison of the NIZK proof resulting to other NIZK proofs and arguments known in the literature (see Sect. 6). The NIZK proof and argument system in the comparison are very different in that they admit so different and disparate relations or can prove general statements through expensive NP-reductions. Nevertheless, it makes sense to compare them in terms of properties achieved. We omit the comparison with the transform of Mittelbach and Venturi that can be instantiated only for specific classes of interactive protocols and uses strong computational assumptions.

The 3rd line in the table refers to a NIZK in the RO constructed from a CRS-based NIZK in the trivial way by replacing the CRS with the string $\mathcal{RO}(1^\lambda)$ and programming the RO in the obvious way. The ZK type is omitted but is implicitly assumed to be (multi-theorem adaptive) computational in the programmable

RO model[5] for works in which the corresponding entry CRS is set to No and (multi-theorem adaptive) computational for the CRS model otherwise.

Efficiency: the Case of Quadratic Residuosity. It is difficult to compare different NIZK proofs and arguments systems for practical statements when they can handle different classes of relations. However, it makes sense to compare FS-transformed NIZK argument to the NIZK proof systems resulting from our transform when both are for the same relation. As an example, we can compare a FS-transformed NIZK argument system for proving that an integer is a quadratic residue to a NIZK proof system resulting from our transformation for the same relation.

The basic sigma protocol for proving quadratic residuosity has soundness error $\frac{1}{2}$. To make the soundness error, let us say $2^{-\lambda}$, it is necessary to repeat the protocol λ times and in turn applying the FS transform to the latter protocol results into just a NIZK argument with computational soundness. Let us now compare the improvement offered by our transform.

As it will be shown in our transform $\mathsf{Trans_{main}}$ of Construction 2, to get soundness error $2^{-\lambda}$ our transform will compute a NIZKP consisting of $p(\lambda)$ repetitions of a 3-round protocol with essentially the same efficiency in terms of communication that the basic sigma protocol for quadratic residuosity, where $p(\lambda)$ has to satisfy the equation (cf. Eq. (1) in Construction 2):

$$2^{2\cdot\lambda+\log(p(\lambda))} \cdot \left(\frac{1}{q} + \left(1 - \frac{1}{q}\right) \cdot \frac{1}{k(\lambda)}\right)^{p(\lambda)} \leq 2^{-\lambda}.$$

As $\frac{1}{q} \approx \frac{3}{4}$, the above equation can be simplified to $3 \cdot \lambda + \log(p(\lambda)) \leq c \cdot p(\lambda)$ where $c \stackrel{\triangle}{=} 3 - \log_2(7) \approx 0.2$.

Then it can be seen that $p(\lambda) \approx 16 \cdot \lambda$ satisfies the equation. Therefore, our transform allows to upgrade from computational to statistical soundness at a cost of a moderate factor of inefficiency.

5 Applications

Efficient NIWI Proofs in the NPRO Model. Yung and Zhao [YZ06] (see also Ciampi *et al.* [CPSV16]) observed that if the original 3-round public-coin HVZK proof system is witness indistinguishable (WI), then the FS-transformed argument is still WI, and the security proof for WI is RO free. Since the same holds for our transform, we get an efficient non-interactive witness indistinguishable (NIWI) *proof* system (also called non-interactive zap in previous work) [GOS06a] [GS08, DN00] in the *non-programmable* RO model. Next we show an application of this primitive.

---

[5] This holds for NIZKAs resulting from the strong FS transform, not for the weak FS one [BPW12].

Unconditional NIWI Proofs in the Ideal-PUF Model. In last decade, there has been a renewed interest about hardware-assisted cryptographic protocols and physically uncloneable functions (PUFs, in short) [PRTG02, GCvD02, TSS+05, Kat07, HL08, GKR08, DORS08, AMS+09, GIS+10, BFSK11, OSVW13, RvD13]. We note that our unconditional NIWI proof system in the NPRO can be turned in an unconditional NIWI *proof* system in the *ideal*-PUF model, in which the PUF acts like a RO.

More specifically, we consider the availability of an *ideal*-PUF. Note that this is different from assuming a RO. In the RO model, all parties need to have access to the same function. In the ideal-PUF model we envision, we just assume that an hardware token acting as an ideal-PUF can be attached to a proof and sent from a party to another (specifically, from the prover to the verifier). We observe that our unconditional NIWI proof system in the NPRO can be turned in an unconditional NIWI *proof* system in the ideal-PUF model.

Table 1. Stat denotes statistical and Comp computational. PV denotes public verifiability: a YES refers to standard NIKZP/NIZKA and a NO to designated verifier ones. CR denotes computational extractability with rewinding extractors and CS denotes computational extractability with straight-line extractors. The ZK type is omitted but is implicitly assumed to be (multi-theorem adaptive) computational in the programmable RO model for works in which the corresponding entry CRS is set to No and (multi-theorem adaptive) computational for the CRS model otherwise. *: When referred to the transforms, a No means that the transform does not *add* any additional computational assumption (beyond assuming the RO model) beyond the ones of the underlying starting protocol (that could even be unconditional). **: Note that the definition of online extractability of Fischlin implicitly assumes that the adversary is possibly computationally unbounded but limited to a polynomial number of RO queries. Thus, according to our terminology, it is still an argument with computational extractability.

Work	Efficiency	Soundness?	CRS?	PV?	Uncondititonal?*	PoK?
NIZKPoK of [GOS06b]	NP-reductions	Stat	Yes	Yes	No	Stat
NIZKPoK of [GS08]	Efficient	Stat	Yes	Yes	No	Stat
NIZKPoK of [GS08] with CRS set to $\mathcal{RO}(1^\lambda)$	NP-reductions	Stat	No	Yes	No	Stat
Transforms of [Lin15, CPSV16]	Efficient	Comp	Yes	Yes	No	No
Transforms of [DFN06, VV09, CG15]	Efficient	Comp	Yes	No	No	No
Transforms of [Pas03, Fis05]	Efficient	Comp	No	Yes	Yes	CS**
Transform of FS	Very efficient	Comp	No	Yes	Yes	CR
Our transform	Efficient	Stat	No	Yes	Yes	CR

6   Related Work

CRS-based NIZK proof and argument systems have been intensively studied in the last 30 years in a sequel of works [BFM88, FLS90, RS92, BY96, Pas03, BCNP04, Ps05, GOS06b, AF07, GS08, Pas13, BFS16]. One of the initial motivations for CRS-based NIZK proof was CCA-security [NY90, CS98, Sah99, CS03, Lin06]. In this setting, the CRS is computed by the receiver, while the NIZK proofs are computed by the sender of ciphertexts. Thus, for CCA-security the CRS model does not pose any issue. However, in e-voting the authority cannot compute the CRS because it must compute proofs that show the correctness of the tally and thus cannot be the same party that computes the CRS that thus has to be setup by a trusted party.

An alternative to the CRS model is the RO model that does not solve the issues of the CRS model but often leads to the design of more efficient protocols. The RO methodology has been introduced in the groundbreaking work of Bellare and Rogaway [BR93]. Canetti *et al.* [CGH98] show that the RO methodology is unsound in general and several works [DNRS99, Bar01, GK03, BLV03, BDSG+13, GOSV14, KRR16] study the security of the FS methodology. The first rigorous analysis of the FS transform (applied to the case of signature schemes) appeared in Pointcheval and Stern [PS00]. Since the introduction of the FS transform [FS87], a lot of works have investigated alternative transformations achieving further properties or mitigating some issues of FS.

Pass [Pas03] and Fischlin [Fis05] introduce new transformations with straight-line extractors to address some problems that arise when using the NIZK argument systems resulting from the FS transform in larger protocols [SG02]. The NIZK systems resulting from the Pass' and Fischlin's transforms share the same limitation of FS of being *arguments*, i.e., sound only against computationally bounded adversaries. Furthermore, as in our case, Fischlin's transform also results in a completeness error.

(Note that the definition of online extractability of Fischlin implicitly assumes that the list of RO queries given to the extractor has polynomial size and thus only withstands adversaries that are possibly computationally unbounded *but* limited to a polynomial number of RO queries; according to our terminology, this limitation brings to an argument system with computational extractability.[6])

Damgård *et al.* [DFN06] propose a new transformation for the standard model but it results in NIZK argument systems that are only *designated verifier*, rests on computational assumptions and has soundness limited to a logarithmic number of theorems. Designated verifier NIZK proofs are sufficient for some applications (e.g., non-malleable encryption [PsV06]) but not for others like e-voting in which public verifiability is a wished property. The limitation on the

---

[6] Note that also the FS transform leads to statistically sound proof systems against computationally unbounded provers constrained to a polynomial number of RO queries. In this paper, we deem a non-interactive system in the RO a proof system only if it enjoys statistical soundness against unbounded adversaries without any limitation on the number of RO queries.

soundness of the Damgård's transformation has been improved in the works of Ventre and Visconti [VV09] and Chaidos and Groth [CG15].

Lindell [Lin15] (see also the improvement of Ciampi *et al.* [CPSV16]) puts forward a new transformation that requires both a *non-programmable* RO and a CRS and has computational complexity only slightly higher than FS. The transformations of Lindell and Ciampi *et al.* are based on computational assumptions whereas ours does not require any unproven hypothesis.

Mittelbach and Venturi [MV16] investigate alternative classes of interactive protocols where the FS transform does have standard-model instantiations but their result yields NIZK argument systems and is based on strong assumptions like indistinguishability obfuscation [GGH+13], and as such is far from being practical. Moreover the result of Mittelbach and Venturi seems to apply only to the weak FS transform in which the statement is not hashed along with the commitment. The weak FS transform is known to be insecure in some applications [BPW12]. In this work, we only consider the strong FS transform.

The work of Mittelbach and Venturi has been improved by Kalai *et al.* [KRR16] that, building on [BLV03,DRV12], have shown how to transform any public-coin interactive proof system into a *two-round* argument system using strong computational assumptions. The latter work does *not* yield non-interactive argument systems.

Sigma protocols, on which efficient NIZK arguments (and our NIZK proofs) in the RO model are based, have been intensively studied [CP93,CDS94,FKI06, BR08,ABB+10,Mau15,GMO16]. Sigma protocols incorporate properties both of interactive proof systems and proofs of knowledge systems [GMR89,BG93]. Faust *et al.* [FKMV12] and Bernhard *et al.* [BFW15] provide a careful study of the definitions and security properties of the NIZK argument systems resulting from the FS transform but they do not investigate the possibility of achieving *statistically* sound proofs. Both works, as well as ours, make use of the general forking lemma of Bellare and Neven [BN06] that extends the forking lemma of Pointcheval and Stern [PS00]. We note that in our NIWI the RO can be replaced by an ideal PUF. In the last decade, a lot of works study constructions and applications of hardware-assisted cryptographic protocols and PUFs [PRTG02, GCvD02,Kat07,HL08,GKR08,DORS08,AMS+09,BFSK11,OSVW13,RvD13].

Roadmap. In Appendix A we provide the necessary background and formal definitions of all the primitives and concepts used in this work, including our new framework of special one-way group homomorphic functions. Additional definitions regarding extractability will be given in Appendix E. In Sect. 7 we present our main transform, in Appendix D we analyze its soundness and in Appendices E-G zero-knowledge, extractability and additional properties. In Appendix B we present several instantiations of special one-way group homomorphic functions.

7 Our Transform

7.1 Step I: From spec-prot to 3-Round Public-Coin HVZK in the ROM

For the sake of exposition, we define our main transform as consisting of two transforms. The first one transforms a spec-prot into a 3-round public-coin HVZK protocol in the RO model.

Specifically, $\mathsf{Trans}(c(\cdot), k(\cdot), q, m(\cdot), f)$ converts a spec-prot SpecP SpecP $=$ (SpecP.Prove, SpecP.Verify) with challenges of length $k(\cdot)$ and commitments of length $c(\cdot)$ for a $(m(\cdot), q)$-SOWGHF f into a 3-round public-coin HVZK proof system $\mathsf{3HVZK}[c(\cdot), k(\cdot), q, m(\cdot), p(\cdot), f]$ $=$ $(\mathsf{3HVZK}[c(\cdot), k(\cdot), q, m(\cdot), p(\cdot), f].$ Prove, $\mathsf{3HVZK}[c(\cdot), k(\cdot), q, m(\cdot), p(\cdot), f].$Verify) with commitments of length $c(\lambda) \cdot p(\lambda)$, space of bad commitments of cardinality $2^{\lambda + \log(p(\lambda))}$, challenges of length $k(\lambda) \cdot p(\lambda)$. Moreover, 3HVZK is associated with a polynomial $\mathsf{poly}_{\mathsf{inp}}(\cdot)$.

The algorithms of $\mathsf{3HVZK}[c(\cdot), k(\cdot), q, m(\cdot), p(\cdot), f]$ when run on an input x with $|x| \triangleq \lambda$ need oracle access to a function $\mathcal{RO}$ with domain $\{0, 1\}^{\mathsf{poly}_{\mathsf{inp}}(\lambda)}$ and co-domain $\{0, 1\}^{c(\lambda)}$, and guarantee soundness bounded by $p(\lambda)$. We next define our transform $\mathsf{Trans}[c(\cdot), k(\cdot), q, m(\cdot), p(\cdot), f]$.

Construction 1. Let SpecP $=$ (SpecP.Prove, SpecP.Verify) be a spec-prot with challenges of length $k(\cdot)$ and commitments of length $c(\cdot)$ for a $(m(\cdot), q)$-SOWGHF f. Note that according to our formulation, SpecP is induced by f, $k(\cdot)$, $m(\cdot)$ and q. Our transform $\mathsf{Trans}(c(\cdot), k(\cdot), q, m(\cdot), p(\cdot), f)$ is a polynomial-time algorithm that takes as input the description of f (and thus implicitly SpecP), the description of functions $c(\cdot), k(\cdot)$, $q, m(\cdot)$ and $p(\cdot)$ and outputs a pair $(\mathsf{poly}_{\mathsf{inp}}(\cdot), \mathsf{3HVZK}[c(\cdot), k(\cdot), q, m(\cdot), p(\cdot), f])$ that consists of the description of a polynomial and the description of a proof system computed as follows.

Compute $\mathsf{poly}_{\mathsf{inp}}(\cdot) = \lambda + \log(p(\cdot))$, and set $\mathsf{3HVZK}[c(\cdot), k(\cdot), q, m(\cdot), p(\cdot), f] =$ (3HVZK$[c(\cdot), k(\cdot), q, m(\cdot), p(\cdot), f].$Prove, 3HVZK$[c(\cdot), k(\cdot), q, m(\cdot), p(\cdot), f].$Verify) according to the description of the following two algorithms that are algorithms with oracle access to a function $\mathcal{RO}$ with domain $\{0, 1\}^{\mathsf{poly}_{\mathsf{inp}}(\lambda)}$ and co-domain $\{0, 1\}^{c(\lambda)}$.

In the following we denote by SpecP.Prove$(y, (x, \mathsf{trap}), f^{-1}(a_i), e_i)$ the output of SpecP.Prove when executed with theorem z, witness (y, trap), first message computed with randomness $f^{-1}(a_i)$ (where the inverse is computed with trapdoor trap) and after having received as challenge e_i from the verifier. Note that the prover of a spec-prot computes its first message as $f(r)$ where r is the chosen randomness, thus the first message corresponds to $f(f^{-1}(a_i)) = a_i$.

3HVZK.Prove, with inputs x, y and the trapdoor trap and 3HVZK.Verify, with input y, performs the following three rounds of communication.

– [Round 1] 3HVZK.Prove$(y, (x, \mathsf{trap})) \rightarrow$ 3HVZK.Verify(y).
  For each $i \in [p(\lambda)]$, **do**
     ∗ **Send** $a_i \leftarrow \mathcal{RO}(y||i)$ to 3HVZK.Verify.
  • **endFor**

- [Round 2] 3HVZK.Verify(y) $\rightarrow$ 3HVZK.Prove(y, (x, trap)).
  - **For each** $i \in [p(\lambda)]$, **do**
    - $*$ $e_i \leftarrow \{0,1\}^{k(\lambda)}$
    - $*$ **Send** e_i to 3HVZK.Prove.
  - $\bullet$ **endFor**
- [Round 3] 3HVZK.Prove(y, (x, trap)) $\rightarrow$ 3HVZK.Verify(y).
  - **For each** $i \in [p(\lambda)]$, **do**
    - $*$ **If** $a_i \notin$ Range(f) **do**
      - $\cdot$ $\pi_i \leftarrow$ Prove(y, trap).
      - $\cdot$ **Send** $z_i = (\bot, \pi_i)$ to 3HVZK.Verify.
    - $*$ **endIf**
    - $*$ **else**
      - $\cdot$ **Send** $z_i \leftarrow$ SpecP.Prove(y, (x, trap), $f^{-1}(a_i)$, e_i) to 3HVZK.Verify.
    - $*$ **endElse**
  - $\bullet$ **endFor.**
- [Acceptance condition] 3HVZK.Verify(y) $\rightarrow \{0,1\}$.
  - **For each** $i \in [p(\lambda)]$, **do**
    - $*$ **If** $a_i \neq \mathcal{RO}(y, i)$ **then return** 0.
    - $*$ **If** $z_i = (\bot, \pi_i)$ **do**
      - $\cdot$ **If** Verify(y, π_i) $= 1$ **then return** 0.
    - $*$ **endIf**
    - $*$ **else**
      - $\cdot$ **If** SpecP.Verify(y, a_i, e_i, z_i) $= 0$ **then return** 0.
    - $*$ **endElse**
    - $*$ **return** 1.
  - $\bullet$ **endFor.**

7.2   Step II: Composing with the FS Transform

Trans($c(\cdot), k(\cdot), q, m(\cdot)p(\cdot), f$) converts a spec-prot SpecP $=$ (SpecP.Prove, SpecP. Verify) with space of bad commitments of cardinality $\leq 2^{b(\cdot)}$, commitments of length $c(\cdot)$, challenges of length $k(\cdot)$ into a proof system in the RO model 3HVZK[$c(\cdot), k(\cdot), q, m(\cdot), p(\cdot), f$] $=$ (3HVZK[$c(\cdot), k(\cdot), q, m(\cdot), p(\cdot), f$]. Prove, 3HVZK[$c(\cdot), k(\cdot), q, m(\cdot), p(\cdot), f$].Verify) with commitments of length $c(\lambda) \cdot p(\lambda)$, space of bad commitments of cardinality $2^{\lambda + \log(p(\lambda))}$ and challenges of length $k(\lambda) \cdot p(\lambda)$. The protocol is associated with a polynomial $\mathsf{poly}_{\mathsf{inp}}(\cdot)$ that dictates the domain of the RO.

By appropriately setting the parameter $p(\cdot)$ and applying the FS transform to 3HVZK we can obtain a NIZK proof system with negligible soundness error (precisely, $p(\cdot)$ and the soundness error will be related). We now show our main transform that uses the previous one and the FS transform to achieve our goal.

Construction 2. Let SpecP $=$ (SpecP.Prove, SpecP.Verify) be a spec-prot with challenges of length $k(\cdot)$ and commitments of length $c(\cdot)$ for a $(m(\cdot), q)$-SOWGHF f. Note that according to our formulation, SpecP is induced by f, $k(\cdot)$, $m(\cdot)$ and q. Our main transform $\mathsf{Trans}_{\mathsf{main}}(c(\cdot), k(\cdot), q, m(\cdot), \delta(\cdot), f)$ is a polynomial-time algorithm that takes as input the description of f (and thus implicitly SpecP), the description of functions $c(\cdot), k(\cdot)$, $q, m(\cdot)$ and a negligible function $\delta(\cdot)$ and outputs a pair $(\mathsf{poly}_{\mathsf{inp}}(\cdot), \mathsf{poly}_{\mathsf{out}}(\cdot), \mathsf{NIZK}[c(\cdot), k(\cdot), q, m(\cdot), \delta(\cdot), f])$ that consists of the description of two polynomials $(\mathsf{poly}_{\mathsf{inp}}(\cdot), \mathsf{poly}_{\mathsf{out}}(\cdot))$ and the description of a NIZKPoK proof system computed as follows.

Firstly, compute a polynomial $p(\cdot)$ satisfying the equation

$$2^{2 \cdot \lambda + \log(p(\lambda))} \cdot \left(\frac{1}{q} + \left(1 - \frac{1}{q}\right) \cdot \frac{1}{k(\lambda)} \right)^{p(\lambda)} \leq \delta(\lambda). \tag{1}$$

We will show in Theorem 10 that it is always possible to find such a polynomial.[7]

Then, apply the transform $\mathsf{Trans}(c(\cdot), k(\cdot), q, m(\cdot)p(\cdot), f)$ of Construction 1 to obtain a 3-round public-coin HVZK proof system in the RO model $3\mathsf{HVZK}[c(\cdot), k(\cdot), q, m(\cdot), p(\cdot), f]$ and a polynomial $\mathsf{poly}'_{\mathsf{inp}}(\cdot)$. Set $\mathsf{poly}_{\mathsf{inp}}(\cdot)$ (resp. $\mathsf{poly}_{\mathsf{out}}(\cdot)$) to the maximum between $\mathsf{poly}'_{\mathsf{inp}}(\cdot)$ and the length of the commitments of 3HVZK (resp. maximum between the length of the commitments and the length of the challenges of 3HVZK).

(In the following we assume that, e.g., if 3HVZK was expecting an RO with domain $\{0,1\}^{m(\lambda)}$ and we execute with an RO with domain $\{0,1\}^{n(\lambda)}$, for $n(\lambda) > m(\lambda)$, the protocol 3HVZK is slightly modified to use the truncation of the output of the RO; similarly for the co-domain. Thus, the previous setting serves to guarantee that the RO has domain and co-domain enough large to be used both for the transform Trans (that uses domain $\{0,1\}^{\lambda + \log((p(\lambda))}$ and co-domain $c(\lambda)$) and the FS transform that uses domain $\{0,1\}^{\lambda + c(\lambda) \cdot p(\lambda)}$ and co-domain $\{0,1\}^{c(\lambda) \times p(\lambda)}$).

Then it applies the FS transform to 3HVZK to get a NIZKPoK proof system $\mathsf{NIZK} = (\mathsf{NIZK.Prove}, \mathsf{NIZK.Verify})$ that uses an RO with domain (resp. co-domain) strings of length $\mathsf{poly}_{\mathsf{inp}}(\cdot)$ (resp. $\mathsf{poly}_{\mathsf{out}}(\cdot)$).

Note that our main transform $\mathsf{Trans}_{\mathsf{main}}$ can be viewed as the composition of Trans with the FS transform.

Remark 1. By defining $\mathsf{Trans}_{\mathsf{main}}$ to be the composition of the two transforms (i.e., Trans and the FS transform), for simplicity we skipped a detail. Namely, the proof system 3HVZK on which we apply the FS transform is a protocol for the RO model and thus care has to be taken in avoiding that the *added* RO queries are in the set of possible RO queries of the original protocol. This issue can be sorted out by letting the RO in the original protocol and in the FS-transformed protocol to query the RO on different prefixes, e.g., 0 and 1; that is, each query x of 3HVZK (resp. each new query added by the FS transform) will invoke the RO on input $(0\|x)$ (resp. $(1\|x)$).

Next, we define the instantiation of a NIZKPoK resulting from our transform with a concrete hash function.

---

[7] Specifically, it does not hold for all negligible functions but does hold for functions like $2^{-c \cdot \lambda}$ for some constant $c > 0$.

Construction 3 [H-instantiation of our transform]. Let $\mathsf{SpecP} = (\mathsf{SpecP}.$
$\mathsf{Prove}, \mathsf{SpecP}.\mathsf{Verify})$ be a spec-prot with challenges of length $k(\cdot)$ and commitments of length $c(\cdot)$ for a $(m(\cdot), q)$-SOWGHF f. Note that according to our formulation, SpecP is induced by f, $k(\cdot)$, $m(\cdot)$ and q.

Let $(\mathsf{poly}_{\mathsf{inp}}(\cdot), \mathsf{poly}_{\mathsf{out}}(\cdot), \mathsf{NIZK}[3\mathsf{HVZK}, c(\cdot), k(\cdot), q, m(\cdot), \delta(\cdot)]) = \mathsf{Trans}$
$(3\mathsf{HVZK}, c(\cdot), k(\cdot), q, m(\cdot), \delta(\cdot))$ be the NIZKPoK system resulting from the transform of Construction 1. Let $H(\cdot)$ be any function with domain $\{0,1\}^*$ and codomain $\{0,1\}^m$ for some integer $m > 0$.

We denote by $\mathsf{Trans}_{\mathsf{main}}^{H(\cdot),m}(3\mathsf{HVZK}, c(\cdot), k(\cdot), q, m(\cdot), \delta(\cdot))$ be the NIZKPoK system resulting from the transform of Construction 1 changed as follows. (In the following we assume for simplicity that $\mathsf{poly}_{\mathsf{out}}(\lambda)$ divides m. It is straightforward to remove the constraint.) When the prover (resp. verifier) needs to access the oracle $\mathcal{RO}(\cdot)$ on an input $y \in \{0,1\}^{\mathsf{poly}_{\mathsf{inp}}(\lambda)}$, the function $H(\cdot)$ is invoked on inputs $H(1^1||0||y), \dots, H(1^{\mathsf{poly}_{\mathsf{out}}(\lambda)/m}||0||y)$ to get respective outputs $e_1, \dots, e_{\mathsf{poly}_{\mathsf{out}}(\lambda)/m}$ and the concatenation of the e_i's as the oracle's answer is returned to the prover (resp. verifier).

With a slight abuse of notation, we call the output of $\mathsf{Trans}^{H(\cdot),m}$ the instantiation of the proof system with function $H(\cdot)$.

References

[AABN02] Abdalla, M., An, J.H., Bellare, M., Namprempre, C.: From identification to signatures via the Fiat-Shamir transform: minimizing assumptions for security and forward-security. In: Knudsen, L.R. (ed.) EUROCRYPT 2002. LNCS, vol. 2332, pp. 418–433. Springer, Heidelberg (2002). https://doi.org/10.1007/3-540-46035-7_28

[AABN08] Abdalla, M., An, J.H., Bellare, M., Namprempre, C.: From identification to signatures via the Fiat-Shamir transform: necessary and sufficient conditions for security and forward-security. IEEE Trans. Inf. Theory **54**(8), 3631–3646 (2008)

[ABB+10] Almeida, J.B., Bangerter, E., Barbosa, M., Krenn, S., Sadeghi, A.-R., Schneider, T.: A certifying compiler for zero-knowledge proofs of knowledge based on Σ-protocols. In: Gritzalis, D., Preneel, B., Theoharidou, M. (eds.) ESORICS 2010. LNCS, vol. 6345, pp. 151–167. Springer, Heidelberg (2010). https://doi.org/10.1007/978-3-642-15497-3_10

[AF07] Abe, M., Fehr, S.: Perfect NIZK with adaptive soundness. In: Vadhan, S.P. (ed.) TCC 2007. LNCS, vol. 4392, pp. 118–136. Springer, Heidelberg (2007). https://doi.org/10.1007/978-3-540-70936-7_7

[AMS+09] Armknecht, F., Maes, R., Sadeghi, A.-R., Sunar, B., Tuyls, P.: Memory leakage-resilient encryption based on physically unclonable functions. In: Matsui, M. (ed.) ASIACRYPT 2009. LNCS, vol. 5912, pp. 685–702. Springer, Heidelberg (2009). https://doi.org/10.1007/978-3-642-10366-7_40

[Bar01] Barak, B.: How to go beyond the black-box simulation barrier. In: 42nd Annual Symposium on Foundations of Computer Science, pp. 106–115. IEEE Computer Society Press, October 2001

[BCNP04] Barak, B., Canetti, R., Nielsen, J.B., Pass, R.: Universally composable protocols with relaxed set-up assumptions. In: 45th Annual Symposium on Foundations of Computer Science, pp. 186–195. IEEE Computer Society Press, October 2004

[BDSG+13] Bitansky, N., et al.: Why "Fiat-Shamir for proofs" lacks a proof. In: Sahai, A. (ed.) TCC 2013. LNCS, vol. 7785, pp. 182–201. Springer, Heidelberg (2013). https://doi.org/10.1007/978-3-642-36594-2_11

[BFM88] Blum, M., Feldman, P., Micali, S.: Non-interactive zero-knowledge and its applications (extended abstract). In: 20th Annual ACM Symposium on Theory of Computing, pp. 103–112. ACM Press, May 1988

[BFS16] Bellare, M., Fuchsbauer, G., Scafuro, A.: NIZKs with an untrusted CRS: security in the face of parameter subversion. In: Cheon, J.H., Takagi, T. (eds.) ASIACRYPT 2016. LNCS, vol. 10032, pp. 777–804. Springer, Heidelberg (2016). https://doi.org/10.1007/978-3-662-53890-6_26

[BFSK11] Brzuska, C., Fischlin, M., Schröder, H., Katzenbeisser, S.: Physically uncloneable functions in the universal composition framework. In: Rogaway, P. (ed.) CRYPTO 2011. LNCS, vol. 6841, pp. 51–70. Springer, Heidelberg (2011). https://doi.org/10.1007/978-3-642-22792-9_4

[BFW15] Bernhard, D., Fischlin, M., Warinschi, B.: Adaptive proofs of knowledge in the random oracle model. In: Katz, J. (ed.) PKC 2015. LNCS, vol. 9020, pp. 629–649. Springer, Heidelberg (2015). https://doi.org/10.1007/978-3-662-46447-2_28

[BG93] Bellare, M., Goldreich, O.: On defining proofs of knowledge. In: Brickell, E.F. (ed.) CRYPTO 1992. LNCS, vol. 740, pp. 390–420. Springer, Heidelberg (1993). https://doi.org/10.1007/3-540-48071-4_28

[BLV03] Barak, B., Lindell, Y., Vadhan, S.P.: Lower bounds for non-black-box zero knowledge. In: 44th Annual Symposium on Foundations of Computer Science, pp. 384–393. IEEE Computer Society Press, October 2003

[BM88] Babai, L., Moran, S.: Arthur-Merlin games: a randomized proof system, and a hierarchy of complexity classes. J. Comput. Syst. Sci. 36(2), 254–276 (1988)

[BN06] Bellare, M., Neven, G.: Multi-signatures in the plain public-key model and a general forking lemma. In: Juels, A., Wright, R.N., De Capitani di Vimercati, S. (eds.) 13th ACM Conference on Computer and Communications Security, CCS 2006 pp. 390–399. ACM Press, October/November 2006

[BPW12] Bernhard, D., Pereira, O., Warinschi, B.: How not to prove yourself: pitfalls of the Fiat-Shamir heuristic and applications to helios. In: Wang, X., Sako, K. (eds.) ASIACRYPT 2012. LNCS, vol. 7658, pp. 626–643. Springer, Heidelberg (2012). https://doi.org/10.1007/978-3-642-34961-4_38

[BR93] Bellare, M., Rogaway, P.: Random oracles are practical: a paradigm for designing efficient protocols. In: Ashby, V. (ed.) 1st ACM Conference on Computer and Communications Security, CCS 1993, pp. 62–73. ACM Press, November 1993

[BR08] Bellare, M., Ristov, T.: Hash functions from sigma protocols and improvements to VSH. In: Pieprzyk, J. (ed.) ASIACRYPT 2008. LNCS, vol. 5350, pp. 125–142. Springer, Heidelberg (2008). https://doi.org/10.1007/978-3-540-89255-7_9

[BY96]   Bellare, M., Yung, M.: Certifying permutations: noninteractive zero-knowledge based on any trapdoor permutation. J. Cryptol. **9**(3), 149–166 (1996)

[CDS94]   Cramer, R., Damgård, I., Schoenmakers, B.: Proofs of partial knowledge and simplified design of witness hiding protocols. In: Desmedt, Y.G. (ed.) CRYPTO 1994. LNCS, vol. 839, pp. 174–187. Springer, Heidelberg (1994). https://doi.org/10.1007/3-540-48658-5_19

[CG15]   Chaidos, P., Groth, J.: Making sigma-protocols non-interactive without random oracles. In: Katz, J. (ed.) PKC 2015. LNCS, vol. 9020, pp. 650–670. Springer, Heidelberg (2015). https://doi.org/10.1007/978-3-662-46447-2_29

[CGH98]   Canetti, R., Goldreich, O., Halevi, S.: The random oracle methodology, revisited (preliminary version). In: 30th Annual ACM Symposium on Theory of Computing, pp. 209–218. ACM Press, May 1998

[CP93]   Chaum, D., Pedersen, T.P.: Wallet databases with observers. In: Brickell, E.F. (ed.) CRYPTO 1992. LNCS, vol. 740, pp. 89–105. Springer, Heidelberg (1993). https://doi.org/10.1007/3-540-48071-4_7

[CPS+16] Ciampi, M., Persiano, G., Scafuro, A., Siniscalchi, L., Visconti, I.: Online/offline OR composition of sigma protocols. In: Fischlin, M., Coron, J.-S. (eds.) EUROCRYPT 2016. LNCS, vol. 9666, pp. 63–92. Springer, Heidelberg (2016). https://doi.org/10.1007/978-3-662-49896-5_3

[CPSV16] Ciampi, M., Persiano, G., Siniscalchi, L., Visconti, I.: A transform for NIZK almost as efficient and general as the Fiat-Shamir transform without programmable random oracles. In: Kushilevitz, E., Malkin, T. (eds.) TCC 2016. LNCS, vol. 9563, pp. 83–111. Springer, Heidelberg (2016). https://doi.org/10.1007/978-3-662-49099-0_4

[CS98]   Cramer, R., Shoup, V.: A practical public key cryptosystem provably secure against adaptive chosen ciphertext attack. In: Krawczyk, H. (ed.) CRYPTO 1998. LNCS, vol. 1462, pp. 13–25. Springer, Heidelberg (1998). https://doi.org/10.1007/BFb0055717

[CS03]   Cramer, R., Shoup, V.: Design and analysis of practical public-key encryption schemes secure against adaptive chosen ciphertext attack. SIAM J. Comput. **33**(1), 167–226 (2003)

[Dam10]   Damgård, I.: On Σ-protocol (2010). http://www.cs.au.dk/~ivan/Sigma.pdf

[DFN06]   Damgård, I., Fazio, N., Nicolosi, A.: Non-interactive zero-knowledge from homomorphic encryption. In: Halevi, S., Rabin, T. (eds.) TCC 2006. LNCS, vol. 3876, pp. 41–59. Springer, Heidelberg (2006). https://doi.org/10.1007/11681878_3

[DG03]   Damgård, I., Groth, J.: Non-interactive and reusable non-malleable commitment schemes. In: 35th Annual ACM Symposium on Theory of Computing, pp. 426–437. ACM Press, June 2003

[DN00]   Dwork, C., Naor, M.: Zaps and their applications. In: 41st Annual Symposium on Foundations of Computer Science, pp. 283–293. IEEE Computer Society Press, November 2000

[DNRS99] Dwork, C., Naor, M., Reingold, O., Stockmeyer, L.J.: Magic functions. In: 40th Annual Symposium on Foundations of Computer Science, pp. 523–534. IEEE Computer Society Press, October 1999

[DORS08] Dodis, Y., Ostrovsky, R., Reyzin, L., Smith, A.D.: Fuzzy extractors: How to generate strong keys from biometrics and other noisy data. SIAM J. Comput. **38**(1), 97–139 (2008)

[DRV12] Dodis, Y., Ristenpart, T., Vadhan, S.: Randomness condensers for efficiently samplable, seed-dependent sources. In: Cramer, R. (ed.) TCC 2012. LNCS, vol. 7194, pp. 618–635. Springer, Heidelberg (2012). https://doi.org/10.1007/978-3-642-28914-9_35

[Fis05] Fischlin, M.: Communication-efficient non-interactive proofs of knowledge with online extractors. In: Shoup, V. (ed.) CRYPTO 2005. LNCS, vol. 3621, pp. 152–168. Springer, Heidelberg (2005). https://doi.org/10.1007/11535218_10

[FKI06] Furukawa, J., Kurosawa, K., Imai, H.: An efficient compiler from Σ-protocol to 2-move deniable zero-knowledge. In: Bugliesi, M., Preneel, B., Sassone, V., Wegener, I. (eds.) ICALP 2006. LNCS, vol. 4052, pp. 46–57. Springer, Heidelberg (2006). https://doi.org/10.1007/11787006_5

[FKMV12] Faust, S., Kohlweiss, M., Marson, G.A., Venturi, D.: On the non-malleability of the Fiat-Shamir transform. In: Galbraith, S., Nandi, M. (eds.) INDOCRYPT 2012. LNCS, vol. 7668, pp. 60–79. Springer, Heidelberg (2012). https://doi.org/10.1007/978-3-642-34931-7_5

[FLS90] Feige, U., Lapidot, D., Shamir, A.: Multiple non-interactive zero knowledge proofs based on a single random string (extended abstract). In: 31st Annual Symposium on Foundations of Computer Science, pp. 308–317. IEEE Computer Society Press, October 1990

[FS87] Fiat, A., Shamir, A.: How to prove yourself: practical solutions to identification and signature problems. In: Odlyzko, A.M. (ed.) CRYPTO 1986. LNCS, vol. 263, pp. 186–194. Springer, Heidelberg (1987). https://doi.org/10.1007/3-540-47721-7_12

[GCvD02] Gassend, B., Clarke, D.E., van Dijk, M., Devadas, S.: Silicon physical random functions. In: Atluri, V. (ed.) 9th ACM Conference on Computer and Communications Security, CCS 2002, pp. 148–160. ACM Press, November 2002

[GGH+13] Garg, S., Gentry, C., Halevi, S., Raykova, M., Sahai, A., Waters, B.: Candidate indistinguishability obfuscation and functional encryption for all circuits. In: 54th Annual Symposium on Foundations of Computer Science, pp. 40–49. IEEE Computer Society Press, October 2013

[GIS+10] Goyal, V., Ishai, Y., Sahai, A., Venkatesan, R., Wadia, A.: Founding cryptography on tamper-proof hardware tokens. In: Micciancio, D. (ed.) TCC 2010. LNCS, vol. 5978, pp. 308–326. Springer, Heidelberg (2010). https://doi.org/10.1007/978-3-642-11799-2_19

[GK03] Goldwasser, S., Kalai, Y.T.: On the (in)security of the Fiat-Shamir paradigm. In: 44th Annual Symposium on Foundations of Computer Science, pp. 102–115. IEEE Computer Society Press, October 2003

[GKR08] Goldwasser, S., Kalai, Y.T., Rothblum, G.N.: One-time programs. In: Wagner, D. (ed.) CRYPTO 2008. LNCS, vol. 5157, pp. 39–56. Springer, Heidelberg (2008). https://doi.org/10.1007/978-3-540-85174-5_3

[GM84] Goldwasser, S., Micali, S.: Probabilistic encryption. J. Comput. Syst. Sci. **28**(2), 270–299 (1984)

[GMO16] Giacomelli, I., Madsen, J., Orlandi, C.: Zkboo: faster zero-knowledge for boolean circuits. In: 25th USENIX Security Symposium, USENIX Security 16, Austin, TX, USA, 10–12 August 2016, pp. 1069–1083 (2016)

[GMR89] Goldwasser, S., Micali, S., Rackoff, C.: The knowledge complexity of interactive proof systems. SIAM J. Comput. **18**(1), 186–208 (1989)

[GMY06] Garay, J.A., MacKenzie, P.D., Yang, K.: Strengthening zero-knowledge protocols using signatures. J. Cryptol. **19**(2), 169–209 (2006)

[Gol01] Goldreich, O.: Foundations of Cryptography: Basic Techniques, vol. 1. Cambridge University Press, Cambridge (2001)

[GOS06a] Groth, J., Ostrovsky, R., Sahai, A.: Non-interactive zaps and new techniques for NIZK. In: Dwork, C. (ed.) CRYPTO 2006. LNCS, vol. 4117, pp. 97–111. Springer, Heidelberg (2006). https://doi.org/10.1007/11818175_6

[GOS06b] Groth, J., Ostrovsky, R., Sahai, A.: Perfect non-interactive zero knowledge for NP. In: Vaudenay, S. (ed.) EUROCRYPT 2006. LNCS, vol. 4004, pp. 339–358. Springer, Heidelberg (2006). https://doi.org/10.1007/11761679_21

[GOSV14] Goyal, V., Ostrovsky, R., Scafuro, A., Visconti, I.: Black-box non-black-box zero knowledge. In: Shmoys, D.B. (ed.) 46th Annual ACM Symposium on Theory of Computing, pp. 515–524. ACM Press, May/June 2014

[GS08] Groth, J., Sahai, A.: Efficient Non-interactive proof systems for bilinear groups. In: Smart, N. (ed.) EUROCRYPT 2008. LNCS, vol. 4965, pp. 415–432. Springer, Heidelberg (2008). https://doi.org/10.1007/978-3-540-78967-3_24

[HL08] Hazay, C., Lindell, Y.: Constructions of truly practical secure protocols using standardsmartcards. In: Ning, P., Syverson, P.F., Jha, S. (eds.) 15th ACM Conference on Computer and Communications Security, CCS 2008, pp. 491–500. ACM Press, October 2008

[Kat07] Katz, J.: Universally composable multi-party computation using tamper-proof hardware. In: Naor, M. (ed.) EUROCRYPT 2007. LNCS, vol. 4515, pp. 115–128. Springer, Heidelberg (2007). https://doi.org/10.1007/978-3-540-72540-4_7

[KRR16] Kalai, Y.T., Rothblum, G.N., Rothblum, R.D.: From obfuscation to the security of Fiat-Shamir for proofs. IACR Cryptology ePrint Archive 2016:303 (2016)

[Lin06] Lindell, Y.: A simpler construction of CCA2-secure public-key encryption under general assumptions. J. Cryptol. 19(3), 359–377 (2006)

[Lin15] Lindell, Y.: An efficient transform from sigma protocols to NIZK with a CRS and Non-programmable random oracle. In: Dodis, Y., Nielsen, J.B. (eds.) TCC 2015. LNCS, vol. 9014, pp. 93–109. Springer, Heidelberg (2015). https://doi.org/10.1007/978-3-662-46494-6_5

[Mau15] Maurer, U.: Zero-knowledge proofs of knowledge for group homomorphisms. Des. Codes Cryptogr. 77(2–3), 663–676 (2015)

[MP03] Micciancio, D., Petrank, E.: Simulatable commitments and efficient concurrent zero-knowledge. In: Biham, E. (ed.) EUROCRYPT 2003. LNCS, vol. 2656, pp. 140–159. Springer, Heidelberg (2003). https://doi.org/10.1007/3-540-39200-9_9

[MV16] Mittelbach, A., Venturi, D.: Fiat–Shamir for highly sound protocols is instantiable. In: Zikas, V., De Prisco, R. (eds.) SCN 2016. LNCS, vol. 9841, pp. 198–215. Springer, Cham (2016). https://doi.org/10.1007/978-3-319-44618-9_11

[NY90] Naor, M., Yung, M.: Public-key cryptosystems provably secure against chosen ciphertext attacks. In: 22nd Annual ACM Symposium on Theory of Computing, pp. 427–437. ACM Press, May 1990

[OPV10] Ostrovsky, R., Pandey, O., Visconti, I.: Efficiency preserving transformations for concurrent non-malleable zero knowledge. In: Micciancio, D. (ed.) TCC 2010. LNCS, vol. 5978, pp. 535–552. Springer, Heidelberg (2010). https://doi.org/10.1007/978-3-642-11799-2_32

[OSVW13] Ostrovsky, R., Scafuro, A., Visconti, I., Wadia, A.: Universally composable secure computation with (Malicious) physically uncloneable functions. In: Johansson, T., Nguyen, P.Q. (eds.) EUROCRYPT 2013. LNCS, vol. 7881, pp. 702–718. Springer, Heidelberg (2013). https://doi.org/10.1007/978-3-642-38348-9_41

[Pas03] Pass, R.: On deniability in the common reference string and random oracle model. In: Boneh, D. (ed.) CRYPTO 2003. LNCS, vol. 2729, pp. 316–337. Springer, Heidelberg (2003). https://doi.org/10.1007/978-3-540-45146-4_19

[Pas13] Pass, R.: Unprovable security of perfect NIZK and non-interactive non-malleable commitments. In: Sahai, A. (ed.) TCC 2013. LNCS, vol. 7785, pp. 334–354. Springer, Heidelberg (2013). https://doi.org/10.1007/978-3-642-36594-2_19

[PRTG02] Pappu, R., Recht, B., Taylor, J., Gershenfeld, N.: Physical one-way functions. Science 297(5589), 2026–2030 (2002)

[PS00] Pointcheval, D., Stern, J.: Security arguments for digital signatures and blind signatures. J. Cryptol. 13(3), 361–396 (2000)

[Ps05] Pass, R., Shelat, A.: Unconditional characterizations of non-interactive zero-knowledge. In: Shoup, V. (ed.) CRYPTO 2005. LNCS, vol. 3621, pp. 118–134. Springer, Heidelberg (2005). https://doi.org/10.1007/11535218_8

[PsV06] Pass, R., Shelat, A., Vaikuntanathan, V.: Construction of a non-malleable encryption scheme from any semantically secure one. In: Dwork, C. (ed.) CRYPTO 2006. LNCS, vol. 4117, pp. 271–289. Springer, Heidelberg (2006). https://doi.org/10.1007/11818175_16

[RS92] Rackoff, C., Simon, D.R.: Non-interactive zero-knowledge proof of knowledge and chosen ciphertext attack. In: Feigenbaum, J. (ed.) CRYPTO 1991. LNCS, vol. 576, pp. 433–444. Springer, Heidelberg (1992). https://doi.org/10.1007/3-540-46766-1_35

[RSA78] Rivest, R.L., Shamir, A., Adleman, L.M.: A method for obtaining digital signature and public-key cryptosystems. Commun. Assoc. Comput. Mach. 21(2), 120–126 (1978)

[RvD13] Rührmair, U., van Dijk, M.: PUFs in security protocols: Attack models and security evaluations. In: 2013 IEEE Symposium on Security and Privacy, pp. 286–300. IEEE Computer Society Press, May 2013

[Sah99] Sahai, A.: Non-malleable non-interactive zero knowledge and adaptive chosen-ciphertext security. In: 40th Annual Symposium on Foundations of Computer Science, pp. 543–553. IEEE Computer Society Press, October 1999

[SG02] Shoup, V., Gennaro, R.: Securing threshold cryptosystems against chosen ciphertext attack. J. Cryptol. 15(2), 75–96 (2002)

[TSS+05] Tuyls, P., Škorić, B., Stallinga, S., Akkermans, A.H.M., Ophey, W.: Information-theoretic security analysis of physical uncloneable functions. In: Patrick, A.S., Yung, M. (eds.) FC 2005. LNCS, vol. 3570, pp. 141–155. Springer, Heidelberg (2005). https://doi.org/10.1007/11507840_15

[VV09] Ventre, C., Visconti, I.: Co-sound zero-knowledge with public keys. In: Preneel, B. (ed.) AFRICACRYPT 2009. LNCS, vol. 5580, pp. 287–304. Springer, Heidelberg (2009). https://doi.org/10.1007/978-3-642-02384-2_18

[YZ06] Yung, M., Zhao, Y.: Interactive zero-knowledge with restricted random oracles. In: Halevi, S., Rabin, T. (eds.) TCC 2006. LNCS, vol. 3876, pp. 21–40. Springer, Heidelberg (2006). https://doi.org/10.1007/11681878_2

[YZ07] Yung, M., Zhao, Y.: Generic and practical resettable zero-knowledge in the bare public-key model. In: Naor, M. (ed.) EUROCRYPT 2007. LNCS, vol. 4515, pp. 129–147. Springer, Heidelberg (2007). https://doi.org/10.1007/978-3-540-72540-4_8

From Quadratic Functions to Polynomials: Generic Functional Encryption from Standard Assumptions

Linru Zhang[1], Yuechen Chen[1], Jun Zhang[2], Meiqi He[1], and Siu-Ming Yiu[1($\boxtimes$)]

[1] Department of Computer Science, The University of Hong Kong,
Pokfulam, Hong Kong SAR, China
{lrzhang,ycchen,mqhe,smyiu}@cs.hku.hk
[2] Educational Technology Department, Shenzhen University,
Shenzhen, Guangdong, China
zhjun@connect.hku.hk

Abstract. The "all-or-nothing" notion of traditional public-key encryptions is found to be insufficient for many emerging applications in which users are only allowed to obtain a functional value of the ciphertext without any other information about the ciphertext. Functional encryption was proposed to address this issue. However, existing functional encryption schemes for generic circuits either have bounded collusions or rely on not well studied assumptions. Recently, Abdalla *et al.* started a new line of work that focuses on specific functions and well-known standard assumptions. Several efficient schemes were proposed for inner-product and quadratic functions. There are still a lot of unsolved problems in this direction, in particular, whether a generic FE scheme can be constructed for quadratic functions and even higher degree polynomials. In this paper, we provide affirmative answers to these questions. First, we show an IND-secure generic functional encryption scheme against adaptive adversary for quadratic functions from standard assumptions. Second, we show how to build a functional encryption scheme for cubic functions (the first in the literature in public-key setting) from a functional encryption scheme for quadratic functions. Finally, we give a generalized method that transforms an IND-secure functional encryption scheme for degree-m polynomials to an IND-secure functional encryption scheme for degree-$(m + 1)$ polynomials.

1 Introduction

Background. Traditional public-key encryption (PKE) allows a user who owns a secret key sk to decrypt a ciphertext CT encrypted with a public key pk. The decryption result is the plaintext of CT if sk matches pk, or nothing otherwise. For many emerging applications, for example, a owner may store her encrypted data in cloud and allow different users to query different functional values of the plaintext without revealing the plaintext, this all-or-nothing concept is insufficient. Functional encryption (FE) was proposed to address this issue, which

© Springer Nature Switzerland AG 2019
C. Carlet et al. (Eds.): C2SI 2019, LNCS 11445, pp. 142–167, 2019.
https://doi.org/10.1007/978-3-030-16458-4_10

enables users to obtain a functional value of a plaintext without any other information about the plaintext. In general, consider a functional encryption scheme for a functionality $F(k, x)$, where $k \in K$ (the key space) and $x \in X$ (the plaintext space). The authority with the master key can generate secret keys sk_k for values k. Given a ciphertext of x, the key holder of sk_k can only learn $F(k, x)$ and nothing else except possibly the length of x.

Before FE was formally defined in [11,26], there were a lot of schemes proposed to overcome the "all-or-nothing" barrier of the traditional public-key encryption. These schemes, including identity-based encryption (IBE) [8,9,28], attribute-based encryption (ABE) [27], searchable encryption [1], and predicate encryption [12,23], are considered as special cases of FE[1].

While there are many exciting results in these special cases, designing FE schemes seems to be more difficult. Existing FE schemes that work for arbitrary circuits either have bounded collusions [21,22], or have to rely on powerful, but impractical and not well understood assumptions (indistinguishable obfuscation (IO) and its variants, or polynomial hardness of simple assumptions on multilinear maps) [13,19,20,31]. Attacks were identified for some constructions that are based on IO and multi-linear map [5,14,15,17].

A Remark on Security Definition. Unlike traditional PKE, [26] showed that simulation-based security (SIM-security) is not always achievable for FE. Indistinguishability-based security (IND-security) is widely used in FE research. We also focus on IND-secure FE schemes. Roughly speaking, IND-security states that the adversary who has the secret keys for functions $f_1, \ldots, f_n$ cannot distinguish which of the challenge messages m_0 or m_1 has been encrypted, under the condition that $f_i(m_0) = f_i(m_1)$, $i \in [1..n]$.

Functional Encryption from Standard Assumptions. Recently, instead of focusing on generic functions, researchers started to design efficient schemes for specific functions using well studied standard assumptions. Abdalla et al. [2] started this line of work by proposing an IND-secure (against selective adversary) functional encryption for inner product (IPFE) based on the decisional Diffie-Hellman assumption. Precisely, given an encrypted vector x in the message space X and a key sk_y based on vector y in the key space K, the decryption algorithm will output the inner product $\langle x, y \rangle$ without revealing any other information about x except the length of it. [4] improved the framework of [2] to achieve IND-security against adaptive adversary, also from standard assumptions. A generic (i.e., one that can instantiate from any PKE scheme) construction of IPFE is given in [3]. The scheme is IND-secure against adaptive adversary.

---

[1] Some classify FE schemes into public index schemes and private index schemes based on the definition of predicate encryption, in which, the message x consists of two parts $(\mathcal{I}, m)$, where $\mathcal{I}$ is an index (e.g. a set of attributes) and m is the actual message. If $\mathcal{I}$ is publicly revealed by the ciphertext and only m is hidden, the corresponding scheme is referred as public index FE, which is commonly known as attributed-based encryption. The scheme is called private index scheme if both $\mathcal{I}$ and m are hidden.

The next step from linear functionality (inner product) is to consider quadratic functions. Note that if one does not care the size of a ciphertext, it is easy to have a generic FE scheme for quadratic function using an inner product scheme as illustrated by the following example. Let $f(x) = 2x_1^2 + 3x_2^2$. We can encrypt every pair of x_i, x_j to obtain $\boldsymbol{x} = (x_1^2, x_1 x_2, x_2 x_1, x_2^2)$. With the vector $\boldsymbol{y} = (2, 0, 0, 3)$, we can easily compute f as the inner product $\langle \boldsymbol{x}, \boldsymbol{y} \rangle$. However, the size of the ciphertext will be $O(n^2)$. Earlier this year, two FE schemes with linear size of ciphertext were proposed in [6]. One is IND-secure against selective adversary based on standard assumptions and the other is IND-secure against adaptive adversary in the generic group model. However, both schemes are not generic and cannot instantiate from any PKE scheme. The question whether it is possible to design a *generic* FE scheme for quadratic functions with linear size ciphertext is still open. And the same question applies to higher finite-degree polynomials[2]. Besides theoretical interest, there are real applications for function encryption for polynomials. For example, cubic functions can be used to calculate volumes; the distance d between two points $\boldsymbol{x}, \boldsymbol{y}$ in L^p space is defined as a p-degree polynomial: $d^p = |x_1 - y_1|^p + |x_2 - y_2|^p + \ldots + |x_n - y_n|^p$ with applications in data mining for high-dimensional data points; and in statistics, measures of central tendency and statistical dispersion, such as mean, median, and standard deviation, are also defined in terms of L^p metrics.

1.1   Our Contributions

In this paper, we provide affirmative answers to the above questions. We focus on the polynomial functionality over Z_p. We list our contributions as follows.

(1) We propose the first generic FE scheme for quadratic functions $LQFE = (Setup, Encrypt, KeyGen, Decrypt)$ with linear-size ciphertexts in the public-key setting. $LQFE$ is proved to be IND-secure against adaptive adversary. Generic functional encryption (proposed in [3]) means that such FE scheme can be instantiated from any PKE scheme with some properties.

(2) We derive a generalized method that transforms an IND-secure degree-m polynomial FE scheme to an IND-secure against selective adversary degree-$(m + 1)$ polynomial FE scheme. We illustrate our method based on our quadratic FE scheme to derive the first FE scheme for cubic functions, $CFE = (Setup, Encrypt, KeyGen, Decrypt)$, in the public-key setting having linear size ciphertext under standard assumptions. Actually, any FE scheme for quadratic functions can be used to build a FE scheme for cubic functions in our construction. For example, [6] can be used in CFE, but then the resulting cubic FE scheme is not generic.

---

[2] Very recently (in June, 2018), [16] provides a polynomial functional encryption scheme with linear ciphertext size. Their scheme is in private-key setting while our scheme is in public-key setting.

1.2   Overview of Our Techniques

In this section, we highlight some of the core ideas underlying our schemes. The details of our schemes will be given in later sections.

Our FE Scheme for Quadratic Functions over Z_p. Our construction is a generic construction, i.e., any public-key encryption scheme that has some structural and homomorphic properties can be used to instantiate it. These properties are similar to the requirements in [3]. Our scheme is efficient in communication and storage size: public keys and ciphertexts are both linear in the size of the encrypted vectors.

To simplify the notation, we may omit the security parameter k in the expression, i.e., instead of writing $f(k, x)$, we may just write $f(x)$ if it is clear from its context. A quadratic function $f(x)$ can be represented[3] as $f(x) = x^T F x$, where $F \in Z_p^{(n+1) \times (n+1)}$ is a matrix with elements $f_{i,j}$, x is a column vector $(x_0, \ldots, x_n) \in Z_p^{n+1}$ and $x_0 = 1$. For our previous example, $f(x) = 2x_1^2 + 3x_2^2$, we can have a column vector $x = (1, x_1, x_2)$ and $F = \begin{pmatrix} 0 & 0 & 0 \\ 0 & 2 & 0 \\ 0 & 0 & 3 \end{pmatrix}$. The input to our scheme is a ciphertext of a vector x, and decryption allows one to obtain $x^T F x$ with the given matrix F.

Our construction works over symmetric bilinear groups G_1, G_2 and G_T and two bilinear maps $e_1(g_1, g_1) = g_T : G_1 \times G_1 \rightarrow G_T, e_2(g_2, g_2) = g_T : G_2 \times G_2 \rightarrow G_T$, where g_1, g_2 and g_T are generators of G_1, G_2 and G_T. The order of G_1, G_2 and G_T is a prime p. The prime order ensures the existence of g_2 (g_1 can be any generator of G_1). The initial idea of the construction is to encrypt each $x_i, i \in \{0, 1, \ldots, n\}$ (denoted by $[n]$ in the rest of the paper) by using the selected PKE scheme ε under certain public key PK_i in group G_1. Then, we can get $\varepsilon.Enc(f_{i,j} x_i x_j)$ with public key PK'_{ij} in group G_T which depends on PK_i and PK_j by computing $e(ct_{x,i}, ct_{x,j})^{f_{i,j}}$, where $ct_{x,i}$ denotes the encrypted x_i. After summing them up and decrypting, we can obtain $f(x) = \sum_{i,j=0}^{n} f_{i,j} x_i x_j = x^T F x$.

However, the result of $e(ct_{x,i}, ct_{x,j})^{f_{i,j}}$ includes not only $\varepsilon.Enc(f_{i,j} x_i x_j)$ in G_T, but also some noisy terms in G_T. The challenge is to carefully design the secret keys and ciphertexts to eliminate these noisy terms while guaranteeing the security.

Notice that the bilinear maps $e_1(\cdot, \cdot)$ and $e_2(\cdot, \cdot)$ are public. If the adversary takes the ciphertexts generated by g_1 (or g_2) as input of $e_1(\cdot, \cdot)$ (or $e_2(\cdot, \cdot)$), it can get new ciphertexts in G_T which are generated by g_T (denote as ct^*). If some parts of ciphertexts in the encryption algorithm are also generated by g_T, then combining such parts of ciphertexts and ct^* would leak information. To avoid this attack, we use the trick that when we need to encrypt something in group G_T, instead of using g_T based public key, we use the public key that is

---

[3] Note that [6] uses a slightly more general representation with two vectors: $f(x, y) = x^T F y$.

based on g_T^q and q is kept secret. And when encrypting vectors in group G_1 (or G_2), we still use g_1 (or g_2) based public key. Therefore, without knowing q, the adversary cannot convert these ciphertexts in G_1 and G_2 to the new ciphertexts which are generated by g_T^q based public key. And the bilinear maps $e_1(\cdot, \cdot)$ and $e_2(\cdot, \cdot)$ cannot help the adversary any more.

The details of this construction can be found in Sect. 3.

Our FE Scheme for Cubic Functions over Z_p and Its Generalization. Our cubic FE scheme is based on any FE scheme for quadratic functions. When building from our generic scheme for quadratic functions, the cubic FE scheme is also generic. The scheme is also efficient: public keys and ciphertexts are both linear in the size of the encrypted vectors.

Similarly, a cubic functionality can be represented as $f(\boldsymbol{x}) =$

$$\sum_{i,j,k \in [n]} f_{i,j,k} x_i x_j x_k = \boldsymbol{x}^T \begin{pmatrix} \boldsymbol{x}^T A_0 \boldsymbol{x} \\ \boldsymbol{x}^T A_1 \boldsymbol{x} \\ \vdots \\ \boldsymbol{x}^T A_n \boldsymbol{x} \end{pmatrix}, \text{ where } A_0, \ldots, A_n \in Z_p^{(n+1) \times (n+1)},$$

$\boldsymbol{x} = (x_0, \ldots, x_n) \in Z_p^{n+1}$ and $x_0 = 1$. After encrypting a vector $\boldsymbol{x}$, the decryption of our scheme is expected to output $\sum_{i,j,k \in [n]} f_{i,j,k} x_i x_j x_k = \sum_{i \in [n]} (x_i \boldsymbol{x}^T A_i \boldsymbol{x})$ with the given coefficients $\{f_{i,j,k}\}_{i,j,k \in [n]}$. Note that there is a requirement for this representation to work and this requirement is easy to satisfy, see Sect. 4.1 for more details.

The initial idea of the construction is to divide the ciphertexts into two parts. The first part will look like $(r_i, t_i^{-1} x_i) W^{-1}$ and the second part will look like $W(a_i, QFE.Enc(x_i))^T$, where $W = \begin{pmatrix} w_{11} & w_{12} \\ w_{21} & w_{22} \end{pmatrix} \in Z_p^{2 \times 2}, w_{12} = u_1^2, w_{22} = u_2^2$ is an invertible matrix and $\boldsymbol{r}, \boldsymbol{a}$ are random vectors in Z_p^{n+1}. The second part can be further divided into two parts, one is $w_{11} a_i, w_{21} a_i$, and the other is $QFE.Enc(u_1 \boldsymbol{x}), QFE.Enc(u_2 \boldsymbol{x})$. For decryption, we call $QFE.Dec(sk_{t_i A_i}, ct)$ to get $w_{12} t_i \boldsymbol{x}^T A_i \boldsymbol{x}$ and $w_{22} t_i \boldsymbol{x}^T A_i \boldsymbol{x}$. The second part becomes $W(a_i, t_i \boldsymbol{x}^T A_i \boldsymbol{x})$. We can multiply both parts of ciphertexts and get $a_i r_i + x_i \boldsymbol{x}^T A_i \boldsymbol{x}$. At last, we sum these up and minus $\sum_{i=0}^{n} a_i r_i$ to get the final value $f(\boldsymbol{x})$. If we have a FE scheme for degree-m polynomial and use degree-m polynomial $f_0(\boldsymbol{x}), \ldots, f_n(\boldsymbol{x})$ instead of matrices in this construction, then we can get a new degree-$(m+1)$ polynomial FE scheme, i.e., this construction can be generalized.

The details of this construction can be found in Sects. 4 and 5.

2   Preliminaries

In this section, we recall some basic definitions that we will use in the remaining sections.

2.1   Bilinear Map

Here we review some facts related to bilinear groups with efficiently computable bilinear maps in [30].

Let G and G_T be two multiplicative cyclic groups of prime order p. Let g be a generator of G and e be a bilinear map, $e : G \times G \to G_T$. The bilinear map e has the following properties:

1. Bilinearity: for all $u, v \in G$ and $a, b \in Z_p$, we have $e(u^a, v^b) = e(u, v)^{ab}$.
2. Non-degeneracy: $e(g, g) \neq 1$.

We say that G is a bilinear group if the group operation in G and the bilinear map $e : G \times G \to G_T$ are both efficiently computable. Notice that the map e is symmetric since $e(g^a, g^b) = e(g, g)^{ab} = e(g^b, g^a)$.

2.2 Functional Encryption

Following Boneh *et al.* [11], we first define the notion of functionality and then the functional encryption scheme FE for functionality $\mathcal{F}$.

Definition 1 (Functionality). *A functionality $\mathcal{F}$ defined over $(K \times M)$ is a function $F : K \times M \to \Sigma \cap \{\bot\}$, where K is the key space, M is the message space and Σ is the output space and $\bot$ is a special string not contained in Σ. Notice that the functionality is undefined when the key is not in the key space or the message is not in the message space.*

Definition 2 (Functional encryption scheme). *For a functionality $\mathcal{F}$, a functional encryption scheme FE for $\mathcal{F}$ is a tuple $FE = (Setup, KeyGen, Encrypt, Decrypt)$ of 4 algorithms:*

1. *$Setup(1^\lambda)$ outputs public key and master secret keys (mpk, msk) for security parameter λ.*
2. *$KeyGen(msk, k)$, on input a master secret key msk and key $k \in K$ outputs secret key sk_k.*
3. *$Encrypt(mpk, m)$, on input public key mpk and message $m \in M$ outputs ciphertext Ct.*
4. *$Decrypt(mpk, Ct, sk_k)$ outputs $y \in \Sigma \times \{\bot\}$*

The correctness requirement is ensured: for all $(mpk, msk) \leftarrow Setup(1^\lambda)$, all $k \in K$ and $m \in M$, for $sk_k \leftarrow KeyGen(msk, k)$ and $Ct \leftarrow Encrypt(mpk, m)$, we have $Decrypt(mpk, Ct, sk_k) = F(k, m)$ whenever $F(k, m) \neq \bot$, except with negligible probability.

Now, we give the IND-FE-CPA and s-IND-FE-CPA security for functional encryption schemes.

Definition 3 (Indistinguishable-based security). *For a functional encryption scheme $FE = (Setup, KeyGen, Encrypt, Decrypt)$ for functionality $\mathcal{F}$, defined over (K, M), we define security against chosen-plaintext attacks (IND-FE-CPA security) via the security game depicted on Table 1. Firstly, the challenger performs **proc Initialize** and returns mpk to the adversary. The adversary can submit function queries f to the challenger, and the challenger returns the output of **proc KeyGen** to the adversary. The adversary can also submit* *two message m_0^*, m_1^* to the challenger, and in response, the challenger returns the output of **proc LR** to the adversary. Finally, the adversary outputs b' and the challenger runs **proc Finalize** to test whether $b = b'$.*

We say that FE is secure against chosen-plaintext attacks if

$$|Pr[Exp_{FE,\lambda}^{ind-fe-cpa-0}] - Pr[Exp_{FE,\lambda}^{ind-fe-cpa-1}]| = negl(\lambda).$$

We also define selective security against chosen-plaintext attacks (s-IND-FE-CPA security) when the challenge message m_0^* and m_1^* have to be chosen before the start of the game (see Table 2).

Table 1. Game $Exp_{FE,\lambda}^{ind-cpa-b}$ define IND-FE-CPA security of FE

proc Initialize(λ)	**proc LR(m_0^*, m_1^*)**
$(mpk, msk) \leftarrow_R Setup(1^\lambda, 1^n)$	$Ct* \leftarrow_R Encrypt(mpk, m_b^*)$
$\mathcal{F} \leftarrow \emptyset$	Return $Ct*$
Return mpk	
proc KeyGen(k)	**proc Finalize(b')**
$\mathcal{F} \leftarrow \mathcal{F} \cup \{k\}$	If $\exists k \in \mathcal{F}$ s.t. $f(k, m_0^*) \neq f(k, m_1^*)$
$sk_k \leftarrow KeyGen(msk, k)$	then return false
Return sk_k	Return (b'=b)

Table 2. Game $Exp_{FE,\lambda}^{s-ind-cpa-b}$ define s-IND-FE-CPA security of FE

proc Initialize(λ, m_0^*, m_1^*)	**proc LR()**
$(mpk, msk) \leftarrow_R Setup(1^\lambda)$	$Ct* \leftarrow_R Encrypt(mpk, m_b^*)$
$\mathcal{F} \leftarrow \emptyset$	Return $Ct*$
Return mpk	
proc KeyGen(k)	**proc Finalize(b')**
$\mathcal{F} \leftarrow \mathcal{F} \cup \{k\}$	If $\exists k \in \mathcal{F}$ s.t. $f(k, m_0^*) \neq f(k, m_1^*)$
$sk_k \leftarrow KeyGen(msk, k)$	then return false
Return sk_k	Return (b'=b)

3   A Generic Functional Encryption Scheme for Quadratic Functions

Now, we present a generic functional encryption scheme for any quadratic functionality over Z_p $LQFE = (Setup, KeyGen, Encrypt, Decrypt)$ based on any public-key encryption scheme $\varepsilon = (Setup, Encrypt, Decrypt)$ that has the some structural and homomorphic properties. These properties are similar to the requirement in [3] and are shown in Supporting Material A. We prove that $LQFE$ is IND-secure against adaptive adversary. Before showing the construction, we give the definitions of quadratic functionality over Z_p.

Quadratic Functionality over Z_p**.** For any quadratic function,

$$f(\boldsymbol{m}) = t_0 + \sum_{i=1}^{n} t_i m_i + \sum_{i,j=1}^{n} t_{i,j} m_i m_j, m_i \in Z_p^n,$$

it can be transformed as $f(\boldsymbol{x}) = \boldsymbol{x}^T F \boldsymbol{x}$ by setting $\boldsymbol{x} = (1, \boldsymbol{m}) \in Z_p^{n+1}$ and the upper triangular matrix $F = (f_{i,j}) \in Z_p^{(n+1) \times (n+1)}$ where: $f_{1,1} = t_0, f_{1,i} = t_{i-1}$ for all $i \in [2, n+1]$, $f_{i,j} = 0$ for all $i > j$, and $f_{i,j} = t_{i-1,j-1}$ for all $i \in [2, n+1]$ and $i \le j$. So we define the quadratic functionality over Z_p that $\mathcal{F}(F, \boldsymbol{x}) = \boldsymbol{x}^T F \boldsymbol{x}$.

3.1   Our FE Scheme for Quadratic Functions over Z_p

Before describing the scheme in full details, we give an informal description of our key ideas. We break the process that get $\varepsilon.Enc(\boldsymbol{x}^T F \boldsymbol{x})$ (which can be used to get the final result $\boldsymbol{x}^T F \boldsymbol{x}$ by calling $\varepsilon.Decrypt$) into following parts:

Firstly, we get $\varepsilon.Enc(f_{i,j} x_i x_j)$ by computing $e_1(ct_{\boldsymbol{x},i}, ct_{\boldsymbol{x},j})$, where $e_1(\cdot, \cdot)$ is a symmetric bilinear map. Secondly, we get $\varepsilon.Enc(\sum_{i,j} f_{i,j} x_i x_j)$ by using the homomorphic properties of ε to sum them up. Then, we eliminate these noisy items by designing secret keys and other ciphertexts. Finally, we set a secret number q to prevent the new attack that the adversary can convert some ciphertexts from one group to another group with the help of bilinear maps $e_1(\cdot, \cdot)$ and $e_2(\cdot, \cdot)$.

Now, here comes the formal description of our construction. Let's consider a PKE scheme $\varepsilon = (Setup, Encrypt, Decrypt)$ with the properties defined above. We define our functional encryption scheme for quadratic functions over Z_p $LQFE = (Setup, KeyGen, Encrypt, Decrypt)$ as follows.

> $Setup(1^\lambda)$: $G_1, G_2, G_T \leftarrow \varepsilon.Setup(1^\lambda)$, the order of G_1, G_2, G_T is a prime p. $e_1(g_1, g_1) = g_T \leftarrow \mathcal{G}^{1^\lambda}$ is a bilinear map $G_1 \times G_1 \rightarrow G_T$, where g_1, g_T are generators of G_1, G_T. Similarly, $e_2(g_2, g_2) = g_T \leftarrow \mathcal{G}^{1^\lambda}$ is a bilinear map $G_2 \times G_2 \rightarrow G_T$, where g_2, g_T are generators of G_2, G_T. Call ε's key generation algorithm to generate $n + 1$ independent secret keys pairs $s_1, ..., s_n, sk$ sharing the same public parameters $params$ and $\boldsymbol{t} = (t_1, ... t_n) \in Z_p^n$. Let $sk_i = s_i + t_i sk, i \in [n]$. Choose $q \leftarrow_R Z_p^*$, then the algorithm sets $g'_T = g_T^q, PK = PKGen(g_1, qsk), PK_i = PKGen(g_1, qsk_i)$. Return $mpk :=$ ($params, PK, \{PK_i\}_{i \in [n]}, g_1, g_2, g_T, g'_T, e(\cdot, \cdot)$) and $msk := (sk, \boldsymbol{s}, \boldsymbol{t}, q)$.
>
> $KeyGen(msk, \{u_{i,j}\}_{i,j \in [n]})$: on input master secret key msk and the coefficients of quadratic function $f(\boldsymbol{x})$, the algorithm first outputs a random matrix $F \in Z_p^{(n+1) \times (n+1)}$, where $f_{i,j} + f_{j,i} = u_{i.j}$. Then, the algorithm computes $sk_{F,1} = q^2 \sum_{i,j \in [n]} f_{i,j}(s_i + t_i sk)(s_j + t_j sk)$. For $i \in [n]$, computes $sk_{F,2,i} = g_2^{q \sum_{j \in [n]} f_{i,j} sk_j}$ and $\hat{sk}_{F,2,i} = g_1^{q \sum_{j \in [n]} f_{i,j} sk_j}$. For $j \in [n]$, computes $sk_{F,3,j} = g_2^{q \sum_{i \in [n]} f_{i,j} sk_i}$ and $\hat{sk}_{F,3,j} = g_1^{q \sum_{i \in [n]} f_{i,j} sk_i}$.
>
> Return $sk_F = (sk_{F,1}, \{sk_{F,2,i}, \hat{sk}_{F,2,i}\}_{i \in [n]}, \{sk_{F,3,j}, \hat{sk}_{F,3,j}\}_{j \in [n]})$

$Encrypt(\boldsymbol{x}, mpk)$: on input master public key mpk and message $\boldsymbol{x} = (x_0, ..., x_n) \in Z_p^{(n+1)}$, chooses shared randomness r and $\boldsymbol{a} = (a_0, ..., a_n)$ in $Z_p^{*(n+1)}$, and computes $ct_0 = \varepsilon.C(r^2, g_T), ct_{x,i} = \varepsilon.E(pk_i.x_i, r)$. For $i \in [n]$, sets $ct_{a,x,i} = \varepsilon.E(pk(g_2, 1)^{x_i}, a_i, r)$ and $ct_{a,i} = \varepsilon.E(pk(g_1, 0), a_i, r)$

Return $ct_x = (ct_0, \{ct_{x,i}, ct_{a,i}, ct_{a,x,i}\}_{i \in [n]})$

$Decrypt(ct_x, sk_F, mpk)$: on input master public key mpk, ciphertext $ct_x = (ct_0, \{ct_{x,i}, ct_{a,i}, ct_{a,x,i}\}_{i \in [n]})$ and secret key sk_F for matrix $F \in Z_p^{(n+1) \times (n+1)}$, returns the output of

$$\varepsilon.Decrypt(sk_{F,1}, ct_0,$$

$$\frac{(\prod_{i,j \in [n]} e_1(ct_{x,i}, ct_{x,j})^{f_{i,j}})(\prod_{i \in [n]} e_1(ct_{a,i}, \hat{sk}_{F,2,i}))(\prod_{j \in [n]} e_1(ct_{a,j}, \hat{sk}_{F,3,j}))}{(\prod_{i \in [n]} e_2(ct_{a,x,i}, sk_{F,2,i}))(\prod_{j \in [n]} e_2(ct_{a,x,j}, sk_{F,3,j}))})$$

Correctness of Our Scheme: We divide the decryption algorithm into the following parts:

$$\mathbf{I} = \prod_{i,j \in [n]} e_1(ct_{x,i}, ct_{x,j})^{f_{i,j}}$$

$$= \prod_{i,j \in [n]} [\varepsilon.E(pk(g_T, q^2 sk_i sk_j), x_i x_j, r^2)\varepsilon.E(pk(g_T, q sk_i)^{x_j},$$

$$0, r)\varepsilon.E(pk(g_T, q sk_j)^{x_i}, 0, r)]^{f_{i,j}}$$

$$= \varepsilon.E(pk(g_T, q^2 \sum_{i,j \in [n]} (f_{i,j} sk_i sk_j)),$$

$$\sum_{i,j \in [n]} f_{i,j} x_i x_j, r^2)\varepsilon.E(pk(g_T, q \sum_{i,j \in [n]} f_{i,j}(x_j sk_i + x_i sk_j)), 0, r).$$

$$\mathbf{II} = (\prod_{i \in [n]} e_2(ct_{a,x,i}, sk_{F,2,i}))(\prod_{j \in [n]} e_2(ct_{a,x,j}, sk_{F,3,j}))$$

$$= \varepsilon.E(pk(g_T, q \sum_{i,j \in [n]} x_i f_{i,j} sk_j), q \sum_{i,j \in [n]} a_i f_{i,j} sk_j, r)\varepsilon.E(pk(g_T,$$

$$q \sum_{i,j \in [n]} x_j f_{i,j} sk_i), q \sum_{i,j \in [n]} a_j f_{i,j} sk_i, r)$$

$$= \varepsilon.E(pk(g_T, q \sum_{i,j \in [n]} (x_i f_{i,j} sk_j + x_j f_{i,j} sk_i)), q \sum_{i,j \in [n]} f_{i,j}(a_i sk_j + a_j sk_i), r)$$

$$\mathbf{III} = (\prod_{i \in [n]} e_1(ct_{a,i}, \hat{sk}_{F,2,i}))(\prod_{j \in [n]} e_1(ct_{a,j}, \hat{sk}_{F,3,j}))$$

$$= \prod_{i \in [n]} \varepsilon.E(pk(g_T, 0), a_i q \sum_{j \in [n]} f_{i,j} sk_j, r) \prod_{j \in [n]} \varepsilon.E(pk(g_T, 0), a_j q \sum_{i \in [n]} f_{i,j} sk_i, r)$$

$$= \varepsilon.E(pk(g_T, 0), q \sum_{i,j \in [n]} (a_i f_{i,j} sk_j + a_j f_{i,j} sk_i), r)$$

So, we can get

$$LQFE.Decrypt(ct_x, sk_F, mpk) = \varepsilon.Decrypt(sk_{F,1}, ct_0, \frac{\mathbf{I} \cdot \mathbf{III}}{\mathbf{II}})$$

$$= \varepsilon.Decrypt(sk_{F,1}, ct_0, \varepsilon.E(pk(g_T, sk_{F,1}), x^T Fx, r^2))$$

$$= x^T Fx$$

Theorem 1. *If the underlying PKE ε has message space, ciphertext space and secret key space of the same order p, if it is IND-CPA and satisfies the properties defined in Sect. 3.1, then LQFE is IND-FE-CP against adaptive adversary.*

The proof of Theorem 1 can be found in Supporting Material B.

4   From Quadratic FE to Cubic FE over Z_p

In this section, we show how to transform our generic FE scheme for quadratic functionality to a generic FE scheme for cubic functionality over Z_p. The method in this section can be generalized to realize a degree-$(m+1)$ polynomial FE from a degree-m polynomial FE, which will be discussed in Sect. 5.

Let $CFE = (Setup, KeyGen, Encrypt, Decrypt)$ be a FE for cubic functionality based on a FE scheme for quadratic functionality $QFE = (Setup, KeyGen, Encrypt, Decrypt)$ which is s-IND-FE-CPA secure. Firstly, we give the definition of cubic functionality over Z_p that is used in our scheme.

4.1   Cubic Functionality over Z_p

For any cubic function $f(x) = \sum_{i,j,k=0}^{n} f_{i,j,k} x_i x_j x_k$, where $x_0 = 1$, we can find

a set of matrices $A_0, \ldots, A_n$, s.t. $f(x) = x^T \begin{pmatrix} x^T A_0 x \\ x^T A_1 x \\ \vdots \\ x^T A_n x \end{pmatrix}$. Actually, there exists

more than one set $\{A_i\}_{i \in [n]}$ that can satisfy this equation.

For security reasons, we define the cubic functionality over Z_p $\mathcal{F}$ in our functional encryption scheme as follows, where $\mathcal{M} \in Z_p^{n+1}$ is the message space:

Definition 4 *(cubic functionality). For any $f_{i,j,k} \in Z_p$, let $\mathcal{F}$ $(\{f_{i,j,k}\}_{i,j,k \in [n]}, x) = \sum_{i,j,k=0}^{n} f_{i,j,k} x_i x_j x_k\}$. For $\forall f(x) \in \mathcal{F}, x_0, x_1 \in \mathcal{M}$ and $f(x_0) = f(x_1)$, there exists an algorithm $ALG(f)$ which could find a*

set of matrices $A_0, \ldots, A_n \in Z_p^{(n+1) \times (n+1)}$, s.t. $f(x) = x^T \begin{pmatrix} x^T A_0 x \\ x^T A_1 x \\ \vdots \\ x^T A_n x \end{pmatrix}$ and

$\forall i \in [n], x_0 A_i x_0 = x_1 A_i x_1.$

This requirement is due to the fact that in any quadratic FE, only if $f(\boldsymbol{x_0}) = f(\boldsymbol{x_1})$, any probabilistic poly(n)-time (PPT) adversary cannot distinguish the ciphertexts of $\boldsymbol{x_0}$ and $\boldsymbol{x_1}$ by IND-security definition of FE.

The message space is decided by how many cubic functions we want to include in the function space. If we just want to use a few fractions of all cubic functions, then the message space could be larger. In the other side, brute-force FE scheme cannot ensure linear-size ciphertext, which is important when constructing FE scheme for higher degree polynomials.

The following theorem shows a special case that if we only have two messages, $\boldsymbol{y_0}, \boldsymbol{y_1}$, such that $f(\boldsymbol{y_0}) = f(\boldsymbol{y_1})$, all cubic functions meet this requirement[4].

Theorem 2. *Given* $\boldsymbol{y_0}, \boldsymbol{y_1} \in Z_p^{n+1}$, $f(\boldsymbol{x}) = \sum_{i \geq j \geq k=0}^{n} f_{i,j,k} x_i x_j x_k$ *and* $f(\boldsymbol{y_0}) =$

$f(\boldsymbol{y_1})$. *There exists* $A_0, \ldots, A_n \in Z_p^{(n+1) \times (n+1)}$, *s.t.* $f(\boldsymbol{x}) = \boldsymbol{x}^T \begin{pmatrix} \boldsymbol{x}^T A_0 \boldsymbol{x} \\ \boldsymbol{x}^T A_1 \boldsymbol{x} \\ \vdots \\ \boldsymbol{x}^T A_n \boldsymbol{x} \end{pmatrix}$ *and*

$\forall i \in [n], \boldsymbol{y_0} A_i \boldsymbol{y_0} = \boldsymbol{y_1} A_i \boldsymbol{y_1}$.

The proof of Theorem 2 can be found in Supporting Material C.

For a given message space $\mathcal{M}$, a natural approach to test whether a cubic function $f(\boldsymbol{x})$ is in $\mathcal{F}$ is that: (1) Find all vector pairs $(\boldsymbol{a}, \boldsymbol{b})$ s.t. $f(\boldsymbol{a}) = f(\boldsymbol{b})$ and sets $\mathcal{V} = \{(\boldsymbol{a}, \boldsymbol{b}) | f(\boldsymbol{a}) = f(\boldsymbol{b})\}$. (2) For each pairs $(\boldsymbol{a}, \boldsymbol{b}) \in \mathcal{V}$, find the system of linear equations and get the solutions $\mathcal{S}_i = \{(A_0, A_1, \ldots, A_n)\}$, where $i = 1, \ldots, |\mathcal{V}|$. (3) Check whether $\mathcal{S}_1 \cap \mathcal{S}_2 \cap \ldots \cap \mathcal{S}_n = \emptyset$.

4.2 Our FE Scheme for Cubic Functions over Z_p

Before describing the scheme in full detail, we give an informal exposition of our key ideas. We use a random invertible matrix $W \in Z_p^{2 \times 2}$ and some random vectors $\boldsymbol{a}, \boldsymbol{r}$ to construct our ciphertexts, which consist of two major parts.

The first part of the ciphertexts seems like $(r_i, t_i^{-1} x_i) W^{-1}$. The second part of the ciphertext seems like $W(a_i, QFE.Enc(x_i))^T$, where QFE is a FE scheme for quadratic functions. Notice that the second part of ciphertexts are not generated directly. The outputs of algorithm ALG is randomized and not unique, so the matrices A_i are not known by the adversary. When doing decryption, firstly, we get $W(a_i, t_i \boldsymbol{x}^T A_i \boldsymbol{x})$ by calling $QFE.Decrypt$. Then, we get $\sum_i a_i r_i + x_i \boldsymbol{x}^T A_i \boldsymbol{x}$ by multiply two parts of ciphertexts and sum them up. Finally, we get the final result $f(\boldsymbol{x}) = \sum_{i,j,k} f_{i,j,k} x_i x_j x_k = \sum_i x_i \boldsymbol{x}^T A_i \boldsymbol{x}$ by substraction $\sum_i a_i r_i$.

Now, here comes the formal description of our construction. Let's consider a quadratic FE scheme $QFE = (Setup, KeyGen, Encrypt, Decrypt)$.

---

[4] A more detailed analysis needs to be carried out to see how practical this requirement is although the requirement and our construction method represent a step towards constructing secure FE schemes for polynomials.

For cubic functions $\mathcal{F}$, we define our functional encryption scheme $CFE = (Setup, KeyGen, Encrypt, Decrypt)$ as follows:

$Setup(1^\lambda, 1^n)$: $(mpk1, msk1) \leftarrow QFE.Setup(1^\lambda, 1^n)$, Randomly choose $t = (t_0, \ldots, t_n) \leftarrow_R Z_p^{n+1}$. Return $mpk := (mpk1, t)$ and $msk := (msk1)$.

$KeyGen(mpk, msk, f = \{f_{i,j,k}\}_{i,j,k \in [n]})$: Call $ALG(f)$ as defined above to obtain the set of matrices $A_0, \ldots, A_n \leftarrow_R ALG(f)$. Then computes $sk_{A_i} = QFE.KeyGen\ (mpk1, msk1, t_i A_i)$. Return $sk_F := \{sk_{A_i}\}_{i \in [n]}$.

$Encrypt(x, mpk)$: Choose a matrix $W = \begin{pmatrix} w_{11} & w_{12} \\ w_{21} & w_{22} \end{pmatrix}$ from $Z_p^{*(2 \times 2)}$, where $w_{12} = u_1^2, w_{22} = u_2^2$ and $WW^{-1} = I$. Randomly choose $r = (r_0, \ldots, r_n), a = (a_0, \ldots, a_n) \in Z_p^{n+1}$. Then computes $Ct_{u_1 x} = QFE.Encrypt(mpk1, u_1 x), Ct_{u_2 x} = QFE.Encrypt(mpk1, u_2 x)$. And sets $Ct_{w,x,i} = (r_i, t_i^{-1} x_i) W^{-1} = (r_i w_{11}^{-1} + t_i^{-1} w_{21}^{-1} x_i, r_i w_{12}^{-1} + t_i^{-1} w_{22}^{-1} x_i)$, $Ct_{a,1,i} = w_{11} a_i, Ct_{a,2,i} = w_{21} a_i, Ct_{ar} = \sum_{i=0}^n a_i r_i$. Return $Ct_x = (Ct_{u_1 x}, Ct_{u_2 x}, \{Ct_{w,x,i}, Ct_{a,i,1}, Ct_{a,2,i}\} i \in [n], Ct_{a,r})$.

$Decrypt(Ct_x, sk_F, mpk)$: Return:

$$\left[\sum_{i=0}^n Ct_{w,x,i} \cdot \begin{pmatrix} Ct_{a,1,i} + QFE.Decrypt(sk_{A_i}, Ct_{u_1 x}, mpk) \\ Ct_{a,2,i} + QFE.Decrypt(sk_{A_i}, Ct_{u_2 x}, mpk) \end{pmatrix} \right] - Ct_{a,r}$$

Correctness of Our Scheme:

$Decrypt(Ct_x, sk_F, mpk)$

$$= \sum_{i=0}^n (r_i w_{11}^{-1} + t_i^{-1} x_i w_{21}^{-1}, r_i w_{12}^{-1} + t_i^{-1} x_i w_{22}^{-1}) \begin{pmatrix} w_{11} a_i + w_{12} t_i x^T A_i x \\ w_{21} a_i + w_{22} t_i x^T A_i x \end{pmatrix} - \sum_{i=0}^n a_i r_i$$

$$= \sum_{i=0}^n (r_i, t_i^{-1} x_i) W^{-1} W \begin{pmatrix} a_i \\ t_i x^T A_i x \end{pmatrix} - \sum_{i=0}^n a_i r_i$$

$$= \sum_{i=0}^n (a_i r_i + x_i \cdot x^T A_i x) - \sum_{i=0}^n a_i r_i$$

$$= x^T \begin{pmatrix} x^T A_0 x \\ \vdots \\ x^T A_n x \end{pmatrix}$$

Theorem 3. *If the underlying functional encryption scheme for quadratic functions QFE has message space and secret key space of the same order p, if it is s-IND-CPA secure, then CFE is s-IND-CPA secure.*

The proof of Theorem 3 can be found in Supporting Material C.

5 Generalization: From Degree-m Polynomial FE to Degree-$(m + 1)$ Polynomial FE

Let $f(x) = \sum_{q_1, \ldots, q_{m+1}=0}^n (f_{q_1, \ldots, q_{m+1}} \Pi_{i=1}^{m+1} x_{q_i})$, where $x_0 = 1$, be a degree-$(m + 1)$ polynomial function, we can find more than one such sets $\{f_0(x), \ldots, f_n(x)\}$

such that, $f(\boldsymbol{x}) = \boldsymbol{x}^T \begin{pmatrix} f_0(\boldsymbol{x}) \\ f_1(\boldsymbol{x}) \\ \vdots \\ f_n(\boldsymbol{x}) \end{pmatrix}$, where $f_0(\boldsymbol{x}), \ldots, f_n(\boldsymbol{x})$ are degree-m polynomial functions.

So our transformation scheme in the above section can be generalized to a degree-$(m+1)$ polynomial FE scheme from any degree-m polynomial FE. For security, the restriction in cubic functionality is also needed in our degree-$(m+1)$ polynomial functionality. Let $\mathcal{M} \in Z_p^{n+1}$ be the message space, then our degree-$(m+1)$ polynomial functionality $\mathcal{F}_{m+1}$ is defined as follows:

Definition 5 (degree-$(m+1)$ polynomial functionality). *For any* $f_{q_1,\ldots,q_{m+1}} \in Z_p$, *let* $\mathcal{F}(\{f_{q_1,\ldots,q_{m+1}}\}_{q_1,\ldots,q_{m+1}\in[n]}, \boldsymbol{x}) = \sum_{q_1,\ldots,q_{m+1}=0}^n (f_{q_1,\ldots,q_{m+1}} \Pi_{i=1}^{m+1} x_{q_i})\}$. $\forall f(\boldsymbol{x}) \in \mathcal{F}_{m+1}$, $\boldsymbol{x_0}, \boldsymbol{x_1} \in \mathcal{M}$ *and* $f(\boldsymbol{x_0}) = f(\boldsymbol{x_1})$, *there exists as algorithm* $ALG(f)$ *which could find a set of degree-m polynomial functions* $f_0(\boldsymbol{x}), \ldots, f_n(\boldsymbol{x})$,

s.t. $f(\boldsymbol{x}) = \boldsymbol{x}^T \begin{pmatrix} f_0(\boldsymbol{x}) \\ f_1(\boldsymbol{x}) \\ \vdots \\ f_n(\boldsymbol{x}) \end{pmatrix}$ *and* $\forall i \in [n], f_i(\boldsymbol{x_0}) = f_i(\boldsymbol{x_1})$.

Similar to our cubic functionality definition, two restrictions on the set of degree-m polynomials $f_0, \ldots, f_n$ are implied by the degree-$(m+1)$ functionality definition. One is that the degree-$(m+1)$ polynomial $f(\boldsymbol{x})$ can be written as $f(\boldsymbol{x}) = \sum_{i=0}^n (x_i f_i(\boldsymbol{x}))$. The other is that for any two vectors $\boldsymbol{x_0}, \boldsymbol{x_1} \in \mathcal{M}$, if $f(\boldsymbol{x_0}) = f(\boldsymbol{x_1})$, then the outputs of each degree-m polynomials $f_i, i \in [n]$ on inputs $\boldsymbol{x_0}, \boldsymbol{x_1}$ are also the same. In the following theorem, we also show that when the message space $\mathcal{M}$ is very small, $\mathcal{F}_{m+1}$ contains all degree-$(m+1)$ polynomials.

Theorem 4. *Given* $\boldsymbol{y_0}, \boldsymbol{y_1} \in Z_p^{n+1}$, $f(\boldsymbol{x}) = \sum_{q_1,\ldots,q_{m+1}=0}^n (f_{q_1,\ldots,q_{m+1}} \Pi_{i=1}^{m+1} x_{q_i})$ *and* $f(\boldsymbol{y_0}) = f(\boldsymbol{y_1})$. *There exists a set of degree-m polynomials* $f_0(\boldsymbol{x}), f_1(\boldsymbol{x}), \ldots,$ $f_n(\boldsymbol{x})$, *s.t.,* $f(\boldsymbol{x}) = \boldsymbol{x}^T \begin{pmatrix} f_0(\boldsymbol{x}) \\ f_1(\boldsymbol{x}) \\ \vdots \\ f_n(\boldsymbol{x}) \end{pmatrix}$ *and* $\forall i \in [n], f_i(\boldsymbol{y_0}) = f_i(\boldsymbol{y_1})$.

Proof. The proof is similar with the proof of Theorem 3.

Intuitively, when m increasing, the number of sets $\{f_0(\boldsymbol{x}), \ldots, f_n(\boldsymbol{x})\}$ where $f(\boldsymbol{x}) = \boldsymbol{x}^T \begin{pmatrix} f_0(\boldsymbol{x}) \\ f_1(\boldsymbol{x}) \\ \vdots \\ f_n(\boldsymbol{x}) \end{pmatrix}$ is increased. Then, the number of equations which are generated by the second restriction $\forall i \in [n], f_i(\boldsymbol{y_0}) = f_i(\boldsymbol{y_1})$ are not change (this system of equations always consists of $n+1$ equations). When $m > 2$, after putting these two restrictions together, it is easier to find a feasible solution than the system of linear equations (3) in the proof of Theorem 3.

Therefore, one can choose a smaller message space $\mathcal{M}$ to achieve larger functionality space $\mathcal{F}_{m+1}$. Or choose smaller functionality space $\mathcal{F}_{m+1}$ to get larger message space $\mathcal{M}$.

5.1   Our FE Scheme for Degree-$(m+1)$ Polynomial over Z_p

Let us consider a degree-m polynomial FE scheme $mFE = (Setup, KeyGen, Encrypt, Decrypt)$. We define our functional encryption scheme for a degree-$(m+1)$ polynomial $\mathcal{F}_{m+1}$ $(m+1)FE = (Setup, KeyGen, Encrypt, Decrypt)$ as follows:

$Setup(1^\lambda, 1^n)$: $(mpk1, msk1) \leftarrow mFE.Setup(1^\lambda, 1^n)$, Randomly choose $t = (t_0, \ldots, t_n) \leftarrow_R Z_p^{n+1}$. Return $mpk := (mpk1, t)$ and $msk := (msk1)$.

$KeyGen(mpk, msk, f = \{f_{q_1,\ldots q_{m+1}}\}_{q_1,\ldots,q_{m+1} \in [n]})$: Call $ALG(f)$ as defined above to obtain the set of m degree polynomial $f_0(x), \ldots, f_n(x) \leftarrow_R ALG(f)$. Then computes $sk_{f_i} = mFE.KeyGen(mpk1, msk1, t_i f_i)$. Return $sk_F := \{sk_{f_i}\}_{i \in [n]}$.

$Encrypt(x, mpk)$: Choose a matrix $W = \begin{pmatrix} w_{11} & w_{12} \\ w_{21} & w_{22} \end{pmatrix}$ from $Z_p^{*(2 \times 2)}$, where $w_{12} = u_1^m, w_{22} = u_2^m$ and $WW^{-1} = I$. Randomly choose $r = (r_0, \ldots, r_n), a = (a_0, \ldots, a_n) \in Z_p^{n+1}$. Then computes $Ct_{u_1 x} = mFE.Encrypt(mpk1, u_1 x), Ct_{u_2 x} = mFE.Encrypt(mpk1, u_2 x)$. And sets $Ct_{w,x,i} = (r_i, t_i^{-1} x_i)W^{-1} = (r_i w_{11}^{-1} + t_i^{-1} w_{21}^{-1} x_i, r_i w_{12}^{-1} + t_i^{-1} w_{22}^{-1} x_i)$, $Ct_{a,1,i} = w_{11} a_i, Ct_{a,2,i} = w_{21} a_i, Ct_{ar} = \sum_{i=0}^n a_i r_i$. Return $Ct_x = (Ct_{u_1 x}, Ct_{u_2 x}, \{Ct_{w,x,i}, Ct_{a,i,1}, Ct_{a,2,i}\} i \in [n], Ct_{a,r})$.

$Decrypt(Ct_x, sk_F, mpk)$: Return:

$$\left[\sum_{i=0}^n Ct_{w,x,i} \cdot \begin{pmatrix} Ct_{a,1,i} + mFE.Decrypt(sk_{A_i}, Ct_{u_1 x}, mpk) \\ Ct_{a,2,i} + mFE.Decrypt(sk_{A_i}, Ct_{u_2 x}, mpk) \end{pmatrix} \right] - Ct_{a,r}$$

The correctness can be easily extended from the proof in our cubic FE scheme.

Theorem 5. *If the underlying functional encryption scheme for a degree-m polynomials, mFE, has message space and secret key space of the same order p, if it is s-IND-CPA secure, then $(m+1)FE$ is s-IND-CPA secure.*

The proof of this theorem can be easily extended from the proof of Theorem 4.

Efficiency Analysis. Notice that in this scheme, the size of secret keys in a degree-$(m+1)$ polynomial FE will become n times the size of secret keys in the degree-m polynomial FE, $m \geq 2$. However, we show that it would not induce more cost in practice. In a cloud application scenario, the data owner stores the encrypted data in a server, and the user has a $m+1$-degree polynomial f and wants to ask the function value $f(x)$. So the user sends all coefficients of monomial in f to the Key Generator, and the Key Generator will return a corresponding secret key sk_f. Then the user sends sk_f to the server, and the server does decryption and returns $f(\boldsymbol{x})$. The size of coefficients is $O(n^{m+1})$. In almost existing public key FE schemes from standard assumptions [2–4,6], the coefficients are used in the Decryption algorithm. So the size of message that the user sends to the server is also $O(n^{m+1})$ in their schemes (the message includes two parts: the coefficients and sk_f). The expansion of the secret key in our transformation scheme is a factor n, but the expansion of the size of coefficients is also a factor n (from degree-m to degree-$(m+1)$). So under the condition that the coefficients are used in the Decryption algorithm, the expansion of secret key can be bounded by the expansion of the size of coefficients. Therefore, our transformation scheme does not lose any efficiency.

6   Conclusions and Discussion

In this paper, we show that constructing generic FE schemes for quadratic functions, cubic functions and finite degree polynomials are achievable. In summary, our generic FE scheme for quadratic functions is IND-secure against adaptive adversary with a linear size ciphertext. This generic scheme can be instantiated from any PKE schemes that satisfy a few structural and homomorphic properties. Our generic FE scheme for cubic functions from our quadratic FE scheme is the first effective scheme for cubic functions. The transformation can be generalized to higher degree polynomials. In particular, we show how to transform an IND-secure degree-m polynomial FE scheme to an IND-secure degree-$(m+1)$ polynomial FE scheme.

There are still quite a number of open questions in this topic. When we use an IND-secure degree-m polynomial FE mFE to build a degree-$(m+1)$ polynomial FE scheme, a natural restriction, i.e., the cubic functionality, on such a degree-$(m+1)$ polynomial appears. It seems that the question of building generic FE scheme for any finite-degree polynomials without this restriction is not feasible. Another question is about function privacy (also known as function hiding, studied in [10,18,24,29]). Intuitively, function privacy requires that decryption keys reveal essentially nothing on their corresponding function. However, in almost existing FE constructions from standard assumptions, the functions are actually a part of their secret keys, i.e., the coefficients are directly used in decryption algorithms without any protection. The question of building functional hiding FE scheme for polynomials from standard assumptions still remains open.

Finally, we conclude the paper by giving a remark on "Indistinguishable obfuscation from Functional encryption." Very recently, some papers [7,25] show that it is possible to construct indistinguishability obfuscation (IO) from FE. They showed that IO can be obtained from constant degree graded encoding schemes or subexponentially-secure weakly-succinct FE for functions in NC^1. In fact, our transformation meets the weakly-succinct condition and may provide a new direction on constructing IO from standard assumptions, although FE for polynomials (i.e., arithmetic circuits) seems not strong enough to get IO yet.

Acknowledgement. This project is partially supported by the Collaborative Research Fund (CRF) of RGC of Hong Kong (Project No. CityU C1008-16G).

Supporting Material

A   Requirements of PKE

Our framework constructs functional encryption scheme for quadratic functions $QFE = (Setup, KeyGen, Encrypt, Decrypt)$ from a public-key encryption scheme $\varepsilon = (Setup, Encrypt, Decrypt)$. In order to prove the correctness and security of the new scheme, we need some structural and homomorphic properties on ε as defined below.

Structure. ε's secret keys and public keys are elements of a group G (with generator g_1), and the message space is $M_x \subset Z$. We require the ciphertexts to consist of two parts $c_0 = C(g_1, r)$ and $ct_1 = E(pk, x, r)$, where $pk(g_1, sk)$ is the public key in G corresponding to the secret key sk. The first part c_0 corresponds to some commitment $C(g_1, r)$ of the randomness r used for the encryption. The second part ct_1 is the encryption of x with randomness r. Computing a from $E(pk(g, 0), a, r)$ can be reduced to some difficult problems.

We also split the **Setup** algorithm for convenience in the following two algorithms to sample secret keys, and to sample corresponding public keys:

$SKGen(1^\lambda)$ takes in input the security parameter and sample a secret key sk from the secret key space according to the same distribution induced by **Setup**. $PKGen(sk, \tau)$ takes in input a secret key sk and parameters τ, and generates a public key pk corresponding to sk according to the distribution induced by τ. We will omit τ when it is clear from the context.

Linear Key Homomorphism. We say that a PKE has linear key homomorphism if for any two secret keys $sk_1, sk_2 \in G$ and any $y_1, y_2 \in Z_p$, the linear combination formed by $y_1 sk_1 + y_2 sk_2$ can be computed efficiently only using public parameters, the secret keys and the coefficients. And this combination $y_1 sk_1 + y_2 sk_2$ also functions as a secret key to a public key that can be computed as $pk_1^{y_1} \cdot pk_2^{y_2}$, where pk_1 (resp. pk_2) is a public key corresponding to sk_1 (resp. sk_2).

Linear Ciphertext Homomorphism Under Shared Randomness. We say that a PKE has linear ciphertext homomorphism under shared randomness if it holds that $E(pk_1, x, r) \cdot E(pk_2, y, r) = E(pk_1 pk_2, x + y, r)$ and $E(pk(g^q, sk), x, r) = E(pk(g, sk), x, r)^q = E(pk(g, qsk), qx, r)$.

Computation Properties in Bilinear Map. Assume that $e(g_1^a, g_1^b) = g_T^{ab}$ is a bilinear map $G \times G \to G_T$, where g_T is a generator of G_T and $e(g_1, g_1) = g_T$. We require that

$$e(E(pk_{(g_1, sk_1)}, x, a), E(pk_{(g_1, sk_2)}, y, b))$$
$$= E(pk_{(g_T, sk_1 sk_2)}, xy, ab) E(pk_{(g_T, sk_1)}, 0, a)^y E(pk_{(g_T, sk_2)}, 0, b)^x$$

And for security, we define two properties via security game. More details can be referred to [3].

l-Public-Key-Reproducibility. For a public-key encryption scheme ε, we define *l*-public-key-reproducibility via the following security game:

Game $Exp_{\varepsilon,\lambda}^{l-ct-rep-b}(\mathcal{A})$
proc Initialize$(\lambda, \mathcal{M})$
$(sk, (\alpha_i, sk_i)_{i \in [l]}) \leftarrow_R \mathcal{D}(1^\lambda)$
If $b = 0$ then $(pk_i = \varepsilon.PKGen(\alpha_i sk + sk_i, \tau))_{i \in [l]}$
else $pk \leftarrow \varepsilon.PKGen(sk, \tau'); (pk_i = pk^{\alpha_i} \cdot \varepsilon.PKGen(sk_i.\tau_i))_{i \in [l]}$
Return $(pk_i, sk_i)_{i \in [l]}$
proc Finalize(b')
Return $(b' = b)$

with $\mathcal{D}$ samples tuples of the form $(sk, (\alpha_i, sk_i)_{i \in [l]})$ where sk and the sk_i's are sampled from $SKGen$, and the α_i's are in $\mathcal{T}$.

Then, we say that ε has *l−public−key−reproducibility* if there exists $\tau, \tau'(\tau_i)_{i \in [l]}$ such that

$$|Pr[Exp_{\varepsilon,\lambda}^{l-pk-rep-0}(\mathcal{A} = 1)]| - |Pr[Exp_{\varepsilon,\lambda}^{l-pk-rep-1}(\mathcal{A}) = 1]| = negl(\lambda)$$

l-Ciphertext-Reproducibility. For a public-key encryption scheme ε, we define *l*-ciphertext-reproducibility via the following security game:

Game $Exp_{\varepsilon,\lambda}^{l-ct-rep-b}(\mathcal{A})$
proc Initialize$(\lambda, \mathcal{M})$
$(a, (\alpha_i, x_i, sk_i)_{i \in [l]}) \leftarrow_R \mathcal{D}(1^\lambda)$
$sk \leftarrow \varepsilon.SKGen(1^\lambda); pk \leftarrow \varepsilon.PKGen(sk, \tau'); (pk_i \leftarrow \varepsilon.PKGen(sk_i, \tau_i))_{i \in [l]}$
$ct_0 = \varepsilon.C(r); ct = \varepsilon.E(pk, a, r)$
If $b = 0$ then $ct_i = ct^{\alpha_i} \cdot \varepsilon.E(pk_i, x_i, r)$
else $ct_i = ct^{\alpha_i} \cdot \varepsilon.E'(sk_i, x_i, ct_0, \tau_i)$
Return $(pk, (\alpha_i, pk_i, sk_i)_{i \in [l]}, ct_0, (ct_i)_{i \in [l]})$
proc Finalize(b')
Return $(b' = b)$

where (1) $\mathcal{D}$ samples tuples of the form $(a, (\alpha_i, x_i, sk_i)_{i \in [l]})$, where sk_i's are sampled from $SKGen$, α_i's are in $\mathcal{T}$ and a and the x_i's are in $\mathcal{M}_x$. (2) E' is an algorithm that takes in input a secret key in H, a message in Z_p, a first part ciphertext $C(r)$ for some r in the randomness space, and the parameters needed to generate public keys, and output a second part ciphertext.

Then, we say that ε has *l−ciphertext−reproducibility* if there exists τ', τ_i's and algorithm E' such that

$$|Pr[Exp_{\varepsilon,\lambda}^{l-ct-rep-0}(\mathcal{A} = 1)]| - |Pr[Exp_{\varepsilon,\lambda}^{l-ct-rep-1}(\mathcal{A}) = 1]| = negl(\lambda)$$

B   Proofs in Our FE Scheme for Quadratic Functions

B.1   Proof of Theorem 1

Proof. We proof the security via a sequence of hybrid experiments, and then we show they are indistinguishable.

Hybrid H1: This is the IND-FE-CPA game:

proc Initialize(λ)	proc LR(x_0, x_1)
$(mpk, msk) \leftarrow_R Setup(1^\lambda, 1^n)$	$Ct* \leftarrow_R Encrypt(mpk, x_b)$
$\mathcal{F} \leftarrow \emptyset$	Return $Ct*$
Return mpk	
proc KeyGen(F)	proc Finalize(b')
$\mathcal{F} \leftarrow \mathcal{F} \cup F$	If $\exists F \in \mathcal{F}$ s.t. $f(F, x_0) \neq f(F, x_1)$
$sk_F \leftarrow KeyGen(msk, F)$	then return false
Return sk_F	Return (b'=b)

Hybrid H2: This is like H1 except that the master public key is generated by invoking the algorithm $H2.Setup$ defined as follows:
$H2.Setup(1^\lambda, 1^n)$: The algorithm samples $sk \leftarrow \varepsilon.SKGen(1^\lambda)$, for $i \in [n]$, PKE secret key $s_i \leftarrow \varepsilon.Setup(1^\lambda)$ and uniformly random scalar $t_i \leftarrow_R Z_P, q \leftarrow_R Z_p^*$ and a bilinear map $e(g_1, g_1) = g_T$, where g_1, g_T are generators of G_1, G_T. Similarly, $e_2(g_2, g_2) = g_T \leftarrow \mathcal{G}^{1^\lambda}$ is a bilinear map $G_2 \times G_2 \rightarrow G_T$, where g_2, g_T are generators of G_2, G_T. Then the algorithm sets: $PK = \varepsilon.PKGen(g_1, qsk, \tau), sk_i = s_i + t_i sk, g_T' = g_T^q$. $PK_{s_i} = \varepsilon.PKGen(g_1, qs_i, \tau_i)$ $PK_i = PK^{t_i} \cdot PK_{s_i}$, where τ is the same as used in the Setup algorithm, and τ_i is such that $PK^{t_i} \cdot PK_{s_i}$ is close to $\varepsilon.PKGen(g_1, qsk_i)$.
The algorithm returns $mpk := (params, PK, \{PK_i\}_{i \in [n]}, g_1, g_2, g_T, g_T', e(\cdot, \cdot))$ and $msk := (s, t, sk, q)$. Under the $l-public-key-reproducibility$ of ε, H1 and H2 are indistinguishable.

Hybrid H3: This is like H2 except that the challenge ciphertext is generated by invoking the algorithm $H3.Encrypt$ defined as follows:
$H3.Encrypt(msk, mpk, x)$: Choose shared randomness r and $a = (a_1, ..., a_n)$ in Z_p, and computes
$ct_0 = \varepsilon.C(r^2, g_1), ct_1 = \varepsilon.E(PK, 0, r), ct_{a,i} = \varepsilon.E(pk(g_1, 0), a_i, r)$
For $i \in [n]$, $ct_{x,i} = ct_1^{t_i} \cdot \varepsilon.E(PK_{s_i}, x_i, r), ct_{a,x,i} = \varepsilon.E(pk(g_2, 1)^{x_i}, a_i, r)$
By linear ciphertext-homomorphism of ε, H2 = H3.

Hybrid H4: This is like H3 except that the challenge ciphertext is generated by invoking the algorithm $H4.Encrypt$ defined as follows:
$H4.Encrypt(msk, mpk, Ct, x)$: Let $Ct = (Ct_0, Ct_1)$. Then the algorithm computes the ciphertext for x in the following way:
$ct_0 = \varepsilon.C(r^2, g_1), ct_{a,i} = \varepsilon.E(pk(g_1, 0), a_i, r)$. For $i \in [n]$, $ct_{x,i} = ct_1^{t_i} \cdot \varepsilon.E'(s_i, x_i, Ct_0, \tilde{r}), ct_{a,x,i} = \varepsilon.E(pk(g_2, 1)^{x_i}, a_i, r)$, where $\varepsilon.E'$ is the alternative encryption algorithm defined in the $l-ciphertext-reproducibility$ game. $\tilde{r}$ is some randomness shared among all the invocation of $\varepsilon.E'$.

proc Initialize(λ)	proc LR(x_0, x_1)
$(mpk, msk) \leftarrow_R H2.Setup(1^\lambda, 1^n)$	$Ct = \varepsilon.E(PK, 0)$
$\mathcal{F} \leftarrow \emptyset$	$Ct* \leftarrow_R H4.Encrypt(msk, mpk, Ct, x_b)$
Return mpk	Return $Ct*$
proc KeyGen(F)	proc Finalize(b')
$\mathcal{F} \leftarrow \mathcal{F} \cup F$	If $\exists F \in \mathcal{F}$ s.t. $f(F, x_0) \neq f(F, x_1)$
$sk_F \leftarrow KeyGen(msk, F)$	then return false
Return sk_F	Return (b'=b)

Under the $l-ciphertext-reproducibility$ of ε, H3 and H4 are indistinguishable.

Hybrid H5: This is like H4 except that the challenge ciphertext is generated by invoking the algorithm $H5.Encrypt$ defined as follows and Ct encrypts a random value in Z_p.

$H5.Encrypt(msk, mpk, Ct, x)$: Let $Ct = (Ct_0, Ct_1)$. Then the algorithm computes the ciphertext for x in the following way:

$ct_0 = \varepsilon.C(r^2, g_1), ct_{a,i} = \varepsilon.E(pk(g_1, 0), a_i, r)$.

For $i \in [n]$, $ct_{x,i} = ct_1^{t_i} \cdot \varepsilon.E'(s_i, x_i, Ct_0, \tilde{r}), ct_{a,x,i} = \varepsilon.E(pk(g_2, 1)^{x_i + t_i}, a_i, r)$.

proc Initialize(λ)	proc LR(x_0, x_1)
$(mpk, msk) \leftarrow_R H2.Setup(1^\lambda, 1^n)$	$Ct = \varepsilon.E(PK, 1)$
$\mathcal{F} \leftarrow \emptyset$	$Ct* \leftarrow_R H5.Encrypt(msk, mpk, Ct, x_b)$
Return mpk	Return $Ct*$
proc KeyGen(F)	proc Finalize(b')
$\mathcal{F} \leftarrow \mathcal{F} \cup F$	If $\exists F \in \mathcal{F}$ s.t. $f(F, x_0) \neq f(F, x_1)$
$sk_F \leftarrow KeyGen(msk, F)$	then return false
Return sk_F	Return (b'=b)

Under the s-IND-CPA security of ε, $\varepsilon.E(PK, 0)$ and $\varepsilon.E(pk, 1)$ are indistinguishable. Now, we need to show that $\varepsilon.E(pk(g_2, 1)^{x_i + t_i}, a_i, r)$ and $\varepsilon.E(pk(g_2, 1)^{x_i}, a_i, r)$ are indistinguishable.

If $\exists w(t_i) \in Z_p$, s.t. $\varepsilon.E(pk(g_2, t_i), 0, r) = \varepsilon.E(pk(g_2, 0), w(t_i), r)$, then

$$\varepsilon.E(pk(g_2, 1)^{x_i + t_i}, a_i, r) = \varepsilon.E(pk(g_2, x_i), a_i, r)\varepsilon.E(pk(g_2, t_i), 0, r)$$
$$= \varepsilon.E(pk(g_2, x_i), a_i, r)\varepsilon.E(pk(g_2, 0), w(t_i), r)$$
$$= \varepsilon.E(pk(g_2, x_i), a_i + w(t_i), r)$$

and $\varepsilon.E(pk(g_2, 1)^{x_i}, a_i, r) = \varepsilon.E(pk(g_2, x_i), a_i, r)$. We can refer to $\varepsilon.E(pk(g_2, 1)^{x_i + t_i}, a_i, r)$ as encryption of a random number, so the ciphertext is a random 'fake' ciphertext. According to the security of PKE ε and the equivalent between IND-security and semantic security of PKE, $\varepsilon.E(pk(g_2, 1)^{x_i}, a_i, r)$ should be indistinguishable from a random number. Therefore $\varepsilon.E(pk(g_2, 1)^{x_i}, a_i, r)$ and $\varepsilon.E(pk(g_2, 1)^{x_i + t_i}, a_i, r)$ are indistinguishable.

Else, $\forall b \in Z_p$, $\varepsilon.E(pk(g_2,0),b,r) \neq \varepsilon.E(pk(g_2,t_i),0,r)$. If $\exists c,d \in Z_p$, $\varepsilon.E(pk(g_2,0),c,r) = \varepsilon.E(pk(g_2,0),d,r)$, then

$$c = \varepsilon.Decrypt(sk,\varepsilon.C(g_2,r),\varepsilon.E(pk(g_2,0),c,r))$$
$$= \varepsilon.Decrypt(sk,\varepsilon.C(g_2,r),\varepsilon.E(pk(g_2,0),d,r))$$
$$= d$$

Since $G_T = p$, we have that $G_T = \{\varepsilon.E(pk(g_2,0),b,r)\}_{b\in Z_p}$. So

$$\{\varepsilon.E(pk(g_2,0),b,r)\}_{b\in Z_p} \cap \varepsilon.E(pk(g_2,t_i),0,r) = G_T \cap \varepsilon.E(pk(g_2,t_i),0,r) \neq \emptyset$$

By contradiction, $\forall t_i \in Z_p$, $\exists b \in Z_p$, s.t. $\varepsilon.E(pk(g_2,0),b,r) = \varepsilon.E(pk(g_2,t_i),0,r)$
Therefore, H4 and H5 are indistinguishable.

Hybrid H6: This is like H5 except that the challenge ciphertext is generated by invoking the algorithm $H6.Encrypt$ defined as follows:
$H6.Encrypt(msk,mpk,\boldsymbol{x})$: The algorithm computes the ciphertext for $\boldsymbol{x}$ in the following way:
$ct_0 = \varepsilon.C(r^2,g_1), ct_1 = \varepsilon.E(PK,1,r), ct_{a,i} = \varepsilon.E(pk(g_1,0),a_i,r)$.
For $i \in [n]$, $ct_{x,i} = ct_1^{t_i} \cdot \varepsilon.E'(s_i,x_i,Ct_0,\tilde{r}), ct_{a,x,i} = \varepsilon.E(pk(g_2,1)^{x_i+t_i},a_i,r)$

proc Initialize(λ)	proc LR($\boldsymbol{x_0},\boldsymbol{x_1}$)
$(mpk,msk) \leftarrow_R H2.Setup(1^\lambda,1^n)$	$Ct* \leftarrow_R H6.Encrypt(msk,mpk,\boldsymbol{x_b})$
$\mathcal{F} \leftarrow \emptyset$	Return $Ct*$
Return mpk	
proc KeyGen(F)	**proc Finalize(b')**
$\mathcal{F} \leftarrow \mathcal{F} \cup F$	If $\exists F \in \mathcal{F}$ s.t. $f(F,\boldsymbol{x_0}) \neq f(F,\boldsymbol{x_1})$
$sk_F \leftarrow KeyGen(msk,F)$	then return false
Return sk_F	Return (b'=b)

Under the $l-ciphertext-reproducibility$ of ε, H5 and H6 are indistinguishable.

Hybrid H7: This is like H8 except that the challenge ciphertext is generated by invoking the algorithm $\varepsilon.Encrypt$

proc Initialize(λ)	proc LR($\boldsymbol{x_0},\boldsymbol{x_1}$)
$(mpk,msk) \leftarrow_R H2.Setup(1^\lambda,1^n)$	$Ct* \leftarrow_R \varepsilon.E(mpk,\boldsymbol{x_b}+t)$
$\mathcal{F} \leftarrow \emptyset$	Return $Ct*$
Return mpk	
proc KeyGen(F)	**proc Finalize(b')**
$\mathcal{F} \leftarrow \mathcal{F} \cup F$	If $\exists F \in \mathcal{F}$ s.t. $f(F,\boldsymbol{x_0}) \neq f(F,\boldsymbol{x_1})$
$sk_F \leftarrow KeyGen(msk,F)$	then return false
Return sk_F	Return (b'=b)

By linear ciphertext homomorphism of ε, H6 = H7.

Hybrid H8: This is like H7 except that the master public key is generated by invoking the algorithm $Setup$.

proc Initialize(λ)	proc LR(x_0, x_1)
$(mpk, msk) \leftarrow_R Setup(1^\lambda, 1^n)$	$Ct* \leftarrow_R \varepsilon.E(mpk, x_b + t)$
$\mathcal{F} \leftarrow \emptyset$	Return $Ct*$
Return mpk	
proc KeyGen(F)	proc Finalize(b')
$\mathcal{F} \leftarrow \mathcal{F} \cup F$	If $\exists F \in \mathcal{F}$ s.t. $f(F, x_0) \neq f(F, x_1)$
$sk_F \leftarrow KeyGen(msk, F)$	then return false
Return sk_F	Return (b' =b)

Under the $l-public-key-reproducibility$ of ε, H7 and H8 are indistinguishable.

Advantage of Any PPT Adversary in H8: Notice that $t + x_b - x_{1-b} \in Z_p^n$. Let $t' = t + x_b - x_{1-b}, s'_i = s_i + (x_{1-b} - x_b)_i sk$. Then (s', t') equally likely as (s, t) that gives exactly the same view by replacing x_b by x_{1-b}.

Moreover, when analyzing $sk_F \leftarrow FE.KeyGen(F, msk)$, since $s'_i + t'_i sk = s_i + x_{1,b,i} sk - x_{b,i} sk + (t_i + x_{b,i} - x_{1-b,i}) sk = s_i + t_i sk$, so the sk_F are same for (s, t) and (s', t'). Therefore, the advantage of the adversary in this game is 0.

C Proofs in Our FE Scheme for Cubic Functions

C.1 Proof of Theorem 2

Proof. Let $a_i = f_{i,j,k}, i = j = k \neq 0$, $b_{i,k} = f_{i,j,k}, i = j \neq k, i, k \neq 0$, $c_{i,j,k} = f_{i,j,k}, i \neq j \neq k, i, j, k \neq 0$, $d_i = f_{i,j,k}, i = j \neq 0, k = 0$, $e_{i,j} = f_{i,j,k}, i \neq j \neq 0, k = 0$, $f_i = f_{i,j,k}, i \neq 0j = k = 0$, $g = f_{i,j,k}, i = j = k = 0$ and

$$A_0 = \begin{pmatrix} a_{00}^0, \dots, a_{0n}^0 \\ a_{10}^0, \dots, a_{1n}^0 \\ \vdots \ddots \vdots \\ a_{n0}^0, \dots, a_{nn}^0 \end{pmatrix}, \dots, A_0 = \begin{pmatrix} a_{00}^n, \dots, a_{0n}^n \\ a_{10}^n, \dots, a_{1n}^n \\ \vdots \ddots \vdots \\ a_{n0}^n, \dots, a_{nn}^n \end{pmatrix}.$$

Since $f(x) = x^T \begin{pmatrix} x^T A_0 x \\ x^T A_1 x \\ \vdots \\ x^T A_n x \end{pmatrix}$, we can get the following equations:

$$\begin{cases} a_{00}^0 = g \\ a_{ii}^i = a_i, i > 0 \\ a_{ii}^0 + (a_{0i}^i + a_{i0}^i) = d_i, i > 0 \\ (a_{i0}^0 + a_{0i}^0) + a_{00}^i = f_i, i > 0 \\ (a_{ij}^0 + a_{ji}^0) + (a_{0i}^j + a_{i0}^j) + (a_{j0}^i + a_{0j}^i) = e_{i,j}, i > j > 0 \\ (a_{ik}^i + a_{ki}^i) + a_{ii}^k = b_{i,k}, i > k > 0 \\ (a_{jk}^i + a_{kj}^i) + (a_{ik}^j + a_{ki}^j) + (a_{ij}^k + a_{ji}^k) = c_{i,j,k}, i > j > k > 0 \end{cases} \quad (1)$$

Since $\forall i \in [n], \boldsymbol{y_0} A_i \boldsymbol{y_0} = \boldsymbol{y_1} A_i \boldsymbol{y_1}$, where $\boldsymbol{y_u} = (y_{u0}, y_{u1}, \ldots, y_{un}), u = 1, 2$ we can get the following equations:

$$
\begin{cases}
\sum_{i=1}^{n}(a_{i0}^0 + a_{0i}^0)(y_{0i} - y_{1i}) + \sum_{i=1}^{n} a_{ii}^0 (y_{0i}^2 - y_{1i}^2) + \sum_{i>j=1}^{n} (a_{ij}^0 + a_{ji}^0)(y_{0i}y_{0j} - y_{1i}y_{1j}) = 0 \\
\vdots \\
\sum_{i=1}^{n}(a_{i0}^n + a_{0i}^n)(y_{0i} - y_{1i}) + \sum_{i=1}^{n} a_{ii}^n (y_{0i}^2 - y_{1i}^2) + \sum_{i>j=1}^{n} (a_{ij}^n + a_{ji}^n)(y_{0i}y_{0j} - y_{1i}y_{1j}) = 0
\end{cases}
\tag{2}
$$

Putting Eqs. (1) and (2) together, we can get that:

$$
\begin{cases}
a_{00}^0 = g \\
a_{ii}^i = a_i, i > 0 \\
\sum_{i=1}^{n}(f_i - a_{00}^i)(y_{0i} - y_{1i}) + \sum_{i=1}^{n}(d_i - (a_{0i}^i + a_{i0}^i))(y_{0i}^2 - y_{1i}^2) + \\
\quad \sum_{i>j=1}^{n} (e_{i,j} - (a_{0i}^j + a_{i0}^j) - (a_{j0}^i + a_{0j}^i))(y_{0i}y_{0j} - y_{1i}y_{1j}) = 0, i > j > 0 \\
\sum_{i=1}^{n}(a_{i0}^1 + a_{0i}^1)(y_{0i} - y_{1i}) + \sum_{i=1}^{n}(b_{i,1} - (a_{i1}^i + a_{1i}^i))(y_{0i}^2 - y_{1i}^2) + \\
\quad \sum_{i>j=1}^{n} (c_{i,j,1} - (a_{j1}^i + a_{1j}^i + a_{i1}^j + a_{1i}^j))(y_{0i}y_{0j} - y_{1i}y_{1j}) = 0, i > j > 0 \\
\vdots \\
\sum_{i=1}^{n}(a_{i0}^n + a_{0i}^n)(y_{0i} - y_{1i}) + \sum_{i=1}^{n}(b_{i,n} - (a_{in}^i + a_{ni}^i))(y_{0i}^2 - y_{1i}^2) + \\
\quad \sum_{i>j=1}^{n} (c_{i,j,n} - (a_{jn}^i + a_{nj}^i + a_{in}^j + a_{ni}^j))(y_{0i}y_{0j} - y_{1i}y_{1j}) = 0, i > j > 0
\end{cases}
\tag{3}
$$

Now, we will show that the system of linear Eq. (3) is solvable, i.e., its coefficient matrix is full rank.

Notice that a_{00}^0 only occurs in the first equation of (3), each a_{ii}^i only occurs in one equation of $\{a_{ii}^i = a_i, i > 0\}$, each a_{00}^i only occurs in one equation of $\{\sum_{i=1}^{n}(f_i - a_{00}^i)(y_{0i} - y_{1i}) + \sum_{i=1}^{n}(d_i - (a_{0i}^i + a_{i0}^i))(y_{0i}^2 - y_{1i}^2) + \sum_{i>j=1}^{n}(e_{i,j} - (a_{0i}^j + a_{i0}^j) - (a_{j0}^i + a_{0j}^i))(y_{0i}y_{0j} - y_{1i}y_{1j}) = 0, i > j > 0\}$, each $(a_{ti}^j + a_{ti}^i)$ only occurs in one equation of $\{\sum_{i=1}^{n}(a_{i0}^t + a_{0i}^t)(y_{0i} - y_{1i}) + \sum_{i=1}^{n}(b_{i,n} - (a_{it}^i + a_{ti}^i))(y_{0i}^2 - y_{1i}^2) + \sum_{i>j=1}^{n}(c_{i,j,n} - (a_{jt}^i + a_{tj}^i + a_{it}^j + a_{ti}^j))(y_{0i}y_{0j} - y_{1i}y_{1j}) = 0, i > j > 0\}$. So the coefficient matrix is full rank.

C.2   Proof of Theorem 3

Proof. We proof security via a sequence of hybrid experiments, and then we show they are indistinguishable.

Hybrid H1: This is the s-IND-CPA game:

proc Initialize($\lambda, \boldsymbol{x_0}, \boldsymbol{x_1}$)	proc LR()
$(mpk, msk) \leftarrow_R Setup(1^\lambda, 1^n)$	$Ct* \leftarrow_R Encrypt(mpk, \boldsymbol{x_b})$
$\mathcal{F} \leftarrow \emptyset$	Return $Ct*$
Return mpk	
proc KeyGen(F)	proc Finalize(b')
$\mathcal{F} \leftarrow \mathcal{F} \cup F$	If $\exists F \in \mathcal{F}$ s.t. $f(F, \boldsymbol{x_0}) \neq f(F, \boldsymbol{x_1})$
$sk_F \leftarrow KeyGen(msk, F)$	then return false
Return sk_F	Return (b'=b)

Hybrid H2: This is like H1 except that the master public key is generated by invoking the algorithm $H2.Setup$ defined as follows:

$H2.Setup(1^\lambda, 1^n, \boldsymbol{x_0}, \boldsymbol{x_1})$: The algorithm samples $(mpk1, msk1) \leftarrow QFE.Setup$ $(1^\lambda, 1^n)$. Randomly choose $\boldsymbol{t} = (t_0, \ldots, t_n) \leftarrow_R Z_p^{n+1}$. Then sets $t_i^0 = (\frac{x_{1i}}{x_{0i}} t_i^{-1})^{-1}$ and $t_i^1 = (\frac{x_{0i}}{x_{1i}} t_i^{-1})^{-1}$. Return $mpk := (mpk1, \boldsymbol{t^b})$ and $msk := (msk1)$.

Z_p is a field, so t_i^0 and t_i^1 are uniformly distributed in Z_p. Therefore, H2 and H1 are indistinguishable.

Hybrid H3: This is like H2 except that the challenge ciphertext is generated by invoking the algorithm $H3.Encrypt(mpk, \boldsymbol{x_b})$ defined as follows:

$H3.Encrypt(mpk, \boldsymbol{x_b})$: Choose a matrix $W = \begin{pmatrix} w_{11} & w_{12} \\ w_{21} & w_{22} \end{pmatrix}$ from $Z_p^{*(2 \times 2)}$, where $w_{12} = u_1^2, w_{22} = u_2^2$ and $WW^{-1} = I$. Randomly choose $\boldsymbol{r} = (r_0, \ldots, r_n), \boldsymbol{a} = (a_0, \ldots, a_n) \in Z_p^{n+1}$. Then computes $Ct_{u_1x} = QFE.Encrypt(mpk1, u_1\boldsymbol{x_{1-b}}, Ct_{u_2x} = QFE.Encrypt(mpk1, u_2\boldsymbol{x_{1-b}})$. Sets $Ct_{w,x,i} = (r_i, (t_i^b)^{-1}x_{bi})W^{-1}$, and $Ct_{a,1,i} = w_{11}a_i, Ct_{a,2,i} = w_{21}a_i, Ct_{ar} = \sum_{i=0}^n a_i r_i$. Return $Ct_x = (Ct_{u_1x}, Ct_{u_2x}, \{Ct_{w,x,i}, Ct_{a,1,i}, Ct_{a,2,i}\}i \in [n], Ct_{a,r})$.

Firstly, we show that $Ct'_{u_1x} = QFE.Encrypt(mpk1, u_1\boldsymbol{x_b})$ and $Ct_{u_1x} = QFE.Encrypt(mpk1, u_1\boldsymbol{x_{1-b}})$ are indistinguishable. For any $f \in \mathcal{F}$, exists a set of matrices $\{A_i\}_{i \in [n]}$, s.t. $f(\boldsymbol{x}) = \sum_{i=0}^n x_i \boldsymbol{x}^T A_i \boldsymbol{x}$ and $\boldsymbol{x_0}^T A_i \boldsymbol{x_0} = \boldsymbol{x_1}^T A_i \boldsymbol{x_1}, i \in [n]$. So,

$$(\boldsymbol{x_{1-b}})^T A_i (\boldsymbol{x_{1-b}}) = \boldsymbol{x_b}^T A_i \boldsymbol{x_b}, i \in [n]$$

By the s-IND-CPA of the QFE scheme, these two should be indistinguishable. Similarly, $Ct'_{u_2x} = QFE.Encrypt(mpk1, u_2\boldsymbol{x_b})$ and $Ct_{u_2x} = QFE.Encrypt(mpk1, u_2\boldsymbol{x_{1-b}})$ are also indistinguishable.

Then, we show that $Ct'_{w,x,i} = (r_i, t_i^{-1}x_{bi})W^{-1}$ and $Ct_{w,x,i} = (r_i, (t_i^b)^{-1}x_{bi})W^{-1}$ are indistinguishable. t_i and t_i^b are hidden by the matrix W, i.e. without knowing about W, the adversary cannot determine whether t_i or t_i^b is used in the encryption. So the only thing we should prove is that the adversary cannot recover W. When considering the ciphertexts $Ct_{a,1,i} = w_{11}a_i$ and $Ct_{a,2,i} = w_{21}a_i$, we find that there exists $\alpha \in Z_p$, s.t. $w_{11} = \alpha w_{21}$. So $Ct_{a,1,i} = w_{11}a_i = \alpha w_{21}a_i = \alpha Ct_{a,2,i}$. Actually, there are $n + 1$ unknown values $(a_1, \ldots, a_n, w_{11})$ but only n effective equations, so w_{11} are not achievable. It is easy to see that w_{11} in other parts of ciphertext is also hidden by some random values.

Therefore, H3 and H2 are indistinguishable.

Hybrid H4: This is like H3 except that the challenge ciphertext is generated by invoking the algorithm $CFE.Encrypt$ as follows:

proc Initialize(λ, x_0, x_1)	proc LR()
$(mpk, msk) \leftarrow_R Setup(1^\lambda, 1^n)$	$Ct* \leftarrow_R Encrypt(mpk, x_{1-b})$
$\mathcal{F} \leftarrow \emptyset$	Return $Ct*$
Return mpk	
proc KeyGen(F)	proc Finalize(b')
$\mathcal{F} \leftarrow \mathcal{F} \cup F$	If $\exists F \in \mathcal{F}$ s.t. $f(F, x_0) \neq f(F, x_1)$
$sk_F \leftarrow KeyGen(msk, F)$	then return false
Return sk_F	Return (b'=b)

In $H3.Encrypt$, $Ct'_{w,x,i} = (r_i, (t_i^b)^{-1}x_{bi})W^{-1} = (r_i, \frac{x_{1-b,i}}{x_{bi}}t_i^{-1}x_{bi})W^{-1} = (r_i,$
$x_{1-b,i}t_i^{-1})W^{-1}$. In $CFE.Encrypt$, $Ct'_{w,x,i} = (r_i, x_{1-b,i}t_i^{-1})W^{-1}$. So H4 = H3.

Advantage of Any PPT Adversary in H4: In H4, the challenge ciphertext is a valid ciphertext for the message x_{1-b}. So it gives the same view by replacing x_b by x_{1-b}. Therefore, the advantage of any adversary in this game is 0. Notice that we only consider the situation that $x_{0i} \neq 0, x_{1i} \neq 0, i \in [n]$. And the proof can be extended when considering 0. We need to modify the construction of t^b and $H3.Encrypt$ as follows:

1. If $x_{0i} = x_{1i} = 0$, then $t_i^0 = t_i^1 = t_i$, and $Ct_{w,x.i} = (r_i, (t_i^b)^{-1}x_{bi})W^{-1}$.
2. If $x_{bi} = 0, x_{1-b,i} \neq 0$, then $t_i^b = x_{1-b,i}t_i^{-1} - x_{bi}$, and $Ct_{w,x,i} = (r_i, t_i^b + x_{bi})W^{-1}$.
3. If $x_{bi} \neq 0, x_{1-b,i} = 0$, then $t_i^b = -x_{bi}t_i^{-1}$, and $Ct_{w,x,i} = (r_i, t_i^b + t_i^{-1}x_{bi})W^{-1}$.

The remaining proof can be easily extended from our proof.

References

1. Abdalla, M., et al.: Searchable encryption revisited: consistency properties, relation to anonymous IBE, and extensions. In: Shoup, V. (ed.) CRYPTO 2005. LNCS, vol. 3621, pp. 205–222. Springer, Heidelberg (2005). https://doi.org/10.1007/11535218_13
2. Abdalla, M., Bourse, F., De Caro, A., Pointcheval, D.: Simple functional encryption schemes for inner products. In: Katz, J. (ed.) PKC 2015. LNCS, vol. 9020, pp. 733–751. Springer, Heidelberg (2015). https://doi.org/10.1007/978-3-662-46447-2_33
3. Abdalla, M., Bourse, F., De Caro, A., Pointcheval, D.: Better security for functional encryption for inner product evaluations. IACR Cryptology ePrint Archive, Report 2016/11 (2016)
4. Agrawal, S., Libert, B., Stehlé, D.: Fully secure functional encryption for inner products, from standard assumptions. In: Robshaw, M., Katz, J. (eds.) CRYPTO 2016. LNCS, vol. 9816, pp. 333–362. Springer, Heidelberg (2016). https://doi.org/10.1007/978-3-662-53015-3_12

5. Apon, D., Döttling, N., Garg, S., Mukherjee, P.: Cryptanalysis of indistinguishability obfuscations of circuits over GGH13. In: LIPIcs-Leibniz International Proceedings in Informatics, vol. 80. Schloss Dagstuhl-Leibniz-Zentrum fuer Informatik (2017)
6. Baltico, C.E.Z., Catalano, D., Fiore, D., Gay, R.: Practical functional encryption for quadratic functions with applications to predicate encryption. In: Katz, J., Shacham, H. (eds.) CRYPTO 2017. LNCS, vol. 10401, pp. 67–98. Springer, Cham (2017). https://doi.org/10.1007/978-3-319-63688-7_3
7. Bitansky, N., Lin, H., Paneth, O.: On removing graded encodings from functional encryption. In: Coron, J.-S., Nielsen, J.B. (eds.) EUROCRYPT 2017. LNCS, vol. 10211, pp. 3–29. Springer, Cham (2017). https://doi.org/10.1007/978-3-319-56614-6_1
8. Boneh, D., Boyen, X.: Efficient selective-ID secure identity-based encryption without random oracles. In: Cachin, C., Camenisch, J.L. (eds.) EUROCRYPT 2004. LNCS, vol. 3027, pp. 223–238. Springer, Heidelberg (2004). https://doi.org/10.1007/978-3-540-24676-3_14
9. Boneh, D., Franklin, M.: Identity-based encryption from the weil pairing. In: Kilian, J. (ed.) CRYPTO 2001. LNCS, vol. 2139, pp. 213–229. Springer, Heidelberg (2001). https://doi.org/10.1007/3-540-44647-8_13
10. Boneh, D., Raghunathan, A., Segev, G.: Function-private identity-based encryption: hiding the function in functional encryption. In: Canetti, R., Garay, J.A. (eds.) CRYPTO 2013. LNCS, vol. 8043, pp. 461–478. Springer, Heidelberg (2013). https://doi.org/10.1007/978-3-642-40084-1_26
11. Boneh, D., Sahai, A., Waters, B.: Functional encryption: definitions and challenges. In: Ishai, Y. (ed.) TCC 2011. LNCS, vol. 6597, pp. 253–273. Springer, Heidelberg (2011). https://doi.org/10.1007/978-3-642-19571-6_16
12. Boneh, D., Waters, B.: Conjunctive, subset, and range queries on encrypted data. In: Vadhan, S.P. (ed.) TCC 2007. LNCS, vol. 4392, pp. 535–554. Springer, Heidelberg (2007). https://doi.org/10.1007/978-3-540-70936-7_29
13. Boyle, E., Chung, K.-M., Pass, R.: On extractability obfuscation. In: Lindell, Y. (ed.) TCC 2014. LNCS, vol. 8349, pp. 52–73. Springer, Heidelberg (2014). https://doi.org/10.1007/978-3-642-54242-8_3
14. Chen, Y., Gentry, C., Halevi, S.: Cryptanalyses of candidate branching program obfuscators. In: Coron, J.-S., Nielsen, J.B. (eds.) EUROCRYPT 2017. LNCS, vol. 10212, pp. 278–307. Springer, Cham (2017). https://doi.org/10.1007/978-3-319-56617-7_10
15. Cheon, J.H., Han, K., Lee, C., Ryu, H., Stehlé, D.: Cryptanalysis of the multilinear map over the integers. In: Oswald, E., Fischlin, M. (eds.) EUROCRYPT 2015. LNCS, vol. 9056, pp. 3–12. Springer, Heidelberg (2015). https://doi.org/10.1007/978-3-662-46800-5_1
16. Cheon, J.H., Hong, S., Lee, C., Son, Y.: Polynomial functional encryption scheme with linear ciphertext size. IACR Cryptology ePrint Archive, Report 2018/585 (2018)
17. Coron, J.-S., Lee, M.S., Lepoint, T., Tibouchi, M.: Cryptanalysis of GGH15 multilinear maps. In: Robshaw, M., Katz, J. (eds.) CRYPTO 2016. LNCS, vol. 9815, pp. 607–628. Springer, Heidelberg (2016). https://doi.org/10.1007/978-3-662-53008-5_21
18. Datta, P., Dutta, R., Mukhopadhyay, S.: Functional encryption for inner product with full function privacy. In: Cheng, C.-M., Chung, K.-M., Persiano, G., Yang, B.-Y. (eds.) PKC 2016. LNCS, vol. 9614, pp. 164–195. Springer, Heidelberg (2016). https://doi.org/10.1007/978-3-662-49384-7_7

19. Garg, S., Gentry, C., Halevi, S., Raykova, M., Sahai, A., Waters, B.: Candidate indistinguishability obfuscation and functional encryption for all circuits. SIAM J. Comput. **45**(3), 882–929 (2016)

20. Garg, S., Gentry, C., Halevi, S., Zhandry, M.: Fully secure attribute based encryption from multilinear maps. Cryptology ePrint Archive, Report 2014/622 (2014)

21. Goldwasser, S., Kalai, Y.T., Popa, R.A., Vaikuntanathan, V., Zeldovich, N.: Reusable garbled circuits and succinct functional encryption. In: Symposium on Theory of Computing Conference, STOC 2013, Palo Alto, California, USA, 1–4 June 2013, pp. 555–564. ACM (2013)

22. Gorbunov, S., Vaikuntanathan, V., Wee, H.: Functional encryption with bounded collusions via multi-party computation. In: Safavi-Naini, R., Canetti, R. (eds.) CRYPTO 2012. LNCS, vol. 7417, pp. 162–179. Springer, Heidelberg (2012). https://doi.org/10.1007/978-3-642-32009-5_11

23. Katz, J., Sahai, A., Waters, B.: Predicate encryption supporting disjunctions, polynomial equations, and inner products. In: Smart, N. (ed.) EUROCRYPT 2008. LNCS, vol. 4965, pp. 146–162. Springer, Heidelberg (2008). https://doi.org/10.1007/978-3-540-78967-3_9

24. Kim, S., Lewi, K., Mandal, A., Montgomery, H.W., Roy, A., Wu, D.J.: Function-hiding inner product encryption is practical. Cryptology ePrint Archive, Report 2016/440

25. Lin, H., Vaikuntanathan, V.: Indistinguishability obfuscation from DDH-like assumptions on constant-degree graded encodings. In: Proceedings of the IEEE 57th Annual Symposium on Foundations of Computer Science, FOCS 2016, Brunswick, New Jersey, USA, 9–11 October 2016, pp. 11–20. IEEE (2016)

26. O'Neill, A.: Definitional issues in functional encryption. Cryptology ePrint Archive, Report 2010/556 (2010)

27. Sahai, A., Waters, B.: Fuzzy identity-based encryption. In: Cramer, R. (ed.) EUROCRYPT 2005. LNCS, vol. 3494, pp. 457–473. Springer, Heidelberg (2005). https://doi.org/10.1007/11426639_27

28. Shamir, A.: Identity-based cryptosystems and signature schemes. In: Blakley, G.R., Chaum, D. (eds.) CRYPTO 1984. LNCS, vol. 196, pp. 47–53. Springer, Heidelberg (1985). https://doi.org/10.1007/3-540-39568-7_5

29. Shen, E., Shi, E., Waters, B.: Predicate privacy in encryption systems. In: Reingold, O. (ed.) TCC 2009. LNCS, vol. 5444, pp. 457–473. Springer, Heidelberg (2009). https://doi.org/10.1007/978-3-642-00457-5_27

30. Waters, B.: Ciphertext-policy attribute-based encryption: an expressive, efficient, and provably secure realization. In: Catalano, D., Fazio, N., Gennaro, R., Nicolosi, A. (eds.) PKC 2011. LNCS, vol. 6571, pp. 53–70. Springer, Heidelberg (2011). https://doi.org/10.1007/978-3-642-19379-8_4

31. Waters, B.: A punctured programming approach to adaptively secure functional encryption. In: Gennaro, R., Robshaw, M. (eds.) CRYPTO 2015. LNCS, vol. 9216, pp. 678–697. Springer, Heidelberg (2015). https://doi.org/10.1007/978-3-662-48000-7_33

Secret Sharing

Efficient Proactive Secret Sharing for Large Data via Concise Vector Commitments

Matthias Geihs$^{(\boxtimes)}$, Lucas Schabhüser, and Johannes Buchmann

Technische Universität Darmstadt, Darmstadt, Germany
mgeihs@cdc.tu-darmstadt.de

Abstract. Proactive secret sharing has been proposed by Herzberg, Jarecki, Krawczyk, and Yung (CRYPTO'95) and is a powerful tool for storing highly confidential data. However, their scheme is not designed for storing large data and communication and computation costs scale linearly with the data size. In this paper we propose a variant of their scheme that uses concise vector commitments. We show that our new scheme, when instantiated with a variant of the Pedersen commitment scheme (CRYPTO'92), reduces computation costs by up to 50% and broadcast communication costs by a factor of L, where L is the length of the commitment message vectors.

1 Introduction

Threshold secret sharing has been proposed independently by Blakley [5] and Shamir [18] and allows to store a piece of secret information x at a set of N shareholders such that any coalition of up to T shareholders obtains no information about the secret. Proactive secret sharing was later proposed by Herzberg, Jarecki, Krawczyk, and Yung [12] and additionally allows the shareholders to update their data shares such that after the update the new shares are independent of the old shares. This property ensures protection against a mobile adversary that gradually obtains data shares over time. Moreover, proactive secret sharing is robust against up to $T < \frac{N}{2}$ malicious shareholders which means that the data owner is guaranteed to retrieve the initially stored data even if up to T shareholders behave arbitrarily bad.

While proactive secret sharing is a powerful tool for storage of highly confidential data, the performance of existing schemes appears insufficient for large data items. For example, storing a data item of size 128 kB at $N = 3$ shareholders and using a threshold of $T = 1$, the scheme described in [12] requires the data owner to broadcast 2 MB of data and to compute more than $16 * 10^3$ modular exponentiations. Moreover, updating the data shares requires 15 MB of data broadcast and each shareholder must compute more than $40 * 10^3$ modular exponentiations. However, securely storing highly confidential data such as legal documents or medical records over long periods of time requires proactive secret

© Springer Nature Switzerland AG 2019
C. Carlet et al. (Eds.): C2SI 2019, LNCS 11445, pp. 171–194, 2019.
https://doi.org/10.1007/978-3-030-16458-4_11

sharing schemes that are capable of efficiently storing data of size several mega bytes or even giga bytes.

In this paper we present a proactive secret sharing scheme that requires significantly less computational resources and immensely less communication than the scheme described in [12] when used for data sizes D that do not fit into the native message space of that scheme, e.g., $D > 32$ B. Our scheme can be instantiated such that in the setting described above, data storage requires the data owner to broadcast only about 16 kB of data and compute only about $8*10^3$ modular exponentiations. Similarly, updating the shares requires only 120 kB of data broadcast and each shareholder must compute only about $20 * 10^3$ modular exponentiations.

We achieve these performance improvements by combining the techniques of [12] with concise vector commitments [10]. While [12] uses cryptographic commitments where a commitment is of the same size as the committed message, concise vector commitments allow for committing to a vector of messages with a commitment that is much smaller than the committed message vector. By using such vector commitment we are able to reduce the broadcast communication costs by a factor of L, where L is the length of the message vectors. Furthermore, we also save up 50% of the computation costs because computing L single commitments requires $2 * L$ modular exponentiations while computing a vector commitment for message vectors of length L requires only $L + 1$ modular exponentiations. We remark that we use the same network model assumptions as [12], i.e., we assume a synchronous authenticated network with broadcast.

1.1 Organization

Our paper is organized as follows. In Sect. 2 we introduce notation and define the notions of a vector commitment scheme and a proactive secret sharing scheme as we will use them in this paper. In contrast to [12] we give a more precise definition of a proactive secret sharing scheme and respective security properties, which we believe is a contribution in its own. Then, in Sect. 3 we present our new vector proactive secret sharing scheme and analyze its security. Finally, in Sect. 4 we show how to instantiate the proposed scheme with a concise vector commitment scheme and then evaluate the theoretical and practical performance of the proposed instantiation.

1.2 Related Work

Since the work of [12] several proactive secret sharing schemes with various properties have been proposed. [11,19] proposed proactive secret sharing schemes where the number N of shareholders and the threshold value T can be changed during a share update. [7,20] proposed proactive secret sharing schemes that work in asynchronous networks where no global clock is available. [17] proposed a scheme which has both properties. However, all of these schemes have high communication and computation costs when storing large data items.

More recently, Baron, Defrawy, Lampkins, and Ostrovsky in [1,2] proposed proactive secret sharing schemes with optimal amortized communication complexity. However, while their schemes enjoy optimal communication costs asymptotically, they do not work well with a small number of shareholders (e.g., $N = 3$) as they require $T < \frac{N}{8}$ and enabling $T < \frac{N}{2}$ requires expensive party virtualization techniques. This approach uses *packed secret sharing* where a set of messages is batched together. The authors propose a batch size of $N - 3T$ which is obviously infeasible for small parameters like $N = 3, T = 1$. They also make use of *double sharings*. For l messages this would require every shareholder to send at least $2l$ shares to every other shareholder. Compared to this our approach based on generalized Pedersen commitments, requires $l + 1$ shares and t commitments to be broadcasted per shareholder. For suitably large l and small t this leads to significantly less bandwidth consumption.

2 Preliminaries

2.1 Notation

We use the convention that $\mathbb{N} = \{1, 2, \ldots\}$ and define $\mathbb{N}_0 = \mathbb{N} \cup \{0\}$. For $(a, b) \in \mathbb{Z}^2$, $a \leq b$, we define $[a, b] = \{x \in \mathbb{Z} : a \leq x \leq b\}$. For $n \in \mathbb{N}$, we define $[n] = [1, n]$ and $\mathbb{Z}_n = [0, n - 1]$. By MODINV we denote an algorithm that on input $(a, m) \in \mathbb{N}_0^2$ outputs the smallest $b \in \mathbb{N}$ such that $(a * b) \bmod m = 1$, or $\perp$ if such b does not exist. For a finite cyclic group $\mathbb{G}$ associated with operator $\circ$, we denote by GEN($\mathbb{G}$) the set of generators of $\mathbb{G}$. Furthermore, we denote by EXP an exponentiation algorithm that on input $(a, b) \in \mathbb{G} \times \mathbb{N}$ outputs a^b such that $a^1 = a$ and $a^{i+1} = a^i \circ a$. For a finite set S, we denote by $U(S)$ the uniform distribution over S. For $\tau \in \mathbb{N}$, we denote by ProbAlgo(τ) the set of probabilistic algorithms that for any input halt after at most τ steps. By $\Im(\mathcal{A})$ we denote the image of algorithm $\mathcal{A}$.

2.2 Network Model

A probabilistic protocol P defines an input-output behavior for a set of communicating parties $\{\mathcal{P}_1, \ldots, \mathcal{P}_n\}$. We write $P\langle \mathcal{P}_1(x_1) \to y_1, \ldots, \mathcal{P}_n(x_n) \to y_n \rangle$ to denote an execution of protocol P, where party $\mathcal{P}_i$ gets input x_i and outputs y_i. Here we assume that each party has a direct communication channel with each other party. In addition, we assume that there exists a broadcast channel with the property that if a party $\mathcal{P}_i$ receives a broadcast message m from party $\mathcal{P}_j$, then it is guaranteed that all other parties $\mathcal{P}_k$ receive the same broadcast message m from $\mathcal{P}_j$. When we write that during a protocol execution $P\langle \{\mathcal{P}_i(x_1) \to y_1\}_{i \in [N]} \rangle$ an adversary $\mathcal{A}$ controls $T \in [0, N]$ parties, we mean that there exists $I \subset [T]$ such that for $i \in I$, the input-output behavior and communication behavior of party $\mathcal{P}_i$ is controlled by $\mathcal{A}$. A majority of the protocol participants can, however, decide to reboot corrupted parties, in which case the adversary loses control over them, their state is cleared, and they return to their specified behavior. We remark that our protocols require the usage of private authenticated channels, which means that messages are always delivered to the correct communication partner, that their content and order cannot be modified, and that no information about the message content can be obtained by tapping the channel.

2.3 Discrete Logarithm Problem

We state the fixed generator discrete logarithm problem [16].

Definition 1 (Discrete logarithm problem). *Let* $\mathbb{G}$ *be a finite cyclic group,* $g \in \mathsf{GEN}(\mathbb{G})$, *and* $\epsilon : \mathbb{N} \to \mathbb{R}$ *be a function. We say* $\mathsf{DLOG}(\mathbb{G}, g)$ *is* ϵ-*hard if for all* τ, *for all* $\mathcal{A} \in \mathsf{ProbAlgo}(\tau)$,

$$\Pr\left[\begin{matrix} \mathsf{EXP}(g, x) = y : \\ U(\mathbb{G}) \to y, \mathcal{A}(y) \to x \end{matrix}\right] \leq \epsilon(\tau).$$

2.4 Vector Commitments

We define vector commitment schemes as we will use them in this paper. We remark that our vector commitment schemes do not support selective opening as opposed to those proposed in [8].

Definition 2 (Vector commitment scheme). *A vector commitment scheme is a tuple* $\mathsf{VC} = (L, \mathcal{P}, \mathcal{M}, \mathcal{C}, \mathcal{D}, \mathsf{Setup}, \mathsf{Commit}, \mathsf{Open})$, *where* $L \in \mathbb{N}$, $\mathcal{P}$, $\mathcal{M}$, $\mathcal{C}$, *and* $\mathcal{D}$ *are sets,* Setup *and* Commit *are probabilistic algorithms, and* Open *is a deterministic algorithm, with the following properties.*

$\mathsf{Setup} : \emptyset \to \mathcal{P}$. *This algorithm gets no input and outputs parameters* $\rho \in \mathcal{P}$.
$\mathsf{Commit} : \mathcal{P} \times \mathcal{M}^L \to \mathcal{C} \times \mathcal{D}$. *This algorithm gets as input parameters* $\rho \in \mathcal{P}$ *and message* $m \in \mathcal{M}^L$, *and outputs a commitment* $c \in \mathcal{C}$ *and a decommitment* $d \in \mathcal{D}$.
Open : $\mathcal{P} \times \mathcal{M}^L \times \mathcal{C} \times \mathcal{D} \to \{0, 1\}$. *This algorithm gets as input parameters* $\rho \in \mathcal{P}$, *message* $m \in \mathcal{M}^L$, *commitment* $c \in \mathcal{C}$, *and decommitment* $d \in \mathcal{D}$, *and outputs* $b \in \{0, 1\}$.

Correct Functionality. *We say* VC *is correct if for all* $m \in \mathcal{M}^L$,

$$\Pr\left[\begin{matrix} \mathsf{Open}(\rho, m, c, d) = 1 : \\ \mathsf{Setup}() \to \rho, \mathsf{Commit}(\rho, m) \to (c, d) \end{matrix}\right] = 1 .$$

Binding Security. *Let* $\epsilon : \mathbb{N} \to \mathbb{R}$ *be a function. We say* VC *is* ϵ-*binding if for all* $\tau \in \mathbb{N}$, $\mathcal{A} \in \mathsf{ProbAlgo}(\tau)$,

$$\Pr\left[\begin{matrix} b = 1 \wedge b' = 1 \wedge m \neq m' : \\ \mathsf{Setup}() \to \rho, \mathcal{A}(\rho) \to (c, m, d, m', d'), \\ \mathsf{Open}(\rho, m, c, d) \to b, \mathsf{Open}(\rho, m, c, d') \to b' \end{matrix}\right] \leq \epsilon(\tau) .$$

Hiding Security. *We say* VC *is perfectly hiding if for all* $\rho \in \mathcal{P}$, $(m_1, m_2) \in \mathcal{M}^{L \times 2}$, $c \in \mathcal{C}$,

$$\Pr\left[\begin{array}{c} c = c' : \\ \mathsf{Commit}(\rho, m_1) \to (c', d') \end{array}\right] = \Pr\left[\begin{array}{c} c = c' : \\ \mathsf{Commit}(\rho, m_2) \to (c', d') \end{array}\right] .$$

Homomorphic Operation. *For* $\rho \in \mathcal{P}$, *define* $\mathsf{COMS}(\rho) = \{(m, c, d) \in \mathcal{M}^L \times \mathcal{C} \times \mathcal{D} : \mathsf{Open}(\rho, m, c, d) = 1\}$. *We say* VC *is homomorphic if there exist binary operations* $+$, $*$, *and* $\circ$ *such that for all* $\rho \in \mathcal{P}$, $(m_1, c_1, d_1) \in \mathsf{COMS}(\rho)$, *and* $(m_2, c_2, d_2) \in \mathsf{COMS}(\rho)$,

$$\mathsf{Open}(\rho, m_1 + m_2, c_1 * c_2, d_1 \circ d_2) = 1 .$$

2.5   Proactive Secret Sharing

We give a definition of proactive secret sharing which will be useful for analyzing the security of the scheme proposed later in this work. We remark that while other authors only sketch syntax and security definitions for proactive secret sharing (e.g., [12]), our definition captures many subtleties of these schemes (e.g., it states exactly when the adversary gains control over parties and when it loses control which is a delicate subject [14]). Such a more precise definition is a valuable contribution in its own.

Informal Description. We first give an overview of the formal definition and then present the precise definition later in Definition 3. A proactive secret sharing scheme consists of a set of protocols that are run between a dealer $\mathfrak{D}$ and a set of shareholders $\mathfrak{S}_1, \ldots, \mathfrak{S}_N$. The goal of the dealer is to store some secret information at the shareholders in a way that none of the shareholders obtains information about the secret. The information can only be reconstructed if a sufficient number of shares are combined together. Protocol Setup is used for initializing the parties. Protocol Share is used for distributing the secret information to the shareholders in terms of secret shares. Protocol Reshare refreshes the secret shares such that the new shares have no correlation with the old shares. Protocol Reconstruct retrieves the shares, asserts their validity, and reconstructs the secret information.

We require several properties of a proactive secret sharing scheme. Correct functionality guarantees that if the scheme is run by honest parties, the original information will be restored. Secrecy guarantees that a coalition of curious shareholders up to a threshold number cannot learn any information about the secret. Robustness guarantees that the scheme tolerates up to a threshold number of shareholders that act maliciously and do not follow the protocol.

The definitions of Secrecy and Robustness are given in terms of games played by an adversary that can corrupt a threshold number of parties and tries to either learn information or destroy the secret information (Figs. 1 and 2). For the secrecy game (Fig. 1), the adversary can choose to learn the secrets of a given set of shareholders I after each round (e.g., sharing or resharing), where the freshly corrupted set of shareholders I' and the previously corrupted set I combined must be of size at most the threshold T. The goal of the adversary is to learn something about the secret information m in terms of a function value $F(m)$ for any function F. The secrecy definition requires that $F(m)$ can be computed equally successful by a simulator B which does not see any of the additional secret information that the adversary may obtain by corrupting certain shareholders. This definition of secrecy follows the ideas of Goldwasser and Micali for defining semantic security [9]. Similarly, for the robustness game (Fig. 2), the adversary can choose to act on behalf of a given set of shareholders during the protocol runs of Share, Reshare, or Reconstruct, but the number of new and old corrupted shareholders must never exceed T. The robustness definition requires that the reconstructed value after the interference of the adversary still corresponds to the value that has been initially stored.

Formal Definition. In the definition we use the following notation. We usually denote the dealer by $\mathfrak{D}$ and shareholder i by $\mathfrak{S}_i$. We write $\mathsf{Share}\langle\rho, m\rangle \to S$ as an abbreviation for $\mathsf{Share}\langle\mathfrak{D}(\rho, m), \{\mathfrak{S}_i(\rho) \to s_i\}_{i\in[N]}\rangle$, $S \leftarrow (s_1, \ldots, s_N)$. For $S = (s_1, \ldots, s_N)$, we write $\mathsf{Reshare}\langle\rho, S\rangle \to S'$ for $\mathsf{Reshare}\langle\{\mathfrak{S}_i(\rho, s_i) \to s'_i\}_{i\in[N]}\rangle$, $S' \leftarrow (s'_1, \ldots, s'_N)$. The game notation that we use follows the notation described in [3,4]. At the start of any game G the special algorithm **Initialize** is executed and its output is handed to the adversary. Afterwards the adversary can call the algorithms specified in the game and obtains the corresponding outputs. The game ends when the adversary calls the special algorithm **Finalize**. The output of the game is defined as the output of that algorithm.

Definition 3 (Proactive secret sharing scheme). *A proactive secret sharing scheme is a tuple* $\mathsf{PSS} = (N, T, \mathcal{P}, \mathcal{M}, \mathcal{S}, \mathsf{Setup}, \mathsf{Share}, \mathsf{Reshare}, \mathsf{Reconstruct})$, *where* $(N, T) \in \mathbb{N} \times \mathbb{N}_0$, $N > 1$, $T < \frac{N}{2}$, $\mathcal{P}$, $\mathcal{M}$, *and* $\mathcal{S}$ *are sets,* Setup *is a probabilistic algorithm, and* Share, $\mathsf{Reshare}$, *and* $\mathsf{Reconstruct}$ *are probabilistic protocols with the following properties:*

$\mathsf{Setup}: \emptyset \to \mathcal{P}$. *This algorithm gets no input and outputs parameters* $\rho \in \mathcal{P}$.
$\mathsf{Share}\langle\mathfrak{D}: \mathcal{P} \times \mathcal{M} \to \emptyset, \{\mathfrak{S}_i: \mathcal{P} \to \mathcal{S}\}_{i\in[N]}\rangle$. *The dealer* $\mathfrak{D}$ *gets as input parameters* $\rho \in \mathcal{P}$, *and message* $m \in \mathcal{M}$. *For* $i \in [N]$, *shareholder* $\mathfrak{S}_i$ *get as input parameters* $p \in \mathcal{P}$, *and outputs a secret share* $s_i \in \mathcal{S}$.
$\mathsf{Reshare}\langle\{\mathfrak{S}_i: \mathcal{P} \times \mathcal{S} \to \mathcal{S}\}_{i\in[N]}\rangle$. *For* $i \in [N]$, *shareholder* $\mathfrak{S}_i$ *gets as input parameters* $\rho \in \mathcal{P}$ *and secret share* $s_i \in \mathcal{S}$, *and outputs a secret share* $s'_i \in \mathcal{S}$.
$\mathsf{Reconstruct}\langle\mathfrak{R}: \mathcal{P} \to \mathcal{M} \cup \{\bot\}, \{\mathfrak{S}_i: \mathcal{P} \times \mathcal{S} \to \emptyset\}_{i\in[N]}\rangle$. *The receiver* $\mathfrak{R}$ *gets as input parameters* $\rho \in \mathcal{P}$. *For* $i \in [N]$, *shareholder* $\mathfrak{S}_i$ *gets as input parameters* $\rho \in \mathcal{P}$ *and secret share* $s_i \in \mathcal{S}$. *The receiver* $\mathfrak{R}$ *outputs a message* $m \in \mathcal{M}$.

Correct Functionality. For $\rho \in \mathcal{P}$ and $m \in \mathcal{M}$, we define

$$
\text{SHARES}(\rho, m) = \left\{ \exists l \in \mathbb{N}_0 : \Pr \left[\begin{array}{l} (s_1, \ldots, s_N) : \\ (s_{l,1}, \ldots, s_{l,n}) = (s_1, \ldots, s_N) : \\ \mathsf{Share}\langle \mathfrak{D}(\rho, m), \{\mathfrak{S}_i(\rho) \to s_{0,i}\}_{i \in [N]}\rangle, \\ \mathsf{Reshare}\langle\{\mathfrak{S}_i(\rho, s_{0,i}) \to s_{1,i}\}_{i \in [N]}\rangle, \\ \ldots, \\ \mathsf{Reshare}\langle\{\mathfrak{S}_i(\rho, s_{l-1,i}) \to s_{l,i}\}_{i \in [N]}\rangle \end{array} \right] > 0 \right\}
$$

as the set of all possible share configurations at which the shareholders can arrive after sharing and resharing m under parameter ρ. We say PSS is correct if for all $\rho \in \mathcal{P}$, $m \in \mathcal{M}$, $(s_1, \ldots, s_N) \in \text{SHARES}(\rho, m)$,

$$
\Pr \left[\begin{array}{c} m = m' : \\ \mathsf{Reconstruct}\langle m' \leftarrow \mathfrak{D}(\rho), \{\mathfrak{S}_i(\rho, s_i)\}_{i \in [N]}\rangle \end{array} \right] = 1 \ .
$$

Secrecy. Let $\epsilon : \mathbb{N}^2 \to \mathbb{R}$ be a function. We say PSS is ϵ-secret if for all probability distributions $\mathcal{D}$ over $\mathcal{M}$, functions $F : \mathcal{M} \to \{0,1\}^*$, $\tau_\mathcal{A}, \tau_\mathcal{B} \in \mathbb{N}$, and $\mathcal{A} \in \mathsf{ProbAlgo}(\tau_\mathcal{A})$, there exists $\mathcal{B} \in \mathsf{ProbAlgo}(\tau_\mathcal{B})$ such that

$$
\Pr \left[\begin{array}{c} F(m) = y : \\ \mathcal{D} \to m, G_1(\mathcal{A}; m) \to y \end{array} \right] \leq \Pr \left[\begin{array}{c} F(m) = y : \\ \mathcal{D} \to m, \mathcal{B} \to y \end{array} \right] + \epsilon(\tau_\mathcal{A}, \tau_\mathcal{B}) \ ,
$$

where $G_1(\mathcal{A}; m)$ is defined in Fig. 1.

Game $G_1(\mathcal{A}; m)$

Initialize

1 : $I \leftarrow \{\}, S \leftarrow \perp$
2 : $\mathsf{Setup}() \to \rho$
3 : **return** ρ

Share (I')

1 : $I \leftarrow (I'$ if $|I'| \leq T$ else $\emptyset)$
   Run $\mathsf{Share}\langle \rho, m\rangle \to S$, where
2 : shareholders I are controlled
   by $\mathcal{A}$ until reboot

Reshare (I')

1 : $I \leftarrow (I'$ if $|I \cup I'| \leq T$ else $\emptyset)$
   Run $\mathsf{Reshare}\langle \rho, S\rangle \to S$, where
2 : shareholders I are controlled
   by $\mathcal{A}$ until reboot

Finalize (y)

1 : **return** y

Fig. 1. The game used in the secrecy definition for proactive secret sharing.

Robustness. Let $\epsilon : \mathbb{N} \to \mathbb{R}$ be a function. We say PSS is ϵ-robust if for all $m \in \mathcal{M}$, $\tau \in \mathbb{N}$, $\mathcal{A} \in \mathsf{ProbAlgo}(\tau)$,

$$
\Pr \left[\begin{array}{c} m \neq m' : \\ G_2(\mathcal{A}, m) \to m' \end{array} \right] \leq \epsilon(\tau) \ ,
$$

where $G_2(\mathcal{A}, m)$ is defined in Fig. 2.

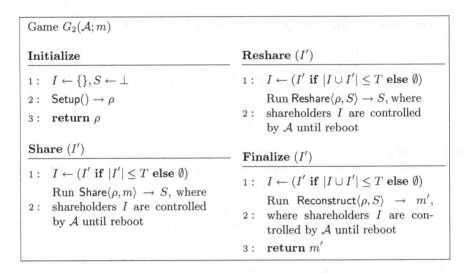

Fig. 2. The game used in the robustness definition for proactive secret sharing.

3   Proactive Secret Sharing with Vector Commitments

We now present our construction of a proactive secret sharing scheme that uses vector commitments for improving efficiency. Our construction is based on the construction of [12] and enhances it so that in each sharing a vector of messages can be stored instead of only a single message. We first present the description of our vector proactive secret sharing scheme in Subsect. 3.1 and then prove its security in Subsect. 3.2.

3.1   Scheme Description

Overview of the Scheme. Our proactive secret sharing scheme follows the construction of [12], but uses a homomorphic vector commitment scheme VC instead of a single message homomorphic commitment scheme. Algorithm Setup of our scheme simply generates commitment parameters ρ by running the setup algorithm of the vector commitment scheme.

   Protocol Share works as follows. On input a message vector $(m_1, \ldots, m_L)$, the dealer first generates secret shares of each m_i using Shamir's Secret Sharing Scheme [18] by sampling $D = N - T - 1$ secret polynomial coefficients, where N is the number of shareholders and T is the corruption threshold. Then, it creates a commitment c_0 to the message vector and a commitment c_i to each of the secret coefficient vectors. The corresponding decommitments $(d_0, \ldots, d_D)$ are used to compute a share of a decommitment r_i corresponding to the message vector. Finally, the dealer broadcasts all the commitments $(c_0, \ldots, c_D)$ and sends share vector $(s_{i,1}, \ldots, s_{i,L})$ and the decommitment share r_i to shareholder $\mathfrak{S}_i$.

   Protocol Reshare works as follows. At first, the shareholders engage in sub protocol ShareRecovery in order to detect parties that hold invalid input shares. If such parties are detected, then these will be rebooted and their shares be recovered so that after the execution of sub protocol ShareRecovery the shareholders hold a consistent share configuration. Now, each of the shareholders creates L verifiable sharings of the identity of the finite field message space using sub protocol ShareIdentity. Next, each shareholder asserts that the received shares of the identity are consistent by verifying the received commitments. If this is the case, then it combines the commitments, decommitments, and shares of the identity sharings with the existing secret shares in a way that the new shares still reconstruct to the original message vector. Here, only commitment c_0 is kept unchanged as an invariant referring to the original message vector. In the other case, i.e., if an inconsistency after ShareIdentity is detected, the faulty parties are determined and rebooted, their shares are recovered, and protocol Reshare is started from the beginning.

Protocol Reconstruct works as follows. The dealer $\mathfrak{D}$ retrieves all shares, commitments, and decommitment shares from the shareholders. It then determines a subset G of parties whose shares are qualified for reconstruction, i.e., with $|G| = D + 1$ and such that the shares are consistent with the commitments and decommitments. If such a subset is found, Lagrange Interpolation is used to reconstruct the message vector. If such a subset is not found, then the protocol aborts and outputs $\bot$. The latter case, however, is guaranteed not to occur if not more than T parties are corrupted.

Detailed Description. We now present our vector proactive secret sharing scheme in detail.

Scheme 1 (VPSS). *Let $(N, T) \in \mathbb{N} \times \mathbb{N}_0$ such that $N < p$ and $T < \frac{N}{2}$. Let $\mathsf{VC} = (L, \mathcal{P}, \mathcal{M}, \mathcal{C}, \mathcal{D}, \mathsf{Setup}, \mathsf{Commit}, \mathsf{Open})$ be a homomorphic vector commitment scheme such that $\mathcal{M}$ is a finite field of prime order p. Let $D = N - T - 1$ and $\mathcal{S} = \mathcal{M}^L \times \mathcal{C}^{1+D} \times \mathcal{D}$. For a given sharing $((s_{i,1}, \ldots, s_{i,L}, c_{i,0}, \ldots, c_{i,D}, r_i))_{i \in [N]} \in \mathcal{S}^n$, we define the subset of parties qualified for reconstruction by*

$$\mathtt{QUALI}(((s_{i,1}, \ldots, s_{i,L}, c_{i,0}, \ldots, c_{i,D}, r_i))_{i \in [N]})$$
$$= \left\{ \begin{array}{c} G \subseteq [N] : \\ |G| = D + 1 \wedge (\forall (i, j, k) \in G \times G \times [0, D] : c_{i,k} = c_{j,k}) \\ \wedge \forall i \in G : \mathsf{Open}(\rho, (s_{i,1}, \ldots, s_{i,L}), \bigodot_{j \in [0,D]} \mathsf{EXP}(c_{i,j}, i^j), r_i) = 1 \end{array} \right\}.$$

We define the proactive secret sharing scheme $\mathsf{VPSS}_{N,T,\mathsf{VC}} = (N, T, \mathcal{P}, \mathcal{M}^L, \mathcal{S}, \mathsf{Setup}, \mathsf{Share}, \mathsf{Reshare}, \mathsf{Reconstruct})$, where Share, Reshare, and Reconstruct are defined with sub protocols ShareRecovery and ShareIdentity as follows:

Main protocols:

$\mathsf{Share}\langle \mathfrak{D}(\rho \in \mathcal{P}, m \in \mathcal{M}^L), \{\mathfrak{S}_i(\rho \in \mathcal{P}) \to s_i \in \mathcal{S}\}_{i \in [N]}\rangle$:

The dealer $\mathfrak{D}$ does the following:

1. *Let $m = (m_1, \ldots, m_L) \in \mathcal{M}^L$.*
2. *For $(i, j) \in [L] \times [D]$, sample $U(\mathcal{M}) \to a_{i,j}$.*

3. For $(i,j) \in [N] \times [L]$, compute $s_{i,j} \leftarrow m_j \bigcirc_{k \in [D]} \mathsf{EXP}(a_{j,k}, i^k)$.
4. Compute $\mathsf{Commit}(\rho, (m_1, \ldots, m_L)) \rightarrow (c_0, d_0)$, and for $i \in [D]$, compute $\mathsf{Commit}(\rho, (a_{1,i}, \ldots, a_{L,i})) \rightarrow (c_i, d_i)$.
5. For $i \in [N]$, compute $r_i \leftarrow d_0 \bigcirc_{j \in [D]} \mathsf{EXP}(d_j, i^j)$.
6. Broadcast $(c_0, \ldots, c_D)$ and for $i \in [N]$, send r_i and $(s_{i,1}, \ldots, s_{i,L})$ to shareholder $\mathfrak{S}_i$.

For $i \in [N]$, shareholder $\mathfrak{S}_i$ sets $s_i \leftarrow (s_{i,1}, \ldots, s_{i,L}, c_0, \ldots, c_D, r_i)$.

$\mathsf{Reshare}\langle\{\mathfrak{S}_i(\rho \in \mathcal{P}, s_i \in \mathcal{S}) \rightarrow s'_i \in \mathcal{S} \cup \{\bot\}\}_{i \in [N]}\rangle$:

Run protocol $\mathsf{ShareRecovery}\langle\{\mathfrak{S}_i(\rho \in \mathcal{P}, s_i \in \mathcal{S}) \rightarrow s_i \in \mathcal{S}\}_{i \in [N]}\rangle$.

For $i \in [N]$, shareholder $\mathfrak{S}_i$ does the following.

1. If $s_i = \bot$, set $s'_i \leftarrow \bot$ and return.
2. Let $s_i = (s_{i,1}, \ldots, s_{i,L}, c_{i,0}, \ldots, c_{i,D}, r_i)$.
3. Run protocol $\mathsf{ShareIdentity}\langle\mathfrak{S}_i(\rho), \{\mathfrak{S}_j(\rho) \rightarrow \hat{s}_{i,j}\}_{j \in [N]}\rangle$ and let $\hat{s}_{i,j} = (\hat{s}_{i,j,1}, \ldots, \hat{s}_{i,j,L}, \hat{c}_{i,j,1}, \ldots, \hat{c}_{i,j,D}, \hat{r}_{i,j})$.
4. Wait until for all $j \in [N]$, $\hat{s}_{j,i}$ has been received or a timeout occurs. In case of a timeout of party j, set $\hat{s}_{j,i} \leftarrow \bot$.
5. For $j \in [N]$, compute $\hat{c}_{i,j} \leftarrow \bigcirc_{k \in [D]} \mathsf{EXP}(\hat{c}_{j,i,k}, i^k)$ and $b_{i,j} \leftarrow \mathsf{Open}(\rho, (\hat{s}_{i,j,1}, \ldots, \hat{s}_{i,j,L}), \hat{c}_{i,j}, \hat{r}_{i,j})$, and broadcast $B_i = (b_{i,1}, \ldots, b_{i,N})$.
6. Wait until for all $j \in [N]$, B_j has been received or a timeout occurs. In case of a timeout of party j, set $B_j \leftarrow 0^N$.
7. If for all $j \in [N]$, $B_j = 1^N$, then all shareholders behaved consistently. In this case, recompute the shares as follows:
   (a) For $j \in [L]$, compute $s'_{i,j} \leftarrow s_{i,j} \bigcirc_{k \in [N]} \hat{s}_{k,i,j}$.
   (b) For $j \in [D]$, compute $c'_{i,j} \leftarrow c_{i,j} \bigcirc_{k \in [N]} \hat{c}_{k,i,j}$.
   (c) Compute $r'_i \leftarrow r_i \bigcirc_{j \in [N]} \hat{r}_{j,i}$.
   (d) Set $s'_i \leftarrow (s'_{i,1}, \ldots, s'_{i,L}, c_{i,0}, c'_{i,1}, \ldots, c'_{i,D}, r'_i)$.
   If there exists $j \in [N]$ such that $0 \in B_j$, then the shareholders behaved inconsistently. In this case, determine the set of faulty shareholders, reboot them, recover their message and decommitment shares as described in [12], and restart the resharing protocol.

$\mathsf{Reconstruct}\langle\mathfrak{D}(\rho \in \mathcal{P}) \rightarrow m \in \mathcal{M}^L \cup \{\bot\}, \{\mathfrak{S}_i(\rho \in \mathcal{P}, s_i \in \mathcal{S})\}_{i \in [N]}\rangle$:

For $i \in [N]$, shareholder $\mathfrak{S}_i$ sends s_i to $\mathfrak{D}$.

The receiver $\mathfrak{D}$ waits until it received s_i for $i \in [N]$ or a timeout occurs. In case of a timeout of party i, set $s_i \leftarrow \bot$. Then, $\mathfrak{D}$ does the following:

1. For $i \in [N]$, let $s_i = (s_{i,1}, \ldots, s_{i,L}, c_{i,0}, \ldots, c_{i,D}, r_i)$.
2. If $\mathtt{QUALI}((s_1, \ldots, s_N)) = \emptyset$, set $m \leftarrow \bot$ and return. Otherwise find $G \in \mathtt{QUALI}((s_1, \ldots, s_N))$.
3. For $i \in G$, compute $l_i \leftarrow \prod_{j \in G \setminus \{i\}} j * \mathsf{MODINV}(j - i, p)$.
4. For $i \in [L]$, compute $m_i \leftarrow \bigcirc_{j \in G} \mathsf{EXP}(s_{j,i}, l_j)$.
5. Set $m \leftarrow (m_1, \ldots, m_L)$.

Sub protocols:

$\mathsf{ShareRecovery}\langle\{\mathfrak{S}_i(\rho \in \mathcal{P}, s_i \in \mathcal{S}) \rightarrow s'_i \in \mathcal{S} \cup \{\bot\}\}_{i \in [N]}\rangle$:

For $i \in [N]$, shareholder $\mathfrak{S}_i$ does the following:

1. Let $s_i = (s_{i,1}, \ldots, s_{i,L}, c_{i,0}, \ldots, c_{i,D}, r_i)$.
2. Broadcast $(c_{i,0}, \ldots, c_{i,D})$.

3. *Wait until for $j \in [N]$, $(c_{j,0}, \ldots, c_{j,D})$ has been received or a timeout occurs. In case of a timeout of party j, set $c_{j,k} \leftarrow \perp$ for $k \in [0, D]$.*
4. *Determine a set $G_i \subseteq [N]$ such that:*
   (a) $|G_i| = D + 1$
   (b) *For $(j, k) \in G_i^2$, $(c_{j,0}, \ldots, c_{j,D}) = (c_{k,0}, \ldots, c_{k,D})$.*
   If such a set G_i does not exist, set $s'_i \leftarrow \perp$ and return.
5. *Let $j \in G_i$ and for $k \in [0, D]$, set $c'_{i,k} \leftarrow c_{j,k}$.*
6. *Compute $\hat{c}_i \leftarrow \bigcirc_{k \in [0,D]} \mathsf{EXP}(c'_{i,k}, i^k)$, $b_i \leftarrow \mathsf{Open}(\rho, s_{i,1}, \ldots, s_{i,L}, \hat{c}_i, r_i)$, and broadcast b_i.*
7. *Wait until for all $j \in [N]$, b_j has been received or a timeout occurs. In case of a timeout of party j, set $b_j \leftarrow 0$.*
8. *Let $B_i = \{j \in [N] : b_j = 0\}$. If $B_i \neq \emptyset$, vote for rebooting shareholders B_i and recover the message and decommitment shares of the rebooted shareholders as described in [12].*
9. *Set $s'_i \leftarrow (s_{i,1}, \ldots, s_{i,L}, c'_{i,0}, \ldots, c'_{i,D}, r_i)$.*

$\mathsf{ShareIdentity}\langle \mathfrak{D}(\rho \in \mathcal{P}), \{\mathfrak{S}_i(\rho \in \mathcal{P}) \rightarrow s_i \in \mathcal{M}^L \times \mathcal{C}^D \times \mathcal{D}\}_{i \in [N]}\rangle$:
   The dealer $\mathfrak{D}$ does the following:
1. *For $(i, j) \in [L] \times [D]$, sample $U(\mathcal{M}) \rightarrow a_{i,j}$.*
2. *For $(i, j) \in [N] \times [L]$, compute $s_{i,j} \leftarrow \bigcirc_{k \in [D]} \mathsf{EXP}(a_{j,k}, i^k)$.*
3. *For $i \in [D]$, compute $\mathsf{Commit}(\rho, (a_{1,i}, \ldots, a_{L,i})) \rightarrow (c_i, d_i)$.*
4. *For $i \in [N]$, compute $r_i \leftarrow \bigcirc_{j \in [D]} \mathsf{EXP}(d_j, i^j)$.*
5. *Broadcast $(c_1, \ldots, c_D)$ and for $i \in [N]$, send r_i and $(s_{i,1}, \ldots, s_{i,L})$ to party $\mathfrak{S}_i$.*

For $i \in [N]$, party $\mathfrak{S}_i$ sets $s_i \leftarrow (s_{i,1}, \ldots, s_{i,L}, c_1, \ldots, c_D, r_i)$.

3.2   Scheme Analysis

We analyze the security of the vector proactive secret sharing scheme VPSS proposed in Subsect. 3.2. We first prove the correct functionality. Then, we show that if the used vector commitment schemes is information-theoretically hiding, our vector proactive secret sharing provides information-theoretic secrecy. Finally, we show that the robustness of our vector commitments scheme can be reduced the binding security of the used vector commitment scheme.

Theorem 1 (Correctness). *Let $(N, T) \in \mathbb{N} \times \mathbb{N}_0$ such that $N < p$ and $T < \frac{N}{2}$. Let $\mathsf{VC} = (L, \mathcal{P}, \mathcal{M}, \mathcal{C}, \mathcal{D}, \mathsf{Setup}, \mathsf{Commit}, \mathsf{Open})$ be a homomorphic vector commitment scheme such that $\mathcal{M}$ is a finite field of prime order. The proactive secret sharing scheme $\mathsf{VPSS}_{N,T,\mathsf{VC}}$ is correct.*

Proof. Let $(N, T) \in \mathbb{N} \times \mathbb{N}_0$ such that $N < p$ and $T < \frac{N}{2}$. Let $\mathsf{VC} = (L, \mathcal{P}, \mathcal{M}, \mathcal{C}, \mathcal{D}, \mathsf{Setup}, \mathsf{Commit}, \mathsf{Open})$ be a homomorphic vector commitment scheme such that $\mathcal{M}$ is a finite field of prime order p. Let $\mathsf{VPSS}_{N,T,\mathsf{VC}} = (N, T, \mathcal{P}, \mathcal{M}^L, \mathcal{S}, \mathsf{Setup}, \mathsf{Share}, \mathsf{Reshare}, \mathsf{Reconstruct})$ and $D = N - T - 1$.

For $\rho \in \mathcal{P}$, $m \in \mathcal{M}$, and $i \in \mathbb{N}_0$, define

$$
\mathsf{SHARES}(\rho, m, l) = \left\{ \Pr \left[\begin{array}{c} (s_1, \ldots, s_N) : \\ (s_{l,1}, \ldots, s_{l,n}) = (s_1, \ldots, s_N) : \\ \mathsf{Share}\langle \mathfrak{D}(\rho, m), \{\mathfrak{S}_i(\rho) \to s_{0,i}\}_{i \in [N]}\rangle, \\ \mathsf{Reshare}\langle\{\mathfrak{S}_i(\rho, s_{0,i}) \to s_{1,i}\}_{i \in [N]}\rangle, \\ \ldots, \\ \mathsf{Reshare}\langle\{\mathfrak{S}_i(\rho, s_{l-1,i}) \to s_{l,i}\}_{i \in [N]}\rangle \end{array} \right] > 0 \right\}.
$$

Let $\rho \in \mathcal{P}$ and $m = (m_1, \ldots, m_L) \in \mathcal{M}^L$. By the definition of protocol Share, we observe that for $(s_1, \ldots, s_N) \in \mathsf{SHARES}(\rho, m, 0)$ we have:

$$\exists A \in \mathcal{M}^{L \times D} : \forall i \in [N] :$$
$$s_i = (s_{i,1}, \ldots, s_{i,L}, c_0, \ldots, c_t, r_i) \in \mathcal{S}$$
$$\wedge \forall j \in [L] : s_{i,j} = m_j \bigcirc_{k \in [D]} \mathsf{EXP}(A_{j,k}, i^k)$$
$$\wedge (c_{i,0}, d_{i,0}) \in \mathsf{Commit}(\rho, (m_1, \ldots, m_L))$$
$$\wedge \forall j \in [D] : (c_{i,j}, d_{i,j}) \in \mathsf{Commit}(\rho, (a_{1,j}, \ldots, a_{L,j}))$$
$$\wedge r_i = \bigcirc_{j \in [0,D]} \mathsf{EXP}(d_{i,j}, i^j)$$

Furthermore, we observe that if the conditions above hold, then $G = [D+1] \in \mathsf{QUALI}((s_1, \ldots, s_n))$ and for $i \in [L]$, we have $m_i = \bigcirc_{j \in G} \mathsf{EXP}(s_{j,i}, l_j)$, where $l_j = \prod_{k \in G \setminus \{j\}} k * \mathsf{MODINV}(k - j, p)$.

Next, we observe that by the definition of Reshare and the homomorphic properties of the shares and the commitments we have $\mathsf{SHARES}(\rho, m, 0) = \mathsf{SHARES}(\rho, m, 1)$. It follows that for all $l \in \mathbb{N}_0$, $\mathsf{SHARES}(\rho, m) = \mathsf{SHARES}(\rho, m, l)$. We obtain that for any $\rho \in \mathcal{P}$, $(s_1, \ldots, s_N) \in \mathsf{SHARES}(\rho, m)$ we have

$$\Pr \left[\begin{array}{c} m = m' : \\ \mathsf{Reconstruct}\langle m' \leftarrow \mathfrak{D}(\rho), \{\mathfrak{S}_i(\rho, s_i)\}_{i \in [N]}\rangle \end{array} \right] = 1 .$$

$\square$

Theorem 2 (Secrecy). *Let $(N, T) \in \mathbb{N} \times \mathbb{N}_0$ such that $N < p$ and $T < \frac{N}{2}$. Let $\mathsf{VC} = (L, \mathcal{P}, \mathcal{M}, \mathcal{C}, \mathcal{D}, \mathsf{Setup}, \mathsf{Commit}, \mathsf{Open})$ be a perfectly hiding homomorphic vector commitment scheme such that $\mathcal{M}$ is a finite field of prime order. Then there exists $\alpha \in \mathbb{R}$ such that $\mathsf{VPSS}_{N,T,\mathsf{VC}}$ is ϵ-secret with*

$$\epsilon(\tau_A, \tau_B) = \begin{cases} 0 & \text{if } \tau_B \geq \alpha * \tau_A, \\ 1 & \text{if } \tau_B < \alpha * \tau_A. \end{cases}$$

Proof. Let $(N, T) \in \mathbb{N} \times \mathbb{N}_0$ such that $N < p$ and $T < \frac{N}{2}$. Let $\mathsf{VC} = (L, \mathcal{P}, \mathcal{M}, \mathcal{C}, \mathcal{D}, \mathsf{Setup}, \mathsf{Commit}, \mathsf{Open})$ be a homomorphic vector commitment scheme such that $\mathcal{M}$ is a finite field of prime order p. Let $\mathsf{VPSS}_{N,T,\mathsf{VC}} = (N, T, \mathcal{P}, \mathcal{M}, \mathcal{S}, \mathsf{Setup}, \mathsf{Share}, \mathsf{Reshare}, \mathsf{Reconstruct})$. Let $\mathcal{D}$ be a probability distribution over $\mathcal{M}$, $F : \mathcal{M} \to \{0, 1\}^*$ be a function, $\tau_A \in \mathbb{N}$, and $\mathcal{A} \in \mathsf{ProbAlgo}(\tau_A)$.

We construct an algorithm $\mathcal{B}$ that simulates $G_1(\mathcal{A}; 0^L)$. First, $\mathcal{B}$ runs $\mathsf{Setup}() \to \rho$ and sets $S \leftarrow \perp$ and $I \leftarrow \{\}$. Then, $\mathcal{B}$ runs $\mathcal{A}^O(\rho)$ and answers oracle calls by $\mathcal{A}$ as follows.

Share(I'): If $|I'| \leq T$ and $S = \bot$, do the following. Set $I \leftarrow I'$ and simulate Share$\langle \rho, 0^L \rangle \rightarrow S$ while giving the control over shareholders I to $\mathcal{A}$ until reboot.

Reshare(I'): If $|I \cup I'| \leq T$ and $S \neq \bot$, do the following. Set $I \leftarrow I'$ and simulate Reshare$\langle \rho, S \rangle \rightarrow S$ while giving the control over shareholders I to $\mathcal{A}$ until reboot.

Finalize(y): Output y.

By the definition of the secrecy game we observe that $\mathcal{A}$ obtains at most T shares per sharing or resharing. Thus, by the perfect secrecy property of Shamir Secret Sharing [18], the distribution of the message shares and decommitment shares observed by $\mathcal{A}$ in game G_1 is independent of m. Furthermore, by the perfect hiding security of VC, the distribution of the commitments observed by $\mathcal{A}$ is also independent of the m. It follows that for all $m \in \mathcal{M}^L$, $y \in \Im(G_1)$,

$$\Pr[G_1(\mathcal{A}; m) = y] = \Pr[G_1(\mathcal{A}; 0^L) = y] . \tag{1}$$

Furthermore, by the definition of $\mathcal{B}$, we have

$$\Pr[G_1(\mathcal{A}; 0^L) = y] = \Pr[\mathcal{B} = y] . \tag{2}$$

By the law of total probability, (1), and (2), we obtain

$$
\Pr\left[\begin{array}{c} F(m) = y : \\ \mathcal{D} \rightarrow m, G_1(\mathcal{A}; m) \rightarrow y \end{array}\right]
$$

$$
= \sum_{\hat{m} \in \Im(\mathcal{D})} \Pr\left[\begin{array}{c} F(m) = y : \\ \mathcal{D} \rightarrow m, G_1(\mathcal{A}; m) \rightarrow y, m = \hat{m} \end{array}\right] * \Pr\left[\begin{array}{c} m = \hat{m} : \\ \mathcal{D} \rightarrow m \end{array}\right]
$$

$$
= \sum_{\hat{m} \in \Im(\mathcal{D})} \Pr\left[\begin{array}{c} F(\hat{m}) = y : \\ G_1(\mathcal{A}; \hat{m}) \rightarrow y \end{array}\right] * \Pr\left[\begin{array}{c} m = \hat{m} : \\ \mathcal{D} \rightarrow m \end{array}\right]
$$

$$
= \sum_{\hat{m} \in \Im(\mathcal{D})} \Pr\left[\begin{array}{c} F(0^L) = y : \\ G_1(\mathcal{A}; 0^L) \rightarrow y \end{array}\right] * \Pr\left[\begin{array}{c} m = \hat{m} : \\ \mathcal{D} \rightarrow m \end{array}\right]
$$

$$
= \sum_{\hat{m} \in \Im(\mathcal{D})} \Pr\left[\begin{array}{c} F(0^L) = y : \\ \mathcal{B} \rightarrow y \end{array}\right] * \Pr\left[\begin{array}{c} m = \hat{m} : \\ \mathcal{D} \rightarrow m \end{array}\right]
$$

$$
= \sum_{\hat{m} \in \Im(\mathcal{D})} \Pr\left[\begin{array}{c} F(m) = y : \\ \mathcal{D} \rightarrow m, \mathcal{B} \rightarrow y, m = \hat{m} \end{array}\right] * \Pr\left[\begin{array}{c} m = \hat{m} : \\ \mathcal{D} \rightarrow m \end{array}\right]
$$

$$
= \Pr\left[\begin{array}{c} F(m) = y : \\ \mathcal{D} \rightarrow m, \mathcal{B} \rightarrow y \end{array}\right] .
$$

Finally, we observe that the running time of $\mathcal{B}$ is upper-bounded by the running time of $\mathcal{A}$ times an upper bound α on the running time of protocols Share and Reshare. We obtain that for all τ_A, $\mathcal{A} \in \mathsf{ProbAlgo}(\tau_A)$, there exists $\mathcal{B} \in \mathsf{ProbAlgo}(\tau_B)$ such that

$$\Pr\left[\begin{matrix} F(m) = y : \\ \mathcal{D} \to m, G_1(\mathcal{A}; m) \to y \end{matrix}\right] \le \Pr\left[\begin{matrix} F(m) = y : \\ \mathcal{D} \to m, \mathcal{B} \to y \end{matrix}\right] + \epsilon(\tau_\mathcal{A}, \tau_\mathcal{B}) \; ,$$

for

$$\epsilon(\tau_\mathcal{A}, \tau_\mathcal{B}) = \begin{cases} 0 & \text{if } \tau_\mathcal{B} \ge \alpha * \tau_\mathcal{A}, \\ 1 & \text{if } \tau_\mathcal{B} < \alpha * \tau_\mathcal{A}. \end{cases}$$

$\square$

Theorem 3 (Robustness). *Let* $(N, T) \in \mathbb{N} \times \mathbb{N}_0$ *such that* $N < p$ *and* $T < \frac{N}{2}$. *Let* $\mathsf{VC} = (L, \mathcal{P}, \mathcal{M}, \mathcal{C}, \mathcal{D}, \mathsf{Setup}, \mathsf{Commit}, \mathsf{Open})$ *be a homomorphic vector commitment scheme such that* $\mathcal{M}$ *is a finite field of prime order* p. *If* VC *is* ϵ-*binding, then the proactive secret sharing scheme* $\mathsf{VPSS}_{N,T,\mathsf{VC}}$ *is* ϵ'-*robust with*

$$\epsilon' : \mathbb{N} \to \mathbb{R}; \tau \mapsto \epsilon(\alpha * \tau) \; .$$

Proof. Let $(N, T) \in \mathbb{N} \times \mathbb{N}_0$ such that $N < p$ and $T < \frac{N}{2}$. Let $\epsilon : \mathbb{N} \to \mathbb{R}$ be a function and $\mathsf{VC} = (L, \mathcal{P}, \mathcal{M}, \mathcal{C}, \mathcal{D}, \mathsf{Setup}, \mathsf{Commit}, \mathsf{Open})$ be an ϵ-binding homomorphic vector commitment scheme such that $\mathcal{M}$ is a finite field of prime order p. Let $\mathsf{VPSS}_{N,T,\mathsf{VC}} = (N, T, \mathcal{P}, \mathcal{M}, \mathcal{S}, \mathsf{Setup}, \mathsf{Share}, \mathsf{Reshare}, \mathsf{Reconstruct})$, $\tau_\mathcal{A} \in \mathbb{N}$, $\mathcal{A} \in \mathsf{ProbAlgo}(\tau_\mathcal{A})$, and $m \in \mathcal{M}$.

We construct an algorithm $\mathcal{B}$ such that

$$\Pr\left[\begin{matrix} m \ne m' : \\ G_2(\mathcal{A}, m) \to m' \end{matrix}\right] = \Pr\left[\begin{matrix} b = 1 \wedge b' = 1 \wedge m \ne m' : \\ \mathsf{Setup}() \to \rho, \mathcal{B}(\rho) \to (c, m, d, m', d'), \\ \mathsf{Open}(\rho, m, c, d) \to b, \mathsf{Open}(\rho, m, c, d') \to b' \end{matrix}\right] \; ,$$

which on input $\rho \in \mathcal{P}$, algorithm $\mathcal{B}$ simulates game $G_2(\mathcal{A}, m)$ as follows. When the game is startet run $G_2.\mathbf{Initialize}$ and replace the output by ρ. When $\mathcal{A}$ calls $\mathbf{Share}(I')$, run $G_2.\mathbf{Share}(I')$ in interaction with $\mathcal{A}$, which controls the corrupted shareholders and denote the output of shareholder i by $s_i = (s_{i,1}, \ldots, s_{i,L}, c_{i,0}, \ldots, c_{i,D}, r_i)$. Then, find $G \in \mathsf{QUALI}((s_1, \ldots, s_N))$ and set $c = c_{i,0}$, for an $i \in G$. For $i \in G$, compute $l_i \leftarrow \prod_{j \in G \setminus \{i\}} j * \mathsf{MODINV}(j - i, p)$, and compute $d \leftarrow \bigcirc_{i \in G} \mathsf{EXP}(r_i, l_i)$. When $\mathcal{A}$ calls $\mathbf{Reshare}$, run $G_2.\mathbf{Reshare}$ in interaction with $\mathcal{A}$. When $\mathcal{A}$ calls $\mathbf{Finalize}$, run $G_2.\mathbf{Finalize}$ in interaction with $\mathcal{A}$ and denote the share sent by shareholder i by $s_i' = (s_{i,1}', \ldots, s_{i,L}', c_{i,0}', \ldots, c_{i,D}', r_i')$ and the output of $G_2.\mathbf{Finalize}$ by m'. Determine a set $G' \in \mathsf{QUALI}((s_1', \ldots, s_N'))$, for $i \in G'$, compute $l_i' \leftarrow \prod_{j \in G' \setminus \{i\}} j * \mathsf{MODINV}(j - i, p)$, and compute $d' \leftarrow \bigcirc_{i \in G'} \mathsf{EXP}(r_i', l_i')$. Output (c, m, d, m', d').

We now derive an upper bound on

$$\Pr\left[\begin{matrix} m \ne m' : \\ G_2(\mathcal{A}, m) \to m' \end{matrix}\right] \; .$$

We observe that by the definition of protocol Share, the properties of the broadcast channel, and because the majority of the shareholders are honest, we have for $i \in [N]$, $\hat{c}_i \leftarrow \bigcirc_{k \in [0, D]} \mathsf{EXP}(c_{i,k}, i^k)$, that $\mathsf{Open}(\rho, (s_{i,1}, \ldots, s_{i,L}), \hat{c}_i, r_i) = 1$. Furthermore, we observe that for $i \in [L]$, $m_i = \bigcirc_{j \in G} \mathsf{EXP}(s_{j,i}, l_j)$, we have $m = (m_1, \ldots, m_L)$, $d = \bigcirc_{j \in G} \mathsf{EXP}(r_j, l_j)$, and $c = \bigcirc_{i \in G} \mathsf{EXP}(\hat{c}_i, l_i)$. Because VC is homomorphic, it follows that $\mathsf{Open}(\rho, m, c, d) = 1$. Analogously we obtain that $\mathsf{Open}(\rho, m', c', d') = 1$. Furthermore, we observe that by the definitions of protocols Reshare and Reconstruct, the properties of the broadcast channel, and the honest majority, we have that for all $i \in G'$, $c = c'$. It follows that

$$\Pr\left[\begin{array}{c} m \neq m' : \\ G_2(\mathcal{A}, m) \to m' \end{array}\right] = \Pr\left[\begin{array}{c} b = 1 \wedge b' = 1 \wedge m \neq m' : \\ \mathsf{Setup}() \to \rho, \mathcal{B}(\rho) \to (c, m, d, m', d'), \\ \mathsf{Open}(\rho, m, c, d) \to b, \mathsf{Open}(\rho, m, c, d') \to b' \end{array}\right] .$$

We observe that for any $\mathcal{A}$, the running time of $\mathcal{B}_\mathcal{A}$ is upper-bounded by the running time of $\mathcal{A}$ times a constant α. Thus, we obtain that $\mathsf{VPSS}_{N,T,\mathsf{VC}}$ is ϵ'-robust with

$$\epsilon' : \mathbb{N} \to \mathbb{R}; \tau \mapsto \epsilon(\alpha * \tau) .$$

$\square$

4   Instantiation, Implementation, and Evaluation

We first describe in Subsect. 4.1 how we instantiate the vector commitment scheme that is necessary for our vector proactive secret sharing scheme described in Sect. 3. Afterwards we describe in Subsect. 4.2 how we implemented our vector proactive secret sharing scheme instantiated with the described vector commitment scheme. Finally, we evaluate the performance of our scheme and its implementation in Subsect. 4.3.

4.1   Instantiation

In the following we describe a vector commitment scheme that has the properties required by our vector proactive secret sharing scheme, i.e., it is perfectly hiding, computationally binding, and homomorphic. In addition, it is concise, which means that commitment and decommitment are potentially much shorter then the committed message vector. The construction is an extension of the commitment scheme proposed in [15] and is sometimes referred to by generalized Pedersen commitment [10]. Here we cast the construction into our definition of a vector commitment scheme and show that its security can be based on the fixed generator discrete logarithm problem.

Scheme 2 (DLVC). *Let $\mathbb{G}$ be a finite cyclic group, p be the order of $\mathbb{G}$, $\circ$ denote the operation associated with $\mathbb{G}$, and $L \in \mathbb{N}$. We define the vector commitment scheme $\mathsf{DLVC}_{\mathbb{G},L} = (L, \mathsf{GEN}(\mathbb{G})^L, \mathbb{Z}_p, \mathbb{G}, \mathbb{Z}_p, \mathsf{Setup}, \mathsf{Commit}, \mathsf{Open})$ as follows.*

$\mathsf{Setup}() \to (g_0, \ldots, g_L)$: *For $i \in [0, L]$, sample $U(\mathsf{GEN}(\mathbb{G})) \to g_i$.*
$\mathsf{Commit}(\rho, m) \to (c, d)$: *Let $\rho = (g_0, \ldots, g_L)$ and $m = (m_1, \ldots, m_L) \in \mathbb{Z}_p^L$. Sample $U(\mathbb{Z}_p) \to d$ and compute $c \leftarrow \mathsf{EXP}(g_0, d) \bigcirc_{i \in [L]} \mathsf{EXP}(g_i, m_i)$.*

Open$(\rho, m, c, d) \rightarrow b$: *Let $\rho = (g_0, \ldots, g_L)$ and $m = (m_1, \ldots, m_L)$. Compute $c' \leftarrow$ EXP$(g_0, d) \bigcirc_{i \in [L]}$ EXP(g_i, m_i). If $c = c'$, set $b \leftarrow 1$. If $c \neq c'$, set $b \leftarrow 0$.*

Theorem 4. *Let $\mathbb{G}$ be a finite cyclic group and $L \in \mathbb{N}$. The vector commitment scheme* DLVC$_{\mathbb{G},L}$ *is correct.*

Theorem 5. *Let $\mathbb{G}$ be a finite cyclic group and $L \in \mathbb{N}$. The vector commitment scheme* DLVC$_{\mathbb{G},L}$ *is perfectly hiding.*

Theorem 6. *Let $\mathbb{G}$ be a finite cyclic group of prime order p, $g \in$ GEN$(\mathbb{G})$, and $L \in \mathbb{N}$. If* DLOG$(\mathbb{G}, g)$ *is ϵ-hard, then there exists $\alpha \in \mathbb{N}$ such that* DLVC$_{\mathbb{G},L}$ *is ϵ'-binding with*

$$\epsilon' : \mathbb{N} \to \mathbb{R}; \tau \mapsto \epsilon(\tau + \alpha) + \frac{1}{p} \ .$$

Theorem 7. *Let $\mathbb{G}$ be a finite cyclic group and $L \in \mathbb{N}$. The commitment scheme* DLVC$_{\mathbb{G},L}$ *is homomorphic.*

The proofs of the theorems can be found in Appendix A.

4.2   Implementation

We implemented a proactive secret sharing system based on the proactive secret sharing scheme VPSS (Subsect. 3.1) instantiated with the vector commitment scheme DLVC (Subsect. 4.1) using the programming language Java 8. In order to support storage of large byte arrays, we use a data encoding that maps byte arrays to message vectors of the secret sharing scheme and then run multiple instances of the scheme per byte array.

System Parameters. Our proactive secret sharing system uses the following parameters:

Number of shareholders N: This parameter specifies the total number of shareholders that are involved in the secret sharing protocols.

Corruption threshold T: This parameters specifies the maximum number of corrupted shareholders that can be tolerated. We require that $T < \frac{N}{2}$.

Vector length L: This parameter specifies the length of the message vectors of the secret sharing scheme and vector commitment scheme.

Message space size M: This parameter represents the size in bytes of an element of a message vector for the secret sharing scheme and the vector commitment scheme. The message space size M is determined by the parameters of the commitment scheme and our implementation supports $M \in \{32, 64\}$. We instantiate the commitment space $\mathbb{G}$ as the unique p-order subgroup of $\mathbb{Z}_q$ for primes p and q with $\log_2(p) > M * 8 \geq 256$, $\log_2(q) \geq 2048$, and $(p - 1) \bmod q = 0$.

Commitment space size C: This parameter represents the size in bytes of commitments and is determined by $C = \lceil \log_2(q)/8 \rceil$.

Data Encoding. We use the following data encoding to map byte arrays to the message space of VPSS. Let $\mathcal{M}^L$ be the message space of the secret sharing scheme. We use the algorithms Encode and Decode for encoding byte arrays of $\mathcal{B} = \{b \in \{0, \ldots, 255\}^* : |b| \leq \mathsf{INTMAX}\}$ to message matrices of $\mathcal{M}^{L \times R^*} = \{m \in \mathcal{M}^{L \times *} : \mathsf{Cols}(m) \leq \lceil \frac{R}{L} \rceil, R = \lceil \frac{\mathsf{INTSIZE} + \mathsf{INTMAX}}{M} \rceil\}$, where $\mathsf{INTSIZE} = 4$ and $\mathsf{INTMAX} = 2^{31} - 1$ for Java 8. Our byte array encoding requires two other types of encodings: $(\mathsf{Encode}_{\mathsf{Integer},\mathbb{B}^{\mathsf{INTSIZE}}}, \mathsf{Decode}_{\mathsf{Integer},\mathbb{B}^{\mathsf{INTSIZE}}})$ is an encoding from Java Integers to byte arrays of length $\mathsf{INTSIZE}$, which is supported natively by Java, and $(\mathsf{Encode}_{\mathbb{B}^M,\mathcal{M}}, \mathsf{Decode}_{\mathbb{B}^M,\mathcal{M}})$ is an encoding from byte arrays of length M to message space elements of $\mathcal{M} = \mathbb{Z}_p$, for $p \in \mathbb{N}$, which we implement using Java Big Integers.

$\mathsf{Encode}(b \in \mathcal{B}) \to m \in \mathcal{M}^{L \times R^*}$:

1. Let $\mathtt{length} = \mathsf{Encode}_{\mathsf{Integer},\mathbb{B}^{\mathsf{INTSIZE}}}(|b|)$ and set $b' \leftarrow \mathtt{length}\|b$.
2. Let $b'' = b'\|0^{|b'| \bmod M}$ and $b'' = a_1\|\ldots\|a_n$ such that for $i \in [n]$, a_i is a byte array of length M.
3. For $i \in [n]$, let $m_i = \mathsf{Encode}_{\mathbb{B}^M,\mathcal{M}}(a_i)$, where $\mathsf{Encode}_{\mathbb{B}^M,\mathcal{M}}$ is an algorithm that encodes elements of $\mathbb{B}^M$
4. Reshape the vector $(m_1, \ldots, m_n) \in \mathcal{M}^n$ into a matrix $m \in \mathcal{M}^{L \times \lceil \frac{n}{L} \rceil}$, that is, let $m = (m_{i,j})_{(i,j) \in [L] \times [\lceil \frac{n}{L} \rceil]}$, where $m_{i,j} = m_k$ for $k = i + (j-1) * L$ and $m_k = 0$ if $k > n$.

$\mathsf{Decode}(m \in \Im(\mathsf{Encode})) \to b \in \mathcal{B}$:

1. Reshape the matrix $m = (m_{i,j}) \in \mathcal{M}^{L \times L'}$ into vector $(m_1, \ldots, m_n) \in \mathcal{M}^{L * L'}$. That is, for $i \in [L * L']$, let $m_i = m_{j,k}$, where $j = i \bmod k$ and $j = \lfloor \frac{i}{L} \rfloor$.
2. For $i \in [L * L']$, let $b_i = \mathsf{Decode}_{\mathbb{B}^M,\mathcal{M}}(m_i)$.
3. Let $b'' = a_1\|\ldots\|a_{L*L'} = b_1\|\ldots\|b_{L*L'*S}$, where $b_i \in \mathbb{B}$ for $i \in [L*L'*M]$.
4. Let $l = \mathsf{Decode}_{\mathsf{Integer},\mathbb{B}^{\mathsf{INTSIZE}}}(b_1\|\ldots\|b_{\mathsf{INTSIZE}})$.
5. Let $b = b_{\mathsf{INTSIZE}+1}\|\ldots\|b_{\mathsf{INTSIZE}+l}$.

This encoding fulfills the requirement that for all $b \in \mathcal{B}$, $\mathsf{Decode}(\mathsf{Encode}(b)) = b$. In our implementation, we store a byte array $b \in \mathcal{B}$ with $m \leftarrow \mathsf{Encode}(B)$ and $\mathsf{Cols}(m) > 1$ by running for each column of m a separate instance of the secret sharing system.

4.3   Evaluation

In this section we evaluate the theoretical and practical performance of our proactive secret sharing system based on the proactive secret sharing scheme VPSS, the vector commitment scheme DLVC, and the data encoding described in Subsect. 4.2. For the theoretical performance evaluation we distinguish between broadcast communication and direct point-to-point communication. For our experimental performance evaluation we focus on measuring the computation time of the protocols. Practical communication times highly depend on the network infrastructure. Our measurements are for honest executions of the protocols. Protocol runs with malicious parties may take longer as they require additional steps for resolving conflicts.

Table 1. Computation and communication complexity of the protocols Share, Reshare, and Reconstruct of our proactive secret sharing system. **COMP** denotes the computation complexity measured in the number of modular exponentiations for modulus $p \approx 2^{8M}$, **BC-OUT** denotes the outgoing broadcast traffic, **BC-IN** denotes the incoming broadcast traffic, **DIR-OUT** denotes the outgoing directed point-to-point traffic, and **DIR-IN** denotes the incoming directed point-to-point traffic, where the traffic is measured in bytes.

	COMP	BC-OUT	BC-IN	DIR-OUT	DIR-IN
Share	$\lceil\frac{D}{LM}\rceil(N-T)$ $*(L+1)$ for $\mathcal{D}$	$\lceil\frac{D}{LM}\rceil(N-T)C$ for $\mathcal{D}$	$\lceil\frac{D}{LM}\rceil(N-T)C$ for $\mathcal{S}_i$	$\lceil\frac{D}{LM}\rceil N(L+1)M$ for $\mathcal{D}$	$\lceil\frac{D}{LM}\rceil(L+1)M$ for $\mathcal{S}_i$
Reshare	$\lceil\frac{D}{LM}\rceil(2N-T)(L+1)$ for $\mathcal{S}_i$	$\lceil\frac{D}{LM}\rceil(2(N-T)+1)C$ for $\mathcal{S}_i$	$\lceil\frac{D}{LM}\rceil N(2(N-T)+1)C$ for $\mathcal{S}_i$	$\lceil\frac{D}{LM}\rceil N(L+1)M$ for $\mathcal{S}_i$	$\lceil\frac{D}{LM}\rceil N(L+1)M$ for $\mathcal{S}_i$
Reconstruct	$\lceil\frac{D}{LM}\rceil(N-T)(L+1)$ for $\mathcal{D}$	0	0	$\lceil\frac{D}{LM}\rceil(L+1)M+(N-T)C$ for $\mathcal{S}_i$	$\lceil\frac{D}{LM}\rceil N((L+1)M+(N-T)C)$ for $\mathcal{D}$

Theoretical Performance. In Table 1 we present the computation and communication complexity of the protocols Share, Reshare, and Reconstruct of our proactive secret sharing system. For the computation complexity, we count the number of modular exponentiations during commitment generation and verification because these typically account for more than 90% of the computation time, as can be seen from the runtime profile of the implementation. For the communication complexity, we count the number of shares and commitments that are transmitted and multiply these counts with the respective sizes of these elements. In Fig. 3 we plot the communication performance as a function of the vector length L. We observe that especially the broadcast communication per party can be drastically reduced by increasing the vector length L. The effect of increasing L on direct communication is noticeable for small L. We observe that in comparison to standard proactive secret sharing (i.e., $L = 1$) our vector proactive secret sharing scheme uses only $\frac{1}{L}$ the communication, that is, for large L the communication complexity is comparable with the optimal communication complexity of standard secret sharing [18].

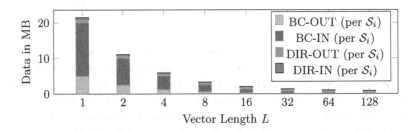

Fig. 3. Network communication during protocol Reshare plotted over the vector length L for $N = 3$, $T = 1$, $D = 128$ kB, $M = 32$ B, where $L = 1$ represents [12].

Experimental Performance. For the experimental performance evaluation we focus on measuring the computation time of the protocols, as practical communication times highly depend on the network infrastructure and would require a more advanced implementation and testbed. In Fig. 4 we show the measured running times for protocols Share, Reshare, and Reconstruct for $M = 32$ and different message vector lengths L. We observe that we reduce the computation time by up to 50% when we increase the vector length L, as predicted by the theoretical complexity evaluation. Increasing the message space size M does not improve performance significantly as modular exponentiations are more expensive for larger M.

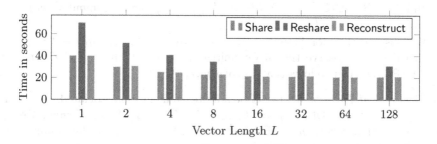

Fig. 4. Measured running times for protocols Share, Reshare, and Reconstruct plotted over the vector length L for $N = 3$, $T = 1$, $D = 128$ kB, $M = 32$ B.

5   Conclusions

We presented a vector proactive secret sharing scheme that allows for drastically reduced communication and computation costs. Concretely, when instantiated with the vector commitment scheme described in Subsect. 4.1 our scheme reduces computation costs by 50% and broadcast communication costs by a factor L, where L is the length of the commitment scheme message vectors, compared to the scheme of [12].

We see several directions for future work. While our scheme achieves almost optimal communication performance, the computation times are still a bottle neck. It would be worthwhile to explore whether there exist suitable vector commitment schemes that are computationally more efficient. Furthermore, the vector commitment scheme used by us is based on the discrete logarithm problem which is susceptible to quantum computer attacks. It would be worthwhile to explore suitable vector commitment schemes that are secure against quantum computers. In [13], Kate, Zaverucha, and Goldberg propose polynomial commitments and show how they can be used to reduce the communication complexity of verifiable secret sharing. However, they do not study the implications for proactive secret sharing. It would be interesting to see whether their techniques can be combined with our techniques in order to further reduce the communication complexity of our vector proactive secret sharing scheme. Besides that, it would be interesting to extend our scheme to the asynchronous network setting where a global clock is not available to the participating network parties.

Acknowledgments. This work has been co-funded by the DFG as part of project S6 within the CRC 1119 CROSSING.

A   Proofs

Proof (Proof of Theorem 4). Let $\mathbb{G}$ be a finite cyclic group, p be the order of $\mathbb{G}$, and $L \in \mathbb{N}$, $\mathsf{DLVC}_{\mathbb{G},L} = (L, \mathsf{GEN}(\mathbb{G})^L, \mathbb{Z}_p, \mathbb{G}, \mathbb{Z}_p, \mathsf{Setup}, \mathsf{Commit}, \mathsf{Open})$, and $m = (m_1, \ldots, m_L) \in \mathbb{Z}_p^L$.

We observe that for $\mathsf{Setup}() \to \rho$, we have $\rho = (g_0, \ldots, g_L) \in \mathsf{GEN}(\mathbb{G})^L$. Furthermore, we observe that if $\mathsf{Commit}(\rho, m) \to (c, d)$, then $c = \mathsf{EXP}(g_0, d) \circ \bigcirc_{i=1}^L \mathsf{EXP}(g_i, m_i)$. It follows that $\mathsf{Open}(\rho, m, c, d) = 1$. ☐

Proof (Proof of Theorem 5). Let $\mathbb{G}$ be a finite cyclic group associated with operation $\circ$, $L \in \mathbb{N}$, and $\mathsf{DLVC}_{\mathbb{G},L} = (L, \mathsf{GEN}(\mathbb{G})^L, \mathbb{Z}_p, \mathbb{G}, \mathbb{Z}_p, \mathsf{Setup}, \mathsf{Commit}, \mathsf{Open})$. We observe that for all $\rho \in \mathsf{GEN}(\mathbb{G})^L$, $m \in \mathbb{Z}_p^L$, $c^* \in \mathbb{G}$, by the definition of Commit and because g is a generator, we have

$$\Pr\left[\begin{array}{c} c = c^* : \\ \mathsf{Commit}(\rho, m) \to (c, d) \end{array}\right]$$

$$= \Pr\left[\begin{array}{c} c = c^* : \\ U(\mathbb{Z}_p) \to d, c \leftarrow \mathsf{EXP}(g_0, d) \bigcirc_{i=1}^L \mathsf{EXP}(g_i, m_i) \end{array}\right]$$

$$= \Pr\left[\begin{array}{c} c = c^* : \\ U(\mathbb{G}) \to c \end{array}\right],$$

where $\rho = (g_0, \ldots, g_L)$ and $m = (m_1, \ldots, m_L)$. ☐

Proof (Proof of Theorem 6). The following proof is adapted from Section 2.3.2 of [6].

Let $\mathbb{G}$ be a finite cyclic group of prime order p, $\mathsf{DLVC}_{\mathbb{G},L} = (L, \mathsf{GEN}(\mathbb{G})^L, \mathbb{Z}_p, \mathbb{G}, \mathbb{Z}_p, \mathsf{Setup}, \mathsf{Commit}, \mathsf{Open})$, $g \in \mathsf{GEN}(\mathbb{G})$, $\tau \in \mathbb{N}$, and $\mathcal{A} \in \mathsf{Algo}(\tau)$. In the following, we prove an upper bound on

$$\Pr\left[\begin{array}{c} \mathsf{Open}(\rho, m, c, d) = 1 \wedge \mathsf{Open}(\rho, m', c, d') = 1 \wedge m \neq m' : \\ \mathsf{Setup}() \to \rho, \mathcal{A}(\rho) \to (c, m, d, m', d') \end{array}\right].$$

Let $\mathcal{B}$ be an algorithm that takes as input $y \in \mathbb{G}$ and works as follows. Sample $U(\mathbb{Z}_p) \to a_0$ and for $i \in [L]$, $U(\mathbb{Z}_p^2) \to (a_i, b_i)$. Compute $g_0 \leftarrow \mathsf{EXP}(g, a_0)$ and for $i \in [L]$, $g_i \leftarrow \mathsf{EXP}(g, a_i) \circ \mathsf{EXP}(y, b_i)$. Run $\mathcal{A}((g_0, \ldots, g_L)) \to (c, m, d, m', d')$. If $\mathsf{Open}(\rho, m, c, d) = 0$ or $\mathsf{Open}(\rho, m', c, d') = 0$, output $\perp$. Otherwise, proceed as follows. Let $m = (m_0, \ldots, m_L) \in \mathbb{Z}_p^L$ and $m' = (m_0', \ldots, m_L') \in \mathbb{Z}_p^L$. Compute $a \leftarrow a_0(d - d') + \sum_{i \in [L]} a_i(m_i - m_i')$ and $b \leftarrow \sum_{i \in [L]} b_i(m_i' - m_i)$. If $b = 0$, output $\perp$. Otherwise, compute $x \leftarrow \frac{a}{b}$ and output x.

We observe that because the a_i's are uniformly distributed and g is a generator, the g_i's are also uniformly distributed. This means that $(g_0, \ldots, g_L)$ has the same distribution as ρ generated by Setup(). It follows that

$$\Pr \begin{bmatrix} \mathsf{Open}(\rho, m, c, d) = 1 \wedge \mathsf{Open}(\rho, m', c, d') = 1 \wedge m \neq m' : \\ \mathsf{Setup}() \to \rho, \mathcal{A}(\rho) \to (c, m, d, m', d') \end{bmatrix}$$

$$= \Pr \begin{bmatrix} \mathsf{Open}(\rho, m, c, d) = 1 \wedge \mathsf{Open}(\rho, m', c, d') = 1 \wedge m \neq m' : \\ U(\mathbb{G}) \to y, \mathcal{B}(y) \to x \end{bmatrix} .$$

Using sigma additivity we write

$$\Pr \begin{bmatrix} \mathsf{Open}(\rho, m, c, d) = 1 \wedge \mathsf{Open}(\rho, m', c, d') = 1 \wedge m \neq m' : \\ U(\mathbb{G}) \to y, \mathcal{B}(y) \to x \end{bmatrix}$$

$$= \Pr \begin{bmatrix} \mathsf{Open}(\rho, m, c, d) = 1 \wedge \mathsf{Open}(\rho, m', c, d') = 1 \wedge m \neq m' \wedge b = 0 : \\ U(\mathbb{G}) \to y, \mathcal{B}(y) \to x \end{bmatrix}$$

$$+ \Pr \begin{bmatrix} \mathsf{Open}(\rho, m, c, d) = 1 \wedge \mathsf{Open}(\rho, m', c, d') = 1 \wedge m \neq m' \wedge b \neq 0 : \\ U(\mathbb{G}) \to y, \mathcal{B}(y) \to x \end{bmatrix} .$$

The first term is upper-bounded by $\frac{1}{p}$, as can be seen as follows:

$$\Pr \begin{bmatrix} \mathsf{Open}(\rho, m, c, d) = 1 \wedge \mathsf{Open}(\rho, m', c, d') = 1 \wedge m \neq m' \wedge b = 0 : \\ U(\mathbb{G}) \to y, \mathcal{B}(y) \to x \end{bmatrix}$$

$$\leq \Pr \begin{bmatrix} m \neq m' \wedge b = 0 : \\ U(\mathbb{G}) \to y, \mathcal{B}(y) \to x \end{bmatrix}$$

$$= \Pr \begin{bmatrix} m \neq m' \wedge \sum_{j \in [L]} b_j (m'_j - m_j) = 0 : \\ U(\mathbb{G}) \to y, \mathcal{B}(y) \to x \end{bmatrix}$$

$$\leq \Pr \begin{bmatrix} \exists i \in [L], m_i \neq m'_i \wedge b_i = \frac{-\sum_{j \in [L] \setminus \{i\}} b_j (m'_j - m_j)}{(m'_i - m_i)} : \\ U(\mathbb{G}) \to y, \mathcal{B}(y) \to x \end{bmatrix} = \frac{1}{p} .$$

Next we prove that the second term is upper-bounded by

$$\Pr \begin{bmatrix} \mathsf{EXP}(g, x) = y : \\ U(\mathbb{G}) \to y, \mathcal{B}(y) \to x \end{bmatrix} .$$

We observe that if $b \neq 0$, then $\mathsf{Open}(\rho, m, c, d) = 1$, $\mathsf{Open}(\rho, m', c, d') = 1$, $m \neq m'$, and

$$\mathsf{EXP}(g_0, d) \bigcirc_{i \in [L]} \mathsf{EXP}(g_i, m_i) = \mathsf{EXP}(g_0, d') \bigcirc_{i \in [L]} \mathsf{EXP}(g_i, m'_i)$$

$$\iff \mathsf{EXP}(g_0, d - d') \bigcirc_{i \in [L]} \mathsf{EXP}(g_i, m_i - m'_i) = e_{\mathbb{G}}$$

$$\iff \mathsf{EXP} \left(g, a_0(d - d') + \sum_{i \in [L]} a_i(m_i - m'_i) \right) \circ \mathsf{EXP} \left(y, \sum_{i \in [L]} b_i(m_i - m'_i) \right) = e_{\mathbb{G}}$$

$$\iff \mathsf{EXP} \left(g, a_0(d - d') + \sum_{i \in [L]} a_i(m_i - m'_i) \right) = \mathsf{EXP} \left(y, \sum_{i \in [L]} b_i(m'_i - m_i) \right)$$

$$\iff \mathsf{EXP} \left(g, \frac{a}{b} \right) = y .$$

It follows that

$$\Pr\begin{bmatrix} \mathsf{EXP}(g, \frac{a}{b}) = y \wedge b \neq 0 : \\ U(\mathbb{G}) \to y, \mathcal{B}(y) \to x \end{bmatrix}$$

$$= \Pr\begin{bmatrix} \mathsf{Open}(\rho, m, c, d) = 1 \wedge \mathsf{Open}(\rho, m', c, d') = 1 \wedge m \neq m' \wedge b \neq 0 : \\ U(\mathbb{G}) \to y, \mathcal{B}(y) \to x \end{bmatrix} .$$

By the fact that $b = 0$ implies $x = \bot$ and $\mathsf{EXP}(g, \bot) \notin \mathbb{G}$, we have

$$\Pr\begin{bmatrix} \mathsf{EXP}(g, x) = y \wedge b \neq 0 : \\ U(\mathbb{G}) \to y, \mathcal{B}(y) \to x \end{bmatrix} = \Pr\begin{bmatrix} \mathsf{EXP}(g, x) = y : \\ U(\mathbb{G}) \to y, \mathcal{B}(y) \to x \end{bmatrix} .$$

In summary, we obtain

$$\Pr\begin{bmatrix} \mathsf{Open}(\rho, m, c, d) = 1 \wedge \mathsf{Open}(\rho, m', c, d') = 1 \wedge m \neq m' : \\ \mathsf{Setup}() \to \rho, \mathcal{A}(\rho) \to (c, m, d, m', d') \end{bmatrix}$$

$$\leq \Pr\begin{bmatrix} \mathsf{EXP}(g, x) = y : \\ U(\mathbb{G}) \to y, \mathcal{B}(y) \to x \end{bmatrix} + \frac{1}{p} .$$

Finally, we observe that the running time of $\mathcal{B}$ is upper-bounded by $\tau + \alpha$, where α is the constant difference between the running time of $\mathcal{B}$ and the running time of $\mathcal{A}$. It follows that if $\mathsf{DLOG}(\mathbb{G}, g)$ is ϵ-hard, then $\mathsf{DLVC}_{\mathbb{G},L}$ is ϵ'-binding-secure with

$$\epsilon' : \tau \mapsto \epsilon(\tau + \alpha) + \frac{1}{p} .$$

$\square$

Proof (Proof of Theorem 7). Let $\mathbb{G}$ be a finite cyclic group, $L \in \mathbb{N}$, and $\mathsf{DLVC}_{\mathbb{G},L} = (L, \mathsf{GEN}(\mathbb{G})^L, \mathbb{Z}_p, \mathbb{G}, \mathbb{Z}_p, \mathsf{Setup}, \mathsf{Commit}, \mathsf{Open})$. Let $\circ$ denote the operation associated with $\mathbb{G}$, $+$ and $*$ denote addition and multiplication over $\mathbb{Z}_p$, and $\oplus$ denote addition over $\mathbb{Z}_p^L$. We observe that for any $\rho \in \mathcal{P}$, $(m_1, c_1, d_1) \in \mathsf{COMS}(\rho)$, and $(m_2, c_2, d_2) \in \mathsf{COMS}(\rho)$ we have that

$$(m_1, c_1, d_1) \in \mathsf{COMS}(\rho) \wedge (m_2, c_2, d_2) \in \mathsf{COMS}(\rho)$$

$$\implies \begin{aligned} & \big(\mathsf{EXP}(g_0, d_1) \bigcirc_{i \in [L]} \mathsf{EXP}(g_i, m_{1,i})\big) = c_1 \\ & \wedge \big(\mathsf{EXP}(g_0, d_2) \bigcirc_{i \in [L]} \mathsf{EXP}(g_i, m_{2,i})\big) = c_2 \end{aligned}$$

$$\implies \begin{aligned} & \big(\mathsf{EXP}(g_0, d_1) \bigcirc_{i \in [L]} \mathsf{EXP}(g_i, m_{1,i})\big) \\ & \circ \big(\mathsf{EXP}(g_0, d_2) \bigcirc_{i \in [L]} \mathsf{EXP}(g_i, m_{2,i})\big) = c_1 \circ c_2 \end{aligned}$$

$$\iff \mathsf{EXP}(g_0, d_1 + d_2) \bigcirc_{i \in [L]} \mathsf{EXP}(g_i, m_{1,i} + m_{2,i}) = c_1 \circ c_2$$

$$\iff \mathsf{Open}(\rho, m_1 \oplus m_2, c_1 * c_2, d_1 \circ d_2) = 1 .$$

$\square$

References

1. Baron, J., Defrawy, K.E., Lampkins, J., Ostrovsky, R.: Communication-optimal proactive secret sharing for dynamic groups. In: Malkin, T., Kolesnikov, V., Lewko, A.B., Polychronakis, M. (eds.) ACNS 2015. LNCS, vol. 9092, pp. 23–41. Springer, Cham (2015). https://doi.org/10.1007/978-3-319-28166-7_2

2. Baron, J., El Defrawy, K., Lampkins, J., Ostrovsky, R.: How to withstand mobile virus attacks, revisited. In: Proceedings of the 2014 ACM Symposium on Principles of Distributed Computing, PODC 2014, pp. 293–302. ACM, New York (2014). https://doi.org/10.1145/2611462.2611474. http://doi.acm.org/10.1145/2611462.2611474

3. Bellare, M., Rogaway, P.: Code-based game-playing proofs and the security of triple encryption. Cryptology ePrint Archive, Report 2004/331 (2004). https://eprint.iacr.org/2004/331

4. Bellare, M., Rogaway, P.: The security of triple encryption and a framework for code-based game-playing proofs. In: Vaudenay, S. (ed.) EUROCRYPT 2006. LNCS, vol. 4004, pp. 409–426. Springer, Heidelberg (2006). https://doi.org/10.1007/11761679_25

5. Blakley, G.R.: Safeguarding cryptographic keys. In: International Workshop on Managing Requirements Knowledge (AFIPS), December 1979. https://doi.org/10.1109/AFIPS.1979.98. doi.ieeecomputersociety.org/10.1109/AFIPS.1979.98

6. Brands, S.A.: Rethinking Public Key Infrastructures and Digital Certificates: Building in Privacy. MIT Press, Cambridge (2000)

7. Cachin, C., Kursawe, K., Lysyanskaya, A., Strobl, R.: Asynchronous verifiable secret sharing and proactive cryptosystems. In: Proceedings of the 9th ACM Conference on Computer and Communications Security, CCS 2002, pp. 88–97. ACM, New York (2002). https://doi.org/10.1145/586110.586124. http://doi.acm.org/10.1145/586110.586124

8. Catalano, D., Fiore, D.: Vector commitments and their applications. In: Kurosawa, K., Hanaoka, G. (eds.) PKC 2013. LNCS, vol. 7778, pp. 55–72. Springer, Heidelberg (2013). https://doi.org/10.1007/978-3-642-36362-7_5

9. Goldwasser, S., Micali, S.: Probabilistic encryption. J. Comput. Syst. Sci. **28**(2), 270–299 (1984). https://doi.org/10.1016/0022-0000(84)90070-9. http://www.sciencedirect.com/science/article/pii/0022000084900709

10. Groth, J.: Linear algebra with sub-linear zero-knowledge arguments. In: Halevi, S. (ed.) CRYPTO 2009. LNCS, vol. 5677, pp. 192–208. Springer, Heidelberg (2009). https://doi.org/10.1007/978-3-642-03356-8_12

11. Gupta, V.H., Gopinath, K.: g_{its}^2 VSR: an information theoretical secure verifiable secret redistribution protocol for long-term archival storage. In: Fourth International IEEE Security in Storage Workshop, pp. 22–33, September 2007. https://doi.org/10.1109/SISW.2007.11

12. Herzberg, A., Jarecki, S., Krawczyk, H., Yung, M.: Proactive secret sharing or: how to cope with perpetual leakage. In: Coppersmith, D. (ed.) CRYPTO 1995. LNCS, vol. 963, pp. 339–352. Springer, Heidelberg (1995). https://doi.org/10.1007/3-540-44750-4_27

13. Kate, A., Zaverucha, G.M., Goldberg, I.: Constant-size commitments to polynomials and their applications. In: Abe, M. (ed.) ASIACRYPT 2010. LNCS, vol. 6477, pp. 177–194. Springer, Heidelberg (2010). https://doi.org/10.1007/978-3-642-17373-8_11

14. Nikov, V., Nikova, S.: On proactive secret sharing schemes. In: Handschuh, H., Hasan, M.A. (eds.) SAC 2004. LNCS, vol. 3357, pp. 308–325. Springer, Heidelberg (2004). https://doi.org/10.1007/978-3-540-30564-4_22

15. Pedersen, T.P.: Non-interactive and information-theoretic secure verifiable secret sharing. In: Feigenbaum, J. (ed.) CRYPTO 1991. LNCS, vol. 576, pp. 129–140. Springer, Heidelberg (1992). https://doi.org/10.1007/3-540-46766-1_9

16. Sadeghi, A.-R., Steiner, M.: Assumptions related to discrete logarithms: why subtleties make a real difference. In: Pfitzmann, B. (ed.) EUROCRYPT 2001. LNCS, vol. 2045, pp. 244–261. Springer, Heidelberg (2001). https://doi.org/10.1007/3-540-44987-6_16

17. Schultz, D., Liskov, B., Liskov, M.: MPSS: mobile proactive secret sharing. ACM Trans. Inf. Syst. Secur. 13(4), 341–3432 (2010). https://doi.org/10.1145/1880022.1880028. http://doi.acm.org/10.1145/1880022.1880028

18. Shamir, A.: How to share a secret. Commun. ACM 22(11), 612–613 (1979). https://doi.org/10.1145/359168.359176. http://doi.acm.org/10.1145/359168.359176

19. Wong, T.M., Wang, C., Wing, J.M.: Verifiable secret redistribution for archive systems. In: Proceedings of the First International IEEE Security in Storage Workshop, pp. 94–105, December 2002. https://doi.org/10.1109/SISW.2002.1183515

20. Zhou, L., Schneider, F.B., Van Renesse, R.: APSS: proactive secret sharing in asynchronous systems. ACM Trans. Inf. Syst. Secur. 8(3), 259–286 (2005). https://doi.org/10.1145/1085126.1085127. http://doi.acm.org/10.1145/1085126.1085127

Secret Sharing Using Near-MDS Codes

Sanyam Mehta[2], Vishal Saraswat[1]([✉]), and Smith Sen[2]

[1] Robert Bosch Engineering and Business Solutions Pvt. Ltd. (RBEI/ESY),
Bangalore, India
vishal.saraswat@gmail.com
[2] Birla Institute of Technology and Science, Pilani, K. K. Birla Goa Campus,
Goa, India
{f20140526,f20140896}@goa.bits-pilani.ac.in

Abstract. We propose a generalized secret sharing scheme based on NMDS codes. The proposed scheme is efficient and the computational complexity for setup and reconstruction phase is only $O(n^3)$, where n is the number of participants. The scheme admits an access structure based on two mutually exclusive sets of participant combinations of sizes t and $t-1$ respectively. The parameter t for the access structure is independent of the field size. The proposed scheme is ideal and perfect and has desirable security features of cheating detection and cheater identification. We also provide a cryptanalysis of the $(t+1, n)$ threshold secret sharing scheme based on NMDS codes proposed in [12]. We show that their scheme is insecure and that there always exists a set of m participants, where $m < t+1$, which can reconstruct the secret.

Keywords: Secret sharing · Generalized access structure · MDS codes · Near-MDS codes

1 Introduction

Secret sharing schemes were independently proposed by Blakley[2] and Shamir[11] in 1979. The scheme by Shamir is based on linear algebra and the standard Lagrange's interpolation while the scheme given by Blakley is built upon the idea of finite geometries, particularly on the concept of intersection of hyperplanes. These were the first threshold secret sharing schemes which allowed a *secret s* to be split into n *shares* which could be distributed among n *participants* (or *users*), $\mathcal{P} = \{P_1, \ldots, P_n\}$, in such a way that for some threshold t, $1 \leq t \leq n$, any group of t or more participants could pool in their shares to *reconstruct* the secret but if the number of participants in a group is less than the threshold t, then that group does not get any extra information about the secret.

Note that a threshold secret sharing scheme makes the authorized sets rigid. Consider a hypothetical situation of a firm, where we have three levels of the workforce, namely, directors, managers and employees. To access the key for a

© Springer Nature Switzerland AG 2019
C. Carlet et al. (Eds.): C2SI 2019, LNCS 11445, pp. 195–214, 2019.
https://doi.org/10.1007/978-3-030-16458-4_12

certain new product launched, the firm does not want every employee to open up the locker. So naturally more power has to be given to the directors and managers than the employees. This in turn means, maybe less directors can pool their shares to find the secret. Comparatively more managers and even more employees should be required to find the secret. This type of flexibility is not directly possible with a threshold access structure.

To overcome the problems arising in the scenario above, Ito et al. [7] introduced the concept of a generalized access structure which contains all the possible sets of participants who can reconstruct the secret. They proposed a secret sharing scheme which admitted a generalized access structure irrespective of the size of each set. Every participant is assigned several shadows of a (t, n)-threshold secret sharing scheme by the dealer. For integers t, m and q satisfying $t \le m < q$, q being a prime power, the dealer

- samples $\alpha_1, \ldots, \alpha_{t-2}$ from GF(q) and α_{t-1} from GF$(q) - \{0\}$ and constructs $f(x) = s + \alpha_1 x + \alpha_2 x^2 + \cdots + \alpha_{t-1} x^{t-1}$, where the secret is $f(0) = s$.
- samples $x_1, \ldots, x_m$ from GF$(q) - \{0\}$ and computes $s_j = f(x_j)$ $(1 \le j \le m)$.
- chooses $S_i \subset \{(x_1, s_1), \ldots, (x_m, s_m)\}$ and assigns S_i to each participant P_i $(1 \le i \le |\mathcal{P}|)$.

In this scheme, the access structure Λ can be defined as the sets in which the union of all the shares of the participants has cardinality greater than t. In case the minimal subsets are big, this scheme turns out to be ineffective. At the same time, for this access structure, Shamir's Scheme gives each party a share equal to the size of the secret.

Later, Benaloh and Leichter [1] proposed a simpler and relatively efficient secret sharing scheme exploiting the *monotonicity* property of access structures in secret sharing schemes. The proposed scheme begins with multiple schemes for simple access structures and creates a scheme for composition of those access structures. Thus, the scheme by Benaloh and Leichter efficiently realizes every access structure that can be described by small monotone formula. Even though this construction is more efficient and generalizes the scheme proposed by Ito et al. [7], the length of shares become exponential in the number of parties.

All the above schemes were linear secret sharing schemes which can be modelled using *monotone span programs* [8]. These are essentially matrices describing a linear mapping of a linear scheme. These variations are very efficient to implement. Around the same time, the following advantages of using linear codes, instead of arbitrary matrices, for designing secret sharing schemes were observed.

- Easier to detect errors and easy transmission.
- Can be defined using a single generator matrix.
- Schemes were still efficient although features for verification and cheating detection and identification were included.

Some of such constructions are based on Maximum Distance Separable (MDS) matrices [10] where the dealer chooses an MDS matrix A of dimension $k \times n$ and a vector $\mathbf{v}$ of dimension $1 \times k$, and computes the codeword $\mathbf{v} \cdot A$ whose first element is the desired secret.

These schemes have been extensively used as they are easier to implement. It has been observed that NMDS matrices have better computational performance than MDS matrices. NMDS matrices require less storage than MDS matrices, do not require additional clock cycles and have sub-optimal branch numbers [9]. Some lightweight block ciphers have already been using NMDS matrices for their diffusion layer which includes ciphers like PRINCE, FIDES, PRIDE and MANTIS due to its benefits of low power, low energy and low latency in implementations. Due to all these, it will be useful to implement a secret sharing scheme using NMDS codes as well. The advantages of using NMDS codes for making a secret sharing scheme are as follows,

- Easy to implement and less space consuming
- Does not require additional clock cycles
- Difficult to identify the generator matrix of the code for an adversary
- Richer access structure than MDS secret sharing
- Has the property of cheating detection and identification like MDS secret sharing

Considering Shamir's secret sharing scheme, one can observe that a dishonest participant cannot find the secret by giving a wrong share but can misguide the honest participants by getting a wrong key which ultimately results in failure for the authorized set of participants to obtain the correct secret. Numerous solutions have been suggested in literature to solve this issue and retrieve the accurate secret. Some propose error correcting codes where a tampered share is treated as an error and is corrected using the error correcting property of code. While, some other propose to use a protocol where dealer validates individual shares in an authorized set to detect and rectify any tampering of shares. One plausible way is to use check vectors that dealer uses as certification for each participant. Some such schemes have been reviewed in Sect. 3.

Most of the initial secret sharing schemes had issues with trusted third parties (dealers and combiners) as well as cheating detection and identification. One of the modifications of Shamir's scheme for cheating detection and correction is proposed by Lein et al. in [5]. It is assumed that $m > t$ number of participants have to come up with their shares, where t is the threshold, giving the participants $\binom{m}{t}$ ways to pool their shares. For each way we get a degree $t - 1$ polynomial by interpolation which can be checked with the original polynomial. Participants who are present in the majority of groups and couldn't recover the same polynomial are grouped as possible cheaters and shares are corrected recursively unless there is no cheater left in the group of participants. They provide the algorithm for cheating detection and cheating correction by trading off the time and space-complexities for computing the secret to prevent cheating.

1.1 Organization

In this paper, we have introduced some essential definitions, problems and assumptions related to the scheme in Sect. 2. Further we have discussed in Sect. 3

some of the previous work done on secret sharing schemes formed using MDS (Maximum Distance Separable) and NMDS (Near-Maximum Distance Separable) codes. In Sect. 4, we have analyzed and discussed the shortcomings of the scheme proposed by Zhou et al. [12]. The proposed secret sharing scheme is presented in Sect. 5 and its security analyzed in Sect. 6. Finally, we provide a concrete instantiation of the proposed scheme in the Appendix A.

2 Preliminaries

The assignment operator is denoted by "$\leftarrow$". In particular, the operation of running a randomized or deterministic algorithm A with input x and storing the result to the variable y is denoted by $y \leftarrow A(x)$. The operation of choosing an element x of a set X randomly at uniform from X is denoted by $x \xleftarrow{\$} X$ and the operation of choosing an element x of X according to a distribution μ on a set X is denoted by $x \xleftarrow{\mu} X$. For a given function $f : N \rightarrow [0, 1]$ is said to be *negligible in n* if $f(n) < 1/p(n)$ for a polynomial p and having sufficiently large n.

2.1 Coding Theory

Definition 1 (Block Codes). *Let $\mathbb{A}^n$ be the set of all strings of length n over $\mathbb{A}$, where $\mathbb{A} = \{a_0, \ldots a_{q-1}\}$. Any nonempty subset $\mathbf{C}$ of $\mathbb{A}^n$ is called a q-ary block code of length n and each string in $\mathbf{C}$ is called a* codeword.

Definition 2 (Hamming Distance). *If $\mathbf{c}$ and $\mathbf{d}$ are two codewords of length n, the* hamming distance $d(\mathbf{c}, \mathbf{d})$ *is the number of positions at which $\mathbf{c}$ and $\mathbf{d}$ differ. The* hamming weight $d(\mathbf{c})$ *of a codeword $\mathbf{c} \in \mathbf{C}$ is defined to the number of its non-zero coordinate positions.*

Definition 3 (Minimum Distance). *The* minimum distance *of a code $\mathbf{C}$ is defined as*

$$d(\mathbf{C}) = \min_{\mathbf{c},\mathbf{d} \in \mathbf{C}} d(\mathbf{c}, \mathbf{d}).$$

Definition 4 (Linear Code). *A linear code, $\mathbf{L}$, of length n is a linear subspace of $\mathbb{F}_q^n$ where $\mathbb{F}_q = \mathrm{GF}(q)$ is the Galois Field of order $q = p^m$ for some prime p and power $m \geq 1$. If $\mathbf{L}$ has a dimension k, we say it is an $[n, k]$ code. Further, if its minimum distance is d, we say $\mathbf{L}$ is an $[n, k, d]$-code.*

Definition 5 (Generator Matrix). *A generator matrix, of a linear $[n, k, d]$ code, $\mathbf{L}$, is a $m \times n$ matrix, $m \geq k$, whose rows span $\mathbf{L}$. That is, every codeword $\mathbf{c} \in \mathbf{L}$ is a linear combination of the rows of the generator matrix, G, and for every $\mathbf{v} \in \mathbb{F}_q^m$, $\mathbf{v} \cdot G$ is a codeword in $\mathbf{L}$.*

Remark 1. For the purposes of this paper, we will assume that the number of rows in generator matrices is equal to the dimension of the code. That is, if G is a generator matrix of a linear $[n, k, d]$ code, $\mathbf{L}$, then G is a $k \times n$ matrix and its rows form a basis of $\mathbf{L}$.

Definition 6 (Standard Form of a Generator Matrix). *A generator matrix, G, of a linear $[n, k, d]$ code, $\mathbf{L}$, is said to be in the* standard form *if $G = [I_k \mid A]$, where I_k is the identity matrix of size $k \times k$ and A is a $k \times (n - k)$ matrix. For such G, the code $\mathbf{L}$ is said to* systematic *in its first k coordinate positions.*

Remark 2. Any $k \times (n-k)$ matrix, A, defines a linear $[n, k, d]$ code, $\mathbf{L}$, completely by defining the standard form of a generator matrix, $G = [I_k \mid A]$, for $\mathbf{L}$.

Definition 7 (Support of a Code). *Let $\mathbf{C}$ be a code over $\mathbb{F}_q$. The support, $\mathrm{Supp}(\mathbf{c})$, of a codeword $\mathbf{c} \in \mathbf{C}$ is defined to be the set of its non-zero coordinate positions. The support, $\mathrm{Supp}(\mathbf{C})$, of the code $\mathbf{C}$ is defined to be*

$$\mathrm{Supp}(\mathbf{C}) = \cup_{\mathbf{c} \in \mathbf{C}} \mathrm{Supp}(\mathbf{c}).$$

Definition 8 (Generalized Hamming Distance). *The minimum cardinality of the supports of the $[n, r]$-subcodes of $\mathbf{C}$, for $1 \leq r \leq k$, is called the rth generalized hamming distance $d_r \mathbf{C}$. That is,*

$$d_r \mathbf{C} = \min\{|\mathrm{Supp}\, \mathbf{D}| : \mathbf{D} \text{ is } [n, r]_q \text{ subcode of } \mathbf{C}\}.$$

Remark 3. Note that $d_1(\mathbf{C}) = d(\mathbf{C})$ is the Hamming Distance of $\mathbf{C}$.

Proposition 1 (Hierarchy of Hamming Weights). *For every linear $[n, k]_q$ code $\mathbf{C}$,*
$$0 < d_1(\mathbf{C}) < d_2(\mathbf{C}) < \cdots < d_k(\mathbf{C}) \leq n.$$

Definition 9 (The Singleton Bound). *The singleton bound states that any $[n, k, d]$-code must satisfy*
$$q^k \leq q^{n-d+1}.$$

In particular, $d \leq n + 1 - k$.

Definition 10 (The Generalized Singleton Bound). *The rth generalized singleton bound is given by $d_r(\mathbf{C})$*

$$d_r(\mathbf{C}) \leq n - k + r \text{ where } r = 1, 2, \ldots, k.$$

Definition 11 (Maximum Distance Separable Codes). *A linear $[n, k, n + 1 - k]$-code, that is, an $[n, k]$-code with largest possible minimum distance, is called a* maximum distance separable (MDS) *code.*

Proposition 2 (Properties of MDS Matrices). *Given an $[n, k, d]$ MDS code, $\mathbf{L}$, over $\mathbb{F}_q$, the accompanying explanations are proportionate.*

1. *If $G = [I_k \mid A]$ is a generator matrix of $\mathbf{L}$ in standard form, then every square submatrix of A is non-singular.*
2. *Any k columns of a generator matrix for $\mathbf{L}$ are linearly independent.*
3. *Any $n - k$ columns of a parity check matrix for $\mathbf{L}$ are linearly independent.*

Definition 12 Almost-MDS Codes). *The class of codes with $d_1(\mathbf{C}) = n - k$ are called* almost-MDS (AMDS) *codes.*

Definition 13 (Near-MDS Codes). *The class of codes with $d_1(\mathbf{C}) = n - k$ and $d_i(\mathbf{C}) = n - k + i$, for $i = 2, 3, \ldots, k$, are called* Near-MDS (NMDS) *codes. Equivalently, a code is NMDS if and only if $d_1(\mathbf{C}) = n - k$ and $d_1(\mathbf{C}^{\perp}) = k$.*

Proposition 3 (Properties of Near-MDS Matrices). *A linear $[n, k]$ code is Near-MDS if and only if its generator matrix satisfies the following conditions*

1. *Any $k - 1$ columns of the generator matrix are linearly independent.*
2. *Any $k + 1$ columns of the generator matrix are of rank k.*
3. *There exists a set of k linearly dependent columns in the generator matrix.*

2.2   Secret Sharing

A secret sharing scheme is a shared control scheme in which a *dealer* D splits a *secret s* into n shares $s_1, \ldots, s_n$ and distributes these to a set $\mathcal{P} = \{P_1, \ldots, P_n\}$ of n *participants* (or *users*) such that while certain *groups* of participants (subsets of $\mathcal{P}$) can reconstruct the secret from their shares (possibly by submitting their shares to a *combiner* C), others cannot.

Definition 14 (Access Structure). *An* access structure Λ *on a set of participants $\mathcal{P}$ is a subset of $2^{\mathcal{P}}$ such that sets in Λ can reconstruct the secret but sets not in Λ cannot. Elements of Λ are termed to be* authorized *sets while the sets not in Λ are called* unauthorized *sets.*

Definition 15 (Monotone Property). *A collection $\Lambda \subseteq 2^{\mathcal{P}}$ is called* monotone *if for all $\mathcal{A} \subseteq \mathcal{B} \subseteq \mathcal{P}$, if $\mathcal{A} \in \Lambda$ then $\mathcal{B} \in \Lambda$. In other words, if $\mathcal{A}$ is in the access structure Λ and $\mathcal{B}$ is a superset of $\mathcal{A}$ then $\mathcal{B}$ is also present in Λ.*

Definition 16 (Distribution Scheme). *A* distribution scheme, $\Pi_{\mathcal{P}, \mathcal{S}, \mathcal{R}, \mu}$, *with a domain of secrets $\mathcal{S}$, a set of strings $\mathcal{R}$ and a probability distribution μ on $\mathcal{R}$, is a system which on input a secret $s \in \mathcal{S}$, chooses a random string $r \xleftarrow{\mu} \mathcal{R}$ sampled in agreement with μ, and computes a vector of shares $\Pi_{\mathcal{P}, \mathcal{S}, \mathcal{R}, \mu}(s) = (s_1, \ldots, s_n)$, and communicates each share s_j to P_j via a secure channel.*

Definition 17 (Secret Sharing Scheme). *A* secret sharing scheme, $\Gamma_{\mathcal{P}, \mathcal{S}, \mathcal{R}, \mu, \Lambda}$, *is a distribution scheme $\Pi_{\mathcal{P}, \mathcal{S}, \mathcal{R}, \mu}$ along with a reconstruction function, RECON, realizing the access structure Λ.*

Remark 4. When any of $\mathcal{P}$, $\mathcal{S}$, $\mathcal{R}$, μ and Λ are clear from the context, we may not specify the respective subscripts in $\Pi_{\mathcal{P}, \mathcal{S}, \mathcal{R}, \mu}$ and $\Gamma_{\mathcal{P}, \mathcal{S}, \mathcal{R}, \mu, \Lambda}$.

Definition 18 (Threshold Secret Sharing Scheme). *If the access structure $\Lambda \subseteq 2^{\mathcal{P}}$ is defined by*

$$\mathcal{A} \in \Lambda \iff |\mathcal{A}| \geq t,$$

for some $t \in \{1, 2, \ldots, n\}$, then we call the secret sharing scheme a (t, n) threshold secret sharing scheme. That is, in a (t, n)-threshold secret sharing scheme, any set of at least t participants should be able to retrieve the secret but any set of $t - 1$ or less participants must not be able to find the secret.

Definition 19 (Generalized Secret Sharing Scheme). *If the access structure $\Lambda \subseteq 2^{\mathcal{P}}$ does not have restrictions such as in the case of threshold secret sharing schemes, then we call the secret sharing scheme a* generalized *secret sharing scheme.*

Definition 20 (Correctness). *A secret sharing scheme $\Gamma_{\mathcal{P},\mathcal{S},\mathcal{R},\mu,\Lambda}$ is said to be* correct *if the secret can be reconstructed by any authorized set of parties by pooling in their shares. That is, for the access structure Λ, for any set $\mathcal{A} \in \Lambda$, and for any key $s \in \mathcal{S}$, $\Pr[\mathsf{RECON}(\mathcal{A}) = s] = 1$.*

Definition 21 (Perfect Secret Sharing). *A secret sharing scheme is said to be* perfect *if, in information theoretic sense, an unauthorized set is unable to learn anything about the secret from their pool of shares. Formally, for every possible pair of secrets $a, b \in \mathcal{S}$, for any set $\mathcal{A} \notin \Lambda$ and a vector of shares $\langle s_j \rangle_{P_j \in \mathcal{A}}$,*

$$\Pr[\Pi(a,r)_{\mathcal{A}} = \langle s_j \rangle_{P_j \in \mathcal{A}}] = \Pr[\Pi(b,r)_{\mathcal{A}} = \langle s_j \rangle_{P_j \in \mathcal{A}}]$$

That is, the probability of finding a secret by an unauthorized set is equivalent to the probability of finding the secret randomly from the set of secrets $\mathcal{S}$.

Definition 22 (Information Rate). *The* information rate, ρ, *of a secret sharing scheme is the ratio between the length of the secret to that of the shares which will be allocated to the participants. That is, if $\mathcal{S}$ is the set of all possible secrets and $\mathcal{T}$ is the set of all possible shares, then*

$$\rho = \frac{\log |\mathcal{S}|}{\log |\mathcal{T}|}.$$

Definition 23 (Ideal Secret Sharing Scheme). *A secret sharing scheme is said to be* ideal *if the key space and the share space are same. More specifically, a scheme is considered to be ideal if information rate is equal to one, that is, the maximum possible value of ρ.*

Definition 24 (Linear Secret Sharing Scheme). *A secret sharing scheme Γ is called* linear *over $\mathrm{GF}(q)$, if there exists a matrix $G \in \mathrm{GF}(q)^{k \times n}$ and a vector $\mathbf{v} = (v_0, v_1, \ldots, v_{k-1}) \in \mathrm{GF}(q)^k$, such that $\mathbf{v} \cdot G = (s_0, s_1, \ldots, s_{n-1})$ gives the vector of shares.*

Definition 25 (Cheating Detection). *In the secret reconstruction phase of the scheme, when a participant or group of participants, $\mathcal{A}_c$, give wrong share(s), an authorized set might fail to retrieve the secret, or an unauthorized set might be able to find the secret. The security against such kind of attacks is known as* cheating detection.

Definition 26 (Cheater Identification). *If any participant P_i produces an incorrect share $s_i' \neq s_i$ during the reconstruction phase of the secret, then with the error probability of ϵ, P_i will be identified as a cheater and will be put in the set of cheaters $\mathcal{A}_c$. This is known as* cheater identification. *Cheater identification claims that the error probability ϵ is negligible.*

3   Related Work

In this section, we review the secret sharing scheme proposed by Zhou et al. [12] which is based on NMDS (Near-Maximum Distance Separable) codes. To the best of our knowledge, this is the first scheme based on NMDS codes. The scheme claims to be perfect and have an access structure such that at least k participants must come together to construct the secret. Unfortunately, the claims are not correct as we show in Sect. 4.

3.1   Share Construction

In this scheme, the dealer constructs the shares for each participant by selecting a generator matrix G of an $[n+1, k, n+1-k]$ NMDS code and a random vector $\mathbf{v} = (v_0, v_1, \ldots, v_{k-1})$ of length k. Using the vector, the dealer calculates the codeword $(s_0, s_1, \ldots, s_n)$ by multiplying $\mathbf{v}$ and G. That is,

$$(s_0, s_1, \ldots, s_n) = (v_0, v_1, \ldots, v_{k-1}) \cdot G.$$

Here s_0 is considered as the secret and s_i's are the shares of participants P_i's, where $1 \leq i \leq n$.

3.2   Secret Reconstruction

The reconstruction of the secret is based on the property of NMDS matrices that in a generator matrix of a NMDS code any $k + 1$ columns have rank k.

Let $P_{j_0}, P_{j_1}, \ldots, P_{j_{m-1}}$, $m > k$, be the participants who come together to find the secret. They pool their shares forming the codeword $(s_{j_0}, s_{j_1}, \ldots, s_{j_{m-1}})$ and construct the corresponding submatrix

$$G' = (\mathbf{g}_{j_0}, \mathbf{g}_{j_1}, \ldots, \mathbf{g}_{j_{m-1}})$$

where $\mathbf{g}_{j_i}$ is the $(j_i + 1)$th column of the matrix G.

Since G is an NMDS matrix and $m \geq k+1$, the submatrix G' is of full rank, the system of linear equations

$$(s_{j_0}, s_{j_2}, \ldots, s_{j_{m-1}}) = (v_0, v_1, \ldots, v_{k-1}) \cdot G'$$

can be uniquely solved for $(v_0, v_1, \ldots, v_{k-1})$.

Then the secret s_0 can be calculated as $\mathbf{s}[0]$ where

$$\mathbf{s} = (v_0, v_1, \ldots, v_{k-1}) \cdot \mathbf{g}_{0G}$$

where $\mathbf{g}_{0G}$ is the first column of G.

Algorithm 1. Secret Reconstruction for the Secret Sharing Scheme in [12]

Input: Generator matrix G, number of participants m, collected set of shares
1: **if** $(m < k + 1)$ **then return** "The secret cannot be recovered!" **end if**
2: $G' \leftarrow$ [columns of G corresponding to first $k + 1$ shares available]
3: $G' \leftarrow$ [first k linearly independent column vectors of G']
4: $(s_{j_0}, s_{j_1}, \ldots, s_{j_{k-1}}) \leftarrow$ [shares corresponding to the columns of G']
5: $(v_0, v_1, \ldots, v_{k-1}) \leftarrow (s_{j_0}, s_{j_1}, \ldots, s_{j_{k-1}}) \cdot (G')^{-1}$
6: $\mathbf{s} \leftarrow (v_0, v_1, \ldots, v_{k-1}) \cdot G'$
7: **secret** $\leftarrow \mathbf{s}[0]$

Output: Secret **secret**

---

4 Attack on the Scheme in [12]

It has been stated in [12] that the scheme is ideal and perfect. This scheme is also claimed to have security characterization of cheating detection and cheating verification. However, we show that the scheme is not perfect and will show that there exist unauthorized sets of participants, that is, sets with k or less number of participants who are able to reconstruct the secret. Since the rank of the submatrix formed using any $k + 1$ columns in an $[n + 1, k, n + 1 - k]$ NMDS matrix is k, there will also exist k participants among the given $k + 1$ participants, who can generate the secret independently. In fact, we show that there may exist sets of only $k - 1$ participants who can generate the secret.

As an illustration of the flaw, we give an instantiation of the scheme formed using the $[12, 6, 6]$ NMDS matrix G in $\mathbb{F}_5$, given in [4].

$$G = \begin{bmatrix} 1 & 0 & 0 & 0 & 0 & 0 & 1 & 1 & 1 & 1 & 1 & 1 \\ 0 & 1 & 0 & 0 & 0 & 0 & 4 & 2 & 0 & 3 & 1 & 2 \\ 0 & 0 & 1 & 0 & 0 & 0 & 1 & 3 & 1 & 0 & 2 & 2 \\ 0 & 0 & 0 & 1 & 0 & 0 & 2 & 4 & 4 & 3 & 3 & 2 \\ 0 & 0 & 0 & 0 & 1 & 0 & 4 & 1 & 2 & 1 & 3 & 2 \\ 0 & 0 & 0 & 0 & 0 & 1 & 0 & 1 & 4 & 2 & 4 & 2 \end{bmatrix}.$$

According to the given scheme, the minimum number of participants in an authorized set is 7 since $k + 1 = 7$. The secret corresponds to the first column. If we denote the $(i+1)$th row by $\mathbf{r}_i$, then a codeword formed from a $[n+1, k, n+1-k]$ NMDS matrix is of the form $\alpha_0 \mathbf{r}_0 + \alpha_1 \mathbf{r}_1 + \cdots + \alpha_{k-1} \mathbf{r}_{k-1}$ where the secret is α_0. Therefore, the codeword $\mathbf{s}$ formed from the matrix G is

$$\mathbf{s} = (\alpha_0, \alpha_1, \alpha_2, \alpha_3, \alpha_4, \alpha_5,$$
$$\alpha_0 + 4\alpha_1 + \alpha_2 + 2\alpha_3 + 4\alpha_4,$$
$$\alpha_0 + 2\alpha_1 + 3\alpha_2 + 4\alpha_3 + \alpha_4 + \alpha_5,$$
$$\alpha_0 + \alpha_2 + 4\alpha_3 + 2\alpha_4 + 4\alpha_5,$$
$$\alpha_0 + 3\alpha_1 + 3\alpha_3 + \alpha_4 + 2\alpha_5,$$
$$\alpha_0 + \alpha_1 + 2\alpha_2 + 3\alpha_3 + 3\alpha_4 + 4\alpha_5,$$
$$\alpha_0 + 2\alpha_1 + 2\alpha_2 + 2\alpha_3 + 2\alpha_4 + 2\alpha_5).$$

Share Reconstruction with only 6 Participants: $\{P_1, P_2, P_3, P_4, P_5, P_7\}$.

The row reduced form of the columns corresponding to these participants is

$$G' = \begin{bmatrix} 1 & 0 & 0 & 0 & 0 & 0 & 3 \\ 0 & 1 & 0 & 0 & 0 & 0 & 2 \\ 0 & 0 & 1 & 0 & 0 & 0 & 1 \\ 0 & 0 & 0 & 1 & 0 & 0 & 4 \\ 0 & 0 & 0 & 0 & 1 & 0 & 4 \\ 0 & 0 & 0 & 0 & 0 & 1 & 1 \end{bmatrix}$$

where the last column corresponds to the secret, that is the first column of G.

Note that, if $\mathbf{g}_i$ denotes the $(i+1)$th column of G', then $\mathbf{g}_0 = 3\mathbf{g}_1 + 2\mathbf{g}_2 + \mathbf{g}_3 + 4\mathbf{g}_4 + 4\mathbf{g}_5 + \mathbf{g}_7$. Therefore the shares corresponding to these columns also satisfy the same equation, that is, $\alpha_0 = 3\alpha_1 + 2\alpha_2 + \alpha_3 + 4\alpha_4 + 4\alpha_5 + \alpha_7$ where $\alpha_7 = \alpha_0 + 2\alpha_1 + 3\alpha_2 + 4\alpha_3 + \alpha_4 + \alpha_5$. Therefore, the secret α_0 can be recovered by the given set of 6 participants.

Share Reconstruction with only 5 Participants: $\{P_1, P_2, P_3, P_4, P_6\}$.

The row reduced form of the columns corresponding to these participants is

$$G' = \begin{bmatrix} 1 & 0 & 0 & 0 & 0 & 1 \\ 0 & 1 & 0 & 0 & 0 & 4 \\ 0 & 0 & 1 & 0 & 0 & 3 \\ 0 & 0 & 0 & 1 & 0 & 1 \\ 0 & 0 & 0 & 0 & 1 & 1 \\ 0 & 0 & 0 & 0 & 0 & 0 \end{bmatrix}.$$

where the last column corresponds to the secret, that is the first column of G.

Note that, here $\mathbf{g}_0 = \mathbf{g}_1 + 4\mathbf{g}_2 + 3\mathbf{g}_3 + \mathbf{g}_4 + \mathbf{g}_6$. Therefore the shares corresponding to these columns also satisfy the same equation, that is, $\alpha_0 = \alpha_1 + 4\alpha_2 + 3\alpha_3 + \alpha_4 + \alpha_6$ where $\alpha_6 = \alpha_0 + 4\alpha_1 + \alpha_2 + 2\alpha_3 + 4\alpha_4$. Therefore, the secret α_0 can be recovered by the given set of 5 participants.

Finally, we observe that, for any secret sharing scheme constructed as in [12], the secret can also be constructed with k or, sometimes even, $k-1$ participants. Thus the mentioned scheme cannot be a perfect secret sharing scheme.

5   Proposed Secret Sharing Scheme

5.1   Motivation for the Scheme

It is observed that according to [12], the minimum number of participants required to find the secret is $k+1$. But in most of the cases, the secret can also be found with either k participants or with $k-1$ participants. This motivates us to make a more generalized access structure for secret sharing scheme based on the properties of Near-MDS matrices which is vaster and has a rich access structure.

5.2   Access Structure

The formation of the access structure is based on the design and properties of the near-MDS matrix [3,4] and is on similar lines as proposed in [12]. Let

$$G = \begin{bmatrix} G[0] & G[1] & \dots & G[k-1] & G[k] & \dots & G[n] \end{bmatrix}$$

be a generator matrix of an $[n+1, k, n+1-k]$ NMDS code over $\mathbb{F}_q$ such that $\mathbf{g}_{iG} := \mathbf{g}_i := G[i] \in \mathbb{F}_q^k$, $0 \leq i \leq n$, is the ith column of G. We assume that G is in the standard form, that is, $G = \begin{bmatrix} I_k \mid A_{k \times (n+1-k)} \end{bmatrix}$.

As noted in [3], since $G[0], G[1], \dots, G[k-1]$ are linearly independent, for all i, $0 \leq i \leq n-k$, there exist $a_j \in \mathbb{F}_q$, such that

$$G[k+i] = \sum_{j=0}^{k-1} a_j G[j].$$

The access structure for the scheme has the monotonicity property and can be defined with the help of two mutually exclusive sets, namely *Group I* and *Group II*. If G is the generator matrix for the scheme, with the first column of G corresponding to the secret and rest of the columns corresponding to the shares of the participants, then the groups can be defined as follows:

Group I consists of all $k-1$-tuples of participants whose corresponding columns in G, along with the first column, form k-linearly dependent columns.

Group II consists of all k-tuples of participants which aren't a superset of a $k-1$-tuple in *Group I*, and their corresponding columns in G are linearly independent.

Let us denote this access structure with Λ_0. Note that due to its monotonicity property, any k participants whose corresponding columns in G are linearly independent as well as any $k+1$ or more participants are authorized to recover the secret. Moreover, Λ_0 has two special groups, namely, *Group I* which needs just $k-1$ participants to generate the secret and *Group II* which need just k participants to generate the secret and no more. This scheme is not a threshold secret sharing scheme but has a more generalized access structure.

5.3   Share Construction

The codeword $(s_0, s_1, \dots, s_n)$ is formed by multiplying G by a chosen vector $(\alpha_0, \alpha_1, \dots, \alpha_{k-1})$ of length k.

$$(s_0, s_1, \dots, s_n) = (\alpha_0, \alpha_1, \dots, \alpha_{k-1}) \cdot G.$$

Here, s_0 forms the secret and rest of the s_i's corresponds to the shares of the participants. Let us denote this distribution algorithm by Π.

Algorithm 2. Pseudocode for Π

Input: Standard Near-MDS Generator matrix G, Secret s_0, Random field element generator $\mathcal{R}$

1: $\alpha[0] \leftarrow s_0$
2: **for** $(i \leftarrow 1; i < k; i \leftarrow i+1)$ **do**
3:     $\alpha[i] \leftarrow \mathcal{R}$
4: **end for**
5: $\mathbf{s} \leftarrow \alpha \cdot G$

Output: Vector $\mathbf{s}$ containing the secret s_0 and the shares $s_1, \ldots, s_n$.

5.4   Secret Reconstruction

The reconstruction of the secret is similar to the way proposed in [12]. Given a set of m participants $\mathcal{A} = \{P_{j_0}, P_{j_1}, \ldots, P_{j_{m-1}}\} \in \Lambda_0$ and their pooled shares forming the *pooled codeword* $\mathsf{pcw} = (s_{j_0}, s_{j_1}, \ldots, s_{j_{m-1}})$, the secret can be reconstructed as follows:

1. Find the submatrix G' corresponding to the shares of the participants, such that $G' = (\mathbf{g}_{j_0}, \mathbf{g}_{j_1}, \ldots, \mathbf{g}_{j_{m-1}}, \mathbf{g}_{0G})$, where $\mathbf{g}_{0G}$ is the first and $\mathbf{g}_{j_i}$ is the $(j_i + 1)$th column of the matrix G.
2. Reduce G' using elementary row operations to make its k (or m, whichever is minimum) rows and columns, an identity matrix and get the modified column $\mathbf{g}'_{0G}$ corresponding to the secret.
3. If $m = k-1$, multiply the pooled codeword $\mathsf{pcw} = (s_{j_0}, s_{j_1}, \ldots, s_{j_{m-1}}, 0)$. Else, multiply its sub-codeword $(s_{j_0}, s_{j_1}, \ldots, s_{j_{k-1}})$ to $\mathbf{g}'_{0G}$ to obtain the secret. Here, $\mathbf{g}_i$'s corresponds to the k columns forming an identity matrix.

Algorithm 3. Pseudocode for RECON

Input: The pooled set of m shares from $\mathcal{A}$

1: **if** $(m < k - 1)$ **then return** "Unauthorized set!" **end if**
2: $G_\mathcal{A} \leftarrow [$ columns of G corresponding to the available shares $]$
3: $G' \leftarrow [G_\mathcal{A} \mid G[0]]$ (where $G[0]$ denotes the first column of G)
4: $G' \leftarrow$ reduced row echelon form of G'
5: **if** $(m = k - 1)$ **then**
6:     **if** $(\mathrm{rank}(G') = k)$ **then return** "Unauthorized set!"
7:     **else** $\mathsf{pcw} \leftarrow [$ shares related to $k - 1$ columns of $G' \mid 0]$ **end if**
8: **else if** $(m = k$ and $\mathrm{rank}(G) = k - 1)$ **then return** "Unauthorized set!"
9: **else** $\mathsf{pcw} \leftarrow [$ shares corresponding to k columns of G' forming identity matrix $]$
10: **end if**
11: $\mathbf{s} \leftarrow \mathsf{pcw} \cdot G'[m - 1]$
12: **secret** $\leftarrow \mathbf{s}[0]$

Output: Secret **secret**

6   Analysis of the Proposed Scheme

Lemma 1. *Given k linearly dependent columns in an $[n+1, k, n+1-k]$ NMDS matrix, each of the remaining $n + 1 - k$ columns will be linearly independent of them.*

Proof. From Property 3 of NMDS matrices, we know that any $k + 1$ columns have rank k. Since the given k columns are linearly dependent, we can write

$$\mathbf{g}_j = \sum_{i=0, i \neq j}^{k-1} a_i \mathbf{g}_i, \text{ not all } a_i = 0 \text{ and } 0 \leq j \leq k - 1.$$

Now, for a column $\mathbf{g}_l$ of the matrix, let's consider $\mathbf{g}_l$ along with given the k columns, $\mathbf{g}_0, \mathbf{g}_1, \dots, \mathbf{g}_{k-1}$. Assuming that $\mathbf{g}_l$ is linearly dependent on given k columns, that is,

$$\mathbf{g}_l = \sum_{i=0}^{k-1} b_i \mathbf{g}_i, \text{ not all } b_i = 0.$$

Substituting the value of $\mathbf{g}_j$, we get

$$\mathbf{g}_l = \sum_{i=0, i \neq j}^{k-1} (a_i + b_i) \mathbf{g}_i, \text{ not all } a_i = 0, \text{ not all } b_i = 0 \text{ and } 0 \leq j \leq k - 1.$$

Note that, the above equation makes $\mathbf{g}_l$ a linear combination of $k-1$ columns. Since both $\mathbf{g}_j$ and $\mathbf{g}_l$ can be expressed as a linear combination of rest of the $k-1$ columns, it makes the rank of these $k + 1$ columns equal to $k - 1$. But, since the rank of these $k + 1$ columns formed needs to be k, our assumption is wrong and $\mathbf{g}_j$ is linearly independent from the given k columns.

Lemma 2. *In the secret sharing scheme Γ_0 on the access structure Λ_0, if a k-participant tuple $\mathcal{A}$ is a superset of a Group I tuple, then columns corresponding to $\mathcal{A}$ will have rank k.*

Proof. Note that, the $k - 1$ columns corresponding to a *Group I* tuple along with the secret's column form k linearly dependent columns. Now, because of Lemma 1, any other column of the matrix will be linearly independent of these k columns and thus, linearly independent of the $k - 1$ columns corresponding to rest $k-1$ participants in $\mathcal{A}$. Therefore, columns corresponding to the participants in $\mathcal{A}$ will have rank k.

Contrapositive: If a set of columns corresponding to k participant tuple $\mathcal{A}$ does not have rank k, then it cannot be a superset of any *Group I* tuple.

Proposition 4. *There exists an unauthorized tuple of $k - 1$ participants.*

Proof. Let us take a tuple $\mathcal{A} = \{P_{j_1}, \ldots, P_{j_{k-1}}\} \in$ *Group I.* By definition, the column corresponding to the secret $\mathbf{g}_0$ is linearly dependent on the $k-1$ columns $\{\mathbf{g}_{j_1}, \mathbf{g}_{j_2}, \ldots, \mathbf{g}_{j_{k-1}}\}$ corresponding to the participants.

Now we will replace one of the participants P_{j_x} in $\mathcal{A}$ with the participant P_{j_y} from rest of the participants. As a result, from Lemma 1, the column $\mathbf{g}_{j_y}$ is linearly independent from the columns $\{\mathbf{g}_0, \mathbf{g}_{j_1}, \ldots, \mathbf{g}_{j_{x-1}}, \mathbf{g}_{j_{x+1}}, \ldots \mathbf{g}_{j_{k-1}}\}$ as well, therefore the secret's column $\mathbf{g}_0$ will also be linearly independent of the new $k-1$ columns, that is, $\{\mathbf{g}_{j_1}, \ldots, \mathbf{g}_{j_{x-1}}, \mathbf{g}_{j_{x+1}}, \mathbf{g}_{j_{k-1}}, \mathbf{g}_{j_y}\}$. Thus, we have constructed an unauthorized set $\mathcal{A}' = \{P_{j_1}, \ldots, P_{j_{x-1}}, P_{j_{x+1}}, \ldots P_{j_{k-1}}, P_{j_y}\}$ consisting of $k-1$ participants.

Proposition 5. *There exists an unauthorized tuple of k participants.*

Proof. From Lemma 1, we know that taking any k linearly dependent columns $\{\mathbf{g}_{j_1}, \mathbf{g}_{j_2}, \ldots, \mathbf{g}_{j_k}\}$, the secret's column $\mathbf{g}_0$ will be linearly independent from them. Thus, the k participants $\{P_{j_1}, \ldots, P_{j_k}\}$ form an unauthorized set.

Theorem 1. *The secret sharing scheme Γ_0 on the access structure Λ_0 is a linear secret sharing scheme.*

Proof. We know that the multiplication by a matrix is a linear operation. From the definition of linearity and construction of the scheme we can conclude that the proposed scheme is linear secret sharing scheme.

Theorem 2. *The secret sharing scheme Γ_0 on the access structure Λ_0 is correct, that is, every authorized set $\mathcal{A}$ in Λ_0 can correctly generate the secret.*

Proof. Let $s_1, \ldots, s_m$ be the shares of the participants in $\mathcal{A}$, and s_0 be the secret.

Case 1: $\mathcal{A}$ is from *Group I*: Note that, the column in G corresponding to the secret s_0 is linearly dependent to the columns corresponding to the participants in $\mathcal{A}$. Therefore, the algorithm of RECON can row reduce the columns to find the coefficients a_i's such that $s_0 = a_1 s_1 + a_2 s_2 + \ldots a_{k-1} s_{k-1}$ and find the secret s_0.

Case 2: $\mathcal{A}$ is from *Group II*: Since participants in $\mathcal{A}$ have linearly independent k columns in G, every other column including the secret's column will be linearly dependent on these k columns. Thus, RECON can row reduce the columns to recover the secret s_0.

Case 3: $\mathcal{A}$ forms a superset of a tuple in *Group I* or *Group I*: Note that if $\mathcal{A}$ is a superset of a tuple from *Group I*, then from Lemma 2, the participants in $\mathcal{A}$ have k linearly independent columns in G. Otherwise, if $\mathcal{A}$ is a superset of a tuple from *Group II*, then since the number of participants is greater than or equal to $k+1$, from Property 3 there exist k linearly independent columns in G corresponding to the participants. Therefore, in both the instances the algorithm RECON will row reduce the columns in a similar way as Case 2 and find the secret s_0. Hence, if $\mathcal{A}$ is an authorized set, then $\Pr[\text{RECON}(\mathcal{A}) = s_0] = 1$ and from Definition 20, the secret sharing scheme $Gamma_0$ is correct.

Proposition 6. *The complexity of the scheme for setup and secret reconstruction phase is of $\mathcal{O}(n^3)$.*

Proof. Note that the algorithm of RECON requires the matrix to be reduced in a reduced row echelon form. This operation is the most complex section of the RECON. Since the number of participants is less than n, the algorithm requires row reduction of an $(k \times n)$ matrix. We know that reduced row echelon form of an $(k \times n)$ matrix requires $\mathcal{O}(k^2 n)$ operations. Since $k \leq n$, the complexity of the reconstruction algorithm RECON is $\mathcal{O}(n^3)$.

Theorem 3. *The secret sharing scheme Γ_0 on the access structure Λ_0 is ideal.*

Proof. Note that both the secret and the shares belong to $\mathrm{GF}(q)$. Therefore, the information rate ρ is

$$\rho = \frac{\log |\mathrm{GF}(q)|}{\log |\mathrm{GF}(q)|} = 1$$

Hence, from Definition 22 of the ideal secret sharing scheme, Γ_0 is ideal.

Theorem 4. *The secret sharing scheme Γ_0 on the access structure Λ_0 is a perfect secret sharing scheme.*

Proof. Let an unauthorized set $\mathcal{A}$ of m participants come together to construct the secret. Note that, since the secret $s_0 \in \mathrm{GF}(q)$, the probability of anyone randomly finding the secret is $1/q$.

Case 1: $m \leq k-2$: Note that columns in G corresponding to these m participants along with the secret's column form less than $k+1$ columns which are linearly independent because of Property 1. Therefore they cannot form the secret s_0 on their own, that is, RECON($\mathcal{A}$) $\neq s_0$. Thus they will need at least one more share to form an authorized set. If they forge one share, the probability of them finding the secret is equal to the probability of them forging a correct secret which is again $1/q$ since the shares also belong to $\mathrm{GF}(q)$. This makes the probability of $\mathcal{A}$ finding the secret greater than or equal to $1/q$.

Case 2: $m = k-1$: Note that since $\mathcal{A}$ is unauthorized, from Lemma 2 we can say that $\mathcal{A}$ does not belong to *Group I*. This implies that the secret's column is linearly independent from the corresponding columns in $\mathcal{A}$ and therefore the participants cannot form the secret s_0 with no additional information. They will need to either forge at least one more share or replace one pooled share with a forged share to form an authorized set. Therefore, the probability of $\mathcal{A}$ finding the secret follows from Case 1 and is at least $1/q$.

Case 3: $m = k$: Since $\mathcal{A}$ is an unauthorized tuple and thus not in *Group II* or a superset of a tuple in *Group I*, from the contrapositive of Lemma 2 we know that columns corresponding to the participants in $\mathcal{A}$ are linearly dependent and the secret's column is linearly independent of these columns. Therefore, in a similar way as Case 2, they also need to either forge one more share or replace one share of their own participant with a forged share to form an authorized set, and the probability of $\mathcal{A}$ finding the secret follows.

Note that, when giving a set of shares as an input to RECON, the probability of RECON generating some other secret $\overline{s_0}$ from the set of secrets $\mathcal{S}$ is $1/q$. That is so because as mentioned in [9], NMDS matrices have a high diffusion property. Therefore, whenever a vector $\mathbf{v} \in \mathrm{GF}(q)^k$ is multiplied to its submatrix, the output generated is uniformly distributed. Therefore,

$$\Pr[\mathsf{RECON}(\mathcal{A}) = s_0] = \Pr[\mathsf{RECON}(\mathcal{A}) = \overline{s_0}].$$

Hence, from Definition 21, no unauthorized set can learn anything about the secret, and the secret sharing scheme Γ_0 is a perfect secret sharing scheme.

6.1   Cheating Detection and Cheating Identification

The proofs for the safety features of cheating detection and cheater identification for the secret sharing scheme Γ_0 are adopted from [12].

We require the following property of linear codes [6] in this work.

Lemma 3. *Let $\mathbf{C}$ be an $[n, k, d]$ linear code over $\mathbb{F}_q$. For any i, $1 \leq i \leq n$, let $\mathbf{C}^\star$ be the code formed by removing the ith coordinate from all codewords of $\mathbf{C}$.*

- *If $d > 1$, $\mathbf{C}^\star$ is an $[n-1, k, d^\star]$ code where $d^\star = d - 1$ if $\mathbf{C}$ has a minimum weight codeword with a nonzero ith coordinate and $d^\star = d$ otherwise.*
- *If $d = 1$, $\mathbf{C}^\star$ is an $[n-1, k, 1]$ code if $\mathbf{C}$ has no codeword of weight 1 whose nonzero entry is in coordinate i.*
- *Otherwise, if $k > 1$, $\mathbf{C}^\star$ is an $[n-1, k-1, d^\star]$ code with $d^\star \geq 1$.*

Remark 5. Note that, the minimum distance between two codewords in $\mathbf{C}^\star$ is at least $d - 1$.

Lemma 4. *Given an $[n+1, k, n+1-k]$ NMDS code with generator matrix G, if*

$$\mathbf{s} = (s_0, s_1, \ldots, s_n) = (\alpha_0, \alpha_1, \ldots, \alpha_{k-1}) \cdot G$$
$$\text{and } \mathbf{s'} = (s'_0, s'_1, \ldots, s'_n) = (\alpha'_0, \alpha'_1, \ldots, \alpha'_{k-1}) \cdot G$$

such that $(\alpha_0, \alpha_1, \ldots, \alpha_{k-1}) \neq (\alpha'_0, \alpha'_1, \ldots, \alpha'_{k-1})$, then

$$d((s_0, s_1, \ldots, s_n), (s'_0, s'_1, \ldots, s'_n)) \geq n + 1 - k.$$

Proof. Since $(\alpha_0, \alpha_1, \ldots, \alpha_{k-1})$ and $(\alpha'_0, \alpha'_1, \ldots, \alpha'_{k-1})$ form different codewords of the NMDS code, the hamming distance between $\mathbf{s}$ and $\mathbf{s'}$ would be greater than or equal to the minimum distance of the code, that is, $n + 1 - k$.

We prove the following results for the secret sharing scheme Γ_0 by applying the same method as in [10].

Theorem 5. *The secret sharing scheme Γ_0 on the access structure Λ_0 has the security characterization of cheating detection when the cheaters are less than $m - k$ where m is the number of active participants.*

Proof. Assume that $P_{j_1}, \ldots, P_{j_m}$ submit their modified shares $s_{j_i}^* = s_{j_i} + \delta_i$, $\delta_i \in \mathrm{GF}(q)$, $1 \leq i \leq m$ to the recovery algorithm. Note that P_{j_i} is honest if and only if $\delta_i = 0$, otherwise he is a cheater. Now consider the $k \times m$ submatrix G' consisting m columns of G, indexed by $j_1, j_2, \ldots j_m$ and let

$$\mathbf{D} = \{(s_1, \ldots, s_m) \mid (s_1, \ldots, s_m) = (\alpha_0, \alpha_1, \ldots, \alpha_{k-1}) \cdot G', \ \alpha_i \in \mathrm{GF}(q)\}.$$

Let $\mathbf{s} = (s_{j_1}, \ldots, s_{j_m})$, $\mathbf{d} = (\delta_1, \ldots, \delta_m)$ and $\mathbf{s}^* = \mathbf{s} + \mathbf{d}$. From Lemma 3, any two distinct shares in $\mathbf{D}$ have a Hamming distance of at least $m - k$. Hence, if $d(\mathbf{d}) = d(\mathbf{s}, \mathbf{s}^*) < m - k$, then $\mathbf{s}^* \in \mathbf{D}$ if and only if $\mathbf{s}^* = \mathbf{s}$, that is, when $\mathbf{d} = 0$. Therefore cheating can be detected if the cheaters are less than $m - k$.

Theorem 6. *In the secret sharing scheme Γ_0 on the access structure Λ_0 cheaters can be identified when their number is less than $\lfloor \frac{m-k}{2} \rfloor$.*

Proof. Using the same notations as in the previous proof let $\mathbf{s} = (s_{j_1}, \ldots, s_{j_m})$, $\mathbf{d} = (\delta_1, \ldots, \delta_m)$ and $\mathbf{s}^* = \mathbf{s} + \mathbf{d}$. Now, if $d(\mathbf{d}) < \lfloor \frac{m-k}{2} \rfloor$, then for $\mathbf{s}' \in \mathbf{D}$, we have the following relation when $\mathbf{s}' \neq \mathbf{s}$

$$d(\mathbf{s}^*, \mathbf{s}') \geq d(\mathbf{s}^*, \mathbf{s}) + d(\mathbf{s}, \mathbf{s}') \geq (m - k) - \left\lfloor \frac{m-k}{2} \right\rfloor = \left\lceil \frac{m-k}{2} \right\rceil.$$

Since $d(\mathbf{s}^*, \mathbf{s}) = \lfloor \frac{m-k}{2} \rfloor$, we get $d(\mathbf{s}^*, \mathbf{s}) = \min\{d(\mathbf{s}^*, \mathbf{s}') \mid \mathbf{s}' \in \mathbf{D}\}$. By decoding $\mathbf{s}^*$ to $\mathbf{s}$ using error decoding algorithms of linear codes and deriving $\mathbf{d} = \mathbf{s}^* - \mathbf{s}$, we can say that the participant P_{j_i} is a cheater if $\delta_i \neq 0$. Therefore when the number of cheaters is less than $\lfloor \frac{m-k}{2} \rfloor$, the secret can be recovered successfully, and the cheaters can be identified.

Acknowledgements. This work has been partially supported by DST-FIST Level-1 Program, Grant No. SR/FST/MSI-092/2013. The authors would like to thank Department of Mathematics, BITS Goa, R. C. Bose Centre for Cryptology and Security, ISI Kolkata, and Indian Institute of Technology, Jammu, for their support.

A   An Instantiation of the Proposed Scheme

Consider the following NMDS matrix G having elements over $\mathbb{F}_5$, as mentioned in [4].

$$G = \begin{bmatrix} 1 & 0 & 0 & 0 & 0 & 0 & 1 & 1 & 1 & 1 & 1 & 1 \\ 0 & 1 & 0 & 0 & 0 & 0 & 4 & 2 & 0 & 3 & 1 & 2 \\ 0 & 0 & 1 & 0 & 0 & 0 & 1 & 3 & 1 & 0 & 2 & 2 \\ 0 & 0 & 0 & 1 & 0 & 0 & 2 & 4 & 4 & 3 & 3 & 2 \\ 0 & 0 & 0 & 0 & 1 & 0 & 4 & 1 & 2 & 1 & 3 & 2 \\ 0 & 0 & 0 & 0 & 0 & 1 & 0 & 1 & 4 & 2 & 4 & 2 \end{bmatrix}.$$

If we denote the i-th row by r_{i-1}, and the chosen vector by $(\alpha_0, \alpha_1, \ldots, \alpha_{k-1})$, then the codeword formed is of the form $\alpha_0 r_0 + \alpha_1 r_1 + \cdots + \alpha_{k-1} r_{k-1}$. Therefore, the codeword c formed from the matrix G is

$$
\begin{aligned}
c = (\alpha_0, \alpha_1, &\alpha_2, \alpha_3, \alpha_4, \alpha_5, \\
&(\alpha_0 + 4\alpha_1 + \alpha_2 + 2\alpha_3 + 4\alpha_4), \\
&(\alpha_0 + 2\alpha_1 + 3\alpha_2 + 4\alpha_3 + \alpha_4 + \alpha_5), \\
&(\alpha_0 + \alpha_2 + 4\alpha_3 + 2\alpha_4 + 4\alpha_5), \\
&(\alpha_0 + 3\alpha_1 + 3\alpha_3 + \alpha_4 + 2\alpha_5), \\
&(\alpha_0 + \alpha_1 + 2\alpha_2 + 3\alpha_3 + 3\alpha_4 + 4\alpha_5), \\
&(\alpha_0 + 2\alpha_1 + 2\alpha_2 + 2\alpha_3 + 2\alpha_4 + 2\alpha_5)) .
\end{aligned}
$$

Hence, the first element of the codeword, that is, α_0 forms the secret while the rest of the elements become the shares for the participants.

A.1   Secret Reconstruction

Now any 5 participants from *Group I* or any 6 participants from *Group II* or more can find the secret.

1. **5 participants:** P_1, P_2, P_3, P_4 and P_6.
   The pooled codeword pcw is $(\alpha_1, \alpha_2, \alpha_3, \alpha_4, \alpha_0 + 4\alpha_1 + \alpha_2 + 2\alpha_3 + 4\alpha_4)$ and the corresponding submatrix G' is:

$$
G' = \begin{bmatrix}
0 & 0 & 0 & 0 & 1 & 1 \\
1 & 0 & 0 & 0 & 4 & 0 \\
0 & 1 & 0 & 0 & 1 & 0 \\
0 & 0 & 1 & 0 & 2 & 0 \\
0 & 0 & 0 & 1 & 4 & 0 \\
0 & 0 & 0 & 0 & 0 & 0
\end{bmatrix} .
$$

After elementary row operations,

$$
(G')' = \begin{bmatrix}
1 & 0 & 0 & 0 & 0 & 1 \\
0 & 1 & 0 & 0 & 0 & 4 \\
0 & 0 & 1 & 0 & 0 & 3 \\
0 & 0 & 0 & 1 & 0 & 1 \\
0 & 0 & 0 & 0 & 1 & 1 \\
0 & 0 & 0 & 0 & 0 & 0
\end{bmatrix} \implies g'_{0G} = \begin{bmatrix}
1 \\
4 \\
3 \\
1 \\
1 \\
0
\end{bmatrix} .
$$

Then

$$
\begin{aligned}
\text{pcw} \cdot g_{0G} &= \alpha_1 + 4\alpha_2 + 3\alpha_3 + \alpha_4 + (\alpha_0 + 4\alpha_1 + \alpha_2 + 2\alpha_3 + 4\alpha_4) \\
&= \alpha_0 + 5\alpha_1 + 5\alpha_2 + 5\alpha_3 + 5\alpha_4 \\
&= \alpha_0 \mod 5 .
\end{aligned}
$$

Hence the secret $s_0 = \alpha_0$ is recovered correctly.

2. 6 participants: P_1, P_2, P_3, P_4, P_5 and P_7.

The pooled codeword pcw is $(\alpha_1, \alpha_2, \alpha_3, \alpha_4, \alpha_5, \alpha_0 + 2\alpha_1 + 3\alpha_2 + 4\alpha_3 + \alpha_4 + \alpha_5)$ and the corresponding submatrix G' is:

$$G' = \begin{bmatrix} 0 & 0 & 0 & 0 & 0 & 1 & 1 \\ 1 & 0 & 0 & 0 & 0 & 2 & 0 \\ 0 & 1 & 0 & 0 & 0 & 3 & 0 \\ 0 & 0 & 1 & 0 & 0 & 4 & 0 \\ 0 & 0 & 0 & 1 & 0 & 1 & 0 \\ 0 & 0 & 0 & 0 & 1 & 1 & 0 \end{bmatrix}.$$

After elementary row operations:

$$(G')' = \begin{bmatrix} 1 & 0 & 0 & 0 & 0 & 0 & 3 \\ 0 & 1 & 0 & 0 & 0 & 0 & 2 \\ 0 & 0 & 1 & 0 & 0 & 0 & 1 \\ 0 & 0 & 0 & 1 & 0 & 0 & 4 \\ 0 & 0 & 0 & 0 & 1 & 0 & 4 \\ 0 & 0 & 0 & 0 & 0 & 1 & 1 \end{bmatrix} \implies g'_{0G} = \begin{bmatrix} 3 \\ 2 \\ 1 \\ 4 \\ 4 \\ 1 \end{bmatrix}.$$

Then

$$\begin{aligned} \text{pcw} \cdot g_{0G} &= 3\alpha_1 + 2\alpha_2 + \alpha_3 + 4\alpha_4 + 4\alpha_5 + \alpha_0 + (2\alpha_1 + 3\alpha_2 + 4\alpha_3 + \alpha_4 + \alpha_5) \\ &= \alpha_0 + 5\alpha_1 + 5\alpha_2 + 5\alpha_3 + 5\alpha_4 + 5\alpha_5 \\ &= \alpha_0 \quad \text{mod } 5. \end{aligned}$$

Hence the secret $s_0 = \alpha_0$ is recovered correctly.

3. 7 or more participants: $P_4, P_5, P_6, P_7, P_8, P_9, P_{10}$ and P_{11}.

The pooled codeword is

$$\begin{aligned} \text{pcw} = (\alpha_4, \alpha_5, \\ &\alpha_0 + 4\alpha_1 + \alpha_2 + 2\alpha_3 + 4\alpha_4, \\ &\alpha_0 + 2\alpha_1 + 3\alpha_2 + 4\alpha_3 + \alpha_4 + \alpha_5, \\ &\alpha_0 + \alpha_2 + 4\alpha_3 + 2\alpha_4 + 4\alpha_5, \\ &\alpha_0 + 3\alpha_1 + 3\alpha_3 + \alpha_4 + 2\alpha_5, \\ &\alpha_0 + \alpha_1 + 2\alpha_2 + 3\alpha_3 + 3\alpha_4 + 4\alpha_5, \\ &\alpha_0 + 2\alpha_1 + 2\alpha_2 + 2\alpha_3 + 2\alpha_4 + 2\alpha_5) \end{aligned}$$

and the corresponding submatrix G' is:

$$\begin{bmatrix} 0 & 0 & 1 & 1 & 1 & 1 & 1 & 1 & 1 \\ 0 & 0 & 4 & 2 & 0 & 3 & 1 & 2 & 0 \\ 0 & 0 & 1 & 3 & 1 & 0 & 2 & 2 & 0 \\ 0 & 0 & 2 & 4 & 4 & 3 & 3 & 2 & 0 \\ 1 & 0 & 4 & 1 & 2 & 1 & 3 & 2 & 0 \\ 0 & 1 & 0 & 1 & 4 & 2 & 4 & 2 & 0 \end{bmatrix}.$$

After elementary row operations:

$$(G')' = \begin{bmatrix} 1 & 0 & 0 & 0 & 0 & 0 & 3 & 1 & 1 \\ 0 & 1 & 0 & 0 & 0 & 0 & 2 & 0 & 1 \\ 0 & 0 & 1 & 0 & 0 & 0 & 1 & 3 & 0 \\ 0 & 0 & 0 & 1 & 0 & 0 & 0 & 1 & 4 \\ 0 & 0 & 0 & 0 & 1 & 0 & 1 & 1 & 3 \\ 0 & 0 & 0 & 0 & 0 & 1 & 4 & 1 & 4 \end{bmatrix} \implies g'_{0G} = \begin{bmatrix} 1 \\ 1 \\ 0 \\ 4 \\ 3 \\ 4 \end{bmatrix}.$$

Then

$$\begin{aligned} \mathsf{pcw} \cdot g_{0G} &= (\alpha_4) + (\alpha_5) + (4\alpha_0 + 3\alpha_1 + 2\alpha_2 + \alpha_3 + 4\alpha_4 + 4\alpha_5) \\ &\quad + (3\alpha_0 + 3\alpha_2 + 2\alpha_3 + \alpha_4 + 2\alpha_5) + (4\alpha_0 + 2\alpha_1 + 2\alpha_3 + 4\alpha_4 + 3\alpha_5) \\ &= 11\alpha_0 + 5\alpha_1 + 5\alpha_2 + 5\alpha_3 + 10\alpha_4 + 10\alpha_5 \\ &= \alpha_0 \mod 5. \end{aligned}$$

Hence the secret $s_0 = \alpha_0$ is recovered correctly.

Hence in every case, the secret s_0 is recovered correctly.

References

1. Benaloh, J., Leichter, J.: Generalized secret sharing and monotone functions. In: Goldwasser, S. (ed.) CRYPTO 1988. LNCS, vol. 403, pp. 27–35. Springer, New York (1990). https://doi.org/10.1007/0-387-34799-2_3
2. George Robert Blakley: Safeguarding cryptographic keys. In: AFIPS, pp. 313–317 (1979)
3. Dodunekov, S., Landgev, I.: On Near-MDS codes. J. Geom. **54**(1), 30–43 (1995)
4. Dodunekov, S.M., Landjev, I.N.: Near-MDS codes over some small fields. Discrete Math. **213**(1–3), 55–65 (2000)
5. Harn, L., Lin, C.: Detection and identification of cheaters in (t, n) secret sharing scheme. Des. Codes Crypt. **52**(1), 15–24 (2009)
6. Huffman, W.C., Pless, V.: Fundamentals of Error-Correcting Codes. Cambridge University Press, New York (2010)
7. Ito, M., Saito, A., Nishizeki, T.: Secret sharing scheme realizing general access structure. Electron. Commun. Jpn. (Part III: Fundam. Electron. Sci.) **72**(9), 56–64 (1989)
8. Karchmer, M., Wigderson, A.: On span programs. In: Structure in Complexity Theory Conference, pp. 102–111. IEEE Computer Society (1993)
9. Li, C., Wang, Q.: Design of lightweight linear diffusion layers from Near-MDS matrices. IACR Trans. Symmetric Cryptol. **2017**(1), 129–155 (2017)
10. Pieprzyk, J., Zhang, X.-M.: Ideal threshold schemes from MDS codes. In: Lee, P.J., Lim, C.H. (eds.) ICISC 2002. LNCS, vol. 2587, pp. 253–263. Springer, Heidelberg (2003). https://doi.org/10.1007/3-540-36552-4_18
11. Shamir, A.: How to share a secret. Commun. ACM **22**(11), 612–613 (1979)
12. Zhou, Y., Wang, F., Xin, Y., Luo, S., Qing, S., Yang, Y.: A secret sharing scheme based on Near-MDS codes. In: NIDC, pp. 833–836. IEEE (2009)

Mathematics for Cryptography

On Plateaued Functions, Linear Structures and Permutation Polynomials

Sihem Mesnager[1] , Kübra Kaytancı[2] , and Ferruh Özbudak[3](✉)

[1] LAGA, UMR 7539, CNRS, University Paris XIII - Sorbonne Paris Cité, University Paris VIII (Department of Mathematics) and Telecom ParisTech, Paris, France
smesnager@univ-paris8.fr
[2] Institute of Applied Mathematics, Middle East Technical University, Ankara, Turkey
kubra.kaytanci@metu.edu.tr
[3] Department of Mathematics and Institute of Applied Mathematics, Middle East Technical University, Ankara, Turkey
ozbudak@metu.edu.tr

Abstract. We obtain concrete upper bounds on the algebraic immunity of a class of highly nonlinear plateaued functions without linear structures than the one was given recently in 2017, Cusick. Moreover, we extend Cusick's class to a much bigger explicit class and we show that our class has better algebraic immunity by an explicit example. We also give a new notion of linear translator, which includes the Frobenius linear translator given in 2018, Cepak, Pasalic and Muratović-Ribić as a special case. We find some applications of our new notion of linear translator to the construction of permutation polynomials. Furthermore, we give explicit classes of permutation polynomials over $\mathbb{F}_{q^n}$ using some properties of $\mathbb{F}_q$ and some conditions of 2011, Akbary, Ghioca and Wang.

Keywords: Plateaued functions · Linear structure · Permutation polynomials

1 Introduction

Plateaued functions are important not only for cryptography but also for some related areas including coding theory and communication. There have been many results in recent years regarding their construction, existence and applications. We refer for example to [2–6,10,14,16–19] and the references therein.

Recently Cusick [9] gave an explicit construction of highly nonlinear plateaued functions without linear structure. In Sect. 3 we obtain a much larger class of explicit functions having all these good properties and including Cusick's class of functions as a very small subclass. Moreover, we prove that Cusick's class have quite low algebraic immunity by concrete upper bounds. We also give an explicit example in our class having better algebraic immunity than the functions in Cusick's class.

© Springer Nature Switzerland AG 2019
C. Carlet et al. (Eds.): C2SI 2019, LNCS 11445, pp. 217–235, 2019.
https://doi.org/10.1007/978-3-030-16458-4_13

For construction of non-trivial mathematical structures it has been shown that linear structures (and linear translators) are useful. There are important connections between linear translators and permutation polynomials over finite fields (see, for example [11]). Recently the authors in [8] gave a generalization of linear translators, which they call the Frobenius linear translator. They also give applications of their generalization to the construction of permutation polynomials. In Sect. 6 we obtain a further and natural generalization of linear translators using additive polynomials. Our generalization also has applications to the construction of permutation polynomials using our generalization different from Frobenius linear translators (see, for example Theorems 5 and 6 and Example 2 below).

Akbary, Ghioca and Wang [1] established a very interesting method in order to construct permutation polynomials over "big" finite fields. If an explicit class of permutation polynomials that satisfies certain criteria is found over a subfield, $\mathbb{F}_q$ it can be used to construct an explicit class of permutation polynomials over an extension field $\mathbb{F}_{q^n}$. For example, the authors in [7] obtained such explicit permutation polynomial classes over $\mathbb{F}_{q^2}$ using certain properties of $\mathbb{F}_q$. By a similar motivation we obtain further explicit permutation polynomial classes over $\mathbb{F}_{q^2}$ via $\mathbb{F}_q$ and also over $\mathbb{F}_{q^n}$ via $\mathbb{F}_q$ with $n \geq 3$ in Sects. 4 and 5, respectively.

We give details of our corresponding contributions and motivations in the beginnings of Sects. 3, 4, 5 and 6 below. We give some background in the next section.

2   Preliminaries

Let q be a power of a prime number and $\mathbb{F}_{q^n}$ be the finite field of order q^n where $n \geq 1$. The extension field $\mathbb{F}_{q^n}$ can be viewed as an n-dimensional vector space over $\mathbb{F}_q$. The trace function Tr_n from $\mathbb{F}_{q^n}$ to $\mathbb{F}_q$ is defined as

$$Tr_n : \mathbb{F}_{q^n} \to \mathbb{F}_q$$
$$\alpha \mapsto \alpha + \alpha^q + \alpha^{q^2} + \cdots + \alpha^{q^{n-1}}.$$

A Boolean function f of n-variables is a function from $\mathbb{F}_2^n$ to $\mathbb{F}_2$.

Definition 1. *Let $f : \mathbb{F}_2^n \to \mathbb{F}_2$ be a Boolean function. Then the Walsh transform $\hat{f}$ of f is defined as*

$$\hat{f} : \mathbb{F}_2^n \to \mathbb{Z}$$
$$w \mapsto \sum_{x \in \mathbb{F}_2^n} (-1)^{f(x)+w \cdot x}$$

where $w = (w_1, w_2, \ldots, w_n)$, $x = (x_1, x_2, \ldots, x_n)$ and $w \cdot x = w_1 x_1 + \cdots + w_n x_n$.

Definition 2. *Let $f : \mathbb{F}_2^n \to \mathbb{F}_2$ be a Boolean function. Then f has linear structure at $a \in \mathbb{F}_2^n$ if and only if either $f(x + a) + f(x) = 0$ for any $x \in \mathbb{F}_2^n$ (a is called a 0-linear structure) or $f(x + a) + f(x) = 1$ for any $x \in \mathbb{F}_2^n$ (a is called a 1-linear structure).*

Definition 3. *Let $f : \mathbb{F}_2^n \to \mathbb{F}_2$ be a Boolean function. Then f is called an s-plateaued function where $0 \leq s \leq n$ if $|\hat{f}(w)|^2 \in \{0, 2^{n+s}\}$ for any $w \in \mathbb{F}_2^n$.*

Definition 4 (See, for example [3]). *Let $f : \mathbb{F}_2^n \to \mathbb{F}_2$ be a Boolean function. The algebraic normal form of f is*

$$f(x) = \bigoplus_{\mathcal{I} \in \mathcal{P}(N)} a_{\mathcal{I}} \left(\prod_{\mathcal{I} \in \mathcal{P}(N)} x^{\mathcal{I}} \right),$$

where $\mathcal{P}(N)$ denotes the power set of $N = \{1, \ldots, n\}$. The degree of the algebraic normal form of f is equal to

$$\max\{|\mathcal{I}| : a_{\mathcal{I}} \neq 0\}$$

where $|\mathcal{I}|$ denotes the size of $\mathcal{I}$.

Definition 5 (See, for example [3]). *Let $f : \mathbb{F}_2^n \to \mathbb{F}$ be a Boolean function. The algebraic immunity $AI(f)$ of f is defined to be the minimal degree of a nonzero function g from $\mathbb{F}_2^n$ to $\mathbb{F}_2$ for which $f \cdot g = 0$ or $(f + 1) \cdot g = 0$, i.e*

$$AI(f) := \min\{\deg g : g \in Ann(f) \cup Ann(f + 1)\}$$

where $Ann(f)$ is the set of annihilators of f. A function g is an annihilator of f if $f \cdot g = 0$.

Remark 1. It is well-known that for any Boolean function f of n-variables, $AI(f) \leq \lceil \frac{n}{2} \rceil$.

For integer $n \geq 1$ and $x = (x_1, \ldots, x_n)$, $y = (y_1, \ldots, y_n) \in \mathbb{F}_2^n$, the inner product $x \cdot y \in \mathbb{F}_2$ is the usual inner product defined as

$$x \cdot y = x_1 y_1 + x_2 y_2 + \cdots + x_n y_n.$$

3 Cusick's Highly Nonlinear Plateaued Functions and Their Modifications

For integers $d \geq 3$ and $k \geq 1$, Cusick introduced an explicit class of Boolean functions of degree d in $n = 2dk - 1$ variables given by

$$f_k(x_1, x_2, \ldots, x_n) = \sum_{j=0}^{k-1} x_{dj+1} \cdots x_{dj+d} + \sum_{j=1}^{m-1} x_j x_{j+m}. \tag{1}$$

where $m = dk$. He proved that these are 1-plateaued, have no linear structure and have nonlinearity $2^{n-1} - 2^{\frac{n-1}{2}}$. They become balanced by adding a concrete linear function. Note that adding a linear function does not change plateauedness, nonlinearity or the set of linear structures. He also states that "... a high algebraic immunity is not to be expected" in [9, page 80, the last paragraph].

In this section we show that indeed algebraic immunity of the functions in (1) is low. Note that the largest degree of the class for a fixed odd integer $n \geq 3$ occurs when $k = 1$. Moreover, if $m = \frac{n-1}{2}$ is a prime, then k may only taken to be 1 in (1). The following result shows in particular that this class has very low algebraic immunity when k is small.

Proposition 1. *For integers $d \geq 3$ and $k \geq 1$, let $n = 2dk - 1$ and $f_k : \mathbb{F}_2^n \to \mathbb{F}_2$ be the Boolean function defined in (1). We have:*

(i) $AI(f_1) \leq 3$.
(ii) For $k \geq 2$, $AI(f_k) \leq \min\{k + 2, \frac{n+1}{2k}\}$.

Proof. We first prove item (i). Put $x = (x_1, x_2, \ldots, x_{m-1})$ and $y = (y_1, \ldots, y_{m-1}) = (x_{m+1}, \ldots, x_{2m-1})$ where $m = dk$. Let

$$h(x) = x_1 x_2 \ldots x_{m-1} \text{ and } g(x, y) = x_1 y_1 + x_2 y_2 + \cdots + x_{m-1} y_{m-1}.$$

Then it is easy to observe that

$$f_1(x_1, \ldots, x_n) = h(x) x_m + g(x, y).$$

It is enough to prove that

$$f_1(x_1, \ldots, x_n)(g(x, y) + 1)(x_m + 1) = 0$$

for all $x, y \in \mathbb{F}_2^{m-1}$ and $x_m \in \mathbb{F}_2$. Indeed, $\deg(g(x, y) + 1)(x_m + 1) = 2 + 1 = 3$. Moreover,

$$\begin{aligned}
f_1(x_1, \ldots, x_n)(g(x, y) + 1)(x_m + 1) &= (h(x) x_m + g(x, y))(g(x, y) + 1)(x_m + 1) \\
&= (h(x) x_m g(x, y) + h(x) x_m + g(x, y) + g(x, y))(x_m + 1) \\
&= (h(x) x_m (g(x, y) + 1))(x_m + 1) \\
&= h(x)(g(x, y) + 1)(x_m(x_m + 1)) = 0,
\end{aligned}$$

as $(x_m(x_m + 1)) = 0$. This completes the proof of item (i).

Next, we consider the proof of item (ii). Note that

$$f_k(x_1, \ldots, x_n) = x_1 \ldots x_d + x_{d+1} \ldots x_{2d} + \cdots + x_{(k-1)(d+1)} \ldots x_{m-1} x_m + g(x, y).$$

Here

$$\begin{aligned}
f_k(x_1, \ldots, x_n)&((x_1 + 1)(x_d + 1) \ldots (x_{(k-1)(d+1)} + 1)(g(x, y) + 1)) \\
&= x_1(x_1 + 1)r_1(x_1, \ldots, x_n) + x_{d+1}(x_{d+1} + 1)r_2(x_1, \ldots, x_n) + \cdots \\
&\quad + x_{(k-1)(d+1)}(x_{(k-1)(d+1)} + 1)r_k(x_1, \ldots, x_n) \\
&\quad + g(x, y)(g(x, y) + 1)r_{k+1}(x_1, \ldots, x_n)
\end{aligned}$$

for some polynomials $r_1(x_1, \ldots, x_n), \ldots, r_{k+1}(x_1, \ldots, x_n)$ in algebraic normal form. As

$$x_1(x_1 + 1) = x_{d+1}(x_{d+1} + 1) = \cdots = x_{(k-1)(d+1)}(x_{(k-1)(d+1)} + 1) = 0$$

and $g(x,y)\,(g(x,y)+1) = 0$ as Boolean functions and

$$\deg\left((x_1+1)(x_{d+1}+1)\ldots(x_{(k-1)(d+1)}+1)\,(g(x,y)+1)\right) = k+2,$$

we have $AI(f_k) \leq k+2$. Also

$$f_k(x_1,\ldots,x_n)\,(f_k(x_1,\ldots,x_n)+1) = 0.$$

And $\deg\left(f_k(x_1,\ldots,x_n)+1\right) = d = \frac{n+1}{2k}$. Hence $AI(f_k) \leq \min\{k+2, \frac{n+1}{2k}\}$.   □

Next, we define a much larger explicit class of Boolean functions containing Cusick's class as defined in (1) as a small subclass. The functions of this class are 1-plateaued, having nonlinearity $2^{n-1} - 2^{\frac{n-1}{2}}$ and balanced up to addition of a concrete linear function as in Cusick's class. Moreover, we also have a characterization whether a function in our class has a linear structure. This condition is easy to apply. Moreover, we give an explicit example demonstrating that the algebraic immunity of a function in our class is much better compared to the class defined in (1).

We first note that if $h : \mathbb{F}_2^{m-1} \to \mathbb{F}_2$ is an arbitrary map, then we have

$$|\{(\alpha_m, \beta) \in \mathbb{F}_2 \times \mathbb{F}_2^{m-1} : h(\beta) + \alpha_m = 0\}| = 2^{m-1}.$$

Now we are ready to give our much larger class of Boolean functions consisting of 1-plateaued, highly nonlinear functions without linear structure. It is easy to make them balanced by adding a linear term as explained in the theorem as well.

Theorem 1. *Let $n \geq 3$ be odd and $n = 2m - 1$. Let $\pi : \mathbb{F}_2^{m-1} \to \mathbb{F}_2^{m-1}$ be a permutation map. Let $g_0, g_1 : \mathbb{F}_2^{m-1} \to \mathbb{F}_2$ be Boolean maps. Let $f : \mathbb{F}_2^n \to \mathbb{F}_2$ be the Boolean map defined as*

$$f : \mathbb{F}_2^{m-1} \times \mathbb{F}_2 \times \mathbb{F}_2^{m-1} \to \mathbb{F}_2$$
$$(x, x_m, y) \mapsto g_0(x) + x_m g_1(x) + \pi(x) \cdot y.$$

Then we have:

(i) f is a 1-plateaued function.
(ii) f has no nonzero linear structure if and only if the subset

$$S = \{(\alpha_m, \beta) \in \mathbb{F}_2 \times \mathbb{F}_2^{m-1} : g_1(\pi^{-1}(\beta)) + \alpha_m = 0\} \subseteq \mathbb{F}_2 \times \mathbb{F}_2^{m-1}$$

is not an affine or linear subset (of dimension m-1).
(iii) The nonlinearity of f is $2^{n-1} - 2^{(n-1)/2}$.
(iv) For $(u, \mu, v) \in \mathbb{F}_2^{m-1} \times \mathbb{F}_2 \times \mathbb{F}_2^{m-1}$, the function

$$f_{u,\mu,v}(x, x_m, y) := f(x, x_m, y) + u \cdot x + \mu \cdot x_m + v \cdot y$$

is balanced if and only if $g_1(\pi^{-1}(v)) + \mu = 1$.

Proof. Let $w = (\alpha, \alpha_m, \beta) \in \mathbb{F}_2^{m-1} \times \mathbb{F}_2 \times \mathbb{F}_2^{m-1}$. We have

$$\hat{f}(w) = \sum_{x \in \mathbb{F}_2^{m-1}} \sum_{x_m \in \mathbb{F}_2} \sum_{y \in \mathbb{F}_2^{m-1}} (-1)^{g_0(x) + x_m g_1(x) + \pi(x) \cdot y + \alpha \cdot x + \alpha_m x_m + \beta \cdot y}$$

$$= \sum_{x \in \mathbb{F}_2^{m-1}} \sum_{x_m \in \mathbb{F}_2} (-1)^{g_0(x) + x_m g_1(x) + \alpha \cdot x + \alpha_m x_m} \sum_{y \in \mathbb{F}_2^{m-1}} (-1)^{(\pi(x) + \beta) \cdot y}$$

$$= 2^{m-1} (-1)^{g_0(\pi^{-1}(\beta)) + \alpha \cdot \pi^{-1}(\beta)} \sum_{x_m \in \mathbb{F}_2} (-1)^{(g_1(\pi^{-1}(\beta)) + \alpha_m) x_m}.$$

Hence

$$\hat{f}(w) = \begin{cases} 2^m (-1)^{g_0(\pi^{-1}(\beta)) + \alpha \cdot \pi^{-1}(\beta)} & \text{if } g_1(\pi^{-1}(\beta)) = \alpha_m, \\ 0 & \text{otherwise.} \end{cases}$$

This completes the proof of the item (i).

It is well-known that the nonlinearity of an arbitrary Boolean function $f : \mathbb{F}_2^n \to \mathbb{F}_2$ is $2^{n-1} - \frac{1}{2} \max_{w \in \mathbb{F}_2^n} |\hat{f}(w)|$. Hence in our case the nonlinearity of our function f is

$$2^{n-1} - \frac{1}{2} \max_{w \in \mathbb{F}_2^n} |\hat{f}(w)| = 2^{n-1} - \frac{1}{2} 2^m = 2^{n-1} - 2^{\frac{n-1}{2}}.$$

This completes the proof of item (iii).

It is also well-known that the Walsh value $\hat{f}_{u,\mu,v}(0,0,0)$ of $\hat{f}_{u,\mu,v}(x, x_m, y)$ is $\hat{f}(u, \mu, v)$. Hence

$$\hat{f}_{u,\mu,v}(0,0,0) = 0 \iff g_1(\pi^{-1}(v)) + \mu = 1.$$

Note that $f_{u,\mu,v}(x, x_m, y)$ is balanced if and only if $\hat{f}_{u,\mu,v}(0,0,0) = 0$. This completes the proof of item (iv).

It only remains to prove the item (ii). Let S_f denote the support of the Walsh spectrum of f, that is $S_f = \{w \in \mathbb{F}_2^{m-1} \times \mathbb{F}_2 \times \mathbb{F}_2^{m-1} : \hat{f}(w) \neq 0\}$. Let $S \subseteq \mathbb{F}_2 \times \mathbb{F}_2^{m-1}$ be the subset defined as

$$S = \{(\alpha_m, \beta) \in \mathbb{F}_2 \times \mathbb{F}_2^{m-1} : g_1(\pi^{-1}(\beta)) + \alpha_m = 0\}. \tag{2}$$

It follows from the proof of item (i) above that $S_f = \mathbb{F}_2^{m-1} \times S$. For $\nu \in \mathbb{F}_2^n$, let $\Delta_f(\nu)$ be the sum

$$\Delta_f(\nu) = \sum_{x \in \mathbb{F}_2^n} (-1)^{f(x+\nu) + f(x)}.$$

It is clear that ν is a linear structure of f if and only if $\Delta_f(\nu) = \pm 2^n$. Moreover, it is not difficult to observe that

$$\sum_{w \in \mathbb{F}_2^n} \hat{f}(w)^2 (-1)^{\nu \cdot w} = 2^n \Delta_f(\nu),$$

which holds for an arbitrary Boolean map $f : \mathbb{F}_2^n \to \mathbb{F}_2$. In our case f is 1-plateaued and hence

$$\sum_{w\in\mathbb{F}_2^n} \hat{f}(w)^2(-1)^{\nu\cdot w} = \sum_{w\in S_f} |\hat{f}(w)|^2(-1)^{\nu\cdot w} = 2^{n+1}\sum_{w\in S_f}(-1)^{\nu\cdot w},$$

where we use our proof of item (i) above. These implies that if $\nu \in \mathbb{F}_2^n$, then we have

$$\Delta_f(\nu) = 2\sum_{w\in S_f}(-1)^{\nu\cdot w}.$$

As $|S_f| = 2^{n-1}$, we conclude that $\nu \in \mathbb{F}_2^n$ is a linear structure of f if and only if $(\nu \cdot w = 0$ for all $w \in S_f)$ or $(\nu \cdot w = 1$ for all $w \in S_f)$. Assume that $v = (a, a_m, b) \in \mathbb{F}_2^{m-1} \times \mathbb{F}_2 \times \mathbb{F}_2^{m-1}$ is a nonzero linear structure of f. Recall that $S_f = \mathbb{F}_2^{m-1} \times S$ where S is defined in (2). First we show that $a = 0$. Indeed otherwise there exist $\alpha, \alpha' \in \mathbb{F}_2^{m-1}$ such that $a \cdot \alpha \neq a \cdot \alpha'$. For fixed $(\alpha_m, \beta) \in S$, both $(\alpha, \alpha_m, \beta)$ and $(\alpha', \alpha_m, \beta)$ are elements of S_f. Then it is impossible that $(a, a_m, b) \cdot (\alpha, \alpha_m, b) = (a, a_m, b) \cdot (\alpha', \alpha_m, b)$ which is a contradiction.

Next, assume that $\nu \cdot w = 0$ for all $w \in S_f$. Then $\nu = (0, a_m, b)$ and $0 = (a_m, b) \cdot (\alpha_m, \beta)$ for all $(\alpha_m, \beta) \in S$. As $\nu \neq 0$, there exist $(c, d) \in \mathbb{F}_2 \times \mathbb{F}_2^{m-1}$ such that $(a_m, b) \cdot (c, d) \neq 0$. We choose such $(c, d) \in \mathbb{F}_2 \times \mathbb{F}_2^{m-1}$. As S is not a linear space and its cardinality is 2^{m-1}, the $\mathbb{F}_2$-span of S is the whole vector space $\mathbb{F}_2 \times \mathbb{F}_2^{m-1}$. In particular, there exist a subset $T \subseteq S$ such that

$$(c, d) = \sum_{(\alpha_m,\beta)\in T}(\alpha_m, \beta).$$

Multiplying both sides by (a_m, b) (as inner product) we get

$$(a_m, b) \cdot (c, d) = \sum_{(\alpha_m,\beta)\in T}(a_m, b) \cdot (c, d) = \sum_{(\alpha_m,\beta)\in T} 0 = 0.$$

However, this is a contradiction as $(a_m, b) \cdot (c, d) \neq 0$ by definition. This completes the proof of item (ii) under the assumption about $\nu \cdot w = 0$ for all $w \in S_f$.

Assume finally that $\nu \cdot w = 1$ for all $w \in S$. We choose $(\alpha_m^{(0)}, \beta^{(0)}) \in S$ and we define

$$S^L = \{(\alpha_m + \alpha_m^{(0)}, \beta + \beta^{(0)}) : (\alpha_m, \beta) \in S\}.$$

Note that S is affine if and only if S^L is linear. Moreover, $\nu = (0, a_m, b)$ is a nonzero linear structure of f if and only if $(a_m, b) \cdot (\alpha_m^L, \beta^L) = 0$ for all $(\alpha_m^L, \beta^L) \in S^L$. The same argument we used in the assumption $\nu \cdot w = 0$ for all $w \in S_f$ applied to S^L completes the proof.   □

Example 1. Let $n = 2m - 1 = 11$. Choose the permutation map

$$\pi : \mathbb{F}_2^5 \to \mathbb{F}_2^5$$
$$x = (x_0, x_1, x_2, x_3, x_4) \mapsto (\pi_1(x), \pi_2(x), \pi_3(x), \pi_4(x), \pi_5(x))$$

where

$$\pi_1(x) = x_0 x_1 x_2 + x_0 x_1 x_4 + x_0 x_2 x_3 + x_0 x_2 x_4 + x_0 x_3 + x_0 + x_1 x_2 x_3 x_4 + x_1 x_2 x_4$$
$$+ x_1 x_2 + x_2 x_3 + x_2 x_4 + x_3 x_4,$$

$$\pi_2(x) = x_0 x_1 x_2 + x_0 x_1 + x_0 x_2 x_3 x_4 + x_0 x_2 x_3 + x_0 x_3 x_4 + x_0 x_3 + x_0 x_4 + x_1 x_2 x_3$$
$$+ x_1 x_3 x_4 + x_1 x_4 + x_1 + x_2 x_3 + x_3 x_4,$$

$$\pi_3(x) = x_0 x_1 x_3 x_4 + x_0 x_1 x_3 + x_0 x_1 x_4 + x_0 x_2 x_4 + x_0 x_2 + x_0 x_3 x_4 + x_1 x_2 x_3 + x_1 x_2$$
$$+ x_1 x_3 x_4 + x_1 x_4 + x_2 x_3 x_4 + x_2 + x_3 x_4,$$

$$\pi_4(x) = x_0 x_1 x_2 x_4 + x_0 x_1 x_2 + x_0 x_1 x_3 + x_0 x_1 x_4 + x_0 x_1 + x_0 x_2 x_4 + x_0 x_2 + x_0 x_3$$
$$+ x_0 + x_1 x_2 x_4 + x_1 x_3 + x_2 x_3 x_4 + x_2 x_3 + x_3,$$

$$\pi_5(x) = x_0 x_1 x_2 x_3 + x_0 x_1 x_2 + x_0 x_1 x_3 + x_0 x_1 x_4 + x_0 x_2 x_3 + x_0 x_3 x_4 + x_0 x_3 + x_0 x_4$$
$$+ x_1 x_2 x_3 + x_1 x_2 x_4 + x_1 x_2 + x_1 x_3 + x_1 x_4 + x_1 + x_2 x_4 + x_3 x_4 + x_4.$$

Then take

$$g_0 : \mathbb{F}_2^5 \to \mathbb{F}_2$$
$$(x_0, x_1, x_2, x_3, x_4) \mapsto x_0 + x_2 + x_3$$

and

$$g_1 : \mathbb{F}_2^5 \to \mathbb{F}_2$$
$$(x_0, x_1, x_2, x_3, x_4) \mapsto x_1 x_2 x_3 + 1.$$

An application of our construction in Theorem 1 gives the map

$$f : \mathbb{F}_2^5 \times \mathbb{F}_2 \times \mathbb{F}_2^5 \to \mathbb{F}_2$$
$$(x, x_5, y) \mapsto g_0(x) + x_5 g_1(x) + \pi(x) y$$
$$(x_0, x_1, x_2, x_3, x_4, x_5, y_0, y_1, y_2, y_3, y_4) \mapsto x_0 + x_2 + x_3 + (x_1 x_2 x_3 + 1) x_5 + y_0 \pi_1(x)$$
$$+ y_1 \pi_2(x) + y_2 \pi_3(x) + y_3 \pi_4(x) + y_4 \pi_5(x)$$

where $\pi_i(x)$ is defined as before for $i = 1, \ldots, 5$. The map is balanced, has no linear structure, has nonlinearity $992 = 2^{10} - 2^5$ and has algebraic immunity 4.

In Example 1, $\pi : \mathbb{F}_2^5 \to \mathbb{F}_2^5$ corresponds to the permutation map $x \mapsto x^{30}$. Note that as $m = 5$ is a prime, there is only one function in Cusick's class, which is f_1 in (1). Moreover, $AI(f_1) \leq 3$. Example 1 gives a concrete example in our class of Theorem 1 improving the algebraic immunity while keeping all the good properties of the maps of Cusick's class: high nonlinearity, 1-plateauedness, absence of having nonzero linear structures, and balancedness. Moreover, using different permutations $\pi : \mathbb{F}_2^5 \to \mathbb{F}_2^5$ and other suitable maps $g_0(x)$, $g_1(x)$ we get a lot of different Boolean functions with algebraic immunity 4 easily satisfying the conditions: 1-plateauedness, absence of having nonzero linear structures, and balancedness.

4   Constructing Permutation Polynomials over $\mathbb{F}_{q^2}$ via $\mathbb{F}_q$

Akbay, Ghioca and Wang [1] recently established a very interesting construction in order to construct polynomials over "big" finite fields using a commutative diagram relating the big field to some smaller subsets and the corresponding conditions on the maps of the commutative diagram. In fact, this construction gives different methods using different commutative diagrams leading to different conditions on different maps and subsets (see, for example [1, Proposition 5.9] and [1, Proposition 5.6]).

They generalized many earlier results and constructed many new permutation polynomial families. They also motivated many research directions in constructing explicit classes of permutation polynomials in "big" finite fields in the following sense: If a class of objects satisfying certain properties can be constructed which are guaranteed to satisfy a full set of conditions of Akbay, Ghioca and Wang in a small set (see, for example [1, Proposition 5.9] or [1, Proposition 5.6]), then it is possible to obtain an explicit class of permutation polynomials in the big finite field.

Recently Cepak, Charpin and Pasalic, among other results, gave such explicit classes in [7]. Namely, in [7, Section 6], they obtain permutation polynomials over $\mathbb{F}_{q^2}$ using certain polynomials over $\mathbb{F}_q$. We refer to Propositions 6, 8, 9 and the corresponding corollaries in [7].

Motivated by these results, we give explicit large class of permutation polynomials over $\mathbb{F}_{q^2}$ starting from polynomials over $\mathbb{F}_q$. We first introduce the notion of b-permutation.

Definition 6. *Let $m(x) \in \mathbb{F}_q[x]$ and $b \in \mathbb{F}_q$ be given. We call $m(x)$ a b-permutation over $\mathbb{F}_q$ if the evaluation mapping $x \mapsto m(x) + bx$ defines a permutation over $\mathbb{F}_q$.*

Remark 2. Note that it is not difficult to construct a b-permutation polynomial starting from a permutation polynomial. Indeed if $x \mapsto h(x)$ is a permutation polynomial, then $x \mapsto h(x) - bx$ is a b-permutation over $\mathbb{F}_q$.

First we present our results in characteristic 2. The following proposition indicates that it is easy to construct the corresponding large families of permutation polynomials over $\mathbb{F}_{q^2}$ as the component $g_0(x) \in \mathbb{F}_q[x]$ may be chosen arbitrarily.

Proposition 2. *Let $q = 2^k$ for some integer k. Let $\theta \in \mathbb{F}_{q^2}/\mathbb{F}_q$ satisfy $\theta^q + \theta = 1$ and $g_0(x) \in \mathbb{F}_q[x]$ be arbitrary. Then we have:*

- *$F(x) = x + g_0(x^q + x) + \theta(x^{2^i q} + x^{2^i} + x^q + x)$ is a permutation over $\mathbb{F}_{q^2}$ for any $i \geq 1$.*
- *If $q \not\equiv 1 \mod 3$, then*

$$F(x) = x + g_0(x^q + x) + \theta(x^{3q} + x^{2q+1} + x^{q+2} + x^3 + x^q + x)$$

is a permutation over $\mathbb{F}_{q^2}$.

- If $q \not\equiv 1 \mod 5$, then

$$F(x) = x + g_0(x^q + x) + \theta(x^{5q} + x^{4q+1} + x^{q+4} + x^5 + x^q + x)$$

is a permutation over $\mathbb{F}_{q^2}$.
- If $r \geq 1$ is an integer such that $\gcd(r, q-1) = 1$, then

$$F(x) = x + g_0(x^q + x) + \theta\left((x^q + x)^r + (x^q + x)\right)$$

is a permutation over $\mathbb{F}_{q^2}$.

In fact, Proposition 2 is just a special subcase of the next theorem. We prefer to state Proposition 2 independently as it shows that the conditions of the next theorem are very easy to satisfy. We do not prove it as it follows from the proof of the next theorem.

Theorem 2. *Let $q = 2^k$ for some integer k. Let $\theta \in \mathbb{F}_{q^2}/\mathbb{F}_q$ satisfying $\theta^q + \theta = 1$. Let $g_0(x) \in \mathbb{F}_q[x]$ be arbitrary and $g_1(x) \in \mathbb{F}_q[x]$ be a 1-permutation over $\mathbb{F}_q$. Then*

$$F(x) = x + g_0(x^q + x) + \theta(g_1(x^q + x))$$

is a permutation over $\mathbb{F}_{q^2}$.

Proof. The proof comes from [1, Proposition 5.9], by taking $g(x)$ of the form $g(x) = g_0(x) + \theta g_1(x) \in \mathbb{F}_{q^2}[x]$, $h(x)$ as a constant function equal to 1 and $\varphi(x) = x$. Observe that $S = \{y^q + y | y \in \mathbb{F}_{q^2}\} = \mathbb{F}_q$ since $\text{char}(\mathbb{F}_q) = 2$. Then

$$h(x)\varphi(x) + g(x)^q + g(x) = x + g_0(x)^q + \theta^q g_1(x)^q + g_0(x) + \theta g_1(x).$$

If $x \in \mathbb{F}_q$, the equality implies

$$h(x)\varphi(x) + g(x)^q + g(x) = x + g_1(x).$$

Since $g_1(x)$ is a 1-permutation over $\mathbb{F}_q$, the function

$$F(x) = x + g_0(x^q + x) + \theta(g_1(x^q + x))$$

is a permutation over $\mathbb{F}_{q^2}$. $\qquad\square$

Next, we present our results in odd characteristic. Again, we first state a special subcase in the next proposition.

Proposition 3. *Let $q = p^k$, where p is any odd prime number. Let $\beta \in \mathbb{F}_{q^2}/\mathbb{F}_q$ and $\gamma = \beta^q - \beta$. Let $g_0(x) \in \mathbb{F}_q[x]$ be arbitrary. Then we have:*

- If $q \not\equiv 1 \mod 3$, then

$$F(x) = x + g_0\left(\frac{x^q}{\gamma^q} - \frac{x}{\gamma}\right) + \beta\left[\frac{x^{3q}}{\gamma^{3q}} - 3\frac{x^{2q+1}}{\gamma^{2q+1}} + 3\frac{x^{q+2}}{\gamma^{q+2}} - \frac{x^3}{\gamma^3} - \frac{x^q}{\gamma^q} + \frac{x}{\gamma}\right]$$

is a permutation over $\mathbb{F}_{q^2}$.

– If $q \not\equiv 1 \mod 5$, *then*

$$F(x) = x + g_0 \left(\frac{x^q}{\gamma^q} - \frac{x}{\gamma} \right)$$

$$+ \beta \left[\frac{x^{5q}}{\gamma^{5q}} - 5\frac{x^{4q+1}}{\gamma^{4q+1}} + 10\frac{x^{3q+2}}{\gamma^{3q+2}} - 10\frac{x^{2q+3}}{\gamma^{2q+3}} + 5\frac{x^{q+4}}{\gamma^{q+4}} - \frac{x^5}{\gamma^5} - \frac{x^q}{\gamma^q} + \frac{x}{\gamma} \right]$$

is a permutation over $\mathbb{F}_{q^2}$.
– *If* $r \geq 1$ *is an integer such that* $\gcd(r, q-1) = 1$, *then*

$$F(x) = x + g_0 \left(\frac{x^q}{\gamma^q} - \frac{x}{\gamma} \right) + \beta \left[\left(\frac{x^q}{\gamma^q} - \frac{x}{\gamma} \right)^r - \left(\frac{x^q}{\gamma^q} - \frac{x}{\gamma} \right) \right]$$

is a permutation over $\mathbb{F}_{q^2}$.

We do not prove Proposition 3 as its proof follows from the next theorem.

Theorem 3. *Let* $q = p^k$, *where* p *is any odd prime number. Let* $\beta \in \mathbb{F}_{q^2}/\mathbb{F}_q$ *and* $\gamma = \beta^q - \beta$. *Let* $g_0(x) \in \mathbb{F}_q[x]$ *be arbitrary and* $g_1(x) \in \mathbb{F}_q[x]$ *be a 1-permutation over* $\mathbb{F}_q$. *Then*

$$F(x) = x + g_0 \left(\frac{x^q}{\gamma^q} - \frac{x}{\gamma} \right) + \beta g_1 \left(\frac{x^q}{\gamma^q} - \frac{x}{\gamma} \right)$$

is a permutation over $\mathbb{F}_{q^2}$.

Proof. The proof comes from [1, Proposition 5.9], by taking $g(x)$ of the form $g(x) = g_0 \left(\frac{x}{\gamma} \right) + \beta g_1 \left(\frac{x}{\gamma} \right) \in \mathbb{F}_{q^2}[x]$, $h(x)$ as a constant function equal to 1 and $\varphi(x) = x$. Observe that $S = \{y^q - y | y \in \mathbb{F}_{q^2}\} = \gamma \mathbb{F}_q$. Now consider the map

$$\gamma y \mapsto \gamma y + g(\gamma y)^q - g(\gamma y).$$

Then

$$\gamma y + g(\gamma y)^q - g(\gamma y) = \gamma y + g_0(y)^q + \beta^q g_1(y)^q - g_0(y) - \beta g_1(y)$$
$$= \gamma y + (\beta^q - \beta) g_1(y)$$
$$= \gamma [y + g_1(y)].$$

Since $g_1(y)$ is a 1-permutation over $\mathbb{F}_q$, the function

$$F(x) = x + g_0 \left(\frac{x^q}{\gamma^q} - \frac{x}{\gamma} \right) + \beta g_1 \left(\frac{x^q}{\gamma^q} - \frac{x}{\gamma} \right)$$

is a permutation over $\mathbb{F}_{q^2}$. □

5   Constructing Permutation Polynomials over $\mathbb{F}_{q^n}$ via $\mathbb{F}_q$ with $n \geq 3$

In Sect. 4 we give explicit classes of permutation polynomials over $\mathbb{F}_{q^2}$ using polynomials over $\mathbb{F}_q$.

In this section we give explicit classes of permutation polynomials over $\mathbb{F}_{q^n}$ using polynomials over $\mathbb{F}_q$ with $n \geq 3$. In fact, it is not easy to give such classes using the conditions of Akbary, Ghioca and Wang [1, Proposition 5.9] since we need to consider the subset $S = \{y^{q^n} - y | y \in \mathbb{F}_{q^n}\}$. This subset is easy to handle if $n = 2$, which we applied in Sect. 4. Hence in this section we use a different method of Akbary, Ghioca and Wang, namely [1, Proposition 5.6].

First we present our result for $n = 3$. The next proposition indicates the corresponding permutation polynomial class is large as the chosen components $g_1, g_2 \in \mathbb{F}_q[x]$ are arbitrary and $g_0 \in \mathbb{F}_q[x]$ has to satisfy a certain condition.

Proposition 4. *Let $\{\theta_0, \theta_1, \theta_2\}$ be a basis of $\mathbb{F}_{q^3}$ over $\mathbb{F}_q$. We assume that $Tr_3(\theta_0) \neq 0$ without loss of generality. We choose $a_0, a_1, a_2 \in \mathbb{F}_q$ satisfying*

$$(a_0 - a_2)^2 + (a_2 - a_0)(a_1 - a_2) + (a_1 - a_2)^2 \neq 0. \tag{3}$$

Let $g_0, g_1, g_2 \in \mathbb{F}_q[x]$ be such that $g_0(x)Tr_3(\theta_0) + g_1(x)Tr_3(\theta_1) + g_2(x)Tr_3(\theta_2)$ is an $(a_0 + a_1 + a_2)$-permutation of $\mathbb{F}_q$. Then

$$F(x) = a_0 x + a_0 x^q + a_2 x^{q^2} + \theta_0 g_0(Tr_3(x)) + \theta_1 g_1(Tr_3(x)) + \theta_2 g_2(Tr_3(x))$$

is a permutation over $\mathbb{F}_{q^3}$.

Proof. We use [1, Proposition 5.6], by taking $g(x)$ of the form

$$g(x) = \theta_0 g_0(x) + \theta_1 g_1(x) + \theta_2 g_2(x)$$

and $h(x)$ as a constant function equal to 1. Let $\varphi(x) = a_0 x + a_1 x^q + a_2 x^{q^2} \in \mathbb{F}_q[x]$ with a_0, a_1, a_2 satisfying (3). For $x \in \mathbb{F}_q$ we have

$$\varphi(x) + Tr_3(g(x)) = a_0 x + a_1 x^q + a_2 x^{q^2} + Tr_3(\theta_0 g_0(x) + \theta_1 g_1(x) + \theta_2 g_2(x))$$
$$= (a_0 + a_1 + a_2)x + g_0(x)Tr_3(\theta_0) + g_1(x)Tr_3(\theta_1) + g_2(x)Tr_3(\theta_2).$$

Since $g_0(x)Tr_3(\theta_0) + g_1(x)Tr_3(\theta_1) + g_2(x)Tr_3(\theta_2)$ is an $(a_0 + a_1 + a_2)$-permutation of $\mathbb{F}_q$, the condition (ii) of [1, Proposition 5.6] is satisfied.

It remains to prove that $\ker \varphi \cap \ker Tr_3 = \{0\}$. As $Tr_3(x) = x + x^q + x^{q^2}$ and $\varphi(x) = a_0 x + a_1 x^q + a_2 x^{q^2} \in \mathbb{F}_q[x]$ considering their q-associates (see, for example, [13, Definition 3.58]) it is enough to prove that

$$\gcd(1 + t + t^2, a_0 + a_1 t + a_2 t^2) = 1. \tag{4}$$

Indeed, if follows from [13, Theorem 3.62] that $\ker \varphi \cap \ker Tr_3 = \{0\}$ if and only if (4) holds. By a simple computation we observe that (3) is equivalent to the condition

$$\gcd(1 + t + t^2, a_0 + a_1 t + a_2 t^2) = 1.$$

$\square$

For $n \geq 3$ in general, the condition

$$(a_0 - a_2)^2 + (a_2 - a_0)(a_1 - a_2) + (a_1 - a_2)^2 \neq 0$$

corresponds to the resultant condition, which is well-known in algebraic geometry. We recall its definition (see, for example, [13, Definition 1.93]).

Definition 7. Let $f(x) = a_0 x^n + a_1 x^{n-1} + \cdots + a_n \in \mathbb{F}_q[x]$ be a polynomial of degree n and $g(x) = b_0 x^m + b_1 x^{m-1} + \cdots + b_m \in \mathbb{F}_q[x]$ be a polynomial of degree m with $n, m \in \mathbb{N}^+$. Then the resultant $Res(f, g)$ of the two polynomials is defined by the determinant

$$R(f, g) = \left. \begin{vmatrix} a_0 & a_1 & \dots & a_n & 0 & & \dots & 0 \\ 0 & a_0 & a_1 & \dots & a_n & 0 & \dots & 0 \\ & \vdots & & & & & & \vdots \\ 0 & \dots & 0 & a_0 & a_1 & & \dots & a_n \\ b_0 & b_1 & \dots & & b_m & 0 & \dots & 0 \\ 0 & b_0 & b_1 & \dots & & b_m & \dots & 0 \\ & \vdots & & & & & & \vdots \\ 0 & \dots & 0 & b_0 & b_1 & & \dots & b_m \end{vmatrix} \right\} \begin{matrix} m \ rows \\ \\ n \ rows \end{matrix}$$

of order $m + n$.

Now we are ready to generalize Proposition 4 in the next theorem.

Theorem 4. Let $\{\theta_0, \theta_1, \dots, \theta_{n-1}\}$ be a basis of $\mathbb{F}_{q^n}$ over $\mathbb{F}_q$. We assume that $Tr_n(\theta_0) \neq 0$ without loss of generality. Let $\varphi(x) = a_0 x + a_1 x^q \cdots + a_{n-1} x^{q^{n-1}}$ be an $\mathbb{F}_q$-linear polynomial over $\mathbb{F}_q$ satisfying the resultant

$$Res(a_0 + a_1 t + \cdots + a_{n-1} t^{n-1}, 1 + t + \cdots + t^{n-1}) \neq 0. \tag{5}$$

Let $g_0, g_1 \dots, g_{n-1} \in \mathbb{F}_q[x]$ be such that $g_0(x)Tr_n(\theta_0) + \cdots + g_{n-1}(x)Tr_n(\theta_{n-1})$ is an $(a_0 + \cdots + a_{n-1})$-permutation of $\mathbb{F}_q$. Then

$$F(x) = \varphi(x) + \theta_0 g_0(Tr_n(x)) + \cdots + \theta_{n-1} g_{n-1}(Tr_n(x))$$

is a permutation over $\mathbb{F}_{q^n}$.

Proof. We use a similar method as in the proof of Proposition 4. Take $g(x)$ of the form

$$g(x) = g_0(x)Tr_n(\theta_0) + \cdots + g_{n-1}(x)Tr_n(\theta_{n-1})$$

and $h(x)$ as the constant function equal to 1. Let

$$\varphi(x) = a_0 x + a_1 x^q \cdots + a_{n-1} x^{q^{n-1}} \in \mathbb{F}_q[x]$$

with $a_0, \dots, a_{n-1}$ satisfying (5). For $x \in \mathbb{F}_q$ we have

$$\varphi(x) + Tr_n(g(x)) = (a_0 + \cdots + a_{n-1})x + g_0(x)Tr_n(\theta_0) + \cdots + g_{n-1}(x)Tr_n(\theta_{n-1}).$$

This is a permutation polynomial over $\mathbb{F}_q$ since

$$g_0(x)Tr_n(\theta_0) + \cdots + g_{n-1}(x)Tr_n(\theta_{n-1})$$

is an $(a_0 + \cdots + a_{n-1})$-permutation of $\mathbb{F}_q$. So condition 2 of [1, Proposition 5.6] holds.

The proof of $\ker \varphi \cap \ker Tr_n = \{0\}$ comes from an important property of the resultant [13, page 36] (see also, [12, Corollary 8.4, page 203]). It indicates that the polynomials $1 + t + \cdots + t^{n-1}$ and $a_0 + a_1 t + \cdots + a_{n-1}t^{n-1}$ do not have common root if and only if (5) holds. Note that we also use q-associates before this argument.   □

6   A Further Generalization of Linear Translators

For an arbitrary $\mathbb{F}_q$ and a map $f : \mathbb{F}_{q^n} \to \mathbb{F}_q$ with $n \geq 2$, the concept of linear structure in Definition 2 corresponds to the notion of linear structure: Let $\gamma \in \mathbb{F}_{q^n}$, $b \in \mathbb{F}_q$. Then γ is called b-linear translator of $f : \mathbb{F}_{q^n} \to \mathbb{F}_q$ if

$$f(x + \gamma u) = f(x) + bu \text{ for all } x \in \mathbb{F}_{q^n} \text{ and } y \in \mathbb{F}_q.$$

Note that if $q = 2$, then b is either 0 or 1 and we have either 0-linear translator or 1-linear translator coinciding with 0-linear structure or 1-linear structure.

Recently Cepak, Pasalić and Muratović-Ribić generalized the notion of linear translators and gave an application for constructing permutation polynomials (see [8]).

In this section we obtain a further and very natural generalization of the notion of linear translators. We also give two different applications of our more general version to permutation polynomials. Theorem 5 is an easy but rather unexpected application. It gives a class of permutation polynomials over $\mathbb{F}_{q^n}$ using a surjective map $f : \mathbb{F}_{q^n} \to S \subseteq \mathbb{F}_q$ and our notion of generalized linear translator.

The proof uses a trick that was used earlier in [15]. Moreover, this method gives the inverse permutation explicitly.

The second application is Theorem 6 below and it shows that under certain conditions one can get permutation polynomials on $\mathbb{F}_{q^n}$ again using $f : \mathbb{F}_{q^n} \to S \subseteq \mathbb{F}_q$ and the corresponding generalized linear translator. Finally, we give an explicit example illustrating that there exist generalized linear translators satisfying the conditions of Theorem 6 and not being Frobenius linear translators, which is the notion expressed in [8].

We start with our generalization of the notion.

Definition 8. *Let $S \subseteq \mathbb{F}_q$ and let $\gamma, b \in \mathbb{F}_{q^n}$. Let $A : \mathbb{F}_{q^n} \to \mathbb{F}_{q^n}$ be an additive map. We say that γ is a (b, A)-linear translator with respect to S for the mapping $f : \mathbb{F}_{q^n} \to S$, if*

$$f(x + \gamma u) = f(x) + bA(u)$$

for all $x \in \mathbb{F}_{q^n}$ and for all $u \in S$.

Now we are ready to present a first application of the notion in Definition 8.

Theorem 5. *Let $S \subseteq \mathbb{F}_{q^n}$ and $f : \mathbb{F}_{q^n} \to S$ be a surjective map. Let $\gamma \in \mathbb{F}_q$ be a (b, A)-linear translator with respect to S for the map f where A is an additive map and $\gamma, b \in \mathbb{F}_{q^n}$. Then for any $g \in \mathbb{F}_{q^n}[x]$ which maps S into S, we have that $F(x) = x + \gamma g(f(x))$ is a permutation over $\mathbb{F}_{q^n}$ if and only if $\psi(z) = z + bA(g(z))$ is a permutation on S.*

Moreover, if F is a permutation over $\mathbb{F}_{q^n}$, then its inverse function F^{-1} is given explicitly as

$$F^{-1}(z) = z - \gamma g(\psi^{-1}(f(z))).$$

Proof. Let x be any element of $\mathbb{F}_{q^n}$. Then we have $F(x) = x + \gamma g(f(x))$ by definition. By applying f to the both sides of the equality we obtain

$$
\begin{aligned}
f(F(x)) &= f(x + \gamma g(f(x))) \\
&= f(x) + bA(g(f(x))) \text{ since } f \text{ is } (b, A)\text{-linear translator} \quad (6) \\
&= \psi(f(x)) \text{ by definition of the map } \psi.
\end{aligned}
$$

Therefore we have $\psi(f(x)) = f(F(x))$.

Assume first that ψ is a permutation over S. Let $F(x_1) = F(x_2)$ for some $x_1, x_2 \in \mathbb{F}_{q^n}$. Then applying f to both sides of the equality we have $f(F(x_1)) = f(F(x_2))$. By using (6), we obtain

$$\psi(f(x_1)) = f(F(x_1)) = f(F(x_2)) = \psi(f(x_2)).$$

Since ψ is a permutation over S, we get $f(x_1) = f(x_2)$. As $F(x_1) = F(x_2)$ we also have

$$x_1 + \gamma g(f(x_1)) = x_2 + \gamma g(f(x_2)).$$

These imply that $x_1 = x_2$. Therefore F is injective and indeed F is bijective.

Conversely, assume that F is a permutation over $\mathbb{F}_{q^n}$. Let s be any element of S. Since f is a surjective map, there exists $\alpha \in \mathbb{F}_{q^n}$ satisfying $f(\alpha) = s$. Because F is permutation over $\mathbb{F}_{q^n}$, there is $x \in \mathbb{F}_{q^n}$ such that $F(x) = \alpha$. By using (6), we have

$$\psi(f(x)) = f(F(x)) = f(\alpha) = s.$$

Therefore ψ is surjective and in fact, ψ is bijective. Then $F(x) = x + \gamma g(f(x))$ is a permutation over $\mathbb{F}_{q^n}$ if and only if $\psi(z) = z + bA(g(z))$ is a permutation over S.

Next, we compute F^{-1} explicitly. Let $y = F(x) = x + \gamma g(f(x))$. Then we have

$$
\begin{aligned}
f(y) &= f(x + \gamma g(f(x))) \\
&= f(x + \gamma u), \text{ where } u = g(f(x)) \in S \\
&= f(x) + bA(u), \text{ since } \gamma \text{ is a } (b, A)\text{-linear translator} \\
&= f(x) + bA(g(f(x))), \text{ recall } u = g(f(x)) \\
&= z + bA(g(z)), \text{ where } f(x) = z \\
&= \psi(z).
\end{aligned}
$$

As ψ is a permutation on S we have that for each y there exists $x = y - \gamma g(\psi^{-1}(f(y)))$ satisfying $F(x) = y$. Therefore, $F(x)$ is surjective and the desired result follows. The converse of the statement is proved similarly.

Moreover, $F^{-1}(z) = z - \gamma g(\psi^{-1}(f(z)))$ since $f^{-1}(z) = x$. □

Next, we give another application of Definition 8.

Theorem 6. *Let f be a function from $\mathbb{F}_{q^n}$ onto $\mathbb{F}_q$, $\gamma \in \mathbb{F}_{q^n}^*$. Let γ be a (b, A)-linear translator of f where $b \in \mathbb{F}_q$ and $A(x) \in \mathbb{F}_{q^n}[x]$ is an additive map satisfying the following conditions:*

1. *A is $\mathbb{F}_q$-linear.*
2. *$A(\gamma) \neq 0$.*
3. *$A(\gamma a) = A(\gamma)A(a)$ for all $a \in \mathbb{F}_q$.*
4. *For any $x \in \mathbb{F}_{q^n}$: If $A(\gamma x) \in A(\gamma)\mathbb{F}_q$, then $x \in \mathbb{F}_q$.*
5. *$A|_{\mathbb{F}_q}$ is onto.*

For any map $h : \mathbb{F}_q \to \mathbb{F}_q$ consider the map

$$G : \mathbb{F}_{q^n} \to \mathbb{F}_{q^n}$$
$$x \mapsto A(x) + A(\gamma)h(f(x)).$$

Then G is a permutation over $\mathbb{F}_{q^n}$ if and only if the following derived map depending on h and b

$$g : \mathbb{F}_q \to \mathbb{F}_q$$
$$u \mapsto u + bh(u)$$

is a permutation over $\mathbb{F}_q$.

Proof. We use a method similar to the ones in [11] or [8]. Let $x, \alpha \in \mathbb{F}_{q^n}$ satisfy $G(x) = G(x + \gamma \alpha)$. Then

$$G(x) = A(x) + A(\gamma)h(f(x)),$$
$$G(x + \gamma \alpha) = A(x + \gamma \alpha) + A(\gamma)h(f(x + \gamma \alpha))$$
$$= A(x) + A(\gamma \alpha) + A(\gamma)h(f(x + \gamma \alpha)) \text{ by condition 1,}$$

and hence

$$A(\gamma)h(f(x)) = A(\gamma \alpha) + A(\gamma)h(f(x + \gamma \alpha)). \tag{7}$$

Divide both sides of Eq. (7) by $A(\gamma)$, since $A(\gamma) \neq 0$ by condition 2. Then we have

$$h(f(x)) = \frac{A(\gamma \alpha)}{A(\gamma)} + h(f(x + \gamma \alpha)).$$

As $f(x), f(x + \gamma \alpha) \in \mathbb{F}_q[x]$, $h \in \mathbb{F}_q[x]$ and $\frac{A(\gamma \alpha)}{A(\gamma)} \in \mathbb{F}_q$, by condition 4 we get $\alpha \in \mathbb{F}_q$. Taking $a = \alpha \in \mathbb{F}_q$, we have

$$h(f(x)) = \frac{A(\gamma a)}{A(\gamma)} + h(f(x + \gamma a)).$$

Note that $A(\gamma a) = A(\gamma)A(a)$ by condition 3, so we get

$$h(f(x)) = A(a) + h(f(x + \gamma a))$$

and hence by using that γ is a (b, A)-linear translator for f, we get

$$h(f(x)) = A(a) + h(f(x) + bA(a)).$$

Then substituting $u = f(x) \in \mathbb{F}_q[x]$, we have

$$h(u) = A(a) + h(u + bA(a)). \tag{8}$$

Consider

$$g(u) = u + bh(u)$$
$$g(u + bA(a)) = u + bA(a) + b(h(u + bA(a)))$$
$$= u + b\,(A(a) + h(u + bA(a)))$$
$$= u + bh(u)$$
$$= g(u).$$

Here as x runs through $\mathbb{F}_{q^n}$, $u = f(x)$ runs through $\mathbb{F}_q$ as f is onto. Then we get

$$g(u) = g(u + bA(a)). \tag{9}$$

Thus the mapping G is a permutation over $\mathbb{F}_{q^n}$ if and only if the only a satisfying Eq. (9) is $a = 0$. If $b = 0$, then we obtain that $A(a) = 0$ as g is permutation. As $A|_{\mathbb{F}_q}$ is one-to-one, we get $a = 0$. If $b = 0$, then from Eq. (8) we have

$$h(u) = A(a) + h(u + bA(a)) = A(a) + h(u).$$

Hence $A(a) = 0$. Therefore, $a = 0$. $\qquad\square$

The next example illustrates a simple situation when the conditions of Theorem 6 hold. Note that the polynomial $A(x)$ in the next example is not in the form of a Frobenius linear translator. Moreover, the next example illustrates that the conditions of Theorem 5 hold easily as its conditions are weaker.

Example 2. Let $q = 2$ and $n = 4$. Take $A(x) = \alpha^2 x + \alpha^7 x^2 + \alpha^3 x^4 + \alpha^5 x^8 \in \mathbb{F}_{2^4}[x]$ where $\alpha^4 = 1 + \alpha$ and $\gamma = \alpha^3 \in \mathbb{F}_{2^4}^*$. Then $A(x)$ satisfies the following conditions:

1. A is $\mathbb{F}_2$-linear since A is additive.
2. $A(\gamma) \neq 0$ since $A(\gamma) = A(\alpha^3) = \alpha^4 \neq 0$.
3. $A(\gamma a) = A(\gamma)A(a)$ for all $a \in \mathbb{F}_2$ since

$$A(a) = \alpha^2 a + \alpha^7 a^2 + \alpha^3 a^4 + \alpha^5 a^8 = a(\alpha^2 + \alpha^7 + \alpha^3 + \alpha^5) = a$$

and

$$A(\gamma a) = \alpha^2(\alpha^3 a) + \alpha^7(\alpha^3 a)^2 + \alpha^3(\alpha^3 a)^4 + \alpha^5(\alpha^3 a)^8 = aA(\gamma) = A(a)A(\gamma).$$

4. For any $x \in \mathbb{F}_{q^n}$: If $A(\gamma x) \in A(\gamma)\mathbb{F}_q$, then $x \in \mathbb{F}_q$. Consider $\theta = \alpha^i \in \mathbb{F}_{2^4}/\mathbb{F}_2$
for $1 \leq i \leq 14$, then we have

$$A(\gamma\theta) = A(\gamma\alpha^i) \notin A(\gamma)\mathbb{F}_2 \text{ where } A(\gamma) = \alpha^4 \text{ for } 1 \leq i \leq 14.$$

Indeed, we have $\{A(\gamma\alpha^i) : 1 \leq i \leq 14\} = \mathbb{F}_{16} \setminus \{0, \alpha^4\}$. For example, $A(\gamma\alpha) = \alpha^8$ and $A(\gamma\alpha^{11}) = \alpha$.

5. $A|_{\mathbb{F}_2}$ is onto.

Let $f : \mathbb{F}_{2^4} \to \mathbb{F}_2$ be the map $x \mapsto Tr_4(x)$. Then α^3 is a $(1, A)$-linear translator of f since we have

$$f(x + \gamma u) = f(x + \alpha^3 u) = Tr_4(x + \alpha^3 u) = Tr_4(x) + uTr_4(\alpha^3)$$
$$= Tr_4(x) + u = f(x) + u$$

for all $x \in \mathbb{F}_{2^4}$ and for all $u \in \mathbb{F}_2$.

7   Conclusion

We define a new class of Boolean functions which includes Cusick's class of functions [9] as a small subclass. We obtain explicit permutation polynomial classes over $\mathbb{F}_{q^2}$ via $\mathbb{F}_q$ and also over $\mathbb{F}_{q^n}$ via $\mathbb{F}_q$ with $n \geq 3$. We give a natural generalization of the notion of linear translators which is called (b,A)-linear translator. By using the connection between linear translators and permutation polynomials over finite fields, we obtain a class of permutation polynomials over $\mathbb{F}_{q^n}$. For applications our class of Boolean functions would be preferable compared to Cusick's class of functions mentioned above as our class is much larger having cryptographic properties as good as (or even better than) the class of Cusick's functions. Using our methods and new notion of (b,A)-linear translator it would be possible to construct further interesting algebraic structures like permutation polynomials or special functions.

Acknowledgments. We thank the reviewers for their insightful and fruitful remarks which greatly improved the presentation of the paper.

The research of the second and third authors has been funded by METU Coordinatorship of Scientific Research Projects via grant for projects GAP-101-2018-2782.

References

1. Akbary, A., Ghioca, D., Wang, Q.: On constructing permutations of finite fields. Finite Fields Appl. **17**(1), 51–67 (2011)
2. Boztaş, S., Özbudak, F., Tekin, E.: Explicit full correlation distribution of sequence families using plateaued functions. IEEE Trans. Inf. Theory **64**(4), 2858–2875 (2018)

3. Carlet, C.: Boolean functions for cryptography and error correcting codes. In: Crama, Y., Hammer, P.L. (eds.) Boolean Models and Methods in Mathematics, Computer Science, and Engineering, pp. 257–397. Cambridge University Press, Cambridge (2010)
4. Carlet, C.: On the properties of vectorial functions with plateaued components and their consequences on APN functions. In: El Hajji, S., Nitaj, A., Carlet, C., Souidi, E.M. (eds.) C2SI 2015. LNCS, vol. 9084, pp. 63–73. Springer, Cham (2015). https://doi.org/10.1007/978-3-319-18681-8_5
5. Carlet, C.: Boolean and vectorial plateaued functions and APN functions. IEEE Trans. Inf. Theory **61**(11), 6272–6289 (2015)
6. Carlet, C., Mesnager, S., Özbudak, F., Sınak, A.: Explicit characterizations for plateaued-ness of p-ary (Vectorial) functions. In: El Hajji, S., Nitaj, A., Souidi, E.M. (eds.) C2SI 2017. LNCS, vol. 10194, pp. 328–345. Springer, Cham (2017). https://doi.org/10.1007/978-3-319-55589-8_22
7. Cepak, N., Charpin, P., Pasalic, E.: Permutations via linear translators. Finite Fields Appl. **45**, 19–42 (2017)
8. Cepak, N., Pasalic, E., Muratović-Ribić, A.: Frobenius linear translators giving rise to new infinite classes of permutations and bent functions. arXiv preprint https://arxiv.org/abs/1801.08460 (2018)
9. Cusick, T.W.: Highly nonlinear plateaued functions. IET Inf. Secur. **11**(2), 78–81 (2017)
10. Cusick, T.W., Stănica, P.: Cryptographic Boolean Functions and Applications, 2nd edn. Academic Press, San Diego (2017). (1st ed., 2009)
11. Kyureghyan, G.M.: Constructing permutations of finite fields via linear translators. J. Comb. Theory Ser. A **118**, 1052–1061 (2011)
12. Lang, S.: Algebra. Graduate Texts in Mathematics, p. 211. Springer-Verlag, New York (2002)
13. Lidl, R., Niederreiter, H.: Finite Fields. Cambridge University Press, Cambridge (1983)
14. Mesnager, S.: Bent Functions: Fundamentals and Results. Springer, Cham (2016)
15. Mesnager, S., Ongan, P., Özbudak, F.: New bent functions from permutations and linear translators. In: El Hajji, S., Nitaj, A., Souidi, E.M. (eds.) C2SI 2017. LNCS, vol. 10194, pp. 282–297. Springer, Cham (2017). https://doi.org/10.1007/978-3-319-55589-8_19
16. Mesnager, S., Özbudak, F., Snak, A.: Linear codes from weakly regular plateaued functions and their secret sharing schemes. Des. Codes Crypt. **87**(2–3), 463–480 (2018). https://doi.org/10.1007/s10623-018-0556-4
17. Riera, C., Solé, P., Stănică, P.: A complete characterization of plateaued boolean functions in terms of their cayley graphs. In: Joux, A., Nitaj, A., Rachidi, T. (eds.) AFRICACRYPT 2018. LNCS, vol. 10831, pp. 3–10. Springer, Cham (2018). https://doi.org/10.1007/978-3-319-89339-6_1
18. Tang, C., Li, N., Qi, Y., Zhou, Z., Helleseth, T.: Linear codes with two or three weights from weakly regular bent functions. IEEE Trans. Inf. Theory **62**(3), 1166–1176 (2016)
19. Tokareva, N.: Bent Functions: Results and Applications to Cryptography. Academic Press, San Diego (2015)

Faster Scalar Multiplication on the x-Line: Three-Dimensional GLV Method with Three-Dimensional Differential Addition Chains

Hairong Yi[1,2(✉)], Guiwen Luo[1,2], and Dongdai Lin[1]

[1] State Key Laboratory of Information Security,
Institute of Information Engineering, Chinese Academy of Sciences,
Beijing 100093, China
{yihairong,luoguiwen,ddlin}@iie.ac.cn
[2] School of Cyber Security, University of Chinese Academy of Sciences,
Beijing 100049, China

Abstract. On the quadratic twist of a GLV curve, we explore faster scalar multiplication on its x-coordinate system utilizing three-dimensional GLV method. We construct and implement two kinds of three-dimensional differential addition chains, one of which is uniform and the other is non-uniform but runs faster. Implementations show that at about 254-bit security level, the triple scalar multiplication using our second differential addition chains runs about 26% faster than the straightforward computing using Montgomery ladder, and about 6% faster that the double scalar multiplication using DJB chains.

Keywords: Scalar multiplication · GLV methods ·
Differential Addition Chains · DJB chains

1 Introduction

Elliptic curve cryptography (ECC) plays an important role in the public key cryptosystems. Various schemes and numerous techniques about ECC have been studied to meet the different needs (basically, efficiency and security) in different settings. In 2014, Costello, Hisil and Smith [6] implemented a very fast elliptic curve scalar multiplication, optimized for Diffie-Hellman Key Exchange at the 128-bit security level. This very efficient scheme involved two crucial ideas: using x-coordinate-only systems and the two-dimensional GLV method on the x-line.

The idea for computing scalar multiplication on elliptic curves by only x-coordinates arose earlier. Montgomery's explicit formulas [14] for the arithmetic on x-coordinate of a Montgomery curve together with his eponymous ladder provided a full solution to its implementation. It is often used as a technique called point compression, for storing or transmitting fewer bits of information in

© Springer Nature Switzerland AG 2019
C. Carlet et al. (Eds.): C2SI 2019, LNCS 11445, pp. 236–253, 2019.
https://doi.org/10.1007/978-3-030-16458-4_14

some specific situation. The Gallant-Lambert-Vanstone (GLV) method [9] is a typical and important technique for speeding up scalar multiplication on certain kinds of elliptic curves. It exploits a fast endomorphism on the curve, replacing a single large scalar multiplication with two scalar multiplications with only a half bit lengths. Then this two-dimensional GLV will result in a twofold performance speedup using parallel computation. Since m-dimensional GLV would probably lead to m-fold performance acceleration by parallel computation, higher dimensional GLV method has also been intensively considered [8,10,12]. In 2009, Galbraith, Lin and Scott [8] proposed the so-called GLS curves and indicated that on restricted GLS curves with j-invariant 0 or 1728, the four-dimensional GLV can be implemented. Further in 2012, Longa and Sica [12] combined the ideas in [9] and [8] and realized the four-dimensional GLV on the quadratic twists of all previous GLV curves appeared in [9].

In [6], Costello et al. have shown a positive effect of applying the two-dimensional GLV method to the scalar multiplication on the x-line. Motivated by the potential acceleration of higher dimensional GLV method, in this paper we investigate the performance of applying the three-dimensional GLV method to the x-coordinate-only systems. We choose the elliptic curves using the approach of [12], which are originally tailored for four-dimensional GLV method but can be transformed to three-dimensional variants as well. The remaining key issue is the chosen of higher dimensional differential addition chains (DACs) used in multi-scalar multiplication, where the "differential" property of the chain is required by the incomplete (pseudo-) operations on the x-line.

The two-dimensional DACs have all kinds of constructions in literature. For example, Schoenmakers' chain in [17], Akishita's chain in [1]. In [6] another three different two-dimensional DACs are implemented: PRAC chains [13,17], AK chains [2] and DJB chains [3]. Each of them offers a different combination of speed, uniformity and constant-time execution. The research about higher dimensional DACs are comparatively less. Early in 2006, Brown [4] extended Bernstein's idea (i.e. DJB chain) to general d-dimensional DACs, but it has been patented. For bypassing it, around 2016 SubramanyaRao tried the three-dimensional analogue of Schoenmakers' chain in [15] and that of Akishita's chain in [16]. The first attempt failed because it was showed to be more expensive than one-dimensional Montgomery ladder. The second one succeeded in competing with Montgomery ladder by about 22% speedup at the 256-bit security level. However there were no results of comparing it with the two-dimensional DACs. The latest progress is made in [11], 2017, by Hutchinson and Karabina. They constructed a d-dimensional DAC which has some similarities with that of Brown's [4], and made specific theoretical comparisons between some known d-point multiplication algorithms showing the algorithm based on their construction to be superior.

In this paper, we propose two kinds of constructions of three-dimensional DACs. The first one is a straightforward extension to higher dimension of the DJB chain, which is totally different from the patented one of Brown's in [4]. It inherits the property of uniformity. The second one comes from our direct observation, which is not a higher dimensional analogue of any two-dimensional DAC.

It is not uniform, but runs very fast. And it runs faster than SubramanyaRao's second chain described in [16] since it saves one more point operation in each iteration. Our final comparison experiments on testing scalar multiplication on the x-coordinate system utilizing different dimensional GLV methods show that at about 254-bit security level, our uniform three-dimensional DAC runs about 9% faster than Montgomery ladder, and the non-uniform one runs about 26% faster than Montgomery ladder and about 6% faster than the two-dimensional DJB chain.

Paper Organization. The rest of the paper is arranged as follows. In Sect. 2, we begin with a brief introduction to the four-dimensional GLV method proposed in [12], and see how to deduce a three-dimensional GLV variant directly in the same settings. In Sect. 3, we describe the basic operations on the x-coordinate system and deploy higher dimensional GLV method on this system. Then in Sect. 4 we describe explicitly the construction of our two three-dimensional DACs, and give some examples. In Sect. 5, from both the theoretic and experimental aspect, we compare the performance of scalar multiplication on the x-coordinate utilizing different dimensional GLV methods together with different DACs. Finally in Sect. 6 we draw our conclusion.

2   Three and Four-Dimensional GLV Method

The 4-dimensional GLV method proposed by Longa and Sica in [12] consists of the chosen of elliptic curves that are equipped with two efficient endomorphisms and 4-dimensional scalar decomposition. They use the quadratic twists of elliptic curves, of which the idea comes from GLS curves, and propose a specific twofold Cornacchia-type algorithm for scalar decomposition. Here we give a brief introduction.

Let $\mathbb{F}_p$ be a finite field where p is prime. A GLV curve over $\mathbb{F}_p$ is an elliptic curve $E/\mathbb{F}_p$ of whom the group of rational points has an almost prime order (cofactor ≤ 4), equipped with an efficiently computable $\mathbb{F}_p$-endomorphism ϕ. Assume that $X^2 + rX + s \in \mathbb{Z}[X]$ is the characteristic polynomial of ϕ, and π is the p-th Frobenius endomorphism of E. Let $E'/\mathbb{F}_{p^2}$ be a quadratic twist of $E(\mathbb{F}_{p^2})$, via the twisting $\mathbb{F}_{p^4}$-isomorphism $t_2 : E \to E'$. We then obtain two efficient endomorphisms on E', $\Phi = t_2 \phi t_2^{-1}$ and $\Psi = t_2 \pi t_2^{-1}$, both defined over $\mathbb{F}_{p^2}$. Suppose that $\langle P \rangle \subset E'(\mathbb{F}_{p^2})$ is a large subgroup of prime order n. Then we have $\Phi^2(P) + r\Phi(P) + sP = \mathcal{O}_{E'}$ and $\Psi^2(P) + P = \mathcal{O}_{E'}$, together with $\Phi(P) = \lambda P$ and $\Psi(P) = \mu P$ where $\lambda, \mu \in [1, n-1]$ is a root of $X^2 + rX + s$ modulo n, $X^2 + 1$ modulo n respectively.

Define the 4-dimensional GLV reduction map w.r.t. $\{1, \Phi, \Psi, \Phi\Psi\}$

$$\mathfrak{f}: \quad \mathbb{Z}^4 \to \mathbb{Z}/n$$
$$(x_1, x_2, x_3, x_4) \mapsto x_1 + x_2\lambda + x_3\mu + x_4\lambda\mu \pmod{n}.$$

Then $\ker \mathfrak{f}$ is a lattice. Applying the twofold Cornacchia-type algorithm [12, 18] to $\ker \mathfrak{f}$, we can find a short basis $\{v_1, v_2, v_3, v_4\}$ to this lattice with $\max_i |v_i| \leq 3.41(\sqrt{1 + |r| + s})n^{1/4}$, where $|\cdot|$ denotes the maximum norm. For any scalar

$k \in [1, n)$, express $(k, 0, 0, 0) = \alpha_1 v_1 + \alpha_2 v_2 + \alpha_3 v_3 + \alpha_4 v_4$ as the $\mathbb{Q}$-linear combination of the basis $\{v_i\}$. Then round α_i to the nearest integers $a_i = \lfloor \alpha_i \rceil$, and let $(k_1, k_2, k_3, k_4) = (k, 0, 0, 0) - \sum_{i=1}^{4} a_i v_i$. Finally we have

$$kP = k_1 P + k_2 \Phi(P) + k_3 \Psi(P) + k_4 \Phi\Psi(P)$$

with

$$\max_i(|k_i|) \leq 6.82(\sqrt{1 + |r| + s})n^{1/4}.$$

For our demand in the following, actually we need the 3-dimensional GLV method. The above way for choosing target curves is exactly what we want. But we delete the dimension controlled by "$\Phi\Psi$" from the 4-dimensional version to obtain a 3-dimensional representation. As for the 3-dimensional scalar decomposition, following the same way as above, then we obtain a 3-dimensional GLV reduction map $\tilde{f}$ w.r.t. $\{1, \Phi, \Psi\}$. For finding a short basis of the lattice $\ker \tilde{f}$, we can apply LLL algorithm. Then using the way described as above we can obtain

$$kP = \ell_1 P + \ell_2 \Phi(P) + \ell_3 \Psi(P) \quad \text{with} \quad \ell_i = O(k^{1/3}).$$

3   Projection to the x-Line

The projective line $\mathbb{P}^1$ can be viewed as a quotient variety of E by the subgroup $\{\pm 1\}$ of the automorphism group $\mathrm{Aut}(E)$ of E. Particularly, if $\{\pm 1\}$ is exactly the whole group $\mathrm{Aut}(E)$ then $\mathbb{P}^1$ is the so-called Kummer variety of E. When E is given by a Weierstrass equation (or Montgomery form as [6] exploited), then the quotient map $E \to \mathbb{P}^1$ is just the projection to x-coordinate.

Some of the operations of E are well-defined on the x-line, like the scalar multiplication. Assume that P is a point of E. Given the x-coordinate $x(P)$ of P and some scalar k, then $x(kP)$ can be computed using the well-known Montgomery ladder. Based on this property, Diffie-Hellman Key Exchange can be executed on the pure x-coordinate settings. Furthermore in [6] Costello et al. require E to be twist-secure, for ensuring the compactness of this system.

However the x-line is not a group. The typical obstruction is that, only given the x-coordinates $x(P), x(Q)$ of two points P, Q of E, one can not distinguish $x(P \oplus Q)$ and $x(P \ominus Q)$. But once one of them is known, then the other is clear.

Basic Pseudo-Operations on the x-Line. In our settings, the target elliptic curve $E'/\mathbb{F}_{p^2}$ as described in Sect. 2 is always defined by a short Weierstrass equation: $y^2 = x^3 + a_4 x + a_6$. For reader's convenience, here we write the explicit formula (in projective coordinate form) for pseudo-doubling and pseudo-addition on the x-line, which one may refer to [5].

Let $x(P_i) = (X_i : Z_i)$, $i = 1, 2$ be the x-coordinates of two points P_1, P_2 on $E'(\mathbb{F}_{p^2})$. Let $x(P_1 \ominus P_2) = (\Delta X : \Delta Z)$. Assume $x(P_1 \oplus P_2) = (X : Z)$. Then

$$X = \Delta Z\big(-4a_6 Z_1 Z_2 (X_1 Z_2 + X_2 Z_1) + (X_1 X_2 - a_4 Z_1 Z_2)^2\big),$$
$$Z = \Delta X\big(X_1 Z_2 - X_2 Z_1\big)^2,$$

and

$$x(2P_1) = \left((X_1^2 - a_4 Z_1^2)^2 - 8a_6 X_1 Z_1^3 : 4Z_1(X_1(X_1^2 + a_4 Z_1^2) + a_6 Z_1^3)\right).$$

Pseudo-Endomorphisms on the x-Line. Every endomorphism of E induces a pseudo-endomorphism of $\mathbb{P}^1$, since it commutes with the negation map of E. On our target curve $E'/\mathbb{F}_{p^2}$, the two endomorphisms Φ and Ψ induce $\Phi_x : x \mapsto \Phi_x(x)$ and $\Psi_x : x \mapsto \Psi_x(x)$ on the x-line. And since they are commutative, we have

$$\Phi_x \Psi_x = (\Phi\Psi)_x = (\Psi\Phi)_x = \Psi_x \Phi_x.$$

Let $\langle P \rangle \subset E'(\mathbb{F}_{p^2})$ be the subgroup with large prime order as in Sect. 2. For any scalar k, we can find (k_1, k_2, k_3, k_4) with only a quater of the bit length of k, such that

$$kP = k_1 P + k_2 \Phi(P) + k_3 \Psi(P) + k_4 \Phi\Psi(P);$$

or we can find (ℓ_1, ℓ_2, ℓ_3) with only one third of the bit length of k, such that

$$kP = \ell_1 P + \ell_2 \Phi(P) + \ell_3 \Psi(P).$$

Denote by x the x-coordinate of P. Then we would like to compute $x(kP)$ using

$$(k_1 + k_2 \Phi + k_3 \Psi + k_4 \Phi\Psi)_x(x) \tag{1}$$

$$\text{or} \quad (\ell_1 + \ell_2 \Phi + \ell_3 \Psi)_x(x). \tag{2}$$

Actually here we only need to consider Eq. (2). We can expect to accelerate the computation of $x(kP)$ using this multi-scalar multiplication. But since there are only pseudo-operations on the x-line, addition chains are not feasible. And it forces us to propose a higher dimensional DAC to this (k_1, k_2, k_3, k_4) or (ℓ_1, ℓ_2, ℓ_3), just as the 2-dimensional case in [6], where computes

$$(m_1 + m_2 \Phi)_x(x) \quad \text{or} \quad (m_1 + m_2 \Psi)_x(x) \tag{3}$$

utilizing a 2-dimensional DAC.

4   Three-Dimensional Differential Addition Chains

A differential addition chain is an addition chain in which each sum is already accompanied by a difference, i.e. whenever a new chain element $M + N$ is formed by adding M and N, the difference $M - N$ was already in the chain. The chain is called n-dimensional, if every element in this chain has the form of n-tuple. For example, the well-known "Montgomery ladder" is a typical one-dimensional DAC.

In this section, we propose two kinds of constructions of 3-dimensional DACs. One is a higher dimensional analogue of the DJB chain. The other comes from observation directly, which is not a higher dimensional analogue of any 2-dimensional DAC.

4.1   A Uniform Three-Dimensional Differential Addition Chain

The DJB chain is a 2-dimensional DAC proposed by Bernstein in 2006. It is uniform, i.e. possesses the same execution pattern: add, double, add in each iteration, and hence can resist side-channel attacks. For more details one can refer to [3]. In the following, we generalize it to the 3-dimensional case.

Let S be the following set

$$\{(0,0,0),(1,0,0),(0,1,0),(0,0,1),(1,1,0),(1,0,1),(0,1,1),(1,1,1)\}.$$

As in the 2-dimensional case, in each iteration we compute part of the eight elements of the set $S(a,b,c) = (a,b,c) + S$.

We find that computing five of them is enough. For ensuring the property of uniform, the element of type (even, even, even) should be reserved. For a pair of elements in $S(a,b,c)$, if every component of them has the opposite parity, then we call them dual to each other. Among the following three dual pairs {(odd, even, even), (even, odd, odd)}, {(even, odd, even), (odd, even, odd)}, {(even, even, odd), (odd, odd, even)}, we omit one of two elements in every pair, and use three parameters d_1, d_2, d_3 to determine which ones are to be omitted, that is

$$
\begin{aligned}
T_1 &= (a + (a + d_1 + 1 \mod 2), b + (b + d_1 \mod 2), c + (c + d_1 \mod 2)), \\
T_2 &= (a + (a + d_2 \mod 2), b + (b + d_2 + 1 \mod 2), c + (c + d_2 \mod 2)), \\
T_3 &= (a + (a + d_3 \mod 2), b + (b + d_3 \mod 2), c + (c + d_3 + 1 \mod 2)).
\end{aligned}
$$

Next we give a recursive definition of the 3-dimensional differential addition chain.

Definition 1. *For a given 3-tuple of nonnegative integers* (A, B, C), *and* $\{D_1, D_2, D_3\}$ *where* $D_1, D_2, D_3 \in \{0,1\}$, *we define the set* $C(\{D_i\}_{i=1}^3; A, B, C)$ *recursively, as the set* $C(\{d_i\}_{i=1}^3; a, b, c)$ *added with the following five elements:*

$$
\begin{aligned}
M_{-1} &= (A + (A + 1 \mod 2), B + (B + 1 \mod 2), C + (C + 1 \mod 2)), \\
M_0 &= (A + (A \mod 2), B + (B \mod 2), C + (C \mod 2)), \\
M_1 &= (A + (A + D_1 \mod 2), B + (B + D_1 + 1 \mod 2), C + (C + D_1 + 1 \mod 2)), \\
M_2 &= (A + (A + D_2 + 1 \mod 2), B + (B + D_2 \mod 2), C + (C + D_2 + 1 \mod 2)), \\
M_3 &= (A + (A + D_3 + 1 \mod 2), B + (B + D_3 + 1 \mod 2), C + (C + D_3 \mod 2)),
\end{aligned}
$$

where $(a, b, c) = (\lfloor A/2 \rfloor, \lfloor B/2 \rfloor, \lfloor C/2 \rfloor)$ *and* (d_1, d_2, d_3) *is taken as*

(d_1, d_2, d_3)	*if* $(a + A, b + B, c + C) \mod 2$
$(1,0,0)$	$(1,0,0)$
$(0,1,1)$	$(0,1,1)$
$(0,1,0)$	$(0,1,0)$
$(1,0,1)$	$(1,0,1)$
$(0,0,1)$	$(0,0,1)$
$(1,1,0)$	$(1,1,0)$
(D_1, D_2, D_3)	$(0,0,0)$
$(1 - D_1, 1 - D_2, 1 - D_3)$	$(1,1,1).$

Specially, for arbitrary D_1, D_2, D_3 let $C(\{D_i\}; 0, 0, 0)$ be the union of the sets

$$S_1 = \{(0,0,0), (1,0,0), (0,1,0), (0,0,1), (1,-1,0), (1,0,-1), (0,1,-1),$$
$$(1,1,-1)\}$$
$$S_2 = \{(1,1,0), (1,0,1), (0,1,1), (1,-1,1), (-1,1,1)\}$$

where S_2 can be computed from S_1.

Remark 1. The elements in S_2 can be computed from S_1. For example, $(1,1,0) = (1,0,0) + (0,1,0)$ with difference $(1,-1,0)$, and $(1,-1,1) = (1,0,0) + (0,-1,1)$ with difference $(1,1,-1)$, where $(1,0,0), (0,1,0), (1,-1,0), (0,-1,1)$ (i.e. $(0,1,-1)$) and $(1,1,-1)$ all belong to S_1.

Proposition 1. *The chain $C(\{D_i\}_{i=1}^3; A, B, C)$ defined above is a uniform DAC, starting from the set $S_1 \cup S_2$.*

Proof. Firstly, we should note that the chain $C(\{D_i\}; A, B, C)$ always contains $(1,1,1)$ when $(A, B, C) \neq (0,0,0)$, since $M_{-1} = (1,1,1)$ is contained in the chain for any $(A, B, C) \in \{0,1\}^3 \setminus (0,0,0)$. And $(1,1,1)$ is the addition of $(1,1,0)$ and $(0,0,1)$ whose difference is contained in S_1.

M_{-1} is the element of type (odd, odd, odd), and is equal to $(2a+1, 2b+1, 2c+1)$ for $(a, b, c) = (\lfloor A/2 \rfloor, \lfloor B/2 \rfloor, \lfloor C/2 \rfloor)$, which is also equal to the addition of any dual pair in the set $S(a, b, c)$, e.g. $(a, b, c) + (a+1, b+1, c+1)$. Note that there are four dual pairs in $S(a, b, c)$, and the definition says at least one complete dual pair is reserved in $C(\{d_i\}_{i=1}^3; a, b, c)$, whose difference is equal to $(1,1,1)$ or contained in S_1 or S_2.

M_0 is the element of type (even, even, even), and is equal to $(2a + 2(A \bmod 2), 2b + 2(B \bmod 2), 2c + 2(C \bmod 2))$, which is a double of the element $(a + (A \bmod 2), b + (B \bmod 2), c + (C \bmod 2))$, denoted by V. Note that $V \equiv (a + A, b + B, c + C) \bmod 2$, and in $C(\{d_i\}; a, b, c)$ the omitted elements modulo 2 are

$$T_1 \equiv (d_1 + 1, d_1, d_1) \bmod 2, T_2 \equiv (d_2, d_2 + 1, d_2) \bmod 2, T_3 \equiv (d_3, d_3, d_3 + 1) \bmod 2.$$

When $(a + A, b + B, c + C) \bmod 2 = (0,0,0)$ or $(1,1,1)$, then V is (even,even,even) or (odd, odd, odd) which must be contained in $C(\{d_i\}; a, b, c)$ by definition. Apart from these two cases, we observe that pairs $(d_1, a + A)$, $(d_2, b + B)$ and $(d_3, c + B)$ have the same parity, which implies that V modulo 2 is not equal to any T_i.

When $D_1 = 0$, $M_1 = (2a + 2(A \bmod 2), 2b + 1, 2c + 1)$, which is equal to

$$(a + (A \bmod 2), b, c) + (a + (A \bmod 2), b + 1, c + 1) \tag{4}$$

or

$$(a + (A \bmod 2), b + 1, c) + (a + (A \bmod 2), b, c + 1) \tag{5}$$

Note that their differences are contained in S_2 or S_1, hence in $C(\{b_i\}; a, b, c)$. Since $a + A$ and $d_1 + 1$ always have the opposite parity, then none of these four elements is equal to T_1. Assume one is equal to T_2 (or T_3), for example

$(a+(A \bmod 2), b, c)$. Then b and c have an opposite parity, in other word, $(b+1, c)$ and $(b, c+1)$ have the same parity, which implies that none of the two elements in (5) is equal to T_3 (or T_2). Therefore they belongs to $C(\{d_i\}; a, b, c)$.

When $D_1 = 1$, $M_1 = (2a+1, 2b+2(B \bmod 2), 2c+2(C \bmod 2))$ which is equal to the addition of $(a, b+(B \bmod 2), c+(C \bmod 2))$ and $(a+1, b+(B \bmod 2), c+(C \bmod 2))$. Their difference is $(1, 0, 0)$ contained in S_1. In the case that $(a + A, b+B, c+C) \bmod 2 = (0, 0, 0)$ or $(1, 1, 1)$, none of these two elements is equal to T_2, T_3 or T_1, and therefore they are contained in $C(\{b_i\}; a, b, c)$. Apart from these two cases, since pairs $(d_2+1, b+B)$ and $(d_3+1, c+C)$ always have the opposite parity, then none of them is equal to T_2 or T_3. If $(a, b+(B \bmod 2), c+(C \bmod 2))$ is equal to T_1, then $(b+B, c+C) \bmod 2 = (0, 0)$ or $(1, 1)$. In the former case, by definition $d_1 = 1$ and then $T_1 = (0, 1, 1)$, which is a contradiction. In the latter case, $d_1 = 0$ and then $T_1 = (1, 0, 0)$ which is also a contradiction.

Similarly, we can show that M_2 and M_3 are additions of some elements in $C(\{b_i\}; a, b, c)$ whose differences are already in this chain.

Finally, it is obviously uniform since each iteration contains 1 double and 4 additions where M_0 is the double and others are additions.   □

Remark 2. Given a 3-tuple (k_1, k_2, k_3), if we want to compute the above 3-dimensional DAC of (k_1, k_2, k_3), the initial D_1, D_2, D_3 should be taken like this:

if $(k_1, k_2, k_3) \bmod 2 = (1, 0, 0)$ or $(0, 1, 1)$, $D_1 \equiv k_1 \bmod 2$; arbitrary D_2, D_3
if $(k_1, k_2, k_3) \bmod 2 = (0, 1, 0)$ or $(1, 0, 1)$, $D_2 \equiv k_2 \bmod 2$; arbitrary D_1, D_3
if $(k_1, k_2, k_3) \bmod 2 = (0, 0, 1)$ or $(1, 1, 0)$, $D_3 \equiv k_3 \bmod 2$; arbitrary D_1, D_2
if $(k_1, k_2, k_3) \bmod 2 = (0, 0, 0)$ or $(1, 1, 1)$, arbitrary D_1, D_2, D_3

Example 1. Here is a simple example of computing the above 3-dimensional DAC of $(199, 331, 513)$, where we set the initial (D_1, D_2, D_3) to be $(1, 1, 1)$.

Stage	M_{-1}	M_0	M_1	M_2	M_3
1		Pre-computation of S_1 and S_2			
2	$(1, 1, 1)$	$(0, 0, 2)$	$(0, 1, 1)$	$(0, 1, 2)$	$(0, 0, 1)$
3	$(1, 1, 3)$	$(0, 2, 2)$	$(1, 2, 2)$	$(0, 1, 2)$	$(1, 1, 2)$
4	$(1, 3, 5)$	$(2, 2, 4)$	$(2, 3, 5)$	$(2, 3, 4)$	$(1, 3, 4)$
5	$(3, 5, 9)$	$(4, 6, 8)$	$(3, 6, 8)$	$(4, 5, 8)$	$(3, 5, 8)$
6	$(7, 11, 17)$	$(6, 10, 16)$	$(6, 11, 17)$	$(6, 11, 16)$	$(7, 11, 16)$
7	$(13, 21, 33)$	$(12, 20, 32)$	$(12, 21, 33)$	$(12, 21, 32)$	$(13, 21, 32)$
8	$(25, 41, 65)$	$(24, 42, 64)$	$(25, 42, 64)$	$(24, 41, 64)$	$(25, 41, 64)$
9	$(49, 83, 129)$	$(50, 82, 128)$	$(50, 83, 129)$	$(50, 83, 128)$	$(49, 83, 128)$
10	$(99, 165, 257)$	$(100, 166, 256)$	$(100, 165, 257)$	$(99, 166, 257)$	$(100, 166, 257)$
11	$(199, 331, 513)$	$(200, 332, 514)$	$(199, 332, 514)$	$(200, 331, 514)$	$(200, 332, 513)$

In this chain, for example, the (D_1, D_2, D_3) in Stage 10 is $(0, 0, 1)$, and hence the omitted elements are {(odd,even,even),(even,odd,even),(odd,odd,even)} = $\{(99, 166, 256), (100, 165, 256), (99, 165, 256)\}$. The five elements in this stage are additions of the elements in Stage 9, e.g. $(99, 165, 257) = (49, 83, 129) + (50, 82, 128)$ with difference $(-1, 1, 1)$ belonging to $S_2, (100, 166, 256) = 2 \cdot$

$(50, 83, 128)$ with difference $(0, 0, 0)$ belonging to S_1, $(100, 165, 257) = (50, 82, 128) + (50, 83, 129)$ with difference $(0, 1, 1)$ belonging to S_2.

4.2   A Faster Three-Dimensional Differential Addition Chain

Now we introduce a new construction of 3-dimensional DAC, which is not uniform but faster than the uniform one described in Sect. 4.1. It only needs four additions or three additions together with one double in each stage of iteration.

Let S be the set defined in Sect. 4.1. We classify part of the sets of four elements of S. We call the set

$$\{(0, 0, 0), (1, 0, 0), (0, 1, 0), (0, 0, 1)\}$$

is of type C_0; the set

$$\{(1, 0, 0), (0, 1, 0), (0, 0, 1), (1, 1, 0)\}$$
$$\text{or } \{(1, 0, 0), (0, 1, 0), (0, 0, 1), (1, 0, 1)\}$$
$$\text{or } \{(1, 0, 0), (0, 1, 0), (0, 0, 1), (0, 1, 1)\}$$

is of type C_1; the set

$$\{(1, 0, 0), (1, 1, 0), (1, 0, 1), (0, 1, 1)\}$$
$$\text{or } \{(0, 1, 0), (1, 1, 0), (1, 0, 1), (0, 1, 1)\}$$
$$\text{or } \{(0, 0, 1), (1, 1, 0), (1, 0, 1), (0, 1, 1)\}$$

is of type C_2; the set

$$\{(1, 0, 0), (0, 1, 0), (1, 1, 0), (1, 0, 1)\} \text{ or } \{(1, 0, 0), (0, 0, 1), (1, 1, 0), (1, 0, 1)\}$$
$$\text{or } \{(1, 0, 0), (0, 1, 0), (1, 1, 0), (0, 1, 1)\} \text{ or } \{(0, 1, 0), (0, 0, 1), (1, 1, 0), (0, 1, 1)\}$$
$$\text{or } \{(1, 0, 0), (0, 0, 1), (1, 0, 1), (0, 1, 1)\} \text{ or } \{(0, 1, 0), (0, 0, 1), (1, 0, 1), (0, 1, 1)\}$$

is of type C_3; the set

$$\{(1, 1, 0), (1, 0, 1), (0, 1, 1), (1, 1, 1)\}$$

is of type C_4.

We use a 3-tuple (a, b, c) of non-negative integers to label each stage of our iteration. In the stage of any given (a, b, c) which is not equal to $(0, 0, 0)$, we compute four elements in $(a, b, c) + S$, of which the set is denoted by $E(a, b, c)$. It has the following form

$$E(a, b, c) = (a, b, c) + \delta,$$

where $\delta \subseteq S$ is of some type C_i for $i = 0, 1, 2, 3$ or 4.

Assume that (a, b, c) is the former stage of (A, B, C), where $a = \lfloor A/2 \rfloor$, $b = \lfloor B/2 \rfloor$, $c = \lfloor C/2 \rfloor$. And assume that $(a, b, c) \neq (0, 0, 0)$. We show in the following that in any case, there exists some set δ of type C_0, C_1, C_2, C_3 or C_4, such that $E(A, B, C)$ can be computed from $(a, b, c) + \delta$. Then we set it to be $E(a, b, c)$. In other word, every element of $E(A, B, C)$ is an addition of two elements of $E(a, b, c)$.

Assume that

$$E(A, B, C) = (A, B, C) + \Delta, \text{ where } \Delta \text{ is of type } C_i.$$

We denote by $t = (A, B, C) - (2a, 2b, 2c)$. Then t is an element of S.

If $i = 0$, i.e. $\Delta = \{(0, 0, 0), (1, 0, 0), (0, 1, 0), (0, 0, 1)\}$, and when $t \in \{(0, 0, 0), (1, 0, 0), (0, 1, 0), (0, 0, 1)\}$, we can set

$$\delta = \{(0, 0, 0), (1, 0, 0), (0, 1, 0), (0, 0, 1)\},$$

which is of type C_0. We can check, for example, when $t = (0, 0, 1)$, then

$$E(A, B, C) = (2a, 2b, 2c) + \{(0, 0, 1), (1, 0, 1), (0, 1, 1), (0, 0, 2)\}$$

can be computed from $E(a, b, c) = (a, b, c) + \delta$ by either additions or double. When $t \in \{(1, 1, 0), (1, 0, 1), (0, 1, 1)\}$, we can set

$$\delta = \{(1, 0, 0), (0, 1, 0), (0, 0, 1)\} \cup \{t\},$$

which is of type C_1. Also we can check, for example when $t = (1, 0, 1)$, then

$$E(A, B, C) = (2a, 2b, 2c) + \{(1, 0, 1), (2, 0, 1), (1, 1, 1), (1, 0, 2)\}$$

can be computed form $E(a, b, c) = (a, b, c) + \delta$ by additions. When $t = (1, 1, 1)$, we can set

$$\delta = \{(1, 0, 0), (1, 1, 0), (1, 0, 1), (0, 1, 1)\},$$

which is of type C_2. In conclusion, we can use the following table to present the δ's in all cases.

$\Delta = \{(0, 0, 0), (1, 0, 0), (0, 1, 0), (0, 0, 1)\}$		
t	δ	Type
$(0, 0, 0)$	Δ	C_0
$(1, 0, 0)/(0, 1, 0)/(0, 0, 1)$	Δ	C_0
$(1, 1, 0)/(1, 0, 1)/(0, 1, 1)$	$\{(1, 0, 0), (0, 1, 0), (0, 0, 1)\} \cup \{t\}$	C_1
$(1, 1, 1)$	$\{(1, 0, 0), (1, 1, 0), (1, 0, 1), (0, 1, 1)\}$	C_2

If $i = 1$, i.e. Δ is of type C_1, assume that $\Delta = \{(1, 0, 0), (0, 1, 0), (0, 0, 1), s\}$ where $s \in \{(1, 1, 0), (1, 0, 1), (0, 1, 1)\}$. Then we can check

Here $s \cdot t$ is the vector with multiplying components, and $s^\perp$ is the vector $(1, 1, 1) - s$, also called the dual vector of s as in Sect. 4.1. Here we only check the case when $t \in \{(1, 1, 0), (1, 0, 1), (0, 1, 1)\} \setminus \{s\}$. Then $E(A, B, C) = (2a, 2b, 2c) + t + \Delta$ and $E(a, b, c) = (a, b, c) + \delta$. Hence we only need to show that

$$t + \Delta = \{t + (1, 0, 0), t + (0, 1, 0), t + (0, 0, 1), t + s\}$$

$\Delta = \{(1,0,0),(0,1,0),(0,0,1),s\}$		
t	δ	Type
$(0,0,0)$	$\{(0,0,0),(1,0,0),(0,1,0),(0,0,1)\}$	C_0
$(1,0,0)/(0,1,0)/(0,0,1)$	Δ	C_1
s	Δ	C_1
$(s \neq)t \in$ $\{(1,1,0),(1,0,1),(0,1,1)\}$	$\{s \cdot t, s^{\perp}, s, t\}$	C_3
$(1,1,1)$	$\{(1,1,0),(1,0,1),(0,1,1),(1,1,1)\}$	C_4

can be computed from $\delta = \{s \cdot t, s^{\perp}, s, t\}$.Obviously, $s \cdot t \neq s^{\perp}$ and both belong to $\{(1,0,0),(0,1,0),(0,0,1)\}$. The remaining element of $\{\{(1,0,0),(0,1,0),(0,0,1)\} \setminus \{s \cdot t, s^{\perp}\}$ can be expressed as $(1,1,1) - s \cdot t - s^{\perp}$, denoted by α. Since $\alpha \cdot t = (s - s \cdot t) \cdot t = s \cdot t - s \cdot t^2 = 0$ and only one component of α is non-zero, it implies that α is dual to t. Then $t + \alpha = (1,1,1) = s^{\perp} + s$ and hence every element of $E(A,B,C)$ is an addition of two elements of $E(a,b,c)$.

If $i = 2$, i.e. Δ is of type C_2, assume that $\Delta = \{s,(1,1,0),(1,0,1),(0,1,1)\}$ where $s \in \{(1,0,0),(0,1,0),(0,0,1)\}$. Also we can check the following

$\Delta = \{s,(1,1,0),(1,0,1),(0,1,1)\}$		
t	δ	Type
$(0,0,0)$	$\{(0,0,0),(1,0,0),(0,1,0),(0,0,1)\}$	C_0
s	Δ	C_2
$(s \neq)t \in$ $\{(1,0,0),(0,1,0),(0,0,1)\}$	$\{s,t,s^{\perp},s+t\}$	C_3
$(1,1,0)/(1,0,1)/(0,1,1)$	Δ	C_2
$(1,1,1)$	$\{(1,1,0),(1,0,1),(0,1,1),(1,1,1)\}$	C_4

If $i = 3$, i.e. Δ is of type C_3, we assume that $\Delta = \{s_1 \cdot s_2, k, s_1, s_2\}$ where $s_1 \neq s_2 \in \{(1,1,0),(1,0,1),(0,1,1)\}$ and $k = s_1^{\perp}$ or $s_2^{\perp}$. We can check

$\Delta = \{s_1 \cdot s_2, k, s_1, s_2\}$		
t	δ	Type
$(0,0,0)$	$\{(0,0,0),(1,0,0),(0,1,0),(0,0,1)\}$	C_0
$s_1 \cdot s_2$ or k	Δ	C_3
the other[a]	$\{(1,0,0),(0,1,0),(0,0,1)\} \cup \{k^{\perp}\}$	C_1
s_1 or s_2	Δ	C_3
the other[b]	$\{k\} \cup \{(1,1,0),(1,0,1),(0,1,1)\}$	C_2
$(1,1,1)$	$\{(1,1,0),(1,0,1),(0,1,1),(1,1,1)\}$	C_4

[a] The remainder in $\{(1,0,0),(0,1,0),(0,0,1)\}$ that is not equal to $s_1 \cdot s_2$ or k.
[b] The remainder in $\{(1,1,0),(1,0,1),(0,1,1)\}$ that is not equal to s_1 or s_2.

If $i = 4$, i.e. $\Delta = \{(1,1,0),(1,0,1),(0,1,1),(1,1,1)\}$, we can check

$\Delta = \{(1,1,0),(1,0,1),(0,1,1),(1,1,1)\}$		
t	δ	Type
$(0,0,0)$	$\{(1,0,0),(0,1,0),(0,0,1),(1,1,0)\}$	C_1
$(1,0,0)/(0,1,0)/(0,0,1)$	$\{t\} \cup \{(1,1,0),(1,0,1),(0,1,1)\}$	C_2
$(1,1,0)/(1,0,1)/(0,1,1)$	Δ	C_4
$(1,1,1)$	Δ	C_4

In conclusion, we have the following

Proposition 2. *In the stage of $(0,0,0)$, we take $E(0,0,0) = S_1 \cup S_2$ where S_1, S_2 are defined in Definition 1. For any given 3-tuple (k_1, k_2, k_3) of non-negative scalars, let $(A, B, C) = (k_1, k_2, k_3)$ and Δ be the set of four elements of type C_0. Then compute recursively the whole chain, denoted by $C(k_1, k_2, k_3)$, using the above method. Then $C(k_1, k_2, k_3)$ is a DAC containing (k_1, k_2, k_3).*

Proof. First, $(k_1, k_2, k_3) \in E(A, B, C) \subseteq C(k_1, k_2, k_3)$. Second, from the above procedure we see that every element (except the elements in the stage of $(0,0,0)$) in this chain is an addition of two former elements (may be the same) in this chain, of which the difference belongs to $S_1 \cup S_2$. Therefore, $C(k_1, k_2, k_3)$ is a DAC. $\qquad\square$

Example 2. Take $(k_1, k_2, k_3) = (9, 10, 11)$. They all have 4 bits. Set $(A_4, B_4, C_4) = (9, 10, 11)$ and $\Delta_4 = \{(0,0,0),(1,0,0),(0,1,0),(0,0,1)\}$ of type C_0. Then
$$E_4 = \{(9,10,11),(10,10,11),(9,11,11),(9,10,12)\}.$$
Set $(A_3, B_3, C_3) = (4, 5, 5)$. In this case $t = (1,0,1)$ and by table lookup $\Delta_3 = \{(1,0,0),(0,1,0),(0,0,1),(1,0,1)\}$ is of type C_1. Then
$$E_3 = \{(5,5,5),(4,6,5),(4,5,6),(5,5,6)\}.$$
Set $(A_2, B_2, C_2) = (2, 2, 2)$. In this case $t = (0,1,1)$ and by table lookup $\Delta_2 = \{(0,1,0),(0,0,1),(1,0,1),(0,1,1)\}$ is of type C_3. Then
$$E_2 = \{(2,3,2),(2,2,3),(3,2,3),(2,3,3)\}.$$
Set $(A_1, B_1, C_1) = (1, 1, 1)$. In this case $t = (0,0,0)$ and by table lookup $\Delta_1 = \{(0,0,0),(1,0,0),(0,1,0),(0,0,1)\}$ is of type C_0. Then
$$E_1 = \{(1,1,1),(2,1,1),(1,2,1),(1,1,2)\}.$$
Finally $(A_0, B_0, C_0) = (0,0,0)$ and $t = (1,1,1)$, and then $\Delta_0 = \{(1,0,0),(1,1,0),(1,0,1),(0,1,1)\}$. Then
$$E_0 = \{(1,0,0),(1,1,0),(1,0,1),(0,1,1)\}.$$
If we denote by $E_i[j]$ the j-th element of E_i, then we have the relations:

$$
\begin{aligned}
&E_4[1] = E_3[1] + E_3[3], \; E_3[1] = E_2[1] + E_2[3], \; E_2[1] = E_1[1] + E_1[3], \; E_1[1] = E_0[1] + E_0[4] \\
&E_4[2] = E_3[1] + E_3[4], \; E_3[2] = E_2[1] + E_2[4], \; E_2[2] = E_1[1] + E_1[4], \; E_1[1] = E_0[2] + E_0[3] \\
&E_4[3] = E_3[2] + E_3[4], \; E_3[3] = E_2[2] + E_2[4], \; E_2[3] = E_1[2] + E_1[3], \; E_1[1] = E_0[2] + E_0[4] \\
&E_4[4] = E_3[3] + E_3[4], \; E_3[4] = E_2[3] + E_2[4], \; E_2[4] = E_1[3] + E_1[4], \; E_1[1] = E_0[3] + E_0[4]
\end{aligned}
$$

5   Comparison

Recall the settings described in Sects. 2 and 3. To compute $x(kP)$, now we can apply different dimensional DACs to different models: Eqs. (2) and (3) or $x(kP)$ directly. In this part, we analyze the performance of scalar multiplication $x(kP)$ utilizing the following four kinds of DACs: 1-dimensional Montgomery ladder (Ladder for short), 2-dimensional DJB chains (DJB), the 3-dimensional uniform differential addition chains (3-Uni.) and the 3-dimensional non-uniform one (3-Non-uni) described in Sect. 4.

5.1   Theoretic Analysis

For an elliptic curve in short Weiestrass form, using the projective coordinates, a general addition (write **A** for short) involves 12 field multiplications (12M) and 2 field squarings (2S), whereas a double (**D**) involves 7M+5S. If we restrict to the operations on x-line, then a pseudo-addition (**PA**) needs 9M+2S and a pseudo-double (**PD**) needs 6M+3S [5, Chap. 13]. Assume that the target group is of 256-bit security level, and the scalar k is a 256-bit number. Then the following table shows the theoretic field operations needed by those five DACs.

Table 1. Theoretical estimate

chain	dim.	rounds	#operations/bit	pre-comp.	#total operations
Ladder	1	256	1**PD** + 1**PA**	0	3840M + 1280S
DJB	2	~ 128	1**PD** + 2**PA**	1A	3084M + 898S
3-Uni.	3	~ 85	1**PD** + 4**PA**	4A + 5**PA**	3663M + 953S
3-Non-uni.	3	~ 85	≤ 4**PA**	4A + 5**PA**	3153M + 698S

Here we note two things. First if we take 1S = 0.8M, our 3-dimensional non-uniform DAC needs 3711.4M, less than 3802.4M of the DJB chain. Second our 3-dimensional non-uniform DAC and the DAC in [11] taking $d = 3$ need almost the same number of field operations in each iteration and precomputation.

5.2   Implementation Results

We make the following experiments with computer algebra package MAGMA. We choose two families of elliptic curves E_1' and E_2' that are quadratic twists of GLV curves chosen from [12]. Let p be a prime. For a non-square element u in $\mathbb{F}_{p^2}$, E_1' and the two efficient $\mathbb{F}_{p^2}$-endomorphisms on the x-line are given by

$$E_1' : y^2 = x^3 - \frac{3}{4}ux^2 - 2u^2x - u^3, \quad \Phi_x(x) = \frac{x^2 - u^2\zeta}{\zeta^2(x - au)}, \quad \Psi_x(x) = u^{1-p}x^p.$$

Their characteristic polynomials are $\Phi^2 - \Phi + 2 = 0$, $\Psi^2 + 1 = 0$. Moreover take $p \equiv 1 \pmod 3$ and $\gamma \in \mathbb{F}_p$ to be an element of order 3. Then E_2' and its efficient $\mathbb{F}_{p^2}$-endomorphisms on the x-line are given by

$$E_2' : y^2 = x^3 + bu^3, \quad \Phi_x(x) = \gamma x, \quad \Psi_x(x) = u^{1-p} x^p$$

with $\Phi^2 + \Phi + 1 = 0$, $\Psi^2 + 1 = 0$. For each $i = 1, 2$, and each of $64, 128$ and 192 bit lengths of primes p, we choose 20 p's such that each $E_i'(\mathbb{F}_{p^2})$ is almost prime with the large prime subgroup of order n, and hence we obtain 20 target elliptic curves. On each curve, we randomly choose 20 pairs (k, P)'s where P is a rational point of the curve of order n and k is a scalar having the same bit length as n. We test the above four DACs in the computation of $x(kP)$. And for each (k, P), we make the following three sets of comparison experiments: 3-Uni versus Ladder, 3-Non-uni. versus Ladder and 3-non-uni. versus DJB[3]. We record their running times and take the average over the $20 \times 20 = 400$ data at each bit length of $64, 128$ and 192. Then we compute the ratio of speedup of the former DAC relative to the latter one. The implementation results are listed in Tables 1 and 2.

Table 2. The ratio of speedup tested in E_1'

p	64-bit	128-bit	192-bit
n	$125 \sim 126$-bit	$253 \sim 254$-bit	$381 \sim 382$-bit
3-Uni. vs Ladder	6.8%	11.2%	11.5%
3-Non-uni. vs Ladder	24.7%	28.7%	29.3%
3-Non-uni. vs DJB	3.9%	8.5%	9.7%

Table 3. The ratio of speedup tested in E_2'

p	64-bit	128-bit	192-bit
n	$125 \sim 126$-bit	$253 \sim 254$-bit	$381 \sim 382$-bit
3-Uni. vs Ladder	4.3%	7.0%	7.4%
3-Non-uni. vs Ladder	22.1%	24.2%	25.3%
3-Non-uni. vs DJB	3.0%	5.7%	6.8%

From the tables, first, we recognise that the performance depends on the GLV model that we choose. However, compared with straightforward computing with Ladder, the triple scalar multiplication using our 3-dimensional DACs runs faster evidently. Moreover, the triple scheme using 3-Non-uni. outperforms the double one using DJB chains. Second, the ratio of speedup increases when the

---

[3] In the two-dimensional GLV, we always utilize the endomorphism Ψ in the testing.

bit length of p grows. The case of 128-bit or equivalently when the security level is about 254-bit may provide more significant reference. In this case, by taking an average of the values in two tables, the triple scheme using 3-Uni. runs about 9% faster than straightforward computing; and that using 3-Non-uni. runs about 26% faster than straightforward computing, and about 6% faster than the double scheme using DJB chains (Table 3).

6   Conclusion and Future Research

We proposed two constructions of 3-dimensional DACs. One is a straightforward extension of the DJB chain to higher dimensional case, and it inherits the property of uniformity. The other is not uniform but runs faster than the uniform one as saving one more point operation in each iteration. On the quadratic twists of GLV curves, we implemented scalar multiplication on the x-coordinate systems, utilizing 1 to 3-dimensional GLV methods with corresponding dimensional DACs. Experiments show that at about 254-bit security level, the triple scalar multiplication using our uniform DACs runs about 9% faster than straightforward computing using Montgomery ladder; and that using our non-uniform DACs runs about 26% faster than that using Montgomery ladder, and about 6% faster than the double scalar multiplication using DJB chains.

As it is pointed out that, it would be more meaningful and we will consider to implement our higher dimensional DACs on the x-coordinate systems of some more advanced curves, such as the complete twisted Edwards curve described in [7], together with optimizing formulas for differential point tripling (or quadrupling) in various forms of curves. The 4-dimensional DACs deserve to be studied as well, since triple scalar multiplication on the x-coordinate performs well and many advanced elliptic curves are originally tailored for 4-dimensional GLV method. We considered the 4-dimensional extension of the uniform case, but found it inefficient for its heavy pre-computation and excessive operations in each iteration, see Appendix A. However, the non-uniform case may provide more possibilities. We leave these topics for future research.

Acknowledgement. We would like to thank Yuqing Zhu for his kind advice and selfless help on the first version of this work. And we would like to thank the anonymous reviewers for their detailed comments and suggestions. This work is supported by National Natural Science Foundation of China (Grant No. 61872359).

A   Four-dimensional Case

If we consider further the straightforward 4-dimensional extension of DJB chains, we found that in each iteration we should compute $2 + (2^4 - 2)/2 = 9$ elements, containing 1 double and 8 additions, which is rather expensive and hence has no practical usage. For completeness, in this part we give its definition and a simple example. Its complex proof of correctness has been done by authors and one can also check it by computers.

For brief of notation we let $e_1 = (1,0,0,0), e_2 = (0,1,0,0), e_3 = (0,0,1,0),$
$e_4 = (0,0,0,1), e_5 = (1,1,0,0), e_6 = (1,0,1,0), e_7 = (1,0,0,1)$. Denote by n^4
the 4-tuple (n,n,n,n). Then the 7 elements omitted from $S(a,b,c,d)^4$ can be
described as $T_i = (a,b,c,d) + (U_i \bmod 2)$ where $U_i = (a,b,c,d) + f_i^4 + e_i$ and
$f_i \in \{0,1\}$ for $i = 1, \cdots, 7$.

Definition 2. *For a given 4-tuple of nonnegative integers (A,B,C,D) and the
set $\{F_1, \cdots, F_7\}$ where $F_i \in \{0,1\}, i = 1, \cdots, 7$, the chain $C(\{F_i\}_{i=1}^7; A, B,$
$C, D)$ is defined recursively, as the set $C(\{f_i\}_{i=1}^7; a, b, c, d)$ added with the following nine elements:*

$$M_{-1} = (A,B,C,D) + ((A+1, B+1, C+1, D+1) \bmod 2),$$
$$M_0 = (A,B,C,D) + ((A, \quad B, \quad C, \quad D) \bmod 2),$$

and for $i = 1, \cdots, 7$,

$$M_i = (A,B,C,D) + (N_i \bmod 2) \quad \text{where } N_i = (A,B,C,D) + (F_i + 1)^4 + e_i.$$

Here $(a,b,c,d) = (\lfloor A/2 \rfloor, \lfloor B/2 \rfloor, \lfloor C/2 \rfloor, \lfloor D/2 \rfloor)$ and $(f_1, \cdots, f_7)$ is taken as

$(f_1, \cdots, f_7)$	$if(a+A, b+B,$ $c+C, d+D) \bmod 2$	$(f_1, \cdots, f_7)$	$if(a+A, b+B,$ $c+C, d+D) \bmod 2$
$(1,0,0,0,1,1,1)$	$(1,0,0,0)$	$(0,1,1,1,0,0,0)$	$(0,1,1,1)$
$(0,1,0,0,1,0,0)$	$(0,1,0,0)$	$(1,0,1,1,0,1,1)$	$(1,0,1,1)$
$(0,0,1,0,0,1,0)$	$(0,0,1,0)$	$(1,1,0,1,1,0,1)$	$(1,1,0,1)$
$(0,0,0,1,0,0,1)$	$(0,0,0,1)$	$(1,1,1,0,1,1,0)$	$(1,1,1,0)$
$(1,1,0,0,1,0,0)$	$(1,1,0,0)$	$(0,0,1,1,0,0,0)$	$(0,0,1,1)$
$(1,0,1,0,0,1,0)$	$(1,0,1,0)$	$(0,1,0,1,0,0,0)$	$(0,1,0,1)$
$(1,0,0,1,0,0,1)$	$(1,0,0,1)$	$(0,1,1,0,0,0,0)$	$(0,1,1,0)$
$(F_1, F_2, F_3, F_4,$ $F_5, F_6, F_7)$	$(0,0,0,0)$	$(1-F_1, 1-F_2, 1-F_3,$ $1-F_4, 1-F_5, 1-F_6,$ $1-F_7)$	$(1,1,1,1).$

Specially, for arbitrary $F_1, \cdots, F_7$, let $C(\{F_i\}; 0,0,0,0)$ be the union of the sets

$S_1 = \{(0,0,0,0), (1,0,0,0), (0,1,0,0), (0,0,1,0), (0,0,0,1),$
$\quad (1,-1,0,0), (1,0,-1,0), (1,0,0,-1), (0,1,-1,0), (0,1,0,-1), (0,0,1,-1),$
$\quad (1,1,-1,0), (1,1,0,-1), (1,0,1,-1), (0,1,1,-1),$
$\quad (1,1,1,-1)\}$

$S_2 = \{(1,1,0,0), (1,0,1,0), (1,0,0,1), (0,1,1,0), (0,1,0,1), (0,0,1,1),$
$\quad (1,1,1,0), (1,1,0,1), (1,0,1,1), (0,1,1,1),$
$\quad (1,-1,1,0), (1,-1,0,1), (1,0,-1,1), (0,1,-1,1),$
$\quad (-1,1,1,0), (-1,1,0,1), (-1,0,1,1), (0,-1,1,1),$
$\quad (1,1,-1,1), (1,-1,1,1), (-1,1,1,1),$
$\quad (1,1,-1,-1), (1,-1,1,-1), (1,-1,-1,1)\}$

where S_2 can be computed from S_1.

---

[4] As the analogous symbol used in Sect. 4.1, $S(a,b,c,d)$ is the set $(a,b,c,d) + \{0,1\}^4$.

We find that as the dimension of the chain increases, the pre-computation part becomes a heavy burden, and it grows exponentially w.r.t. the dimension. In some situation, this maybe a main disadvantage of computing scalar multiplication using higher dimensional DACs.

Example 3. Given a simple 4-tuple $(10, 9, 8, 7)$. The uniform 4-dimensional DAC of $(10, 9, 8, 7)$ is: $S_1 \cup S_2 \cup S_3$ where $S_3 =$

$\{(1, 1, 1, 1), (2, 2, 2, 0), (2, 1, 1, 1), (2, 1, 1, 2, 0), (2, 2, 1, 1, 0), (2, 2, 2, 1), (2, 2, 1, 1), (2, 1, 2, 1), (2, 1, 1, 0),$
$(3, 3, 3, 1), (2, 2, 2, 2), (3, 2, 2, 2), (3, 2, 3, 1), (3, 3, 3, 2, 1), (3, 3, 3, 2), (3, 3, 2, 2), (3, 2, 3, 2), (3, 2, 2, 1),$
$(5, 5, 5, 3), (6, 4, 4, 4), (5, 4, 4, 4), (6, 5, 4, 4), (5, 5, 4, 3), (5, 5, 5, 4), (5, 5, 4, 4), (5, 4, 5, 4), (5, 4, 4, 3),$
$(11, 9, 9, 7), (10, 10, 8, 8), (10, 9, 9, 7), (11, 10, 9, 7), (11, 9, 8, 7), (11, 9, 9, 8), (10, 10, 9, 7), (10, 9, 8, 7),$
$(10.9.9.8)\}$

References

1. Akishita, T.: Fast simultaneous scalar multiplication on elliptic curve with montgomery form. In: Vaudenay, S., Youssef, A.M. (eds.) SAC 2001. LNCS, vol. 2259, pp. 255–267. Springer, Heidelberg (2001). https://doi.org/10.1007/3-540-45537-X_20

2. Azarderakhsh, R., Karabina, K.: A new double point multiplication algorithm and its application to binary elliptic curves with endomorphisms. IEEE Trans. Comput. **63**(10), 2614–2619 (2014)

3. Bernstein, D.J.: Differential addition chains. Technical Report (2006). http://cr.yp.to/ecdh/diffchain-20060219.pdf

4. Brown, D.R.: Multi-dimensional montgomery ladders for elliptic curves. Cryptology ePrint Archive, Report 2006/220 (2006). https://eprint.iacr.org/2006/220

5. Cohen, H., et al.: Handbook of Elliptic and Hyperelliptic Curve Cryptography. CRC Press (2005)

6. Costello, C., Hisil, H., Smith, B.: Faster compact diffie–hellman: endomorphisms on the x-line. In: Nguyen, P.Q., Oswald, E. (eds.) EUROCRYPT 2014. LNCS, vol. 8441, pp. 183–200. Springer, Heidelberg (2014). https://doi.org/10.1007/978-3-642-55220-5_11

7. Costello, C., Longa, P.: FourQ: four-dimensional decompositions on a Q-curve over the mersenne prime. In: Iwata, T., Cheon, J.H. (eds.) ASIACRYPT 2015. LNCS, vol. 9452, pp. 214–235. Springer, Heidelberg (2015). https://doi.org/10.1007/978-3-662-48797-6_10

8. Galbraith, S.D., Lin, X., Scott, M.: Endomorphisms for faster elliptic curve cryptography on a large class of curves. In: Joux, A. (ed.) EUROCRYPT 2009. LNCS, vol. 5479, pp. 518–535. Springer, Heidelberg (2009). https://doi.org/10.1007/978-3-642-01001-9_30

9. Gallant, R.P., Lambert, R.J., Vanstone, S.A.: Faster point multiplication on elliptic curves with efficient endomorphisms. In: Kilian, J. (ed.) CRYPTO 2001. LNCS, vol. 2139, pp. 190–200. Springer, Heidelberg (2001). https://doi.org/10.1007/3-540-44647-8_11

10. Zhi, H., Longa, P., Maozhi, X.: Implementing the 4-dimensional GLV method on GLS elliptic curves with j-invariant 0. Des. Codes Crypt. **63**(3), 331–343 (2012)

11. Hutchinson, A., Karabina, K.: Constructing multidimensional differential addition chains and their applications. J. Cryptographic Eng. 1–19 (2017)

12. Longa, P., Sica, F.: Four-dimensional gallant-lambert-vanstone scalar multiplication. In: Wang, X., Sako, K. (eds.) ASIACRYPT 2012. LNCS, vol. 7658, pp. 718–739. Springer, Heidelberg (2012). https://doi.org/10.1007/978-3-642-34961-4_43
13. Montgomery, P.L.: Evaluating recurrences of form $X_{m+n} = f(X_m, X_n, X_{m-n})$ via lucas chains (1983). ftp.cwi.nl:/pub/pmontgom/lucas.ps.gz
14. Montgomery, P.L.: Speeding the pollard and elliptic curve methods of factorization. Math. Comput. **48**(177), 243–264 (1987)
15. Rao, S.R.S.: A note on Schoenmakers algorithm for multi exponentiation. In: 2015 12th International Joint Conference on e-Business and Telecommunications (ICETE), vol. 4, pp. 384–391 (2015)
16. Subramanya Rao, S.R.: Three dimensional montgomery ladder, differential point tripling on montgomery curves and point quintupling on weierstrass' and edwards curves. In: Pointcheval, D., Nitaj, A., Rachidi, T. (eds.) AFRICACRYPT 2016. LNCS, vol. 9646, pp. 84–106. Springer, Cham (2016). https://doi.org/10.1007/978-3-319-31517-1_5
17. Stam, M.: Speeding up subgroup cryptosystems. Technische Universiteit Eindhoven (2003)
18. Yi, H., Zhu, Y., Lin, D.: Refinement of the four-dimensional GLV method on elliptic curves. In: Adams, C., Camenisch, J. (eds.) SAC 2017. LNCS, vol. 10719, pp. 23–42. Springer, Cham (2018). https://doi.org/10.1007/978-3-319-72565-9_2

Codes and Their Applications

On Good Polynomials over Finite Fields
for Optimal Locally Recoverable Codes

Sihem Mesnager[✉]

LAGA, Department of Mathematics, University of Paris VIII and Paris XIII,
UMR 7539; CNRS and Telecom ParisTech,
2 rue de la liberté, 93526 Saint-Denis cedex 02, France
smesnager@univ-paris8.fr

Abstract. [This is an extended abstract of the paper [3]] A locally recoverable (LRC) code is a code that enables a simple recovery of an erased symbol by accessing only a small number of other symbols. LRC codes currently form one of the rapidly developing topics in coding theory because of their applications in distributed and cloud storage systems. In 2014, Tamo and Barg have presented in a very remarkable paper a family of LRC codes that attain the maximum possible (minimum) distance (given code length, cardinality, and locality). The key ingredient for constructing such optimal linear LRC codes is the so-called r-good polynomials, where r is equal to the locality of the LRC code. In this extended abstract, we review and discuss good polynomials over finite fields for constructing optimal LRC codes.

Keywords: Finite fields · Good polynomials ·
Locally recoverable codes · Coding theory · Storage

1 Introduction

Locally recoverable codes (LRC codes) have recently been a very attractive subject in research in coding theory due to their theoretical appeal and applications in large-scale distributed storage systems, where a single storage node erasure is considered as a frequent error-event. An LRC code is said to have *locality* r if the value at any codeword coordinate can be recovered by accessing at most r other coordinates. By an (n, k, r) LRC code over finite field $\mathbb{F}_q$, we mean a code of length n, which has q^k codewords and locality r. For LRC codes, if a symbol is lost due to a node failure, its value can be recovered by accessing the value of at most r other symbols. A linear (n, k, r) LRC code $\mathcal{C}$ is said to be *optimal* if its minimum distance $d(\mathcal{C})$ satisfies $d(\mathcal{C}) = n - k - \lceil k/r \rceil + 2$. One of the most interesting constructions of optimal LRC codes is due to Tamo and Barg [8] and is realised via constructing polynomials of degree $r + 1$ which are constant on subsets of $\mathbb{F}_q$ of cardinality $r + 1$. These polynomials are called *good polynomials*. Construction of good polynomials are provided in [3,4] and [8]. All the constructions in [3] and [8] are essentially based on algebraic properties of the

© Springer Nature Switzerland AG 2019
C. Carlet et al. (Eds.): C2SI 2019, LNCS 11445, pp. 257–268, 2019.
https://doi.org/10.1007/978-3-030-16458-4_15

base field $\mathbb{F}_q$. The constructions provided in [4] explore properties of Dickson polynomials. Very recently, Micheli [5] has provided a Galois theoretical framework which allows to produce good polynomials and showed that the construction of good polynomials can be reduced to a Galois theoretical problem over global function fields. The present paper (which is an extended abstract of the paper [3]) is devoted to good polynomials for the construction of optimal LRC codes. The manuscript is structured as follows. In Sect. 2, we introduce the needed definitions related to LRC codes and good polynomials. In Sect. 3, we review and discuss the main constructions of good polynomials over finite fields for building optimal LRC codes.

2 Preliminaries

For a finite set A, $\#A$ denotes the cardinality of A and $A^\star = A \setminus \{0\}$. Throughout this paper, we always assume that p is a prime. Let $\mathbb{F}_q$ be a finite field of order q and with characteristic p. For positive integers t and s satisfying $t|s$, let $Tr_t^s(\cdot) : \mathbb{F}_{p^s} \to \mathbb{F}_{p^t}$ be the *trace function* defined as

$$Tr_t^s(x) = x + x^{p^t} + x^{p^{2t}} + \cdots + x^{p^{s-t}}.$$

In particular, for $x \in \mathbb{F}_{p^s}$, $Tr_1^s(\cdot)$ denotes the *absolute trace* function.

A code $\mathcal{C} \subseteq \mathbb{F}_{q^n}$ is called *locally recoverable (LRC)* code if every coordinate of the codeword $c = (c_1, \ldots, c_n) \in \mathcal{C}$ can be recovered from a subset of r other coordinates of c. Such a LRC code is said to have *locality* r. Mathematically, it gives the following definition.

Definition 1 (LRC codes). *Code $\mathcal{C}$ has locality r if for every $i \in [1, \cdots, n]$ there exists a subset $R_i \subset [1, \cdots, n] \setminus \{i\}$, $\#R_i \leq r$ and a function ϕ_i such that for every codeword $c \in \mathcal{C}$:*

$$c_i = \phi_i(\{c_j, j \in R_i\}).$$

An (n, k, r) LRC code $\mathcal{C}$ over $\mathbb{F}_q$ is of code length n, cardinality q^k, and locality r. The parameters of an (n, k, r) LRC code have been studied.

Theorem 2 ([1,7]). *Let $\mathcal{C}$ be an (n, k, r) LRC code of cardinality q^k over an alphabet of size q, then the minimum distance of $\mathcal{C}$ satisfies*

$$d \leq n - k - \lceil k/r \rceil + 2.$$

The rate of $\mathcal{C}$ satisfies

$$\frac{k}{n} \leq \frac{r}{r+1}.$$

Note that if $r = k$ then the upper bound given in the above theorem coincides with the well-known Singleton bound ($d \leq n - k + 1$).

In view of the above upper bound on the minimal distance, optimal (resp. almost optimal) LRC codes have been defined as follows.

Definition 3 (Optimal-Almost optimal LRC codes). *Codes for which $d = n - k - \lceil k/r \rceil + 2$ are called* optimal codes. *We refer to* almost optimal codes *when the minimum distance differs by at most one from the optimal value.*

We now recall the concept of r-good polynomials which is the key ingredient for constructing optimal linear LRC codes.

Definition 4 (Good polynomials) ([8]). *A polynomial F over $\mathbb{F}_{p^s}$ is said to be an r-good polynomial if and only if*

1. *the degree of F is $r + 1$,*
2. *there exist pairwise disjoint subsets $\{A_1, \ldots, A_l\}$ of $\mathbb{F}_{p^s}$ with cardinality $\#A_i = r + 1$ for $i = 1, \ldots, l$, such that the restriction of F to each subset A_i is constant. Namely for all $i = 1, \ldots, l$, and any α, $\beta \in A_i$, $F(\alpha) = F(\beta)$.*

Good polynomials produce optimal LRC codes according to the construction due to Tamo and Barg [8] given in the next theorem.

Theorem 5 ([8]). *For $r \geq 1$, let $g(x)$ be an r-good polynomial over $\mathbb{F}_{p^s}$. Set $n = (r + 1)l$ and $k = rt$, where $t \leq l$. For $a = (a_{ij}, i = 0, \ldots, r - 1; j = 0, \ldots, t - 1) \in (\mathbb{F}_{p^s})^k$, let*

$$f_a(x) = \sum_{i=0}^{r-1} \sum_{j=0}^{t-1} a_{ij} g(x)^j x^i.$$

Set $A = \bigcup_{i=1}^{l} A_i$, and define

$$\mathcal{C} = \left\{ (f_a(x), x \in A) \mid a \in (\mathbb{F}_{p^s})^k \right\}.$$

Then, $\mathcal{C}$ is an optimal linear (n, k, r) LRC code over $\mathbb{F}_{p^s}$.

In the above theorem, the elements of the set A are called *localisations* and the elements of the vector $f_a(x))$ are called *symbols* of the codeword. The local recovery is accomplished as follows. Suppose that the erased symbol corresponds to the localisation $\alpha \in A_j$ where A_j is one of the sets in the partition A. Let $(c_\beta, \beta \in A_j \setminus \{\alpha\})$ denote the remaining r symbols in the localisations of the set A_j. To find the value $c_\alpha = f_a(\alpha)$, find the unique polynomial $\delta(x)$ of degree less than r such that $\delta(\beta) = c_\beta$ for all $\beta \in A_j \setminus \{\alpha\}$, that is,

$$\delta(x) = \sum_{\beta \in A_j \setminus \{\alpha\}} c_\beta \prod_{\beta' \in A_j \setminus \{\alpha, \beta\}} \frac{x - \beta'}{\beta - \beta'} \tag{1}$$

and set $c_\alpha = \delta(\alpha)$. Hence, to find one erased symbol, we need to perform polynomial interpolation from r known symbols in its recovery set.

Example 6. Parameters of the constructed LRC code: $n = 9$, $k = 4$, $r = 2$, $q = 13$.

Set of points: $A = \{P_1, \cdots, P_9\} \subset \mathbb{F}_{13}$; $A = \{A_1 = (1, 3, 9), A_2 = (2, 6, 5), A_3 = (4, 12, 10)\}$;

Code construction: $ev_A : f_a \mapsto (f_a(P_i), i = 1, \cdots 9)$.

Set $g(x) = x^3$. We have $g(1) = g(3) = g(9) = 1$, $g(2) = g(6) = g(5) = 8$, $g(4) = g(12) = g(10) = 12$. Therefore g is constant on A_1, A_2 and A_3.

Let $a = (a_{00}, a_{01}, a_{10}, a_{11})$ be the information vector of length 4 over $\mathbb{F}_{13}$.

$f_a(x) = (a_{00} + a_{01}g(x)) + x(a_{10} + a_{11}g(x)) = a_{00} + a_{10}x + a_{01}x^3 + a_{11}x^4$.

Let take $a = (1111)$ then

$$c := ev_A(f_a) = (f_a(1), f_a(3), f_a(9)|f_a(2), f_a(6), f_a(5)|f_a(4), f_a(2), f_a(10))$$
$$= (4, 8, 7|1, 11, 2|0, 0, 0).$$

Suppose $f_a(1)$ is erased. By the construction of Tamo and Barg, it can be recovered by accessing 2 other codeword symbols; namely the symbols at the localisation corresponding to 3 and 9. Using Formula (1), we find that $\delta(x) = 2x + 2$ and compute $\delta(1) = 4$, which is the required value.

3   Constructions of r-good Polynomials

In this section, we are going to consider r-good polynomials over $\mathbb{F}_{p^s}$ with $r = mp^t - 1$, where $\gcd(m, p) = 1$.

3.1   Known Constructions of Good Polynomials

First of all, it is easy to remark that if F is an r-good polynomial over $\mathbb{F}_{p^s}$, then γF and $F - \alpha$ are again r-good polynomials over $\mathbb{F}_{p^s}$ for every $\gamma \in \mathbb{F}_{p^s}^*$ and every $\alpha \in \mathbb{F}_{p^s}$.

Recall that a function from $\mathbb{F}_q$ to itself is called q-ary function. A q-ary function of the form $F(x) = \sum_{i=0}^{n} a_i x^{p^i}$ with $a_i \in \mathbb{F}_q$ is called *linear*, where p is the characteristic of $\mathbb{F}_q$.

The following constructions are known.

1. If $t = 0$ and $p^s \equiv 1 (\text{mod } m)$, then the p^s-ary power function

$$G_\gamma(x) = \gamma x^m \tag{2}$$

is an r-good polynomial, where $\gamma \in \mathbb{F}_{p^s}^*$. Note that $\mathbb{F}_{p^s}^*$ can be split into pairwise disjoint multiplicative cosets of the form bU_m, where $b \in \mathbb{F}_{p^s}^*$ and $U_m = \{x \in \mathbb{F}_{p^s} \mid x^m = 1\}$. Observe next that, for every $x \in bU_m$, $G_\gamma(x) = G_\gamma(b)$ (see [8, Proposition 3.2]).

2. If $t > 0$ and $m = 1$, then the p^s-ary linear function

$$F_a(x) = \sum_{i=0}^{t} a_i x^{p^i} \tag{3}$$

is an r-good polynomial, where $a = (a_0, \ldots, a_t) \in (\mathbb{F}_{p^s})^{t+1}$, $a_0 \neq 0$, $a_t \neq 0$.
Note that $\mathbb{F}_{2^s}$ can be split into pairwise disjoint additive cosets of the form
$b + E_a$, where $b \in \mathbb{F}_{p^s}$ and $E_a = \{x \in \mathbb{F}_{p^s} \mid F_a(x) = 0\}$. Observe next that,
for every $x \in b + E_a$, $F_a(x) = F_a(b)$ (see [8, Proposition 3.2]).

3. If $t > 0$, $m > 1$, $p^s \equiv 1 \pmod m$, and $p^t \equiv 1 \pmod m$, then the p^s-ary function

$$F(x) = \left(\sum_{i=0}^{t/e} a_i x^{p^{ei}} \right)^m$$

is an r-good polynomial, where e is a divisor of t satisfying $p^e \equiv 1 \pmod m$,
$a_i \in \mathbb{F}_{p^s}$ satisfying $\sum_{i=0}^{t/e} a_i = 0$, $a_0 \neq 0$, and $a_{t/e} \neq 0$ (see [8, Theorem 3.3]).
In fact, the r-good polynomial defined above can be written as

$$F(x) = \prod_{i=1}^{m} \prod_{h \in H} (x + h + \alpha_i)$$

$$= \prod_{h \in H} (x + h)^m = \left(\sum_{i=0}^{t/e} a_i x^{p^{ei}} \right)^m,$$

where H is the set of roots of linearized polynomial $\sum_{i=0}^{t/e} a_i x^{p^{ei}}$ satisfying
$\sum_{i=0}^{t/e} a_i = 0$, $a_0 \neq 0$, $a_{t/e} \neq 0$, and $\alpha_1, \ldots, \alpha_m$ are the m-th degree roots of
unity in $\mathbb{F}_{p^s}$. Note that H is an additive subgroup of $\mathbb{F}_{p^s}$ that is closed under
the multiplication by $\mathbb{F}_{p^e}$, and $\alpha_1, \ldots, \alpha_m \in \mathbb{F}_{p^e} \subseteq H$ (since $\sum_{i=0}^{t/e} a_i = 0$
implies $1 \in H$, then $\mathbb{F}_{p^e} \subseteq H$).

3.2 More Constructions of Good Polynomials

In this subsection, we present more constructions of r-good polynomials by using
function composition. We mainly consider the more general case that $m > 1$,
$p^s \equiv 1 \pmod m$, and t does not necessarily satisfy $p^t \equiv 1 \pmod m$. For more
details, we invite the reader to consult the full paper [3].

Theorem 7 ([3]). *Denote by* $\text{Im}(F) = \{F(x) \mid x \in \mathbb{F}_{p^s}\}$ *the image set of* F. *Let*
G_γ *and* F_a *be defined as in (2) and (3) respectively. Suppose that* $\mathbb{F}_{p^s}$ *contains
all the roots of* F_a.
Set $H(x) = F_a(G_\gamma(x)) = \sum_{i=0}^{t} a_i \gamma^{p^i} x^{m p^i}$. *Then,* H *is an* $(mp^t - 1)$-*good
polynomial over* $\mathbb{F}_{p^s}$ *if and only if* $\mathcal{A} = \{b \in \mathbb{F}_{p^s} \setminus E_a \mid b + E_a \subseteq \text{Im}(G_\gamma)\}$ *is non
empty, where* $E_a = \{x \in \mathbb{F}_{p^s} \mid F_a(x) = 0\}$.

One can rewrite the above result as follows.

Theorem 8 ([3]). *Let* p *be a prime,* $r = mp^t - 1$, *where* $t \geq 1$ *and* $\gcd(m, p) = 1$.
Let F_a *be defined as in (3), where integer* s *satisfies* $p^s \equiv 1 \pmod m$. *Suppose that*
$\mathbb{F}_{p^s}$ *contains all the roots of* F_a. *Denote by* $E_a = \{0, \beta_1, \ldots, \beta_{p^t - 1}\} \subseteq \mathbb{F}_{p^s}$ *the set*

of p^t roots of F_a. For $\gamma \in \mathbb{F}_{p^s}^*$, let N be the number of solutions $(x_1, \ldots, x_{p^t}) \in (\mathbb{F}_{p^s}^*)^{p^t}$ of the equations $\gamma x_i^m - \gamma x_1^m = \beta_{i-1}$, $i = 2, \ldots, p^t$. Then,

$$H(x) = \sum_{i=0}^{t} a_i \gamma^{p^i} x^{mp^i} \tag{4}$$

is an r-good polynomial over $\mathbb{F}_{p^s}$ if and only if $N \geq p^t m^{p^t}$.

Denote by U_m the set of all m-th roots of unity over $\mathbb{F}_{p^s}$ and by cU_m a multiplicative coset of U_m, where $c \in \mathbb{F}_{p^s}^*$. Then, the r-good polynomial $H(x)$ in Theorem 8 is constant on $\bigcup_{i=1}^{p^t} x_i U_m$, where each $x_i \in \mathbb{F}_{p^s}^*$, and $\{\gamma x_1^m, \ldots, \gamma x_{p^t}^m\}$ is an additive coset of the form $b + E_a$. Moreover, it is easy to see that the r-good polynomial H in (4) is constant on $l_H = N/p^t m^{p^t}$ pairwise disjoint subsets of $\mathbb{F}_{p^s}$ with cardinality $r + 1$.

One can consider a specific p^s-ary linear function $F_a(x) = x^{p^t} - \alpha^{p^t-1}x$. Then one gets:

Corollary 9 ([3]) *[Construction-1]. Let p be a prime, $r = mp^t - 1$, where $t \geq 1$ and $\gcd(m, p) = 1$. Let s be a multiple of t satisfying $p^s \equiv 1 \pmod{m}$, $\alpha, \gamma \in \mathbb{F}_{p^s}^*$, and denote by N the number of solutions $(x_1, \ldots, x_{p^t}) \in (\mathbb{F}_{p^s}^*)^{p^t}$ of the equations $\gamma x_i^m - \gamma x_1^m = \alpha \eta^{i-2}$, $i = 2, \ldots, p^t$, where η is a primitive element of $\mathbb{F}_{p^t}$. Then,*

$$H(x) = \gamma^{p^t} x^{mp^t} - \alpha^{p^t-1} \gamma x^m \tag{5}$$

is an r-good polynomial over $\mathbb{F}_{p^s}$ if and only if $N \geq p^t m^{p^t}$.

Now, recall that for $c \in \mathbb{F}_q$, the function $\chi_c : \mathbb{F}_q \to \mathbb{C}$ defined by

$$\chi_c(x) = \zeta_p^{Tr_1^q(cx)}, \quad \text{where } \zeta_p = e^{2\pi i/p}$$

is a *character* of the additive group of $\mathbb{F}_q$. We refer to [6, Chapter 5] for background on characters of finite abelian group.

The *Walsh-Hadamard transform* of a q-ary function F is defined as the complex function

$$\mathcal{W}_F(v, c) = \sum_{x \in \mathbb{F}_q} \zeta_p^{Tr_1^q(vF(x))} \chi_c(x), \quad v \in \mathbb{F}_q^*, \ c \in \mathbb{F}_q.$$

where Tr_1^q denotes the absolute trace function from $\mathbb{F}_q$ ($q = p^s$) to $\mathbb{F}_p$.

Using a classical result on exponential sums (namely, for a finite field $\mathbb{F}_q$, $\sum_{c \in \mathbb{F}_q} \chi_c(x) = 0$ if $x \neq 0$ and q otherwise) one can express the integer N involved in the above corollary in terms of exponential sums (or more specifically, the Walsh transform of a power function) as follows:

$$N = \frac{1}{p^{s(p^t-1)}} \sum_{\substack{c \in \mathbb{F}_{p^s} \\ \gamma c^m \notin \alpha \mathbb{F}_{p^t}}} \prod_{i=0}^{p^t-2} \left(p^s + \sum_{b \in \mathbb{F}_{p^s}^*} \chi_b \left(-\gamma c^m - \alpha \eta^i\right) \mathcal{W}_{x^m}(\gamma b, 0) \right),$$

which can be rewritten as

$$N = \sum_{\substack{c \in \mathbb{F}_{p^s} \\ \gamma c^m \notin \alpha \mathbb{F}_{p^t}}} \prod_{i=0}^{p^t-2} \left(1 + \frac{1}{mp^s} \sum_{j=0}^{m-1} \mathcal{W}_{x^m} \left(\gamma \xi^j, 0 \right) \mathcal{W}_{x^m} \left(\left(-\gamma c^m - \alpha \eta^i \right) \xi^j, 0 \right) \right),$$

where η is a primitive element of $\mathbb{F}_{p^t}$, and ξ is a primitive element of $\mathbb{F}_{p^s}$.

Combining two results due to Hou [2] dealing with the explicit evaluation of Walsh-Hadamard transform of binary quadratic functions, one can derive the following explicit construction of good polynomials valid in the case where $m = 2^a + 1$ ($a \geq 1$).

Corollary 10 ([3]). *Let $m = 2^a + 1$, where $a \geq 1$. Integer s satisfies $2^s \equiv 1 \pmod{m}$ and $s \geq 4a + 2$. Then, for any $\alpha, \gamma \in \mathbb{F}_{2^s}^*$, $H(x) = \gamma^2 x^{2m} + \alpha \gamma x^m$ is a $(2m-1)$-good polynomial over $\mathbb{F}_{2^s}$. More explicitly, $H(x)$ is constant on l_H pairwise disjoint subsets with cardinality $2m$, where*

$$l_H = \begin{cases} \left(2^s + 2^{s/2+a}(2^a - 1) - 3 \cdot 2^a - 2 \right) / 2(2^a + 1)^2, \\ \quad \text{if } v_2(s) = v_2(a) + 1 \text{ and } \gamma^{-1}\alpha \in \{x^m \mid x \in \mathbb{F}_{2^s}^*\}; \\ \left(2^s - (2^{s/2} + 1)(2^a - 1) - 1 \right) / 2(2^a + 1)^2, \\ \quad \text{if } v_2(s) = v_2(a) + 1 \text{ and } \gamma^{-1}\alpha \notin \{x^m \mid x \in \mathbb{F}_{2^s}^*\}; \\ \left(2^s - 2^{s/2+a}(2^a - 1) - 3 \cdot 2^a - 2 \right) / 2(2^a + 1)^2, \\ \quad \text{if } v_2(s) > v_2(a) + 1 \text{ and } \gamma^{-1}\alpha \in \{x^m \mid x \in \mathbb{F}_{2^s}^*\}; \\ \left(2^s + (2^{s/2} - 1)(2^a - 1) - 1 \right) / 2(2^a + 1)^2, \\ \quad \text{if } v_2(s) > v_2(a) + 1 \text{ and } \gamma^{-1}\alpha \notin \{x^m \mid x \in \mathbb{F}_{2^s}^*\}, \end{cases}$$

where $v_2(\cdot)$ denotes the 2-adic order function, i.e., $v_2(n)$ is the highest exponent e such that 2^e divides n.

The good polynomials described in the above corollary are constant on the union of (disjoint) multiplicative cosets of $U_m := \{x \in \mathbb{F}_{2^s} \mid x^m = 1\}$. Moreover, Corollary 10 leads to (n, k, r) LRC codes over $\mathbb{F}_{2^s}$, where $r = 2m - 1$, $n = (r+1)l_H$, and $k \leq r l_H$.

Example 11. From Corollary 10, we get that $H(x) = x^6 + x^3$ is a 5-good polynomial over $\mathbb{F}_{2^s}$, where s is even and $s \geq 6$.

– If $s = 6$, then $l_H = 4$. Let $U_3 = \{x \in \mathbb{F}_{2^6} \mid x^3 = 1\}$ and ξ be a primitive element of $\mathbb{F}_{2^6}$, then the 2^6-ary function $H(x) = x^6 + x^3$ is constant on the following 4 pairwise disjoint subsets

$$\left\{ \{\xi^3 U_3, \xi^9 U_3\}, \ \{\xi^6 U_3, \xi^{18} U_3\}, \ \{\xi^7 U_3, \xi^{14} U_3\}, \right.$$
$$\left. \{\xi^{12} U_3, \xi^{15} U_3\} \right\} \subseteq \mathbb{F}_{2^6}.$$

- If $s = 8$, then $l_H = 12$. Let $U_3 = \{x \in \mathbb{F}_{2^8} \mid x^3 = 1\}$ and ξ be a primitive element of $\mathbb{F}_{2^8}$, then the 2^8-ary function $H(x) = x^6 + x^3$ is constant on the following 12 pairwise disjoint subsets

$$\Big\{ \{\xi^3 U_3, \xi^{40} U_3\}, \ \{\xi^5 U_3, \xi^{11} U_3\},$$
$$\{\xi^6 U_3, \xi^{80} U_3\}, \ \{\xi^{10} U_3, \xi^{22} U_3\},$$
$$\{\xi^{12} U_3, \xi^{75} U_3\}, \ \{\xi^{20} U_3, \xi^{44} U_3\},$$
$$\{\xi^{24} U_3, \xi^{65} U_3\}, \ \{\xi^{37} U_3, \xi^{82} U_3\},$$
$$\{\xi^{41} U_3, \xi^{61} U_3\}, \ \{\xi^{45} U_3, \xi^{48} U_3\},$$
$$\{\xi^{63} U_3, \xi^{73} U_3\}, \ \{\xi^{74} U_3, \xi^{79} U_3\} \Big\} \subseteq \mathbb{F}_{2^8}.$$

The pairwise disjoint subsets are found by MAGMA.

In Theorem 12, we provide another possible constructions of r-good polynomials by considering the composition $G_1 \circ F_a(x) = \left(\sum_{i=0}^{t} a_i x^{p^i} \right)^m$.

Theorem 12 ([3]). *Denote by $\mathrm{Im}(F) = \{F(x) \mid x \in \mathbb{F}_{p^s}\}$ the image set of F. Let G_γ and F_a be defined as in (2) and (3) respectively. Suppose that $\mathbb{F}_{p^s}$ contains all the roots of F_a. Set $I(x) = G_1(F_a(x)) = \left(\sum_{i=0}^{t} a_i x^{p^i} \right)^m$. Then, I is an $(mp^t - 1)$-good polynomial over $\mathbb{F}_{p^s}$ if and only if $\mathcal{A}' = \{b \in \mathbb{F}_{p^s}^* \mid b U_m \subseteq \mathrm{Im}(F_a)\}$ is non empty, where $U_m = \{x \in \mathbb{F}_{p^s} \mid x^m = 1\}$.*

One can rewrite the above theorem as follows.

Theorem 13 ([3]). *Let p be a prime, $r = mp^t - 1$, where $t \geq 1$ and $\gcd(m, p) = 1$. Let F_a be defined as in (3), where integer s satisfies $p^s \equiv 1 \pmod{m}$. Suppose that $\mathbb{F}_{p^s}$ contains all the roots of F_a. Denote by N the number of integers $0 \leq i \leq p^s - 2$ such that for every $j = 0, 1, \ldots, m - 1$,*

$$F_a(x) = \xi^{i + j(p^s - 1)/m}$$

has solutions on $\mathbb{F}_{p^s}$, where ξ is a primitive element of $\mathbb{F}_{p^s}$. Then,

$$I(x) = \left(\sum_{i=0}^{t} a_i x^{p^i} \right)^m \tag{6}$$

is an r-good polynomial over $\mathbb{F}_{p^s}$ if and only if $N \geq m$.

Note that the r-good polynomial in Theorem 13 is constant on $\bigcup_{i=1}^{m} (x_i + E_a)$, where $E_a = \{x \in \mathbb{F}_{p^s} \mid F_a(x) = 0\}$, and $\{F_a(x_1), \ldots, F_a(x_m)\}$ is a coset of U_m. Moreover, it is not difficult to see that the r-good polynomial I in (6) is constant on $l_I = N/m$ pairwise disjoint subsets of $\mathbb{F}_{p^s}$ with cardinality $r + 1$.

Now, we consider the case of a special p^s-ary linear function $F_a(x) = x^{p^t} - \alpha^{p^t - 1} x$.

We know that $x^{p^t} - \alpha^{p^t-1}x = \xi^{i+j(p^s-1)/m}$ has solutions in $\mathbb{F}_{p^s}$ if and only if

$$Tr_t^s \left(\alpha^{-p^t} \xi^{i+j(p^s-1)/m} \right) = 0,$$

where $t|s$, $0 \leq i \leq p^s - 2$ and $0 \leq j \leq m - 1$. Note that $E_a = \{x \in \mathbb{F}_{p^s} \mid x^{p^t} - \alpha^{p^t-1}x = 0\} = \alpha \mathbb{F}_{p^t}$, then $\mathbb{F}_{p^s}$ contains all the roots of $x^{p^t} - \alpha^{p^t-1}x$. Then, the following construction can be obtained from Theorem 13.

Corollary 14 ([3]) *[Construction-2]. Let p be a prime, $r = mp^t - 1$, where $t \geq 1$ and $\gcd(m, p) = 1$. Let s be a multiple of t satisfying $p^s \equiv 1 \pmod{m}$, $\alpha \in \mathbb{F}_{p^s}^*$, and denote by N the number of integers $0 \leq i \leq p^s - 2$ such that*

$$Tr_t^s \left(\alpha^{-p^t} \xi^{i+j(p^s-1)/m} \right) = 0 \tag{7}$$

holds for every $j = 0, 1, \ldots, m - 1$, where ξ is a primitive element of $\mathbb{F}_{p^s}$. Then,

$$I(x) = \left(x^{p^t} - \alpha^{p^t-1}x \right)^m$$

is an r-good polynomial over $\mathbb{F}_{p^s}$ if and only if $N \geq m$.

The r-good polynomial described in Corollary 14 is constant on $\bigcup_{i=1}^{m} (x_i + \alpha \mathbb{F}_{p^t})$, where $\{x_1^{p^t} - \alpha^{p^t-1}x_1, \ldots, x_m^{p^t} - \alpha^{p^t-1}x_m\}$ is a coset of U_m. Now, we notice that $N = \#\mathcal{N}'$ where

$$\mathcal{N}' := \left\{ x \in \mathbb{F}_{p^s}^* \;\middle|\; Tr_t^s \left(x\alpha^{-p^t} \xi^{j(p^s-1)/m} \right) = 0 \right.$$

$$\left. \text{for all } j = 0, \ldots, m - 1 \right\}.$$

Then we deduce the following corollary.

Corollary 15 ([3]). *Let p be a prime, $r = mp^t - 1$, where $t \geq 1$ and $\gcd(m, p) = 1$. Let s be a multiple of t satisfying $p^s \equiv 1 \pmod{m}$. Then, for any $\alpha \in \mathbb{F}_{p^s}^*$, $I(x) = \left(x^{p^t} - \alpha^{p^t-1}x \right)^m$ is an r-good polynomial over $\mathbb{F}_{p^s}$ if and only if $N' \geq m$, where*

$$N' = \frac{1}{p^{tm}} \sum_{x \in \mathbb{F}_{p^s}^*} \prod_{i=1}^{m} \left(\sum_{b \in \mathbb{F}_{p^t}} \chi_{b\alpha^{-p^t} \xi^{i(p^s-1)/m}}(x) \right), \tag{8}$$

and ξ is a primitive element of $\mathbb{F}_{p^s}$.

From corollary 15, we get the more precise following result.

Corollary 16 ([3]). *Let p be a prime, $r = mp^t - 1$, where $t \geq 1$ and $\gcd(m, p) = 1$. Let s be a multiple of t satisfying $p^s \equiv 1 \pmod{m}$ and $s > t(m-1)$. Then, for any $\alpha \in \mathbb{F}_{p^s}^*$, $I(x) = \left(x^{p^t} - \alpha^{p^t-1}x \right)^m$ is an r-good polynomial over $\mathbb{F}_{p^s}$. More explicitly, $I(x)$ is constant on at least $\lceil (p^{s-t(m-1)} - 1)/m \rceil$ pairwise disjoint subsets with cardinality $r + 1$.*

Corollary 16 leads to (n, k, r) LRC codes over $\mathbb{F}_{p^s}$, where $r = mp^t - 1$, $n = (r+1)l_I$, $k \leq rl_I$, and $l_I = \lceil (p^{s-t(m-1)} - 1)/m \rceil$.

Example 17. Let $p = 2$, $m = 3$, and $t = 1$ (in this case, $p^t \not\equiv 1 \pmod{m}$). From Corollary 16, we get that $I(x) = (x^2 + x)^3$ is a 5-good polynomial over $\mathbb{F}_{2^s}$, where s is even and $s > 2$.

If $s = 6$, then $l_I \geq \lceil (p^{s-t(m-1)} - 1)/m \rceil = 5$. Let ξ be a primitive element of $\mathbb{F}_{2^6}$, then the 2^6-ary function $I(x) = (x^2 + x)^3$ is constant on the following 5 pairwise disjoint subsets

$$\left\{ \{\xi + \mathbb{F}_2, \xi^7 + \mathbb{F}_2, \xi^9 + \mathbb{F}_2\}, \right.$$
$$\{\xi^2 + \mathbb{F}_2, \xi^{14} + \mathbb{F}_2, \xi^{18} + \mathbb{F}_2\},$$
$$\{\xi^4 + \mathbb{F}_2, \xi^{28} + \mathbb{F}_2, \xi^{36} + \mathbb{F}_2\},$$
$$\{\xi^5 + \mathbb{F}_2, \xi^{17} + \mathbb{F}_2, \xi^{20} + \mathbb{F}_2\},$$
$$\left. \{\xi^{10} + \mathbb{F}_2, \xi^{15} + \mathbb{F}_2, \xi^{40} + \mathbb{F}_2\} \right\} \subseteq \mathbb{F}_{2^6}.$$

The pairwise disjoint subsets are found by MAGMA. In fact, l_I is exactly 5.

In the following, we consider another special function. More precisely, the p^s-ary linear function in the form $F_a(x) = Tr_1^{t+1}(\alpha x)$ (where $\alpha \in \mathbb{F}_{p^s}^*$ and s is a multiple of $t+1$). The reader can notice that $\mathbb{F}_{p^s}$ contains all the roots of $Tr_1^{t+1}(\alpha x)$. Then, the following construction is obtained from Theorem 13.

Corollary 18 ([3]) *[Construction-3]. Let p be a prime, $r = mp^t - 1$, where $t \geq 1$ and $\gcd(m, p) = 1$. Let s be a multiple of $t+1$ satisfying $p^s \equiv 1 \pmod{m}$. If there exist $\gamma \in \mathbb{F}_{p^s}^*$ and integer $k < s$ such that $p^k \equiv 1 \pmod{m}$ and $\gamma \mathbb{F}_{p^k} \subseteq \mathrm{Im}\left(Tr_1^{t+1}(x)\right)$, then for any $\alpha \in \mathbb{F}_{p^s}^*$,*

$$I(x) = \left(Tr_1^{t+1}(\alpha x)\right)^m \tag{9}$$

is an r-good polynomial over $\mathbb{F}_{p^s}$. Moreover, $I(x)$ is constant on at least $(p^k - 1)/m$ pairwise disjoint subsets with cardinality $r + 1$.

For any $\alpha \in \mathbb{F}_{p^s}^*$, $I(x) = \left(Tr_1^{t+1}(\alpha x)\right)^m$ is constant on the following pairwise disjoint subsets with cardinality $r + 1$,

$$A_i = \left\{ x \in \mathbb{F}_{p^s} \mid Tr_1^{t+1}(\alpha x) = \xi^{c+i(p^s-1)/(p^k-1)+j(p^s-1)/m}, \right.$$
$$\left. j = 0, \ldots, m-1 \right\},$$

where $i = 0, 1, \ldots, (p^k - 1)/m - 1$.

Example 19. Let $p = 2$, $m = 5$, $t = 2$ (in this case, $p^t \not\equiv 1 \pmod{m}$), and $s = 12$. It can be easily checked that $\mathbb{F}_{2^4} \subseteq \mathrm{Im}\left(Tr_1^3(x)\right)$. Then, from Corollary 18, for any $\alpha \in \mathbb{F}_{2^{12}}^*$, $I(x) = \left(Tr_1^3(\alpha x)\right)^5$ is a 19-good polynomial over $\mathbb{F}_{2^{12}}$, which is constant on at least 3 pairwise disjoint subsets as follows,

$$A_i = \left\{ x \in \mathbb{F}_{2^{12}} \mid Tr_1^3(\alpha x) = \xi^{273i+819j}, j = 0, \dots, 4 \right\},$$

where $i = 0, 1, 2$, and ξ is a primitive element of $\mathbb{F}_{2^{12}}$. By using MAGMA, we find $l_I = 3$.

Corollary 20 ([3]). *Let p be a prime, $r = mp^t - 1$, where $\gcd(m, p) = 1$ and integer $t \geq 1$ satisfies $p^{t+1} \equiv 1 \pmod{m}$. Let s be a multiple of $2(t + 1)$. Then, for any $\alpha \in \mathbb{F}_{p^s}^*$,*

$$I(x) = \left(Tr_1^{t+1}(\alpha x)\right)^m$$

is an r-good polynomial over $\mathbb{F}_{p^s}$. Moreover, $I(x)$ is constant on at least $(p^{t+1} - 1)/m$ pairwise disjoint subsets with cardinality $r + 1$.

Example 21. Due to Corollary 20, we can provide some examples of r-good polynomials in the form (9).

- Let $p = 2$, $m = 5$, $t = 3$ (in this case, $p^{t+1} \equiv 1 \pmod{m}$), and $s = 8$. It can be easily checked that $\mathbb{F}_{2^4} \subseteq \text{Im}\left(Tr_1^4(x)\right)$. Then, for any $\alpha \in \mathbb{F}_{2^8}^*$, $I(x) = \left(Tr_1^4(\alpha x)\right)^5$ is a 39-good polynomial over $\mathbb{F}_{2^8}$, which is constant on the following 3 pairwise disjoint subsets,

$$A_i = \left\{ x \in \mathbb{F}_{2^8} \mid Tr_1^4(\alpha x) = \xi^{17i+51j}, j = 0, \dots, 4 \right\},$$

where $i = 0, 1, 2$, and ξ is a primitive element of $\mathbb{F}_{2^8}$. By using MAGMA, we find $l_I = 3$.
- Let $p = 3$, $m = 5$, $t = 3$ (in this case, $p^{t+1} \equiv 1 \pmod{m}$), and $s = 8$. It can be easily checked that $\xi^{41}\mathbb{F}_{3^4} \subseteq \text{Im}\left(Tr_1^4(x)\right)$. Then, for any $\alpha \in \mathbb{F}_{3^8}^*$, $I(x) = \left(Tr_1^4(\alpha x)\right)^5$ is a 134-good polynomial over $\mathbb{F}_{3^8}$, which is constant on the following 16 pairwise disjoint subsets,

$$A_i = \left\{ x \in \mathbb{F}_{3^8} \mid Tr_1^4(\alpha x) = \xi^{41+82i+1312j}, \right.$$
$$\left. j = 0, \dots, 4 \right\},$$

where $i = 0, 1, \dots, 15$, and ξ is a primitive element of $\mathbb{F}_{3^8}$. By using MAGMA, we find $l_I = 16$.

Acknowledgements. The author is very grateful to Jian Liu for her valuable help. She also thanks the co-chairs program (in particular Claude Carlet for his careful reading) and the organizers of the conference C2SI 2019 for their nice invitation.

References

1. Gopalan, P., Huang, C., Simitci, H., Yekhanin, S.: On the locality of codeword symbols. IEEE Trans. Inf. Theory **58**(11), 6925–6934 (2012)
2. Hou, X.-D.: Explicit evaluation of certain exponential sums of binary quadratic functions. Finite Fields Appl. **13**(4), 843–868 (2007)
3. Liu, J., Mesnager, S., Chen, L.: New constructions of optimal locally recoverable codes via good polynomials. IEEE Trans. Inf. Theory **62**(2), 889–899 (2018)
4. Liu, J., Mesnager, S., Tang, D.: Constructions of optimal locally recoverable codes via Dickson polynomials. In: Workshop WCC 2019: The Eleventh International Workshop on Coding and Cryptography (2019)
5. Micheli, G.: Constructions of locally recoverable codes which are optimal. arXiv:1806.11492 [cs.IT] (2018)
6. Lidl, R., Niederreiter, H.: Finite Fields, Encyclopedia of Mathematics and its Applications, vol. 20. Cambridge University Press, Cambridge (1997)
7. Papailiopoulos, D.S., Dimakis, A.G.: Locally repairable codes. IEEE Trans. Inf. Theory **60**(10), 5843–5855 (2014)
8. Tamo, I., Barg, A.: A family of optimal locally recoverable codes. IEEE Trans. Inf. Theory **60**(8), 4661–4676 (2014)

A New Gabidulin-Like Code
and Its Application in Cryptography

Terry Shue Chien Lau$^{(\boxtimes)}$ and Chik How Tan

Temasek Laboratories, National University of Singapore,
5A Engineering Drive 1, #09-02, Singapore 117411, Singapore
{tsltlsc,tsltch}@nus.edu.sg

Abstract. We introduce a new rank-metric code, namely λ-Gabidulin code by multiplying each of the columns of the generator of Gabidulin codes with entries from $\lambda = (\lambda_1, \ldots, \lambda_n) \in \mathbb{F}_{q^m}^n$. We discuss the motivation of introducing λ-Gabidulin code and prove some of its properties. Then, we design a new McEliece type rank metric based encryption scheme on λ-Gabidulin code, with a scrambler matrix depending on λ. We show that this new cryptosystem is secure against the existing attacks on Gabidulin codes based encryption, in particularly how it resists Overbeck's structural attack, annulator polynomial attack and the Frobenius weak attack. Finally, we also propose some parameters for the new cryptosystem and show that our proposal has smaller key size than the Loi17 Encryption [29] using Gabidulin codes proposed in PQCrypto 2017.

Keywords: Post-quantum cryptography · McEliece · Gabidulin code · Public-key encryption

1 Introduction

In 1978, McEliece [31] proposed a public-key cryptosystem based on Goppa codes in the Hamming metric. The idea of McEliece cryptosystem is to hide the structure of the generator matrix for the decodable codes with random invertible matrix S and random permutation matrix P, and publish the matrix $G_{\mathsf{pub}} = SGP$. Although his design has efficient encryption and decryption, it involves a significantly large public key size. To tackle this problem, several modifications of the scheme have been proposed. One of the approaches to overcome the large public key size for schemes in Hamming metric, is to consider an alternative metric, namely the rank metric. In 1985 Gabidulin [8] introduced the rank metric and the Gabidulin codes with efficient decoding algorithm. Gabidulin codes are usually seen as equivalent of Reed-Solomon codes in the Hamming metric which both are highly structured. Later on, Gabidulin, Paramanov, and Tretjakov used the Gabidulin codes and proposed the first rank metric based cryptosystem, namely GPT [11].

However, due to the well-structuredness of Gabidulin codes, proposals of cryptosystems based on Gabidulin codes have alternately been attacked and modified. The first structural attack on the initial GPT system was suggested by Gibson

© Springer Nature Switzerland AG 2019
C. Carlet et al. (Eds.): C2SI 2019, LNCS 11445, pp. 269–287, 2019.
https://doi.org/10.1007/978-3-030-16458-4_16

[18] through exploiting the structure of Gabidulin codes and the distortion matrix in GPT. Modifications have been made to produce GPT's variants to resist Gibson's attack. To counter Gibson's attack, a modified GPT with right scrambler was proposed in [10,34]. However, this modified GPT with right scrambler was cryptanalyzed by Overbeck by extending Gibson's attacks [36]. A modified cryptosystem, namely generalized GPT (GGPT) was introduced by Overbeck in the same paper to resist Gibson's attacks. Yet, as the Gabidulin codes contains huge vector space invariant under the Frobenius automorphism, Overbeck [37] was successful in cryptanalyze all the previous Gabidulin codes based cryptosystems. Despite the efforts of other variants of GGPT proposed in [9,12,28,39] to secure against Overbeck's attack, these GGPT variants were shown to be insecure against more recent structural attacks such as extension of Overbeck's attack [20], reduction attack to GGPT [33], and Frobenius weak attack [21].

More recently, there are several encryption schemes based on Gabidulin codes being proposed. Loidreau [29] considered a McEliece type cryptosystem based on Gabidulin codes with a scrambler matrix P which its inverse P^{-1} over a w-dimensional subspace of $\mathbb{F}_{q^m}$. This cryptosystem is then implemented in DRANKULA [1]. Also, Lau and Tan [25,26] introduced a new technique to construct McEliece type encryption scheme based on any generic decodable codes. Apart from these McEliece type cryptosystems based on Gabidulin codes, there are some other encryption schemes such as [2,13] that do not hide the structure of the generator matrix and use other techniques to construct the encryption. Moreover, there are some other encryption schemes that combines the idea of McEliece and Niederreiter cryptosystem, such as [17,27].

Although there are other techniques in constructing code-based encryption scheme, the question of the possibility to construct secure McEliece type cryptosystem by considering alternative rank codes is still of interest in the research community. In 2014, the Low Rank Parity Check codes (LRPC) were proposed to construct a McEliece type encryption scheme [15]. Later in 2018, Kim et al. [22] extended the LRPC codes into a new LRPC-Kronecker product codes and proposed a McEliece type encryption based on this code.

The main task of this paper is to propose a new rank metric code, namely λ-Gabidulin code which is an extension of Gabidulin code. This λ-Gabidulin code is analogous to the generalized Reed-Solomon codes in rank metric settings, which is obtained by multiplying the columns of the generator matrix with some elements in $\mathbb{F}_{q^m}$. We show that λ-Gabidulin code is decodable when certain conditions are met, and use this property to construct a new code-based cryptosystem based on λ-Gabidulin code. In this paper, we first review in Sect. 2 some basic facts and definitions in rank metric and Gabidulin codes. We introduce a new rank metric code, namely λ-Gabidulin code in Sect. 3. Based on λ-Gabidulin code, we propose a new Gabidulin-like code public-key encryption in Sect. 4. In Sect. 5, its security against existing attacks is discussed. In Sect. 6, we suggest some parameters for our proposal and shows that the our proposal has smaller public key size than Loidreau's proposal in [29] and DRANKULA in [1]. Finally, we conclude this paper in Sect. 7.

2   Background on Rank Metric and Gabidulin Codes

In this section we recall the definition of rank metric and some related results, which are the core of rank metric based cryptosystems.

2.1   Rank Metric

Let $\mathbb{F}_{q^m}$ be a finite field with q^m elements and let $\{\beta_1, \ldots, \beta_m\}$ be a basis of $\mathbb{F}_{q^m}$ over the base field $\mathbb{F}_q$, where q is power of prime.

Definition 1. Let $\boldsymbol{x} = (x_1, \ldots, x_n) \in \mathbb{F}_{q^m}^n$. The *rank* of $\boldsymbol{x}$ in $\mathbb{F}_q$, denoted by $\mathrm{rk}_q(\boldsymbol{x})$ is the rank of the matrix $X = [x_{ij}] \in \mathbb{F}_q^{m \times n}$ where $x_j = \sum_{i=1}^{m} x_{ij} \beta_i$.

Equivalently, the rank of $\boldsymbol{x}$ is the dimension over $\mathbb{F}_q$ of the subspace of $\mathbb{F}_{q^m}$ which is spanned by the coordinates of $\boldsymbol{x}$. Note that the rank of a vector is a norm and is independent of the chosen basis.

Definition 2. The *rank distance* between $\boldsymbol{x}, \boldsymbol{y} \in \mathbb{F}_{q^m}$ is defined to be

$$d_R(\boldsymbol{x}, \boldsymbol{y}) = \mathrm{rk}_q(\boldsymbol{x} - \boldsymbol{y}).$$

If $\mathcal{C}$ is a linear code, the minimum rank distance of $\mathcal{C}$, is defined by

$$d_R^{\min}(\mathcal{C}) := \min_{\boldsymbol{c} \in \mathcal{C}} \{d_R(\boldsymbol{c}, \boldsymbol{0}) \mid \boldsymbol{c} \neq \boldsymbol{0}\}.$$

The Singleton bound for rank-metric codes is given by the inequality

$$d_R^{\min}(\mathcal{C}) \leq n - \dim(\mathcal{C}) + 1.$$

Definition 3. A rank-metric code satisfying the Singleton bound is called a *maximum rank-distance* (MRD) code.

We now state a few results related to the rank metric, in particular the concepts of Grassmann support which are important for security analysis in Sect. 5.

Lemma 1. Let $\boldsymbol{x} \in \mathbb{F}_{q^m}^n$ such that $\mathrm{rk}_q(\boldsymbol{x}) = r \leq n$, then there exists $\hat{\boldsymbol{x}} \in \mathbb{F}_{q^m}^r$ with $\mathrm{rk}_q(\hat{\boldsymbol{x}}) = r$ and $U \in \mathbb{F}_q^{r \times n}$ with $\mathrm{rk}(U) = r$ such that $\boldsymbol{x} = \hat{\boldsymbol{x}}U$. This decomposition is unique up to $\mathrm{GL}_r(\mathbb{F}_q)$-operation between $\hat{\boldsymbol{x}}$ and U.

Notation. We denote $[i] := q^i$ as the ith Frobenius power. Let $M = [M_{a,b}] \in \mathbb{F}_{q^m}^{k \times n}$, we denote $M^{([i])} := \left[M_{a,b}^{[i]}\right] \in \mathbb{F}_{q^m}^{k \times n}$. Also, for any set $S \subset \mathbb{F}_{q^m}^n$, we denote $S^{([i])} := \{s^{([i])} \mid s \in S\}$. For a matrix U over $\mathbb{F}_q$, we denote $\langle U \rangle_{\mathbb{F}_{q^m}}$ as the row span of a matrix U over $\mathbb{F}_{q^m}$. By abuse of notation, for vector $\boldsymbol{u}_1, \ldots, \boldsymbol{u}_j$ over $\mathbb{F}_{q^m}$, we denote $\langle \boldsymbol{u}_1, \ldots, \boldsymbol{u}_j \rangle_{\mathbb{F}_{q^m}}$ as $\mathbb{F}_{q^m}$ span of the vectors $\boldsymbol{u}_1, \ldots, \boldsymbol{u}_j$.

Definition 4. Let $\boldsymbol{x} \in \mathbb{F}_{q^m}^n$ with $\mathrm{rk}_q(\boldsymbol{x}) = r \leq n$ and decomposition $\boldsymbol{x} = \hat{\boldsymbol{x}}U$ as in Lemma 1. We call U a *Grassman support matrix* for $\boldsymbol{x}$ and $\langle U \rangle_{\mathbb{F}_{q^m}}$ the *Grassman support* of $\boldsymbol{x}$.

Lemma 2 ([20,21]). *Let $x \in S \subseteq \mathbb{F}_{q^m}^n$ with $\mathrm{rk}_q(x) = r \leq n$, and s be an integer such that $\gcd(s, m) = 1$. Then*

$$\mathrm{supp}(x) = \left\langle x, x^{([s])}, \ldots, x^{([s(r-1)])} \right\rangle_{\mathbb{F}_{q^m}} \subseteq \sum_{i=0}^{r-1} S^{([si])}.$$

Horlemann-Trautmann et al. [20] efficiently computed the elements of rank one in an $\mathbb{F}_{q^m}$-linear code $\mathcal{C} \subseteq \mathbb{F}_{q^m}^n$ with the following lemma:

Lemma 3 ([20]). *Let $G \in \mathbb{F}_{q^m}^{k \times n}$ be a generator matrix for a code $\mathcal{C}$ in reduced row echelon form. Denote G_i as the ith row of G. Then*

– All elements of rank one in $\langle G \rangle_{\mathbb{F}_{q^m}}$ are multiples of the elements in

$$\mathcal{C}^* := \langle G \rangle_{\mathbb{F}_{q^m}} \cap \mathbb{F}_q^n.$$

– The elements in $\mathcal{C}^*$ are in one-to-one correspondence to the solution of

$$\sum_{i=1}^{k} a_i \left[G_i^{([1])} - G_i \right] = 0, \quad \text{where } a_i \in F_q.$$

– Computing the solutions of this system requires $O(kmn^2)$ operations in $\mathbb{F}_q$.

2.2 Gabidulin Codes

We now give the definition and some properties of Gabidulin codes as they will be used to construct our new code in Sect. 3.

Definition 5 (Gabidulin Codes, [8]). *Let $g = (g_1, \ldots, g_n) \in \mathbb{F}_{q^m}^n$ be linearly independent over $\mathbb{F}_q$. The Gabidulin code, $\mathrm{Gab}_{n,k}(g)$ over $\mathbb{F}_{q^m}$ of dimension k and generator vector g is the code generated by matrix G of the form*

$$G = \begin{bmatrix} g_1 & g_2 & \cdots & g_n \\ g_1^{[1]} & g_2^{[1]} & \cdots & g_n^{[1]} \\ \vdots & \vdots & \ddots & \vdots \\ g_1^{[k-1]} & g_2^{[k-1]} & \cdots & g_n^{[k-1]} \end{bmatrix}. \tag{1}$$

Gabidulin [8] showed that the error-correcting capability of $\mathrm{Gab}_{n,k}(g)$ is $r = \lfloor \frac{n-k}{2} \rfloor$. Moreover, it was also shown that Gabidulin code is an MRD code if and only if $m \geq n$. Gabidulin also provided an efficient decoding algorithms for Gabidulin codes up to the rank error correcting capability in [8]. The most updated complexity to decode an $[n, k]$-Gabidulin code is $O\left(n^{1.69} \log^2(n)\right)$ operations in $\mathbb{F}_{q^m}$ [38, Theorem 17].

Definition 6. *A linearized polynomial $F(z)$ over $\mathbb{F}_{q^m}$ is a polynomial of the form $F(z) = \sum_{i=0}^{k} f_i z^{[i]}$ where $f_i \in \mathbb{F}_{q^m}$ for $0 \leq i \leq k$. We refer k as the q-degree of $F(z)$, $\deg_q F(z)$.*

With $F(z) = \sum_{i=0}^{k-1} f_i z^{[i]}$, we can now rewrite a codeword $\boldsymbol{c} = (f_0, \ldots, f_{k-1})G \in$ $\mathrm{Gab}_{n,k}(\boldsymbol{g})$ as:

$$
\begin{aligned}
\boldsymbol{c} &= (f_0, \ldots, f_{k-1})
\begin{bmatrix}
g_1 & \cdots & g_n \\
\vdots & \ddots & \vdots \\
g_1^{[k-1]} & \cdots & g_n^{[k-1]}
\end{bmatrix} \\
&= \left(\sum_{i=0}^{k-1} f_i g_1^{[i]}, \ldots, \sum_{i=0}^{k-1} f_i g_n^{[i]} \right) = (F(g_1), \ldots, F(g_n)).
\end{aligned}
\tag{2}
$$

Gabidulin codes contains huge vector space invariant under the Frobenius automorphism, which subjects the cryptosystem based on Gabidulin codes to Overbeck's attack. To be more precise, we now define an $\mathbb{F}_q$-linear operator Λ_i on a matrix M as the following:

Definition 7 (Frobenius Map). For any integer $i \geq 0$, let $\Lambda_i : \mathbb{F}_{q^m}^{k \times n} \to \mathbb{F}_{q^m}^{ik \times n}$ be the $\mathbb{F}_q$-linear operator that maps any matrix $M \in \mathbb{F}_{q^m}^{k \times n}$ to $\Lambda_i(M)$:

$$
\Lambda_i(M) := \begin{bmatrix} M^{[0]} \\ \vdots \\ M^{[i]} \end{bmatrix}.
\tag{3}
$$

As a consequence, the Gabidulin codes contains huge vector space invariant under the Frobenius automorphism:

Lemma 4. Let G be the generator matrix of $\mathrm{Gab}_{n,k}(\boldsymbol{g})$. For integer $i \geq 0$ and $1 \leq j \leq m - 1$, we have $\dim_{\mathbb{F}_{q^m}} (\Lambda_i(G)) = k + i$ and

$$
\dim_{\mathbb{F}_{q^m}} \left(\mathrm{Gab}_{n,k}(\boldsymbol{g})^{[j]} \cap \mathrm{Gab}_{n,k}(\boldsymbol{g})^{[j-1]} \right) = k - 1.
$$

Proof. Recall from (3) that

$$
\Lambda_i(G) = \begin{bmatrix} G^{[0]} \\ \vdots \\ G^{[i]} \end{bmatrix} = \begin{bmatrix} \boldsymbol{g}^{[0]} \\ \vdots \\ \boldsymbol{g}^{[k-1]} \\ \vdots \\ \boldsymbol{g}^{[i]} \\ \vdots \\ \boldsymbol{g}^{[k+i-1]} \end{bmatrix} \quad \Rightarrow \quad \mathrm{rk}(\Lambda_i(G)) = k + i.
$$

Also, since $\mathrm{Gab}_{n,k}(\boldsymbol{g})^{[j]} = \left\{ \boldsymbol{x} \begin{bmatrix} \boldsymbol{g}^{[j]} \\ \vdots \\ \boldsymbol{g}^{[j+k-1]} \end{bmatrix} : \boldsymbol{x} \in \mathbb{F}_{q^m}^k \right\}$, then

$$\mathrm{Gab}_{n,k}(\boldsymbol{g})^{[j]} \cap \mathrm{Gab}_{n,k}(\boldsymbol{g})^{[j-1]} = \left\{ \boldsymbol{x} \begin{bmatrix} \boldsymbol{g}^{[j]} \\ \vdots \\ \boldsymbol{g}^{[j+k-2]} \end{bmatrix} : \boldsymbol{x}' \in \mathbb{F}_{q^m}^{k-1} \right\}$$

$$\Rightarrow \quad \dim_{\mathbb{F}_{q^m}} \left(\mathrm{Gab}_{n,k}(\boldsymbol{g})^{[j]} \cap \mathrm{Gab}_{n,k}(\boldsymbol{g})^{[j-1]} \right) = k - 1.$$

$\square$

2.3 General Decoding of Rank Metric Codes

In the case of rank metric, the rank syndrome decoding problem is analogous to the classical syndrome decoding problem with Hamming metric, as described in the following:

Definition 8. Rank Syndrome Decoding Problem (RSD). Let H be a full rank $(n - k) \times n$ matrix over $\mathbb{F}_{q^m}$, $\boldsymbol{s} \in \mathbb{F}_{q^m}^{n-k}$ and w an integer. The *Rank Syndrome Decoding Problem* $\mathsf{RSD}(q, m, n, k, w)$ needs to determine $\boldsymbol{x} \in \mathbb{F}_{q^m}^n$ such that $\mathrm{rk}_q(\boldsymbol{x}) = w$ and $H\boldsymbol{x}^T = \boldsymbol{s}^T$.

Recently, Gaborit and Zémor [16] showed that if there were efficient probabilistic algorithms for solving the RSD problem, then there exist efficient probabilistic algorithm to solve the syndrome decoding problem in Hamming metric. Therefore, RSD problem is a good candidate for the hard problem which our cryptosystem is based on.

There are generally two types of generic attacks on the RSD problem, namely the combinatorial attack and algebraic attack. The combinatorial approach depends on counting the number of possible supports of size r for a rank code of length n over $\mathbb{F}_{q^m}$, which corresponds to the number of subspaces of dimension r in $\mathbb{F}_{q^m}$. For the algebraic approach, the nature of the rank metric favors algebraic attacks using Gröbner bases, as they are largely independent of the value q. These attacks became efficient when q increases. There are mainly three approaches in translating the notion of rank into algebraic setting. The first approach [24] considers directly the RSD problem, but the complexity of solving the quadratic system from their attack is hard to evaluate, especially when $r \geq 4$. The second approach reduces RSD problem into MinRank problem [7], but such reduction only works for certain type of MinRank parameters and not for usual parameters used with rank codes based cryptography. While the third approach is proposed by Gaborit et al. [14] by considering the linearized q-polynomials introduced by Ore [32].

We summarize the existing combinatorial and algebraic attacks with their conditions and complexities in Tables 1 and 2 respectively.

Table 1. Combinatorial attacks on RSD with their corresponding solving complexities

Attacks	Complexity
CS [4]	$O\left((nr+m)^3 q^{(m-r)(r-1)}\right)$
GRS-I [14]	$\begin{cases} O\left((n-k)^3 m^3 q^{r\min\left\{k,\lfloor\frac{km}{n}\rfloor\right\}}\right) & \text{if } s \neq 0, \\ O\left((n-k)^3 m^3 q^{(r-1)\min\left\{k,\lfloor\frac{km}{n}\rfloor\right\}}\right) & \text{if } s = 0. \end{cases}$
OJ-I [35]	$O\left(r^3 m^3 q^{(r-1)(k+1)}\right)$
OJ-II [35]	$O\left((k+r)^3 r^3 q^{(m-r)(r-1)}\right)$
GRS-II [14]	$O\left((n-k)^3 m^3 q^{(r-1)\min\left\{k+1,\frac{(k+1)m}{n}\right\}}\right)$
AGHT [3]	$O\left((n-k)^3 m^3 q^{r\frac{(k+1)m}{n}-m}\right)$

Table 2. Algebraic attacks on RSD with their corresponding solving complexities

Attacks	Conditions	Complexity
MinRank–FLP [7]	$m = n$ $(n-r)^2 = nk$	$O\left((\log q)\, n^{3(n-r)^2}\right)$
CG-Kernel [19]		$O\left(k^3 m^3 q^{r\lceil\frac{km}{n}\rceil}\right)$
GRS-Basic [14]	$n \geq (r+1)(k+1)-1$	$O\left(((r+1)(k+1)-1)^3\right)$
GRS-Hybrid [14]	$\left\lceil\frac{(r+1)(k+1)-(n+1)}{r}\right\rceil \leq k$	$O\left(r^3 k^3 q^{r\left\lceil\frac{(r+1)(k+1)-(n+1)}{r}\right\rceil}\right)$

Post-quantum Security. Bernstein [5] showed that the exponential term in the decoding complexity should be square rooted using Grover's algorithm with Quantum computer. Therefore, we use this method to evaluate the post-quantum security of our scheme in Sect. 6.

3   A New Code: λ-Gabidulin Codes

In this section, we discuss the motivation to construct a new rank code, λ-Gabidulin codes. We also prove some of its properties and propose a decoding algorithm for λ-Gabidulin codes.

3.1   λ-Gabidulin Codes Construction

Our construction of λ-Gabidulin codes is in a linearized polynomial settings which is similar to the construction of the generalized Reed-Solomon codes in polynomial settings. We recall the definition of Reed-Solomon codes and generalized Reed-Solomon codes.

Definition 9 (Reed-Solomon (RS). Codes [40] & Generalized RS Codes [30, Ch. 10, Sec. 8]). Let $g' = (g_1', \ldots, g_n') \in \mathbb{F}_q^n$ where each g_i' are pairwise distinct and $\lambda = (\lambda_1, \ldots, \lambda_n) \in \mathbb{F}_q^n$ where each of $\lambda_i \neq 0$. The *Reed-Solomon codes* $RS_{n,k}(g')$ over $\mathbb{F}_q$ of dimension k and generator vector g' is the code generated by matrix G_{RS} of the form

$$
G_{RS} = \begin{bmatrix} (g_1')^0 & (g_2')^0 & \cdots & (g_n')^0 \\ (g_1')^1 & (g_2')^1 & \cdots & (g_n')^1 \\ \vdots & \vdots & \ddots & \vdots \\ (g_1')^{k-1} & (g_2')^{k-1} & \cdots & (g_n')^{k-1} \end{bmatrix}. \tag{4}
$$

The *generalized Reed-Solomon codes* $GRS_{n,k}(g_\lambda')$ over $\mathbb{F}_q$ of dimension k associated with g' and λ is the code generated by matrix G_{GRS} of the form

$$
G_{GRS} = \begin{bmatrix} \lambda_1(g_1')^0 & \lambda_2(g_2')^0 & \cdots & \lambda_n(g_n')^0 \\ \lambda_1(g_1')^1 & \lambda_2(g_2')^1 & \cdots & \lambda_n(g_n')^1 \\ \vdots & \vdots & \ddots & \vdots \\ \lambda_1(g_1')^{k-1} & \lambda_2(g_2')^{k-1} & \cdots & \lambda_n(g_n')^{k-1} \end{bmatrix}. \tag{5}
$$

For all $(f_0', \ldots, f_{k-1}') \in \mathbb{F}_q^k$, we can rewrite a codeword $c_{RS} \in RS_{n,k}(g')$ as

$$
c_{RS} = (f_0', \ldots, f_{k-1}')G_{RS} = (F'(g_1), \ldots, F'(g_n)) \tag{6}
$$

where $F'(z) = \sum_{i=0}^{k-1} f_i' z^i$. Using similar notation, $c_{GRS} \in GRS_{n,k}(g', v)$ can be written as

$$
c_{GRS} = (f_0', \ldots, f_{k-1}')G_{GRS} = (\lambda_1 F'(g_1), \ldots, \lambda_n F'(g_n)). \tag{7}
$$

Recall that a codeword $c \in Gab_{n,k}(g)$ can be written in the form of (2):

$$
c = (f_0, \ldots, f_{k-1}) \begin{bmatrix} g_1 & \cdots & g_n \\ \vdots & \ddots & \vdots \\ g_1^{[k-1]} & \cdots & g_n^{[k-1]} \end{bmatrix} = (F(g_1), \ldots, F(g_n))
$$

where $F(z) = \sum_{i=0}^{k-1} f_i z^{[i]}$. Comparing (2) and (6), we notice that the difference between them is the involvement of linearized polynomial $F(z)$ in (2) and polynomial $F'(z)$ in (6).

We can now construct a code which has codewords of the form similar as (7), except that the polynomial $F'(z)$ is replaced with linearized polynomial $F(z)$.

Definition 10 (**λ**-Gabidulin Codes). Let $\boldsymbol{g} = (g_1, \ldots, g_n) \in \mathbb{F}_{q^m}^n$ be linearly independent over $\mathbb{F}_q$ and $\boldsymbol{\lambda} = (\lambda_1, \lambda_2, \ldots, \lambda_n) \in \mathbb{F}_{q^m}^n$. The $\boldsymbol{\lambda}$-*Gabidulin code* $\mathrm{Gab}_{n,k}(\boldsymbol{g_\lambda})$ over $\mathbb{F}_{q^m}$ of dimension k associated with vector $\boldsymbol{g}$ and $\boldsymbol{\lambda}$ is the code generated by matrix G_λ of the form

$$
G_\lambda = \begin{bmatrix}
\lambda_1 g_1 & \lambda_2 g_2 & \cdots & \lambda_n g_n \\
\lambda_1 g_1^{[1]} & \lambda_2 g_2^{[1]} & \cdots & \lambda_n g_n^{[1]} \\
\vdots & \vdots & \ddots & \vdots \\
\lambda_1 g_1^{[k-1]} & \lambda_2 g_2^{[k-1]} & \cdots & \lambda_n g_n^{[k-1]}
\end{bmatrix}. \tag{8}
$$

Now, we can rewrite a codeword $\boldsymbol{c} = (f_0, \ldots, f_{k-1}) G_\lambda \in \mathrm{Gab}_{n,k}(\boldsymbol{g_\lambda})$ as

$$
\boldsymbol{c} = (\lambda_1 F(g_1), \ldots, \lambda_n F(g_2)) \tag{9}
$$

where $F(z) = \sum_{i=0}^{k-1} f_i z^{[i]}$. Notice from (9) that such construction replaces the polynomial $F'(z)$ in (7) with linearized polynomial $F(z)$.

Table 3 summarizes the relations between $\boldsymbol{\lambda}$-Gabidulin codes, Gabidulin codes, Reed-Solomon Codes and generalized Reed-Solomon Codes:

Table 3. Relations between $\mathrm{Gab}_{n,k}(\boldsymbol{g})$, $\mathrm{Gab}_{n,k}(\boldsymbol{g_\lambda})$, $RS_{n,k}(\boldsymbol{g})$, $GRS_{n,k}(\boldsymbol{g_\lambda})$

	Codewords of the form	
	$(F(g_1), \ldots, F(g_n))$	$(\lambda_1 F(g_1), \ldots, \lambda_n F(g_n))$
Polynomial $F(z)$	$RS_{n,k}(\boldsymbol{g})$	$GRS_{n,k}(\boldsymbol{g_\lambda})$
	$\boldsymbol{g} \in \mathbb{F}_q^n$	$\boldsymbol{g}, \boldsymbol{\lambda} \in \mathbb{F}_q^n$
Linearized	$\mathrm{Gab}_{n,k}(\boldsymbol{g})$	$\mathrm{Gab}_{n,k}(\boldsymbol{g_\lambda})$
Polynomial $F(z)$	$\boldsymbol{g} \in \mathbb{F}_{q^m}^n$	$\boldsymbol{g}, \boldsymbol{\lambda} \in \mathbb{F}_{q^m}^n$

3.2 λ-Gabidulin Codes Construction

Our construction of **λ**-Gabidulin codes in fact does not have similar weakness as Gabidulin code (Lemma 4), i.e., it does not contain huge vector space invariant under the Frobenius automorphism as defined in Definition 7.

Consider a generator G_λ for $\mathrm{Gab}_{n,k}(\boldsymbol{g_\lambda})$ and the map Λ_i on G_λ, we have

$$
\Lambda_i(G_\lambda) = \begin{bmatrix} G_\lambda^{[0]} \\ \vdots \\ G_\lambda^{[i]} \end{bmatrix} = \begin{bmatrix}
\lambda_1 g_1 & \cdots & \lambda_n g_n \\
\vdots & \ddots & \vdots \\
\lambda_1 g_1^{[k-1]} & \cdots & \lambda_n g_n^{[k-1]} \\
\vdots & \ddots & \vdots \\
\lambda_1^{[i]} g_1^{[i]} & \cdots & \lambda_n^{[i]} g_n^{[i]} \\
\vdots & \ddots & \vdots \\
\lambda_1^{[i]} g_1^{[i+k-1]} & \cdots & \lambda_n^{[i]} g_n^{[i+k-1]}
\end{bmatrix}.
$$

It is possible for us to choose some $\lambda \in \mathbb{F}_{q^m}^n$ such that

$$\dim_{\mathbb{F}_{q^m}} \left(\mathrm{Gab}_{n,k}(g_\lambda)^{([j])} \cap \mathrm{Gab}_{n,k}(g_\lambda)^{([j-1])} \right) = 0$$

for $1 \le j \le n-1$ and $\dim(\ker(\Lambda_i(G_\lambda))) \ne 1$ for all $i \le n$. Therefore, the Overbeck's attack [37] is not useful against $\mathrm{Gab}_{n,k}(g_\lambda)$ with this property.

We now deduce a parity check matrix for G_λ.

Proposition 1. Let $H \in \mathbb{F}_{q^m}^{(n-k) \times n}$ in the form of

$$H = \begin{bmatrix} h_1 & h_2 & \cdots & h_n \\ h_1^{[1]} & h_2^{[1]} & \cdots & h_n^{[1]} \\ \vdots & \vdots & \ddots & \vdots \\ h_1^{[n-k-1]} & h_2^{[n-k-1]} & \cdots & h_n^{[n-k-1]} \end{bmatrix}$$

be a parity check matrix for G (as in (1)) which generates $\mathrm{Gab}_{n,k}(g)$. Then

$$H_\lambda = \begin{bmatrix} \lambda_1^{-1} h_1 & \lambda_2^{-1} h_2 & \cdots & \lambda_n^{-1} h_n \\ \lambda_1^{-1} h_1^{[1]} & \lambda_2^{-1} h_2^{[1]} & \cdots & \lambda_n^{-1} h_n^{[1]} \\ \vdots & \vdots & \ddots & \vdots \\ \lambda_1^{-1} h_1^{[n-k-1]} & \lambda_2^{-1} h_2^{[n-k-1]} & \cdots & \lambda_n^{-1} h_n^{[n-k-1]} \end{bmatrix}$$

is a parity check matrix for G_λ.

Proof. Given H a parity check matrix for G, we have $GH^T = 0$. Rewrite $G_\lambda = G\Delta$, $H_\lambda = H\Delta^{-1}$ where $\Delta = \begin{bmatrix} \lambda_1 & & 0 \\ & \ddots & \\ 0 & & \lambda_n \end{bmatrix}$. Then $G_\lambda H_\lambda^T = G\Delta(H\Delta^{-1})^T = G\Delta(\Delta^{-1})^T H^T = GH^T = 0.$ □

In fact, there exist $\lambda \in \mathbb{F}_{q^m}^n$ such that λ-Gabidulin code is not an MRD code.

Proposition 2. Let $\alpha \in \mathbb{F}_{q^m}$ and $\lambda = (\lambda_1, \ldots, \lambda_n)$ be a vector over $\mathbb{F}_{q^m}$ such that $(\lambda_1^{-1}\alpha d_1, \ldots, \lambda_n^{-1}\alpha d_n) \in \mathrm{Gab}_{n,k}(g)$ where $(d_1, \ldots, d_n) \in \mathbb{F}_q^n$, then λ-Gabidulin code is not an MRD code. In particular, $d_R^{\min}(\mathrm{Gab}_{n,k}(g_\lambda)) = 1$.

Proof. Suppose that $\alpha \in \mathbb{F}_{q^m}$ and $\lambda = (\lambda_1, \ldots, \lambda_n)$ is a vector over $\mathbb{F}_{q^m}$ such that $(\lambda_1^{-1}\alpha d_1, \ldots, \lambda_n^{-1}\alpha d_n) \in \mathrm{Gab}_{n,k}(g)$ where $(d_1, \ldots, d_n) \in \mathbb{F}_q^n$, then there exists $m \in \mathbb{F}_{q^m}^k$ such that

$$(\lambda_1^{-1}\alpha d_1, \ldots, \lambda_n^{-1}\alpha d_n) = mG = \left(\sum_{i=0}^{k-1} m_i g_1^{[i]}, \ldots, \sum_{i=0}^{k-1} m_i g_n^{[i]} \right).$$

Consider $c = mG_\lambda$, a code in $\mathrm{Gab}_{n,k}(g_\lambda)$, then

$$c = \sum_{i=0}^{k-1} m_i \left(\lambda_1 g_1^{[i]}, \ldots, \lambda_n g_n^{[i]} \right)$$

$$= \left(\lambda_1 \sum_{i=0}^{k-1} m_i g_1^{[i]}, \ldots, \lambda_n \sum_{i=0}^{k-1} m_i g_n^{[i]} \right)$$

$$= \left(\lambda_1 \lambda_1^{-1} \alpha d_1, \ldots, \lambda_n \lambda_n^{-1} \alpha d_n \right) = \alpha(d_1, \ldots, d_n).$$

This implies that $\mathrm{rk}_q(c) = 1 < n - k + 1$. Such λ-Gabidulin code is not an MRD code. □

Recall from (9) that a codeword $c = fG_\lambda \in \mathrm{Gab}_{n,k}(g_\lambda)$ can be written as $(\lambda_1 F(g_1), \ldots, \lambda_n F(g_n))$ where $F(z) = \sum_{i=0}^{k-1} f_i z^{[i]}$. Therefore, the decoding of λ-Gabidulin code is not the same as decoding Gabidulin codes (for examples, using Berlekamp-Massey algorithm or Euclidean algorithm). We need the following result to decode λ-Gabidulin codes:

Proposition 3. Let $\lambda = (\lambda_1, \lambda_2, \ldots, \lambda_n) \in \mathbb{F}_{q^m}^n$ with $\mathrm{rk}_q(\lambda) = u$ and $x = (x_1, \ldots, x_n) \in \mathbb{F}_{q^m}^n$ with $\mathrm{rk}_q(x) = w$. Then

$$\mathrm{rk}_q((\lambda_1 x_1, \ldots, \lambda_n x_n)) \le uw.$$

Proof. Let $X = \mathrm{span}\{x_1, \ldots, x_n\} = \mathrm{span}\{y_1, \ldots, y_w\}$ where $\{y_1, \ldots, y_w\}$ is linearly independent. Also, let $L = \mathrm{span}\{\lambda_1, \ldots, \lambda_n\} = \mathrm{span}\{\gamma_1, \ldots, \gamma_u\}$ where $\{\gamma_1, \ldots, \gamma_u\}$ is linearly independent. For $(\lambda_1 x_1, \ldots, \lambda_n x_n)$, each entry $\lambda_i x_i$ is a linear combinations of elements in $\{y_i \gamma_j : 1 \le i \le w, 1 \le j \le u\}$, which has dimension at most uw. □

Our new code $\mathrm{Gab}_{n,k}(g_\lambda)$ has a decoding algorithm as described in the following:

Proposition 4. Let $g \in \mathbb{F}_{q^m}^n$ with $\mathrm{rk}_q(g) = n$, $\lambda \in \mathbb{F}_{q^m}^n$ with $\mathrm{rk}_q(\lambda) = u$ and $r = \lfloor \frac{n-k}{2} \rfloor \ge u$, there exists decoding algorithm for $\mathrm{Gab}_{n,k}(g_\lambda)$ with error-correcting capabilities up to $\frac{r}{u}$ and decoding complexities of $O\left(n^{1.69} \log^2(n)\right)$ operations in $\mathbb{F}_{q^m}$.

Proof. There are two parts in the decoding algorithm for $\mathrm{Gab}_{n,k}(g_\lambda)$, the first part is to multiply each coordinates of the received vector $y = (y_1, \ldots, y_n)$ with λ_i^{-1}. Then we can apply any decoding algorithm for the Gabidulin codes $\mathrm{Gab}_{n,k}(g)$ on $(y_1 \lambda_1^{-1}, \ldots, y_n \lambda_n^{-1})$. To be more precise, let c be a codeword in $\mathrm{Gab}_{n,k}(g_\lambda)$ and $e \in \mathbb{F}_{q^m}^n$ with $\mathrm{rk}_q(e) \le \frac{r}{u}$. Then there exists $f \in \mathbb{F}_{q^m}^k$ such that $c = fG_\lambda$. Let $F(z) = \sum_{i=0}^{k-1} f_i z^{[i]}$, then the received vector, y can be written as

$$(y_1, \ldots, y_n) = fG_\lambda + e = (\lambda_1 F(g_1), \ldots, \lambda_n F(g_n)) + (e_1, \ldots, e_n).$$

Multiplying each entry of y with λ_i^{-1} for $i = 1, \ldots, n$:

$$\hat{y} := (\lambda_1^{-1} y_1, \ldots, \lambda_n^{-1} y_n) = (F(g_1), \ldots, F(g_n)) + (\lambda_1^{-1} e_1, \ldots, \lambda_n^{-1} e_n).$$

Notice that $\hat{c} := (F(g_1), \ldots, F(g_n))$ is a codeword in $\text{Gab}_{n,k}(g)$. If the vector $\hat{e} := (\lambda_1^{-1} e_1, \ldots, \lambda_n^{-1} e_n)$ has rank less than or equal to r, then we can decode $\hat{y}$ and recover $\hat{c}$. By Proposition 3, $\text{rk}_q(\hat{e}) \leq \text{rk}_q(e) \times \text{rk}_q(\lambda) \leq \frac{r}{u} \times u = r$. Therefore we can recover $\hat{c}$ and thus recover c by multiplying each entry with λ_i.

Since the first part consists of n multiplications in $\mathbb{F}_{q^m}$, the complexity of the first part is $O(n)$. For the second part, the complexity is $O\left(n^{1.69} \log^2(n)\right)$ operations in $\mathbb{F}_{q^m}$ by using sub-quadratic decoding of Gabidulin codes in [38]. Therefore, the total complexity to decode λ-Gabidulin codes is $O\left(n^{1.69} \log^2(n)\right)$ operations in $\mathbb{F}_{q^m}$. □

4   New Public-Key Encryption on λ-Gabidulin Codes

The λ-Gabidulin code does not contain huge vector space invariant under the Frobenius automorphism with proper choices of λ, hence we propose a new Gabidulin-like code encryption, namely LG encryption based on λ-Gabidulin codes with a scrambler matrix from elements in λ. We first prove a result that is related to the choice of our scrambler matrix, P:

Proposition 5. Let $\gamma \in \mathbb{F}_{q^m} \setminus \mathbb{F}_q$ and $\lambda = (\lambda_1, \lambda_2, \ldots, \lambda_n)$ such that for $i = 1, \ldots, n$, $\lambda_i \in \{\gamma, \gamma^{-1}\}$. Define $P := [P_1, \ldots, P_n]$ an $n \times n$ invertible matrix consisting entries of the form $c\gamma$ or $c\gamma^{-1}$ where $c \in \mathbb{F}_q$ and Δ be a diagonal matrix with entries $\Delta_{ii} = \lambda_i$ for $i = 1, \ldots, n$. Let $x = (x_1, \ldots, x_n) \in \mathbb{F}_{q^m}^n$ such that $\text{rk}_q(x) = t$. Then $\text{rk}_q\left(xP^{-1}\Delta^{-1}\right) \leq 3t$.

Proof. Consider the matrix $P^{-1}\Delta^{-1}$, each entries in $P^{-1}\Delta^{-1}$ is a linear combination of the elements from the set

$$\left\{\gamma \times \gamma, \gamma \times \gamma^{-1}, \gamma^{-1} \times \gamma^{-1}, \gamma^{-1} \times \gamma\right\} = \left\{\gamma^2, 1, \gamma^{-2}\right\}.$$

Let $X = \text{span}\{x_1, \ldots, x_n\}$ generated by $\{y_1, \ldots, y_t\}$, since $\text{rk}_q(x) = t$. Then each entries in $xP^{-1}\Delta^{-1}$ belongs to the span of elements in

$$\left\{y_i \gamma^2, y_i, y_i \gamma^{-2}\right\}_{i=1,\ldots,t}$$

which has dimension at most $3t$. □

We also need the following properties for our public-key encryption scheme:

Definition 11. An $[n, k]$-linear code $\mathcal{C} \subseteq \mathbb{F}_{q^m}^n$ is called an (s, t, l)-*intersecting code* if

$$\dim_{\mathbb{F}_{q^m}} \left(\bigcup_{i=0}^{t-1} \mathcal{C}^{([si])} \right) = \min\{n, tk - l\}.$$

Remark. Note that for $1 \leq t \leq n - k - 1$, $\text{Gab}_{n,k}(g)$ is a $(1, t, (t-1)(k-1))$-intersecting code, since

$$\dim_{\mathbb{F}_{q^m}} \left(\bigcup_{i=0}^{t-1} \text{Gab}_{n,k}(g)^{([i])} \right) = k + t - 1 = tk - (t-1)(k-1) < n.$$

4.1   Description of the Encryption Scheme

$\boxed{\textbf{Setup, } \mathcal{S}_{\text{PE}}}$ Generates global parameters $m \geq n > k$ and parameters r and a such that $k \nmid n - 1$, $r = \lfloor \frac{n-k}{2} \rfloor$, $a = \lfloor \frac{r}{3} \rfloor$ and $ak \geq n$. The plaintext space is $\mathbb{F}_{q^m}^k$. Outputs parameter $= (m, n, k, r, a)$.

$\boxed{\textbf{Key generation, } \mathcal{K}_{\text{PE}}}$ Generate random $S \in \text{GL}_k(\mathbb{F}_{q^m})$. Form $G_\lambda P$ by

i. generate randomly $\gamma \in \mathbb{F}_{q^m} \setminus \mathbb{F}_q$ such that $\gamma^2 \neq 1$, $(\gamma^{-1})^2 \neq 1$ and $\gamma \neq \gamma^{-1}$. Form $\boldsymbol{\lambda} = (\lambda_1, \ldots, \lambda_n)$ where each λ_i is picked randomly from $\{\gamma, \gamma^{-1}\}$;
ii. generate randomly $\boldsymbol{g} \in \mathbb{F}_{q^m}^n$ with $\text{rk}_q(\boldsymbol{g}) = n$. Then construct G_λ in the form of (8) as a generator of length n and dimension k;
iii. generate randomly P an $n \times n$ invertible matrix such that its inverse P^{-1} consisting entries from $\{c\gamma, c\gamma^{-1} : c \in \mathbb{F}_q\}$;

such that for all s relatively prime to m, the code generated by $G_\lambda P$ is $(s, a, 0)$-intersecting. Compute

$$G_{\text{pub}} := SG_\lambda P. \tag{10}$$

Outputs public key, $\kappa_{pub} = (G_{\text{pub}}, r)$ and secret key $\kappa_{pvt} = (S, \boldsymbol{g}, \boldsymbol{\lambda}, P)$.

$\boxed{\textbf{Encryption, } \mathcal{E}_{\text{PE}}(\kappa_{pub}, \boldsymbol{m})}$ Given the plaintext $\boldsymbol{m} \in \mathbb{F}_{q^m}^k$ to be encrypted, choose a random vector $\boldsymbol{e} \in \mathbb{F}_{q^m}^n$ such that $\text{rk}_q(\boldsymbol{e}) = a$. Compute and output the ciphertext $\boldsymbol{y} = \boldsymbol{m}G_{\text{pub}} + \boldsymbol{e}$.

$\boxed{\textbf{Decryption, } \mathcal{D}_{\text{PE}}(\kappa_{pvt}, \boldsymbol{y})}$ Given $\boldsymbol{y}$ the received ciphertext. Let Δ be a diagonal matrix with entries $\Delta_{ii} = \lambda_i$ for $i = 1, \ldots, n$. Compute P^{-1} and $\boldsymbol{y}P^{-1}\Delta^{-1}$. Perform decoding on $\boldsymbol{y}P^{-1}\Delta^{-1}$ with respect to $\text{Gab}_{n,k}(\boldsymbol{g})$ to recover $\boldsymbol{m}S$. We can then recover $\boldsymbol{m}$ by multiplying S^{-1}.

Correctness. The correctness of our encryption scheme relies on the decoding capability of the code $\text{Gab}_{n,k}(\boldsymbol{g})$. Let $\hat{\boldsymbol{e}} := \boldsymbol{e}P^{-1} = (\hat{e}_1, \ldots, \hat{e}_n)$ and G be of the form of (1), then

$$\boldsymbol{y}P^{-1}\Delta^{-1} = (\boldsymbol{m}G_{\text{pub}} + \boldsymbol{e}) P^{-1}\Delta^{-1} = \boldsymbol{m}SG_\lambda\Delta^{-1} + \boldsymbol{e}P^{-1}\Delta^{-1}$$
$$= \boldsymbol{m}SG + \left(\lambda_1^{-1}\hat{e}_1, \ldots, \lambda_n^{-1}\hat{e}_n\right).$$

By Proposition 5, we have $\text{rk}_q\left((\lambda_1^{-1}\hat{e}_1, \ldots, \lambda_n^{-1}\hat{e}_n)\right) \leq a \times 3 \leq r$ where r is the error correcting capability of $\text{Gab}_{n,k}(\boldsymbol{g})$, then we can decode $\boldsymbol{y}P^{-1}\Delta^{-1}$ correctly to recover $\boldsymbol{m}S$. Finally, compute $\boldsymbol{m} = \boldsymbol{m}SS^{-1}$ to recover $\boldsymbol{m}$.

4.2   A Toy Example of $G_\lambda P$ in LG Encryption

Let $(m, n, k, r, a) = (29, 25, 13, 6, 2)$. Let z be the primitive element in $\mathbb{F}_{q^m}$. Generate random

$$\gamma = z^{27} + z^{25} + z^{23} + z^{22} + z^{21} + z^{19}$$
$$+ z^{18} + z^{17} + z^{13} + z^{12} + z^8 + z^6 + z^4 + z^3$$
$$\gamma^{-1} = z^{28} + z^{27} + z^{26} + z^{25} + z^{18} + z^{16}$$
$$+ z^{15} + z^{13} + z^{12} + z^{11} + z^{10} + z^9 + z^7 + z^4 + z^2.$$

and $\boldsymbol{g} = (g_1, g_1^{[1]}, \ldots, g_1^{[24]})$ where $\mathrm{rk}_q(\boldsymbol{g}) = n$ and

$$g_1 = z^{27} + z^{25} + z^{24} + z^{20} + z^{19} + z^{15} + z^{12} + z^8 + z^7 + z^2 + z + 1.$$

Let P be the $n \times n$ circulant matrix induced by the vector

$$\boldsymbol{p} = [\gamma^{-1}\,0\,0\,\gamma\,\gamma\,\gamma^{-1}\,\gamma^{-1}\,0\,0\,\gamma^{-1}\,0\,0\,\gamma\,0\,0\,\gamma\,\gamma^{-1}\,0\,0\,0\,\gamma\,0\,\gamma\,0\,0].$$

We can verify that the code generated by matrix $G_\lambda P$ is $(s, a, 0)$-intersecting for all s relatively prime to m.

5   Security Against Structural Attacks

We now show that the new encryption scheme with public key (10) is able to resist the structural attacks on the cryptosystems based on Gabidulin codes.

5.1   Overbeck's Attack

Overbeck's attack exploits the properties of Gabidulin codes which contains huge vector space invariant under the Frobenius automorphism. We consider the Frobenius map Λ_i on the G_{pub}:

$$\Lambda_i(G_{\mathsf{pub}}) = \begin{bmatrix} (SG_\lambda P)^{[0]} \\ \vdots \\ (SG_\lambda P)^{[i]} \end{bmatrix} = \begin{bmatrix} S^{[0]} & & 0 \\ & \ddots & \\ 0 & & S^{[i]} \end{bmatrix} \begin{bmatrix} G_\lambda^{[0]} P^{[0]} \\ \vdots \\ G_\lambda^{[i]} P^{[i]} \end{bmatrix}$$

Let $G^{**} = \begin{bmatrix} G_\lambda^{[0]} P^{[0]} \\ \vdots \\ G_\lambda^{[i]} P^{[i]} \end{bmatrix}$. The code generated by $G_\lambda P$ is $(1, a, 0)$-intersecting.

If $(i + 1)k \geq n$, then $\dim(G^{**}) \geq n$, which implies that $\dim(G^{**}) = n$. If $(i + 1)k < n$, then $\dim(G^{**}) = (i + 1)k$. Since $k \nmid n - 1$, there does not exist i such that $(i + 1)k = n - 1$. Hence we know that $\dim(G^{**}) \neq n - 1$. Since $\dim(G^{**}) \neq n - 1$ for all i, we have $\dim(\ker(G^{**})) \neq 1$. Overbeck's attack will then fail.

5.2   Annulator Polynomial Attack

An adversary will consider an annulator polynomial for $\boldsymbol{e} \in \mathbb{F}_{q^m}^n$ and try to reconstruct $\boldsymbol{e}$ from $f(\boldsymbol{e})$. Since $\mathrm{rk}_q(\boldsymbol{e}) = a \leq \lfloor \frac{r}{3} \rfloor$, then there exists a linearized polynomial with $f(x)$ of degree q^a of the form:

$$f(\boldsymbol{x}) = \boldsymbol{x}^{[a]} + \sum_{i=0}^{a-1} f_i \boldsymbol{x}^{[i]}$$

for some $f_i \in \mathbb{F}_{q^m}$, such that

$$f(e) = f(y - mG) = 0$$

$$(y - mG)^{[a]} + \sum_{i=0}^{a-1} f_i(y - mG) = 0. \tag{11}$$

The linear system (11) consists of n equations with k variables of m, a variables f_i and $a \times k$ variables of $f_i m_j$ for $i = 0, \ldots, a-1$, $j = 1, \ldots, k$, giving us a total of $ak + k + a$ variables to be determined. Since $ak \geq n$ as in our choices of the cryptosystem, we have $ak + k + n > n$, thus the complexity of solving RSD problem for G_{pub} is exponential.

5.3   Frobenius Weak Attack

Let $\mathcal{C}$ be the code generated by G_{pub}, $y = mG_{\mathsf{pub}} + e$ with $\mathrm{rk}_q(e) = a$. Consider $s < m$ such that $\gcd(s, m) = 1$. First of all, an adversary will try to construct the matrix

$$G_{\mathsf{pub}_j} = \begin{bmatrix} G_{\mathsf{pub}}^{([s(0)])} \\ y^{([s(0)])} \\ \ldots \\ G_{\mathsf{pub}}^{([s(j-1)])} \\ y^{([s(j-1)])} \end{bmatrix}.$$

If $j < a$, then by Lemma 2, we have $\langle e, e^{([s])}, \ldots, e^{([s(j-1)])} \rangle \neq \mathrm{supp}(e)$. Therefore, the adversary cannot obtain a parity check matrix H for $\mathcal{U}$, where $\mathcal{U}$ is the span of all elements of rank one in $\mathcal{C}_{ext} := \sum_{i=0}^{a-1} (\mathcal{C} + \langle e \rangle)^{[si]}$ such that $eH^T = 0$.

Hence, an adversary will consider to construct G_{pub_j} with $j = a$, so that $\langle e^{([0])}, \ldots, e^{([s(a-1)])} \rangle = \mathrm{supp}(e) \subseteq \mathcal{U}$. The adversary will compute the space $\mathcal{U}$ generated by the elements of rank one in $\mathcal{C}_{ext}$ using Lemma 3. Since $\bigcup_{i=0}^{a-1} \mathcal{C}^{([si])} \subset \mathcal{C}_{ext}$ and $\mathcal{C}$ is a $(s, a, 0)$-intersecting code, then

$$\dim_{\mathbb{F}_{q^m}} (\mathcal{C}_{ext}) \geq \dim_{\mathbb{F}_{q^m}} \left(\bigcup_{i=0}^{a-1} \mathcal{C}^{([si])} \right) \geq ak \geq n.$$

Therefore we have $\dim_{\mathbb{F}_{q^m}} (\mathcal{C}_{ext}) = n$. Let $\bar{G}$ be the generator matrix for $\mathcal{C}_{ext}$ in reduced row echelon form. We then have

$$\bar{G} = \begin{bmatrix} I_n \\ 0 \end{bmatrix} =: \begin{bmatrix} \bar{G}_1 \\ \bar{G}_2 \\ \vdots \\ \bar{G}_{a(k+1)} \end{bmatrix} \in \mathbb{F}_{q^m}^{(a(k+1)) \times n}$$

where $\bar{G}_i$ denotes the ith row of $\bar{G}$. Then for each i, $\bar{G}_i^{([1])} - \bar{G}_i = 0$. Thus the adversary is not able to compute the space $\mathcal{U}$ using Lemma 3, and not able to determine its parity check matrix H. The Frobenius weak attack fails.

Remark. Since the structure of our λ-Gabidulin codes is similar as Gabidulin codes, therefore we do not consider other attacks on the cryptosystems based on LRPC codes, such as attacks from [6,27], as these attacks are not relevant to our cryptosystem.

6   Proposed Parameters

We performed simulation on Magma by generating 1000 random sets of λ, G_λ, P and $G_\lambda P$ with parameters $(q, m, n, k, a) = (2, 83, 79, 31, 8)$ and conditions in Key Generation $\mathcal{K}_{\mathsf{PE}}$. We found that all of the codes with generator matrix $G_\lambda P$ in the simulation are $(s, a, 0)$-intersecting, for all s relatively prime to m. This indicates that such $G_\lambda P$ with the required properties is easy to be generated.

Recall that Tables 1 and 2 give the complexity to solve RSD problem using combinatorial attacks and algebraic attacks. We replace the term r in the formulas with a in the calculations. In addition, we square root the exponential term in evaluating the post-quantum complexity in solving RSD problem. We suggest two sets of parameters for 2^{128} and 2^{256} bits post quantum security respectively in Table 4. We consider the public key matrix G_{pub} in systematic form, which gives us key size of $\frac{k(n-k)m}{8} \log_2(q)$ bytes. We denote the achieved post-quantum security as "PQ.Sec".

Table 4. Parameters for 2^{128} and 2^{256} bits post quantum security

Encryption	q	m	n	k	a	Key size	PQ.Sec
LG-I	2	83	79	31	8	15.43 KB	128
LG-II	2	85	83	29	9	16.64 KB	128
LG-III	2	97	89	23	10	18.41 KB	128
LG-IV	2	117	115	49	11	47.30 KB	256
LG-V	2	129	127	36	15	52.83 KB	256
LG-VI	2	133	131	34	16	54.83 KB	256

We consider and compare the Loi17 and DRANKULA encryption with our encryption scheme as these encryption schemes are structurally similar (McEliece type), except that the codes used are different. We also include the formula $m^3 2^{\frac{a-1}{2} \lfloor (k \min(m,n))/n \rfloor}$ to evaluate the complexity of attack on RSD in Table 5 (as this formula is used in [29] to evaluate the complexity in Quantum computer).

Our LG Encryption using λ-Gabidulin codes has smaller public key size (17.85 KB) than public key size of Loidreau's proposal (Loi17 of 21.50 KB in [29]), and smaller public key size than public key size of DRANKULA (27.65 KB in [1]) at similar post quantum security of 2^{140}.

Table 5. Comparison on parameters for LG encryption, Loi17 and DRANKULA

Encryption	q	m	n	k	a	Key size	PQ.Sec
LG-VII	2	85	83	35	8	17.85 KB	140
LG-VIII	2	91	89	28	10	19.43 KB	140
Loi17-I	2	128	90	24	11	21.50 KB	140
Loi17-II	2	128	120	80	4	52.83 KB	141
DRANKULA	2	96	96	48	6	27.65 KB	139

7   Conclusion

This paper has proposed a new rank metric code, λ-Gabidulin code and a new
McEliece type cryptosystem based on λ-Gabidulin code as an alternative to the
current rank metric code based cryptosystem. In particular, we consider a public
key matrix with generator matrix of λ-Gabidulin code multiplied with a scrambler
matrix associated to λ. In fact, we can convert our encryption scheme to IND-CCA2
encryption scheme via security conversions proposed in [23]. As such we do not
present security proofs but rather discuss more on the scheme's structural security in resisting the Overbeck's attack, annulator polynomial attack and Frobenius weak attack. Moreover, our proposal has smaller public key size (17.85 KB)
than Loidreau's proposal (21.50 KB) in [29], and smaller public key size than
DRANKULA (27.65 KB) in [1] at similar post quantum security of 2^{140}.

References

1. Abdouli, A., et al.: DRANKULA: a McEliece-like rank metric based cryptosystem
   implementation. In: The Proceedings of the 15th International Joint Conference on
   e-Business and Telecommunications (ICETE) 2018, vol. 2, pp. 64–75. SECRYPT
   (2018)
2. Aguilar, C., Blazy, O., Deneuville, J., Gaborit, P., Zémor, G.: Efficient encryption
   from random quasi-cyclic codes. IEEE Trans. Inf. Theory **64**(5), 3927–3943 (2018)
3. Aragon, N., Gaborit, P., Hauteville, A., Tillich, J.-P.: A new algorithm for solving
   the rank syndrome decoding problem. In: The Proceedings of IEEE International
   Symposium on Information Theory (ISIT) 2018, pp. 2421–2425 (2018)
4. Chabaud, F., Stern, J.: The cryptographic security of the syndrome decoding problem for rank distance codes. In: Kim, K., Matsumoto, T. (eds.) ASIACRYPT 1996.
   LNCS, vol. 1163, pp. 368–381. Springer, Heidelberg (1996). https://doi.org/10.
   1007/BFb0034862
5. Bernstein, D.J.: Grover vs. McEliece. In: Sendrier, N. (ed.) PQCrypto 2010. LNCS,
   vol. 6061, pp. 73–80. Springer, Heidelberg (2010). https://doi.org/10.1007/978-3-
   642-12929-2_6
6. Debris-Alazard, T., Tillich, J.-P.: Two attacks on rank metric code-based schemes:
   RankSign and an IBE scheme. In: Peyrin, T., Galbraith, S. (eds.) ASIACRYPT
   2018. LNCS, vol. 11272, pp. 62–92. Springer, Cham (2018). https://doi.org/10.
   1007/978-3-030-03326-2_3

7. Faugère, J.-C., Levy-dit-Vehel, F., Perret, L.: Cryptanalysis of MinRank. In: Wagner, D. (ed.) CRYPTO 2008. LNCS, vol. 5157, pp. 280–296. Springer, Heidelberg (2008). https://doi.org/10.1007/978-3-540-85174-5_16

8. Gabidulin, E.M.: Theory of codes with maximum rank distance. Probl. Peredachi Informatsii **21**(1), 3–16 (1985)

9. Gabidulin, E.M.: Attacks and counter-attacks on the GPT public key cryptosystem. Des. Codes Cryptogr. **48**(2), 171–177 (2008)

10. Gabidulin, E.M., Ourivski, A.V.: Modified GPT PKC with right scrambler. Electron. Notes Discret. Math. **6**, 168–177 (2001)

11. Gabidulin, E.M., Paramonov, A.V., Tretjakov, O.V.: Ideals over a noncommutative ring and their application in cryptology. In: Davies, D.W. (ed.) EUROCRYPT 1991. LNCS, vol. 547, pp. 482–489. Springer, Heidelberg (1991). https://doi.org/10.1007/3-540-46416-6_41

12. Gabidulin, E.M., Rashwan, H., Honary, B.: On improving security of GPT cryptosystems. In: The Proceedings of IEEE International Symposium on Information Theory (ISIT) 2009, pp. 1110–1114 (2009)

13. Gaborit, P., Hauteville, A., Phan, D.H., Tillich, J.-P.: Identity-based encryption from codes with rank metric. In: Katz, J., Shacham, H. (eds.) CRYPTO 2017. LNCS, vol. 10403, pp. 194–224. Springer, Cham (2017). https://doi.org/10.1007/978-3-319-63697-9_7

14. Gaborit, P., Ruatta, O., Schrek, J.: On the complexity of the rank syndrome decoding problem. IEEE Trans. Inf. Theory **62**(2), 1006–1019 (2016)

15. Gaborit, P., Ruatta, O., Schrek, J., Zémor, G.: New results for rank-based cryptography. In: Pointcheval, D., Vergnaud, D. (eds.) AFRICACRYPT 2014. LNCS, vol. 8469, pp. 1–12. Springer, Cham (2014). https://doi.org/10.1007/978-3-319-06734-6_1

16. Gaborit, P., Zémor, G.: On the hardness of the decoding and the minimum distance problems for rank codes. IEEE Trans. Inf. Theory **62**(12), 7245–7252 (2016)

17. Galvez, L., Kim, J., Kim, M.J., Kim, Y., Lee, N.: McNie: compact McEliece-Niederreiter Cryptosystem. https://csrc.nist.gov/CSRC/media/Projects/Post-Quantum-Cryptography/documents/round-1/submissions/McNie.zip

18. Gibson, J.K.: Severely denting the Gabidulin version of the McEliece public-key cryptosystem. Des. Codes Cryptogr. **6**(1), 37–45 (1995)

19. Goubin, L., Courtois, N.T.: Cryptanalysis of the TTM cryptosystem. In: Okamoto, T. (ed.) ASIACRYPT 2000. LNCS, vol. 1976, pp. 44–57. Springer, Heidelberg (2000). https://doi.org/10.1007/3-540-44448-3_4

20. Horlemann-Trautmann, A., Marshall, K., Rosenthal, J.: Extension of Overbeck's attack for Gabidulin based cryptosystems. Des. Codes Cryptogr. **86**(2), 319–340 (2018)

21. Horlemann-Trautmann, A., Marshall, K., Rosenthal, J.: Considerations for rank-based cryptosystems. In: IEEE International Symposium on Information Theory (ISIT) 2016, pp. 2544–2548 (2016)

22. Kim, J., Galvez, L., Kim, Y.-S., Lee, N.: A new LRPC-Kronecker product codes based public-key cryptography. In: The Proceedings of the 5th ACM on Asia Public-Key Cryptography Workshop (APKC) 2018, pp. 25–33 (2018)

23. Kobara, K., Imai, H.: Semantically secure McEliece public-key cryptosystems - conversions for McEliece PKC -. In: Kim, K. (ed.) PKC 2001. LNCS, vol. 1992, pp. 19–35. Springer, Heidelberg (2001). https://doi.org/10.1007/3-540-44586-2_2

24. Levy-dit-Vehel, F., Perret, L.: Algebraic decoding of rank metric codes. In: The Proceedings of Yet Another Conference on Cryptography (YACC) 2006, pp. 142–152 (2006)

25. Lau, T.S.C., Tan, C.H.: A new encryption scheme based on rank metric codes. In: Susilo, W., Yang, G. (eds.) ACISP 2018. LNCS, vol. 10946, pp. 750–758. Springer, Cham (2018). https://doi.org/10.1007/978-3-319-93638-3_43

26. Lau, T.S.C., Tan, C.H.: A new technique in rank metric code-based encryption. Cryptography **2**(4), 32 (2018)

27. Lau, T.S.C., Tan, C.H.: Key recovery attack on McNie based on low rank parity check codes and its reparation. In: Inomata, A., Yasuda, K. (eds.) IWSEC 2018. LNCS, vol. 11049, pp. 19–34. Springer, Cham (2018). https://doi.org/10.1007/978-3-319-97916-8_2

28. Loidreau, P.: Designing a rank metric based McEliece cryptosystem. In: Sendrier, N. (ed.) PQCrypto 2010. LNCS, vol. 6061, pp. 142–152. Springer, Heidelberg (2010). https://doi.org/10.1007/978-3-642-12929-2_11

29. Loidreau, P.: A new rank metric codes based encryption scheme. In: Lange, T., Takagi, T. (eds.) PQCrypto 2017. LNCS, vol. 10346, pp. 3–17. Springer, Cham (2017). https://doi.org/10.1007/978-3-319-59879-6_1

30. MacWilliams, F.J., Sloane, N.J.A.: The Theory of Error-Correcting Codes. Elsevier, North-Holland, Amsterdamm (1977)

31. McEliece, R.J.: A public-key cryptosystem based on algebraic coding theory. The Deep Space Network Progress Report 42-44, Jet Propulsion Laboratory, Pasedena, pp. 114–116 (1978)

32. Ore, O.: On a special class of polynomials. Trans. Am. Math. Soc. **35**(3), 559–584 (1933)

33. Otmani, A., Kalachi, H.T., Ndjeya, S.: Improved cryptanalysis of rank metric schemes based on Gabidulin codes. Des. Codes Cryptogr. **86**(9), 1983–1996 (2018)

34. Ourivski, A.V., Gabidulin, E.M.: Column scrambler for the GPT cryptosystem. Discret. Appl. Math. **128**, 207–221 (2003)

35. Ourivski, A.V., Johansson, T.: New technique for decoding codes in the rank metric and its cryptography applications. Probl. Inf. Transm. **38**(3), 237–246 (2002)

36. Overbeck, R.: Extending Gibson's attacks on the GPT cryptosystem. In: Ytrehus, Ø. (ed.) WCC 2005. LNCS, vol. 3969, pp. 178–188. Springer, Heidelberg (2006). https://doi.org/10.1007/11779360_15

37. Overbeck, R.: Structural attacks for public key cryptosystems based on Gabidulin codes. J. Cryptol. **21**(2), 280–301 (2008)

38. Puchinger, S., Wachter-Zeh, A.: Sub-quadratic decoding of Gabidulin codes. In: IEEE International Symposium on Information Theory (ISIT) 2016, pp. 2554–2558 (2016)

39. Rashwan, H., Gabidulin, E.M., Honary, B.: Security of the GPT cryptosystem and its applications to cryptography. Secur. Commun. Netw. **4**(8), 937–946 (2011)

40. Reed, I.S., Solomon, G.: Polynomial codes over certain finite fields. J. Soc. Ind. Appl. Math. (SIAM) **8**(2), 300–304 (1960)

Perfect, Hamming and Simplex Linear Error-Block Codes with Minimum π-distance 3

Soukaina Belabssir, Edoukou Berenger Ayebie, and El Mamoun Souidi[✉]

Faculty of Sciences, Laboratory of Mathematics, Computer Science,
Applications and Information Security, Mohammed V University in Rabat,
BP 1014 RP, 10 000 Rabat, Morocco
soukainabelabssir@gmail.com, berenger.ayebie@gmail.com, emsouidi@gmail.com

Abstract. Linear error-block codes were introduced in 2006 as a generalization of linear block codes. In this paper we construct two new families of perfect binary linear error-block codes of π-distance 3, namely, $[n_1]\ldots[n_t][2]^s$ (where $t \geq 1$), and $[n_1][n_t][3]^s$ (where $t = 1$ or $t = 2$), we also introduce the notions of Hamming and Simplex linear error-block codes, and we give a method to construct Hamming LEB codes from its parity check matrix. We also prove that Hamming LEB codes are perfect, and the constructed perfect codes are Hamming.

Keywords: Linear error-block codes · Simplex codes ·
Hamming code · Hamming bound and perfect codes

1 Introduction

Linear error-block codes (or LEB code for abbreviation) were initiated by Feng, Xu and Hickernell [1] in 2006 as a generalization of linear block codes. They held that these codes yield mixed-level orthogonal arrays and have applications in experimental design and high-dimensional numerical integration. Likewise, these codes may be used in cryptography. Dariti and Souidi [4] showed that using LEB codes in public key cryptography can allow obtaining small keys while keeping the same level of security as in the classical case. Also, in [3] they showed that the use of LEB codes in steganography can help to increase the embedding capacity of hidden information than the classical codes.

The topic of perfect codes is an interesting topic in the theory of error-correcting codes. Perfect codes correct every word within the space. The Golay codes, the Hamming codes and the repetition codes of odd length are shown in [8,9] to be the unique existing perfect code in the classical case.

In [1], some algebraic aspects and fields of applications of linear error-block codes are given, and a number of results about bounds, perfects and MDS LEB codes are treated in [7]. A generalization of some results on the packing and the covering radii to the error-block case is done, and some bounds on the packing

© Springer Nature Switzerland AG 2019
C. Carlet et al. (Eds.): C2SI 2019, LNCS 11445, pp. 288–306, 2019.
https://doi.org/10.1007/978-3-030-16458-4_17

and the covering radii of these codes are given in [5]. Optimal linear error-block codes are investigated in [6]. New families of perfect linear error-block codes are constructed in [2].

In this paper, we construct two new families of perfect binary linear error-block codes of minimum π-distance 3, of type $[n_1] \ldots [n_t][2]^s$ $(t \geq 1)$, and of type $[n_1][n_t][3]^s$ $(t = 1$ or $2)$. Furthermore, the notions of Hamming and Simplex linear error-block codes are introduced and a construction method is given of Hamming LEB codes from its parity check matrix. We also prove that Hamming LEB codes are perfect.

This paper is organized as follows. In this introduction we continue by introducing some definitions and known results about LEB codes. In Sect. 2 we construct perfect binary LEB codes of type $\pi = [n_1] \ldots [n_t][2]^s$ $(n_1 \geq \ldots \geq n_t \geq 2)$. We determine all possible parameters and sufficient conditions for these codes to be perfect. In Sect. 3 we construct perfect LEB codes of type $\pi = [n_1][n_t][3]^s$ for $t = 1, 2$. In Sect. 4 we extend the definition of Hamming codes to linear error-block case, then we give some properties of LEB Hamming codes and we show that these codes are perfect. Section 5 is devoted to Simplex LEB codes. The conclusion and perspective of this work are discussed in Sect. 6.

Following Feng *et al.* [1], a partition π of a positive integer n, is a sequence of nonnegative integers denoted by $\pi = [n_1][n_2] \ldots [n_s]$, where s is an integer ≥ 1,

$$n = n_1 + n_2 + \ldots + n_s \tag{1}$$

and $n_1 \geq n_2 \geq \ldots \geq n_s \geq 1$, If $n = \sum_{i=1}^{s} n_i = l_1 m_1 + l_2 m_2 + \ldots + l_r m_r$ where $m_1 > m_2 > \ldots > m_r \geq 1$, then π will be denoted by $\pi = [m_1]^{l_1}[m_2]^{l_2} \ldots [m_r]^{l_r}$.

Let $\pi = [n_1] \ldots [n_s]$ $(s \geq 1)$ be a partition of an integer n, $\mathbb{F}_q$ the finite field of q (q is a prime power) elements, $V_i = \mathbb{F}_q^{n_i} (1 \leq i \leq s)$, and the direct some

$$V = V_1 \oplus V_2 \oplus \ldots \oplus V_s \simeq \mathbb{F}_q^n. \tag{2}$$

Each vector in V can be written uniquely as $v = (v_1, v_2, \ldots, v_s)$, where v_i is in V_i (*for* $1 \leq i \leq s$). For $u = (u_1, u_2, \ldots, u_s)$ and $v = (v_1, v_2, \ldots, v_s)$ in V, the π-weight $w_\pi(u)$ and respectively the Hamming π-distance $d_\pi(u, v)$ are defined by:

$$w_\pi(u) = \#\{i/1 \leq i \leq s, \ 0 \neq u_i \in V_i\}$$

and

$$d_\pi(u, v) = w_\pi(u - v) = \#\{i/1 \leq i \leq s, \ u_i, \ v_i \in V_i \ and \ u_i \neq v_i\}. \tag{3}$$

A linear error-block code (LEB code for short) over $\mathbb{F}_q$ of type π where π is a partition of n is an $\mathbb{F}_q$-linear subspace C of V defined by (2). The integer n is called the length of C, $k = dim_{\mathbb{F}_q} C$ is its dimension and

$$d_\pi = \min\{d_\pi(c, c')/c, c' \in C, c \neq c'\} = \min\{w_\pi(c)/0 \neq c \in C\}, \tag{4}$$

is its minimal π-distance. Such an LEB code is denoted by $[n, k, d_\pi]_q$ code.

Linear error-block codes (LEB) are a generalization of classical codes. In fact, classical linear error-correcting code is a linear error-block code of type $\pi = [1]^n$.

Definition 1. *A generator matrix of an $[n, k]$ code, regardless of its type, is a $k \times n$ matrix whose rows form a basis of the code.*

Before going further, note that there are two possible ways to define the orthogonality of two vectors in V, as shown in Definition 2.

Definition 2. *Let $\pi = [n_1] \ldots [n_s]$ a partition of a positive integer n and C an LEB codes of type π and $u = (u_1, \ldots, u_s)$ and $v = (v_1, \ldots, v_s)$ in C.*
We say that u and v are (strongly)orthogonal if

$$u_i.v_i = 0 \ for \ all \ i = 1, \ldots, s \tag{5}$$

We say that u and v are orthogonal if

$$\sum_{i=1}^{s} u_i.v_i = 0 \tag{6}$$

where $u_i.v_i$ denotes the classical scalar product in $V_i = \mathbb{F}_q^{n_i}$.

Equation (5) is a strong condition of orthogonality. We use (6) to specify the orthogonality in V thereafter.

Let C be an $[n, k]$ code of type $\pi = [n_1][n_2] \ldots [n_s]$, whose generator matrix is G and whose parity-check matrix is H, the dual of C is an $[n, n - k]$ code of type $\pi = [n_1][n_2] \ldots [n_s]$, whose generator matrix is H and whose parity-check matrix is G, and is denoted by $C^{\perp} = \{u.H/u \in V\}$.

Definition 3. *A parity-check matrix of an $[n, k]$ code, regardless of its type, is an $(n - k) \times n$ matrix whose rows are linearly independent and are orthogonal with the code.*

An LEB code is completely defined by a generator matrix or a parity check matrix. As in the classical case, the minimum π-distance of a linear error-block code is straightforwardly determined using a parity-check matrix as follows:

Theorem 1 ([1]). *Let $H = [H_1, H_2, \ldots, H_s]$ be a parity-check matrix for an $[n, k, d_\pi]$ code C over $\mathbb{F}_q$ of type $\pi = [n_1][n_2] \ldots [n_s]$. Then the minimum π-distance is d_π if and only if the union of columns of any $d_\pi - 1$ blocks of H are $\mathbb{F}_q$-linearly independent and there exist d_π blocks columns of H which are linearly dependent.*

Example 1. Let C be a $[7, 2, 2]$ binary code of type $\pi = [3][2][1]^2$ defined as follows:

$$C = \{000|00|0|0, 101|10|1|0, 011|11|0|0, 110|01|1|0\}.$$

Then C is generated by the matrix

$$G = \begin{pmatrix} 1 & 0 & 1 & 1 & 0 & 1 & 0 \\ 0 & 1 & 1 & 1 & 1 & 0 & 0 \end{pmatrix}.$$

Hereafter we recall the Hamming and Singleton bounds for LEB codes which are introduced by Feng *et al.* [1].

Theorem 2. *Let C be an $[n, k, d_\pi]_q$ LEB code over $\mathbb{F}_q$ of type $\pi = [n_1]$ $[n_2] \ldots [n_s]$. Then*

$$
\begin{aligned}
q^{n-k} &\geq b_\pi(l) \ if \ d_\pi = 2l + 1, \\
q^{n-k} &\geq b'_\pi(l) \ if \ d_\pi = 2l \geq 2.
\end{aligned}
\tag{7}
$$

where

$$
b_\pi(l) = 1 + \sum_{\alpha=1}^{l} \sum_{1 \leq i_1 \leq i_2 \leq \ldots \leq i_\alpha \leq s} (q^{n_{i_1}} - 1)(q^{n_{i_2}} - 1) \ldots (q^{n_{i_\alpha}} - 1),
$$

$$
b'_\pi(l) = q^{n_1} \left(1 + \sum_{\alpha=1}^{l-1} \sum_{2 \leq i_1 \leq i_2 \leq \ldots \leq i_\alpha \leq s} (q^{n_{i_1}} - 1)(q^{n_{i_2}} - 1) \ldots (q^{n_{i_\alpha}}) - 1 \right)
$$

and

$$
n - k \geq n_1 + n_2 + \ldots + n_{d_\pi - 1}.
\tag{8}
$$

The inequality (7) is called the Hamming bound and the inequality (8) is called the Singleton bound.

Definition 4. *An $[n, k, d_\pi]_q$ LEB code of type π is said to be perfect if it attains the Hamming bound (7) and is said to be MDS if it attains the Singleton bound (8).*

According to Eq. (7), an $[n, k, d_\pi]_2$ binary LEB code of type $\pi = [n_1] \ldots [n_s]$ is said to be perfect if it satisfies the Hamming bound that is in this case:

$$
2^{n-k} = b_\pi(1) = 1 + \sum_{i=1}^{s} (2^{n_i} - 1)
\tag{9}
$$

Proposition 1. [1] *Assume that there exists an $[n, k, 3]_2$ code C of type $\pi = [n_1][n_2] \ldots [n_s]$. Then there exists an $[n + N, k + N, 3]_2$ code C' of type $\pi = [n_1][n_2] \ldots [n_s][1]^N$, where $N = 2^{n-k} - 1 - \sum_{i=1}^{s}(2^{n_i} - 1)$ is positive. Moreover, C' is perfect.*

Example 2. Let C be a $[5, 1, 3]_2$ code of type $\pi = [2][2][1]$ with parity-check matrix

$$
H = \begin{pmatrix} 1 \, 0 & 1 \, 0 & 0 \\ 0 \, 1 & 0 \, 1 & 0 \\ 0 \, 0 & 1 \, 0 & 1 \\ 0 \, 0 & 0 \, 1 & 0 \end{pmatrix}.
$$

The code C is not perfect. In fact, using the inequality (7) we have $N = 2^{n-k} - \sum_{i=1}^{3}(2^{n_i} - 1) - 1 = 2 > 0$. So according to Proposition 1, the $[5 + 2, 1 + 2, 3]_2$ code of type $\tilde{\pi} = [2][2][1][1]^2$ and parity-check matrix

$$H = \begin{pmatrix} 1 & 0 & 1 & 0 & 0 & 0 & 0 & 1 & 0 & 1 \\ 0 & 1 & 0 & 1 & 0 & 0 & 1 & 0 & 0 & 1 \\ 0 & 0 & 1 & 0 & 1 & 0 & 1 & 1 & 1 & 0 \\ 0 & 0 & 0 & 1 & 0 & 1 & 1 & 1 & 1 & 1 \end{pmatrix}$$

is perfect.

More constructions of perfect and MDS codes of type $\pi = [n_1][n_2]\ldots[n_t][1]^N$ and π-distance 3 are given in [7], and generalized to a larger class of partitions.

2   Perfect LEB Codes of Type $\pi = [n_1]\ldots[n_t][2]^s, t \geq 1$ with $d_\pi = 3$

To provide new technical constructions of LEB codes, we are interested in the formal characterization of binary codes with π-distance 3. In [2], Dariti *et al.* have characterized perfect LEB codes.

Algorithm 1. Generation of parity check matrix H of LEB code $\pi = [n_1]\cdots[n_t]^s$

Notations

getCanonicalBasis(r): give a set of columns which make the canonical basis of $\mathbb{F}_2^r$.

NextComb($2^r, p$): draw the next set of P vectors in $\mathbb{F}_2^r$

Rank(G): give the Rank of G.

Size(A): give the number of blocks of A

Require: $A = [n_1, \cdots, n_m]$, $r \geq n_1 + \cdots + n_m + 2$, $s \neq 0$

Ensure: H

  $H \leftarrow []$

  $Basis \leftarrow getCanonicalBasis(r)$

  $k \leftarrow 0$

  for all $i \in [0, m]$ **do**

    $H[i] \leftarrow basis[k : k + A[i]]$

    $k \leftarrow A[i]$

  end for

  while $Size(H) < s + m$ and $NextComb(2^r, 2) \neq Null$ **do**

    $x \leftarrow NextComb(2^r, 2)$

    for all $y \in H$ **do**

      if $Rank([y, x]) == Size([y, x])$ **then**

        $i \leftarrow i + 1$

        $H[i] \leftarrow x$

      end if

    end for

  end while

Algorithm 1 takes as input an $[n, k, 3]$ LEB code of type $\pi = [n_1]\ldots[n_t]^s$ where $n = n_1 + \ldots + n_t$ and outputs its corresponding parity check matrix.

We start by generating the canonical basis of the vector subspace $\mathbb{F}_2^r$ that will form the first column vectors of our parity check matrix. We generate afterwards a linear combination of all the blocks of vectors of size $n_1, n_2, \ldots, n_t$ until obtaining exactly s blocks of size n_t and a block of size n_i $(1 \leq i \leq t)$ which are all pairwise linearly independent.

2.1   Construction of Perfect LEB Codes of Type $\pi = [n_1][2]^s (n_1 \geq 2)$ with $d_\pi = 3$

According to Definition 4, a code C of type π is said to be perfect if and only if it reaches the Hamming bound described in Theorem 2. Theorem 3 below, gives conditions of existence of perfect binary LEB codes of type $\pi = [n_1][2]^s$:

Theorem 3. *Let n be a positive integer and $\pi = [n_1][2]^s$ where $n_1 \geq 2$ a partition of n. An $[n, k, 3]_2$ LEB code of type π exists and is perfect if and only if n_1 and $r = n - k$ are even and $s = \frac{2^r - 2^{n_1}}{3}$ is an integer.*

Proof. 1. According to Definition 2, C is perfect if and only if

$$2^r = 1 + (2^{n_1} - 1) + s(2^2 - 1)$$

that is

$$s = \frac{2^r - 2^{n_1}}{3}$$

and since s is an integer, then $2^{n_1} \equiv 2^r [3]$. Hence $s = \frac{2^r - 2^{n_1}}{3}$ is an integer and r and n_1 have the same parity.

2. Existence of C: let C be an $[n, k, 3]_2$ LEB code of type $\pi_1 = [n_1]$ and let $H = [H_1]$ be a parity-check matrix of C. If $2^{n-k} - 1 > 2^{n_1} - 1$ then there exist $u_i, u_j \in \mathbb{F}_q^r$ $(1 \leq i \neq j \leq 2s, \ u_i \neq u_j)$ such that $\{u_i\} \cup H_1$ are linearly independent and $\{u_i\} \cup \{u_j\}$ are linearly independent. Then we obtain $H' = [H_1][H_2] \cdots [H_{s+1}]$ where $H_k = [u_i][u_j]$ (concatenation of two vectors u_i and u_j) for all $1 \leq k \leq s + 1$. The blocks H_k are pairwise linearly independent.

Let C' be a linear error-block code with H' as a parity-check matrix. Then C' is an $[N, K, 3]_2$ code (where $N = n + 2s$ and $K = N - r = n + 2s - (n - k) = k + 2s$) of type $\pi = [n_1][2]^s$. Hence C' is perfect. $\qquad\qquad\square$

Example 3. 1. The binary LEB code C of length $n = 10$, dimension $k = 6$, and type $\pi = [2]^5$; and whose parity-check matrix is:

$$H = \begin{pmatrix} 1 & 0 & 0 & 0 & 0 & 1 & 1 & 0 & 1 & 1 \\ 0 & 1 & 0 & 0 & 1 & 0 & 1 & 1 & 0 & 1 \\ 0 & 0 & 0 & 1 & 0 & 1 & 0 & 1 & 0 & 1 \\ 0 & 0 & 1 & 0 & 1 & 0 & 1 & 0 & 1 & 0 \end{pmatrix}$$

is perfect and MDS. In fact, The columns of any two block are linearly independent and $2^{10-6} = 1 + 5(2^2 - 1)$ and $n - k = 10 - 6 = 2 + 2 = n_1 + n_2$.

Proposition 2. *There exists no perfect LEB code C of type $\pi = [n_1][2]^s$ with $d_\pi = 3$ and n_1 odd.*

Proof. Assume the existence of an $[n, k, 3]_2$ perfect binary LEB code C over $\mathbb{F}_2^n$ with type $\pi = [n_1][2]^s$ $(n_1 \geq 2)$ and $d_\pi = 3$ where n_1 is odd. The code C is of length $n = n_1 + 2s$ and dimension $k \leq n - n_1 = 2(s - 1)$.
Let X be the set of $x \in \mathbb{F}_2^n$ which are of the form:

$$x = (\overbrace{0000000 \dots 000010000000 \dots 000000000000}^{\text{one 1 is randomly dispersed in the first block}}, 01, 00, \dots, 00)$$

Then $\omega_\pi(x) = 2$ and $\mid X \mid = n_1 - 2$ is the number of elements of X.
Since C is perfect, for all $x \in X$ there exists a unique $c \in C$ such that $d_\pi(c, x) = 1$. We have

$$1 = d_\pi(C) - \omega_\pi(x) \leq \omega_\pi(c) - \omega_\pi(x) \leq \omega_\pi(c - x) = 1 \qquad (10)$$

i.e. $\omega_\pi(c) - \omega_\pi(x) = 1$. Then $\omega_\pi(c) = \omega_\pi(x) + 1 = 3$, this means that c must have the digit "1" in the block where x has.
Let $Y \subset C$ the set of y which are of the form:

$$y = (\overbrace{0000000 \dots 000010000000 \dots 0000100 \dots 00000}^{\text{two 1 are randomly dispersed in the first block}}, 01, 11, \dots, 00, \dots, 00)$$

We have $\omega_\pi(y) = 3$ and for all $x \in X$ there exists a unique y *in* Y such that the number of one in $x - y$ equals to 2, then

$$\mid \{(x, y) \in X \times Y \setminus \text{ the number of one in } x - y \text{ equals to } 2\} \mid = n_1.$$

However, for each $x \in X$ there exist exactly two vectors in X such that the number of one in $x - y$ equals to 2 indeed $2 \mid Y \mid = n_1$. Absurd since n_1 is odd. In conclusion, there exist no perfect LEB code C of type $\pi = [n_1][2]^s$ over $\mathbb{F}_2^n$ with $d_\pi = 3$ and n_1 odd. $\square$

2.2 Binary Perfect LEB Codes of Type $\pi = [n_1][n_2][2]^s$ with $d_\pi = 3$

Let C be an $[n, k, 3]_2$ code of type $\pi = [n_1][n_2][2]^s (n_1 \geq n_2 \geq 2)$. Set $r = n - k$. If C is perfect, then its parameters satisfy

$$2^r = 1 + (2^{n_1} - 1) + (2^{n_2} - 1) + s(2^2 - 1) = 2^{n_1} + 2^{n_2} - 1 + 3s, \qquad (11)$$

which means that $s = \frac{2^r - 2^{n_1} - 2^{n_2} + 1}{3}$. Since s must be an integer, then $2^r - 2^{n_1} - 2^{n_2} + 1 \equiv 0$ [3]. Therefore, the existence of s and C is related to r, n_1 and n_2 by the following facts:

- If r is even:
    If n_1 and n_2 are both even then $2^r - 2^{n_1} - 2^{n_2} + 1 \equiv 0$ [3] and s is an integer. Therefore, C is perfect.

If n_1 and n_2 are both odd then $2^r - 2^{n_1} - 2^{n_2} + 1 \equiv -2$ [3] and s is not an integer. Therefore, C is not perfect.

If n_1 or n_2 is odd then $2^r - 2^{n_1} - 2^{n_2} + 1 \equiv -1$ [3] and so s is not an integer. Therefore, C is not perfect.

- If r is odd:

If n_1 and n_2 are both odd then $2^r - 2^{n_1} - 2^{n_2} + 1 \equiv -1$ [3] and s is not an integer. Therefore, C is not perfect.

If n_1 and n_2 are both even then $2^r - 2^{n_1} - 2^{n_2} + 1 \equiv 1$ [3] and s is not an integer. Therefore, C is not perfect.

If n_1 is even or n_2 is odd then $2^r - 2^{n_1} - 2^{n_2} + 1 \equiv 0$ [3]. Therefore, C is perfect.

Thus we have proved the following result:

Theorem 4. *Let C be an $[n, k, 3]_2$ code of type $\pi = [n_1][n_2][2]^s (n_1 \geq n_2 \geq 2)$. Set $r = n - k$, the code C is perfect if and only if $s = \frac{2^r - 2^{n_1} - 2^{n_2}}{3}$ and [(r, n_1 and n_2 are even) or (r is odd and n_1 or n_2 is even)].*

We use Algorithm 1 to generate codes of type $\pi = [n_1][n_2][2]^s (n_1 \geq n_2 \geq 2)$, with $d_\pi = 3$ and for which parameters verify the conditions of Theorem 4. We have the following result:

Theorem 5. *Let n be a positive integer and $\pi = [n_1][n_2][2]^s (n_1 \geq n_2 \geq 2)$ be a partition of n where s is a positive integer such that $s = \frac{2^r - 2^{n_1} - 2^{n_2}}{3}$. Set $r = n - k$. An $[n, k, 3]_2$ binary code of type π exists only if r, n_1 and n_2 are both even.*

Proof. Assume r, n_1 are even, and n_2 is odd. We proceed as in Proposition 2 except that in this case, the first block of both $x \in X$ and $y \in Y$ are null and the remaining blocks are similar to those of $x \in X$ and $y \in Y$ respectively.   □

Example 4. The binary LEB code C of length $n = 36$, dimension $k = 30$, and type $\pi = [4][2][2]^{15}$ whose parity-check matrix is $H = (H_1|H_2|H_3)$ is perfect and MDS where

$$H_1 = \begin{pmatrix} 1\,0\,0\,0 & 0\,0 & 1\,0 & 0\,1 & 1\,1 \\ 0\,1\,0\,0 & 0\,0 & 0\,1 & 1\,1 & 1\,0 \\ 0\,0\,1\,0 & 0\,0 & 0\,0 & 0\,0 & 0\,0 \\ 0\,0\,0\,1 & 0\,0 & 0\,0 & 0\,0 & 0\,0 \\ 0\,0\,0\,0 & 1\,0 & 1\,0 & 1\,0 & 1\,0 \\ 0\,0\,0\,0 & 0\,1 & 0\,1 & 0\,1 & 0\,1 \end{pmatrix}, \quad H_2 = \begin{pmatrix} 0\,0 & 1\,0 & 0\,1 & 1\,1 & 0\,0 & 1\,0 \\ 0\,0 & 0\,1 & 1\,1 & 1\,0 & 0\,0 & 0\,1 \\ 1\,0 & 1\,0 & 1\,0 & 1\,0 & 0\,1 & 0\,1 \\ 0\,1 & 0\,1 & 0\,1 & 0\,1 & 1\,1 & 1\,1 \\ 1\,0 & 1\,0 & 1\,0 & 1\,0 & 1\,0 & 1\,0 \\ 0\,1 & 0\,1 & 0\,1 & 0\,1 & 0\,1 & 0\,1 \end{pmatrix},$$

and

$$H_3 = \begin{pmatrix} 0\,1 & 1\,1 & 0\,0 & 1\,0 & 0\,1 & 1\,1 \\ 1\,1 & 1\,0 & 0\,0 & 0\,1 & 1\,1 & 1\,0 \\ 0\,1 & 0\,1 & 1\,1 & 1\,1 & 1\,1 & 1\,1 \\ 1\,1 & 1\,1 & 1\,0 & 1\,0 & 1\,0 & 1\,0 \\ 1\,0 & 1\,0 & 1\,0 & 1\,0 & 1\,0 & 1\,0 \\ 0\,1 & 0\,1 & 0\,1 & 0\,1 & 0\,1 & 0\,1 \end{pmatrix}.$$

2.3 Binary Perfect LEB Codes of Type $\pi = [n_1]\ldots[n_t][2]^s\,(t \geq 2)$ and $d_\pi = 3$

In this subsection we aim to generalize results about the existence of LEB codes of type $\pi = [n_1]\ldots[n_t][2]^s$ where $n_1 \geq \ldots \geq n_t \geq 2$. We have the following result:

Theorem 6. *Let C be an $[n,k,3]_2$ LEB code of type $\pi = [n_1]\ldots[n_t]$ where $n_1 \geq n_2 \geq \ldots \geq n_t \geq 2$. Let $r = n - k$. If r and n_i are even for $i = 1,\ldots,t$ then $s = \frac{2^r - \sum_{i=1}^{t} 2^{n_i} + t - 1}{3}$ is a positive integer and there exists an $[n + 2s, k + 2s, 3]_2$ LEB code C' of type $\pi = [n_1]\ldots[n_t][2]^s$. Moreover, C' is perfect.*

Proof. 1. Since r and n_i are even for $i = 1,\ldots,t$ so $2^r \equiv 1$ [3], we have $2^r - \sum_{i=1}^{t} 2^{n_i} + t - 1 \equiv 0$ [3]. Hence, s is an integer, and s is positive since $2^r - 1 \geq \sum_{i=1}^{t}(2^{n_i} - 1)$.

2. Existence of C': Let $H = [H_1]\ldots[H_t]$ be a parity-check matrix of C. If $2^r - 1 > \sum_{i=1}^{t}(2^{n_i} - 1)$ then there exist $u_i, u_j \in \mathbb{F}_q^r$ $(1 \leq i \neq j \leq 2s,\ u_i \neq u_j)$ such that $\{u_i\} \cup H_l$ where $(1 \leq l \leq t)$ are linearly independent and $\{u_i\} \cup \{u_j\}$ are linearly independent. Then we obtain $H' = [H_1]\ldots[H_t][H_{t+1}]\ldots[H_{t+s}]$ where $H_k = [u_i][u_j]$ (concatenation of two vectors u_i and u_j) for all $t + 1 \leq k \leq t + s$. The blocks H_k are pairwise linearly independent.

3. Let C' be the linear error-block code with H' as a parity-check matrix. Then C' is an $[N, K, 3]_2$ (where $N = n + 2s$ and $K = k + 2s$) code of type $\pi' = [n_1]\ldots[n_t][2]^s$. Hence C' is perfect. $\qquad\square$

Using Theorem 6 we can construct binary LEB codes of type $\pi = [n_1]\ldots[n_t][2]^s$ where simply by taking an LEB code of type $\pi = [n_1]\ldots[n_t]$ where $n_1 \geq \ldots \geq n_t$ and then adding to $2s$ matrices H of length $(r \times 1)$ such that the union of the columns of each matrix and the columns of each block of H are linearly independent. Besides, this family of codes is infinite.

We now construct codes of type $\pi = [n_1][n_t][3]^s\,(n_1 \geq n_t \geq 3)$ and minimum π-distance 3.

3 Perfect LEB Codes of Type $\pi = [n_1][n_t][3]^s$, $t = 1$ or $t = 2$ with $d_\pi = 3$

We now construct codes of type $\pi = [n_1][n_t][3]^s\,(n_1 \geq n_t \geq 3)$ and minimum π-distance 3.

3.1 Perfect LEB Codes of Type $\pi = [n_1][3]^s\,(n_1 \geq 3)$ and $d_\pi = 3$

The following lemma gives necessary conditions for an LEB code C of type $\pi = [n_1][3]^s$ to be perfect, in other words, conditions when parameters of C achieve the Hamming bound.

Lemma 1. *If C is an $[n, k, 3]_2$ perfect code of type $\pi = [n_1][3]^s$, and $r = n - k$ then $r \geq n_1 + 3$, $s = \frac{2^r - 2^{n_1}}{7}$ and $n_1 - r \equiv 0$ [3].*

Proof. Let C be an $[n, k, 3]_2$ perfect code of type $\pi = [n_1][3]^s$. Set $r = n - k$ then $r \geq n - 1 + 3$ and

$$2^r = 1 + (2^{n_1} - 1) + s(2^3 - 1) = 2^{n_1} + 7s. \tag{12}$$

Then, $s = \frac{2^r - 2^{n_1}}{7}$. Since s is an integer, then $2^r \equiv 2^{n_1}[7]$. Therefore, the existence of s and that of C is related to r and n_1 by the following relationship:

- Since, $2^3 \equiv 1[7]$. Therefore, if $n_1 - r \equiv 0$ [3], then $2^r \equiv 2^{n_1}$ [7] and so s is an integer. Then, C is perfect.
- If $n_1 - r \not\equiv 0 \equiv 3$, then $2^r \not\equiv 2^{n_1}[7]$, and so s is not an integer. Then, C is not perfect.   □

Using Lemma 1, we can define parameters of $[n, k, 3]_2$ perfect codes of type $\pi = [n_1][3]^s$. We list here some parameters of $[n, k, 3]_2$ perfect codes of type $\pi = [n_1][3]^s$ $(n_1 \geq 3)$.

Example 5

1. $k = 21$, $n = 27$, $r = 6$, $\pi = [3]^9$.
2. $k = 45$, $n = 52$, $r = 7$, $\pi = [4][3]^{16}$.

Using Algorithm 1, we have been unable to generate the parity check matrices of the $[n, k, 3]_2$ codes of type $\pi = [n_1][3]^s$ where:

1. Length $n = 101$, dimension $k = 93$ and type $\pi = [5][3]^{32}$;
2. Length $n = 198$, dimension $k = 185$ and type $\pi = [6][3]^{64}$;
3. Length $n = 3463$, dimension $k = 3450$ and type $\pi = [7][3]^{1152}$.

Based on computation results, we conjecture the following:

Conjecture 1. 1. There exists no $[n, k, d_\pi]_2$ perfect code of type $\pi = [n_1][3]^s$ if $n_1 > 4$ (where $s = \frac{2^r - 2^{n_1}}{7}$, $r = n - k$ and $n_1 - r \equiv 0[3]$).
2. There exists a $[27, 21, 3]_2$ perfect LEB code of type $\pi = [3]^9$ and parity-check matrix $H = (H_1|H_2)$ where

$$H_1 = \begin{pmatrix} 1\,0\,0 & 0\,0\,0 & 1\,0\,0 & 0\,0\,1 & 1\,0\,1 \\ 0\,1\,0 & 0\,0\,0 & 0\,1\,0 & 1\,0\,1 & 1\,1\,1 \\ 0\,0\,1 & 0\,0\,0 & 0\,0\,1 & 0\,1\,0 & 0\,1\,1 \\ 0\,0\,0 & 1\,0\,0 & 1\,0\,0 & 1\,0\,0 & 1\,0\,0 \\ 0\,0\,0 & 0\,1\,0 & 0\,1\,0 & 0\,1\,0 & 0\,1\,0 \\ 0\,0\,0 & 0\,0\,1 & 0\,0\,1 & 0\,0\,1 & 0\,0\,1 \end{pmatrix}, H_2 = \begin{pmatrix} 0\,1\,0 & 1\,1\,0 & 0\,1\,1 & 1\,1\,1 \\ 0\,1\,1 & 0\,0\,1 & 1\,1\,0 & 1\,0\,0 \\ 1\,0\,1 & 1\,0\,0 & 1\,1\,1 & 1\,1\,0 \\ 1\,0\,0 & 1\,0\,0 & 1\,0\,0 & 1\,0\,0 \\ 0\,1\,0 & 0\,1\,0 & 0\,1\,0 & 0\,1\,0 \\ 0\,0\,1 & 0\,0\,1 & 0\,0\,1 & 0\,0\,1 \end{pmatrix}.$$

3. There exists a $[52, 45, 3]_2$ perfect LEB code of type $\pi = [4][3]^{16}$ and parity-check matrix $(H_1|H_2|H_3|H_4)$ where,

$$H_1 = \begin{pmatrix} 1\,0\,0\,0 & 0\,0\,0 & 1\,0\,0 & 0\,1\,0 & 1\,1\,0 \\ 0\,1\,0\,0 & 0\,0\,0 & 0\,1\,0 & 1\,1\,0 & 1\,0\,0 \\ 0\,0\,1\,0 & 0\,0\,0 & 0\,0\,1 & 0\,0\,0 & 0\,0\,1 \\ 0\,0\,0\,1 & 0\,0\,0 & 0\,0\,0 & 0\,0\,1 & 0\,0\,1 \\ 0\,0\,0\,0 & 1\,0\,0 & 1\,0\,0 & 1\,0\,0 & 1\,0\,0 \\ 0\,0\,0\,0 & 0\,1\,0 & 0\,1\,0 & 0\,1\,0 & 0\,1\,0 \\ 0\,0\,0\,0 & 0\,0\,1 & 0\,0\,1 & 0\,0\,1 & 0\,0\,1 \end{pmatrix}, H_2 = \begin{pmatrix} 0\,0\,0 & 1\,0\,0 & 0\,1\,0 & 1\,1\,0 \\ 0\,0\,1 & 0\,1\,1 & 1\,1\,1 & 1\,0\,1 \\ 1\,0\,1 & 1\,0\,0 & 1\,0\,1 & 1\,0\,0 \\ 0\,1\,0 & 0\,1\,0 & 0\,1\,1 & 0\,1\,1 \\ 1\,0\,0 & 1\,0\,0 & 1\,0\,0 & 1\,0\,0 \\ 0\,1\,0 & 0\,1\,0 & 0\,1\,0 & 0\,1\,0 \\ 0\,0\,1 & 0\,0\,1 & 0\,0\,1 & 0\,0\,1 \end{pmatrix},$$

$$H_3 = \begin{pmatrix} 0\,0\,1 & 1\,0\,1 & 0\,1\,1 & 1\,1\,1 \\ 0\,0\,1 & 0\,1\,1 & 1\,1\,1 & 1\,0\,1 \\ 0\,1\,0 & 0\,1\,1 & 0\,1\,0 & 0\,1\,1 \\ 1\,1\,1 & 1\,1\,1 & 1\,1\,0 & 1\,1\,0 \\ 1\,0\,0 & 1\,0\,0 & 1\,0\,0 & 1\,0\,0 \\ 0\,1\,0 & 0\,1\,0 & 0\,1\,0 & 0\,1\,0 \\ 0\,0\,1 & 0\,0\,1 & 0\,0\,1 & 0\,0\,1 \end{pmatrix}, H_4 = \begin{pmatrix} 0\,0\,1 & 1\,0\,1 & 0\,1\,1 & 1\,1\,1 \\ 0\,0\,0 & 0\,1\,0 & 1\,1\,0 & 1\,0\,0 \\ 1\,1\,1 & 1\,1\,0 & 1\,1\,1 & 1\,1\,0 \\ 1\,0\,1 & 1\,0\,1 & 1\,0\,0 & 1\,0\,0 \\ 1\,0\,0 & 1\,0\,0 & 1\,0\,0 & 1\,0\,0 \\ 0\,1\,0 & 0\,1\,0 & 0\,1\,0 & 0\,1\,0 \\ 0\,0\,1 & 0\,0\,1 & 0\,0\,1 & 0\,0\,1 \end{pmatrix}.$$

3.2   Perfect LEB Codes of Type $\pi = [n_1][n_2][3]^s$ with $d_\pi = 3$

The following lemma gives necessary conditions for an LEB code C of type $\pi = [n_1][n_2][3]^s$ to be perfect, in other words, conditions when the parameters of C achieve the Hamming bound.

Lemma 2. *If C is an $[n, k, 3]_2$ perfect code of type $\pi = [n_1][3]^s$, and $r = n - k$ then $r \geq n_1 + 3$, $s = \frac{2^r - 2^{n_1} - 2^{n_2} + 1}{7}$ and the parameters r and n_1 and n_2 verify one of the following conditions:*

- $r \equiv 1\ [3]$ *and* $[(n_1 \equiv 0\ [3]$ *and* $n_2 \equiv 1\ [3])$ *or* $(n_1 \equiv 1\ [3]$ *and* $n_2 \equiv 0\ [3])]$
- $r \equiv 0\ [3]$ *and* $n_1 \equiv 0\ [3]$ *and* $n_2 \equiv 0\ [3]$
- $r \equiv 2\ [3]$ *and* $[(n_1 \equiv 0\ [3]$ *and* $n_2 \equiv 2\ [3])$ *or* $(n_1 \equiv 2\ [3]$ *and* $n_2 \equiv 0\ [3])]$

Proof. Let C be an $[n, k, 3]_2$ perfect code of type $\pi = [n_1][n_2][3]^s$. Set $r = n - k$ then $r \geq n - 1 + 3$ and

$$2^r = 1 + (2^{n_1} - 1) + (2^{n_2} - 1) + s(2^3 - 1) = 2^{n_1} + 2^{n_2} - 1 + 7s. \qquad (13)$$

Hence $s = \frac{2^r - 2^{n_1} - 2^{n_2} + 1}{7}$. Since s is an integer, then $2^r + 1 \equiv 2^{n_1} + 2^{n_2}\ [7]$.
Therefore, the existence of s and C is related to r, n_1 and n_2 by the following:

- If $r \equiv 0\ [3]$ then $2^{n_1} + 2^{n_2} \equiv 2\ [3]$ which means that $n_1 \equiv 0\ [3]$ and $n_2 \equiv 0\ [3]$.
- If $r \equiv 1\ [3]$ then $2^{n_1} + 2^{n_2} \equiv 3[3]$ which means that $n_1 \equiv 0\ [3]$ and $n_2 \equiv 1\ [3]$ or $n_1 \equiv 1\ [3]$ and $n_2 \equiv 0\ [3]$.
- If $r \equiv 2\ [3]$ then $2^{n_1} + 2^{n_2} \equiv 5\ [3]$ which means that $n_1 \equiv 0\ [3]$ and $n_2 \equiv 2\ [3]$ or $n_1 \equiv 2\ [3]$ and $n_2 \equiv 0\ [3]$.

In the three cases cited above, s is an integer, with these parameters of C satisfying the Hamming bound. $\qquad \square$

Example 6. The $[n, k, 3]_2$ code where $k = 13797$, $n = 13812$ and $\pi = [9][6][3]^{4599}$ is perfect. In fact, $r \equiv 0\ [3]$ *and* $n_1 \equiv 0\ [3]$ *and* $n_2 \equiv 0\ [3]$.

The question that arises now is the existence of code of type $\pi = [n_1][n_2][3]^s$ ($n_1 \geq n_2 \geq 3$) and with $d_\pi = 3$. Using Algorithm 1, and by computation we have been unable to generate the parity check matrices of some codes like:

- The $[n, k, 3]_2$ code where $k = 13797$, $n = 13812$ and $\pi = [9][6][3]^{4599}$.
- The $[1146, 1134, 3]_2$ code of type $\pi = [6][6][3]^{567}$.

Based on computation results we conjecture the following:

Conjecture 2. There exist no $[n, k, d_\pi]_2$ perfect code of type $\pi = [n_1][n_2][3]^s$ (where s and r and n_1 verify the conditions of Lemma 2).

4 Hamming LEB Codes

In this section, we introduce Hamming codes for the error-block case, and we give some related results.

Lemma 3. *Let m and r be two integers where $m \geq 1$, and $r \geq 2m$. Set $s = \frac{q^r-1}{q^m-1}$. Then, s is an integer if and only if $r = \lambda m$ where $\lambda \geq 1$.*

Proof. – If s is an integer, then $q^r - 1 \equiv 0 \ [q^m - 1]$, write $r = \lambda m + \alpha$ where $0 \leq \alpha < m$. Since, $q^m \equiv 1 \ [q^m - 1]$. Then, $(q^m)^\lambda \equiv 1 \ [q^m - 1]$, and $q^{\lambda m + \alpha} \equiv q^\alpha \ [q^m - 1]$. Therefore $q^r - 1 \equiv q^\alpha - 1 \ [q^m - 1]$. Thus $\alpha = 0$ which means $r = \lambda m$.
- Conversely, if $r = \lambda m$, then $q^r \equiv 1 \ [q^m - 1]$. i. e. $q^r - 1 \equiv 0 \ [q^m - 1]$. So s is an integer.

$\square$

Definition 5. *Let $\mathbb{F}_q$ be the finite field of q elements, and m and λ be integers where $m \geq 1$ and $\lambda \geq 1$. A Hamming LEB code denoted by π-Ham(r,q) over $\mathbb{F}_q$ of length $n = m\frac{q^r-1}{q^m-1}$ where $r = \lambda m \geq 2$ is the code whose parity check matrix H is an $r \times n$ matrix for which the union of columns of any two blocks is linearly independent.*

Remark 1. In a parity check-matrix of a $\pi - Ham(r, q)$ code there exists

- no null column.
- no column which is a multiple of an other one.

Remark 2. Let m be an integer ≥ 1.
   A classical Hamming code $Ham(r, q)$ over $\mathbb{F}_q$ of length $n = \frac{q^r-1}{q-1}$ is a $\pi - Ham(r, q)$ code of type $\pi = [1]^s$ where $s = n$ and $m = 1$.

Theorem 7. *Let m be an integer ≥ 1. The π-Ham(r,q) Hamming codes are perfect LEB codes over $\mathbb{F}_q$ with parameters $[n = m\frac{q^r-1}{q^m-1}, k = m\frac{q^r-1}{q^m-1} - r, d_\pi = 3]$.*

Proof. Let C be a $\pi - Hamm(r, q)$ code where $s = \frac{q^r-1}{q^m-1} \in \mathbb{N}$, and let H be a parity check matrix of C. Therefore $n = m\frac{q^r-1}{q^m-1}$ is the length of C.
   Since r is the number of rows of H, then by Definition 3, $r = n - k = \lambda m$. Thus

$$dim_{\mathbb{F}_q}(C) = k = n - r = m\frac{q^r - 1}{q^m - 1} - r.$$

By Definition 5 and Proposition 1, the union of columns of any two blocks in H is linearly independent, then $d_\pi = 3$. Since $r = n - k = \lambda m$, and $n = sm$.
   We have
$$\begin{aligned}
1 + \textstyle\sum_{i=1}^{s}(q^{n_i} - 1) &= 1 + \textstyle\sum_{i=1}^{s}(q^m - 1) \\
&= 1 + s(q^m - 1) \\
&= 1 + \tfrac{q^r-1}{q^m-1}(q^m - 1) \\
&= 1 + q^r - 1 \\
&= q^r.
\end{aligned}$$

Therefore, the Hamming bound (7) is satisfied and then C is perfect. $\square$

Example 7. The binary LEB code C of length $n = 10$, dimension $k = 6$, and type $\pi = [2]^5$ and whose parity check matrix is

$$H = \begin{pmatrix} 1 & 0 & 0 & 0 & 0 & 1 & 1 & 0 & 1 & 1 \\ 0 & 1 & 0 & 0 & 1 & 0 & 1 & 1 & 0 & 1 \\ 0 & 0 & 0 & 1 & 0 & 1 & 0 & 1 & 0 & 1 \\ 0 & 0 & 1 & 0 & 1 & 0 & 1 & 0 & 1 & 0 \end{pmatrix}$$

is a $[2]^5 - Ham(4,2)$ code, and it is perfect because $2^4 = 1 + 5(2^2 - 1)$.

Definition 6. *Let* $v = (v_1, \ldots, v_l)$ *be a vector in* $\mathbb{F}_q^l$. *A block extension of* v *is an* $l \times l$ *matrix* M *defined as follows*

- *The columns of* M *are linearly independent.*
- *The sum of all columns of* M *is equal to* v^T *(transpose of* v*).*

Example 8. A possible block extension of the vector $v = (0,1,1) \in \mathbb{F}_2^3$ is the matrix

$$\begin{pmatrix} 0 & 1 & 1 \\ 1 & 0 & 0 \\ 0 & 1 & 0 \end{pmatrix}$$

Remark 3. If M and M' are two blocks extensions of two different vectors v and v' in $\mathbb{F}_q^m$, then, the columns of the matrix

$$\begin{pmatrix} M & M' \\ I_m & I_m \end{pmatrix}$$

are linearly independent where I_m is the matrix identity of size m.

Theorem 8. *Let* m *be an integer* ≥ 1 *and* $\pi = [m]^s$ *where* $s = \frac{q^r - 1}{q^m - 1} \geq 2$.

Consider a $\pi - Ham(r, q)$ *code* C *over the field* $\mathbb{F}_q$ *of type* π, $r = \lambda m$ *and* $\lambda \geq 2$. *The matrix* H_λ *defined recursively as follows:*

$$H_2 = \begin{pmatrix} I_m & E_1 & \cdots\cdots & E_{q^m-1} & 0_m \\ 0_{m-1} & I_m & \cdots\cdots & I_m & I_m \end{pmatrix} \tag{14}$$

and for $\lambda \geq 3$

$$H_\lambda = \begin{pmatrix} I_m & A_1 & \cdots\cdots & A_{q^m-1} & A_0 \\ 0_{m(\lambda-1)} & H_{\lambda-1} & \cdots\cdots & H_{\lambda-1} & H_{\lambda-1} \end{pmatrix} \tag{15}$$

where

- $E_1, \ldots, E_{q^m-1}$ *are the extensions of non-zero vectors in* $\mathbb{F}_q^m$.
- *For all* $1 \leq i \leq q^m - 1$, $A_i = \underbrace{(E_i, \ldots, E_i)}_{s_\lambda-1 \ time}$ *where* $s_{\lambda-1} = \frac{q^{(\lambda-1)m}-1}{q^m-1}$.
- $A_0 = \underbrace{(0_m, \ldots, 0_m)}_{s_\lambda-1 \ time}$ *where* 0_m *is the* $m \times m$ *null matrix.*

is a parity check matrix of C.

Proof. Considering

$$H_2 = \begin{pmatrix} I_m & E_1 & \cdots\cdots & E_{q^m-1} & 0_m \\ 0_m & I_m & \cdots\cdots & I_m & I_m \end{pmatrix}$$

and for $\lambda \geq 3$, define inductively H_λ by:

$$H_\lambda = \begin{pmatrix} I_m & A_1 & \cdots\cdots & A_{q^m-1} & A_0 \\ 0_{m(\lambda-1)} & H_{\lambda-1} & \cdots\cdots & H_{\lambda-1} & H_{\lambda-1} \end{pmatrix}$$

As a matrix generating a LEB code S_λ.

We state that S_λ is the dual code of a $\pi - Ham(r,q)$ code of type $\pi = [m]^{s_\lambda}$ where $s_\lambda = \frac{q^{m\lambda}-1}{q^m-1}$ and $\lambda \geq 2$.

To prove that H_λ generates the $(\pi - Ham(r,q))^\perp$, we will prove that H_λ has r rows, $s_\lambda = \frac{q^{\lambda m}-1}{q^m-1}$ blocks, and the union of columns of any two blocks are linearly independent.

– Clearly, H_λ has m more rows than $H_{\lambda-1}$, and H_2 has $2m$ rows, then H_λ has $r = m\lambda$ rows.
– It is clear that

$$s_2 = 1 + q^m = \frac{q^{2m}-1}{q^m-1}.$$

We assume that $s_{\lambda-1} = \frac{q^{(\lambda-1)m}-1}{q^m-1}$. By definition of H_λ we deduce

$$s_\lambda = q^m . s_{\lambda-1} + 1$$
$$= q^m . \frac{q^{(\lambda-1)m}-1}{q^m-1} + 1$$
$$= \frac{q^{\lambda m} - q^m + q^m - 1}{q^m-1}$$
$$= \frac{q^{\lambda m}-1}{q^m-1}$$

– The columns of any block of H_2 are pairwise distinct, and the columns of any two blocks of H_2 are linearly independent. Clearly by construction, the columns of any block of H_λ are pairwise distinct, and the columns of any two blocks of H_λ are linearly independent if the columns of any block of $H_{\lambda-1}$ are pairwise distinct, and the columns of any two blocks of $H_{\lambda-1}$ are linearly independent. Then by induction, H_λ generates the dual S_λ of a $\pi - Ham(r,q)$ code of type $\pi = [m]^{s_\lambda}$ where $s_\lambda = \frac{q^{\lambda m}-1}{q^m-1}$ and $\lambda \geq 2$. Thus, H_λ is a parity check matrix of a $\pi - Ham(r,q)$ code of type $\pi = [m]^{s_\lambda}$ where $s_\lambda = \frac{q^{\lambda m}-1}{q^m-1}$.

□

Example 9. The dual of the $\pi - Ham(6, 2)$ code of type $\pi = [3]^9$ is generated by the matrix G defined by

$$G = (G_1 | G_2)$$

where,

$$G_1 = \begin{pmatrix} 1\,0\,0 & 1\,0\,0 & 0\,0\,1 & 1\,0\,1 \\ 0\,1\,0 & 0\,1\,0 & 1\,0\,1 & 1\,1\,1 \\ 0\,0\,1 & 0\,0\,1 & 0\,1\,0 & 0\,1\,1 \\ 0\,0\,0 & 1\,0\,0 & 1\,0\,0 & 1\,0\,0 \\ 0\,0\,0 & 0\,1\,0 & 0\,1\,0 & 0\,1\,0 \\ 0\,0\,0 & 0\,0\,1 & 0\,0\,1 & 0\,0\,1 \end{pmatrix}, G_2 = \begin{pmatrix} 0\,1\,0 & 1\,1\,0 & 0\,1\cdot1 & 1\,1\,1 & 0\,0\,0 \\ 0\,1\,1 & 0\,0\,1 & 1\,1\,0 & 1\,0\,0 & 0\,0\,0 \\ 1\,0\,1 & 1\,0\,0 & 1\,1\,1 & 1\,1\,0 & 0\,0\,0 \\ 1\,0\,0 & 1\,0\,0 & 1\,0\,0 & 1\,0\,0 & 1\,0\,0 \\ 0\,1\,0 & 0\,1\,0 & 0\,1\,0 & 0\,1\,0 & 0\,1\,0 \\ 0\,0\,1 & 0\,0\,1 & 0\,0\,1 & 0\,0\,1 & 0\,0\,1 \end{pmatrix}$$

Theorem 9. *Perfect codes of type $\pi = [m]^s (m \geq 1, s \geq 2)$ and with minimum π-distance $d_\pi = 3$ over $\mathbb{F}_q$ are π-Hamming codes.*

Proof. Let m be an integer ≥ 1. Let C be an $[n, k, 3]_q$ perfect code of type $\pi = [m]^s$ where $s \geq 1$ over $\mathbb{F}_q$. Set $r = n - k$. Then by Definition 4, C satisfies the equation

$$q^r = 1 + s(q^m - 1). \tag{16}$$

Hence,

$$s = \frac{q^r - 1}{q^m - 1}.$$

Since s is an integer, then by Lemme 3, $r = m\lambda$ where λ is an integer ≥ 1. Thus

$$n = ms = m\frac{q^r - 1}{q^m - 1},$$

and

$$k = n - r = m\frac{q^r - 1}{q^m - 1} - r.$$

Since $d_\pi = 3$ then the union of columns of any two blocks of H the parity check matrix of C is linearly independent.

Finally, C is a $\pi - Ham(r, q)$ code of type $\pi = [m]^s$ where $s = \frac{q^r - 1}{q^m - 1}$ and $r = n - k$. □

Corollary 1. *Perfect codes of types $[n_1] \dots [n_t][2]^s$ (where $t \geq 1$), and $[n_1]$ $[n_t][3]^s$ (where $t = 1$ or $t = 2$) and with minimum π-distance $d_\pi = 3$ over $\mathbb{F}_q$ are π-Hamming codes if $[n_i] = [n_j]$ where $1 \leq i \leq t$ and $j = 1, 2$.*

Proof. This is yielded by direct analogy to the proof of Theorem 9. □

5 Simplex LEB Codes

Definition 7. *A code is said to be simplex if all its non-zero codewords have the same weight.*

Example 10. The binary LEB code C of length $n = 10$, dimension $k = 6$, and type $\pi = [2]^5$; and whose generator matrix:

$$G = \begin{pmatrix} 1 & 0 & 0 & 0 & 0 & 1 & 1 & 0 & 1 & 1 \\ 0 & 1 & 0 & 0 & 1 & 0 & 1 & 1 & 0 & 1 \\ 0 & 0 & 0 & 1 & 0 & 1 & 0 & 1 & 0 & 1 \\ 0 & 0 & 1 & 0 & 1 & 0 & 1 & 0 & 1 & 0 \end{pmatrix}$$

is simplex. In fact, all non-zero codewords of C have only one nul block. Then, the π-weight of any codeword of C is 4.

Theorem 10. *Let π-ham(r,q) be a Hamming code of type $\pi = [m]^s$. The dual code $(\pi\text{-}Ham(r,q))^\perp$ is a Simplex code and the common π-weight of its non-zero codewords is $w_\lambda = 2^{r-m} = 2^{(\lambda-1)m}$ where $\lambda = \frac{r}{m}$ is an integer ≥ 1.*

Proof. Let C' be a dual code of a $\pi - Ham(r,q)$ code C of type $\pi = [m]^s$. Then by Theorem 8, C' is generated by H_λ, where

$$H_2 = \begin{pmatrix} I_m & E_1 & \cdots & E_{q^m-1} & 0_m \\ 0_m & I_m & \cdots & I_m & I_m \end{pmatrix}$$

For $\lambda \geq 3$

$$H_\lambda = \begin{pmatrix} I_m & A_1 & \cdots & A_{q^m-1} & A_0 \\ 0_{m(\lambda-1)} & H_{\lambda-1} & \cdots & H_{\lambda-1} & H_{\lambda-1} \end{pmatrix}$$

- Set s_λ and w_λ where $r = n - k = m\lambda$ and $t \geq 2$ respectively the number of blocks of H_λ and the weight of a codeword c in S_λ.
- The non-zero codewords generated by H_2, have the weight $w_2 = s_2 - 1 = \frac{q^{2m}-1}{q^m-1} - 1 = q^m - 1 + 1 = q^{(2-1)m}$. In fact, they have one of the following forms: $c = (e \mid a_1 \mid a_2 \mid \ldots \mid a_{q^m} \mid 0)$ or $c = (0 \mid e_1 \mid e_2 \mid \ldots \mid e_{q^m})$ where for all $i = 1, \ldots, q^m$, a_i is a codeword generated by $H_{\lambda-1}$, e_i is in $\mathbb{F}_q^m$ and e is an element of the canonic basis of $\mathbb{F}_q^m$.
- We assume that the non-zero codewords generated by $H_{\lambda-1}$ have the weight $w_{\lambda-1} = q^{r-2m} = q^{r(\lambda-2)}$.
- Then, the non-zero codewords of the sub-code generated by the last $(r - m)$ rows of H_λ have the form $c = (0 \mid a_1 \mid a_2 \mid \ldots \mid a_{q^m})$ where for all $i = 1, \ldots, q^m$, a_i is a codeword generated by $H_{\lambda-1}$. Therefore,

$$w_\lambda = q^m.w_{\lambda-1} = q^m(q^{r-2m}) = q^{r-m}.$$

- The remaining non-zero codewords generated by $H_{\lambda-1}$ have the form $c = (e \mid a_1 \mid a_2 \mid \ldots \mid a_{q^m-1}, \underbrace{0 \ldots 0}_{s_{\lambda-1} time})$ where for all $i = 1, \ldots, q^m$, $a_i \neq 0$ and e is an element of the canonic basis of $\mathbb{F}_q^m$. These codewords have the weight

$$w_\lambda = s_\lambda - s_{\lambda-1}$$
$$= \frac{q^{m\lambda} - 1}{q^m - 1} - \frac{q^{m(\lambda-1)} - 1}{q^m - 1}$$
$$= \frac{q^{m\lambda} - q^{m(\lambda-1)}}{q^m - 1}$$
$$= q^{m(\lambda-1)} \left(\frac{q^m - 1}{q^m - 1} \right)$$
$$= q^{m(\lambda-1)} = q^{r-m}$$

- Thus by induction, all the non-zero codewords of C' have the weight

$$w_\lambda = q^{r-m} = q^{(\lambda-1)m}.$$

$\square$

Example 11. The non-zero codewords of the simplex code C' of type $\pi = [4]^{17}$ generated by the matrix

$$G = (G_1 \mid G_2)$$

where,

$$G_1 = \begin{pmatrix} 1\,0\,0\,0 & 0\,0\,0\,0 & 1\,0\,0\,0 & 0\,1\,0\,0 & 1\,1\,0\,0 & 0\,0\,0\,1 & 1\,0\,0\,1 & 0\,1\,0\,1 & 1\,1\,0\,1 & 0\,0\,1\,1 & 1\,0\,1\,1 \\ 0\,1\,0\,0 & 0\,0\,0\,0 & 0\,1\,0\,0 & 1\,1\,0\,0 & 1\,0\,0\,0 & 0\,0\,1\,1 & 0\,1\,1\,1 & 1\,1\,1\,1 & 1\,0\,1\,1 & 0\,0\,1\,0 & 0\,1\,1\,0 \\ 0\,0\,1\,0 & 0\,0\,0\,0 & 0\,0\,1\,0 & 0\,0\,0\,1 & 0\,0\,1\,1 & 1\,0\,1\,0 & 1\,0\,0\,0 & 1\,0\,1\,1 & 1\,0\,0\,1 & 0\,1\,0\,1 & 0\,1\,1\,1 \\ 0\,0\,0\,1 & 0\,0\,0\,0 & 0\,0\,0\,1 & 0\,0\,1\,1 & 0\,0\,1\,0 & 0\,1\,0\,1 & 0\,1\,0\,0 & 0\,1\,1\,0 & 0\,1\,1\,1 & 1\,1\,1\,1 & 1\,1\,1\,0 \\ 0\,0\,0\,0 & 1\,0\,0\,0 & 1\,0\,0\,0 & 1\,0\,0\,0 & 1\,0\,0\,0 & 1\,0\,0\,0 & 1\,0\,0\,0 & 1\,0\,0\,0 & 1\,0\,0\,0 & 1\,0\,0\,0 & 1\,0\,0\,0 \\ 0\,0\,0\,0 & 0\,1\,0\,0 & 0\,1\,0\,0 & 0\,1\,0\,0 & 0\,1\,0\,0 & 0\,1\,0\,0 & 0\,1\,0\,0 & 0\,1\,0\,0 & 0\,1\,0\,0 & 0\,1\,0\,0 & 0\,1\,0\,0 \\ 0\,0\,0\,0 & 0\,0\,1\,0 & 0\,0\,1\,0 & 0\,0\,1\,0 & 0\,0\,1\,0 & 0\,0\,1\,0 & 0\,0\,1\,0 & 0\,0\,1\,0 & 0\,0\,1\,0 & 0\,0\,1\,0 & 0\,0\,1\,0 \\ 0\,0\,0\,0 & 0\,0\,0\,1 & 0\,0\,0\,1 & 0\,0\,0\,1 & 0\,0\,0\,1 & 0\,0\,0\,1 & 0\,0\,0\,1 & 0\,0\,0\,1 & 0\,0\,0\,1 & 0\,0\,0\,1 & 0\,0\,0\,1 \end{pmatrix}$$

and

$$G_2 = \begin{pmatrix} 0\,1\,1\,1 & 1\,1\,1\,1 & 0\,0\,1\,0 & 1\,0\,1\,0 & 0\,1\,1\,0 & 1\,1\,1\,0 \\ 1\,1\,1\,0 & 1\,0\,1\,0 & 0\,0\,0\,1 & 0\,1\,0\,1 & 1\,1\,0\,1 & 1\,0\,0\,1 \\ 0\,1\,0\,0 & 0\,1\,1\,0 & 1\,1\,1\,1 & 1\,1\,0\,1 & 1\,1\,1\,0 & 1\,1\,0\,0 \\ 1\,1\,0\,0 & 1\,1\,0\,1 & 1\,0\,1\,0 & 1\,0\,1\,1 & 1\,0\,0\,1 & 1\,0\,0\,0 \\ 1\,0\,0\,0 & 1\,0\,0\,0 & 1\,0\,0\,0 & 1\,0\,0\,0 & 1\,0\,0\,0 & 1\,0\,0\,0 \\ 0\,1\,0\,0 & 0\,1\,0\,0 & 0\,1\,0\,0 & 0\,1\,0\,0 & 0\,1\,0\,0 & 0\,1\,0\,0 \\ 0\,0\,1\,0 & 0\,0\,1\,0 & 0\,0\,1\,0 & 0\,0\,1\,0 & 0\,0\,1\,0 & 0\,0\,1\,0 \\ 0\,0\,0\,1 & 0\,0\,0\,1 & 0\,0\,0\,1 & 0\,0\,0\,1 & 0\,0\,0\,1 & 0\,0\,0\,1 \end{pmatrix}$$

have all the weight $2^{8-4} = 16$

6   Conclusion and Perspectives

In this work, we aimed to construct perfect binary linear error-block codes with $d_\pi = 3$ and types $\pi = [n_1] \ldots [n_t][2]^s$ where $n_1 \geq \ldots \geq n_t \geq 2$ and $t \geq 1$ and $s \geq 1$ and $\pi = [n_1][n_t][3]^s$ where $n_1 \geq n_t \geq 3$, $t = 1$ or 2 and $s \geq 1$ and to define Hamming and Simplex codes.

Firstly, we showed the conditions for a binary LEB code with π-distance three and type $\pi = [n_1] \ldots [n_t][2]^s$ where $n_1 \geq \ldots \geq n_t \geq 2$ and $t \geq 1$ and $s \geq 1$ (and respectively $\pi = [n_1][3]^s$ and $\pi = [n_1][n_2][3]^s$) to reaches this bound.

Secondly, we have given conditions of existence of perfect binary LEB codes, then we have shown that there exists an infinite family of codes of type $\pi = [n_1] \ldots [n_t][2]^s$ where $n_1 \geq \ldots \geq n_t \geq 2$, $t \geq 1$ and $s \geq 1$.

Thirdly, we have constructed large families of Hamming codes of types $\pi = [m]^{\frac{q^r-1}{q^m-1}}$ using their parity check matrix. We have showed that LEB Hamming codes are perfect and have given conditions to the constructed perfect codes to be Hamming codes.

Finally, we have given conditions of existence of simplex codes. Ten we have showed that the dual of a Hamming code of type $\pi = [m]^{\frac{q^r-1}{q^m-1}}$ is a Simplex LEB code.

We list hereafter some open interesting problems from our point of view.

- Provide a complete classification of perfect LEB codes.
- Show that we can construct an infinite family of perfect binary $[n + 2p.s, k + 2p.s, 3]$ (with p any) codes of type $\pi = [n_1] \ldots [n_t][2p]^s$ where $n_1 \geq \ldots \geq n_t \geq 2p$ and $t \geq 1$ and $s \geq 1$, with specification of necessary conditions to these codes.
- Construct binary perfect LEB codes with π-distance 4 and 5.
- Determine some particular bounds for LEB codes like the Griesmer bound and a decoding algorithm for Hamming codes.

References

1. Feng, K., Xu, L., Hickernell, F.J.: Linear error-block codes. Finite Fields Appl. **12**, 638–652 (2006)
2. Dariti, R., Souidi, E.M.: New families of perfect linear error-block codes. Int. J. Inf. Coding Theory **2**(2/3), 84–95 (2013)
3. Dariti, R., Souidi, E.M.: An application of linear error-block codes in steganography. Int. J. Digit. Inf. Wirel. Commun. **1**, 426–433 (2012)
4. Dariti, R., Souidi, E.M.: Cyclicity and decoding of linear error-block codes. J. Theorecal Appl. Inf. Technol. **25**, 39–42 (2011)
5. Dariti, R., Souidi, E.M.: Packing and covering radii of linear error-block codes. Int. J. Math. Sci. **7**, 13–17 (2013)
6. Udomkavanich, P., Jitman, S.: Bounds and modifications on linear error-block codes. Int. Math. Forum **5**, 35–50 (2010)
7. Dariti, R.: Linear error-block codes and applications. Thèse de Doctorat, Université Mohammed V-Agdal, Faculté des Sciences (2012)

8. Tietäväinen, A.: On the nonexistence of perfect codes over finite fields. SIAM J. Appl. Math. **24**(1), 88–96 (1973)
9. Zinovev, V.A., Leontev, V.K.: Nonexistence of perfect codes over Galois fields. Probl. Control. Inf. Theory **2**(2), 123–132 (1973)

Quasi-Dyadic Girault Identification Scheme

Brice Odilon Boidje[(✉)], Cheikh Thiecoumba Gueye, Gilbert Ndollane Dione,
and Jean Belo Klamti

Faculté des Sciences et Techniques, DMI, LACGAA, Université Cheikh Anta Diop,
Dakar, Senegal
{briceodilon.boidje,cheikht.gueye,gilbertndollane.dione,
jeanbelo.klamti}@ucad.edu.sn

Abstract. Zero-knowledge identification schemes allow a prover to convince a verifier that a certain fact is true, while not revealing any additional information.

In this paper, we propose a scheme whose security relies on the hardness of the Quasi-Dyadic Subcode Equivalence and the Quasi-dyadic syndrome decoding problems. Our code-based scheme is an improvement of the code-based identification scheme devised by Girault. Our construction uses quasi-dyadic subcode with a cheating probability of 1/2. Using quasi-dyadic subcode allows to reduce matrix size and also the communication cost by sending lower data.

Keywords: Code-based cryptography · Identification scheme ·
Syndrome decoding problem · Zero-knowledge · Quasi-dyadic subcode

1 Introduction

An identification scheme can be obtained by using a zero-knowledge interactive protocol, in which a party called prover tries to prove its identity without revealing anything secret to another party called verifier. In zero-knowledge schemes, no secret information belonging to the prover should be revealed from the protocol, except for the fact that the prover knows the secret. The main hardness assumptions for our identification scheme are the syndrome decoding problem for quasi-dyadic code and the quasi-dyadic subcode equivalence (QD-ES).

Our Contribution: In this paper, we propose an improvement of the Girault Identification Scheme by using code with compact matrices. In our proposal, we use particularly quasi-dyadic subcodes to decrease the communication cost in each round. Indeed, instead of sending the whole matrix, we just send some rows consisting of its signatures. We end with a discussion on the security parameters of our protocol and we compare its performances with previous Girault identification protocols variants one.

Organization of the Paper: In Sect. 2 we introduce some background concepts that we will use for the construction of our identification scheme. In Sect. 3, we

© Springer Nature Switzerland AG 2019
C. Carlet et al. (Eds.): C2SI 2019, LNCS 11445, pp. 307–321, 2019.
https://doi.org/10.1007/978-3-030-16458-4_18

discuss the problems on whose our scheme is based. In Sect. 4, we describe the original code-based identification scheme proposed by Girault. We present our improved identification scheme in Sect. 5. We follow up in Sect. 6, where we prove completeness, zero-knowledge and soundness of our scheme. Then, in Sect. 7, we analyze the performance of our proposal. Finally, we conclude in Sect. 8.

2   Background

2.1   Notation

$\mathbb{F}_q$ denotes the finite field with q elements, $w_H()$ denotes the Hamming weight. By QD-ES, we denote Quasi-Dyadic Equivalence Subcode.

2.2   Coding Theory

Definition 1. *A $[n, k]$-linear code on $\mathbb{F}_q$ is a subspace of $\mathbb{F}_q^n$ of dimension k. A codeword is an element of the code.*

Definition 2. *The Hamming weight $w_H(y)$ of a word $y \in \mathbb{F}_q^n$ is the number of non-zero coordinates of y.*

Definition 3. *The generator matrix G of a $[n, k]$-linear code $\mathcal{C}$ is a $k \times n$ matrix such that:*

$$\mathcal{C} = \{mG : m \in \mathbb{F}_q^k\}$$

Definition 4. *The parity check matrix H of a $[n, k]$-linear code $\mathcal{C}$ is a $r \times n$ matrix with $r = n - k$ such that:*

$$\mathcal{C} = \{c \in \mathbb{F}_q^n : Hc^T = 0\}$$

Proposition 1. *Let $\mathcal{C}$ be a (n, k)-linear code over $\mathbb{F}_q$ of minimal distance d. Then each subcode (vector subspace of dimension $k' \leq k$) $\mathcal{C}'$ of $\mathcal{C}$, verifies:*

$$d' \geq d$$

where d' is the minimal distance of $\mathcal{C}'$.

Proposition 2. *Let $\mathcal{C}$ a (n, k)-linear code over $\mathbb{F}_q$ of minimal distance d and with generator matrice G. We can construct an arbitrary subcode $\mathcal{C}'$ with dimension $k' \leq k$ of $\mathcal{C}$ as following:*
by choosing arbitrary a $k' \times k$ matrix S of rank k' then the generator matrix G' of the subcode $\mathcal{C}'$ is given by:
$$G' = SG$$

Let $n = 2^r$ be an integer with $r \in \mathbb{N}$. We have the following definitions:

Definition 5. *The m-dyadic shift, $m = 0, 1, \cdots, n - 1$, of a vector $(a_0, a_1, \cdots, a_{n-1})$ is the vector: $(a_{0 \oplus m}, a_{1 \oplus m}, \cdots, a_{(n-1) \oplus m})$, where the operation $\oplus$ is the bitwise XOR.*

Definition 6. *A linear code of length $n = 2^r$ over a finite field $\mathbb{F}_q$ is a dyadic code if the m-dyadic shift on each codeword is a codeword $\forall m \in \{0, \cdots, n - 1\}$.*

Definition 7. *Given a ring R and a vector $h = (h_0, \cdots, h_{n-1}) \in R^n$, the dyadic matrix $\Delta(h) \in R^{n \times n}$ is the symmetric matrix with components $\Delta_{ij} = h_{i \oplus j}$. The sequence h is called its signature.*

Definition 8. *A quasi-dyadic matrix is a (possibly non-dyadic) block matrix whose component blocks are dyadic sub-matrices.*

Definition 9. *A dyadic permutation matrix is a dyadic matrix whose signature admits a single non-zero element and equal to 1.*
Therefore, a quasi-dyadic permutation matrix is a square binary block matrix that has exactly one entry of identity matrix in each row quasi-dyadic block and each row quasi-dyadic block quasi-dyadic block and null matrix elsewhere.
thus

$$
\begin{bmatrix}
\begin{bmatrix} 1 & 0 \\ 0 & 1 \end{bmatrix} & \begin{bmatrix} 0 & 0 \\ 0 & 0 \end{bmatrix} & \begin{bmatrix} 0 & 0 \\ 0 & 0 \end{bmatrix} & \begin{bmatrix} 0 & 0 \\ 0 & 0 \end{bmatrix} \\[4mm]
\begin{bmatrix} 0 & 0 \\ 0 & 0 \end{bmatrix} & \begin{bmatrix} 0 & 0 \\ 0 & 0 \end{bmatrix} & \begin{bmatrix} 1 & 0 \\ 0 & 1 \end{bmatrix} & \begin{bmatrix} 0 & 0 \\ 0 & 0 \end{bmatrix} \\[4mm]
\begin{bmatrix} 0 & 0 \\ 0 & 0 \end{bmatrix} & \begin{bmatrix} 0 & 0 \\ 0 & 0 \end{bmatrix} & \begin{bmatrix} 0 & 0 \\ 0 & 0 \end{bmatrix} & \begin{bmatrix} 1 & 0 \\ 0 & 1 \end{bmatrix} \\[4mm]
\begin{bmatrix} 0 & 0 \\ 0 & 0 \end{bmatrix} & \begin{bmatrix} 1 & 0 \\ 0 & 1 \end{bmatrix} & \begin{bmatrix} 0 & 0 \\ 0 & 0 \end{bmatrix} & \begin{bmatrix} 0 & 0 \\ 0 & 0 \end{bmatrix}
\end{bmatrix}
$$

is a quasi-dyadic permutation matrix.

Definition 10. *A quasi-dyadic code is a linear error-correcting code that admits a quasi-dyadic parity-check matrix. A quasi-dyadic code of length $n = \ell n_0$ is defined by its index $n_0 \in \mathbb{N}^*$ and its order $\ell = 2^s$, with $s \geq 2$. n_0 is the number of dyadic blocks and ℓ the size of each dyadic block.*

The parameters of quasi dyadic codes are: its length $n = \ell n_0$ with $\ell = 2^s \in \mathbb{N}^*, s \in \mathbb{N}$ and its dimension $k = (n_0 - m_0)\ell$ with $m_0 \in \mathbb{N}^*$ and $\ell > m$

2.3   NP-Complete Problem

Definitions

Definition 11. *NP-class*
The NP-class is the set of all problems that can be solved by Non deterministic Polynomial time algorithms.

Definition 12. *NP-problem*
A problem in the NP-class is called a NP-problem.
To show that a problem is in the NP-class, it is sufficient to find an algorithm which verifies if a given solution is valid in polynomial time.

Definition 13. *NP-complete*
An NP-problem is said to be NP-complete if the existence of a polynomial time solution for that problem implies that all NP-problems have a polynomial time solution.
A problem is called NP-complete problem if all problem of the NP-class is polynomially reducible to it.

Polynomial Reduction
To prove that a problem A is NP-complete, we must do a polynomial reduction of the problem A to an NP-complete problem B. For that it is necessary:

 – To assume an algorithm γ is able to solve any instance of A
 – To start from an instance U of B
 – To convert this instance U to an instance V of A
 – To solve A with input V using γ to obtain a solution S
 – To convert this solution S to a solution T of B
 – The conversions (transformations) must be done in polynomial time.

Therefore if one day, it exists a polynomial time algorithm to solve A it implies the existence of an algorithm (polynomial) to solve B. That proves that A is NP-complete.

NP-Complete Problems in Coding Theory

Definition 14 *(Syndrome decoding (SD)).*
Let (H, w, s) be a triple consisting of a matrix $H \in \mathbb{F}_q^{r \times n}$, an integer $w < n$, and a vector $s \in \mathbb{F}_q^r$.
Does there exist a vector $e \in \mathbb{F}_q^n$ of Hamming weight $w_H(e) \leq w$ such that $He^T = s^T$?

Definition 15 *(Equivalence Subcode (ES)).*
Given two linear codes $\mathcal{C}$ and $\mathcal{D}$ of length n and respective dimension k' and k, $k' \geq k$, over the same finite field $\mathbb{F}_q$, is there a permutation σ of the support such $\sigma(\mathcal{C})$ be a subcode of $\mathcal{D}$?

3   Quasi-Dyadic Equivalence Subcode (QD-ES)

In this section, we will state the problems on which the security of our schema is based.

3.1   Statement of Problems

Problem 1 **Quasi-Dyadic Syndrome Decoding (QD-SD).**

Input: Let $\mathbb{F}_q$ be a finite field, and let (H, w, S) be a triple consisting of a quasi-dyadic matrix $H \in [\Delta(\mathbb{F}_q^\ell)]^{r_0 \times n_0}$, an integer $w < \ell n_0$, and a vector $S \in \mathbb{F}_q^{\ell r_0}$.
Question: Does there exist a vector $e \in \mathbb{F}_q^{\ell n_0}$ of Hamming weight $w_H(e) \leq w$ such that $He^T = S^T$?

Problem 2 **Quasi-Dyadic Equivalence Subcode (QD-ES).**

Input: Let $\mathcal{C}$ and $\mathcal{D}$ are two random quasi-dyadic linear codes of length $n = \ell n_0$ and respective dimension $k' = (n_0 - r_0')\ell$ and $k = (n_0 - r_0)\ell$, over the same finite field $\mathbb{F}_q$.
Question: Does it exist a dyadic permutation σ such $\sigma(C)$ be a subcode quasi-dyadic of $\mathcal{D}$?

3.2   Some Remarks About These Problems

It is important to emphasize that Problem 1 was demonstrated NP-complete by Barreto in [16]. He did a reduction of the SD problem on random codes to the QD-SD problem. Barreto, in his proof, fixes a quasi-dyadic order ℓ, and shows that the problem SD is NP-complete for ℓ fixed (and n tending towards infinity). The proof consists of concatenating ℓ occurrences of random code, reordering the coefficients so as to make the code quasi-dyadic.

The approach used consists of constructing from a $r_0 \times n_0$ parity check matrix H of a random code C, another $\ell r_0 \times \ell n_0$ parity check matrix H' of a quasi-dyadic random code by replacing each entrie 1 by the identity matrix of size $\ell \times \ell$ and each entrie 0 by null matrix of the same size.

The same approach can be used to show the NP-completeness of Problem 2. We did it in Appendix A. However, instead of setting the order l, if we fix the index n_0, then l increases linearly as a function of n, and the reduction proposed by Baretto becomes exponential in n. To our knowledge, no fixed-index reduction has been proposed to prove the NP-completeness of these problems. In the case where we fix the index n_0, we make the following security assumptions:

Assumption 1. *The QD-SD Problem is $\mathcal{NP}$-complete.*

Assumption 2. *The QD-ES problem is $\mathcal{NP}$-complete.*

4   The Girault Identification Protocol

In this subsection, after making the history of code-based identification protocols, we briefly describe Girault's three-pass identification protocol.

4.1   Overview of Code-Based Identification Protocols

Stern, in 1993, was the first one to propose a zero-knowledge identification scheme based on the hardness of the syndrome decoding problem [12]. His scheme has a soundness error of $2/3$, where the soundness error is the probability that the verifier accepts an incorrect input. In order to guarantee that an honest prover is accepted, it is necessary to repeat the scheme a large number of times. In 1996, another code-based identification scheme was designed by Véron based on the same hard problem [13]. Véron's scheme improved Stern's scheme by using a "dual" construction. Moreover, the scheme has lower communication cost but has larger key size.

In 2010 Cayrel, Véron and El Yousfi [6] devised a code-based identification scheme, which is an improvement of Stern's construction. They were able to decrease the cheating probability of Véron's scheme to nearly $1/2$.

In 2011 Gaborit et al. [1] proposed a double circulant scheme which reduce the matrix size and the communication cost.

In [8], Han et al. proposed an identification scheme related to Véron's one and based on the general decoding problem. The protocol uses quasi-dyadic matrix, which consequently decrease the matrix size. The protocol decreases the cheating probability to about $\frac{1}{2}$ and it also has low communication cost by sending fewer commitments.

Finally, in 2016, Gueye et al. presented a new version of the Girault identification scheme [14]. Their protocol is based on the hardness of subcode equivalence and the syndrome decoding problem.

4.2   Description of Girault Identification Protocol

Key Generation Algorithm. Let H be a parity check matrix $(n - k) \times n$ common to all users. The prover chooses randomly, as his secret key, a vector $e \in \mathbb{F}_q^n$ of weight w.

To get his public key, the prover computes $s = He^T$; the public is $p_k = (H, s)$ (Figs. 1 and 2).

KEYGEN:
$e \xleftarrow{\$} \mathbb{F}_q^n,\ w_H t(e) = w$
H parity check matrix $(n - k) \times n$
$s \leftarrow He^T$
$s_k = e,\ p_k = (H, s)$

Fig. 1. Girault key generation scheme

Identification Scheme

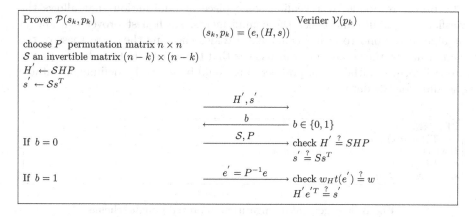

Fig. 2. Girault identification scheme

5   Version Improved of the Girault Identification Scheme Using Quasi-Dyadic Subcode

In this subsection we propose the improved Girault identification protocol using quasi-Dyadic Subcode.

5.1   Key Generation Algorithm

We choose our parameters such that $n = \ell n_0$; $k = \ell k_0, q = 2^m$, where $m \geq 1$, $\ell = 2^p$, with $p \geq 1$ and $n_0 \geq 2k_0$.

Let be $t = n_0 - k_0$.

Let $H \in \mathbb{F}_q^{r \times n}$, $r = n - k = \ell t$, be a parity check matrix of a $C[n, k]$ quasi-dyadic code of order ℓ. H is common to all users (in particular the prover $\mathcal{P}$ and the verifier $\mathcal{V}$).

Let be w an integer, the prover chooses randomly a vector $e \in \mathbb{F}_q^n$ of weight at least equal to w as his secret key. His public key consists of $p_k = (H, s)$ where $s = He^T$.

5.2   Improved Identification Scheme

In Fig. 4, the identification describes the interaction between prover and verifier. In this protocol, the former tries to prove his identity to the latter (Fig. 3).

In the commitment phase, the prover commits to two values H', s'. As the matrix H' is quasi-dyadic, only t' lines $H'_{ip}, i = 0 \cdots t' - 1$, consisting of the signatures, need to be sent instead of the whole matrix. Those commitments are sent to the verifier. Upon reception of these values, the verifier makes a challenge to the prover, picking a value uniformly at random from the set $\{0, 1\}$. The prover responds by revealing some piece of information that allows the verifier to compute and check the commitments. An honest prover will always be able to respond to either challenge. Besides checking the correctness of the commitments, the verifier must also check that the values disclosed by the prover are well-formed, although in practice this would be solved by defining a suitable encoding for the data.

KEYGEN:

$e \xleftarrow{\$} \mathbb{F}_q^n,\ w_H t(e) \leq w$

H a quasi-dyadic parity check matrix of size $r \times n$

$s \leftarrow He^T$

$s_k = e,\ p_k = (H, s)$

Fig. 3. Key generation algorithm improved girault scheme

Prover $\mathcal{P}(s_k, p_k)$ Verifier $\mathcal{V}(p_k)$

$$(s_k, p_k) = (e, (H, s, w))$$

choose randomly

P_σ : a $n \times n$ quasi-dyadic permutation matrix

an integer $t' < t$ for arbitrary $\ell t' \times r$

quasi-dyadic matrix S of rank lt'

$H' = SHP_\sigma$ and $s' = Ss^T$

$\xrightarrow{\quad H'_{i\ell}, i = 0 \cdots t' - 1 \text{ and } s' \quad}$

$\xleftarrow{\qquad\qquad b \qquad\qquad}$ $b \in \{0, 1\}$

If $b = 0$ $\xrightarrow{\quad S_{i\ell}, i = 0 \cdots t' - 1 \text{ and } \sigma \quad}$ check $H' \overset{?}{=} SHP_\sigma$

$s' \overset{?}{=} Ss^T$

If $b = 1$ $\xrightarrow{\qquad e' = P_\sigma^{-1} e \qquad}$

check $w_H t(e') \overset{?}{=} w$

$s' \overset{?}{=} H' e'^T$

Fig. 4. Improved Girault identification scheme

6   Security

In this section, we give our proof for completeness, zero-knowledge and soundness of the scheme.

6.1   Completeness

We have to show that our protocol is complete, i.e. that the prouver will always be "accepted" by the Verifier if the two partners correctly follow the protocol. If $b = 0$, after receiving the values σ and $S_{il}, i = 0 \cdots t' - 1$ from the prover, the verifier first reconstructs the matrices P_σ and S. Then, he can easily check that $H' = SHP_\sigma$ and $Ss = s'$
If $b = 1$, the prover sends $e' = P_\sigma^{-1}e$, then the verifier is convinced of the equality $H'e' = s'$ and also that $w_H(e') = w$.

6.2   Soundness

We will show that a dishonest prover has a negligible probability of convincing a verifier, by showing that a dishonest prover is able to cheat a verifier with a probability of $\frac{1}{2}$.

Let's assume that a dishonest prover wants to answer all the challenges where $b = 0$. He just picks a quasi-dyadic permutation matrix P_σ and an invertible quasi-dyadic matrix S and then computes $H' = SHP_\sigma$ and $s' = Ss^T$.

To answer to the challenge $b = 1$, the cheating prover chooses a vector $\hat{e} \in \mathbb{F}_q^n$ such that $w_H(\hat{e}) = w$.

Now, let's assume that the cheating prover can prepare H', s' so that he can answer to both challenges $b = 0$ and $b = 1$. It means that he found P_σ, S and $\hat{e}$ so that these equalities hold: $H' = SHP_\sigma$; $s' = Ss^T$; $H'\hat{e}'^T = s'$ and $w_H(\hat{e}') = w$.

This implies that $SHP_\sigma\hat{e} = Ss^T$ and $w_H(\hat{e}') = w$. Let be $\tilde{e} = P_\sigma\hat{e}'$. Since S is full rank matrix and P_σ is a permutation matrix, $H\tilde{e} = s$ and $w_H(\tilde{e}) = w$.

In other words, the cheating prover has found $\tilde{e}$ such that $H\tilde{e} = s$ with $w_H(\tilde{e}) = w$. This means that the cheating prover has solved an instance of the syndrome decoding problem, in other words our assumption according to which QD-SDP is a NP-complete problem is violated.

6.3   Zero-Knowledge

No private information can be deduced in polynomial time from an execution of the protocol except the knowledge of the public data, i.e the verifier can know nothing else except what the prover reveals to him.

Just like in [14], the protocol leaks or not any information about the prover's secret key if and only if it's computationally infeasible to deduce anything about the permutation P_σ and the matrix S of rank $\ell t'$ from H' and s'. On the one hand, one cannot retrieve the matrices P_σ and S from H' according to one of the underlined problems (QD-ES).

On the other hand, the knowledge of one of the unknown matrices leads to the knowledge of the other one. Then knowing S allows to obtain P_σ and then e via the equality $e' = P_\sigma^{-1}e^T$. But retreiving S from $s' = Ss^T$ consists of resolving a linear system of $\ell t'$ equations and $\ell^2 tt'$ unknowns.

7   Performance Analysis of the Scheme

7.1   Parameters

The random permutation σ and the other random elements included in the protocol are usually generated from random seeds of size ℓ_σ. Instead of sending the whole permutation σ, the prover can send just the seed after agreeing with the verifier on the common algorithm to generate σ and the other random values [7]. Hence, for a security of 2^{100}, only the 100 bits required for the seed are sent, instead of the whole permutation σ.

The cheating probability is $\dfrac{1}{2}$. Then, to achieve a soundness error of 2^{-16}, the protocol has to be run 16 times.

According to the way we construct the quasi-dyadic permutation matrix, there are $n_0!$ diffrent matrices. So, we choose n_0 such that $n_0! \approx 2^{100}$.

We use the following parameters: $n_0 = 29$, $\ell = 8$, $k_0 = 4$, $m = 8$, $t' = 21$. Hence, $n = 232$, $k = 116$; $q = 256$.

7.2   Communication Cost

At each round, we have:

- **Commitments:** $t' \times n \times m + (n - k) \times m = m \times n \times (t' + 1) - k \times m$ bits
- **Challenge:** 1 bit
- **Answers average:** $\frac{1}{2}\left[t \times (n - k) \times m + \ell_\sigma + n \times m\right] = \frac{1}{2}\left[n \times m \times (t' + 1) + \ell_\sigma - t' \times k \times m\right]$ bits

T_i: $\frac{3}{2} \times \left[n \times m \times (t' + 1)\right] - k \times m \times (1 + \frac{t'}{2}) + \frac{\ell_\sigma}{2} + 1$ bits

Let **T** be the whole communication cost of the protocol. Then we have:

$$\mathbf{T} = \textbf{Number of rounds} \times T_i$$

The whole communication cost of our scheme is $\mathbf{T} = 98.88\,\text{kB}$.

- Girault's scheme communication cost [14]:
  $\mathbf{t} = m \times (n - k) \times \left[\frac{3n}{2} - \frac{k}{2} + 1\right] + \frac{\ell_\sigma}{2} + \frac{m \times n}{2} + 1$
- Sendrier *et al.* scheme communication cost [11]:
  $\mathbf{t} = m \times (n - k) \times \left[\frac{3n}{2} - \frac{k}{2} + 1\right] + \frac{\ell_\sigma}{2} + \frac{m \times n}{2} + 1$
- Gueye *et al.* scheme communication cost [3]:
  $\mathbf{t} = m \times (n - k - \ell) \times \left[\frac{3n}{2} - \frac{k}{2} + 1\right] + \frac{\ell_\sigma}{2} + \frac{m \times n}{2} + 1$

In the binary case: $q = 2$, with the same parameters we have (Tables 1 and 2):

Table 1. Communication cost with parameters: $n = 232$, $k = 116$, $q = 256$ (non binary case)

Scheme	Rounds	Total communication cost (Kb)
Girault [14]	16	529.35
Sendrier [11]	16	529.35
Gueye *et al.* [3]	16	483.88
Ours	16	98.88

Table 2. Communication cost with parameters: $n = 232$, $k = 116$, $q = 2$ (binary case)

Scheme	Rounds	Total communication cost (Kb)
Girault [14]	16	66.25
Gueye *et al.* [3]	16	60.57
Ours	16	12.45

7.3 Performance

As an improvement of Girault's identification protocol, our scheme is also a three-pass identification protocol.

The security of our scheme is guaranteed on one hand by the QD-SD problem, and on the other hand by the QD-ES problem. So breaking our scheme would lead to either finding a solution for QD-SD or to finding a solution for QD-ES. Compared to [11,14] and [3], our scheme has lower communication cost and public key size. The most important improvement is in the commitment and the response phases when the challenge is equal to 1. Actually, the prover commits to two values H', s' and must send S when the challenge is equal 1. As the matrices H' and S are quasi-dyadic, only $2t$ lines $H'_{i\ell}, S'_{i\ell}$, $i = 0 \cdots t' - 1$, consisting of the signatures of H' and S, need to be sent instead of the whole two matrices.

8 Conclusion

In this paper, we presented an identification scheme whose security is based on the assumption that the QD-SD and QD-ES problems are NP-complete. This scheme is an improvement of the code-based identification scheme of Girault [14]. Our construction is based of the quasi-dyadic subcode, which permits to reduce the size of the public key and the communication cost as well by sending fewer data. In the future, it will be interesting to study a constructive polynomial reduction of QD-SD problem and QD-ES problem to a NP-complete one while fixing the quasi-dyadicity index to prove their NP-complexity.

Acknowledgments. This work is supported by CEA-MITIC/Project CBC and the government of Senegal's Ministry of Higher Education and Research for ISPQ project.

A   Proof of the NP-Completeness of the QD-ES Problem when We Fix the Order

A.1   Definitions

Four Dimensional Matching Problem (FDMP)

Definition 16.

Input: a subset $U \subseteq T \times T \times T \times T$ where T is a finite set.
Question: Does it exist a set $W \subseteq U$ such that $|W| = |T|$ and every two vectors of W have different i-th coordinate, $i \in \{1,2,3,4\}$?

The Kronecker Product

Let A be a $k \times \ell$ matrix, and B be a $m \times n$ matrix.

Definition 17. *The Kronecker product of A and B (denoted $(A \otimes B)$ is the $km \times \ell n$ matrix:*

$$A \otimes B = \begin{pmatrix} a_{11}B & a_{12}B & \cdots & a_{1\ell}B \\ a_{21}B & a_{22}B & \cdots & a_{2\ell}B \\ \vdots & \vdots & \ddots & \vdots \\ a_{k1}B & a_{k2}B & \cdot & a_{k\ell}B \end{pmatrix}$$

Note that the Kronecker product of two matrices is another matrix, usually a much larger one.

A.2   Relation Between ES Problem and FDMP

Through the following illustration, we show the relation between the ES problem and the FDMP.

Let $T = \{1,2,3,4\}$ and $U = \{U_1, U_2, U_3, U_4, U_5, U_6\}$ with $U_1 = (1,2,3,4)$; $U_2 = (4,1,3,2)$; $U_3 = (2,1,4,3)$; $U_4 = (3,4,1,2)$; $U_5 = (4,3,2,1)$; $U_6 = (4,4,3,4)$.

A solution for the FDMP is the set W consisting of the elements U_1, U_3, U_4 et U_5.

We apply differents transformations $\mathcal{T}$ to U in order to obtain an $|U| \times 4|T|$ matrix M:

– For each $x = (x_1, x_2, x_3, x_4) \in U$, we give the vector $l(x) = (y_1, \cdots, y_{4n})$ such that $y_i = 0$ for all i except $y_{x_1} = y_{n+x_2} = y_{2n+x_3} = y_{3n+x_4} = 1$.
For our example, we obtain:

$$l((1,2,3,4)) = (1,0,0,0,\ 1,0,0,0,\ 1,0,0,0,\ 1,0,0,0)$$
$$l((4,1,3,2)) = (0,0,0,1,\ 1,0,0,0,\ 0,0,1,0,\ 0,1,0,0)$$
$$l((2,1,4,3)) = (0,1,0,0,\ 1,0,0,0,\ 0,0,0,1,\ 0,0,1,0)$$
$$l((3,4,1,2)) = (0,0,1,0,\ 0,0,0,1,\ 1,0,0,0,\ 1,0,0,0)$$
$$l((4,3,2,1)) = (0,0,0,1,\ 0,0,1,0,\ 0,1,0,0,\ 1,0,0,0)$$
$$l((4,4,3,4)) = (0,0,0,1,\ 0,0,0,1,\ 0,0,1,0,\ 0,0,0,1)$$

- We construct the matrix M of size $|U| \times 4|T|$ by keeping the vectors $l(x)$ of the ordered elements of U as following:

$$M = \begin{pmatrix} 1\ 0\ 0\ 0 & 0\ 1\ 0\ 0 & 0\ 0\ 1\ 0 & 0\ 0\ 0\ 1 \\ 0\ 0\ 0\ 1 & 1\ 0\ 0\ 0 & 0\ 0\ 1\ 0 & 0\ 1\ 0\ 0 \\ 0\ 1\ 0\ 0 & 1\ 0\ 0\ 0 & 0\ 0\ 0\ 1 & 0\ 0\ 1\ 0 \\ 0\ 0\ 1\ 0 & 0\ 0\ 0\ 1 & 1\ 0\ 0\ 0 & 0\ 1\ 0\ 0 \\ 0\ 0\ 0\ 1 & 0\ 0\ 1\ 0 & 0\ 1\ 0\ 0 & 1\ 0\ 0\ 0 \\ 0\ 0\ 0\ 1 & 0\ 0\ 0\ 1 & 0\ 0\ 1\ 0 & 0\ 0\ 0\ 1 \end{pmatrix}$$

With this new representation of U, a valid FDMP solution corresponds to the existence of $|T|$ rows of M forming a matrix

$$M_{sol} = \begin{pmatrix} 1\ 0\ 0\ 0 & 0\ 1\ 0\ 0 & 0\ 0\ 1\ 0 & 0\ 0\ 0\ 1 \\ 0\ 1\ 0\ 0 & 1\ 0\ 0\ 0 & 0\ 0\ 0\ 1 & 0\ 0\ 1\ 0 \\ 0\ 0\ 1\ 0 & 0\ 0\ 0\ 1 & 1\ 0\ 0\ 0 & 0\ 1\ 0\ 0 \\ 0\ 0\ 0\ 1 & 0\ 0\ 1\ 0 & 0\ 1\ 0\ 0 & 1\ 0\ 0\ 0 \end{pmatrix}$$

Since M_{sol} contains only one 1 on each of its columns, it is equivalent by permutation to a matrix of the form $(I_4|I_4|I_4|I_4)$.

Now, let consider $\mathcal{D}$ and $\mathcal{C}$, linear codes over $\mathbb{F}_q$ of respective generator matrices $G_{\mathcal{D}}$ and $G_{\mathcal{C}}$ defined by:

$$G_{\mathcal{D}} = (I_6|I_6|I_6|I_6|M)$$

$$G_{\mathcal{C}} = (I_4|0_{4\times 2}|I_4|0_{4\times 2}|I_4|0_{4\times 2}|I_4|0_{4\times 2}|I_4|0_{4\times 2}|I_4|I_4|I_4|I_4)$$

where $0_{4\times 2}$ is the 4×2 null matrix and I_4 the 4×4 identity matrix.

So, for the same reasons as before, finding a valid FDMP solution is such as to determine a permutation σ such as $\sigma(G_{\mathcal{C}})$ is a subcode of $G_{\mathcal{D}}$. This corresponds to the ES problem.

A.3   Proof

We make a reduction of FDMP to QD-ES.

- Let us assume an algorithm γ is able to solve any instance of the QD-ES Problem.
- Let $U \subset T \times T \times T \times T$ with T, a finite set of cardinality n. (n, U) is the inputs of FDMP.
- Let U be a set such that:

$$U = \{u_1, u_2, \cdots, u_r\} \text{ with } r = |U|.$$

we apply the transformations $\mathcal{T}$, view in the previous section, to U and obtain an $|U| \times 4|T|$ matrix M. Let G be a $r \times 4r + 4n$ matrix defined as follows:

$$G = (I_r|I_r|I_r|I_r|M)$$

From this matrix G we construct the quasi-dyadic matrix $\mathbf{G}_{\mathcal{D}}$ of size $2r \times 8r + 8n$:

$$\mathbf{G}_{\mathcal{D}} = G \otimes I_2$$

(where I_2 the identity matrix of size 2×2)

Let $\mathcal{D}$ be the $[8r + 8n, 2r]$ linear code over $\mathbb{F}_q$ generated by the matrix $\mathbf{G}_{\mathcal{D}}$. $\mathcal{D}$ is a quasi-dyadic code.

Lemma 1. *The minimum distance of $\mathcal{D}$ is exactly 8. In addition, the minimum codewords are exactly the rows of $\mathbf{G}_{\mathcal{D}}$.*

Proof. The rows of $\mathbf{G}_{\mathcal{D}}$ correspond to codewords of weight 8. Since all the rows of M are distinct, it is the same with rows of $M \otimes I_2$. Then the weight of the sum of two rows of $\mathbf{G}_{\mathcal{D}}$ is at least 10. Finally, the weight of the sum of t distinct rows is at least $4t$, which is greater than 12 for $t \geq 3$.

- We transform a solution of the QD-ES into a solution of the FDMP.
  Let $\mathbf{G}_{\mathcal{C}}$ be a $2n \times 8r + 8n$ quasi-dyadic matrix defined by

$$\mathbf{G}_{\mathcal{C}} = (I_n|0_{n\times(r-n)}|I_n|0_{n\times(r-n)}|I_n|0_{n\times(r-n)}|I_n|0_{n\times(r-n)}|I_n|I_n|I_n|I_n) \otimes I_2$$

A solution to QD-ES Problem, with $\mathbf{G}_{\mathcal{D}}$ and $\mathbf{G}_{\mathcal{C}}$ as inputs, is a quasi-dyadic permutation σ such that $\sigma(\mathcal{C})$ be a quasi-dyadic subcode of $\mathcal{D}$.

The image of any rowgroups of $\mathbf{G}_{\mathcal{C}}$ by σ is rowgroups whose rows are codewords of $\mathcal{D}$ of weight exactly 8. From Lemma 1, these elements are rows of $\mathbf{G}_{\mathcal{D}}$. Thus, we obtain n distinct row quasi-dyadic block of $\mathcal{D}$. We choose the first rows of each row quasi-dyadic block and we get n distinct rows with the particularity that no two rows agree on any coordinate. This leads directly to a matching W of U.

References

1. Aguilar, C., Gaborit, P., Schrek, J.: A new zero-knowledge code-based identification scheme with reduced communication scheme. In: IEEE Information Theory Workshop 2011, pp. 648–652 (2011)
2. Berger, T., Gueye, C.-T., Klamti, J.-B.: Generalized subspace subcodes with application in cryptology
3. Berger, T.P., Gueye, C.T., Klamti, J.B.: A NP-complete problem in coding theory with application to code based cryptography. In: El Hajji, S., Nitaj, A., Souidi, E.M. (eds.) C2SI 2017. LNCS, vol. 10194, pp. 230–237. Springer, Cham (2017). https://doi.org/10.1007/978-3-319-55589-8_15
4. Cayrel, P.-L., Lindner, R., Rückert, M., Silva, R.: Improved zero-knowledge identification with lattices. Tatra Mountains Math. Publ. **53**(1), 33–63 (2012)
5. Cayrel, P.-L., Lindner, R., Rückert, M., Silva, R.: A lattice-based threshold ring signature scheme. In: Abdalla, M., Barreto, P.S.L.M. (eds.) LATINCRYPT 2010. LNCS, vol. 6212, pp. 255–272. Springer, Heidelberg (2010). https://doi.org/10.1007/978-3-642-14712-8_16

6. Cayrel, P.-L., Véron, P., El Yousfi Alaoui, S.M.: A zero-knowledge identification scheme based on the q-ary syndrome decoding problem. In: Biryukov, A., Gong, G., Stinson, D.R. (eds.) SAC 2010. LNCS, vol. 6544, pp. 171–186. Springer, Heidelberg (2011). https://doi.org/10.1007/978-3-642-19574-7_12

7. Dambra, A., Gaborit, P., Roussellet, M., Schrek, J., Tafforeau, N.: Improved secure implementation of code-based signature schemes on embedded devices'. In: IACR Cryptology ePrint Archive, p. 163 (2014)

8. Han, M., Feng, X., Ma, S.: An improved zero-knowledge identification scheme based on quasi-dyadic codes. Int. J. Secur. Appl. 10(10), 181–190 (2016)

9. Cayrel, P.-L., Diagne, M.K., Gueye, C.T.: NP-completeness of the Goppa parameterised random binary quasi-dyadic syndrome decoding problem. IJICoT 4(4), 276–288 (2017)

10. Lyubashevsky, V.: Lattice-based identification schemes secure under active attacks. In: Cramer, R. (ed.) PKC 2008. LNCS, vol. 4939, pp. 162–179. Springer, Heidelberg (2008). https://doi.org/10.1007/978-3-540-78440-1_10

11. Sendrier, N., Simos, D.E.: The hardness of code equivalence over $\mathbb{F}_q$ and its application to code-based cryptography. In: Gaborit, P. (ed.) PQCrypto 2013. LNCS, vol. 7932, pp. 203–216. Springer, Heidelberg (2013). https://doi.org/10.1007/978-3-642-38616-9_14

12. Stern, J.: A new identification scheme based on syndrome decoding. In: Stinson, D.R. (ed.) CRYPTO 1993. LNCS, vol. 773, pp. 13–21. Springer, Heidelberg (1994). https://doi.org/10.1007/3-540-48329-2_2

13. Véron, P.: Improved identification schemes based on error-correcting codes. Appl. Algebra Eng. Commun. Comput. 8(1), 5769 (1996)

14. Girault, M.: A (non-practical) three-pass identification protocol using coding theory. In: Seberry, J., Pieprzyk, J. (eds.) AUSCRYPT 1990. LNCS, vol. 453, pp. 265–272. Springer, Heidelberg (1990). https://doi.org/10.1007/BFb0030367

15. Berger, T.P., Cayrel, P.-L., Gaborit, P., Otmani, A.: Reducing key length of the McEliece cryptosystem. In: Preneel, B. (ed.) AFRICACRYPT 2009. LNCS, vol. 5580, pp. 77–97. Springer, Heidelberg (2009). https://doi.org/10.1007/978-3-642-02384-2_6

16. Misoczki, R., Barreto, P.S.L.M.: Compact McEliece keys from Goppa codes. In: Jacobson, M.J., Rijmen, V., Safavi-Naini, R. (eds.) SAC 2009. LNCS, vol. 5867, pp. 376–392. Springer, Heidelberg (2009). https://doi.org/10.1007/978-3-642-05445-7_24

Homomorphic Encryption

Securely Aggregating Testimonies with Threshold Multi-key **FHE**

Gerald Gavin[✉] and Stephane Bonnevay

Laboratory ERIC, University of Lyon, Lyon, France
{gerald.gavin,stephane.bonnevay}@univ-lyon1.fr

Abstract. Many data management applications, such as setting up Web portals, managing enterprise data, managing community data, and sharing scientific data, require integrating data from multiple sources. Each of these sources provides a set of values and different sources can often provide conflicting values. To discover the true values, data integration systems should resolve conflicts. In this paper, we present a formal probabilistic framework in the expert/authority setting. Each expert has a partial and maybe imperfect view of a binary target vector b that an authority wishes recovering. The goal of this paper consists of proposing a multi-party aggregating function of experts' views to recover b with an error rate as small as possible. In addition, it is assumed that some of the experts are corrupted by an adversary $\mathcal{A}$. This adversary controls and coordinates the behavior of the corrupted experts and can thus perturb the aggregating process. In this paper, we present a simple aggregating function and we provide a formal upper-bound over of the output vector error expectation in the worst case, i.e. whatever the behavior of the adversary is. We then propose to securely implement this aggregating function in order to preserve the privacy of experts' views. A natural secure implementation could be achieved with recent powerful cryptographic tools, i.e. Threshold Multi-key Fully Homomorphic Encryptions schemes (**TMFHE**). Finally, trade-off between the time complexity and the number of interaction rounds are proposed.

1 Introduction

Fusion of conflicting data, when for instance several experts have very different ideas about the same phenomenon, has long been identified as a challenging task in the data fusion community. The inherent imperfection of data is the most fundamental challenging problem of data fusion systems, and thus the bulk of research work has been focused on tackling this issue. In [DN09], the authors distinguish two kinds of data conflict: (a) uncertainty about the attribute value, caused by missing information; and (b) contradictions, caused by different attribute values.

There are a number of mathematical theories [KKKR13] available to represent data imperfection [She91], such as probability theory [DWH08], fuzzy set theory [Zad65], possibility theory [NZZ78], rough set theory [Paw92], and

© Springer Nature Switzerland AG 2019
C. Carlet et al. (Eds.): C2SI 2019, LNCS 11445, pp. 325–348, 2019.
https://doi.org/10.1007/978-3-030-16458-4_19

Dempster-Shafer evidence theory (DSET) [Fin77]. Most of these approaches are capable of representing specific aspect(s) of imperfect data. For example, a probabilistic distribution expresses data uncertainty, fuzzy set theory can represent vagueness of data, and evidential belief theory can represent uncertain as well as ambiguous data.

In [DBES09], the authors present a novel approach that considers dependence between data sources in truth discovery. Intuitively, if two data sources provide a large number of common values and many of these values are rarely provided by other sources (e.g., particular false values), it is very likely that one copies from the other. They apply bayesian analysis to decide dependence between sources and design an algorithm that iteratively detects dependence and discovers truth from conflicting information. They also extend their model by considering accuracy of data sources and similarity between values.

In this paper, each source/expert has a partial and maybe imperfect view of a target binary database b which can be seen as a binary vector. For concreteness, each expert only knows a subset of components of b with maybe some errors. In our model, the views of the experts are drawn according to a probability distribution D. In addition, we consider the existence of an unique entity, called an adversary, totally controlling a minority of sources/experts: in particular, it knows each corrupted expert view but not the views of uncorrupted experts (called honest experts). This adversary can be seen as an active noise generator. This paper aims to build a way to aggregate expert views in order to recover b whatever the behavior of the adversary is. As far as we know, it is the first time that such an assumption is considered in data fusion. The novelty of our approach makes difficult comparisons with other existing solutions. In our opinion, the main interest of the paper is that the proposed solution is totally formalized making clear the assumptions and the results.

We finally propose to securely implement this process in order to preserve privacy of experts' views. We propose a natural implementation with recent powerful cryptographic tools, i.e. Threshold Multi-key Fully Homomorphic Encryptions schemes (TMFHE) [LTV13,BHP17,MW15].

2   Problem Statement

Just to illustrate this problem from a police investigation perspective, let us consider T witnesses which have partially seen a crime scene and have identified a set $\mathcal{N}$ of n suspects. One of these witnesses is assumed to be the police. We consider the vector $b = (b_1, ..., b_n) \in \{-1, 1\}^n$ by $b_i = 1$ if and only if Suspect i is guilty. Witness j knows (maybe erroneously) the culpability or non-culpability of a subset $S_j \subset \mathcal{N}$ of the suspects, i.e., Witness j knows $(b_i)_{i \in S_j}$. An adversary $\mathcal{A}$ has corrupted some of the witnesses. The adversary $\mathcal{A}$ can change the testimony of any corrupted witness. Those witnesses which have not been corrupted are said to be honest. The challenge consists in elaborating a multi-party aggregating function allowing the police to recover b (or something close).

Let us consider now an other example in the user/server setting. The server wishes recovering a binary vector $b = (b_1, ..., b_n) \in \{-1, 1\}^n$. For instance, the server could be an online encyclopedia. In order to index its pages, some questions could be asked to the users. For instance, does the ith page contains pornographic pictures? Each user sends this information for a subset of pages. One can imagine that some users are corrupted by an adversary $\mathcal{A}$. How can the server fight against any adversary $\mathcal{A}$ to recover the truth about its pages?

Typically, an authority wishes recovering a binary vector $\boldsymbol{b}$ partially and imperfectly known by a set $\mathcal{J}$ of T experts. The knowledge of the jth expert can be represented by a vector $\varepsilon_j \in \{-1, 0, 1\}^n$ where $\varepsilon_{ji} = 0$ means that Expert j does not know b_i. Moreover, if $b_i\varepsilon_{ji} < 0$ means that b_i is erroneously known by Expert j. In this paper, we assume that $\varepsilon = (\varepsilon_1, \ldots, \varepsilon_T)$ is randomly drawn according to a probability distribution D. Each expert j sends its vector ε_j to the authority. The objective of the authority is to recover $\boldsymbol{b}$ from the values ε_{ji}. At this step, the problem is trivial for some probability distributions D. Indeed, if the experts do not input too many incorrect values ε_{ji} (i.e. $b_i\varepsilon_{ji} < 0$) then the majority vote is relevant, i.e. $(\text{sign}(\sum_{j \in \mathcal{J}} \varepsilon_{ji}))_{i=1,\ldots n} \approx \boldsymbol{b}$.

However, the majority vote strategy could be not relevant anymore if some experts misbehave by sending malicious values ε_{ji}. Worse, one can assume the existence of a coalition of experts aiming to perturb the recovering of $\boldsymbol{b}$. For concreteness, these experts decide to collaborate by elaborating a common malicious strategy. A simple way to represent this scenario consists of assuming the existence of an adversary $\mathcal{A}$ which has corrupted a minority $\mathcal{C} \subset \mathcal{J}$ of experts. $\mathcal{A}$ can be seen as an external unique entity which totally controls and coordinates the behavior of the corrupted experts[1]. In our problem, its power consists in arbitrarily modifying the vectors ε_j sent by the corrupted experts. The challenge consists in elaborating an aggregating function Aggregate allowing the authority to recover $\boldsymbol{b}$ (or something close) whatever the behavior of $\mathcal{A}$ is.

Clearly, for some probability distributions D, our problem cannot be solved. Indeed, let us assume that the sets $S_j = \{i \in \{1, \ldots n\}|\varepsilon_{ji} \neq 0\}$ do not overlap. In this case, each component b_i is known by at most one expert and it is not possible to distinguish a corrupted value from an honest one. Consequently, the adversary $\mathcal{A}$ could generate $\sum_{j \in \mathcal{C}} |S_j|$ errors in the recovering of $\boldsymbol{b}$ and nothing can be done to prevent this (without any other assumption). Thus, only probability distributions D ensuring overlapping makes our problem relevant.

In the next section we propose a formalization of this problem. In Sect. 4, we propose a function Aggregate exploiting the redundancy of the knowledge of the experts. The principle of this function is very simple. The experts which disagree on too many instances i with too many other experts are eliminated. It follows that a corrupted expert which inputs too many incorrect values is eliminated. Consequently, it should behave almost honestly to not be eliminated. In Sect. 5, we provide an upper-bound for the expectation error of the vector output by Aggregate in the worst case, i.e., independent of the adversary $\mathcal{A}$. In Sect. 6, numerical values dealing with simple probability distributions D are given.

---

[1] The definition and the properties of the adversaries considered in this paper are directly inspired from the Secure Multiparty Computation framework see ([OSA87, CDN01]).

The analysis of these results shows that Aggregate dramatically outperforms the naive approach consisting of taking a majority vote.

In Sect. 7, we propose the protocol SAggregate which securely implements Aggregate. The ideal implementation of SAggregate dealing with a trusted party $\mathfrak{T}$ is presented in Fig. 1.

Ideal implementation of SAggregate

Private inputs. Each expert $j \in \mathcal{J}$ has a secret vector $\varepsilon_j \in \{-1, 0, 1\}^n$

1. Each party $j \in \mathcal{J}$ sends ε_j to $\mathfrak{T}$
2. $\mathfrak{T}$ computes $o = \mathsf{Aggregate}(\varepsilon_1, \ldots, \varepsilon_T)$ and sends it to the authority.
3. The authority outputs o

Fig. 1. Ideal implementation of SAggregate assuming the existence of a trusted party $\mathfrak{T}$.

Our function Aggregate can be optimally represented by a boolean circuit. It follows that fully homomorphic encryptions (FHE) are natural tools to implement this function. More precisely, Threshold Multi-key FHE (TMFHE) will be considered in order to minimize the interactions between parties (the experts and the authority), i.e. two rounds of interactions can be achieved (with some additional cryptographic assumptions). However, the performance of current FHE are prohibitive for many real applications. We propose ways to reduce time complexity by accepting to slightly increase the number of communication rounds.

3   Formalization

Let n, T, ϑ be positive integers s.t. $\vartheta < T/2$, let $\mathcal{N} = \{1, \ldots, n\}$ and let $\Delta = \{-1, 0, 1\}^{n \times T}$. The target vector is denoted by $b \in \{-1, 1\}^n$ and $\mathcal{J} = \{1, \ldots, T\}$ refers to the set of the T experts. The set of the subsets $\mathcal{C} \subset \mathcal{J}$ s.t. $|\mathcal{C}| \leq \vartheta$ is denoted by $P_\vartheta(\mathcal{J})$.

3.1   Definition of $\mathcal{D}_\perp$

Definition 1. Let $\mathcal{V}$ be the set of probability distributions defined over $\{-1, 0, 1\}^n$ and let $\mathcal{D}$ denote the family of probability distributions over Δ defined by

$$\mathcal{D}_\perp = \{D_1 \times \cdots \times D_T | D_i \in \mathcal{V}\}$$

Throughout this paper, we will only consider probability distributions $D \in \mathcal{D}_\perp$ (defined over Δ). Let $(\varepsilon_1, \ldots, \varepsilon_T) \in \Delta$ be randomly drawn according to $D \in \mathcal{D}_\perp$. By definition of $\mathcal{D}_\perp$, it is ensured that the T vectors $\varepsilon_1, \ldots, \varepsilon_T$ are independent. In the setting of this paper, it means that each expert j has generated its vector ε_j independently of the vectors of the other experts. For instance, one can imagine that the experts are anonymous and do not know each other. It can make sense in an open network such as the Web. This will be used to simplify the adversary model by reducing its power. Conversely, one can easily imagine some settings where this assumption is not relevant and further investigations should be done to remove or at least to restrict it.

3.2   Overview

Let $\mathcal{K} \subseteq \mathcal{D}_\perp \times \{-1, 1\}^n$, let $(D, \boldsymbol{b}) \in \mathcal{K}$ and let $\varepsilon = (\varepsilon_1, \ldots, \varepsilon_T) \in \Delta$ be drawn according to D. The objective is to elaborate a function Aggregate : $\Delta \rightarrow \{-1, 1\}^n$ (computing by the authority) inputting ε and outputting a binary vector $\boldsymbol{o} \in \{-1, 1\}^n$ as close as possible to $\boldsymbol{b}$. More precisely, it is desired to minimize the error rate $er(\boldsymbol{o})$ defined as the Hamming distance between $\boldsymbol{b}$ and $\boldsymbol{o}$ divided by $2n$, i.e.,

$$er(\boldsymbol{o}) = \frac{1}{2n}\|\boldsymbol{o} - \boldsymbol{b}\|_1$$

In order to elaborate this function, the authority is not assumed to know $D, \boldsymbol{b}$ but only $\mathcal{K}$. As suggested in the introduction, we assume the existence of an adversary $\mathcal{A}$ able to corrupt a chosen subset $\mathcal{C}$ of experts. The set of uncorrupted experts (also called honest) is denoted by $\mathcal{H} = \mathcal{J} \setminus \mathcal{C}$. We propose to overestimate the real-life adversary power by assuming that it knows everything except the honest vectors ε_j (input by honest experts). In particular, it can be assumed that $\mathcal{A}$ knows the target vector $\boldsymbol{b}$, the probability distribution $D \in \mathcal{K}$, the function Aggregate and can replace corrupted expert inputs by arbitrary values in $\{-1, 0, 1\}$. In other words, $\mathcal{A}$ can arbitrarily modify at most ϑ vectors ε_j. Roughly speaking, $\mathcal{A}$ can be seen as an active noise generator. The vector $\boldsymbol{o}$ outputs by Aggregate should be as close as possible to $\boldsymbol{b}$ regardless of the behavior of $\mathcal{A}$. The authority wishes building a function Aggregate robust against any adversary $\mathcal{A}$ for families $\mathcal{K}$ as large as possible.

3.3   The Adversary Model

First, we consider an adversary $\mathcal{A}$ which can control at most $\vartheta < T/2$ experts: we do not see how to fight against adversaries corrupting a majority of experts. It is a quite restricting assumption for some realistic applications but it seems difficult to overcome it.

Moreover, in this paper we only consider probability distributions $D \in \mathcal{D}_\perp$. The adversary $\mathcal{A}$ is assumed to know $D, \boldsymbol{b}$ before to corrupts a subset $\mathcal{C} \subset \mathcal{J}$ of at most θ experts chosen arbitrarily. By definition of $\mathcal{D}_\perp$, the vectors $\varepsilon_1, \cdots, \varepsilon_T$ are independent. It means that the knowledge of the vectors $(\varepsilon_j)_{j \in \mathcal{C}}$

is not informative about the *honest* vectors $(\varepsilon_j)_{j \in \mathcal{H}}$. This can be used to restrict the power of the adversary $\mathcal{A}$ by assuming that it chooses the vectors[2] $(\varepsilon_j^*)_{j \in \mathcal{C}}$ *a priori*, i.e. before to know the vectors $(\varepsilon_j)_{j \in \mathcal{C}}$. In other words, $\mathcal{A}$ can be seen as a pair $(\mathcal{C}, \delta) \in P_\vartheta(\mathcal{J}) \times \Delta$ where $\mathcal{C}$ refers to the set of corrupted experts and δ contains the malicious values, i.e. for any $j \in \mathcal{C}$, Expert j inputs the jth row δ_j of δ. It should be noted that the number of adversary is finite.

3.4 The Objective

Consider a target vector $\boldsymbol{b}$, a probability distribution $D \in \mathcal{D}_\perp$, a function $\mathsf{Aggregate} : \Delta \to \{-1, 1\}^n$ and an adversary $\mathcal{A} = (\mathcal{C}, \delta)$. We define

$$er_\mathcal{A}^{\mathsf{Aggregate}}(D, \boldsymbol{b}) \stackrel{\text{def}}{=} E(er(\boldsymbol{o}))$$

as the expectation of $er(\boldsymbol{o}) = \frac{1}{2n} \|\boldsymbol{o} - \boldsymbol{b}\|_1$ where $\boldsymbol{o}$ is the vector output by the following protocol:

Protocol 1.

// In this protocol, it is assumed that all the communications are done via secure channels.

Parameters: n, T, θ

1. $\mathcal{A}$ corrupts a subset $\mathcal{C} \subset \mathcal{J}$ of at most θ experts,
2. Let $(\varepsilon_1, \ldots, \varepsilon_T)$ be drawn according to D,
3. Each expert $j \in \mathcal{J}$ receives[3] ε_j and sends a vector ε_j^* to the authority defined as follows:
$$\begin{cases} \varepsilon_j^* = \varepsilon_j \text{ if } j \in \mathcal{H} \\ \varepsilon_j^* = \delta_j \text{ if } j \in \mathcal{C} \end{cases}$$
4. The authority outputs $\boldsymbol{o} = \mathsf{Aggregate}(\varepsilon_1^*, \ldots, \varepsilon_T^*)$

The authority is interested in building a function $\mathsf{Aggregate}$ minimizing

$$er^{\mathsf{Aggregate}}(\mathcal{K}) = \sup_{\mathcal{A} \in P_\vartheta(\mathcal{J}) \times \Delta; (D, b) \in \mathcal{K}} er_\mathcal{A}^{\mathsf{Aggregate}}(D, \boldsymbol{b}) \tag{1}$$

for families $\mathcal{K}$ as large and realistic as possible[4].

---

[2] That it will send to the authority.

[3] For instance from real-life.

[4] As explained in the introduction, $\mathcal{K}$ cannot contain all probability distributions but only *redundant* ones.

4   A Proposal for **Aggregate**

4.1   Case of Perfect Honest Experts

We first assume that the experts do not receive incorrect values, i.e. $\varepsilon_{ji}b_i \geq 0$ for any $(i,j) \in \mathcal{N} \times \mathcal{J}$. Consequently, honest experts do not input incorrect values. Because of this assumption, we can define a natural elimination strategy where the honest experts cannot be eliminated and the corrupted experts cannot input too many incorrect values without being eliminated. Our solution exploits the fact that honest experts only input correct values and that the corrupted experts are in a minority. We say that two experts j and j' are **compatible** if they do not disagree on at least one instance $i \in \mathcal{N}$. For any $j \in \mathcal{J}$, $\alpha(j)$ refers to the subset of experts $j' \in \mathcal{J}$ which are compatible with j.

$$\alpha(j) = \{j' \in \mathcal{J} \mid \forall i \in \mathcal{N} \ \varepsilon^*_{ji}\varepsilon^*_{j'i} \geq 0\}.$$

Clearly, for each $j \in \mathcal{H}$

$$|\alpha(j)| \geq |\mathcal{H}| \geq T - \vartheta.$$

The definition of the function **Aggregate** is based on this fact. It simply consists of eliminating experts $j \in \mathcal{J}$ verifying $|\alpha(j)| < T - \vartheta$ before estimating b by a majority vote (See Table 1). In other words, the weight w_j of Expert j in the majority vote is defined by

$$w_j = \begin{cases} 1 \text{ if } |\alpha(j)| \geq T - \vartheta \\ 0 \text{ otherwise.} \end{cases}$$

According to the previous discussion, honest experts are not eliminated. Intuitively, if a corrupted expert inputs many incorrect values, then it becomes incompatible with almost all honest experts, implying that it is eliminated because $|\alpha(j)| \approx \vartheta < T - \vartheta$. As a corollary, a corrupted expert should behave "almost honestly" in order to avoid elimination. This naturally leads to the following definition of **Aggregate**.

$$\text{Aggregate}(\varepsilon^*_1, \ldots, \varepsilon^*_T) = \left(\text{sign} \left(\sum_{j \in \mathcal{J}} w_j \ \varepsilon^*_{ji} \right) \right)_{i \in \mathcal{N}}$$

4.2   General Case

In this section, we extend the previous study by assuming that honest experts can input incorrect values ε_{ji}, i.e. $\varepsilon_{ji}b_i < 0$. The function **Aggregate** should be adapted to not exclude too many honest experts. To achieve this, it suffices to strengthen the definition of incompatibility between two experts and to relax the strategy of elimination. The new function **Aggregate** is parameterized by two new positive integers $0 \leq \sigma \leq n$ and $0 \leq \tau \leq T - 2\vartheta$. Two experts j and j' are **compatible** if they do not disagree on more than σ instances $i \in \mathcal{N}$ and an expert will be eliminated if it is compatible with less than $T - \vartheta - \tau$ experts.

Table 1. Table illustrating the Majority Vote (MV) and Aggregate (Agg) in the case $n = 5, T = 5, \theta = 2$. The sets $\alpha(j)$ computed in Aggregate$(\varepsilon_1^*, \ldots, \varepsilon_5^*)$ are equal to $\alpha(1) = \alpha(2) = \alpha(5) = \{1, 2, 5\}$ and $\alpha(3) = \alpha(4) = \{3, 4\}$. As $|\alpha(3)| = |\alpha(4)| \leq T - \theta = 3$, Expert 3 and Expert 4 are eliminated, i.e. $w_3 = w_4 = 0$. It follows that Aggregate$(\varepsilon_1^*, \ldots, \varepsilon_5^*)$ consists of taking a majority vote over $\varepsilon_1^*, \varepsilon_2^*$ and ε_5^*. We see that Aggregate outperforms the majority vote in this example.

ε_1^*	ε_2^*	ε_3^*	ε_4^*	ε_5^*	b	MV	Agg
-1	0	1	1	0	-1	1	-1
0	-1	1	1	0	-1	1	-1
1	1	1	0	0	1	1	1
1	0	1	0	1	1	1	1
1	1	0	0	1	1	1	1
0	1	0	0	1	1	1	1

Aggregate$_{\sigma, \tau}\left(\varepsilon_1^*, \ldots, \varepsilon_T^*\right)$

---

1. $I(j, j') := \{i \in \mathcal{N} \mid \varepsilon_{ji}^* \varepsilon_{j'i}^* < 0\}$
   //$I(j, j')$ is the set of components of b where the experts j and j' disagree

2. $\alpha(j) := \{j' \in \mathcal{J} \mid |I(j, j')| \leq \sigma\}$
   //$\alpha(j)$ is the set of the experts compatible with Expert j

3. $w_j := \begin{cases} 1 \text{ if } |\alpha(j)| \geq T - \vartheta - \tau \\ 0 \text{ otherwise.} \end{cases}$
   // w_j is the weight of Expert j in the final vote

4. Output $\left(\text{sign}\left(\sum_{j \in \mathcal{J}} w_j \; \varepsilon_{ji}^*\right)\right)_{i \in \mathcal{N}}$

The previous section deals with the case $\sigma = \tau = 0$. In practice, σ, τ are chosen as large as possible ensuring that the honest experts are eliminated with a very small probability. The running-time of Aggregate is

$$O(nT^2)$$

5   Analysis

Let $\mathcal{K} \subset \mathcal{D}_\perp \times \{-1, 1\}^n$. In this section, we propose an upper bound of $er^{\text{Aggregate}_{\sigma, \tau}}(\mathcal{K})$ which can be efficiently computed for some families of probability distributions $\mathcal{K}$. Given $(D, b) \in \mathcal{K}$ and a subset $\mathcal{H} \subset \mathcal{J}$ of honest experts, we consider the two quantities $\Gamma_{D,b,\mathcal{H}}(u,v)$ and $\rho_{D,b,\mathcal{H}}^{\sigma,\tau}$ defined as follows (these quantities are formally defined in Appendix A):

- $\Gamma_{D,b,\mathcal{H}}(u,v)$ is the probability that (strictly) more than u components of b are (correctly) known[5] by (strictly) less than v honest experts.
- $\rho_{D,b,\mathcal{H}}^{\sigma,\tau}$ is the probability there is at least one honest expert incompatible with more than τ other honest experts. Note that $\rho_{D,b,\mathcal{H}}^{\sigma,\tau}$ upper-bounds the probability that at least one honest expert is eliminated.

We then consider the suprema $\Gamma_{\mathcal{K}}(u,v)$, $\rho_{\mathcal{K}}^{\sigma,\tau}$ of these quantities over the choices of $(D,b) \in \mathcal{K}$ and $\mathcal{H} \subset \mathcal{J}$ s.t. $|\mathcal{H}| \geq T - \vartheta$.

$$\Gamma_{\mathcal{K}}(u,v) = \max_{(D,b)\in\mathcal{K};H\subset\mathcal{J}:|\mathcal{H}|\geq T-\vartheta} \Gamma_{D,b,\mathcal{H}}(u,v)$$

$$\rho_{\mathcal{K}}^{\sigma,\tau} = \max_{(D,b)\in\mathcal{K};H\subset\mathcal{J}:|\mathcal{H}|\geq T-\vartheta} \rho_{D,b,\mathcal{H}}^{\sigma,\tau}$$

Moreover, the number of incorrect values ε_{ji}^* sent to the authority by the corrupted experts which are not eliminated[6] is denoted by $\Omega_{\mathcal{A},D,b}^{\sigma,\tau}$ (see Appendix A to get a formal definition). The supremum of the expectation of this quantity is denoted by $\Omega_{\mathcal{K}}^{\sigma,\tau}$, i.e.

$$\Omega_{\mathcal{K}}^{\sigma,\tau} = \max_{\mathcal{A}\in P_\vartheta(\mathcal{J})\times\Delta,(D,b)\in\mathcal{K}} E(\Omega_{\mathcal{A},D,b}^{\sigma,\tau})$$

These three suprema can be used to upper-bound $er^{\mathsf{Aggregate}_{\sigma,\tau}}(\mathcal{K})$.

Proposition 1. *We have,*

$$er^{\mathsf{Aggregate}_{\sigma,\tau}}(\mathcal{K}) \leq \rho_{\mathcal{K}}^{\sigma,\tau}$$

$$+ \min_{0\leq u\leq n;0\leq v\leq T} \left(\Gamma_{\mathcal{K}}(u,v) + \frac{u}{n} + \frac{\Omega_{\mathcal{K}}^{\sigma,\tau}}{nv} \right)$$

Proof (Sketch). See Appendix B for details. Let u,v be integers arbitrarily chosen. Let us consider the event "$E \equiv$ *no honest expert is eliminated and there are at least u components $I = \{i_1,\ldots,i_{t\leq u}\}$ such that $\sum_{j\in\mathcal{H}}\varepsilon_{ji_k} \leq v$ for any $k = 1,\ldots,t$*". E is not satisfied with a probability smaller that than $\rho_{\mathcal{K}}^{\sigma,\tau} + \Gamma_{\mathcal{K}}(u,v)$. In this case, we upper-bound the error rate by 1. Assume now that E is satisfied. In this case, the error can be upper-bounded by $\frac{u}{n} + \frac{\Omega}{nv}$ where Ω is the number of input malicious values: it suffices to assume that the components $b_{i\in I}$ are erroneously predicted and to notice that at most $\frac{\Omega}{v}$ components of $\mathcal{N} \setminus I$ can be erroneously predicted. We conclude by using the fact that $E(\Omega) \leq \Omega_{\mathcal{K}}^{\sigma,\tau}$.

For some families of probability distributions $\mathcal{K}$, there exists σ,τ such that this upper-bound is small and can be efficiently computed. This is the object of the next section.

---

[5] We say that a component b_i is correctly known by v honest experts if $b_i \sum_{j\in\mathcal{H}}\varepsilon_{ji} = v$.
[6] We say that Expert j is eliminated when $w_j = 0$. An eliminated expert does not participate in the majority vote.

6   Numerical Application

Notation. $\mathcal{B}_{p,m}$ denotes the cdf of the binomial distribution with parameters p, m. Let $X_1, \ldots, X_m$ be m independent random variables belonging to $\{-1, 0, 1\}$ drawn according to the same probability distribution, i.e. $\Pr(X_i = k) = p_k$. The cdf of the probability distribution of $Z = X_1 + \cdots + X_m$ is denoted by $\mathcal{B}_{p_{-1}, p_0, m}$.

Let $p, p_e \in [0, 1]$ such that $p_e < p$. In this section, we consider a very simple family $\mathcal{K}_{p,p_e} \subset \mathcal{D}_\perp \times \{-1, 1\}^n$ where any $(D, \boldsymbol{b}) \in \mathcal{K}_{p,p_e}$ satisfies the following properties. Each component of $\boldsymbol{b}$ is correctly known by an expert with a probability larger than $p - p_e$ and incorrectly known with a probability smaller than p_e. Roughly speaking, an expert has an opinion over a component of $\boldsymbol{b}$ with a probability larger than p. We formally define $\mathcal{K}_{p,p_e}$ as follows.

Definition 2. Let $D \in \mathcal{D}_\perp$, $\boldsymbol{b} \in \{-1, 1\}^n$ and $(\boldsymbol{c}_1, \ldots, \boldsymbol{c}_T)$ drawn according to D. The family $\mathcal{K}_{p,p_e}$ contains all the pairs $(D, \boldsymbol{b})$ satisfying

- ε_{ji} and $\varepsilon_{j'i'}$ are independent if $(i, j) \neq (i', j')$.
- $\Pr(\varepsilon_{ji} \neq 0) \geq p$
- $\Pr(b_i \varepsilon_{ji} < 0) \leq p_e$.

The quantities $\Gamma_{\mathcal{K}_{p,p_e}}(u, v)$, $\rho_{\mathcal{K}_{p,p_e}}^{\sigma,\tau}$ and $\Omega_{\mathcal{K}_{p,p_e}}^{\sigma,\tau}$ can be easily computed or at least upper-bounded.

Lemma 1. We have,

1. $\Omega_{\mathcal{K}_{p,p_e}}^{\sigma,\tau} \leq \vartheta \cdot \max_{i \in U} \left(i \mathcal{B}_{1 - \mathcal{B}_{p-p_e, i}(\sigma), T - \vartheta}(\vartheta + \tau) \right)$
2. $\Gamma_{\mathcal{K}_{p,p_e}}(u, v) = 1 - \mathcal{B}_{\mathcal{B}_{p_e, 1-p, T-\vartheta}(v-1), n}(u)$
3. $\rho_{\mathcal{K}_{p,p_e}}^{\sigma,\tau} \leq T \cdot \left(1 - \mathcal{B}_{1 - \mathcal{B}_{2p_e(p-p_e), n}(\sigma), T-\vartheta-1}(\tau) \right)$

Proof. See Appendix C

$\square$

By injecting these upper-bounds in the inequality of Proposition 1, we get an upper-bound $UB_{p,p_e,\sigma,\tau}$ of $er^{\mathsf{Aggregate}_{\sigma,\tau}}(\mathcal{K}_{p,p_e})$. Evaluating $UB_{p,p_e,\sigma,\tau}$ requires computing a "min" over a finite set. To achieve this, we propose a brute force computation by considering all the possible cases. For the parameters used in our experiments, no optimizations are needed[7]. Let us recall that σ, τ are parameters of Aggregate and thus they can be arbitrarily chosen. Let σ^*, τ^* minimizing $UB_{p,p_e,\sigma,\tau}$, i.e.

$$(\sigma^*, \tau^*) \overset{\text{def}}{=} \underset{0 \leq \sigma \leq n; 0 \leq \tau \leq T-2\vartheta}{\arg\min} UB_{p,p_e,\sigma,\tau}$$

Recovering σ^*, τ^* requires computing a "min" over a finite set. To achieve this, we propose a brute force computation by considering all the possible cases.

---

[7] In fact, $\Gamma_{D,\mathcal{H}}(u, v)$ converges quickly to 0 when u, v grow. Thus, only "small" values of u and v need considered.

Table 2. Computation of $UB_{p,0,0,0}$ for several values of n, T, ϑ, p.

$(n, T, p) \setminus \vartheta/T$	0.10	0.20	0.25	0.30	0.35	0.40
$(10^2, 10^3, 0.2)$	0.0%	1.3%	2.1%	4.8%	9.0%	18.8%
$(10^3, 10^3, 0.1)$	0.2%	1.0%	1.8%	3.5%	6.2%	10.0%
$(10^3, 10^2, 0.1)$	0.8%	3.8%	6.3%	9.7%	15.2%	23.0%
$(10^4, 10^2, 0.1)$	0.1%	0.4%	0.7%	1.2%	2.0%	3.4%
$(10^4, 50, 0.1)$	0.9%	1.7%	2.1%	3.0%	3.9%	5.8%
$(10^4, 50, 0.2)$	0.0%	0.1%	0.1%	0.3%	0.4%	0.9%

Results. Computations of $UB_{p,0,0,0}$ are proposed (see Table 2) for several values of n, T, ϑ, p. For instance when $n = 1000$, $T = 1000$, $p = 0.1$, $p_e = 0$ and $\vartheta = T/4 = 250$, the error rate $er^{\mathsf{Aggregate}_{0,0}}(\mathcal{K}_{p,0})$ is less than 2% on average against any adversary $\mathcal{A}$. These results could be compared to the naive approach consisting of a simple majority vote. In (almost) all our experiments, $\vartheta \geq p(T - \vartheta)$ ensuring that this naive strategy leads to an error rate larger than 50% in the worst case, i.e. each corrupted experts sends n incorrect values. Indeed, in this case, the number of honest inputs is, in mean, smaller than the number of corrupted inputs making the majority vote fail.

Moreover, for several pairs (n, T), we fixed $\vartheta = T/5$ and we searched[8] p ensuring that $UB_{p,0,0,0} \approx 1\%$ (see Table 3). We observe that p decreases with both n and T. For instance, it suffices that each honest expert knows each component of b with a probability larger than 7.7% to allow the authority to recover b with an error smaller (in mean) than 1% when the number of experts is larger than 1600 and the size of b is larger than 1600.

Table 3. Given $n, T, \vartheta = T/5$, we give a value of p ensuring that $UB_{p,0,0,0} = 1 \pm 0.1\%$. This value was obtained by a dichotomic search.

$n \setminus T$	200	400	800	1600	3200	6400
200	27.3%	24.1%	24.1%	24.1%	24.1%	24.1%
400	23.0%	17.5%	14.2%	13.4%	13.3%	13.3%
800	18.6%	12.6%	12.0%	10.9%	9.8%	9.3%
1600	14.2%	9.8%	8.5%	7.7%	7.7%	7.1%
3200	12.3%	7.7%	6.3%	5.5%	5.5%	5.2%
6400	9.8%	6.0%	4.9%	4.4%	3.8%	3.8%
12800	6.0%	4.4%	3.8%	3.2%	3.0%	2.8%

Computations of $UB_{p,p_e,\sigma^*,\tau^*}$ for different values of ϑ, p, p_e are presented in Table 4. As expected, we see that σ^*, τ^* grow with p_e and ϑ.

---

[8] With a dichotomic search.

Table 4. Fix $n = 2000$ and $T = 500$, we computed $\mathsf{UB}_{p,p_e,\sigma^*,\tau^*}$ for different values of ϑ, p, p_e. The optimal parameters τ^*, σ^* are given in subscript.

$(p, p_e) \setminus \vartheta/T$	0.10	0.20	0.30	0.40
$(5\%, 0.15\%)$	$2.3\%_{100,0}$	$7.0\%_{90,0}$	$18.2\%_{80,0}$	$51.8\%_{50,0}$
$(10\%, 0.30\%)$	$1.2\%_{250,0}$	$3.5\%_{80,1}$	$7.9\%_{70,1}$	$19.2\%_{60,1}$
$(15\%, 0.45\%)$	$0.8\%_{220,1}$	$2.4\%_{200,1}$	$5.3\%_{90,2}$	$12.3\%_{70,2}$
$(20\%, 0.60\%)$	$0.7\%_{240,2}$	$1.9\%_{60,1}$	$4.1\%_{110,3}$	$8.6\%_{200,4}$
$(p, p_e) \setminus \vartheta/T$	0.10	0.20	0.30	0.40
$(5\%, 0.3\%)$	$3.3\%_{160,0}$	$9.9\%_{140,0}$	$25.2\%_{120,0}$	$65.7\%_{30,1}$
$(10\%, 0.6\%)$	$1.9\%_{190,1}$	$5.3\%_{170,1}$	$12.2\%_{70,2}$	$26.7\%_{60,2}$
$(15\%, 0.9\%)$	$1.6\%_{260,2}$	$4.0\%_{150,3}$	$8.4\%_{130,3}$	$17.2\%_{60,4}$
$(20\%, 1.2\%)$	$1.4\%_{270,4}$	$3.3\%_{170,5}$	$6.6\%_{100,6}$	$13.3\%_{50,7}$
$(p, p_e) \setminus \vartheta/T$	0.10	0.20	0.30	0.40
$(5\%, 0.45\%)$	$4.4\%_{200,0}$	$12.9\%_{180,0}$	$32.7\%_{50,1}$	$72\%_{40,1}$
$(10\%, 0.9\%)$	$2.7\%_{270,1}$	$7.1\%_{40,1}$	$15.2\%_{120,1}$	$32.7\%_{50,3}$
$(15\%, 1.35\%)$	$2.1\%_{190,4}$	$5.4\%_{170,4}$	$11.1\%_{90,5}$	$23.0\%_{80,5}$
$(20\%, 1.8\%)$	$1.9\%_{340,5}$	$4.6\%_{180,7}$	$9.1\%_{110,8}$	$17.8\%_{70,9}$

7   The Protocol **SAggregate**

Notation. $n, T, \theta, \sigma, \tau$ *will refer to the parameters of* **Aggregate** *as defined in the previous sections. They might be omitted in notation. The addition and the multiplication over* $\mathbb{Z}/2\mathbb{Z}$ *will be denoted respectively by* $\oplus$ *and* $\otimes$.

This section aims at proposing a protocol **SAggregate** which securely implements the multi-party functionality **Aggregate** described in Sect. 4. For concreteness, we wish to implement the ideal model (see Fig. 1) dealing with a truted party $\mathfrak{T}$. In this ideal model, each expert/party $j \in \mathcal{J}$ sends its private vector ε_j to $\mathfrak{T}$. Then, $\mathfrak{T}$ evaluates $o := \mathsf{Aggregate}(\varepsilon_1, \ldots, \varepsilon_T)$ and sends it to the authority. In this section, we propose to remove the trusted party $\mathfrak{T}$ and to build a protocol **SAggregate** between the $T + 1$ parties (the T parties of $\mathcal{J}$ and the authority) offering the same security guarantees as the ideal model. For instance, **SAggregate** should ensure that the output vector o is correct and that the input vectors ε_j are not revealed to other parties. As done in previous sections, we consider an adversary $\mathcal{A}$ controlling a subset of parties (See Sect. 3.3). This adversary can control and coordinate the behaviour of corrupted parties. The implementation of **SAggregate** is required to be secure against any subset of corrupted parties[9] while **Aggregate** is relevant in the case of an honest majority. Such security requirements are nevertheless useful. Indeed, this will ensure, for instance, that the honest input ε_{ji} remain private even if the adversary controls a majority.

---

[9] At least one party should be honest.

7.1   Secure Multi-party Computation

Yao [Yao86] has proved that any multi-party functionality can be securely computed. Several MPC models allowing to securely realize any multi-party functionality are proposed in the literature. Some of these models are based on oblivious transfer protocols, others are based on threshold homomorphic scheme, verifiable secret sharing or homomorphic secret sharing. A fundamental theorem says that any multi-party problem can be securely computed:

- Computational setting: for any number of corruptions and assuming trapdoor permutations,
- Information theoretic setting: for a 2/3 majority (or regular majority given a broadcast channel).

Secure MPC protocols complexities are measured in rounds of interaction, number of communicated bits and computational overhead. Optimizing these three complexities at the same time is challenging and trade-off are often required. Many identified applications of SAggregate deal with internet where stable communications between a large number of parties is not guaranteed. Ideally, it would be suitable to develop a *on-the-fly* protocol ([LTV13]) in which the set of parties who contribute inputs to the computation, and even the computation itself, need not be fixed in advance, and can even be chosen adaptively. In addition, there is no interaction among the parties: any user whose data might potentially be used simply uploads her encrypted input to a central server in advance, and can then go offline. The server then uses the uploaded data to compute (or continue computing) a desired function, and when finished, outputs an encrypted output. Finally, the parties whose inputs were used in the computation and only those parties run an interactive protocol to jointly decrypt the ciphertext and obtain the output. Minimizing the number of rounds of interaction is clearly crucial to reach this ideal setting (requiring two rounds).

Round Complexity of MPC. We refer the reader to [AJL+12] for a comprehensive overview of prior work on round complexity of MPC. Brakerski et al. [BHP17] recently propose a 4-round MPC without setup. However, with a common random string (CRS), there is only a simple lower bound of 2-rounds [HLP11]. Asharov et al. [AJL+12] showed how to achieve a 3-round MPC protocol in the CRS model, by relying on techniques from threshold fully homomorphic encryption (TFHE). Their construction achieves semi-honest security under the learning with errors (LWE) assumption, and fully malicious security by assuming the existence of non-interactive zero knowledge arguments (NIZKs).

In order to reach two rounds, multi-key threshold fully homomorphic encryptions (MTFHE) were recently introduced in order to remove the round of interactions required to generate keys [MW15]. Indeed, a MTFHE scheme allows parties to independently encrypt their data under different individually chosen keys, while still allowing homomorphic computations over such ciphertexts.

7.2 Threshold Multi-key Fully Homomorphic Encryption (TMFHE)

TMFHE are natural tools [MW15], [BHP17] for constructing MPC based on fully homomorphic encryption (FHE). At a high level, this approach is based on the following simple template:

1. Each party individually chooses its own TMFHE key pair (pk_i, sk_i), encrypts its input x_i under pk_i, and broadcasts the resulting ciphertext(s). At the end of this round, each party can homomorphically compute the desired function f on the received ciphertexts and derive common multi-key ciphertexts which encrypt the output $(y_1, \ldots, y_n) = f(x_1, \ldots, x_T)$.
2. The parties run a secure distributed protocol for *threshold decryption* using their secret keys sk_i to decrypt the multi-key ciphertext and recover the output y in plaintext.

Secure protocols for threshold decryption can be implemented generically for any FHE scheme by using general MPC techniques, but this would require many rounds. Based on the LWE assumption (and auxiliary general cryptographic assumptions detailed later), the above template results in a 2-round MPC protocol.

High-level Description of TMFHE. Below we call any ciphertext/encryption which is associated with multiple keys an expanded ciphertext/encryption. Also, the ciphertexts that are generated by the encryption procedure (and thus corresponds to a single key) are called fresh ciphertexts, and the expanded ciphertexts that are output by the homomorphic evaluations are called evaluated ciphertexts or simply evaluations.

Definition 3 (Threshold Multi-key FHE). *A threshold multi-key FHE is a tuple of algorithms/protocols* MTFHE = (Setup, Keygen, Encrypt, Expand, Eval, Decrypt) *described as follows:*

- *params* ← *Setup*(1^λ): *Setup takes as input the security parameter* λ *and outputs the system parameters* **params**. *We assume that all the other algorithms take params as an input implicitly.*
- (sk, pk) ← *Keygen*(*params*): *Output secret key* sk *and public key* pk.
- c ← *Encrypt*(pk, x, pk): *On input* pk *and some message* $x \in \mathbb{Z}_2$ *output a ciphertext* c.
- $\widehat{c}$:= *Expand*(($pk_1, \ldots, pk_T$), i, c): *Given a sequence of* T *public-keys and a fresh ciphertext* c *under the* i^{th} *key* pk_i, *it outputs an expanded ciphertext* $\widehat{c}$.
- $\widehat{c}$:= *Eval*($\mathcal{C}$, ($\widehat{c}_1, \ldots, \widehat{c}_m$)): *Given a boolean circuit* $\mathcal{C} : \mathbb{Z}_2^m \to \mathbb{Z}_2^\ell$ *along expanded ciphertexts* ($\widehat{c}_1, \ldots, \widehat{c}_m$), *outputs evaluated ciphertexts* ($\widehat{c}_1', \ldots, \widehat{c}_\ell'$).
- x := *Decrypt*(($sk_1, \ldots, sk_T$), $\widehat{c}$): *On input some ciphertext* $\widehat{c}$ *and a sequence of* T *secret keys output a message* $x \in \mathbb{Z}_2$.

In addition, we will consider the auxiliary protocol PrivateDecrypt (straightforwardly derived from Decrypt).

- x := PrivateDecrypt(($sk_1, \ldots, sk_T$), $\widehat{c}, j$): *On input some ciphertext* $\widehat{c}$ *and a sequence of* T *secret keys, Party* j *outputs a message* $x \in \mathbb{Z}_2$.

Correctness and Security (Informal). We classically say that a public-key encryption scheme is semantically secure (or equivalently IND-CPA secure) if there does not exist any p.p.t. algorithm able to distinguish between encryptions of 0 and encryptions of 1, knowing params and the public key pk used to encrypt.

MTFHE.Expand is correct if the decryption of the output expanded ciphertext $\widehat{c}$ is equal to the value encrypted by the input fresh ciphertext c.

Finally MTFHE.Eval and MTFHE.Decrypt are correct if the evaluated ciphertexts $(\widehat{c}'_1, \ldots, \widehat{c}'_\ell)$ encrypt $(x'_1, \ldots, x'_\ell) = C(x_1, \ldots, x_m)$, where $(x_1, \ldots, x_m)$ are the values encrypted by the input expanded ciphertexts $(\widehat{c}_1, \ldots, \widehat{c}_m)$[10].

TMFHE in MPC. Let us detail the template presented at the beginning of this section. Each involved party j locally generates (pk_j, sk_j) with MTFHE.KeyGen, encrypts its private data x_j with pk_j and broadcasts it with pk_j. Then, each party applies MTFHE.Expand on all the received ciphertexts and (locally) evaluates C with MTFHE.Eval over the expanded ciphertexts previously built. At this step each party as the same tuple of evaluated ciphertexts $\widehat{c}_1, \ldots, \widehat{c}_\ell$. Finally, MTFHE.Decrypt is invoked over $\widehat{c}_1, \ldots, \widehat{c}_\ell$ to recover the expected plaintexts.

Intrinsic limits of TMFHE in MPC. Any boolean function $f(x_1, \ldots, x_m)$ can be written as a boolean circuit $C(x_1, \ldots, x_m)$. However, some functionalities f cannot be efficiently represented by arithmetic circuits C. For concreteness, some functionalities f could be evaluated in polynomial-time while there does not exit any polynomial-size boolean circuit C representing f. Typically, branching algorithms are required to implement such functionalities. This represents a serious restriction of FHE in MPC. Nevertheless, this is not a problem here because Aggregate can be optimally represented by an arithmetic (or boolean) circuit.

7.3   LWE-Based (TM)FHE

LWE [Reg05] is a famous cryptographic problem allowing to efficiently implement many cryptographic primitives such as FHE, signatures, etc. Roughly speaking, this problem relies on the difficulty to solve noisy linear systems. Typically, ciphertexts/evaluations of LWE-based FHE are noisy and the noise level grows with the size of the evaluated circuit C. Decryption becomes incorrect when noise becomes too large. It follows that noise should be controlled to achieve unlimited numbers of homomorphic operations. LWE-based FHE are currently the most efficient [GSW13] and some of them can be adapted in one-round decryption TMFHE leading to the following result.

Proposition 2 *(in [MW15]). Assume LWE is hard, there exist TMFHE leading to 2-round MPC protocols assuming the CRS model and the existence of NIZKs.*

---

[10] Decrypt(params, $(sk_1, \ldots, sk_T)$, Eval(params, C, $(\widehat{c}_1, \ldots, \widehat{c}_m)$))) $= C$(Decrypt(params, $(sk_1, \ldots, sk_T), \widehat{c}_1), \ldots,$ Decrypt(params, $(sk_1, \ldots, sk_T), \widehat{c}_m)$).

The CRS model is required in the choice of common parameters between the involved parties (without the CRS model, corrupted parties might get an advantage in this phase). Finally, (NIZKs) are required to ensure fulfilment of the decryption without any additional round.

7.4 SAggregate

As FHE can locally evaluate any arithmetic circuit or equivalently any boolean circuit, it suffices to write the output vector o as a boolean circuit defined over the input vectors $\varepsilon_1, \ldots, \varepsilon_T$. Let us re-write Aggregate in this sense. As the plaintext space is $\mathbb{Z}_2$, we propose to re-write each input $\varepsilon_{ji} \in \{-1, 0, 1\}$ as a pair $(\varepsilon_{1ji}, \varepsilon_{2ji}) \in \mathbb{Z}_2^2$ such that

$$(\varepsilon_{1ji}, \varepsilon_{2ji}) = \begin{cases} (0, 1), \text{ if } \varepsilon_{ji} = -1 \\ (1, 1), \text{ if } \varepsilon_{ji} = 1 \\ (\cdot, 0), \text{ if } \varepsilon_{ji} = 0 \end{cases}$$

If follows that $\varepsilon_{ji}\varepsilon'_{ji} < 0$ if and only if $(\varepsilon_{1ji} \oplus \varepsilon'_{1ji}) \otimes \varepsilon_{2ji}\varepsilon'_{2ji} = 1$. We then consider the functions:

- SUM$((b_0, \ldots, b_r)) \in \{0, 1\}^r)$ outputs the binary representation $x_0, \ldots, x_{\lfloor \log_2 r \rfloor + 1}$ of $b_1 + \ldots + b_r$ (integer sum).
- COMPARE$((b_0, \ldots, b_r) \in \{0, 1\}^r, (b'_0, \ldots, b'_r) \in \{0, 1\}^r)$ outputs 1 if[11] $(b_0, \ldots, b_r)_2 \geq (b'_0, \ldots, b'_r)_2$ and 0 otherwise.

These functions can be optimally evaluated by boolean circuits or equivalently by $(\oplus, \otimes)$-circuits.

Lemma 2. *The function SUM can be represented by a size-$O(r \log r)$ boolean circuit and COMPARE by a size-$O(r)$ boolean circuit.*

Proof. High school exercise.

$\square$

It then suffices to write Aggregate as a $(\oplus, \otimes)$-circuit $C_{\mathsf{Aggregate}}$ by using these simple circuits (see Fig. 2). By exploiting the fact that SUM and COMPARE can be optimally implemented by boolean circuits, Aggregate can be implemented by a $(\oplus, \otimes)$-circuit $C_{\mathsf{Aggregate}}$ with $O(T^2 n \log n + T^2 \log T)$ gates. This is optimal (neglecting logarithmic factors) in the sense that the running-time of any algorithm implementing Aggregate is $\Omega(nT^2)$. To implement SAggregate with TMFHE, it then suffices to evaluate $C_{\mathsf{Aggregate}}$ by following the general template presented at the beginning of Sect. 7.2 (see Fig. 3).

Proposition 3. *SAggregate securely realizes Aggregate assuming IND-CPA security of TMFHE.*

Proof. Aggregate exactly follows MPC constructions based on TMFHE.

$\square$

---

[11] $(b_1, \ldots, b_r)_2$ refers to the integer whose binary representation is $(b_1, \ldots, b_r)$.

$\mathcal{C}_{\mathsf{Aggregate}}\left((\varepsilon_{1ji}, \varepsilon_{2ji})_{(j,i)\in\mathcal{J}\times\mathcal{N}}\right)$

Notation. The binary representation of an integer x is denoted by $(x)_2$

Parameters: $n, T, \theta, \sigma, \tau$

1. **for** any $(j, j') \in \mathcal{J}^2$
   for any $i \in \mathcal{N}$
   $$x_{ijj'} := (\varepsilon_{1ji} \oplus \varepsilon'_{1ji}) \otimes \varepsilon_{2ji}\varepsilon'_{2ji}$$
   $$z_{jj'} := \mathsf{SUM}(x_{1jj'}, \ldots, x_{njj'}) \ // \ z_{jj'} \text{ is a boolean tuple}$$
   $$y_{jj'} := \mathsf{COMPARE}((\sigma)_2, z_{jj'}) \ // \ y_{jj'} \text{ is a boolean tuple}$$

2. **for** any $j \in \mathcal{J}$
   $$p_j := \mathsf{SUM}(y_{j1}, \ldots, y_{jT})$$
   $$w_j := \mathsf{COMPARE}(p_j, (T - \theta - \tau)_2)$$

3. **for** any $i \in \mathcal{N}$
   $$u_i := \mathsf{SUM}(w_1 \otimes \varepsilon_{11i} \otimes \varepsilon_{21i}, \ldots, w_T \otimes \varepsilon_{1Ti} \otimes \varepsilon_{2Ti})$$
   $$v_i := \mathsf{SUM}(w_1 \otimes (\varepsilon_{11i} \oplus 1) \otimes \varepsilon_{21i}, \ldots, w_T \otimes (\varepsilon_{1Ti} \oplus 1) \otimes \varepsilon_{2Ti})$$
   $$o_i := \mathsf{COMPARE}(u_i, v_i)$$

Fig. 2. Implementing $\mathsf{Aggregate}$ as a $(\oplus, \otimes)$-circuit $\mathcal{C}_{\mathsf{Aggregate}}$. The running-time of 1, 2 and 3 are respectively $O(T^2 n \log n)$, $O(T^2 \log T)$ and $O(nT \log T)$.

Assuming the CRS model and the existence of NIZKs, $\mathsf{SAggregate}$ can be achieved in two rounds according to Proposition 2. Morever, $O(nT^2)$ homomorphic additions and multiplications are required. However, the size of ciphertexts (due to MTFHE.Expand) and thus the cost of homomorphic operations grows with T for all existing MTFHE. For instance, an expanded ciphertext is a matrix whose size is proportional to $T + 1$ in the MTFHE based on GSW [MW15] implicitly considered. As a homomorphic multiplication is a matrix multiplication (of ciphertexts), the running-time of $\mathsf{SAggregate}$ is

$$O(nT^{2+\omega})$$

with $\omega < 2.38$.

7.5 Running-Time *vs* Round Complexity

Performance of existing MTFHE are prohibitive to implement $\mathsf{SAggregate}$ with $n = T = 100$ for instance. In this section, we propose to see how to reduce running-time by accepting to increase the number of rounds. In this section, $\mathcal{J}$ refers to the set of involved parties (the experts and the authority). To simplify notation, we will assume that $|\mathcal{J}| = T$ (instead of $T + 1$).

Using TFHE Instead of TMFHE. LWE-based TFHE achieves 3-rounds [AJL+12] (assuming the CRS model and the existence of NIZKs). Indeed, one

---

Protocol SAggregate

Notations. $\mathcal{C}_{\mathsf{Aggregate}}$ refers to the optimal circuit evaluating **Aggregate**

Involved parties. The authority and each expert $j \in \mathcal{J}$

Public inputs. $n, T, \theta, \sigma, \tau$

Private inputs. Each expert $j \in \mathcal{J}$ inputs a private vector $(\varepsilon_{1j}, \varepsilon_{2j}) \in (\{0,1\} \times \{0,1\})^n$.

- The authority generates $(pk_0, sk_0) \leftarrow \mathsf{TMFHE.KeyGen}(1^\lambda)$ and then broadcasts pk_0
- Each expert $j \in \mathcal{J}$ generates $(pk_j, sk_j) \leftarrow \mathsf{TMFHE.KeyGen}(1^\lambda)$ and then broadcasts pk_j and $(c_{kji} \leftarrow \mathsf{TMFHE.Encrypt}(pk_j, \varepsilon_{kji}))_{k \in \{1,2\}; i \in \mathcal{N}}$
- Each party computes $\widehat{c}_{kji} := \mathsf{TMFHE.Expand}(pk_0, \ldots, pk_T, c_{kji})$ for any $k \in \{1,2\}$; $i \in \mathcal{N}$; $j \in \mathcal{J}$ and then $(\widehat{o}_i)_{i \in \mathcal{N}} := \mathsf{TMFHE.Eval}(\mathcal{C}_{\mathsf{Aggregate}}, (\widehat{c}_{kji})_{k \in \{1,2\}; (i,j) \in \mathcal{N} \times \mathcal{J}})$
- Authority outputs $o_i := \mathsf{TMFHE.PrivateDecrypt}(sk_0, \ldots, sk_T, \widehat{o}_i, \mathsf{Authority})$ for any $i \in \mathcal{N}$

Fig. 3. Implementing SAggregate with a TMFHE consisting of evaluating $\mathcal{C}_{\mathsf{Aggregate}}$.

additional round is required to generate keys. However, the size of ciphertexts and thus the cost of homomorphic operations does not depend anymore on the number T of involved parties. It follows that the running-time of SAggregate using such schemes is asymptotically optimal, i.e. $O(nT^2)$. An interesting open problem is to build a 2-round protocol asymptotically optimal.

Parallelizing Computations+TFHE. The execution of Aggregate can be highly parallelized. Indeed, each party j can evaluate (get an encryption of) its weight w_j by itself and then broadcast it. Then, each party $j \in \mathcal{J}$ can obtain $\widehat{o}_i$ for a subset of $E_j \subset \mathcal{N}$. Consequently, by adding one round in the protocol, the running-time is divided by T, i.e. the running-time per party is $O(nT)$. However, this way to proceed is not secure because malicious parties are not controlled. To palliate this, parallelization should be achieved between subsets S_k of parties ensuring that each subset contains at least one honest party. By assuming that the number of corrupted parties $\theta < T/2$, it suffices to choose at random cardinal-λ subsets to ensure that they contain at least one honest party with overwhelming probability. The running-time per party becomes $O(\lambda nT)$.

Refreshing Encryptions. While implementing SAggregate with TFHE is asymptotically optimal, the computational overhead is large making the protocol impractical for many applications. Indeed, all existing FHE consider a Somewhat Homomorphic Encryption SWHE which is transformed in a FHE by bootstrapping technics (consisting of evaluating the decryption circuit [Gen09]). However, boostrapping is very costly. Some FHE can be obtained without boostrapping ([GSW13, BGV12]). However, the parametrization of such schemes depends on the circuit $\mathcal{C}$ which should be evaluated. In other words, such schemes are just SWHE which can be parameterized to efficiently evaluate any polynomial-size circuit $\mathcal{C}$. It follows that the cost of a homomorphic operation is strongly impacted by the (multiplicative) depth of $\mathcal{C}$. We propose here to build a protocol Refresh aiming at reducing the noise level of encryptions (similarly to boostrapping procedure except that our procedure requires a round of communication.). For concreteness, Refresh input an encryption c and output an encryption c' encrypting the same value whose noise level does not depend on the noise level of c (in our case, c' is a fresh ciphertext in the sense that its noise level is identical (neglecting logarithm factors) to the one of ciphertexts output by Encrypt).

Protocol Refresh

Notation. $\mathcal{S}_r : \mathbb{Z}_2^r \to \mathbb{Z}_2$ is a $\{\oplus, \otimes\}$-circuit such that $\mathcal{S}_r(x_1, \ldots, x_r) = x_1 \oplus \cdots \oplus x_r$. Let ONE $\leftarrow$ TFHE.Encrypt$_{pk}(1)$ be an arbitrary public fresh encryption of 1.

Require. The parties invokes TFHE.KeyGen to get keys (pk, sk) and each party $j \in \mathcal{J}$ publicizes $B_j \leftarrow$ TMFHE.Encrypt(b_j) where b_j is a bit chosen at random by Party j. It follows that each party receives T encryptions $B_1, \ldots, B_T$

Public inputs. An evaluation c

1. $B :=$ TFHE.Eval$(\mathcal{S}_T, B_1, \cdots, B_T)$

2. $D :=$ TFHE.Eval$(\mathcal{S}_2, B, c)$

3. $d :=$ TFHE.Decrypt$_{sk}(D)$

4. Output $c' = \begin{cases} B, & \text{if } d = 0 \\ \text{TMFHE.Eval}(\mathcal{S}_2, \text{ONE}, B) & \text{if } d = 1 \end{cases}$

Clearly, c and c' encrypt the same plaintext meaning that Refresh is correct. We easily show that this protocol is secure assuming the semantic security of TMFHE. Intuitively, the adversary cannot recover the encrypted value by B (assuming there is at least one honest party). It follows that d does not reveal anything over the value encrypted by D. Moreover, the noise level of c' is equal to the noise level of B and thus it does not depend on the noise level of c.

How to use Refresh in Aggregate? First, the encryptions $B_1, \ldots, B_T$ of random bits required by Refresh are generated at the same time that the encryptions of private data. By choosing to *refresh* the evaluations of $y_{jj'}$ and the ones of w_j, we add two rounds of communication (assuming Decrypt requires only one round of communication). The benefit is that only degree-$O(T \log T + n \log n)$ circuits should be evaluated instead of $O(n \log n \times T \log T)$. This could represent a major improvement in terms of running-time paid by two supplementary rounds of communication.

8   Conclusion and Future Work

Relevant upper-bounds over $er^{\mathsf{Aggregate}}(\mathcal{K})$ were proposed in this paper. We proposed a numerical application dealing with simple families $\mathcal{K}_{p,p_e}$ of probability distributions ensuring that each component of b is (maybe imperfectly) known by each (honest) expert with a probability larger than p. These families could make sense for some applications. Other families $\mathcal{K}$ could be considered. However, it could be difficult to give an analytic upper-bound of $er^{\mathsf{Aggregate}}(\mathcal{K})$. Nevertheless, approximations can be obtained by sampling worst-case probability distributions $D \in \mathcal{K}$.

Moreover, we are convinced that Aggregate and its analysis (under the specific conditions of this paper) can be improved. Furthermore, the target vector b is binary but natural extensions to numerical vectors $b \in \mathbb{R}^n$ could be provided by applying threshold γ, i.e. c_{ji} and $c_{j'i}$ are said to be equal if $|c_{ji} - c_{j'i}| < \gamma$. The new parameter γ should be carefully chosen in order that most of honest experts input the same values c_{ji} within γ. In [DP94], Dubois et al. propose that each expert sends an interval I_i containing the true value b_i. Investigations should be done to adapt our work to this setting.

While TMFHE are very powerful tools in theory, their induced computational overhead which could be prohibitive in practice. Moreover, achieving two rounds of interactions is subject to two cryptographic assumptions (CRS model and NIZKs). Without these assumptions only four rounds can be expected.

Acknowledgment. The authors would like to thank the BAG members for their helpful discussions always around a coffee.

A   Formal Definition of Quantities Considered in Sect. 5

- Let u, v be positive integers s.t. $u \leq n$ and $v \leq T$. Let $I_v = \{i \in \mathcal{N}|b_i \sum_{j \in \mathcal{H}} \varepsilon_{ji} < v\}$. $\Gamma_{D,b,\mathcal{H}}(u, v)$ denotes the probability under D that the cardinality of I_v is strictly larger than u, i.e.

$$\Gamma_{D,b,\mathcal{H}}(u, v) = \mathsf{Pr}(|I_v| > u)$$

- Let $I(j, j') := \{i \in \mathcal{N} - \varepsilon_{ji}^* \varepsilon_{j'i}^* < 0\}$ and let $\alpha_{D,b,\mathcal{H}}(j) = \{j' \in \mathcal{H}||I(j, j')| > \sigma\}$.

$$\rho_{D,b,\mathcal{H}}^{\sigma,\tau} = \mathsf{Pr}(\exists j \in \mathcal{H}, |\alpha_{D,b,\mathcal{H}}(j)| > \tau)$$

- $\Omega_{\mathcal{A},D,b}^{\sigma,\tau} = \sum_{j \in \mathcal{C}} w_j |\{i \in \mathcal{N}|\varepsilon_{ji}^* b_i < 0\}|$

B   Proof of Proposition 1

Proof. According to notation of Sect. 3, o denotes the random vector output by Aggregate$_{\sigma,\tau}$. For the sake of simplicity, $er_{\mathcal{A}}^{\mathsf{Aggregate}_{\sigma,\tau}}(D, b)$ will be denoted by er.

The event G refers to the fact that no honest expert is eliminated[12], i.e. $w_j = 1$ for any $j \in \mathcal{H}$. By definition, $\Pr(\overline{G}) \leq \rho_{\mathcal{K}}^{\sigma,\tau}$.

Let u, v be arbitrary positive integers s.t. $u \leq n$ and $v \leq T$. Let $I_v = \{i \in \mathcal{N} | b_i \sum_{j \in \mathcal{H}} \varepsilon_{ji} \leq v\}$. The event $|I_v| \geq u$ will be denoted by F. By definition,

$$\Pr(F) = \Gamma_{D,b,\mathcal{H}}(u,v) \leq \Gamma_{\mathcal{K}}(u,v)$$

In the following of the proof, er' denotes the expectation of the error of o assuming that $G, \overline{F}$ are realized, i.e.,

$$er' = \frac{1}{2n} E(\|b - o\|_1 | G, \overline{F})$$

Clearly, $er \leq \Pr(\overline{G}) + \Pr(F, G) + \Pr(\overline{F}, G) er'$ implying that

$$er \leq \rho_{\mathcal{K}}^{\sigma,\tau} + \Gamma_{\mathcal{K}}(u,v) + \Pr(\overline{F}, G) er'$$

Let us focus on er' by assuming that the events $G, \overline{F}$ are realized. According to the definition of $\overline{F}$, the cardinality of I_v is smaller than u implying that

$$|\{i \in I_v | o_i \neq b_i\}| \leq u$$

By definition, for each $i \in \overline{I_v}$, $b_i \sum_{j \in \mathcal{H}} \varepsilon_{ji} \geq v$. It follows that

$$|\{i \in \overline{I_v} | o_i \neq b_i\}| \leq \frac{\Omega_{\mathcal{A},D,b}^{\sigma,\tau}}{v}$$

Consequently, the error of o is smaller than $\frac{1}{n}(u + \frac{\Omega_{\mathcal{A},D,b}^{\sigma,\tau}}{v})$, implying that

$$er' \leq \frac{u}{n} + \frac{1}{nv} E(\Omega_{\mathcal{A},D,b}^{\sigma,\tau} | G, \overline{F})$$

As $\Omega_{\mathcal{A},D,b}^{\sigma,\tau}$ is a positive random variable,

$$E(\Omega_{\mathcal{A},D,b}^{\sigma,\tau} | G, \overline{F}) \leq \frac{E(\Omega_{\mathcal{A},D,b}^{\sigma,\tau})}{\Pr(G, \overline{F})} \leq \frac{\Omega_{\mathcal{K}}^{\sigma,\tau}}{\Pr(G, \overline{F})}$$

It follows that

$$er \leq \rho_{\mathcal{K}}^{\sigma,\tau} + \Gamma_{\mathcal{K}}(u,v) + \Pr(G, \overline{F}) \left(\frac{u}{n} + \frac{\Omega_{\mathcal{K}}^{\sigma,\tau}}{nv \Pr(G, \overline{F})} \right)$$

$$\leq \rho_{\mathcal{K}}^{\sigma,\tau} + \Gamma_{\mathcal{K}}(u,v) + \frac{u}{n} + \frac{\Omega_{\mathcal{K}}^{\sigma,\tau}}{nv}$$

As u, v were arbitrarily chosen, $er \leq \rho_{\mathcal{K}}^{\sigma,\tau} + \min_{0 \leq u \leq n; 0 \leq v \leq T} (\Gamma_{\mathcal{K}}(u,v) + \frac{u}{n} + \frac{\Omega_{\mathcal{K}}^{\sigma,\tau}}{nv})$. This concludes the proof.

---

[12] The fact that G is realized means that all the values input by the honest experts are considered by $\mathsf{Aggregate}_{\sigma,\tau}$.

C   Proof of Lemma 1

To prove this lemma, we consider the worst[13] probability distribution $D \in \mathcal{K}_{p,p_e}$ defined by $\Pr(\varepsilon_{ji} \neq 0) = p$ and $\Pr(b_i \varepsilon_{ji} < 0) = p_e$. Moreover, we assume that the adversary controls exactly ϑ experts.

1 - The set S_j of correct values ε_{ji} received by each honest expert $j \in \mathcal{H}$ is denoted by

$$S_{j \in \mathcal{H}} = \{i \in \mathcal{N} | b_i \varepsilon_{ji} > 0\}$$

The set M_j of incorrect values input by a corrupted expert $j \in \mathcal{C}$ is denoted by

$$M_{j \in \mathcal{C}} = \{i \in \mathcal{N} | b_i \varepsilon_{ji}^* < 0\}$$

Let us upper-bound the probability p_j that Expert j is not eliminated, i.e. $w_j = 1$. It suffices that $|S_k \bigcap M_j| > \sigma$ to ensure that an honest Expert k and Expert j are incompatible. For each $i \in M_j$, the probability that $b_i \varepsilon_{ki} > 0$ is equal to $p - p_e$. Consequently, as ε_{ji} and $\varepsilon_{ki'}$ are independent, the probability that Expert j and Expert k are incompatible is smaller than

$$\rho_{M_j} \stackrel{\text{def}}{=} \Pr_D(|S_k \bigcap M_j| > \sigma) = 1 - \mathcal{B}_{p - p_e, |M_j|}(\sigma)$$

and as Expert j is eliminated if it is incompatible with more than $\vartheta + \tau$ honest experts,

$$\Pr_D(w_j = 1) \leq \mathcal{B}_{\rho_{|M_j|}, T - \vartheta}(\vartheta + \tau)$$

It follows that the number of incorrect values input by Expert j is upper-bounded, in mean, by

$$|M_j|(\mathcal{B}_{\rho_{|M_j|}, T - \vartheta}(\vartheta + \tau)) \leq \max_{i \in U} (i \mathcal{B}_{\rho_i, T - \vartheta}(\vartheta + \tau))$$

Thus,

$$\Omega_{A,D}^{\sigma,\tau} \leq \vartheta \cdot \max_{i \in U} (i \mathcal{B}_{\rho_i, T - \vartheta}(\vartheta + \tau))$$

2 - Let $h_i = b_i \sum_{j \in \mathcal{H}} \varepsilon_{ji}$. As ε_{ji} and $\varepsilon_{j'i'}$ are independent,

$$\Pr(h_i < v) = \mathcal{B}_{p_e, 1 - p, T - \vartheta}(v - 1) = \rho_v$$

and the random variables h_i are independent. Thus, the probability that the number of instances $i \in \mathcal{N}$ satisfying $h_i < v$ is strictly larger than u is equal to

$$\Gamma_{D,\mathcal{H}}(u, v) = 1 - \mathcal{B}_{\rho_v, n}(u)$$

3 - Let j and j' be two honest experts and let $i \in \mathcal{N}$.

$$\Pr_D(\varepsilon_{ji} \varepsilon_{j'i} < 0) = 2p_e(p - p_e)$$

---

[13] It is the probability distribution where the probability that an honest expert inputs correct values is the smallest and the probability that it inputs incorrect values is the largest.

It follows that the probability that Expert j is incompatible with Expert j' is equal to

$$\rho = 1 - \mathcal{B}_{2p_e(p-p_e),n}(\sigma)$$

As the values input by honest experts are independent, the probability that Expert j is incompatible with more than τ other honest experts is equal to $1 - \mathcal{B}_{\rho,T-\vartheta-1}(\tau)$ implying that

$$\rho_{D,\mathcal{H}}^{\sigma,\tau} \leq T \cdot (1 - \mathcal{B}_{\rho,T-\vartheta-1}(\tau))$$

$\square$

References

[AJL+12] Asharov, G., Jain, A., López-Alt, A., Tromer, E., Vaikuntanathan, V., Wichs, D.: Multiparty computation with low communication, computation and interaction via threshold FHE. In: Pointcheval, D., Johansson, T. (eds.) EUROCRYPT 2012. LNCS, vol. 7237, pp. 483–501. Springer, Heidelberg (2012). https://doi.org/10.1007/978-3-642-29011-4_29

[BGV12] Brakerski, Z., Gentry, C., Vaikuntanathan, V.: (Leveled) fully homomorphic encryption without bootstrapping. In: Innovations in Theoretical Computer Science 2012, Cambridge, MA, USA, 8–10 January 2012, pp. 309–325 (2012)

[BHP17] Brakerski, Z., Halevi, S., Polychroniadou, A.: Four round secure computation without setup. In: Kalai, Y., Reyzin, L. (eds.) TCC 2017. LNCS, vol. 10677, pp. 645–677. Springer, Cham (2017). https://doi.org/10.1007/978-3-319-70500-2_22

[CDN01] Cramer, R., Damgård, I., Nielsen, J.B.: Multiparty computation from threshold homomorphic encryption. In: Pfitzmann, B. (ed.) EUROCRYPT 2001. LNCS, vol. 2045, pp. 280–300. Springer, Heidelberg (2001). https://doi.org/10.1007/3-540-44987-6_18

[DBES09] Dong, X.L., Berti-Equille, L., Srivastava, D.: Integrating conflicting data: the role of source dependence. Proc. VLDB Endow. 2(1), 550–561 (2009)

[DN09] Dong, X.L., Naumann, F.: Data fusion - resolving data conflicts for integration. PVLDB 2(2), 1654–1655 (2009)

[DP94] Dubois, D., Prade, H.: Possibility theory and data fusion in poorly informed environments. Control Eng. Pract. 2(5), 811–823 (1994)

[DWH08] Durrant-Whyte, H., Henderson, T.C.: Multisensor data fusion. In: Siciliano, B., Khatib, O. (eds.) Springer Handbook of Robotics, pp. 585–610. Springer, Heidelberg (2008). https://doi.org/10.1007/978-3-540-30301-5_26

[Fin77] Fine, T.L.: Review: Glenn Shafer, a mathematical theory of evidence. Bull. Am. Math. Soc. 83(4), 667–672 (1977)

[Gen09] Gentry, C.: Fully homomorphic encryption using ideal lattices. In: STOC, pp. 169–178 (2009)

[GSW13] Gentry, C., Sahai, A., Waters, B.: Homomorphic encryption from learning with errors: conceptually-simpler, asymptotically-faster, attribute-based. In: Canetti, R., Garay, J.A. (eds.) CRYPTO 2013, part I. LNCS, vol. 8042, pp. 75–92. Springer, Heidelberg (2013). https://doi.org/10.1007/978-3-642-40041-4_5

[HLP11] Halevi, S., Lindell, Y., Pinkas, B.: Secure computation on the web: computing without simultaneous interaction. In: Rogaway, P. (ed.) CRYPTO 2011. LNCS, vol. 6841, pp. 132–150. Springer, Heidelberg (2011). https://doi.org/10.1007/978-3-642-22792-9_8

[KKKR13] Khaleghi, B., Khamis, A., Karray, F.O., Razavi, S.N.: Multisensor data fusion: a review of the state-of-the-art. Inf. Fusion 14(1), 28–44 (2013)

[LTV13] López-Alt, A., Tromer, E., Vaikuntanathan, V.: On-the-fly multiparty computation on the cloud via multikey fully homomorphic encryption. In: IACR Cryptology ePrint Archive 2013:94 (2013)

[MW15] Mukherjee, P., Wichs, D.: Two round MPC from LWE via multi-key FHE. In: IACR Cryptology ePrint Archive 2015:345 (2015)

[NZZ78] Negoita, C.V., Zadeh, L.A., Zimmermann, H.J.: Fuzzy sets as a basis for a theory of possibility. Fuzzy Sets Syst. 1, 3–28 (1978)

[OSA87] Goldreich, O., Michali, S., Wigderson, A.: How to play any mental game or a completeness theorem for protocols with honest majority. In: STOC, pp. 218–229 (1987)

[Paw92] Pawlak, Z.: Rough Sets: Theoretical Aspects of Reasoning About Data. Kluwer Academic Publishers, Norwell (1992)

[Reg05] Regev, O.: On lattices, learning with errors, random linear codes, and cryptography. In: Proceedings of the 37th Annual ACM Symposium on Theory of Computing, Baltimore, MD, USA, 22–24 May 2005, pp. 84–93 (2005)

[She91] Sheridan, F.K.J.: A survey of techniques for inference under uncertainty. Artif. Intell. Rev. 5(1–2), 89–119 (1991)

[Yao86] Yao, A.C.-C.: How to generate and exchange secrets (extended abstract). In: 27th Annual Symposium on Foundations of Computer Science, Toronto, Canada, 27–29 October 1986, pp. 162–167 (1986)

[Zad65] Zadeh, L.A.: Fuzzy sets. Inf. Control 8(3), 338–353 (1965)

Improved Efficiency of a Linearly Homomorphic Cryptosystem

Parthasarathi Das[1(✉)], Michael J. Jacobson Jr.[1], and Renate Scheidler[2]

[1] Department of Computer Science, University of Calgary,
2500 University Drive NW, Calgary, AB T2N 1N4, Canada
{parthasarathi.das,jacobs}@ucalgary.ca
[2] Department of Mathematics and Statistics, University of Calgary,
2500 University Drive NW, Calgary, AB T2N 1N4, Canada
rscheidl@ucalgary.ca

Abstract. We present an extended version of the Castagnos and Laguillaumie linearly homomorphic cryptosystem [5] in which the non-maximal imaginary quadratic order is allowed to have conductor equal to a product of prime powers as opposed to a single prime. Numerical results obtained with an optimized C implementation demonstrate that this variation improves performance when large messages and exponents are used. When compared to the cryptosystems of Paillier [11] and Bresson et al. [3] at the same security levels, the basic version of Castagnos and Laguillaumie is the fastest at high security levels for small messages.

Keywords: Linearly homomorphic encryption ·
Public key cryptography · Ideal class group · Electronic voting ·
Encryption switching protocol

1 Introduction

A *linearly homomorphic cryptosystem* is one for which linear combinations of ciphertexts can be computed in such a way that the result is the encryption of the same linear combination of the corresponding plaintexts. Such cryptosystems have a number of applications. For example, when used for electronic voting, encrypted votes (encrypting 1 for "yes" and 0 for "no") can be tallied with a single decryption by homomorphically adding the ciphertexts and decrypting the result. Two well-known examples of linearly homomorphic encryption systems are due to Paillier [11] and Bresson et al. [3]. In both cases, the security relies on the presumed intractability of integer factorization.

In [5], Castagnos and Laguillaumie presented a linearly homomorphic encryption scheme whose security is based on the hardness of the decision Diffie-Hellman (DDH) problem in a group that has a subgroup in which the discrete logarithm (DL) problem can be solved easily; this setting is referred to as a "DDH group with an easy DL subgroup". Assuming the existence of such groups, they

The second and third authors' research is supported by NSERC.

C. Carlet et al. (Eds.): C2SI 2019, LNCS 11445, pp. 349–368, 2019.
https://doi.org/10.1007/978-3-030-16458-4_20

described a linearly homomorphic encryption scheme that is provably one-way and semantically secure subject to relatively standard hardness assumptions. They also gave an instantiation of their cryptosystem using the ideal class group of a non-maximal imaginary quadratic order with prime conductor as the DDH group with easy DL subgroup. Subsequently, this cryptosystem was used in combination with a variant of ElGamal in an encryption switching protocol [4], providing an efficient setting for a secure two-party computation protocol.

The cryptosystem of [5] has two main novel features. Firstly, it is the only purely linearly homomorphic cryptosystem (not counting the fully homomorphic cryptosystems based on the learning with errors problem) whose security does not depend on integer factorization—all hardness assumptions are versions of Diffie-Hellman and discrete logarithm problems. The second feature is that the size of the message space can be chosen independently of the security parameter. This is especially attractive in electronic voting applications, as the message space can be chosen just large enough to handle the required number of votes. In contrast, [11] and [3] are both defined in terms of RSA moduli, and the number of messages that can be encrypted is of the same size as the modulus. When appropriate security levels are used, these allow far more messages than necessary for typical voting scenarios.

Castagnos and Laguillaumie [5] also presented numerical results using an implementation of their cryptosystem, which suggested that it has advantages over Pailler and Bresson et al. at the 112- and 128-bit security levels. However, the implementation was done using a general-purpose computer algebra system as opposed to a more specialized and optimized implementation. In addition, two possible improvements were suggested, designed to allow larger messages without increasing the security level, and to speed up decryption via the Chinese Remainder Theorem. These improvements arise from using conductors that are prime powers and products of distinct primes, respectively, as opposed to primes. Exploring both these ideas was left as future work.

In this paper, we fully explore the efficiency of the cryptosystem of Castagnos and Laguillaumie [5]. Our first contribution is a complete description of the cryptosystem using conductors that are products of prime powers, thereby covering both the suggested improvements in [5]. We present a detailed benchmarking of the cryptosystem at the 128-, 192-, and 256-bit security levels, and compare its performance to both the Pailler [11] and the Bresson et al. [3] cryptosystems. Our implementation makes use of a state-of-the-art C implementation of class group arithmetic in imaginary quadratic orders due to Sayles [12]. We use both the original version of [5] where group elements are sampled from the entire group, as well as standard short exponent versions that also have provable security properties but under variations of the intractability assumptions that are restricted to short exponents, based on the results of Koshiba and Kurosawa [10]. The variations of Castagnos and Laguillaumie considered here offer performance improvements when using large exponents and large messages. When compared to the cryptosystems of Paillier [11] and Bresson et al. [3] at the same security levels, our results show that the basic version of Castagnos and Laguillaumie is the fastest at high security levels for small messages.

2   The Castagnos and Laguillaumie Cryptosystem

2.1   The Basic System

As mentioned in the previous section, Castagnos and Laguillaumie presented a linearly homomorphic encryption scheme based on a DL related problem, effectively solving a thirty-year-old open problem. Their scheme [5] is based on the hardness of the DDH problem in certain groups $\mathcal{G}$ that contain a subgroup $\mathcal{F}$ where solving the DL problem is easy. Castagnos and Laguillaumie call such a setting a DDH group with an easy DL subgroup and instantiate an example of one such group-subgroup pair as the class group of a non-maximal imaginary quadratic order with prime conductor [5]. The following is a simplified version of Definition 1 in [5], with unused parameters omitted.

Definition 1 ([5, Definition 1]). *A* DDH *group with an easy* DL *subgroup is a pair of algorithms* Gen *and* Solve. *The* Gen *algorithm takes as input two parameters* λ *and* μ *and outputs a tuple* $(B, f, \mathfrak{g}, \mathfrak{f}, \mathcal{G}, \mathcal{F})$. *Here,* $\mathcal{G}$ *is a finite cyclic group generated by* $\mathfrak{g}$, $\mathcal{F}$ *is a subgroup of* $\mathcal{G}$ *of order* f *generated by* $\mathfrak{f}$, $|\mathcal{G}|/f$ *is a* λ-*bit integer bounded above by* B, *and* f *is a* μ-*bit integer. The* Solve *algorithm is an efficient algorithm for solving the* DL *problem in* $\mathcal{F}$ *which is assumed to be easy, while the* DDH *problem in* $\mathcal{G}$ *is assumed to be hard even with access to the* Solve *algorithm.*

In addition, random powers $\mathfrak{g}^r$ with $0 \le r \le Bf - 1$ are assumed to be statistically indistinguishable from the uniform distribution on $\mathcal{G}$, and both images and pre-images under the canonical surjection $\mathcal{G} \to \mathcal{G}/\mathcal{F}$ are assumed to be efficiently computable. In slight abuse of terminology, we will refer to $\mathcal{G}$ as a DDH group and $\mathcal{F}$ an easy DL subgroup of $\mathcal{G}$, with an implicit assumption of the associated Gen and Solve algorithms.

For the scheme of [5], we let $f, \Delta_K \in \mathbb{Z}$ where $f > 0$, $\Delta_K < -4$, Δ_K is square-free and $\Delta_K \equiv 1 \pmod 4$. Then Δ_K is a fundamental discriminant that defines an imaginary quadratic field K. Let $C(\mathcal{O}_{\Delta_K})$ and $C(\mathcal{O}_{\Delta_f})$ denote the class group of the maximal order $\mathcal{O}_{\Delta_K}$ of K of discriminant Δ_K and the non-maximal suborder $\mathcal{O}_{\Delta_f}$ of $\mathcal{O}_{\Delta_K}$ of discriminant $\Delta_f = f^2 \Delta_K$ and conductor f, respectively. Arithmetic in $C(\mathcal{O}_{\Delta_f})$ is conducted on reduced ideals, uniquely represented by a pair (a, b) where a, b are bounded integers and $a > 0$. There is an efficiently computable canonical injection $\psi_f : C(\mathcal{O}_{\Delta_K}) \to C(\mathcal{O}_{\Delta_f})$ and a corresponding canonical surjection $\bar{\varphi}_f : C(\mathcal{O}_{\Delta_f}) \to C(\mathcal{O}_{\Delta_K})$ whose kernel has order

$$|\mathrm{ker}(\bar{\varphi}_f)| = f \prod_{p \mid f} \left(1 - \left(\frac{\Delta_K}{p} \right) \frac{1}{p} \right) ,$$

where the product runs over the prime factors p of f and (Δ_K/p) is the Kronecker symbol. If every prime factor of f divides Δ_K, then $|\mathrm{ker}(\bar{\varphi}_f)| = f$. If in addition $\mathrm{ker}(\bar{\varphi}_f)$ is cyclic, then one can put $\mathcal{F} = \mathrm{ker}(\bar{\varphi}_f)$ and take $\mathcal{G}$ to be a suitable large cyclic subgroup of $C(\mathcal{O}_{\Delta_f})$.

Castagnos and Laguillaumie specifically chose $\Delta_K = -pq$ and $f = p$, where p is prime and q is a positive integer not divisible by p such that $q > 4p$. Then the ideal class of $\mathfrak{f} = (p^2, p)$ generates $\mathcal{F}$, and the DL in $\mathcal{F}$ is easy since for all $m \in \{1, 2, \ldots, p-1\}$, the ideal class of $\mathfrak{f}^m$ is given by $(p^2, L(m)p)$ where $L(m)$ is the unique odd inverse of $m \pmod{p}$ in the interval $[-p, p]$; see Proposition 1 of [5]. In Algorithms 1 and 2, we present the Gen algorithm that constructs the DDH group $\mathcal{G}$ with an easy DL subgroup $\mathcal{F}$ and the Solve algorithm that solves the DL problem in $\mathcal{F}$ in this setting; see [5, Figure 2]. For security reasons, as explained in Subsect. 2.2, we assume that q is also prime and that $(p/q) = (q/p) = -1$. The map $\psi = \psi_f$ in Gen is the aforementioned injection from $C(\mathcal{O}_{\Delta_K})$ into $C(\mathcal{O}_{\Delta_f})$; see [5, Lemma 3] and [8, Algorithm 9] for a method to efficiently compute this map. The call to $\mathrm{Red}(\cdot)$ in Algorithm 2 outputs the two-integer representation of the unique reduced ideal equivalent to the input.

Algorithm 1. Gen

Input: λ, μ with $\lambda \geq \mu + 2$.
Output: $B, f, \mathfrak{g}, \mathfrak{f}, \mathcal{G}, \mathcal{F}$
1. Pick random integers p and q such that p is a μ-bit prime, q is a $(2\lambda - \mu)$-bit prime, $pq \equiv 3 \pmod{4}$ and $(p/q) = (q/p) = -1$
2. Set $\Delta_K \leftarrow -pq$
3. Set $f \leftarrow p$
4. Set $\Delta_f \leftarrow f^2 \Delta_K$
5. Set $\mathfrak{f} \leftarrow [(f^2, f)]$ in $C(\mathcal{O}_{\Delta_f})$
6. Choose a small prime r such that $\gcd(r, f) = 1$ and $(\Delta_K/r) = 1$. Set $\mathfrak{r}$ to a prime ideal of $\mathcal{O}_{\Delta_K}$ lying above r
7. Pick $k \xleftarrow{\$} (\mathbb{Z}/f\mathbb{Z})^*$ and set $\mathfrak{g} \leftarrow [\psi(\mathfrak{r}^2)] \cdot \mathfrak{f}^k$ in $C(\mathcal{O}_{\Delta_f})$
8. Set $B \leftarrow f \cdot \left\lceil \frac{\log(|\Delta_K|) \cdot \sqrt{|\Delta_K|}}{4\pi} \right\rceil$
9. Return $(B, f, \mathfrak{g}, \mathfrak{f}, \mathcal{G}, \mathcal{F})$

Algorithm 2. Solve

Input: $f, \mathfrak{f}, \mathfrak{m}$
Output: m such that $\mathfrak{m} = \mathfrak{f}^m$
1. Parse $\mathrm{Red}(\mathfrak{m})$ as $(f^2, \tilde{x}f)$
2. Return $\tilde{x}^{-1} \pmod{f}$

Algorithm 3. KeyGen

Input: λ
Output: Public key pk, secret key sk
1. $(B, f, \mathfrak{g}, \mathfrak{f}) \xleftarrow{\$} \mathrm{Gen}(\lambda, \mu)$
2. $x \xleftarrow{\$} (\mathbb{Z}/Bf\mathbb{Z})$ and $\mathfrak{h} \leftarrow \mathfrak{g}^x$
3. $pk \leftarrow (B, f, \mathfrak{g}, \mathfrak{h}, \mathfrak{f})$ and $sk \leftarrow x$
4. Return (pk, sk)

Algorithms 3–7 present the linearly homomorphic encryption system first given in [5]. While we use the notation associated with the specific setting of class groups, this description applies to the generic setting of a DDH group with an easy DL subgroup of Definition 1. Here, plaintexts are integers modulo f, while ciphertexts are pairs of elements in $\mathcal{G}$. Thus, the size of the message space is completely determined by the size of the easy DL subgroup $\mathcal{F}$; in the class group setting, this is precisely the conductor f of the non-maximal order $\mathcal{O}_{\Delta_f}$.

Algorithm 4. Encrypt

Input: λ, pk, message m
Output: Ciphertext (c_1, c_2)
  1. Pick $r \xleftarrow{\$} \{0, \cdots, Bf - 1\}$
  2. Compute $c_1 \leftarrow \mathfrak{g}^r$
  3. Compute $c_2 \leftarrow \mathfrak{f}^m \mathfrak{h}^r$
  4. Return (c_1, c_2)

Algorithm 5. Decrypt

Input: $\lambda, pk, sk, (c_1, c_2)$
Output: Message m
  1. Compute $\mathfrak{m} \leftarrow c_2/c_1^x$
  2. $m \leftarrow \mathtt{Solve}(f, \mathfrak{f}, \mathcal{F}, \mathfrak{m})$
  3. Return m

Algorithm 6. EvalSum

Input: λ, pk,
  $(c_1, c_2) = \mathtt{Encrypt}(pk, m)$,
  $(c'_1, c'_2) = \mathtt{Encrypt}(pk, m')$
Output: (C_1, C_2) such that
  $\mathtt{Decrypt}(sk, (C_1, C_2)) = m + m'$
  1. Compute $c''_1 \leftarrow c_1 c'_1$, $c''_2 \leftarrow c_2 c'_2$
  2. Pick $r \xleftarrow{\$} \{0, \cdots, Bf - 1\}$
  3. Return $(c''_1 \mathfrak{g}^r, c''_2 \mathfrak{h}^r)$

Algorithm 7. EvalScal

Input: λ, pk, α,
  $(c_1, c_2) = \mathtt{Encrypt}(pk, m)$
Output: (C_1, C_2) such that
  $\mathtt{Decrypt}(sk, (C_1, C_2)) = \alpha m$
  1. Compute $c'_1 \leftarrow c_1^\alpha$, $c'_2 \leftarrow c_2^\alpha$
  2. Pick $r \xleftarrow{\$} \{0, \cdots, Bf - 1\}$
  3. Return $(c'_1 \mathfrak{g}^r, c'_2 \mathfrak{h}^r)$

2.2 Security

It is easy to see that if one can solve the discrete logarithm problem in $\mathcal{G}$, then one can recover the secret key sk and totally break the scheme of [5]. Castagnos and Laguillaumie show that the DL problem in $\mathcal{G}$ is at least as hard as the DL problem in $\mathcal{G}/\mathcal{F}$.

Theorem 1 ([5, Theorem 2]). *Let $\mathcal{G}$ be a DDH group with an easy DL subgroup. Then the DL problem in $\mathcal{G}/\mathcal{F}$ reduces to the DL problem in $\mathcal{G}$.*

The DDH problem in our context reads as follows.

Definition 2 (Decisional Diffie Hellman Problem). *Let $\mathcal{G}$ be a DDH group of order n with an easy DL subgroup $\mathcal{F}$ and $\mathfrak{g}$ a generator of $\mathcal{G}$. Let x, y, z be integers such that $x, y, z \xleftarrow{\$} \mathbb{Z}/n\mathbb{Z}$. The Decisional Diffie Hellman Problem consists of deciding whether $\mathfrak{g}^{xy} = \mathfrak{g}^z$, given $(\mathfrak{g}, \mathfrak{g}^x, \mathfrak{g}^y, \mathfrak{g}^z)$ and access to the $\mathtt{Solve}$ algorithm.*

Theorem 2 ([5, Theorem 4]). *The scheme described in Algorithms 1–7 is semantically secure under chosen plaintext attacks (ind-cpa) if and only if the DDH problem is hard in $\mathcal{G}$.*

The following problems were introduced by Bresson et al. in [3] and Paillier in [11] respectively, and were then adapted by Castagnos and Laguillaumie in [5].

Definition 3 (Lift Diffie-Hellman Problem). *Let $\mathcal{G}$ be a* DDH *group of order n with an easy* DL *subgroup $\mathcal{F}$ and $\mathfrak{g}$ a generator of $\mathcal{G}$. Let $x, y \xleftarrow{\$} \mathbb{Z}/n\mathbb{Z}$ and let $\pi \colon \mathcal{G} \to \mathcal{G}/\mathcal{F}$ be the canonical surjection. The Lift Diffie-Hellman (*LDH*) problem consists of computing g^{xy}, given $(\mathfrak{g}, g^x, g^y, \pi(g^{xy}))$ and access to the* Solve *algorithm.*

Definition 4 (Partial Discrete Logarithm Problem). *Let $\mathcal{G}$ be a* DDH *group of order n with an easy* DL *subgroup $\mathcal{F}$ and $\mathfrak{g}$ a generator of $\mathcal{G}$. Let $x \xleftarrow{\$} \mathbb{Z}/n\mathbb{Z}$. The Partial Discrete Logarithm (*PDL*) problem consists of computing $x \pmod{|\mathcal{F}|}$, given $\mathfrak{g}$ and $\mathfrak{g}^x$ and access to the* Solve *algorithm.*

Theorem 3 ([5, Theorem 3]). *The scheme described in Algorithms 1–7 is one-way under chosen plaintext attacks (*ow-cpa*) if and only if the* LDH *problem (equivalently, the* PDL *problem) is hard.*

Castagnos and Laguillaumie show that the LDH and PDL problems are equivalent [5, Theorem 1]. They also show that knowledge of the order n of $\mathcal{G}$ makes it possible to solve the PDL problem efficiently [5, Lemma 1].

For security reasons, it is desirable to work in a cyclic subgroup of $C(\mathcal{O}_{\Delta_f})$ that is as large as possible. To that end, Hamdy and Möller [7] recommend to choose a fundamental Δ_K for which the 2-Sylow subgroup of the class group $C(\mathcal{O}_{\Delta_K})$, and hence the even part of the class number $h(\Delta_K) = |C(\mathcal{O}_{\Delta_K})|$, is minimal. The construction in [5] achieves this, since for $\Delta_K = -pq$, the even part of the class number is exactly 2 if p, q are primes with $(p/q) = (q/p) = -1$, and that value is as small as possible for non-prime discriminants. In addition, Castagnos and Laguillaumie also require $\mu > 80$ in order to ensure that the probability of the conductor p dividing the odd part of $h(\Delta_K)$ is extremely low according to the Cohen-Lenstra heuristics. A large cyclic subgroup of $C(\mathcal{O}_{\Delta_K})$ of order s, where s is a large factor of $h(\Delta_K)$, thus produces a large cyclic subgroup $\mathcal{G}$ of $C(\mathcal{O}_{\Delta_f})$ of order ps, and s is the security parameter for the scheme. The Cohen-Lenstra heuristics in fact predict that the odd part of $C(\mathcal{O}_{\Delta_K})$ is itself cyclic with very high probability. Under these assumptions, finding the order $|\mathcal{G}|$ is believed to be intractable.

2.3 A Variant of the Basic System

Castagnos and Laguillaumie proposed a variant that aims to reduce the size of the first component c_1 of a ciphertext (c_1, c_2) [5, Section 4.2]. They suggested constructing the generator $\mathfrak{g}$ of $\mathcal{G}$ in $C(\mathcal{O}_{\Delta_K})$ so that $\mathfrak{h} \in C(\mathcal{O}_{\Delta_K})$ and hence $c_1 \in C(\mathcal{O}_{\Delta_K})$. The ciphertext c_2 can then be generated by lifting $\mathfrak{h}$ to $C(\mathcal{O}_{\Delta_p})$ using the ψ map. Thus, we have the following changes for this variant. Note that the semantic security of this variant now relies on the intractability of a different, less standard modification of the DDH problem.

Modification to Algorithm 1
7. Set $\mathfrak{g} \leftarrow [\mathfrak{r}^2]$ in $C(\mathcal{O}_{\Delta_K})$

Algorithm 8. Encrypt
Input: λ, pk, message m
Output: Ciphertext (c_1, c_2)
1. Pick $r \xleftarrow{\$} \{0, \cdots, Bf - 1\}$
2. Compute $c_1 \leftarrow \mathfrak{g}^r$
3. Compute $c_2 \leftarrow \mathfrak{f}^m \psi(\mathfrak{h}^r)$
4. Return (c_1, c_2)

Algorithm 9. Decrypt
Input: $\lambda, pk, sk, c_1, c_2$
Output: Message m
1. Compute $\mathsf{m} \leftarrow c_2 / \psi(c_1^x)$
2. $m \leftarrow \mathsf{Solve}(B, f, \mathfrak{g}, \mathfrak{f}, \mathsf{m})$
3. Return m

2.4 Expanding the Message Space

The condition $q > 4p$ implies $|\Delta_K| > 4p^2$ and hence $p^2 < \sqrt{\Delta_p}/2$, which ensures that $\mathsf{Red}(\mathfrak{f}) = (p^2, p)$ is a reduced ideal in $\mathcal{O}_{\Delta_f}$ [9, Theorem 5.6]. This restriction allows for a polynomial time Solve algorithm, but it also introduces a fixed upper bound on the size of the message space for a given security level. To see this more clearly, consider a factorization based linearly homomorphic scheme such as the Paillier cryptosystem. Its hardness is based on the factorization of the RSA modulus and thus, the size of the message space is the size of the modulus which is the security parameter. In the CL schemes described above, the message space has size p, so the bound $q > 4p$ forces $\Delta_K > 4p^2$. For example, based on [1, Table 4], a security level of 128 bits corresponds to factoring a modulus of bit size 3072 and computing discrete logarithms in a class group corresponding to a 1828-bit discriminant Δ_K. In the Paillier scheme, a security level of 3072 bits thus corresponds to messages of bit length of 3072. Yet, in the Castanos-Laguilliomie scheme, messages whose length is equal to the corresponding security level of 1828 bits necessitate using a discriminant of size at least $2 \cdot 1828 + 2 = 3658$ bits, far larger than what is required at the same security level. Thus, the CL variants discussed so far lose their advantage over factoring based schemes.

To solve this problem, Castagnos and Laguillaumie proposed a variant of their scheme that drops the requirement $q > 4p$ and has no restriction on the size of q in Gen (Algorithm 1). In this case, however, the ideal (p^2, p) of $\mathcal{O}_{\Delta_p}$ and its powers may no longer be reduced. In order to still guarantee a polynomial time Solve algorithm, one solution is to lift the ideal (p^2, p) to the order $\mathcal{O}_{\Delta_{p^2}}$ of discriminant $\Delta_{p^2} = p^4 \Delta_K$ where the lifted ideal is reduced since $p^2 < \sqrt{|\Delta_{p^2}|}/2$ if $|\Delta_K| > 4$. The class $\mathfrak{f} = [(p^2, p)] \in C(\mathcal{O}_{\Delta_p})$ lifts to the ideal class $\mathfrak{f}_l \in c(\mathcal{O}_{\Delta_{p^2}})$ whose unique reduced representative is again $[(p^2, p)]$, where the lift is now effected by the map $\psi : C(\mathcal{O}_{\Delta_p}) \rightarrow C(\mathcal{O}_{\Delta_{p^2}})$.

Castagnos and Laguillaumie show that $\mathfrak{f}_l$ belongs to the cyclic subgroup of $C(\Delta_{p^2})$ generated by $[(p^2, p)]$ where $\mathfrak{f}_l = \psi(\mathfrak{f})$ is the lift of $\mathfrak{f}$ under the lifting map ψ that maps elements in $\mathcal{O}_{\Delta_p}$ to elements in $\mathcal{O}_{\Delta_{p^2}}$ [5, Section 4.1]. So we precompute the discrete logarithm z of $\mathfrak{f}_l$ with respect to $[(p^2, p)]$ in Gen using a technique analogous to that used in Solve, but computing inside $C(\Delta_{p^2})$. Our computations show that $z = 1$ almost always. We have the following Gen and Solve algorithms for this variant.

Algorithm 10. Gen

Input: λ, μ with $\lambda \geq \mu + 2$.

Output: $B, f, z, \mathfrak{g}, \mathfrak{f}, \mathcal{G}, \mathcal{F}$

1. Pick random integers p and q such that p is a μ-bit prime, q is a $(2\lambda - \mu)$-bit prime, $pq \equiv 3 \pmod 4$ and $(p/q) = (q/p) = -1$ if $q \neq 1$
2. Set $\Delta_K \leftarrow -pq$
3. Set $f \leftarrow p$
4. Set $\Delta_f \leftarrow f^2 \Delta_K$
5. Set $\mathfrak{f} \leftarrow [(f^2, f)]$ in $C(\mathcal{O}_{\Delta_f})$
6. Parse $\mathrm{Red}(\psi(\mathfrak{f}))$ as $(f^2, \tilde{z}f)$
7. $z \leftarrow \tilde{z}^{-1} \pmod f$
8. Choose a small prime r such that $\gcd(r, f) = 1$ and $(\Delta_K/r) = 1$. Set $\mathfrak{r}$ to be a prime ideal of $\mathcal{O}_{\Delta_K}$ lying above r
9. Pick $k \xleftarrow{\$} (\mathbb{Z}/f\mathbb{Z})^*$ and set $\mathfrak{g} \leftarrow [\psi(\mathfrak{r}^2)] \cdot \mathfrak{f}^k$ in $C(\mathcal{O}_{\Delta_f})$
10. Set $B \leftarrow f \cdot \left\lceil \frac{\log(|\Delta_K|) \cdot \sqrt{|\Delta_K|}}{4\pi} \right\rceil$
11. Return $(B, f, z, \mathfrak{g}, \mathfrak{f}, \mathcal{G}, \mathcal{F})$

Algorithm 11. Solve

Input: $z, f, \mathfrak{f}, \mathfrak{m}$

Output: m such that $\mathfrak{m} = \mathfrak{f}^m$

1. Compute $\mathfrak{m}' \leftarrow \psi(\mathfrak{m})$
2. Parse $\mathrm{Red}(\mathfrak{m}')$ as $(f^2, \tilde{y}f)$
3. Return $z\tilde{y}^{-1} \pmod f$

In this version, p can be chosen independently of the security level, subject to the restriction that it is large enough so p does not divide q with very high probability (e.g. at least 80 bits). We note that this idea can also be applied to the variant presented in Subsect. 2.3.

3   Extensions

The original probabilistic encryption scheme in [5] and its modifications presented in Sect. 2 all use a prime conductor p. Castagnos and Laguillaumie also suggested the use of a composite conductor f, which could potentially improve the efficiency of their schemes, and to allow the message space to be increased arbitrarily without increasing the security level (governed by the size of the fundamental discriminant Δ_K). Specifically, they proposed $f = \prod_{i=1}^{N} p_i$ or

$f = p^t$ where $N, t \in \mathbb{Z}_{\geq 1}$ and p_i, p are primes. In this section, we describe modified versions of the algorithms presented Sect. 2 for the more general conductor $f = \prod_{i=1}^{N} p_i^t$ that includes the two proposed forms as the special cases $t = 1, N > 1$ and $t > 1, N = 1$ and the original scheme as the case $N = t = 1$. To ensure that the kernel of the surjection $\bar{\varphi}_f : C(\mathcal{O}_{\Delta_f}) \to C(\mathcal{O}_{\Delta_K})$ is f, we put $\Delta_K = -p_1 p_2 \cdots p_N q$. It is easy to deduce that the ideal (f^2, f) is reduced in $\mathcal{O}_{\Delta_f}$ when $q > 4(p_1 p_2 \cdots p_N)^{2t-1}$. If this is not the case, we need to proceed as in Subsect. 2.4 and lift the class $\mathfrak{f}$ of (f^2, f) to $C(\mathcal{O}_{\Delta_{f^2}})$ via the map $\psi : C(\mathcal{O}_{\Delta_f}) \to C(\mathcal{O}_{\Delta_{f^2}})$. In order to focus entirely on the differences arising in all our algorithms when replacing a prime conductor $f = p$ by a composite conductor $f = \prod_{i=1}^{N} p_i^t$, we assume that no such lifting is necessary. The Gen algorithm for this extension is as follows. The KeyGen algorithm remains unchanged. We present modified versions of Encrypt, Decrypt and Solve separately for the cases $t = 1$ and $t > 1$.

Algorithm 12. Gen

Input: λ, μ
Output: $B, f, \mathfrak{g}, \mathfrak{f}, \mathcal{G}, \mathcal{F}$
1. Pick random primes $p_1, p_2, \cdots, p_N, q$ such that $p_1 p_2 \cdots p_N$ is a μ-bit integer, q is a $(2\lambda - \mu)$-bit prime, $p_1 p_2 \cdots p_N q \equiv 3 \pmod 4$ and $(p_i/p_j) = 1$ and $(p_i/q) = (q/p_i) = -1$ for $1 \leq i, j \leq N$
2. Set $\Delta_K \leftarrow -p_1 p_2 \cdots p_N q$
3. Pick $t \xleftarrow{\$} \mathbb{Z}_{>0}$ and set $f \leftarrow (p_1 p_2 \cdots p_N)^t$
4. Set $\Delta_f \leftarrow f^2 \Delta_K$
5. Set $\mathfrak{f} \leftarrow [(f^2, f)]$ in $C(\mathcal{O}_{\Delta_f})$
6. Choose a small prime r such that $\gcd(r, f) = 1$ and $(\Delta_K/r) = 1$. Set $\mathfrak{r}$ a prime ideal lying above r
7. Pick $k \xleftarrow{\$} (\mathbb{Z}/f\mathbb{Z})^*$ and set $\mathfrak{g} \leftarrow [\psi(\mathfrak{r}^2)] \cdot \mathfrak{f}^k$ in $C(\mathcal{O}_{\Delta_f})$
8. Set $B \leftarrow |\mathcal{M}| \cdot \left\lceil \frac{\log(|\Delta_K|) \cdot \sqrt{|\Delta_K|}}{4\pi} \right\rceil$
9. Return $(B, f, \mathfrak{g}, \mathfrak{f}, \mathcal{G}, \mathcal{F})$

3.1 Case $t > 1$

Note that since $\ker(\bar{\varphi}_f)$ contains subgroups of order p_i^t for all i, one could also encrypt $m_i \pmod{p_i^t}$. The resulting decryption simply needs to solve the simultaneous congruences $m \equiv m_i \pmod{p_i^t}$ via Chinese remaindering. This yields the following modifications.

Modification to Algorithm 12

---

5. Set $\mathfrak{f}_i \leftarrow [(p_i^{2t}, p_i^t)]$ in $C(\mathcal{O}_{\Delta_f})$ $\forall i \in \{1, \cdots, N\}$

Algorithm 13. Encrypt

Input: λ, pk, m
Output: Ciphertext (c_1, c_2)

1. Pick $r \xleftarrow{\$} \{0, \cdots, Bf - 1\}$
2. Compute $m_i \leftarrow m \pmod{p_i}$
3. Compute $c_1 \leftarrow \mathfrak{g}^r$
4. Compute $\hat{c}_i \leftarrow \mathfrak{f}_i^{m_i} h^r$
5. Return $c_1, \hat{c}_1, \cdots, \hat{c}_n$

Algorithm 14. Decrypt

Input: $\lambda, pk, sk, c_1, \hat{c}_1, \cdots, \hat{c}_n$
Output: Message m

1. Compute $\mathfrak{m}_i \leftarrow \hat{c}_i / c_1^x$
2. Compute $m_i \leftarrow \texttt{Solve}(p_i^t, \mathfrak{f}_i, \mathfrak{m}_i)$
3. Solve $m \equiv m_i \pmod{p_i}$
4. Return m

Algorithm 15. Solve

Input: $f, \mathfrak{f}, \mathfrak{m}$
Output: m such that $\mathfrak{f}^m = \mathfrak{m}$

1. **for** $i = 1$ to N **do**
2.   Compute $\mathfrak{f}_i \leftarrow \mathfrak{f}^{f/p_i^t}$
3.   Compute $\mathfrak{m}_i \leftarrow \mathfrak{m}^{f/p_i^t}$
4.   Set $x_0 \leftarrow 0$
5.   Compute $\gamma \leftarrow \mathfrak{f}_i^{p_i^{t-1}}$
6.   **for** $k = 0$ to $t - 1$ **do**
7.   Compute $\mathfrak{m}'_k \leftarrow (\mathfrak{f}_i^{-x_k} \mathfrak{m}_i)^{p_i^{t-1-k}}$
8.   Compute $d_k \leftarrow \texttt{Solve}(p_i, \gamma, \mathfrak{m}'_k)$
9.   Set $x_{k+1} \leftarrow x_k + p^k d_k$
10.   **end for**
11.   Set $m_i \leftarrow x_t$
12. **end for**
13. Solve $m \equiv m_i \pmod{p_i^t}$ $\quad \forall i \in \{1, \cdots, N\}$ using CRT
14. Return m

3.2 $t = 1$

If $t = 1$, we have $f = p_1 p_2 \cdots p_N$. If we assume $q > 4f$ as before, *i.e.*, $\lambda \geq \mu + 2$ in
Gen, then the reduced representative of the ideal class $\mathfrak{f} \in C(\mathcal{O}_{\Delta_f})$ is (f^2, f) and
$\mathfrak{f}$ generates a cyclic group of order f in $C(\mathcal{O}_{\Delta_f})$. Thus, our Encrypt, Decrypt
and Solve algorithms remain unchanged from their original versions. However,
since the Solve algorithm is essentially an inversion modulo f (a prime in the
CL schemes) and f is now composite, we can perform computations modulo
the individual prime factors of f and retrieve the message modulo f using the
Chinese Remainder Theorem (CRT). This can be done in three ways:

1. The first CRT modification is straightforward: we simply compute inversions
   modulo each prime divisor of f and use CRT to retrieve the message modulo f.
   The modified Solve algorithm is as follows:

Algorithm 16. Solve

Input: $f, \mathfrak{f}, \mathfrak{m}$
Output: m such that $\mathfrak{m} = \mathfrak{f}^m$
1. Parse $\mathtt{Red}(\mathfrak{m})$ as $(f^2, \tilde{x}f)$
2. Compute $m_i \leftarrow \tilde{x}^{-1} \pmod{p_i}$
3. Solve $m \equiv m_i \pmod{p_i}$
4. Return m

---

2. The second CRT modification utilizes the idea that $\mathcal{F}$ contains order p_i subgroups for each i that are generated by the elements $\mathfrak{f}_i = \mathfrak{f}^{(f/p_i)}$ represented by the ideals (p_i^2, p_i). Thus, one can compute $m_i \equiv m \pmod{p_i}$ and encrypt $\mathfrak{m} = \prod_{i=1}^{n} \mathfrak{f}_i^{m_i}$. Clearly, $\mathfrak{m}$ is of form $(f^2, \tilde{x}f)$ i.e., $\mathfrak{m} \in \langle \mathfrak{f} \rangle$ and we have the following modifications.

Modification to Algorithm 12

---

5. Set $\mathfrak{f}_i \leftarrow [(p_i^2, p_i)]$ in $C(\mathcal{O}_{\Delta_f})$

Algorithm 17. Encrypt

Input: λ, pk, m
Output: Ciphertext (c_1, c_2)
1. Pick $r \xleftarrow{\$} \{0, \cdots, Bf - 1\}$
2. Compute $m_i \leftarrow m \pmod{p_i}$
3. Compute $c_1 \leftarrow \mathfrak{g}^r$
4. Compute $c_2 \leftarrow \mathfrak{f}_1^{m_1} \mathfrak{f}_2^{m_2} \cdots \mathfrak{f}_N^{m_N} h^r$
5. Return c_1, c_2

Algorithm 18. Solve

Input: $f, \mathfrak{f}, \mathfrak{m}$
Output: m such that $\mathfrak{m} = \mathfrak{f}^m$
1. Parse $\mathtt{Red}(\mathfrak{m})$ as $(f^2, \tilde{x}f)$
2. $m_i \leftarrow (\tilde{x}f/p_i)^{-1} \pmod{p_i}$
3. Solve $m \equiv m_i \pmod{p_i}$
4. Return m

---

3. The third CRT variant also uses the fact that $\mathfrak{f}_i = [(p_i^2, p_i)]$ is cyclic of order p_i and generates N ciphertexts $\mathfrak{m}_i = \mathfrak{f}_i^{m_i}$ where $m_i \equiv m \pmod{p_i}$. The modification to the Gen algorithm is identical to that of the previous variant, and the modified Encrypt and Decrypt algorithms take the following form:

Algorithm 19. Encrypt

Input: λ, pk, m
Output: Ciphertext $(c_1, \tilde{c}_1, \ldots, \tilde{c}_n)$
1. Pick $r \xleftarrow{\$} \{0, \cdots, Bf - 1\}$
2. Compute $m_i \leftarrow m \pmod{p_i}$
3. Compute $c_1 \leftarrow \mathfrak{g}^r$
4. Compute $\hat{c}_i \leftarrow \mathfrak{f}_i^{m_i} h^r$
5. Return $c_1, \hat{c}_1, \cdots, \hat{c}_n$

Algorithm 20. Decrypt

Input: $\lambda, pk, sk, c_1, \hat{c}_1, \cdots, \hat{c}_n$
Output: Message m
1. Compute $\mathfrak{m}_i \leftarrow \hat{c}_i / c_1^x$
2. Compute $m_i \leftarrow \mathtt{Solve}(p_i, \mathfrak{f}_i, \mathfrak{m}_i)$
3. Solve $m \equiv m_i \pmod{p_i}$
4. Return m

3.3 Security Considerations for the Extensions

It is easy to verify that the extensions presented in Sect. 3 preserve the linearly homomorphic properties. Moreover, the security considerations for the original CL scheme remain unchanged throughout these extensions, with the appropriate conditions on the Legendre symbols (p_i/p_j), (p_i/q) and (q/p_i) as stated in Algorithm 12. As described in Subsect. 2.2, the fundamental discriminants Δ_K should be chosen such that 2-Sylow subgroup of the class group $C(\mathcal{O}_{\Delta_K})$ is as small as possible.

If N is the number of prime factors of Δ_K, then the 2-rank of $C(\mathcal{O}_{\Delta_K})$ is $N - 1$, and 2^{N-1} divides $h(\Delta_K)$. We wish to ensure that this is in fact the highest power of 2 dividing $h(\Delta_K)$. For discriminants of the form $\Delta_K = -pq$ as in Algorithm 1, we have $N = 2$, so $h(\Delta_K)$ is even. The conditions $(p/q) = (q/p) = -1$ guarantee that $h(\Delta_K)/2$ is odd. Similarly, when $\Delta_K = -p_1 p_2 \cdots p_N q$, we see that 2^{N-1} divides $h(\Delta_K)$. If $(p_i/p_j) = 1$ and $(p_i/p_N) = (p_N/p_i) = -1$ for $1 \le i, j < N$, then no higher power of 2 divides $h(\Delta_K)$ (see, for example, [2]).

4   Parameter Choices

As described in [5], the main concern with selecting parameters is that it should be computationally infeasible to compute $h(\Delta_K)$, the class number of the maximal order $\mathcal{O}_{\Delta_K}$, as knowledge of the class number in this setting enables the computation of discrete logarithms in $C(\mathcal{O}_{\Delta_f})$. Biasse et al. in [1] gave estimates of discriminant sizes to provide various levels of security using the best-known index calculus algorithms of subexponential complexity. In Table 1, we give these sizes for the 128-, 192-, and 256-bit security levels, along with the corresponding RSA modulus sizes required for Paillier [11] and Bresson et al. [3]. Note that generic group algorithms do not play a role here, as their complexity is worse than the index calculus algorithms.

Table 1. Parameter sizes (in bits)

Security level	RSA modulus	Δ_K	Δ_f (for n-bit messages)			
			16	80	256	32768
128	3072	1828	1860	1988	2340	67364
192	7680	3598	3630	3758	4110	69134
256	15360	5972	6004	6132	6484	71508

We also list, in Table 1, the sizes of the non-fundamental discriminants Δ_f required to provide the given security level for various message sizes. As mentioned earlier, Paillier and Bresson et al. can encrypt messages of up to the same size as the RSA modulus used, which is determined by the desired security level. The variants of the Castagnos and Laguillaumie cryptosystem have their security level fixed primarily by the size of the fundamental discriminant Δ_K, and can work with different message sizes by varying the conductor. We see that smaller message spaces should be quite favorable for the Castagnos and Laguillaumie system and its variations, as even the non-maximal discriminans are quite small compared to the RSA moduli required Paillier and Bresson et al. at the same security levels. We also see that larger message spaces can be used at a fixed security level, but note that the extensions involving prime power conductors are necessary, since all primes dividing the conductor must also divide Δ_K. Even with this extension, the CL cryptosystems would not be very efficient on such large messages, as the discriminants required are very large.

The two other considerations for security parameter choices are the sizes of primes dividing the conductor f and the upper bound for selecting random exponents in the protocol. We now discuss these two considerations.

4.1   Restrictions on Prime Factors of f

Castagnos and Laguillaumie insisted on using a conductor (a prime p) of size at least 80 bits to ensure $\gcd(p, h(\Delta_K)) = 1$ with high probability implying that the odd part of the class number is completely unknown. This is important as the odd part of $h(\Delta_K)$ is the security parameter and knowing the size of the odd part, s, leads to a total break of the scheme as shown in Subsect. 2.2. If a divisor of s is known, then computing s itself may be easier. Extrapolating this idea to our extension in which the conductor is a product of prime powers would then imply that the prime divisors of the conductor be at least 80 bits. This restriction is detrimental to the performance of both the original and extended versions of the cryptosystem.

However, we believe that this is an unnecessary restriction when one considers how a known factor of $h(\Delta_K)$ could be exploited in practice. The best known algorithms to compute the class number are subexponential index-calculus algorithms and generic group algorithms. There is no known way to speed up the index calculus algorithms given a divisor of the class number, as the complexity depends on the discriminant as opposed to the class number. Thus, the discriminant sizes recommended by Biasse et al. in [1] offer enough protection against index calculus algorithms even if a divisor of the class number is known.

When considering generic algorithms, on the other hand, a known divisor of the class number does improve the running time, as one can target the unknown part directly. We consider the worst case that the entire conductor f divides the odd part of the class number (note that f itself is odd). Let 2^{k_1} be the even and $s = f \cdot s'$ be the odd factors of $h(\Delta_K)$ where $k_1 \in \mathbb{Z}_{\geq 0}$ and s' is the unknown part of the odd part s. Since $h(\Delta_K) < \frac{1}{\pi} \log(|\Delta_K|)\sqrt{\Delta_K}$ (see, for example, [6, §5.10]), we have,

$$s' < \frac{1}{2^{k_1} \cdot f \cdot \pi} \log(|\Delta_K|)\sqrt{|\Delta_K|}. \qquad (1)$$

Generic group algorithms can be used to compute s' in time $O(\sqrt{s'})$. Ignoring constants and lower-order terms, in order to provide b bits of security, we require that $\sqrt{s'} > 2^b$. Combining this with (1) yields the following upper bound on $\log_2 f$:

$$\log_2 f \leq \log_2(\log(|\Delta_K|)) + \frac{1}{2}\log_2(|\Delta_K|) - k_1 - 2 - 2b. \qquad (2)$$

For example, following the recommendations in [1], Castagnos and Laguillaumie chose a discriminant of size 1828 bits at the 128-bit security level to prevent index calculus attacks in $C(\mathcal{O}_{\Delta_K})$. Substituting these values in Eq. 2 results in

$$\log_2 f \leq 667 - k_1,$$

meaning that we can tolerate known divisors of the conductor of size over 600 bits before the generic attacks would work in fewer than 2^b operations. Note that using conductors with prime divisors larger than this bound is also highly unlikely to be an issue, because, as discussed in [5], the probability that primes of this size divide the class number is negligible—indeed, in [5], using primes larger than 2^{80} was deemed to be sufficient. Thus, we conclude that based on the current state of knowledge of possible attacks on the cryptosystem, prime divisors of any size in the conductor are unlikely to result in any loss of security. This is because the discriminant sizes required to avoid index calculus attacks result in class numbers that are sufficiently large to prevent the generic algorithms, which could exploit a known factor of the class number, from working in fewer than 2^b operations.

4.2   Selection of Random Exponents

The bound B on exponents in Algorithm 1, taken directly from [5], is designed to ensure that the resulting group elements are selected from the entire class group uniformly at random, a necessary condition for the security proofs to hold. In [5], the formula for B has a factor of 2^{80} in order to ensure statistical distance of 2^{-80} from the uniform distribution; in our exposition above, we instead use the size of the message space f, thus allowing the resulting statistical distance $1/f$ to vary with the size of the message space. In the following section, in which we benchmark the practical performance of their version as well as our extensions, we will consider this version of the cryptosystem.

However, it is also known that one can obtain similar security proofs using much shorter exponents if one is willing to use slightly non-standard versions of the intractability assumptions, a critical performance optimization. There is no known way to take advantage of knowledge that discrete logarithms are small in the index calculus algorithms, so these have no bearing on the exponent bounds. The only concern is with generic algorithms of square root complexity, which imply that all exponents should be chosen with at least $2b$ bits for a b-bit security level. Koshiba and Kurosawa [10] proved that security proofs relying on Diffie-Hellman problems also hold assuming that such short exponent versions of the discrete logarithm problem are intractable. Thus, it is at least plausible that the security proofs of [5] also hold under similarly modified intractability assumptions. We will also consider short exponent versions of our cryptosystems, as is typically done in practice, in the benchmarks presented in the next section, using exponents of $2b$ bits.

5   Numerical Results

In this section we present numerical results from benchmarking our extended version of the cryptosystem of Castagnos and Laguillaumie [5]. Our first set of experiments were designed to determine which variation and parameter selection yields the fastest encryption and decryption times for different combinations of security level and message size. The second set of experiments compares the best versions against the Paillier [11] and Bresson et al. [3] cryptosystems.

Our experiments were carried out on a standard desktop with 4 Intel Core i5-2400 CPUs, each CPU with 4 cores, running at 3.10 GHz, and 8 GB RAM, running Fedora 28. Our programs are written in C/C++ (using gcc version 8.1.1) with GMP (version 6.1.2) and NTL (version 11.3.2) support for arbitrary precision arithmetic. We used Maxwell Sayles's optimized binary quadratic forms library [12] for ideal arithmetic. Generic single ideal exponentiations were computed using the 8-NAF method while double exponentiations were computed using the interleaving method with window size 8. However, the exponentiations of $\mathfrak{f} = [(f^2, f)]$ were performed by simply computing the inverse of the exponent modulo the order of the ideal class of $\mathfrak{f}$ and setting $\mathfrak{f}^x$ as $[(f^2, x^{-1}f)]$.

5.1   Comparison of Variations of the Castagnos and Laguillaumie Cryptosystem

The objective of these experiments was to find the fastest CL variation among different choices of the conductor at each security level. Since the message space can be chosen independently of the security parameter, we considered message space sizes of 16, 80 and 256 bits, as well as the same message size of the Pailler [11] cryptosystem at the same security level. We considered 80 bits as Castagnos and Laguillaumie promote 80 bits of message space for practical applications in their paper, and the remaining message sizes were selected to illustrate performance with smaller and larger message sizes at fixed security levels. As one can select short exponents in the CL and BCP schemes, we performed each experiment twice for these cryptosystems, once with full domain exponents and next with shorter exponents.

We used conductors of the general form $f = (p_1 \cdots p_N)^t$, and varied N and t to find the optimal (N, t) pair for each security level, message space size, and variant. We performed some preliminary experiments to find the maximum values of N and t that one should consider during these experiments. Our observations showed that the bounds $N = 9$ and $t' \leq t < t' + 5$ were sufficient to find the optimal (N, t) pairs for a message space at a given security level. Here, $t' = \lceil |\mathcal{M}|/\Delta_K \rceil$ is the minimum t value required to achieve the message space size at a security level. The choice of $N = 9$ and five more values of t were merely to see the effect of increasing N and t values on the performance. We generated

10 different parameters (f, Δ_K) for each of the 45 combinations of N and t. As N and t increase, it is difficult to maintain exact conductor sizes as desired and so we made sure that the conductor has at least the required minimum number of bits, but at most 3 bits more.

We considered all four variations of the cryptosystem of Castagnos and Laguillaumie described in Sect. 2 as well as the modifications to the original conductor choice in Sect. 3. We denote the four schemes as Basic, Variant, BasicPlus and VariantPlus, where "Variant" denotes the version described in Subsect. 2.3 with smaller ciphertexts, and the latter two are the Basic and Variant with the expansion technique from Subsect. 2.4 applied. We also used all the CRT-based encryption and decryption variations described in Sect. 3.

In summary, for every combination of security level, message size, conductor decomposition (N and t), and specific cryptosystem variant, we computed the average encryption and decryption times in milliseconds taken over the same set of 1000 messages. Table 2 contains a summary of these experiments. For each security level and message size pair, we list the average encryption and decryption times for the fastest variant along with the corresponding N and t values. We record this for both full domain exponents and short exponents. The variants are specified using the short-hand notation B, V, BP, and VP, for Basic, Variant, BasicPlus, and VariantPlus, respectively. ED denotes encryption and decryption, 2ED denotes decryption with CRT2 and its corresponding encryption and 3ED denotes encryption with CRT3 and its corresponding encryption.

Table 2. Summary of best performances by CL schemes (in ms)

Security	Message	Short exponents					Full exponents				
		N	t	Scheme	Enc.	Dec.	N	t	Scheme	Enc.	Dec.
128	16	1	1	B-ED	14	9	1	1	B-ED	58	28
	80	1	1	B-ED	15	9	1	1	B-ED	63	33
	256	1	1	B-ED	18	11	1	1	V-ED	96	50
	3072	1	1	B-ED	156	98	6	2	VP-ED	964	794
192	16	1	1	B-ED	47	27	1	1	B-ED	223	115
	80	1	1	B-ED	47	27	1	1	B-ED	249	128
	256	1	1	B-ED	54	31	1	1	B-ED	**320**	166
							2	1	V-ED	328	**160**
	7680	1	1	B-ED	871	508	6	3	VP-ED	7276	6702
256	16	1	1	B-ED	116	65	1	1	B-ED	672	342
	80	1	1	B-ED	118	66	1	1	B-ED	728	370
	256	1	1	B-ED	126	70	2	1	B-2ED	**865**	440
							2	1	V-2ED	955	**432**
	15360	5	1	B-ED	4449	2436	6	3	VP-ED	35790	34551

We see that conductors with multiple prime divisors ($N > 1$) only improve performance for sufficiently large messages and large exponents. Using prime powers ($t > 1$) does not generally improve performance, but is necessary to handle messages that are larger than the fundamental discriminant. In that case, the smallest required value of t was optimal. Among the cryptosystem variations, the basic version was optimal when using short exponents and/or small messages, while the small ciphertext variation and some of the CRT modifications came out on top when using full exponents and larger security levels and messages.

5.2   Comparison to Paillier and Bresson et al.

We next compare the best versions of the Castagnos and Laguillaumie cryptosystem to the Paillier [11] and Bresson et al. [3] schemes. Paillier mentioned two encryption schemes in his paper [11] and presented CRT improvements for both decryption routines. We implemented the schemes along with their CRT improvements and observed that *Scheme 1* with CRT gives the best encryption and decryption results with small message sizes and the best decryption result with large message sizes. *Scheme 3* with CRT gives the best encryption results with large message sizes. Since the BCP scheme is also based on the DDH problem, we have two versions of the BCP scheme as well, one with full domain exponents and the other with short exponents. Note that contrary to BCP, Paillier encryption performs operations with the message as an exponent. Thus, for a fixed security level, we expect that Pailler encryption times should vary slightly with different message sizes, whereas the other operations should remain relatively constant.

We compare below these results with those of the best results from the Castagnos and Laguillaumie variants in Tables 3, 4 and 5. For the Castagnos and Laguillaumie timings, we list the best observed encryption and decryption times amongst all the variants we implemented. Note that for the largest message spaces, no single variant results in both optimal encryption and decryption; in practice, we recommend the version with faster decryption, as the difference in encryption times relative to the optimal version is much smaller than the corresponding difference between decryption times.

At the 128-bit security level, Paillier was the fastest when using full exponents and BCP was the fastest for short exponents, for all message sizes considered. BCP was fastest for short exponents at the 192-bit level, while the Castagnos and Laguillaumie variants were superior when using full exponents for 16- and 80-bit messages; the results were mixed for larger messages. At the 256-bit security level, Castagnos and Laguillaumie variants are fastest for the three smallest message sizes when using full and short exponents. Among the Castagnos and Laguillaumie cryptosystem variations under consideration here, the basic version from [5] proved to be the best for small messages and exponents, but other variations and conductor decompositions were advantageous once the messages and exponents were sufficiently large.

Table 3. Summary of best performance (in ms)—128-bit security

Message	System	Short exponents		Full exponents	
		Encryption	Decryption	Encryption	Decryption
16	Pai			37	12
	BCP	7	3	147	73
	CL	14	9	58	28
80	Pai			38	12
	BCP	7	3	147	73
	CL	14	9	63	33
256	Pai			40	12
	BCP	7	3	147	73
	CL	18	11	96	50
3072	Pai			74	12
	BCP	7	3	145	72
	CL	156	98	964	794

Table 4. Summary of best performance (in ms)—192-bit security

Message	System	Short exponents		Full exponents	
		Encryption	Decryption	Encryption	Decryption
16	Pai			376	128
	BCP	38	18	1508	754
	CL	47	27	223	115
80	Pai			381	129
	BCP	38	18	1508	754
	CL	47	27	249	128
256	Pai			393	129
	BCP	38	18	1508	754
	CL	54	31	**320**	166
				328	**160**
7680	Pai			**745**	254
				755	**129**
	BCP	38	18	1487	743
	CL	871	508	7276	6702

Table 5. Summary of best performance (in ms)—256-bit security

Message	System	Short exponents		Full exponents	
		Encryption	Decryption	Encryption	Decryption
16	Pai			2069	753
	BCP	146	77	8306	4154
	CL	116	65	672	342
80	Pai			2079	752
	BCP	146	77	8298	4152
	CL	116	65	728	370
256	Pai			2104	751
	BCP	146	77	8295	4151
	CL	126	70	**865**	440
				955	**432**
15360	Pai			**4072**	1475
				4125	**751**
	BCP	141	74	8170	4087
	CL	4449	2436	35790	34551

6   Further Work

Our results show that, as expected, the Castagnos and Laguillaumie cryptosystem has some performance advantages as compared to Paillier and BCP for small messages and at high security levels. The variations described in this paper provide improvements when large exponents and message sizes are used.

One further optimization that could be considered to improve the extended versions is to take advantage of the fact that sufficiently small prime divisors of the conductor can be handled without multiprecision. This was not done in our experiments and could potentially make these versions more competitive.

We remark that the short exponent versions of the cryptosystems, as expected, are quite efficient. It would be of interest to revise and complete the security proofs in this context, where the intractability assumptions are all replaced by their short exponent analogues.

References

1. Biasse, J.-F., Jacobson Jr., M.J., Silvester, A.K.: Security estimates for quadratic field based cryptosystems. In: Steinfeld, R., Hawkes, P. (eds.) ACISP 2010. LNCS, vol. 6168, pp. 233–247. Springer, Heidelberg (2010). https://doi.org/10.1007/978-3-642-14081-5_15
2. Bosma, W., Stevenhagen, P.: On the computation of quadratic 2-class groups. J. Théor. Nombres Bordeaux 8(2), 283–313 (1996). http://jtnb.cedram.org/item?id=JTNB_1996__8_2_283_0

3. Bresson, E., Catalano, D., Pointcheval, D.: A simple public-key cryptosystem with a double trapdoor decryption mechanism and its applications. In: Laih, C.-S. (ed.) ASIACRYPT 2003. LNCS, vol. 2894, pp. 37–54. Springer, Heidelberg (2003). https://doi.org/10.1007/978-3-540-40061-5_3

4. Castagnos, G., Imbert, L., Laguillaumie, F.: Encryption switching protocols revisited: switching modulo p. In: Katz, J., Shacham, H. (eds.) CRYPTO 2017. LNCS, vol. 10401, pp. 255–287. Springer, Cham (2017). https://doi.org/10.1007/978-3-319-63688-7_9

5. Castagnos, G., Laguillaumie, F.: Linearly homomorphic encryption from DDH − DL. In: Topics in Cryptology - CT-RSA 2015, The Cryptographer's Track at the RSA Conference 2015, San Francisco, CA, USA, 20–24 April 2015. Proceedings, pp. 487–505 (2015). https://doi.org/10.1007/978-3-319-16715-2_26

6. Cohen, H.: A Course in Computational Algebraic Number Theory. Graduate Texts in Mathematics, vol. 138. Springer, Berlin (1993). https://doi.org/10.1007/978-3-662-02945-9

7. Hamdy, S., Möller, B.: Security of cryptosystems based on class groups of imaginary quadratic orders. In: Okamoto, T. (ed.) ASIACRYPT 2000. LNCS, vol. 1976, pp. 234–247. Springer, Heidelberg (2000). https://doi.org/10.1007/3-540-44448-3_18

8. Hühnlein, D., Jacobson Jr., M.J., Paulus, S., Takagi, T.: A cryptosystem based on non-maximal imaginary quadratic orders with fast decryption. In: Nyberg, K. (ed.) EUROCRYPT 1998. LNCS, vol. 1403, pp. 294–307. Springer, Heidelberg (1998). https://doi.org/10.1007/BFb0054134

9. Jacobson Jr., M.J., Williams, H.C.: Solving the Pell Equation. CMS Books in Mathematics/Ouvrages de Mathématiques de la SMC. Springer, New York (2009). https://doi.org/10.1007/978-0-387-84923-2

10. Koshiba, T., Kurosawa, K.: Short exponent Diffie-Hellman Problems. In: Bao, F., Deng, R., Zhou, J. (eds.) PKC 2004. LNCS, vol. 2947, pp. 173–186. Springer, Heidelberg (2004). https://doi.org/10.1007/978-3-540-24632-9_13

11. Paillier, P.: Public-key cryptosystems based on composite degree residuosity classes. In: Stern, J. (ed.) EUROCRYPT 1999. LNCS, vol. 1592, pp. 223–238. Springer, Heidelberg (1999). https://doi.org/10.1007/3-540-48910-X_16

12. Sayles, M.: Optarith and qform libraries for fast binary quadratic forms arithmetic (2013). http://github.com/maxwellsayles

Applied Cryptography

On the Tracing Traitors Math

Dedicated to the Memory of Bob Blakley - Pioneer of Digital Fingerprinting and Inventor of Secret Sharing

Grigory Kabatiansky[✉]

Skolkovo Institute of Science and Technology (Skoltech),
Moscow 143025, Russia
g.kabatyansky@skoltech.ru

Abstract. We give an overview of the most important mathematical results related to different types of tracing traitors schemes, or schemes with identifiable parent property, especially for the case when the scheme's "length" goes to infinity.

1 Introduction

The interest in protecting digital content from unauthorized copying and distribution can be traced from the mid 80s of the last century, see [1,2]. A well-developed mathematical approach to this problem firstly appeared in the paper "Tracing traitors" by [3]. This paper introduced many important notions. Among them two types of tracing traitors systems capable to trace at least one guity user (under an attack of unknown) were proposed and considered in [3]: *open* systems, with zero-error probability, which later leaded to the notion of IPP (identifiable parent property) systems [4], and *secret* systems, which later became a basis of so-called collusion resistant digital fingerprinting code, see [5].

In this paper we shall review different types of IPP systems and some related objects. There are two the following mostly explored particular cases of IPP systems, namely, codes with the identifiable parent property (IPP codes), coined in [4], and set systems with the identifiable parent property (IPP set systems) introduced in [7]. These IPP systems are based on perfect *secret sharing schemes* (SSS, for short) independently invented in [8] and [9]. Namely, IPP codes are based on the simplest n-out-of-n threshold perfect SSS, and IPP set systems are based on general w-out-of-n threshold perfect SSS.

One of tracing traitor systems proposed in [3] is a particular case of IPP codes with an additional property, called *"traceability"*, which allow to find (to trace) a guilty user as the nearest (in the Hamming distance) code vector to the given unauthorized copy (vector). This property makes "tracing" (decoding) much feasible than in a general case. We shall discuss such systems as well as other approaches to constructing IPP systems with feasible decoding.

© Springer Nature Switzerland AG 2019
C. Carlet et al. (Eds.): C2SI 2019, LNCS 11445, pp. 371–380, 2019.
https://doi.org/10.1007/978-3-030-16458-4_21

2   IPP Codes and IPP Set Systems - How Do They Work?

Following [3] we consider a broadcasting scenario when a dealer distributes some digital content x to M legal users. In order to prevent illegal redistribution the dealer sends the content x in an encrypted form $y = E(x, k)$ obtained by usage of some secret key k. The key k serves as a session key and should be changed for distribution another portion of a digital content. In order to distribute secretly the key k to users the dealer firstly apply n-out-of-n threshold perfect SSS and generate the corresponding shares $s_1, \ldots, s_n$. We assume that the session key k belongs to the finite field $GF(q)$ of q elements. The corresponding shares $s_1, \ldots, s_n$ are random uniformly distributed variables with values from $GF(q)$ such that

$$s_1 + \ldots + s_n = k \tag{1}$$

It is well-known (and easy to check) that knowledge of all s_i allows to anyone uniquely reveal k from (1) and, on the other hand, it is impossible to recover k (except of guessing) if not all shares are known.

The dealer encrypts every share s_j on q different encryption keys, which form the set $F^{(j)}$, $|F^{(j)}| = q$. The corresponding nq encrypted shares

$$a_{11}, a_{12}, \ldots, a_{1q}; a_{21}, a_{21}, \ldots, a_{1q}; a_{n1}, a_{n2}, \ldots, a_{nq}$$

are transmitted by the dealer along with the encrypted portion of digital content (this sequence of nq encrypted shares is called in [3] as *enabling block*). During the initialization phase a given i-th user receives from the dealer the set of decryption keys $\{d_{1i}, \ldots, d_{ni}\}$, where d_{ji} is the decryption key for the encryption key $f_{ji} \in F^{(j)}$ (this set of decryption keys is called in [3] as *user personal key*). Since for every $j = 1, 2, \ldots, n$ there are exactly q decryption keys $D^{(j)} = \{d_{j1}, \ldots, d_{jq}\}$ we shall enumerate them and consider the ordered set of decryption keys $(d_{1i}, \ldots, d_{ni})$ assigned to the i-th user as a q-ary vector $\mathbf{d}_i \in GF(q)^n$. The set of all such vectors $C \subset GF(q)^n$ is called a *fingerprinting code*. From now we won't distinguish between a given user i and assigned to it codevector $\mathbf{d}_i \in C$.

Let a coalition of malicious users (traitors) $U \subset C$ want to create a "device" ("decoder") which will be able to decrypt every transmitted encrypted portion of digital content. It means that the coalition has to create a new sequence $\mathbf{z} = (z_1, \ldots, z_n)$ of decryption keys with the property that $z_j \in D^{(j)}$ for all $j \in \{1, 2, \ldots, n\}$. It is very important to note that $z_j \in \{d_{ju} : u \in U\}$, i.e. that the coalition can choose keys only from the set of the decryption keys (in digital fingerprinting it is called *marking assumption*, see [5,6]). Hence the resulting problem can be formulated in the language of coding theory as it was first done in [4].

For any set $U \subset GF(q)^n$ and any coordinate i define its i-th projection $P_i(U)$ as

$$P_i(U) = \bigcup_{\mathbf{u} \in U} u_i \tag{2}$$

Remind that for a fingerprinting code C we shall denote by U a coalition of malicious users (traitors) as well as the corresponding to them set of codevectors. Denote by $<U>$ the set of all false fingerprints (also called descendants [4]) that the coalition U can create, namely,

$$<U> \; = \; \{\mathbf{z} = (z_1, \ldots, z_n) \in GF(q)^n : \forall i \; z_i \in P_i(U)\} \tag{3}$$

Let

$$E_t(C) = \cup_{U \subset C: \, |U| \le t} <U>$$

denote the set of all false fingerprints which can be created by all coalitions U of size at most t.

Definition 1 ([4]). *A q-ary code C is called a code with identifiable parent property of order t, or C is a t-IPP code for short, if for all $\mathbf{z} \in E_t(C)$*

$$C_t(\mathbf{z}) := \bigcap_{U: \, \mathbf{z} \in <\varphi(U)>, \, |U| \le t} U \ne \emptyset \tag{4}$$

Hence, if the dealer uses a t-IPP code then from any false fingerprint $\mathbf{z}$ created by a coalition U, at least one user from U will be identified with probability 1 (without accusing any innocent user).

For a given q-ary code C of length n let us define its *rate* as $R(C) = n^{-1} \log_q |C|$. And let us denote $M_q(n, t)$ the maximal possible cardinality of a q-ary t-IPP code of length n. Then

$$R_q(n, t) := n^{-1} \log_q M_q(n, t) \tag{5}$$

is the largest possible rate of q−ary t-IPP codes of length n.

As usual in coding theory a family of codes $C^{(i)}$ called *good* if their rate is separated from zero, i.e. $R(C^{(i)}) \ge \gamma > 0$. It is easy to see that $M_q(n, q) \le q$ and hence good q−ary t-IPP codes do not exist for $q \le t$.

First construction of good t-IPP codes was proposed in [3] based on the following simple observation:

Lemma 1. *[3] A q-ary code of length n with the minimal code distance*

$$d(C) > n(1 - t^{-2}) \tag{6}$$

is a t-IPP code.

Moreover codes with the minimal code distance satisfying the inequality (6) posses the following stronger property called *traceability*:
for any false fingerprint $\mathbf{z}$ created by a coalition U the closest (in the Hamming metric $d(.,.)$) codevector belongs to U.

Definition 2. *A code C is called a t-traceability code if for any coalition $U \subset C : \; |U| \le t$ and any vector $\mathbf{z} \in <U>$ the following inequality holds for all $c \in C \setminus U$*

$$d(\mathbf{c}, \mathbf{z}) > \min_{u \in U} d(\mathbf{u}, \mathbf{z}) \tag{7}$$

Hence the complexity of tracing a guilty user in this case has the order M instead of M^t for general t-IPP codes. The following question is open: *what is the minimal alphabet size q_t for which there exist family of good t-IPP codes with traceability?*

It follows immediately from Plotkin and GV bounds [11] that the Eq. (6) guaranties existence of such codes when (and only) $q > t^2$. On the other hand, we have remarked already that good q-ary t-IPP codes do not exist for $q \le t$. It is known [12,13] that $q_2 = 3$ and for larger t it was proved in [14] that $q_t \le t^2 - \lceil \frac{t}{2} \rceil + 1$. Hence first unknown value is q_3 for which I *conjecture that* $q_3 = 4$.

Let us note that the aforementioned results were proved by the probabilistic method [15], also known in information theory as random coding technique. And we know even less about feasible (i.e. with polynomial in n complexity) constructions of good t-IPP codes with traceability. In contrary, there is known explicit construction of good t-IPP codes with polynomial in n complexity of encoding and decoding (i.e. tracing) for all $q > t$. This construction is based on algebraic-geometry codes and concatenated construction [16].

Another class of schemes with IPP was proposed in [7] based on W-out-of-N threshold perfect SSS, which were constructed in [8,9]. Namely, the dealer firstly apply W-out-of-N threshold perfect SSS to the key k and generates N shares $s_1, \ldots, s_N$ which allow anyone who has W or more shares uniquely recover k and at the same time having less than W shares provides no a posteriori information about the key k. The dealer encrypts every share s_j on its unique encryption key f_j. The corresponding N encrypted shares $\alpha_1, \alpha_2, \ldots, \alpha_N$ are transmitted by the dealer along with the encrypted portion of digital content. During the initialization phase the dealer sends to a given i-th user the corresponding set X_i of W decryption keys. Hence every legal user can recover the key k (and then to "open" the corresponding digital content).

According to the properties of W-out-of-N threshold perfect SSS, a coalition U of malicious users in order to create a "device" ("decoder"), which will be able to decrypt every transmitted encrypted portion of digital content, have to create a set of decryption keys $X^{(U)} \subset \cup_{u \in U} X_u$ of the cardinality at least W. For this model the corresponding marking assumption is that the coalition have to create a set of decryption keys of size at least W and only keys from the union of sets of the decryption keys provided to the coalition's members can be chosen. Denote by $< U >_{ss}$ all subsets that can be generated by the coalition U under this marking assumption, namely,

$$< U >_{ss} = \{X \subset [N] : |X| \ge W, X \subset \cup_{u \in U} X_u\} \tag{8}$$

The goal of the dealer (as always) is, for any given forged $\ge w$−subset of the decryption keys be able to identify at least one user from the malicious coalition. It leads to the following definition of the t-IPP (W, N)-set system.

Definition 3 [10]. *A family $X = \{X_1, \ldots, X_M\}$ of W-subsets of $\{1, \ldots, N\}$ is called a t-IPP (W, N)-set system if for every $S \subseteq \{1, \ldots, N\}$, $|S| \ge W$ the intersection* *of all coalitions of size $\leq t$ that can generate S is either non empty, i.e.*

$$\bigcap_{U:|U|\leq t, S \in <U>_{ss}} U \neq \emptyset, \tag{9}$$

or there is no $\leq t$-coalition U such that $S \in <U>_{ss}$.

There is a natural one-to-one correspondance between (W, N)-set systems and binary constant-weight code of weight W and length N. Indeed, let us substitute to a (W, N)-set system $X = \{X_1, ..., X_M\}$ the corresponding binary constant-weight code C_X of weight W and length N consisting of characteristic vectors $c_1, ..., c_M$ of sets $X_1, ..., X_M$. If a (W, N)-set system is the t-IPP then we call the corresponding binary code as t-IPP set system code. The rate of the corresponding binary constant weight code we will also call the rate of t-IPP (W, N)-set system.

Let us denote $M(W, N, t)$ the maximal possible cardinality of a binary t-IPP set system code of weight W and length N, and denote by

$$R(W, N, t) := N^{-1} \log_2 M(W, N, t) \tag{10}$$

is the largest possible rate of a (W, N)-set system. The relationship between t-IPP (W, N)-set systems and binary constant weight codes was firstly observed and investigated in [17], but unfortunately main results of [17], concerning t-IPP (W, N)-set systems, appeared to be incorrect as it was shown in [18]. The correct application of coding results to t-IPP (W, N)-set systems was done in [19], which provides some best known rates of t-IPP (W, N)-set systems. We shall compare IPP-codes and IPP (W, N)-set systems later.

Note that the original paper [7], in which (W, N)-set systems were introduced, contains the definition with additional property of traceability. On the language of set systems the traceability property means that for any coalition $U : |U| \leq t$ and any set S "generated" by the coalition, i.e. $S \subset \cup_{u \in U} X_u$ and $|S| \geq W$, the set from the family which has the largest intersection with S belongs to U.

Definition 4 *A family $X = \{X_1, ..., X_M\}$ of W-subsets of $\{1, ..., N\}$ is called a t-traceability (W, N)-set system if for any coalition $U : |U| \leq t$ and any set $S \in <U>_{ss}$ the following inequality holds for all $j \notin U$*

$$|S \cap X_j| < \max_{u \in U} |S \cap X_u| \tag{11}$$

The following simple lemma is an analog of Lemma 1 for t-traceability (W, N)-set systems.

Lemma 2 *If $|X_i \cap X_j| < W/t^2$ for any $X_i, X_j \in X, i \neq j$, then the family X is a t-traceability set system.*

The binary code corresponding to a t-traceability (W, N)-set system we shall call a t-traceability constant weight code. We shall say that a binary vector $\mathbf{a} = (a_1, ..., a_N)$ covers a binary vector $\mathbf{b} = (b_1, ..., b_N)$ and denote it $\mathbf{a} \succ \mathbf{b}$

if $a_i \geq b_i$ for all i. Equivalently, $\mathbf{a} \succ \mathbf{b}$ if $\mathbf{a} \vee \mathbf{b} = \mathbf{a}$. For any set U of binary vectors let us denote $\mathbf{U}^* = \vee_{u \in U} \mathbf{u}$. Then the Definition 4 and Lemma 2 can be rewritten in the following way.

Definition 5 *A binary constant weight code C of weight W and length N is a t-traceability code if for any t-subset $U \subset C$ and any $\mathbf{z} : \mathbf{U}^* \succ \mathbf{z}$ of weight $wt(\mathbf{z}) \geq W$ the following inequality holds for all $\mathbf{c} \in C \setminus U$*

$$d(\mathbf{c}, \mathbf{z}) > \min_{u \in U} d(\mathbf{u}, \mathbf{z}) \tag{12}$$

Lemma 3 *A binary constant weight code C of weight W is a t-traceability code if*

$$d(C) > 2W(1 - t^{-2}) \tag{13}$$

The similarity between (6) and (13) is obvious.

3   Existence of Good t-IPP Codes

In this section we consider asymptotic behavior of rate $R_q(n,t) := n^{-1} \log_q M_q(n,t)$ of the best t-IPP codes when q is fixed and n goes to infinity (it is traditional for coding theory).

Lemma 1 says that any ordinary error-correcting code C with enough large normalized minimal code distance $\delta(C) := n^{-1} d(C) > 1 - t^{-2}$ is t-IPP code. It follows from Singleton bound [11] that rate of such code is upper bounded by t^{-2}. On the other hand, if we choose $q = 2t^2$ then the rate of codes achieving GV-bound with $\delta(C) > 1 - t^{-2}$ has order $1/t^2$. Hence for $q \geq 2t^2$

$$R_q(n,t) = \Omega(t^{-2}) \tag{14}$$

For a particular case $t = 2$ a better lower bound was obtained for all $q > 2$ in [4]

$$R_q(n,2) \geq 1 - 3^{-1} \log_q(4q^2 - 6q + 3) + o(1) \tag{15}$$

from which follows that good family of ternary 2-IPP codes exists. It generates an intriguing question if it is true for any t which was affirmatively solved in [20] and later numerically improved in [21]. Unfortunately the rate of codes from [20,21] (obtained by the random coding technique) for q closer to t appeared to be exponentially small with t. For instance, for the most interesting case $q = t+1$ it was proved in [21] that

$$R_{t+1}(n,t) \geq t^{-t(1+o(1))} \tag{16}$$

In fact, it is not a defect of the random coding technique but an inevitable drawback as we shall see it now.

Recall that a q-ary code C called a (t,t)-separating code if for any two nonintersecting subsets U and V of C there is at least one coordinate j which *separate* them, i.e. $U_j \cap V_j = \emptyset$, see [22–24]. This notion, known in coding theory for half a century, was rediscovered under the name "secure frame-proof codes", see [5,25]. Obviously any t-IPP code is at the same time a (t,t)-separating code. Denote by $R_q^{sep}(t,t;n)$ the maximal rate of a q-ary (t,t)-separating code of length n. Recently received in [26] the following upper bound for the rate of separating codes says that

$$R_q^{sep}(t,t;n) \le c\frac{2^q}{2^{2t}\log_2 q} + o(1), \tag{17}$$

where c is some constant does not depending on q and t ($c < 2.1$, see [26]). Hence for the most interesting case $q = t+1$

$$R_{t+1}(n,t) \le \frac{2c}{2^t \log_2 t} + o(1) = 2^{-t(1+o(1))} \tag{18}$$

4   How to Compare Different Systems with IP Property?

How to compare two t-IPP codes but over different alphabet size, or how to compare a t-IPP code and t-IPP family of sets?

There are the following two main parameters of such systems defined in [3]. Namely, the size of enabling block and the size of personal key.

The size of a personal key is equal to n for IPP code of length n and it equals W for IPP (W,N)-set system. It plays a secondary role in analysis of effectiveness of IPP systems.

The size of enabling block plays the key role as an analog of redundancy for error-correcting codes. Indeed, the dealer should transmit this block, consisting of encrypted shares, along with each portion of encrypted digital content. Denote by N the size of enabling block measured in the number of encrypted shares. Hence, for a q-ary t-IPP code of length n it equals to $N = nq$, and for a t-IPP (W,N)-set system it equals to N. For a q-ary t-IPP code C of length n let us define its *effective* (or normalized) rate

$$R^*(C) = N^{-1}\log_2 |C| = R(C)q^{-1}\log_2 q$$

And define the best asymptotical effective rate of q-ary t-IPP codes as

$$R_q^*(t) := \frac{\log_2 q}{q} \lim_{n\to\infty} R_q(n,t) \tag{19}$$

Note. We cannot prove that the limit in (19) exist and use it just to simplify notations instead of usage lim sup *and* lim inf.

Our goal is to construct t-IPP codes with the largest possible effective rate, i.e., to find q for which $R_q^*(t)$ is the maximal possible. Note that it is inefficient to choose a very large value of q. Indeed $R_q(n,t) \le 1$ and hence $R_q(n,t)q^{-1}\log_2 q$ tends to zero with growing q. Then define the best effective rate of t-IPP codes as

$$R^*(t) = \max_q R_q^*(t)$$

Consider this notion in the simplest case $t = 2$. It follows from (15) that for the minimal possible of $q = 3$

$$R_3^*(2) \geq 9^{-1} \log_2 3(2 - \log_3 7) = 0.04028$$

The corresponding lower bound from (15) achieves its maximum at $q = 7$ what gives $R^*(2) \geq 0.0536$

Now let us set $q = 2t^2$. Then it follows immediately from (14) that the best normalized rate

$$R^*(t) = \Omega(\frac{\log t}{t^4}) \tag{20}$$

On the other hand,

$$R^*(t) = O(\frac{\log t}{t^2}) \tag{21}$$

as it was noticed in [3] since a t-IPP code is a t-superimposed code [27], [28], also called t-*cover-free* family [29]. One can see that lower and upper bounds of (20) and (21) differ very significantly. One of explanations of such a big difference could be that fact that the lower bound was obtained for t-IPP codes with the additional property of traceability. For IPP set systems the following remarkable result was proved in [30]: a t-traceability set system is a t^2-superimposed code (i.e. t^2-cover-free family). If this result is valid to IPP-codes also then we will get the upper bound being very close to the lower bound (20). It is an interesting open problem.

Finally let us draw your attention to the following abandoned IPP system which is based on perfect SSS with more complicated access structure than threshold. It is so-called open two level scheme from [3]. This t-IPP scheme has effective rate $R^* = (t^3 \log^4(t))^{-1}$ what gives roughly rate of order t^{-3} and it is much better than we know for t-IPP codes and set systems. So, the main open problem of IPP systems:

What is the order of maximal possible effective rate for t-IPP systems?

Acknowledgements. I am very grateful to Alexander Barg, Marcel Fernandez and Elena Egorova for very fruitful collaboration in the area of tracing traitors and around!

References

1. Wagner, N.R.: Fingerprinting. In: Proceedings of the Symposium on Security and Privacy, Oakland, CA, pp. 18–22, April 1983
2. Blakley, G.R., Meadows, C., Purdy, G.B.: Fingerprinting long forgiving messages. In: Williams, H.C. (ed.) CRYPTO 1985. LNCS, vol. 218, pp. 180–189. Springer, Heidelberg (1986). https://doi.org/10.1007/3-540-39799-X_15
3. Chor, B., Fiat, A., Naor, M.: Tracing traitors. In: Desmedt, Y.G. (ed.) CRYPTO 1994. LNCS, vol. 839, pp. 257–270. Springer, Heidelberg (1994). https://doi.org/10.1007/3-540-48658-5_25
4. Hollmann, H.D., van Lint, J.H., Linnartz, J.P., Tolhuizen, L.M.: On codes with the identifiable parent property. J. Comb. Theory Ser. A **82**(2), 121–133 (1998)

5. Boneh, D., Shaw, J.: Collusion-secure fingerprinting for digital data. IEEE Trans. Inf. Theory **44**, 1897–1905 (1998)
6. Barg, A., Blakley, G.R., Kabatiansky, G.: Digital fingerprinting codes: problems statements, constructions, identification of traitors. IEEE Trans. Inf. Theory **49**(4), 852–865 (2003)
7. Stinson, D.R., Wei, R.: Combinatorial properties and constructions of traceability schemes and frameproof codes. SIAM J. Discrete Math. **11**(1), 41–53 (1998)
8. Blakley, G.R.: Safeguarding cryptographic keys. In: Proceedings of the National Computer Conference, vol. 48, pp. 313–317 (1979)
9. Shamir, A.: How to share a secret. Commun. ACM **22**(11), 612–613 (1979)
10. Collins, M.J.: Upper bounds for parent-identifying set systems. Des. Codes Crypt. **51**(2), 167–173 (2009)
11. MacWilliams, F.J., Sloane, N.J.A.: The Theory of Error-Correcting Codes, vol. 16, North-Holland Mathematical Library (1977)
12. Kabatiansky, G.A.: Good ternary 2-traceability codes exist. In: Proceedings of the IEEE Symposium on Information Theory, Chicago, IL, p. 203 (2004)
13. Kabatiansky, G.A.: Codes for copyright protection: the case of two pirates. Probl. Inf. Transm. **41**, 182–186 (2005)
14. Blackburn, S.R., Etzion, T., Ng, S.-L.: Traceability codes. J. Comb. Theory Ser. A **117**(8), 1049–1057 (2010)
15. Alon, N., Spencer, J.H.: The Probabilistic Method, 4th edn., Wiley Series in Discrete Mathematics and Optimization (2016)
16. Barg, A., Kabatiansky, G.: Class of I.P.P codes with effective tracing algorithm. J. Complex. **20**(2–3), 137–147 (2004)
17. Safavi-Naini, R., Wang, Y.: New results on frame-proof codes and traceability schemes. IEEE Trans. Inf. Theory **47**(7), 3029–3033 (2001)
18. Lofvenberg, J., Larsson, J.-A.: Comments on "new results on frame-proof codes and traceability schemes". IEEE Trans. Inf. Theory **56**(11), 5888–5889 (2010)
19. Egorova, E., Kabatiansky, G.: Analysis of two tracing traitor schemes via coding theory. In: Barbero, Á.I., Skachek, V., Ytrehus, Ø. (eds.) ICMCTA 2017. LNCS, vol. 10495, pp. 84–92. Springer, Cham (2017). https://doi.org/10.1007/978-3-319-66278-7_8
20. Barg, A., Cohen, G., Encheva, S., Kabatiansky, G., Zémor, G.: A hypergraph approach to the identifying parent property: the case of multiple parents. SIAM J. Discrete Math. **14**(3), 423–431 (2001)
21. Alon, N., Cohen, G., Krivelevich, M., Litsyn, S.: Generalized hashing and parent-identifying codes. J. Comb. Theory Ser. A **104**(1), 207–215 (2003)
22. Friedman, A.D., Graham, R.L., Ullman, J.D.: Universal single transition time asynchronous state assignments. IEEE Trans. Comput. **18**(6), 541–547 (1969)
23. Sagalovich, Y.L.: Separating systems. Prob. Inf. Transm. **30**(2), 105–123 (1994)
24. Cohen G.D., Schaathun H.G.: Asymptotic overview on separating codes. Technical report 248, Department of Informatics, University of Bergen, Bergen, Norway (2003)
25. Staddon, J.N., Stinson, D.R., Wei, R.: Combinatorial properties of frameproof and traceability codes. IEEE Trans. Inf. Theory **47**, 1042–1049 (2001)
26. Vorob'ev, I.V.: Bounds on the rate of separating codes. Prob. Inf. Transm. **53**(1), 30–41 (2017)
27. Kautz, W., Singleton, R.: Nonrandom binary superimposed codes. IEEE Trans. Inf. Theory **10**(4), 363–377 (1964)
28. Dyachkov, A.G., Rykov, V.V.: Bounds on the length of disjunctive codes. Prob. Inf. Transm. **18**(2), 166–171 (1982)

29. Furedi, Z., Erdos, P., Frankl, P.: Families of finite sets in which no set is covered by the union of r others. Israel J. Math. **51**(1), 79–89 (1985)
30. Gu, Y., Miao, Y.: Bounds on traceability schemes. IEEE Trans. Inf. Theory **64**(5), 3450–3460 (2018)

Reusable Garbled Turing Machines Without FHE

Yongge Wang[1][✉] and Qutaibah M. Malluhi[2]

[1] Department of Software and Information Systems, UNC Charlotte,
9201 University City Blvd., Charlotte, NC 28223, USA
yonwang@uncc.edu
[2] Department of Computer Science and Engineering, Qatar University, Doha, Qatar
qmalluhi@qu.edu.qa

Abstract. Since Yao introduced the garbled circuit concept in 1980s, it has been an open problem to design efficient reusable garbled Turing machines/circuits. Recently, Goldwasser et al. and Garg et al. answered this question affirmatively by designing reusable garbled circuits and reusable garbled Turing machines. Both of these reusable garbling schemes use fully homomorphic encryption (FHE) schemes as required building components. Here, we use multilinear maps to design a reusable Turing machine garbling scheme that will not need any FHE schemes. Though it is not clear whether our multilinear map based garbling approach could be more efficient than FHE based garbling approach, the goal of this paper is to develop alternative techniques for resuable garbling schemes to stimulate further research in this direction.

1 Introduction

Yao [24] introduced the garbled circuit concept which allows computing a function f on an input x without leaking any information about the input x or the circuit used for the computation of $f(x)$. Since then, garbled circuit based protocols have been used in numerous places and it has become one of the fundamental components of secure multi-party computation protocols. Yao's garbled circuits could be used to evaluate the circuit on one input value only.

Since Yao's work in 1980s, it has been an open problem to design efficient reusable garbled Turing machines. Traditionally, a Turing machine M is first converted to a circuit C_M which is then converted to a garbled circuit $\overline{C}_M$ using Yao's technique. However, using a garbled circuit to evaluate an algorithm on encrypted data takes the worst-case runtime of the algorithm on all inputs of the same length since Turing machines are simulated by circuits via unrolling loops to their worst-case runtime, and via considering all branches of a computation. It is preferred that the runtime of the garbled algorithm on garbled input $\overline{x}$ (of x) should be approximately the same as that of the corresponding

The work reported in this paper is supported by Qatar Foundation Grants NPRP8-2158-1-423 and NPRP X-063-1-014.

un-garbled algorithm on input x. To be more specific, the open problem is to design garbled Turing machines that are efficient from following two aspects: (1) the garbled Turing machine $\overline{M}$ has smaller size than $\overline{C}_M$; (2) For each input x, the evaluation of $\overline{M}$ on $\overline{x}$ takes approximately the same time that M takes on x. In this paper, we answer this open problem affirmatively by showing that for each Turing machine M, we can construct a reusable garbled Turing machine $\overline{M}$ approximately the same size of M without using fully homomorphic encryption schemes.

Recently, Goldwasser et al. [17] and Garg et al. [12] constructed reusable garbled circuits by using techniques of computing on encrypted data such as fully homomorphic encryption (FHE) schemes and attribute-based encryption (ABE) schemes for arbitrary circuits. Goldwasser et al. [16] also constructed reusable garbled Turing machines by employing techniques of FHE, witness encryption (WE) schemes, and the existence of SNARKs (Succinct Non-interactive Arguments of Knowledge). It would be interesting to know whether one can design reusable garbled Turing machines without using FHE schemes.

Using Garg et al.'s indistinguishability obfuscators for NC^1 [12], this paper designs a Turing machine garbling scheme without using FHE schemes. Though it is not clear whether multilinear maps based indistinguishability obfuscators could be more efficient than FHE, the goal of this paper is to develop alternative techniques for resuable garbling schemes to stimulate further research in this direction. The techniques that we used to construct garbled Turing machines could also be used to construct indistinguishability obfuscators for all polynomial size circuits without FHE schemes. Though it has been shown (see, e.g., [1]) that several proposed cryptographic multilinear map construction techniques are insecure, there has been a promising trend (see, e.g., Huang [18,19]) of using Weil descent to design secure trilinear maps. If the security of these Weil descent based trilinear maps could be verified, they should be sufficient for our garbled Turing machine design.

Independently of this work, Koppula, Lewko, and Waters [21] recently designed indistinguishability obfuscation for Turing machines using Garg et al.'s indistinguishability obfuscators, one-way functions and injective pseudo random generators. Some other recent related works on iterated circuit based garbling schemes could be found in Lin and Pass [22], Bitansky, Garg, and Telang [6], Canetti and Holmgren [10], Garg, Lu, Ostrovsky, and Scafuro [14], and Cannetti, Holmgren, Jain, and Vaikuntanathan [9]. It should also be noted that Boyle, Chung, and Pass [7] and Ananth, Boneh, Garg, Sahai, and Zhandry [2] showed how to transform Garg et al.'s indistinguishability obfuscators into one that operates on Turing machines with a strong security assumption called differing input obfuscation.

We conclude this section with the introduction of some notations. A Turing machine is defined as a 5-tuple $M = \langle Q, \Gamma, \delta, q_0, q_F \rangle$ with the properties:

- Q is a finite, non-empty set of states.
- Γ is a finite, non-empty set of tape alphabet symbols. Among symbols in Γ, a special symbol $B \in \Gamma$ is the blank symbol.

- $q_0 \in Q$ is the initial state, and $q_F \in Q$ is the final accepting state.
- $\delta : (Q \setminus \{q_F\}) \times \Gamma \rightarrow Q \times \Gamma \times \{L, R\}$ is the transition function, where L is left shift, R is right shift.

A Turing machine M is called oblivious (OTM) if there exists a function $s(t)$ such that M's head is at cell position $s(t)$ at time t regardless of M's input values. Since every $T(n)$-time bounded Turing Machine can be simulated by an $O(T(n)\log(T(n)))$-time bounded OTM (see, Pippenger and Fischer [23]) all along this paper all TMs are oblivious.

For our garbled Turing machine $\overline{M}$, it takes approximately the same time for $\overline{M}$ to stop on an encrypted input $\bar{x}$ as that the un-garbled M to stop on the un-encrypted input x. If the running time of Turing machines on specific inputs needs to be protected, then one can easily modify Turing machines in such a way that it takes the same time to stop on all inputs of the same length. The details are omitted in this paper.

For a string $x \in \Gamma^*$, we use $x[i]$ to denote the ith element of x. That is, $x = x[0] \cdots x[n-1]$ where n is the length of x. We use $x \in_R \Gamma$ to denote that x is randomly chosen from Γ with the uniform distribution. We use κ to denote the security parameter, $p(\cdot)$ to denote a function p that takes one input, and $p(\cdot, \cdot)$ to denote a function p that takes two inputs. A function f is said to be negligible in an input parameter κ if for all $d > 0$, there exists n_0 such that for all $\kappa > n_0$, $f(\kappa) < \kappa^{-d}$. For convenience, we write $f(\kappa) = \text{negl}(\kappa)$. Two ensembles, $X = \{X_\kappa\}_{\kappa \in N}$ and $Y = \{Y_\kappa\}_{\kappa \in N}$, are said to be computationally indistinguishable if for all probabilistic polynomial-time algorithm D, we have

$$|\text{Prob}[D(X_\kappa, 1^\kappa) = 1] - \text{Prob}[D(Y_\kappa, 1^\kappa) = 1]| = \text{negl}(\kappa).$$

Throughout the paper, we use probabilistic experiments and denote their outputs using random variables. For example, $\text{Exp}_{E,A}^{\text{real}}(1^\kappa)$ represents the output of the real experiment for scheme E with adversary A on security parameter κ. Throughout the paper, $\text{E} = (\text{E.KeyGen}, \text{E.Enc}, \text{E.Dec})$ denotes a semantically secure symmetric-key encryption scheme and $\text{PK} = (\text{PK.KeyGen}, \text{PK.Enc}, \text{PK.Dec})$ denotes a semantically secure public-key encryption scheme.

The structure of this paper is as follows. In Sect. 2, we briefly present the intuition for our construction of reusable garbled Turing machines. Section 3 reviews the reusable circuit garbling scheme for NC^1 circuits. Section 4 presents the construction of reusable garbled Turing machines with ABE_2. Section 5 presents the construction of reusable garbled Turing machines without ABE_2.

2   Overview of Our Construction

In this section, we describe the intuition underlying our constructions. Assuming the hardness of multilinear Jigsaw puzzles (that is, in the generic multilinear encoding model), Garg et al. [12] constructed functional encryption schemes for NC^1 circuits with succinct ciphertexts. Garg et al. then extended their results to all polynomial size circuits using fully homomorphic encryption (FHE) schemes.

As a corollary, for each circuit $C \in NC^1$, one can construct a reusable garbled circuit $\overline{C}$ without using FHE schemes. After Garg et al.'s [12] work, several other obfuscators for complexity class NC^1 have been proposed. For example, Brakerski and Rothblum [8] and Barak et al. [3] designed virtual black-box obfuscators for NC^1 without using FHE.

In the following, we present our idea of constructing reusable Turing machines garbling schemes without using FHE schemes. This construction can also be used to design succinct ciphertext functional encryption schemes for all Turing machines without employing FHE schemes. Based on Pippenger and Fischer's results [23], we assume that the given Turing machine M is oblivious. In order to garble a Turing machine M, the transition function δ of M is converted to a circuit C_δ.

The circuit C_δ takes three inputs: the current head tape symbol b, the current state q of M, and a special session control tape that contains the session information and seed for pseudorandom generators. This session control tape is used to provide session information for C_δ to check whether the current head tape symbol and the current state of M are consistent. There are several reasons for including this additional tape. For example, it could be used to prevent the adversary from feeding tape symbols and Turing machine states from one execution of $\overline{M}(x)$ to another execution of $\overline{M}(y)$ and to prevent the adversary from replaying the execution of $\overline{M}(x)$ on an early or later stage of the tape cell contents. Given these inputs, C_δ checks whether these inputs are consistent (e.g., all of them contain the same random session identification string, the counters are consistent, and the tape cell is the most recently updated one). If the inputs are consistent, C_δ finds the matching transition rule and outputs the next head state q' and changes the current tape symbol to b'. Since C_δ will be converted to Garg et al.'s reusable garbled circuit $\overline{C}_\delta$ and $\overline{C}_\delta$ only accepts appropriately encoded inputs, both q' and b' need to be appropriately encoded by C_δ before output. Using information from the three inputs, C_δ updates the session control tape and uses the encoding key (that is, the public key of a public key encryption scheme, this key could either be included as part of the input to the circuit C_δ or be built-in C_δ itself) for Garg et al.'s NC^1 circuit garbling scheme to encode the session control tape, the tape symbol b', and the state q' respectively. The encoding process consists of encrypting the corresponding values using two public keys at the same time and constructing a statistically simulation sound NIZK proof that the two cipher texts are the encryption of the same plain text[1]. Furthermore, if the output state is q_F, C_δ may output the Turing machine state q_F in clear text without encoding so that the evaluator knows that the Turing machine M stops. Gentry et al. [15] showed that it is possible to check whether a memory cell value is the most recently updated one using NC^1 circuits, and Ishai et al. [20] showed that general cryptographic primitives such as encryptions and commitments could be constructed in NC^1 assuming the existence of

---

[1] Note that if we use recent virtual black-box obfuscators by Brakerski and Rothblum [8] and Barak et al. [3], then it is sufficient to encode the input using one public key and no NIZK proof is needed.

NC^0 pseudorandom generators. Thus C_δ could be easily constructed in NC^1 with reasonable assumptions. Indeed, Garg et al.'s construction [12] requires the existence of an NC^1 decryption circuit for a public key encryption scheme. In a summary, circuit C_δ could be constructed in NC^1. Thus Garg et al.'s approach [12] implies a reusable garbled circuit $\overline{C}_\delta$ for C_δ without FHE.

Depending on the application scenario, the evaluator may or may not need to decrypt the encrypted final output of the Turing machine execution $M(x)$. For example, if a client submits the garbled Turing machine to a cloud data server to carry out computation on his encrypted data at the cloud, the cloud only needs to return the encrypted output to the client without decryption. However, in functional encryption schemes or other applications, the evaluator needs to learn the decrypted output $M(x)$. In this case, the innovative ideas by Goldwasser et al. [16] can be used to decrypt the output. That is, an ABE_2 scheme for Turing machines is used to provide keys for Yao's one-time garbled circuit to decrypt the output. The details are presented in Sect. 4.

Attribute-Based Encryption scheme ABE_2 for Turing machines are relatively slow. In order to improve the efficiency, we can design another reusable garbled circuit to decrypt the encrypted output $\overline{M(x)}$. For this approach, special caution needs to be taken. For example, an active adversary may manipulate the encoded input tape $\bar{x}$ by swapping/repeating tape cells for $\bar{x}$ to obtain a valid encoded tape for $x' \neq x$. The adversary may then run $\overline{M}$ on $\bar{x}'$ to obtain $\overline{M}(x')$ and run the reusable decryption circuit to decrypt $\overline{M}(x')$. In order to address these challenges, we use Chaitin's universal self-delimiting Turing machines [11]. The input to a self-delimiting Turing machine must be encoded in a prefix-free domain. Without proper encoded prefix-free input, the self-delimiting Turing machine would not enter the q_F state. secure message authentication tags for inputs. Furthermore, we also revise the Turing machine in such a way that before entering the state q_F, it selects a random secret key $\mathsf{sk_o}$ and encrypts the output $M(x)$. That is, the output tape contains encoded $\mathsf{sk_o}||\mathsf{E.Enc}(\mathsf{sk_o}, M(x))$. An NC^1 circuit C_d is constructed to decrypt the output tape to $\mathsf{sk_o}||\mathsf{E.Enc}(\mathsf{sk_o}, M(x))$ first and then use $\mathsf{sk_o}$ to decrypt the actual output $M(x)$. Since such kind of circuits exist in NC^1, Garg et al.'s approach [12] can be used to obtain a reusable garbled circuit $\overline{C}_d$. The detailed construction of C_d is presented in Sect. 5.

In a summary, for each evaluation of a Turing machine M on an input x, Turing machine owner pads each bit $x[i]$ with appropriate session control information to $x[i]||\mathsf{session}_b||i||0$ and uses encoding keys for Garg's NC^1 reusable garbling scheme to encode it to $\mathsf{RGC_{nc^1}.Enc}(\mathsf{gsk}, x[i]||\mathsf{session}_b||i||0)$ as the content of the i-th tape cell. The padded suffix 0 denotes that this cell value is an input value. When a cell value is modified at Turing machine step j, the value j is placed in the suffix. The Turing machine owner also encodes the session control information (e.g., $\mathsf{session}$ and random seeds) and provides them in the session control tape and encodes the Turing machine initial state q_0. The evaluator uses $\overline{C}_\delta$ to simulate the Turing machine M and uses an ABE_2 scheme or another reusable garbled circuit to decrypt the output.

3 Reusable Garbled Circuits for NC^1

In this section, we review necessary techniques that are required for our construction. We first present the formal definition of one-time and reusable garbling schemes for circuits and Turing machines.

Definition 1. *Let* $\mathcal{M} = \{\mathcal{M}_n\}_{n \in N}$ *be a family of circuits/Turing machines such that* $\mathcal{M}_n$ *is a set of functions that take n-bit inputs. A garbling scheme for* $\mathcal{M}$ *is a tuple of probabilistic polynomial time algorithms* GS = (GS.Garble, GS.Enc, GS.Eval) *with the following properties*

- $(\overline{M}, \mathsf{gsk}) = \mathsf{GS.Garble}(1^\kappa, M)$ *outputs a garbled circuit/Turing machine* $\overline{M}$ *and a secret key* gsk *for* $M \in \mathcal{M}_n$ *on the security parameter input* κ.
- $c_x = \mathsf{GS.Enc}(\mathsf{gsk}, x)$ *outputs an encoding* c_x *for an input* $x \in \{0,1\}^*$.
- $y = \mathsf{GS.Eval}(\overline{M}, c_x)$ *outputs a value* y *which should equal to* $M(x)$.

The garbling scheme GS is *correct* if the probability that $\mathsf{GS.Eval}(\overline{M}, c_x) \neq M(x)$ is negligible. The garbling scheme GS is *efficient* if the size of $\overline{M}$ is bounded by a polynomial and the run-time of $c_x = \mathsf{GS.Enc}(\mathsf{gsk}, x)$ is also bounded by a polynomial.

Throughout this paper, we will use GT = (GT.Garble, GT.Enc, GT.Eval) and GC = (GC.Garble, GC.Enc, GC.Eval) to denote a garbling scheme for Turing machines and a garbling scheme for circuits respectively. Similarly, we will use RGT = (RGT.Garble, RGT.Enc, RGT.Eval) and RGC = (RGC.Garble, RGC.Enc, RGC.Eval) to denote reusable garbling schemes for Turing machines and circuits respectively.

The security of garbling schemes is defined in terms of input and circuit privacy in the literature. The following security definition for one-time garbling schemes based on Bellare, Hoand, and Rogaway [4] captures the intuition that for any circuit or input chosen by the adversary, one can simulate the garbled circuit and the encoding based on the computation result in polynomial time. In the definition, the variable α represents any state that A may want to give to D.

Definition 2. *(Input and circuit privacy for one-time garbling schemes) A garbling scheme* GS *for a family of circuits/Turing machine* $\mathcal{M}$ *is said to be input and circuit private if there exists a probabilistic polynomial time simulator* $\mathsf{Sim}_{\mathsf{GS}}$ *such that for all probabilistic polynomial time adversaries* A *and* D *and all large* κ, *we have*

$$\left| \mathrm{Prob}[D(\alpha, x, M, \overline{M}, c) = 1 | \mathrm{REAL}] - \mathrm{Prob}[D(\alpha, x, M, \tilde{M}, \tilde{c}) = 1 | \mathrm{SIM}] \right| = \mathrm{negl}(\kappa)$$

where REAL *and* SIM *are the following events*

REAL :	SIM :
$(x, M, \alpha) \leftarrow A(1^\kappa)$	$(x, M, \alpha) \leftarrow A(1^\kappa)$
$(\overline{M}, \mathsf{gsk}) \leftarrow \mathsf{GS.Garble}(1^\kappa, M)$	$(\tilde{M}, \tilde{c}_x) \leftarrow \mathsf{Sim}_{\mathsf{GS}}(M(x), 1^{\max\{\kappa, |M|, |x|\}})$
$c_x \leftarrow \mathsf{GS.Enc}(\mathsf{gsk}, x)$	

The privacy for reusable garbling schemes is defined also in terms of circuit and input privacy and the reader is referred to Goldwasser et al. [17] for details.

Definition 3. *(Private reusable garbling schemes, adapted from Goldwasser et al. [17]) Let* RGS *be a reusable garbling scheme for a family of Turing machines/circuits* $\mathcal{M} = \{\mathcal{M}_n\}_{n \in N}$ *and* $M \in \mathcal{M}_n$ *be a Turing machine/circuit with n-bits inputs. For a pair of probabilistic polynomial time algorithms* $A = (A_0, A_1)$ *and a probabilistic polynomial time simulator* $S = (S_0, S_1)$, *define two experiments:*

$$
\begin{array}{ll}
\mathrm{Exp}_{\mathrm{RGS},A}^{\mathrm{real}}(1^\kappa): & \mathrm{Exp}_{\mathrm{RGS},A,S}^{\mathrm{ideal}}(1^\kappa): \\
(M, \mathsf{state}_A) = A_0(1^\kappa) & (M, \mathsf{state}_A) = A_0(1^\kappa) \\
(\mathsf{sk}, \overline{M}) = \mathrm{RGS.Garble}(1^\kappa, M) & (\tilde{M}, \mathsf{state}_S) = S_0(1^\kappa, M) \\
\alpha = A_1^{\mathrm{RGS.Enc}(\mathsf{sk}, \cdot)}(M, \overline{M}, \mathsf{state}_A) & \alpha = A_1^{O(\cdot, M)[[\mathsf{state}_S]]}(M, \tilde{M}, \mathsf{state}_A)
\end{array}
$$

In the above experiments, $O(\cdot, M)[[\mathsf{state}_S]]$ *is an oracle that on input* x *from* A_1, *runs* S_1 *with inputs* $1^{|x|}$, $M(x)$, *and the latest state of* S; *it returns the output of* S_1 *(storing the new simulator state for the next invocation). The garbling scheme* RGS *is said to be* private *with reusability if there exists a probabilistic polynomial time simulator* S *such that for all pairs of probabilistic polynomial time adversaries* $A = (A_0, A_1)$, *the following two distributions are computationally indistinguishable:*

$$
\left\{\mathrm{Exp}_{\mathrm{RGS},A}^{\mathrm{real}}(1^\kappa)\right\}_{\kappa \in N} \approx_c \left\{\mathrm{Exp}_{\mathrm{RGS},A,S}^{\mathrm{ideal}}(1^\kappa)\right\}_{\kappa \in N} \tag{1}
$$

The recent virtual black-box obfuscators for NC^1 by Brakerski-Rothblum [8] and Barak et al. [3] require generic multilinear encoding model. Though Garg et al.'s [12] indistinguishability obfuscator for NC^1 is constructed using generic multilinear encoding also, it does not rule out the possibility of constructing indistinguishability obfuscators in the plain model with weaker assumptions. Garg et al. [12] showed the following theorem.

Theorem 1. *Assuming the existence of an indistinguishability obfuscator, there is a garbling scheme* RGC$_{nc^1}$ *for* NC^1 *circuits that is secure according to the definition in Goldwasser et al. [17].*

Based on witness encryption (WE) schemes by Garg et al. [13] and the existence of SNARKs (Succinct Non-interactive Arguments of Knowledge) by Bitansky et al. [5], Goldwasser et al. [16] designed attribute-based encryption (ABE) schemes for Turing machines[2]. The single-outcome ABE schemes for Turing machines in [16] could be converted to two-outcome attribute-based encryption schemes (ABE$_2$) for Turing machines using the techniques from Goldwasser et al. [17].

Goldwasser et al. [17] introduced the following concept of two-outcome attribute-based encryption schemes (ABE$_2$) for Turing machines.

---

[2] Note that the **correctness** definition of Definition 3 for ABE in [16] is messed up.

Definition 4. *A two-outcome attribute-based encryption scheme* ABE$_2$ *for a class of Turing machines* $\mathcal{M}$ *is a tuple of four algorithms* (ABE$_2$.Setup, ABE$_2$.Enc, ABE$_2$.KeyGen, ABE$_2$.Dec*):*

- (mpk, msk) = ABE$_2$.Setup(1^κ)*: On the security parameter input* 1^κ, *outputs the master public key* mpk *and the master secret key* msk.
- sk$_M$ = ABE$_2$.KeyGen(msk, M)*: On input* msk *and a Turing machine* M, *outputs a secret key* sk$_M$ *corresponding to* M. *Note that* M *is public.*
- c = ABE$_2$.Enc(mpk, x, b_0, b_1)*: On input the master public key* mpk, *an attribute* $x \in \{0,1\}^*$, *and two messages* b_0, b_1, *outputs a ciphertext* c.
- b_i = ABE$_2$.Dec(sk$_M$, c)*: On input a secret key* sk$_M$ *for the Turing machine* M *and a ciphertext* c, *outputs* b_i *if* $M(x) = i$ *for* $i = 0, 1$.

Correctness (informal). *The correctness of an* ABE$_2$ *scheme means* ABE$_2$.Dec(sk$_M$, c) *fails with a negligible probability (for a formal definition, it is referred to* [17]*).*

The security of an ABE$_2$ scheme means that if one has the secret key sk$_M$ for a Turing machine M, then one can decrypt one of the two encrypted messages based on the value of $M(x)$ where x is the attribute, but learns zero information about the other message. The formal definition could be found in Goldwasser et al. [17].

Formally, the security can be defined as follows.

Definition 5. *(Goldwasser et al.* [17]*) Let* ABE$_2$ *be a two-outcome attribute-based encryption scheme for a class of Turing machines* $\mathcal{M}$. *Let* $A = (A_1, A_2, A_3)$ *be a tuple of probabilistic polynomial time adversaries. Define the experiment* Exp$_{\text{ABE}_2}$(1^κ)*:*

1. (mpk, msk) = ABE$_2$.Setup(1^κ)
2. (M, state$_1$) = A_1(mpk)
3. sk$_M$ = ABE$_2$.KeyGen(msk, M)
4. (a, a_0, a_1, x, state$_2$) = A_2(state$_1$, sk$_M$) *where* a, a_0, a_1 *are bits*
5. *Choose a random bit* b *and let*

$$c = \begin{cases} \text{ABE}_2.\text{Enc}(\text{mpk}, x, a, a_b), & \text{if } M(x) = 0, \\ \text{ABE}_2.\text{Enc}(\text{mpk}, x, a_b, a), & \text{otherwise.} \end{cases}$$

6. $b' = A_3$(state$_2$, c). *If* $b = b'$, *then output 1, else output 0.*

The scheme is said to be a single-key fully-secure two-outcome ABE$_2$ *if for all probabilistic polynomial time adversaries* A *and for all sufficiently large security parameters* κ, *we have*

$$\text{Prob}[\text{Exp}_{\text{ABE}_2, A}(1^\kappa) = 1] \leq 1/2 + \text{negl}(\kappa).$$

The scheme is said to be single-key selectively secure if A *needs to provide* x *before receiving* mpk.

4   Reusable Garbled Turing Machines with ABE$_2$

The construction of a garbling scheme RGT = (RGT.Garble, RGT.Enc, RGT.Eval) for Turing machines M proceeds as follows.

$(\text{gsk}, \overline{M}) = \text{RGT.Garble}(1^\kappa, M)$:

– sk = E.KeyGen(1^κ), $(\text{psk}_i, \text{ppk}_i)$ = PK.KeyGen(1^κ) for $i = 0, 1$.
– Let E_M = E.Enc(sk, M) and $\overline{\text{sk}}$ = PK.Enc(ppk_0, sk).
– Let U_M be an oblivious universal Turing machine and let $s(t)$ be the head position function for U_M. On input x, U_M first decrypts sk = PK.Dec(psk_0, $\overline{\text{sk}}$) and M = E.Dec(sk, E_M). U_M then runs M on x to output $M(x)$.
– Let δ be the transition function of U_M and $C_\delta \in NC^1$ be the following circuit:

> **Input:** head sate $q||\text{session}_q||j_q$, tape cell $b||\text{session}_b||j_c||j_b$, and control tape ctape = $\text{ppk}_0||\text{ppk}_1||\text{state}||\text{session}_s||j_q$.
>
> 1. use information from session_s to extract the current Turing machine step j_1, expected current head position $j_2 = s(j_1)$, and the most recent time j_3 that the cell j_c has been updated.
> 2. if $j_1 \neq j_q + 1$ or $j_2 \neq j_c$ or $j_3 \neq j_b$, go to step 11.
> 3. if $\text{session}_s, \text{session}_b$, and session_q are inconsistent, go to step 11.
> 4. if $q = q_F$, output the state q_F in clear and exit.
> 5. if $q = q_{\text{noop}}$, go to step 11.
> 6. compute the next state and tape symbols $(q', b') = \delta(q, b)$.
> 7. update ideal cipher E state, public key cipher PK state, and the values in $\text{session}_s, \text{session}_b, \text{session}_q$, and state.
> 8. let $e_i^{q'}$ = PK.Enc($\text{ppk}_i, q'||\text{session}_q||j_1$) for $i = 0, 1$, and $\pi^{q'}$ be a statistically simulation sound non-interactive zero knowledge (NIZK) proof for the following NP statement: $e_0^{q'}$ and $e_1^{q'}$ are encryptions of a same message using public keys ppk_0 and ppk_1.
> 9. Similarly, compute $(e_0^{b'}, e_1^{b'}, \pi^{b'})$ for tape cell $b'||\text{session}_b||j_c||j_1$ and $(e_0^{\text{ctape}}, e_1^{\text{ctape}}, \pi^{\text{ctape}})$ for ctape = $\text{ppk}_0||\text{ppk}_1||\text{state}||\text{session}_s||j_1$
> 10. write $(e_0^{b'}, e_1^{b'}, \pi^{b'})$ to tape cell, output next state $(e_0^{q'}, e_1^{q'}, \pi^{q'})$, and update control tape as $(e_0^{\text{ctape}}, e_1^{\text{ctape}}, \pi^{\text{ctape}})$. Exit.
> 11. let $q' = q_{\text{noop}}$, $b' = 0$, and go to step 8.

– Let $\overline{C}_\delta = \text{RGC}_{nc^1}.\text{Garble}(1^\kappa, \text{ppk}_0, \text{ppk}_1, \text{psk}_0, C_\delta)$. Here we provide the parameters $\text{ppk}_0, \text{ppk}_1$, and psk_0 to $\text{RGC}_{nc^1}.\text{Garble}$ to overwrite the corresponding internal key generation process within $\text{RGC}_{nc^1}.\text{Garble}$.
– Let $\overline{U}_M = (s(t), \overline{C}_\delta)$ be a Turing machine that uses $\overline{C}_\delta$ to simulate the transition function δ of U_M.
– Let $\omega = \omega(\kappa)$ be the length of the total garbled outputs in the $\overline{U}_M$ under the security parameter κ.
– Run ABE$_2$.Setup(1^κ) algorithm ω times: $(\text{mpk}_i, \text{msk}_i) \leftarrow$ ABE$_2$.Setup(1^κ) for $i < \omega$ and let

$$\text{msk} = (\text{msk}_0, \cdots, \text{msk}_{\omega-1}) \text{ and } \text{mpk} = (\text{mpk}_0, \cdots, \text{mpk}_{\omega-1}).$$

- Let $\overline{U}_M^i(\cdot)$ be the ith bit of the output of running $\overline{U}_M$ on an encoded input.
- Run $\mathsf{ABE}_2.\mathsf{KeyGen}(\mathsf{msk}, \cdot)$ for each of the function $\overline{U}_M^i(\cdot)$ under the different master secret keys to construct secret keys:

$$\mathsf{gM}_i \leftarrow \mathsf{ABE}_2.\mathsf{KeyGen}(\mathsf{msk}_i, \overline{U}_M^i(\cdot)) \text{ for } i < \omega.$$

- Output $\overline{M} = (\mathsf{gM}_0, \cdots, \mathsf{gM}_{\omega-1})$ and $\mathsf{gsk} = (\mathsf{ppk}_0, \mathsf{ppk}_1, \mathsf{psk}_0, \mathsf{mpk})$.

$c_x = \mathsf{RGT.Enc}(\mathsf{gsk}, x)$:

- Generate state uniformly at random for the input string x.
- Update session identification values $\mathsf{session}_s, \mathsf{session}_b, \mathsf{session}_q$.
- For each input tape cell j, let $e_i^j = \mathsf{PK.Enc}(\mathsf{ppk}_i, x[j]\|\mathsf{session}_b\|j\|0)$ for $i = 0, 1$, and π^j be a statistically simulation sound non-interactive zero knowledge (NIZK) proof for the following NP statement: e_0^j and e_1^j are encryptions of a same message using public keys ppk_0 and ppk_1.
- Similarly, compute $(e_0^{q_0}, e_1^{q_0}, \pi^{q_0})$ for the initial head state $q_0\|\mathsf{session}_q\|0$ and $(e_0^{\mathsf{ctape}}, e_1^{\mathsf{ctape}}, \pi^{\mathsf{ctape}})$ for $\mathsf{ctape} = \mathsf{ppk}_0\|\mathsf{ppk}_1\|\mathsf{state}\|\mathsf{session}_s\|0$.
- Let $c = \left\{ (e_0^{q_0}, e_1^{q_0}, \pi^{q_0}), (e_0^{\mathsf{ctape}}, e_1^{\mathsf{ctape}}, \pi^{\mathsf{ctape}}), (e_0^j, e_1^j, \pi^j) : 0 \le j \le n-1 \right\}$.
- Let $C_d \in NC^1$ be the following circuit:

> **Input:** encoded output tape $\overline{\mathsf{otape}}$ and encoded control tape $\overline{\mathsf{ctape}}$.
>
> 1. decrypt output tape $(\mathsf{otape}, \mathsf{session}_b) = \mathsf{PK.Dec}(\mathsf{psk}_0, \overline{\mathsf{otape}})$ and current control tape $(\mathsf{state}, \mathsf{session}_s) = \mathsf{PK.Dec}(\mathsf{psk}_0, \overline{\mathsf{ctape}})$.
> 2. if $\mathsf{session}_s$ and $\mathsf{session}_b$ are inconsistent, exit.
> 3. write otape to output tape and exit.

- Run Yao's one-time garbled circuit generation algorithm to produce a garbled circuit $\Lambda: \{0,1\}^\omega \to \{0,1\}$ together with 2ω labels L_i^b for $i < \omega$ and $b \in \{0,1\}$.

$$\left(\Lambda, \{L_i^0, L_i^1\}_{i=0}^{\omega-1}\right) = \mathsf{GC.Garble}(1^\kappa, C_d).$$

- Produce ABE_2 ciphertexts $c_0, \cdots, c_{\omega-1}$ as follows:

$$c_i \leftarrow \mathsf{ABE}_2.\mathsf{Enc}(\mathsf{mpk}_i, c, L_i^0, L_i^1) \text{ for } i < \omega.$$

- Output the cipher texts $c_x = (\Lambda, c_0, \cdots, c_{\omega-1})$.

$M(x) = \mathsf{RGT.Eval}(\overline{M}, c_x)$:

- Run ABE_2 decryption algorithm on ciphertexts $c_0, \cdots, c_{\omega-1}$ to calculate the labels for Yao's garbled circuit Λ for $d_i = \overline{M}^i(c_x)$:

$$L_i^{d_i} \leftarrow \mathsf{ABE}_2.\mathsf{Dec}(\mathsf{gM}_i, c_i) \text{ for } i < \omega$$

- Evaluate the garbled circuit Λ with labels $L_i^{d_i}$ to compute the output $M(x)$

$$M(x) = \mathsf{GC.Eval}(\Lambda, L_i^{d_0}, \cdots, L_{\omega-1}^{d_{\omega-1}})$$

Proof of Security

The correctness and efficiency of the reusable Turing machine garbling scheme RGT in the preceding paragraph is straightforward. In the following, we show that the scheme RGT is private with reusability according to the definition in Goldwasser et al. [17].

Assume that a Turing machine M is selected with the security parameter κ. We need to construct a simulator $S = (S_0, S_1)$ such that (1) holds for the reusable garbled Turing machine $\overline{M} = (\mathrm{gM}_0, \cdots, \mathrm{gM}_{\omega-1})$, assuming that there are a simulator $S_\delta = (S_{\delta,0}, S_{\delta,1})$ satisfying the security definition in Goldwasser et al. [17]. reusable garbled circuits $\overline{C}_\delta$ and a simulator $\mathrm{Sim}_{\mathrm{GS}}$ satisfying Definition 2 for Yao's one-time garbling scheme.

To generate a simulated garbled Turing machine $\tilde{M} = (\tilde{\mathrm{gM}}_0, \cdots, \tilde{\mathrm{gM}}_{\omega-1})$ for the Turing machine M, S_0 runs the following procedures:

1. Generate fresh mpk and msk as in RGT.Garble process.
2. Run simulators S_δ to generate a reusable garbled circuit $\tilde{C}_\delta$.
3. Run $\mathrm{ABE}_2.\mathrm{KeyGen}(\mathrm{msk}, \cdot)$ to generate $\tilde{M} = (\tilde{\mathrm{gM}}_0, \cdots, \tilde{\mathrm{gM}}_{\omega-1})$.

During the simulation, S_1 receives the latest simulator's state, $1^{|x|}$, $\tilde{C}_\delta$, and a Turing machine output $M(x)$ for some input x without seeing the value of x. S_1 needs to output a simulated encoding $\tilde{c} = (\tilde{\Lambda}, \tilde{c}_0, \cdots, \tilde{c}_{\omega-1})$ for the RGT.Eval process without access to C_d. Let $\mathrm{Sim}_{\mathrm{GS}}$ be the simulator from Definition 2 for Yao's one-time garbling scheme. Run $\mathrm{Sim}_{\mathrm{GS}}$ to produce a simulated garbled circuit $\tilde{\Lambda}$ for the circuit C_d together with the simulated encoding consisting of ω labels $\tilde{L}_i$ for $i = 0, \cdots, \omega - 1$. That is, we have

$$\left(\tilde{\Lambda}, \tilde{L}_0, \cdots, \tilde{L}_{\omega-1} \right) = \mathrm{Sim}_{\mathrm{GS}}(1^\kappa, M(x), 1^\omega).$$

S_1 can invoke the above simulation since it knows $M(x)$ and the size of input to C_d (that is, the output size of $\tilde{C}_\delta$). S_1 can then produce the simulated ABE_2 ciphertexts $\tilde{c}_0, \cdots, \tilde{c}_{\omega-1}$ as follows:

$$\tilde{c}_i \leftarrow \mathrm{ABE}_2.\mathrm{Enc}(\mathrm{mpk}_i, \tilde{c}_x, \tilde{L}_i, \tilde{L}_i) \text{ for } i < \omega.$$

Note that we used the label $\tilde{L}_i$ for two times. In a summary, S_1 can now output the simulated encoding $(\tilde{\Lambda}, \tilde{c}_0, \cdots, \tilde{c}_{\omega-1})$.

Now it suffices to show that the simulation satisfies the security definition in Goldwasser et al. [17]. for any adversary $A = (A_0, A_1)$. Without loss of generality, we may assume that A_1 output α equals to its entire view. That is, all information that A_1 has received during the protocol run. Note that if we could prove that the real and ideal experiment outputs are computationally indistinguishable with this kind of output, it will be computationally indistinguishable with any other kind of outputs since A_1 is a probabilistic polynomial time algorithm. That is, any output should be probabilistic polynomial time computable from this view. In the following, we define five games first.

Game 0: The ideal game $\text{Exp}^{\text{ideal}}_{\text{RGT},A,S}(1^\kappa)$ of the security definition in Goldwasser et al. [17] with simulator S. The output distribution for this game is:

$$M, \text{gsk}, \text{state}_A, \text{ABE}_2.\text{KeyGen}(\text{msk}, \cdot),$$

$$\left\{ x_i, \tilde{c}_{x_i}, \text{Sim}_{\text{Garble}}(1^\kappa, M(x_i), 1^\omega), \left\{ \text{ABE}_2.\text{Enc}(\text{mpk}_i, \tilde{c}_{x_i}, \tilde{L}_{i,j}, \tilde{L}_{i,j}) \right\}_{j=0}^{\omega-1} \right\}_{i=0}^{t-1}$$

Game 1: The same as Game 0 except that the Turing machine M is replaced with the reusable garbled circuit $\overline{C}_\delta$ and the circuit C_d. That is, the output distribution for this game is:

$$\overline{C}_\delta, C_d, \text{gsk}, \text{state}_A, \text{ABE}_2.\text{KeyGen}(\text{msk}, \cdot),$$

$$\left\{ x_i, \tilde{c}_{x_i}, \text{Sim}_{\text{Garble}}(1^\kappa, M(x_i), 1^\omega), \left\{ \text{ABE}_2.\text{Enc}(\text{mpk}_i, \tilde{c}_{x_i}, \tilde{L}_{i,j}, \tilde{L}_{i,j}) \right\}_{j=0}^{\omega-1} \right\}_{i=0}^{t-1}$$

Game 2: The same as Game 1 except that the simulated input encoding $\tilde{c}_{x_i}$ is replaced with the actual encoding c_{x_i} of x_i by encoding x_i using gsk. Note that we keep $\tilde{c}_{x_i}$ unchanged within the $\text{ABE}_2.\text{Enc}$ procedure. That is, the output distribution for this game is:

$$\overline{C}_\delta, C_d, \text{gsk}, \text{state}_A, \text{ABE}_2.\text{KeyGen}(\text{msk}, \cdot),$$

$$\left\{ x_i, c_{x_i}, \text{Sim}_{\text{Garble}}(1^\kappa, M(x_i), 1^\omega), \left\{ \text{ABE}_2.\text{Enc}(\text{mpk}_i, \tilde{c}_{x_i}, \tilde{L}_{i,j}, \tilde{L}_{i,j}) \right\}_{j=0}^{\omega-1} \right\}_{i=0}^{t-1}$$

Game 3: The same as Game 2 except the simulated garbled circuit $\tilde{\Lambda}$ is replaced with the real garbled circuit Λ: $\left(\Lambda, \{L_j^0, L_j^1\}_{j=0}^{\omega-1}\right) = \text{GC.Garble}(1^\kappa, C_d)$. The output distribution for this game is:

$$\overline{C}_\delta, C_d, \text{gsk}, \text{state}_A, \text{ABE}_2.\text{KeyGen}(\text{msk}, \cdot),$$

$$\left\{ x_i, c_{x_i}, \text{GC.Garble}(1^\kappa, C_d), \left\{ \text{ABE}_2.\text{Enc}(\text{mpk}_i, \tilde{c}_{x_i}, \tilde{L}_{i,j}, \tilde{L}_{i,j}) \right\}_{j=0}^{\omega-1} \right\}_{i=0}^{t-1}$$

Game 4: The same as Game 3 except that the $\text{ABE}_2.\text{Enc}$ ciphertext is replaced with the real ABE_2 ciphertext. In other words, this is the real experiment $\text{Exp}^{\text{real}}_{\text{RGT},A}(1^\kappa)$ of the security definition in Goldwasser et al. [17]. The output distribution for this game is:

$$\overline{C}_\delta, C_d, \text{gsk}, \text{state}_A, \text{ABE}_2.\text{KeyGen}(\text{msk}, \cdot),$$

$$\left\{ x_i, c_{x_i}, \text{GC.Garble}(1^\kappa, C_d), \left\{ \text{ABE}_2.\text{Enc}(\text{mpk}_i, c_{x_i}, L_{i,j}^0, L_{i,j}^1) \right\}_{j=0}^{\omega-1} \right\}_{i=0}^{t-1}$$

We prove that the outputs of each pair of games are computationally indistinguishable in the following lemmas. Thus our reusable garbled circuits are circuit and input private with reusability.

Lemma 1. *Assume that* $\overline{C}_\delta$ *is a secure reusable garbled circuit for* C_δ *in the simulation-based security model. Then the outputs of Game 0 and Game 1 are computationally indistinguishable.*

Proof (sketch). The proof is by contradiction. Assume that the outputs of Game 0 and Game 1 could be distinguished by a probabilistic polynomial time algorithm D. Then one can use D to construct a probabilistic polynomial time distinguisher D_1 to show that Theorem 1 is not true. Details are omitted here. □

Lemma 2. *Assume that both ciphers* E.Enc *and* PK.Enc *are semantically secure. Then the outputs of Game 1 and Game 2 are computationally indistinguishable.*

Proof (sketch). Assume that there exist probabilistic polynomial time adversaries $A = (A_1, A_2)$ and a probabilistic polynomial time distinguisher D armed with A that distinguishes outputs of Game 1 and Game 2 with a non-negligible probability. Then one can use the standard hybrid argument to construct a probabilistic polynomial time distinguisher D_1 to distinguish the cipher texts c_{x_i} from the simulated cipher text $\tilde{c}_{x_i}$ with a non-negligible probability for some $i_0 = 0, \cdots, t-1$. This is a violation that both ciphers E.Enc and PK.Enc are semantically secure. □

Lemma 3. *Assume that the one-time garbling scheme is secure in the sense of Definition 2. Then the outputs of Game 2 and Game 3 are computationally indistinguishable.*

Proof (sketch). Assume that there exist probabilistic polynomial time adversaries $A = (A_1, A_2)$ and a probabilistic polynomial time distinguisher D armed with A that distinguishes outputs of Game 2 and Game 3 with a non-negligible probability. Then one can build a probabilistic polynomial time distinguisher D_1 to distinguish the outputs of the simulator $\mathtt{Sim_{Garble}}$ and $\mathtt{GC.Garble}$. This contradicts Definition 2. The details for the construction of D_1 are omitted here. □

Lemma 4. *Assume that the* ABE$_2$ *scheme is secure in the sense of Goldwasser et al.* [17]. *Then the outputs of Game 3 and Game 4 are computationally indistinguishable.*

Proof (sketch). Assume that there exist probabilistic polynomial time adversaries $A = (A_1, A_2)$ and a probabilistic polynomial time distinguisher D armed with A that distinguishes outputs of Game 3 and Game 4 with a non-negligible probability. Then one can build a probabilistic polynomial time adversary $A = (A_1, A_2, A_3)$ such that

$$\mathtt{Prob}[\mathtt{Exp}_{\mathtt{ABE_2}, A}(1^\kappa) = 1] > 1/2 + \mathtt{negl}(\kappa).$$

This contradicts the security definition of ABE$_2$. Details for the construction of A are omitted here. □

Theorem 2. *Assume that the one-time garbling scheme is secure, the* ABE$_2$ *scheme is secure, both ciphers* E.Enc *and* PK.Enc *are semantically secure, and* RGC$_{nc^1}$ *is secure according to Definition 2. Then the reusable garbling scheme* RGT *in Sect. 4 is secure according to the security definition in Goldwasser et al.* [17].

Proof. This follows from Lemmas 1, 2, 3 and 4. □

5   Reusable Garbled Turing Machines Without ABE$_2$

In Sect. 4, we used Yao's one-time garbled circuits for C_d and Attribute Based Encryption (ABE$_2$) schemes for Turing machines to decrypt the garbled Turing machine output $\overline{U}_M(\overline{x})$. ABE$_2$ cipher text is relatively expensive to construct and the size of Yao's one-time garbled circuit for C_d is too large to be included in each garbled input. Thus it is preferred to use a reusable garbled circuit to decrypt the output of $\overline{U}_M(\overline{x})$. As mentioned in early sections, the challenge to use a garbled version $\overline{C}_d$ directly is that the adversary may use $\overline{C}_d$ to calculate $M(x')$ for input x' whose encoding is not provided by the Turing machine owner. To address these challenges, we use secure message authentication tags.

Let MAC = (MAC.KeyGen, MAC.Enc, MAC.Veri) be a secure message authentication scheme. The Turing machine M is revised to a new Turing machine M_{mac} as follows. The input to M_{mac} is first authenticated using a MAC scheme key and then encrypted using the semantically secure ideal cipher. That is, M_{mac} takes an input in format of $\overline{x} = $ E.Enc($sk_{mac}, x\|tag$) where x is the supposed input to M and $tag = $ MAC.Enc(ask, x). On an input $\overline{x}$, M_{mac} uses the built-in key sk_{mac} to decrypt $(x, tag) = $ E.Dec($sk_{mac}, \overline{x}$) and uses the built-in key ask to verify that MAC.Veri(ask, x, tag) is true. If the verification fails, M_{mac} enters q_{noop} state and keeps doing nothing until it stops. Otherwise, M_{mac} computes the value of $M(x)$, chooses a random key $sk_o = $ E.KeyGen(1^κ) and outputs $M_{mac}(\overline{x}) = sk_o\|$E.Enc($sk_o, M(x)$).

The garbling scheme RGT$_1$ = (RGT$_1$.Garble, RGT$_1$.Enc, RGT$_1$.Eval) for Turing machines M without ABE$_2$ is then constructed as follows. $(gsk, \overline{M}) = $ RGT$_1$.Garble($1^\kappa, M$):

- sk_{mac} = E.KeyGen(1^κ), ask = MAC.KeyGen(1^κ), and (psk_i, ppk_i) = PK.KeyGen(1^κ) for $i = 0, 1$.
- Construct M_{mac} from M.
- Define $U_{M_{mac}}$ and design the reusable garble garbled circuit $\overline{C}_\delta$ for $U_{M_{mac}}$'s transition function δ as in the process RGT.Garble($1^\kappa, U_{M_{mac}}$) of Sect. 4. Let $\overline{U}_{M_{mac}} = (s(t), \overline{C}_\delta)$ be the resulting Turing machine.
- Let $C_d \in NC^1$ be the following circuit:

Input: $U_{M_{mac}}$'s decrypted output tape (otape, session$_b$) and decrypted control tape (state, session$_s$).

1. if session$_s$ and session$_b$ are inconsistent then exit.
2. let $(sk_o, \overline{y}) = $ otape.
3. compute $y = $ E.Dec($sk_o, \overline{y}$) and output y.

- Let $\overline{C}_d = \text{RGC}_{\text{nc}^1}.\text{Garble}(1^\kappa, \text{ppk}_0, \text{ppk}_1, \text{psk}_0, C_d)$. Here we provide the parameters $\text{ppk}_0, \text{ppk}_1$, and psk_0 to RGC_{nc^1} to overwrite the corresponding internal key generation process within $\text{RGC}_{\text{nc}^1}.\text{Garble}$. By overwriting the key generation process for RGC_{nc^1}, the output of $\overline{U}_{M_{\text{mac}}}$ is in the correct encoding format according to $\text{RGC}_{\text{nc}^1}.\text{Enc}$ and is ready for $\overline{C}_d$ to process.
- Output $\overline{M} = (s(t), \overline{C}_\delta, \overline{C}_d)$ and $\text{gsk} = (\text{ppk}_0, \text{ppk}_1, \text{psk}_0, \text{sk}_{\text{mac}}, \text{ask})$.

$c_x = \text{RGT}_1.\text{Enc}(\text{gsk}, x)$:

- Let $\bar{x} = \text{E.Enc}(\text{sk}_{\text{mac}}, x \| \text{MAC.Enc}(\text{ask}, x))$.
- Let c_x be constructed for $\bar{x}$ as in the process $\text{RGT.Enc}(\text{gsk}, \bar{x})$.

$M(x) = \text{RGT}_1.\text{Eval}(\overline{M}, c_x)$:

- Run the Turing machine $\overline{U}_{M_{\text{mac}}} = (s(t), \overline{C}_\delta)$ on input c_x until it stops.
- Run $\overline{C}_d$ on the output tape and control tape of $\overline{U}_{M_{\text{mac}}}$ to obtain $M(x)$.

Comments: We have two comments for the construction of RGT_1.

- The circuit C_d in RGT_1 takes the entire tape as input and decrypts it at the same time. In practice, it may be more efficient to define C_d in a way that it only takes one cell and decrypts the cell separately. In order to achieve this, Turing machine M_{mac} needs to be revised further so that the output cells are encrypted separately.
- For the convenience of presenting constructions of RGT and RGT_1 in a compatible way, we constructed C_δ and C_d separately. Indeed, for the construction of RGT_1, C_δ and C_d can be defined as one circuit which is then garbled using Garg et al.'s NC^1 garbling scheme.

We can then prove the following theorem in a similar way as that of Theorem 2. The proof is omitted in this extended abstract.

Theorem 3. *Assume that the one-time garbling scheme* GC *is secure, both ciphers* E.Enc *and* PK.Enc *are semantically secure, the message authentication scheme* MAC *is secure, and* RGC_{nc^1} *is secure according to Definition 2. Then the reusable garbling scheme* RGT_1 *for Turing machines is secure according to the security definition in Goldwasser et al. [17].*

6   Discussions and Oblivious Turing Machines

In the construction of RGT_1, we used a secure message authentication scheme to protect adversaries from swapping/inserting/deleting/duplicating input tape cells. Some other techniques could also be used to achieve this same goal. For example, one may use Chaitin's universal self-delimiting Turing machines [11]. A universal self-delimiting Turing machine U takes the input px and outputs $U(px) = M_p(x)$ where p is the encoding of a self-delimiting Turing machine M_p. For a self-delimiting Turing machine M_p, if $M_p(x)$ is defined, then $M_p(y)$ is not defined for all strings y with y being a prefix of x or x being a prefix of y. Before

Turing machine stops, it needs to mark each cell on the output tape as final by inserting a special symbol such as FIN to each cell on the output tape. The circuit C_d would only decrypt cells marked as final.

It should also be noted that the black cell "B" could be encoded in advance so that for each input, the Turing machine owner does not need to encode the entire working tape cells. The self-delimiting Turing machines could be used to defeat the attacks that the adversary copies some input cells to some "B" cells and potentially runs the garbled Turing machine on inputs that are not provided by the machine owner.

In our construction of RGT and RGT$_1$, oblivious Turing machines are used to determine the next cell that the Turing machine needs to process. If Turing machine head movement pattern does not need to be protected, this requirement could be dropped since the circuit C_δ could output the head movement symbol "R" or "L" in plain text.

In Goldwasser et al.'s garbling scheme [16], the owner of a Turing machine M first converts M to an oblivious Turing machine M_O using the Pippenger-Fischer transformation [23], where an oblivious Turing machine is a Turing machine whose head movement is independent of the current cell content. From M_O, a new Turing machine M_{FHE} is constructed to perform the FHE evaluation of M_O. The owner of the Turing machine M gives M_{FHE} to the evaluator. Each time when the Turing machine owner wants the evaluator to calculate $M(x)$, the Turing machine owner creates a homomorphic encryption scheme public key hpk and a corresponding private key hsk. Using the newly created public key hpk, the Turing machine owner calculates the homomorphic encryption cipher texts $c_x = (E_{\text{hpk}}(x[0]), \cdots, E_{\text{hpk}}(x[n-1]))$ for the input $x = x[0] \cdots x[n-1]$ bit by bit and constructs a Yao's one-time garbled circuit D for decrypting the homomorphic encryption scheme by integrating the private key hsk within D. The Turing machine owner then gives (c_x, D, hpk) to the evaluator. The evaluator runs M_{FHE} on c_x homomorphically step by step. During the evaluation, each cell of M_O's tape corresponds to the FHE ciphertext of M_{FHE}'s cell value and M_{FHE} maintains the FHE ciphertext $\overline{\text{state}}_i$ of M_O's current state. At step i, M_{FHE} takes as input the encrypted cell $\bar{b}$ from the input tape that the head currently points at and the current encrypted state $\overline{\text{state}}_i$. Then M_{FHE} outputs an encrypted new state $\overline{\text{state}}_{i+1}$ and a new content $\bar{b}'$. M_{FHE} updates the current cell with $\bar{b}'$ and then moves its head left or right according to the oblivious head movement definition. Though [16] did not describe how to get the value $(\overline{\text{state}}_{i+1}, \bar{b}')$ from $(\overline{\text{state}}_i, \bar{b})$. We assume that it uses the straightforward circuit simulation of the Turing machine transition functions. That is, a circuit Π_δ with inputs (state_i, b) and outputs (state_{i+1}, b') is constructed from M_O's transition function δ and M_{FHE} homomorphically evaluates Π_δ to obtain $(\overline{\text{state}}_{i+1}, \bar{b}')$ from $(\overline{\text{state}}_i, \bar{b})$. After the evaluation, the evaluator obtains the homomorphic encryption ciphertext $E_{\text{hpk}}(M(x))$ of $M(x)$. In order for the evaluator to decrypt $E_{\text{hpk}}(M(x))$, the circuit owner uses an attribute based encryption scheme for Turing machines (constructed from the witness encryption scheme) to send corresponding labels for the garbled circuit D so that the evaluator will be able to decrypt $E_{\text{hpk}}(M(x))$

to $M(x)$. In the above scheme, the Turing machine M_O's transition function is leaked via the circuit Π_δ. Though [16] provides no details on how to avoid this leakage, we assume that the authors used the same approach as in Goldwasser et al. [17] to protect the privacy of Turing machine M's transition function. That is, M_{FHE} is constructed for a universal oblivious Turing machine U_O and the description of M is encrypted using an ideal cipher scheme E such as AES. The evaluator only holds the encrypted version $\text{E.Enc}(\text{sk}, M)$ of M. For each evaluation of M on x, the Turing machine owner needs to give both $E_{\text{hpk}}(x)$ and $E_{\text{hpk}}(\text{sk})$ to the evaluator.

7   Conclusion

Using multilinear maps, Garg et al. showed the existence of reusable garbling schemes for NC^1 circuits. By further using FHE schemes, Garg et al. showed the existence of reusable garbling schemes for all polynomial size circuits. This paper constructed reusable garbling schemes for Turing machines (that is, for all polynomial size circuits also) only assuming the existence of secure multilinear maps. Though it is not clear whether multilinear maps based indistinguishability obfuscators could be more efficient than FHE, the goal of this paper is to develop alternative techniques for resuable garbling schemes to stimulate further research in this direction.

References

1. Albrecht, M., Davidson, A.: Are graded encoding schemes broken yet? https://malb.io/are-graded-encoding-schemes-broken-yet.html
2. Ananth, P., Boneh, D., Garg, S., Sahai, A., Zhandry, M.: Differing-inputs obfuscation and applications. IACR Cryptology ePrint Archive, 2013:689 (2013)
3. Barak, B., Garg, S., Kalai, Y.T., Paneth, O., Sahai, A.: Protecting obfuscation against algebraic attacks. In: Nguyen, P.Q., Oswald, E. (eds.) EUROCRYPT 2014. LNCS, vol. 8441, pp. 221–238. Springer, Heidelberg (2014). https://doi.org/10.1007/978-3-642-55220-5_13
4. Bellare, M., Hoang, V., Rogaway, P.: Foundations of garbled circuits. In: Proceedings 2012 ACM CCS, pp. 784–796. ACM (2012)
5. Bitansky, N., Canetti, R., Chiesa, A., Tromer, E.: Recursive composition and bootstrapping for SNARKs and proof-carrying data. In: Proceedings of 45th ACM STOC, pp. 111–120. ACM (2013)
6. Bitansky, N., Garg, S., Telang, S.: Succinct randomized encodings and their applications. Technical report, Cryptology ePrint Archive, Report 2014/771 (2014). http://eprint.iacr.org
7. Boyle, E., Chung, K.-M., Pass, R.: On extractability obfuscation. In: Lindell, Y. (ed.) TCC 2014. LNCS, vol. 8349, pp. 52–73. Springer, Heidelberg (2014). https://doi.org/10.1007/978-3-642-54242-8_3
8. Brakerski, Z., Rothblum, G.N.: Virtual black-box obfuscation for all circuits via generic graded encoding. In: Lindell, Y. (ed.) TCC 2014. LNCS, vol. 8349, pp. 1–25. Springer, Heidelberg (2014). https://doi.org/10.1007/978-3-642-54242-8_1

9. Canetti, R., Holmgren, J., Jain, A., Vaikuntanathan, V.: Indistinguishability obfuscation of iterated circuits and ram programs. In: Proceedings of STOC 15, New York, NY, USA. ACM (2015)
10. Canetti, R., Holmgren, J.: Fully succinct garbled ram (2015)
11. Chaitin, G.J.: On the length of programs for computing finite binary sequences. J. Assoc. Comput. Math. **13**, 547–569 (1966)
12. Garg, S., Gentry, C., Halevi, S., Raykova, M., Sahai, A., Waters, B.: Candidate indistinguishability obfuscation and functional encryption for all circuits. In: Proceedings of IEEE 54th FOCS, pp. 40–49. IEEE (2013)
13. Garg, S., Gentry, C., Sahai, A., Waters, B.: Witness encryption and its applications. In: Proceedings of 45th ACM STOC, pp. 467–476. ACM (2013)
14. Garg, S., Lu, S., Ostrovsky, R., Scafuro, A.: Garbled RAM from one-way functions. In: Proceedings of STOC 15, New York, NY, USA. ACM (2015)
15. Gentry, C., Halevi, S., Lu, S., Ostrovsky, R., Raykova, M., Wichs, D.: Garbled RAM revisited. In: Nguyen, P.Q., Oswald, E. (eds.) EUROCRYPT 2014. LNCS, vol. 8441, pp. 405–422. Springer, Heidelberg (2014). https://doi.org/10.1007/978-3-642-55220-5_23
16. Goldwasser, S., Kalai, Y.T., Popa, R.A., Vaikuntanathan, V., Zeldovich, N.: How to run turing machines on encrypted data. In: Canetti, R., Garay, J.A. (eds.) CRYPTO 2013. LNCS, vol. 8043, pp. 536–553. Springer, Heidelberg (2013). https://doi.org/10.1007/978-3-642-40084-1_30
17. Goldwasser, S., Kalai, Y., Popa, R., Vaikuntanathan, V., Zeldovich, N.: Reusable garbled circuits and succinct functional encryption. In: Proceedings of 45th STOC, pp. 555–564. ACM (2013)
18. Huang, M.-D.A.: Trilinear maps for cryptography. arXiv preprint arXiv:1803.10325 (2018)
19. Huang, M.-D.A.: Trilinear maps for cryptography ii. arXiv preprint arXiv:1810.03646 (2018)
20. Ishai, Y., Kushilevitz, E., Ostrovsky, R., Sahai, A.: Cryptography with constant computational overhead. In: Proceedings of 40th ACM STOC, pp. 433–442. ACM (2008)
21. Koppula, V., Lewko, A., Waters, B.: Indistinguishability obfuscation for turing machines with unbounded memory. In: Proceedings of STOC 15, New York, NY, USA. ACM (2015)
22. Lin, H., Pass, R.: Succinct garbling schemes and applications. Technical report, Cryptology ePrint Archive, Report 2014/766 (2014). http://eprint.iacr.org
23. Pippenger, N., Fischer, M.: Relations among complexity measures. J. ACM **26**(2), 361–381 (1979)
24. Yao, A.: How to generate and exchange secrets. In: Proceedings of 27th IEEE FOCS, pp. 162–167. IEEE (1986)

An Extension of Formal Analysis Method with Reasoning: A Case Study of Flaw Detection for Non-repudiation and Fairness

Jingchen Yan, Yating Wang, Yuichi Goto[(⊠)], and Jingde Cheng

Department of Information and Computer Sciences,
Saitama University, Saitama 338-8570, Japan
{jingchenyan,wangyating,gotoh,cheng}@aise.ics.saitama-u.ac.jp

Abstract. Formal analysis is used to find out flaws of cryptographic protocols. A formal analysis method with reasoning for cryptographic protocols has been proposed. In the method, behaviors of participants and behaviors of an intruder are used as premises of forward reasoning to deduce formulas, then analysts check whether the deduced formulas are related to flaws. However, the method only can detect the flaws related to confidentiality and authentication but is unable to detect the flaws related to non-repudiation and fairness. This paper proposes an extension of the formal analysis method with reasoning, which can deal with the flaws related to non-repudiation and fairness. This paper also shows a case study of flaw detection for non-repudiation and fairness in ISI protocol with the proposed method. The result shows that the proposed method is effective to find out flaws that related to the two security properties above.

Keywords: Cryptographic protocol ·
Formal analysis method with reasoning · Non-repudiation · Fairness

1 Introduction

Formal analysis is used to find out flaws of cryptographic protocols [9,18,19]. Model checking and automated theorem proving [2,3,8,21] are proving methods of formal analysis for cryptographic protocols. In these methods, analysts first need to strictly, completely and correctly describe the security specifications that a cryptographic protocol should satisfy as formulas or theorems, and use them as the targets of verification, and then check the enumerated formulas or theorems hold or not in the protocol. However, if the security specifications are not listed completely, or the formulas or theorems are not described completely, some flaws cannot be found.

To solve the problem of enumerating verification targets, a formal analysis method with reasoning for cryptographic protocols has been proposed [6,24,25].

© Springer Nature Switzerland AG 2019
C. Carlet et al. (Eds.): C2SI 2019, LNCS 11445, pp. 399–408, 2019.
https://doi.org/10.1007/978-3-030-16458-4_23

In this method, analysts do not need to enumerate the verification targets but use the formalized participants' behaviors and an intruder's behaviors as premises to perform forward reasoning. By forward reasoning, all possible executed result of the protocol will be deduced. Analysts check whether the deduced formulas are related to flaws to determine the security of the protocol. However, this method only can detect flaws related to confidentiality and authentication but not detect flaws related to non-repudiation and fairness.

This paper proposes the extension of formal analysis method with reasoning for cryptographic protocols which can detect flaws related to the security of non-repudiation and fairness. The paper also shows a case study of flaw detection for non-repudiation and fairness in ISI protocol. By the result of analyzing ISI protocol, it can be said that the extended method is valid to detect flaws that related to the security properties of non-repudiation and fairness.

The rest of the paper is organized as follows. Section 2 explains the basic notions about non-repudiation and fairness. Section 3 presents the extension of formal analysis method with reasoning. Section 4 describes the case study in ISI protocols. Section 5 discuss the problems of the extension of formal analysis method with reasoning. Finally, concluding remarks are given in Sect. 6.

2 Basic Notions

A cryptographic protocol is a protocol which performs a security-related function using cryptography [14]. Security-related function means prevention of or protection against (a) access to information by an unauthorized entity or (b) the intentional but unauthorized destruction or alteration of that information [4].

Entity is an independent unit which performs one or more operations in a cryptographic protocol. There are two types of entity, *Agent* and *Sever*. *Agent* is an independent unit which actively performs each operation. *Sever* is an independent system which passively returns an answer to the request.

Participant is an authorized entity who executes the cryptographic protocols.

Participant is divided into two types. One is an honest participant who sends or receives data in strict accordance with the steps of a cryptographic protocol. The other is a dishonest participant who may lie in the execution of a cryptographic protocol or not execute the cryptographic protocol at all, trying to impersonate or deceive the other participant to achieve various illegal purposes. In this paper, we assumed that participant A and B may be dishonest participants, while CS (currency server) and TTP (trusted third party) are always honest participants. *Intruder* is an unauthorized entity who participates in or interfere with the execution of cryptographic protocols.

The execution of each message of a cryptographic protocol is related to the security of the environment. If the message is not executed or is not executed correctly, we consider that the message is interruptible. If a message should be sent by a dishonest participant, it is interruptible because the dishonest participant may choose to stop sending a message for his/her own benefit. If a message should be sent by an honest participant, the message is uninterruptible in a situation of secure environment because an honest participant will always follow the protocol process. If the environment is not secure, the message sent by the honest participant may be lost, so that the message is interruptible. This paper only considers the interruption in a secure environment.

Non-repudiation [12,13,15] and fairness [1,11,15] are the security properties of cryptographic protocols. Non-repudiation means that the participants of a cryptographic protocol should be responsible for their actions, the sender cannot deny the messages they have sent, and the receiver cannot deny any messages received. In the event of a dispute, a participant can provide the necessary evidence to protect its own interests. Non-repudiation is achieved by the sender having the receiver's non-repudiation evidence and the receiver having the sender's non-repudiation evidence [22,23]. The sender's non-repudiation evidence is used to prove that the sender did send the message, and the receiver's non-repudiation evidence to prove that the receiver did receive the message.

Fairness means that at any stage of the operation of a cryptographic protocol, any participant will not have more privilege in the operation. It includes implementation fairness, acquired fairness and retrospective fairness [1,20]. Implementation fairness means any participant has the same control over the execution of the cryptographic protocol. In other words, the participants have the right to choose whether to continue or give up the execution of the protocol step and to exercise such rights without affecting the rights of other participants. Acquired fairness means in the case of normal termination of the cryptographic protocols, participants can be guaranteed the information they should have obtained. In the case of abnormal suspension, all participants did not receive anything. Retrospective fairness means no participant can escape the responsibilities associated with the exchange of information. In this paper, we focused on the realization of acquired fairness, which is also the most important aspect of fairness.

3 An Extension of Formal Analysis Method with Reasoning

3.1 Formalization of Cryptographic Protocols

Overview of Formalization. In the previous formal analysis method with reasoning, analysts formalize the "behaviors of participants", "behaviors of an intruder", "common behaviors among participants and an intruder" and "irregular case" as targets of formalization [25]. In the extended method, to detect the flaws that caused by dishonest participants, we have added "confirm behaviors" and some new tasks in "common behaviors". Below we only provide a formal description of behaviors to perform flaws detection of non-repudiation and fairness.

Analysts formalize "behaviors of participants", "common behaviors" and "confirm behaviors" as targets of formalization. "behavior of participants" means a set of rules of participants." "common behaviors" represents rules except for the behaviors of sending and receiving data by participants. "confirm behaviors" represents a set of rules that participants judge whether the signatures or keys are true.

To formalize the behaviors above, we defined following predicates, functions, and individual constants that represents participants' behavior or data in cryptographic protocols.

Predicates

- $Parti(p)$: p is a participant of a protocol.
- $Eq(x_1, x_2)$: x_1 and x_2 are equal.
- $Cof(p_1, p_2, x)$: p_1 confirms that p_2 has responsibility of x.
- $Recv(p, x)$: p receives x.
- $Send(p_1, p_2, x)$: p_1 sends x to p_2.
- $Start(p_1, p_2)$: p_1 and p_2 start a communication process.

Functions

- $data(x_1, \cdots, x_n)$ $(n \in \mathbb{N})$: A data set that consists of sent and received $x_1, \ldots,$ and x_n.
- $enc(k, x_1, \cdots, x_n)$: A data set that consists of encrypted $x_1, \cdots,$ and x_n by k.
- $id(p)$: Identifier of p.
- $nonce(p)$: Nonce of p.
- $old(x)$: Old data of x.
- $pk(p)$: Public key of p.
- $plus(x)$: Incremented data of x.
- $sig(p, x_1, \cdots, x_n)$: A data set that consists of $x_1, \cdots,$ and x_n with p's signature.
- $symk(p_1, p_2)$: Symmetric key of p_1 and p_2.
- $tstamp(p)$: Timestamp of p.

Constants

- a, b $(n \in \mathbb{N})$: Persons
- ttp: Trusted third sever.

In addition, there are uniquely defined functions and individual constants that are assigned to each data in a cryptographic protocol.

Behaviors of Participants. Behaviors of participants are to describe the specification of a cryptographic protocol. Generally, in specification of cryptographic protocols, sending and receiving in step M are represented as $M.X_1 \rightarrow X_2$: $Y_1, Y_2, \cdots, Y_z$, it means that X_1 sends data $Y_1, Y_2, \cdots, Y_z$ $(z \in \mathbb{N})$ to X_2 in step M.

1. Represent participants' behaviors in each step of a cryptographic protocol by formulas. p_i and x_i are individual variables, n and m are the number of sent or received data.

a. As step 1 of the protocol,

$$Start(p_1, p_2) \Rightarrow Send(p_1, p_2, data(x_1, \ldots, x_n)) \tag{1}$$

means "if a cryptographic protocol starts with p_1 and p_2, p_1 sends data $x_1, \ldots, x_n$ to p_2".

b. As step 2 of the protocol,

$$Recv(p_1, data(x_1, \ldots, x_m)) \Rightarrow (Parti(p_1) \Rightarrow$$
$$Send(p_1, p_2, data(x_1, \ldots, x_n))) \tag{2}$$

means "if a participant p_1 receives data, p_1 sends the next data to p_2." p_i, x_i are individual variables, and n, m are the number of sent or received data.

2. Replace individual variables p_1 and p_2 in formulas (1) and (2) with ttp or p_i respectively in the previous task. For example, if sender of corresponding step is a third trusted party ttp, individual variable p_1 is replaced with the individual constant ttp.

3. Replace individual variables $x_1, \cdots, x_n$ in formulas (1) and (2) with terms according to following rules corresponding step of the specification.
   a. If sent data Y_i is not encrypted, substitute a function $f(p_i)$ or $f(ttp)$ respectively or an individual variable that is uniquely defined.
   b. If Y_i is incremented data, substitute $plus(x_i')$. x_i' is replaced as well as previous task 3-a.
   c. If Y_i is encrypted data, substitute $enc(k, x_1', \cdots, x_n')$ and replace k depending on key types such as public key or symmetric key.
   d. If Y_i is signed data, substitute $sig(p_i, x_1', \cdots, x_n')$ and replace p_i with $p_1, p_2, \ldots, p_n$ or ttp.

4. In part of formulas $A_1 \Rightarrow A_2$ (A_1, A_2 is formulas), if a variable is included only in A_1 or A_2, define an individual constant and replace the variable into the constant.

5. Add quantifier $\forall$ corresponded to individual variables k, x_i, and p_i in those formulas.

6. Generate a formula $Start(p_1, p_2)$ with substituting an individual constant of participants to p_1 and p_2.

Common Behaviors. Common behaviors mainly describe implicit behaviors such as encryption or decryption behaviors of participants.

1. Generate $\forall p((Recv(p, data_1) \wedge \cdots \wedge Recv(p, data_n) \Rightarrow Recv(p, data')))$ represents if p receives multiple data, p receives another data.

2. Generate the formula that means if p receives data encrypted by p's symmetric key or public key, p gets original data. $\forall p_1 \forall p_2 \forall x_1 \ldots \forall x_n (Recv(p_1, enc(symk(p_1, p_2), x_1, \cdots, x_n)) \Rightarrow Recv(p_1, data(x_1, \cdots, x_n)))$, and $\forall p \forall x_1 \ldots \forall x_n (Recv(p, enc(pk(p), x_1, \cdots, x_n)) \Rightarrow Recv(p, data(x_1, \cdots, x_n)))$.

3. Generate the formula that means if p receives data encrypted by a session key that p knows, p gets original data. $\forall p_1 \forall x_1 \ldots \forall x_n(Recv(p_1, enc(sesk(p_1), x_1, \cdots, x_n)) \Rightarrow Recv(p_1, data(x_1, \cdots, x_n)))$.
4. $\forall p_1 \forall p_2(Eq(symk(p_1, p_2), symk(p_2, p_1)))$ represents $symk(p_1, p_2)$ and $symk(p_2, p_1)$ are equal.
5. $Parti(\alpha)$ where α represents a person or the third trusted server.

Confirm Behaviors. Confirm behaviors are the basis for the participants to judge whether the received message is correct or not.

1. Generate formulas of the public key other participants that each participant have confirmed before the cryptographic protocol executing. $\forall p_1 \forall p_2(Cof(p_1, p_2, pk(p_2)))$, which means p_1 have confirmed that p_2 has responsible for the $pk(p_2)$.
2. If participant p_1 receives the data $\{x\}_{sig_{p_2}}$, and p_1 confirms that p_2 has the public key which can decrypt the signature, then p_1 can confirm p_2 has responsibility of data x. $\forall p_1 \forall p_2 \forall x(Recv(p_1, \{x\}_{sig_{p_2}}) \wedge Cof(p_1, p_2, pk(p_2)) \Rightarrow Cof(p_1, p_2, x))$.
3. If participant p_1 receives the data $\{x\}_k$, and p_1 confirms that k is the key of p_2, p_1 can confirm p_2 has responsibility of data x. $\forall p_1 \forall p_2 \forall x(Recv(p_1, \{x\}_k) \wedge Cof(p_1, p_2, k) \Rightarrow Cof(p_1, p_2, x))$.
4. If participant p_1 confirms the data $\{x\}_k$, and p_1 confirms that k is the key of p_2, p_1 can confirm p_2 has responsibility of data x. $\forall p_1 \forall p_2 \forall x(Cof(p_1, \{x\}_k) \wedge Cof(p_1, p_2, k) \Rightarrow Cof(p_1, p_2, x))$.
5. If participant p_1 confirms that p_2 has responsibility to data set (x, y, z), p_1 can confirm p_2 has responsibility of each data, same if vice versa. They are represented as $\forall p_1 \forall p_2 \forall x_1 \ldots \forall x_n(Cof(p_1, p_2, \{x_1 \ldots x_n\}) \Rightarrow Cof(p_1, p_2, x_1) \wedge \cdots \wedge Cof(p_1, p_2, x_n))$ and $\forall p_1 \forall p_2 \forall x_1 \ldots \forall x_n(Cof(p_1, p_2, x_1) \wedge \cdots \wedge Cof(p_1, p_2, x_n) \Rightarrow Cof(p_1, p_2, \{x_1 \ldots x_n\}))$.
6. TTP and CS are always honest participants. If participants p_1 and p_2 exchange data through TTP or CS, and p_1 confirms TTP or CS has responsibility to data m, p_1 can confirm p_2 has responsibility to data m. $\forall p_1 \forall p_2 \forall x(Cof(p_1, ttp, x_1) \Rightarrow Cof(p_1, p_2, x_1))$.

3.2   Forward Reasoning

In the method, analysts use FreeEnCal [7] to perform forward reasoning automatically. Strong relevant logic [5,6] is used when forward reasoning. It stipulates conclusions that are not related to the premise are not deduced, thus greatly reducing the useless deduced data. In the extended method, the number of forward reasoning executions depends on the number of steps of the cryptographic protocol to be detected. Analysts put generated logical formulas of "common behaviors", "confirm behaviors" into FreeEncal, and put the first step of the "behaviors of participants" into FreeEnCal for the first execution of forward reasoning, and then add the formula that represents the second step of the protocol to the result of first execution of forward reasoning to perform forward reasoning the second time. Add the formula that represents each step of the protocol in turn. If the added formula is represented as the final step of the cryptographic protocol, forward reasoning is finished.

3.3   Analysis

Analysts check the deduced formulas in each execution result of forward reasoning. If in the final execution result, all participant have confirmed the data they should receive, the cryptographic protocol has no flaws related to non-repudiation. Because according to the "confirm behaviors", if one participant deceives the other in the protocol, the other participant cannot confirm the data he/she has received. If in the middle execution results, one participant has confirmed the target data but the other has not, it indicates that the cryptographic protocol has the flaw related to fairness.

4   Case Study in ISI Protocol

To validate the extension of formal analysis method with reasoning is valid of detecting flaws related to non-repudiation and fairness, we use ISI protocol as a case to analyze the security. ISI protocol is proposed by Medvinsky and Neuman [17], the purpose of the protocol is participant A pays participant B, then B gives the receipt to A.

The specification of the protocol is as follows. In step 1, participant A sends the symmetric key to ask the public key of B, and then B answers. Then A sends the electronic money, the service identification number to be obtained and password to B. By checking the signature of the CS, B can confirm the validity of the electronic money. In the fourth step, B transmits the electronic money to CS (currency server). Then CS will pay B in step 5. After receiving the money, B sends the receipt to A. In this protocol, CS is an honest participant. Here, $coins, id, passward, transaction, new - coins, amount, tid$ and $date$ are data that is uniquely defined in the protocol.

Specification

1. $A \rightarrow B : K_{ab}$
2. $B \rightarrow A : \{K_b\}_{K_{ab}}$
3. $A \rightarrow B : \{\{coins\}_{Sig_{cs}}, SK_a, id, password\}_{K_b}$
4. $B \rightarrow CS : \{\{coins\}_{Sig_{cs}}, SK_b, transaction\}_{K_{cs}}$
5. $CS \rightarrow B : \{\{new - coins\}_{Sig_{cs}}\}_{SK_b}$
6. $B \rightarrow A : \{\{amount, tid, date\}_{Sig_b}\}_{SK_a}$

This protocol has been pointed out that it does not satisfy the security of non-repudiation and fairness [16]. In the fifth step, B receives the currency signed by CS, but at this time A does not receive the receipt. If B stops the cryptographic protocol, A has no way to get the receipt. Therefore, according to the definition of fairness, the cryptographic protocol has a flaw of not satisfying fairness. In the sixth step of the protocol, A receives the signed receipt, but A cannot confirm whether this is the signature of B, so according to the definition of non-repudiation, the protocol has the flaw of not satisfying non-repudiation.

As the result of formal analysis by the extended method, 2435 logical formulas were deduced. After the fourth step of the protocol is executed, $Cof(B, A, new-coins)$ was deduced which means that participant B can confirm that A has responsibility of $new-coins$, that is, B received the currency. After the last step of the protocol is executed, formula $Recv(A, data(sig(b, amount, tid, date)))$ was deduced which means that A only cannot confirm whether the signature is from B. Therefore, this protocol has the flaw that does not satisfy non-repudiation. Since A did not get a receipt when the currency was obtained by B on the 18th path, the protocol has a flaw that does not satisfy fairness.

If we use the previous formal analysis method with reasoning [25] to analysis the protocol, we can get 2938 logical formulas. In the deduced formulas, $Recv(A, data(enc(seak(a), sig(i, amount', tid', date'))))$ and $Get(A, data(amount', tid', date'))$ were deduced, which means participant A gets the falsified data. Therefore, according to the flaw analysis criteria [26], the ISI protocol also does not satisfy the security properties of authentication.

The attack process is as follows.

Attack

1. $A \to I(B) : K_{ab}$
2. $I(A) \to B : K_{ab}$
3. $B \to I(A) : \{K_b\}_{K_{ab}}$
4. $I(B) \to A : \{K_i\}_{K_{ab}}$
5. $A \to I(B) : \{\{coins\}_{Sig_{cs}}, SK_a, id, password\}_{K_i}$
6. $I(A) \to B : \{\{coins\}_{Sig_{cs}}, SK_a, id, password\}_{K_b}$
7. $B \to CS : \{\{coins\}_{Sig_{cs}}, SK_b, transaction\}_{K_{cs}}$
8. $CS \to B : \{\{new-coins\}_{Sig_{cs}}\}_{SK_b}$
9. $B \to I(A) : \{\{amount, tid, date\}_{Sig_b}\}_{SK_a}$
10. $I(B) \to A : \{\{amount', tid', date'\}_{Sig_i}\}_{SK_a}$

Based on the two results above, it can be said that the formal analysis method with reasoning can deal with flaws related to authentication, non-repudiation and fairness.

5   Discussions

Although we have successfully proved that the extension of formal analysis method with reasoning can find flaws related to confidentiality, authentication [25], non-repudiation and fairness, there are still two problems with this method.

The first problem is that only limited types of flaws can be detected. In the method, we use Dolev-Yao model [10] to describe the intruder's capabilities and use the confirm behaviors to restrict participant's capabilities. But it cannot describe the ability of all honest participants, dishonest participants and intruders to cross-combine, so the formulas associated with certain flaws may not be deduced.

Second, a large number of logical formulas have been deduced by using the extended method, obviously, it is difficult for analysts to analyze them one by one. In the case study of ISI protocol, the meaning of other logical representations has not yet been analyzed. Therefore we need to find some ways to exclude the formulas that considered secure in the generated formulas, narrow the scope of the analysis.

6   Concluding Remarks

In this paper, we have made an extension of formal analysis method with reasoning for cryptographic protocols in order to detect the flaws that related to the security of non-repudiation and fairness. We also have analyzed the ISI protocol by using the proposed method and the known flaw was detected. Therefore, based on the ability to detect flaws related to confidentiality and authentication, the extended method can detect flaws related to the security properties of confidentiality and authentication, non-repudiation and fairness.

In the future, we will analyze more cryptographic protocols to verify the validity of the extended method. We will also more fully describe the capabilities of intruders and dishonest participants, and we will find some ways to narrow the scope of the deduced formulas and analyze the formulas automatically.

References

1. Asokan, N.: Fairness in electronic commerce. Ph.D. thesis, Department of Mathematics, University of Waterloo, Canada (1998)
2. Avalle, M., Alfredo, P., Bogdan, W.: Formal verification of security protocol implementations: a survey. Formal Aspects Comput. **26**(1), 99–123 (2014)
3. Bau, J., Mitchell, J.C.: Security modeling and analysis. IEEE Secur. Priv. **9**(3), 18–25 (2011)
4. Butterfield, A., Ngondi, G.: Oxford Dictionary of Computer Science. Oxford University Press, Oxford (2016)
5. Cheng, J.: A strong relevant logic model of epistemic processes in scientific discovery. In: Information Modelling and Knowledge Bases XI, Frontiers in Artificial Intelligence and Applications, vol. 61, pp. 136–159 (2000)
6. Cheng, J., Miura, J.: Deontic relevant logic as the logical basis for specifying, verifying, and reasoning about information security and information assurance. In: 1st International Conference on Availability, Reliability and Security, pp. 601–608. IEEE Computer Society, Vienna, Austria (2006)
7. Cheng, J., Nara, S., Goto, Y.: FreeEnCal: a forward reasoning engine with general-purpose. In: Apolloni, B., Howlett, R.J., Jain, L. (eds.) KES 2007. LNCS (LNAI), vol. 4693, pp. 444–452. Springer, Heidelberg (2007). https://doi.org/10.1007/978-3-540-74827-4_56
8. Clarke Jr., E.M., Grumberg, O., Peled, D.: Model Checking. MIT Press, Cambridge (1999)

9. Cortier, V., Kremer, S., Warinschi, B.: A survey of symbolic methods in computational analysis of cryptographic systems. J. Autom. Reasoning **46**(3–4), 225–259 (2011)

10. Dolev, D., Andrew, C.Y.: On the security of public key protocols. IEEE Trans. Inf. Theory **29**(2), 198–208 (1983)

11. Hauser, R., Steiner, M., Waidner, M.: Micro-payments based on IKP. IBM Zurich Research Laboratory, IBM Research Division Report RZ279, Zurich, Switzerland (1996)

12. International Organization for Standardization: ISO/IEC 13888–3: Information security techniques - non-repudiation - Part: Mechanisms using asymmetric techniques (1997)

13. International Organization for Standardization: ISO/IEC 13888–2: Information security techniques - non-repudiation - Part: Mechanisms using symmetric techniques (1998)

14. International Organization for Standardization: ISO/IEC 29128: Information technology - Security techniques - Verification of cryptographic protocols (2011)

15. Kremera, S., Markowitcha, O., Zhoub, J.: An intensive survey of fair non-repudiation protocols. Comput. Commun. **25**(17), 1606–1621 (2002)

16. Liu, Y., Zhang, H.: Stand spaces analysis of electronic commerce protocols. Comput. Sci. **35**(2), 109–114 (2008)

17. Medvinsky, G., Neuman, C.: NetCash: a design of practical electronic currency on the internet. In: 1st ACM Conference on Computer and Communications Security, Fairfax, Virginia, USA, pp. 102–106 (1993)

18. Meadows, C.A., Meadows, C.A.: Formal verification of cryptographic protocols: a survey. In: Pieprzyk, J., Safavi-Naini, R. (eds.) ASIACRYPT 1994. LNCS, vol. 917, pp. 133–150. Springer, Heidelberg (1995). https://doi.org/10.1007/BFb0000430

19. Meadows, C.: Formal methods for cryptographic protocol analysis: emerging issues and trends. IEEE J. Sel. Areas Commun. **21**(1), 44–54 (2003)

20. Markowitch, O., Gollmann, D., Kremer, S.: On fairness in exchange protocols. In: Lee, P.J., Lim, C.H. (eds.) ICISC 2002. LNCS, vol. 2587, pp. 451–465. Springer, Heidelberg (2003). https://doi.org/10.1007/3-540-36552-4_31

21. Paulson, L.C.: The inductive approach to verifying cryptographic protocols. J. Comput. Secur. **6**(1), 85–128 (1998)

22. Roe, M.: Cryptography and evidence. Ph.D. thesis, Computer Laboratory, University of Cambridge (1997)

23. Zhou, J., Gollmann, D.: Evidence and non-repudiation. J. Network Comput. Appl. **20**(30), 267–281 (1997)

24. Wagatsuma, K., Goto, Y., Cheng, J.: A formal analysis method with reasoning for key exchange protocols. IPSJ J. **56**(3), 903–910 (2015). (in Japanese)

25. Yan, J., Wagatsuma, K., Gao, H., Cheng, J.: A formal analysis method with reasoning for cryptographic protocols. In: 12th International Conference on Computational Intelligence and Security, pp. 566–570. IEEE Computer Society, Wuxi (2016)

26. Yan, J., Ishibashi, S., Goto, Y., Cheng, J.: A study on fine-grained security properties of cryptographic protocols for formal analysis method with reasoning. In: 2018 IEEE SmartWorld, Ubiquitous Intelligence, Computing, Advanced, Trusted Computing, Scalable Computing, Communications, Cloud, Big Data Computing, Internet of People and Smart City Innovations, pp. 210–215. IEEE-CS, Guangzhou (2018)

A Practical and Insider Secure Signcryption with Non-interactive Non-repudiation

Augustin P. Sarr[✉], Papa B. Seye, and Togdé Ngarenon

Lacca, UFR SAT, Université Gaston Berger de Saint-Louis, Saint-Louis, Senegal
aug.sarr@gmail.com

Abstract. Signcryption with non-interactive non-repudiation is a public key primitive which aims at combining the functionalities of encryption and signature schemes, while offering to a judge the ability to settle a repudiation dispute without engaging in a costly multi-round protocol. We propose a new RSA based identification scheme together with a strongly unforgeable signature scheme. We derive a practical and efficient signcryption scheme with non-interactive non-repudiation we show to be insider secure, under the RSA assumption and the Random Oracle model. The communication overhead of our signcryption scheme, compared to the corresponding signature scheme is one group element.

Keywords: Identification · Signature · Signcryption ·
Insider security · Non-interactive non-repudiation ·
Signed quadratic residues

1 Introduction

Signcryption is a public key primitive introduced by Zheng [23], with the aim of combining the functionalities of encryption and signature schemes. Since Zheng's seminal work, many security models and constructions have been proposed [3]. In a recent work, Badertscher *et al.* [2] consider, from an application-centric perspective, the security goals a signcryption scheme should achieve depending on the secret keys the attacker knows. They conclude, in opposition to [3, p. 29], that insider security should be considered as the standard security goal.

An important attribute which is not considered in the "standard" insider security model is *non-interactive non-repudiation*. As discussed in [2], the natural usage of signcrytion is to achieve a confidential and authenticated channel between two parties over an insecure network. The same can be achieved using non-interactive or one pass-key exchange protocols, which often outperform signcryption schemes. So, a major benefit of signcryption schemes compared

---

This Research was supported by the African Center of Excellence in Mathematics, Computer Science and ICT of UGB.

C. Carlet et al. (Eds.): C2SI 2019, LNCS 11445, pp. 409–429, 2019.
https://doi.org/10.1007/978-3-030-16458-4_24

to non-interactive and one-pass key exchange is non-interactive non-repudiation (NINR), *i.e.* a non-repudiation attribute wherein a judge does not have to engage in a costly multi-round interactive protocol to settle a repudiation dispute.

A first attempt to achieve NINR in a signcryption design was proposed by Bao and Deng [6]. Unfortunately their scheme fails in providing both NINR and confidentiality [17,22]. In [17], Malone–Lee propose a design with NINR. However, he analyses his design, under the Gap Diffie–Hellman Assumption [19] and the Random Oracle (RO) model [8], in a security definition which is closer to the outsider model than to the insider one [3, Chap. 2–4]. Fan *et al.* [11] propose a strengthening of Malone–Lee's security model which considers, not only confidentiality and unforgeability in the insider model, but also soundness and unforgeability of non-repudiation evidence. They propose a design they show to be insider secure under the Decisional Bilinear Diffie–Hellman assumption, without resorting to the RO model.

In this paper, we propose a new identification scheme, inspired from the FXCR [20,21] and Guillou–Quisquater (GQ) [13] schemes, over the group of signed quadratic residues [14].

We derive a signature scheme which is strongly unforgeable against chosen message attacks. A significant advantage of our signature scheme, compared to the FXCR or GQ schemes is that it is defined over a group wherein the strong Diffie–Hellman assumption is known to hold under the factoring assumption [14]. Then, using a variant of Cash *et al.*'s trapdoor test technique [10], we derive a signcryption scheme with non-interactive non-repudiation (SCNINR) we show to be insider secure, under the RSA assumption and the RO model, in a variant of Fan *et al.*'s security definition [11].

This paper is organized as follows. In Sect. 2, we present some preliminaries. In Sect. 3, we propose the identification scheme, discuss its attributes, and derive the signature scheme. We present the new SCNINR scheme and its security arguments in Sect. 4.

2   Preliminaries

Notations. If n is an integer, $|n|$ denotes its bit-length and $[n]$ denotes the set $\{0, \cdots, n\}$. For a real l, $\lceil l \rceil$ denotes the smallest integer which is greater than or equal to l. We refer to the length of a list $\mathcal{L}$ by $|\mathcal{L}|$, and to the cardinality of a set S by $|S|$. If P is a probabilistic algorithm which takes as parameters $u_1, \cdots, u_n$ and outputs a result V which belongs to a set $\mathbf{V}$, we write $V \leftarrow_{\mathrm{R}} P(u_1, \cdots, u_n)$. We denote by $\{P(u_1, \cdots, u_n)\}$ the set $\{v \in \mathbf{V} : \Pr(V = v) \neq 0\}$. If S is a set, the notation $a \leftarrow_{\mathrm{R}} S$ means that a is chosen uniformly at random from S. $\mathsf{Exp}(\mathbb{Z}_N, t, l)$ denotes the computational effort required to perform t exponentiations with l bit exponents in $\mathbb{Z}_N$; $\mathsf{Exp}(\mathbb{Z}_N, l)$ stands for $\mathsf{Exp}(\mathbb{Z}_N, 1, l)$. $\mathsf{Jcb}(\mathbb{Z}_N)$ denotes the effort required to compute a Jacobi symbol in $\mathbb{Z}_N$. For two bit strings m_1 and m_2, $m_1 \| m_2$ denotes their concatenation; ϵ denotes the empty string. If $x_1, x_2, \cdots, x_k$ are objects belonging to different structures (group, bit-string, etc.) $(x_1, x_2, \cdots, x_k)$ denotes a representation of the tuple such that each component can be unequivocally parsed.

RSA Public Key Generator. Let k be a security parameter, $n(k)$ be a function of k and $0 \leqslant \delta < 1/2$ be a constant. An algorithm RSAGen (which may be distributed) is said to be a $(n(k), \delta)$ RSA public key generator if on input 1^k, it outputs a $n(k)$ bit Blum integer $N = pq$ together with a public exponent e such that all the prime factors of $\phi(N)/4$ are: *(i)* pairwise distinct, and *(ii)* at least δn bit integers, and *(iii)* e is a $(k+1)$ bit prime.

RSA and Factoring Assumptions. Let $\mathcal{A}$ be an algorithm. We define the quantity

$$\mathsf{Adv}^{\mathsf{RSA}}_{\mathcal{A},\mathsf{RSAGen}}(k) = \Pr\left[\begin{array}{l} (N, e) \leftarrow_{\mathrm{R}} \mathsf{RSAGen}(1^k); x \leftarrow_{\mathrm{R}} \mathbb{Z}_N; \\ y \leftarrow x^e \mod N; \hat{x} \leftarrow_{\mathrm{R}} \mathcal{A}(N, e, y) \end{array} : \hat{x} = x \right].$$

The RSA assumption for an $(n(k), \delta)$ RSA public key generator is said to hold if for all efficient adversary $\mathcal{A}$, $\mathsf{Adv}^{\mathsf{RSA}}_{\mathcal{A},\mathsf{RSAGen}}(k)$ is negligible. For an instance $(N, e) \leftarrow_{\mathrm{R}} \mathsf{RSAGen}(1^k)$ and an efficiently sampleable and recognizable subset J of $\mathbb{Z}_N$, we say that the RSA problem is $(t(k), \varepsilon(k))$ hard in J, if for all $\mathcal{A}$ running in time at most t, $\Pr\left[x \leftarrow_{\mathrm{R}} \mathsf{J}; y \leftarrow x^e \mod N; \hat{x} \leftarrow_{\mathrm{R}} \mathcal{A}(N, e, y) : \hat{x} = x \right] \leqslant \varepsilon$.

Let $\mathcal{A}$ be a factoring algorithm and

$$\mathsf{Adv}^{\mathsf{fac}}_{\mathcal{A},\mathsf{RSAGen}}(k) = \Pr\left[\begin{array}{l} (N, e) \leftarrow_{\mathrm{R}} \mathsf{RSAGen}(k); \\ p \leftarrow_{\mathrm{R}} \mathcal{A}(N, e) \end{array} : p \mid n \text{ and } p \notin \{\pm N, \pm 1\} \right].$$

The factoring assumption for an (n, δ) RSA public key generator is said to hold if for all efficient adversary $\mathcal{A}$, $\mathsf{Adv}^{\mathsf{fac}}_{\mathcal{A},\mathsf{RSAGen}}(k)$ is negligible.

Diffie–Hellman Assumptions. Let $\mathcal{G} = \langle G \rangle$ be a cyclic group, which order is a function of the security parameter k and is not necessarily known. For $X \in \mathcal{G}$, $\log_G X$ denotes the smallest non-negative integer x such that $G^x = X$. For, $X, Y \in \mathcal{G}$, we denote $G^{(\log_G X)(\log_G Y)}$ by $\mathrm{CDH}(X, Y)$. The *computational Diffie–Hellman (CDH) Assumption* is said to hold in $\mathcal{G}$ if for all efficient algorithm $\mathcal{A}$,

$$\mathsf{Adv}^{\mathsf{CDH}}_{\mathcal{A}}(\mathcal{G}) = \Pr\left[X \leftarrow_{\mathrm{R}} \mathcal{G}; Y \leftarrow_{\mathrm{R}} \mathcal{G}; Z \leftarrow_{\mathrm{R}} \mathcal{A}(G, X, Y) : Z = \mathrm{CDH}(X, Y) \right]$$

is negligible in k. The *strong Diffie–Hellman (sCDH) assumption* is said to hold in $\mathcal{G}$ if the CDH assumption holds even if $\mathcal{A}$ is endowed with a decisional Diffie–Hellman oracle $\mathcal{O}_{\mathrm{DDH},X}(\cdot, \cdot)$ for a some fixed X, which on input $U, V \in \mathcal{G}$ outputs 1 if $V = \mathrm{CDH}(X, U)$ and 0 otherwise.

Signed Quadratic Residues. For an odd integer N, we consider $\{-(N-1)/2, \cdots, (N-1)/2\}$ as a set of representatives of the residue classes modulo N. We denote by $\mathbb{J}_N$ the subgroup of elements of $\mathbb{Z}_N^*$ with Jacobi symbol 1, and consider the quotient group $\mathbb{J}_N/\{-1, 1\}$. We define $\mathbb{J}_N^+ = \mathbb{J}_N \cap \{1, \cdots, (N-1)/2\}$, and the binary operation $\circ$ over $\mathbb{J}_N^+$ by $X \circ Y = |X \cdot Y \mod N|$. For $X \in \mathbb{J}_N^+$ and

$$t \in \mathbb{N}, \text{ we write } X^{\underline{t}} \text{ for } \overbrace{X \circ \cdots \circ X}^{t \text{ times}} = |X^t \mod N| \in \mathbb{J}_N^+.$$

Then $(\mathbb{J}_N^+, \circ)$ is a group, termed group of signed quadratic residues. Moreover the mapping which associates $\{-X, X\} \in \mathbb{J}_N/\{-1, 1\}$ to $|X| \in \mathbb{J}_N^+$ is an isomorphism. We identify the quotient group $\mathbb{J}_N/\{-1, 1\}$ with $\mathbb{J}_N^+$. From [14], we have the following Lemma.

Lemma 1. *If N is a Blum integer then (a) $(\mathbb{J}_N^+, \circ)$ is a subgroup of $\mathbb{Z}_N^*$ of order $\phi(N)/4$; (b) $\mathbb{J}_N^+$ is efficiently recognizable given only N; and (c) if $\mathbb{J}_N$ is cyclic then so is $\mathbb{J}_N^+$.*

Canonical Identification Schemes

Definition 1. *A canonical identification scheme $\mathcal{I} = (\mathsf{Gen}, \mathsf{P}, \mathsf{V}, \mathsf{ChSet})$ is a triple of algorithms together with a challenge set, such that:*

- *Gen is a probabilistic algorithm which takes as input a domain parameters dp and returns a key pair (sk, pk).*
- *$\mathsf{P} = (\mathsf{P}_1, \mathsf{P}_2)$ is a pair of algorithms such that: (i) P_1 takes as input a secret key sk and outputs a commitment X together with a state st; and (ii) P_2 takes as inputs a private key sk, a commitment X, a challenge $c \in \mathsf{ChSet}$, and a state st and outputs a response $s \in \{0,1\}^*$.*
- *V is a deterministic verification algorithm which takes as inputs a public key pk, a commitment X, a challenge c, and a response s and outputs $d \in \{0,1\}$.*
- *And, for all $(sk, pk) \in \{\mathsf{Gen}(dp)\}$, all $(X, st) \in \{\mathsf{P}_1(sk)\}$, all $c \in \mathsf{ChSet}$, and all $s \in \{\mathsf{P}_2(sk, X, c, st)\}$, $\mathsf{V}(pk, X, c, s) = 1$.*

A transcript (X, c, s) is said to be *accepting* with respect to pk if $\mathsf{V}(pk, X, c, s) = 1$.

An identification scheme is said to be *unique* if for all $(sk, pk) \in \{\mathsf{Gen}(dp)\}$, all $(X, st) \in \{\mathsf{P}_1(sk)\}$, and all $c \in \mathsf{ChSet}$, there is at most one $s \in \{0,1\}^*$ such that $\mathsf{V}(pk, X, c, s) = 1$. It is said to have α-bits of min entropy if for all $(sk, pk) \in \{\mathsf{Gen}(dp)\}$, the commitments generated through $\mathsf{P}_1(sk)$ are chosen from a distribution with min entropy at least α; *i.e.*, for all commitment X_0, if $(X, st) \leftarrow_R \mathsf{P}_1(sk)$ was honestly generated then $\Pr(X = X_0) \leqslant 2^{-\alpha}$.

Definition 2. *Let $\mathcal{I} = (\mathsf{Gen}, \mathsf{P}, \mathsf{V}, \mathsf{ChSet})$ be a canonical identification scheme.*

(a) *$\mathcal{I}$ is said to provide* special soundness (SpS) *if there exists an efficient deterministic algorithm Ext (an extractor) such that for all accepting conversations with respect to a public key pk, (X, c, s) and (X, c', s'), if $c \neq c'$ then $sk^* \leftarrow \mathsf{Ext}(pk, X, c, s, c', s')$ is such that $(sk^*, pk) \in \{\mathsf{Gen}(dp)\}$.*

(b) *It is said to be* honest verifier zero knowledge (HVZK) *if there exists an efficient probabilistic algorithm sim (a simulator) such that for all $(sk, pk) \in \{\mathsf{Gen}(dp)\}$, the output distribution of sim on input pk is identical to that of a real transcript between $\mathsf{P}(sk)$ and $\mathsf{V}(pk)$.*

(c) *It is said to be* random self reducible (RSR) *if there is a probabilistic algorithm Rerand together with two deterministic algorithms Tran and Derand such that for all $(sk, pk) \in \{\mathsf{Gen}(dp)\}$:*
  - *if $(\tau, pk_1) \leftarrow_R \mathsf{Rerand}(pk)$ and $(sk_2, pk_2) \leftarrow_R \mathsf{Gen}(dp)$ then pk_1 and pk_2 have the same distribution;*
  - *for all $(sk_1, pk_1) \in \{\mathsf{Gen}(dp)\}$, for all τ such that $(\tau, pk_1) \in \{\mathsf{Rerand}(pk)\}$, if $sk^* \leftarrow \mathsf{Derand}(pk, pk_1, sk_1, \tau)$ then $(sk^*, pk) \in \{\mathsf{Gen}(dp)\}$;*

– *for all* $(sk_1, pk_1) \in \{\text{Gen}(dp)\}$ *and all* (X, c, s_1) *such that* $\mathsf{V}(pk_1, X, c, s_1) = 1$, *if* $(X, c, s) \leftarrow \mathsf{Tran}(pk, pk_1, \tau, (X, c, s_1))$ *then* $\mathsf{V}(pk, X, c, s) = 1$.

Definition 3. *A canonical identification scheme* $\mathcal{I} = (\text{Gen}, \mathsf{P}, \mathsf{V}, \mathsf{ChSet})$ *is said to be* (t, ε)-*secure against Key Recovery against Key Only Attacks (KR-KOA), if for all adversary* $\mathcal{A}$ *running in time at most* t

$$\Pr\left[(sk, pk) \leftarrow_R \text{Gen}(dp); sk^* \leftarrow_R \mathcal{A}(pk) : (sk^*, pk) \in \{\text{Gen}(dp)\}\right] \leqslant \varepsilon.$$

Symmetric Encryption, Digital Signature

Definition 4. *A symmetric encryption scheme* $\mathcal{E} = (\mathsf{E}, \mathsf{D}, \mathbf{K}(k), \mathbf{M}(k), \mathbf{C}(k))$ *is a pair of efficient algorithms* (E, D) *together with a triple of sets* $(\mathbf{K}(k), \mathbf{M}(k), \mathbf{C}(k))$ *such that for all* $\tau \in \mathbf{K}$ *and all* $m \in \mathbf{M}$, $\mathsf{E}(\tau, m) \in \mathbf{C}$, $m = \mathsf{D}(\tau, \mathsf{E}(\tau, m))$.

Definition 5. *Let* $\mathcal{A}$ *be an adversary against an encryption scheme* $\mathcal{E}$; *its semantic security advantage is*

$$\mathsf{Adv}_{\mathcal{A}, \mathcal{E}}^{\mathsf{ss}}(k) = \left| \Pr\left[\begin{matrix} (m_0, m_1) \leftarrow_R A(1^k); \tau \leftarrow_R \mathbf{K}; b \leftarrow_R \{0, 1\}; \\ c \leftarrow \mathsf{E}(\tau, m_b); \hat{b} \leftarrow_R \mathcal{A}(1^k, c) \end{matrix} : \hat{b} = b \right] - \frac{1}{2} \right|,$$

where $m_0, m_1 \in \mathbf{M}$ *are distinct equal length messages. The scheme* $\mathcal{E}$ *is said to be* (t, ε)-*semantically secure if for all adversary* $\mathcal{A}$ *running in time* t $\mathsf{Adv}_{\mathcal{A}, \mathcal{E}}^{\mathsf{ss}}(k) \leqslant \varepsilon$.

Definition 6. *A signature scheme* $\mathcal{S} = (\text{Gen}, \text{Sign}, \text{Vrfy})$ *is a triple of efficient algorithms together with a message space* $\mathbf{M}$, *such that:*

– Gen *is probabilistic algorithm which takes as input a domain parameter* dp *and returns a key pair* (sk, pk);
– Sign *is a probabilistic algorithm which takes as inputs a secret key* sk *and a message* $m \in \mathbf{M}$ *and outputs a signature* σ;
– Vrfy *is a deterministic algorithm which takes as inputs a public key* pk, *a message* m, *and a signature* σ *and outputs* $d \in \{0, 1\}$; *and*
– *for all* $(sk, pk) \in \{\text{Gen}(dp)\}$, *all* $m \in \mathbf{M}$, $\Pr[\text{Vrfy}(pk, m, \text{Sign}(sk, m)) = 1] = 1$.

Game 1. MU-SUF-CMA security game

1) For $i \in [U]$, $(sk_i, pk_i) \leftarrow_R \text{Gen}(dp)$;
2) $(i_0, m_0, \sigma_0) \leftarrow_R \mathcal{A}^{\mathcal{O}_H(\cdot), \mathcal{O}_{\text{Sign}}(\cdot, \cdot)}(pk_1, \cdots, pk_U)$, wherein $\mathcal{O}_H(\cdot)$ is a hashing oracle and $\mathcal{O}_{\text{Sign}}(\cdot, \cdot)$ a signing oracle which takes as inputs an index $j \in [U]$ together with a message m and outputs $\sigma \leftarrow_R \text{Sign}(sk_j, m)$.
3) $\mathcal{A}$ succeeds if : (a) $i_0 \in [U]$ and $\text{Vrfy}(pk_{i_0}, m_0, \sigma_0) = 1$, and (b) σ_0 was not received from the oracle $\mathcal{O}_{\text{Sign}}(\cdot, \cdot)$ on a query on (i_0, m_0).

Definition 7. *Let* $\mathcal{S} = (\text{Gen}, \text{Sign}, \text{Vrfy})$ *be a signature scheme such that the execution of* Sign *involves the computation of one digest value, at least.* $\mathcal{S}$ *is said to be* $(t, U, Q_{\text{Sign}}, Q_H, \varepsilon)$ *multi-user strongly unforgeable against chosen message* *attacks (MU-SUF-CMA) in the RO model, if for all adversary $\mathcal{A}$ playing Game 1 (wherein we consider U and dp as implicit parameters), if $\mathcal{A}$ runs in time at most t, issues at most Q_{Sign} and Q_H queries to the signing and hashing oracles respectively, the probability it succeeds is at most ε.*

Signcryption Schemes

Definition 8. *A signcryption scheme is a quintuple of algorithms $\mathcal{SC} = ($Setup, $\mathsf{Gen}_S, \mathsf{Gen}_R, \mathsf{Sc}, \mathsf{Usc})$ wherein:*

(a) Setup *is a probabilistic algorithm which takes a security parameter 1^k as input, and outputs a domain parameter dp.*

(b) Gen_S *is a probabilistic algorithm which takes as input a domain parameter dp and outputs a sender key pair (sk_S, pk_S) wherein sk_S is the signing key.*

(c) Gen_R *is a probabilistic algorithm which takes dp as input and outputs a receiver key pair (sk_R, pk_R).*

(d) Sc *is a probabilistic algorithm which takes as inputs dp, a sender private key sk_S and a receiver public key pk_R, and outputs a signcrypted text C. We consider dp as an implicit parameter and write $C \leftarrow_R \mathsf{Sc}(sk_S, pk_R, m)$.*

(e) Usc *is a deterministic algorithm which takes as input dp, a sender public key pk_S, a receiver secret key sk_R and outputs either a message $m \in \mathcal{M}$ or an error symbol $\perp \notin \mathcal{M}$.*

The above algorithms are such that for all $dp \in \{\mathsf{Setup}(1^k)\}$, all $m \in \mathcal{M}$, all $(sk_S, pk_S) \in \{\mathsf{Gen}_S(dp)\}$, and all $(sk_R, pk_R) \in \{\mathsf{Gen}_R(dp)\}$, $m = \mathsf{Usc}(sk_R, pk_S,$ $\mathsf{Sc}(sk_S, pk_R, m))$. The scheme is said to provide NINR if there is a non-repudiation evidence generation algorithm N together with a pubic verification algorithm PV such that:

- N *takes as inputs a receiver secret key sk_R, a sender public key pk_S, and a signcrypted text C, and outputs a non-repudiation evidence nr or a failure symbol $\perp$; we write $nr \leftarrow \mathsf{N}(sk_R, pk_S, C)$.*

- PV *takes as inputs a signcryptext C a message m, a non-repudiation evidence nr, and two public keys pk_S and pk_R and outputs, a decision $d \in \{0,1\}$; we write $d \leftarrow \mathsf{PV}(C, m, nr, pk_S, pk_R)$.*

- *And, for all $dp \in \{\mathsf{Setup}(1^k)\}$, all $C \in \{0,1\}^*$, all $(sk_S, pk_S) \in \{\mathsf{Gen}_S(dp)\}$, and all $(sk_R, pk_R) \in \{\mathsf{Gen}_R(dp)\}$, if $\perp \neq m \leftarrow \mathsf{Usc}(sk_R, pk_S, C)$ and $nr \leftarrow \mathsf{N}(sk_R, pk_S, C)$ then $1 = d \leftarrow \mathsf{PV}(C, m, nr, pk_S, pk_R)$.*

Confidentiality. We propose in Game 2 an extension of the Secret Key Ignorant Multi-User (SKI-MU) insider confidentiality in the Flexible Signcryption/Unsigncryption Oracle (FSO/FUO) model [4,5] geared to SCNINR.

Game 2. SKI–MU Insider Confidentiality in the FSO/FUO–IND–CCA2 sense

$\mathcal{A} = (\mathcal{A}_1, \mathcal{A}_2)$ is a two–stage adversary against $\mathcal{SC}$; dp is the domain parameter.
1) The challenger computes $(sk_R, pk_R) \leftarrow_R \mathsf{Gen}_R(dp)$;
2) $\mathcal{A}_1$ is provided with dp and pk_R together with two oracles: (a) $\mathcal{O}_{\mathsf{Usc}}(\cdot, \cdot)$, which takes as inputs a public key pk and a signcrypted text C and outputs $m \leftarrow \mathsf{Usc}(sk_R, pk, C)$; (b) $\mathcal{O}_{\mathsf{N}(\cdot, \cdot)}$ which takes as inputs a public key pk and a signcrypted text C and outputs $nr \leftarrow \mathsf{N}(sk_R, pk, C)$.
3) $\mathcal{A}_1$ outputs a four–tuple $(m_0, m_1, st, pk_S) \leftarrow_R \mathcal{A}_1^{\mathcal{O}_{\mathsf{Usc}}(\cdot, \cdot), \mathcal{O}_{\mathsf{N}}(\cdot, \cdot)}(pk_R)$ wherein $m_0, m_1 \in \mathcal{M}$ are distinct equal length messages, st is a state, and pk_S is the attacked sender public key.
4) The challenger chooses $b \leftarrow_R \{0, 1\}$, computes $C^* \leftarrow_R \mathsf{Sc}(sk_S, pk_R, m_b)$.
5) $\mathcal{A}_2$ outputs $b' \leftarrow_R \mathcal{A}_2^{\mathcal{O}_{\mathsf{Sc}}(\cdot, \cdot), \mathcal{O}_{\mathsf{Usc}}(\cdot, \cdot), \mathcal{O}_{\mathsf{N}}(\cdot, \cdot)}(C^*, st)$, where $\mathcal{O}_{\mathsf{Usc}}(\cdot, \cdot)$ and $\mathcal{O}_{\mathsf{N}}(\cdot, \cdot)$ are as in step 2, and $\mathcal{O}_{\mathsf{Sc}}(\cdot, \cdot)$ takes as inputs $pk \in \{\mathsf{Gen}_R(dp)\}$ and $m \in \mathcal{M}$ and outputs $C \leftarrow_R \mathsf{Sc}(sk_S, pk, m)$.
6) $\mathcal{A}$ wins the game if: (a) $\mathcal{A}_2$ never issued $\mathcal{O}_{\mathsf{Usc}}(pk_S, C^*)$ or $\mathcal{O}_{\mathsf{N}}(pk_S, C^*)$, and (b) $b = b'$.

We denote by $\mathsf{Succ}_{\mathcal{A}}^{\mathsf{cca2}}$ the event "conditions (6a) and (6b) are satisfied", and define $\mathcal{A}$'s advantage by $\mathsf{Adv}_{\mathcal{A}, \mathcal{SC}}^{\mathsf{cca2}}(1^k) = | \Pr(\mathsf{Succ}_{\mathcal{A}}^{\mathsf{cca2}}) - 1/2 |$.

Definition 9. *A SCNINR SC is said to be $(t, q_{\mathsf{Sc}}, q_{\mathsf{Usc}}, q_{\mathsf{N}}, \varepsilon)$-secure in the SKI-MU insider confidentiality in the FSO/FUO-IND-CCA2 sense if for all adversary $\mathcal{A}$ playing Game 2, if $\mathcal{A}$ runs in time t, and issues respectively $q_{\mathsf{Sc}}, q_{\mathsf{Usc}},$ and q_{N} queries to the signcryption, unsigncryption, and non-repudiation evidence generation oracles then $\mathsf{Adv}_{\mathcal{A}, \mathcal{SC}}^{\mathsf{cca2}}(1^k) \leqslant \varepsilon$.*

Unforgeability. We recall here the multi-user insider unforgeability in the FSO/FUO-sUF-CMA sense for SCNINR.

Game 3. Multi–User insider Unforgeability in the FSO/FUO–sUF–CMA sense

$\mathcal{A}$ is a forger against $\mathcal{SC}$, dp is the domain parameter.
1) The challenger computes $(sk_S, pk_S) \leftarrow_R \mathsf{Gen}_S(dp)$.
2) $\mathcal{A}$ takes pk_S as input and is given access to a FSO $\mathcal{O}_{\mathsf{Sc}}(\cdot, \cdot)$, as in step 5 of Game 2.
3) $\mathcal{A}$ outputs $((sk_R, pk_R), C^*) \leftarrow_R \mathcal{A}^{\mathcal{O}_{\mathsf{Sc}}(\cdot, \cdot)}(pk_S)$. He wins the game if: (a) $\perp \neq m \leftarrow \mathsf{Usc}(sk_R, pk_S, C^*)$, and (b) $\mathcal{A}$ never received C^* from the oracle $\mathcal{O}_{\mathsf{Sc}}(\cdot, \cdot)$ on a query on (pk_R, m).

$\mathsf{Adv}_{\mathcal{A}, \mathcal{SC}}^{\mathsf{suf}}(1^k) = \Pr(\mathsf{Succ}_{\mathcal{A}}^{\mathsf{suf}})$ denotes the probability that $\mathcal{A}$ wins the game.

Definition 10. *A SCNINR is said to be $(t, q_{\mathsf{Sc}}, \varepsilon)$ multi-user insider unforgeable in the FSO/FUO-sUF-CMA sense if for all attacker $\mathcal{A}$ playing Game 3, if $\mathcal{A}$ runs in time t and issues q_{Sc} signcryption queries then $\mathsf{Adv}_{\mathcal{A}, \mathcal{SC}}^{\mathsf{suf}}(1^k) \leqslant \varepsilon$.*

Soundness of Non-repudiation. This attribute ensures that public verification always yields a correct result.

Game 4. Soundness of non–repudiation

$\mathcal{A} = (\mathcal{A}_1, \mathcal{A}_2)$ is an attacker against $\mathcal{SC}$, dp is the domain parameter.

1) $\mathcal{A}_1$ executes with parameter dp and outputs $(st, pk_S) \leftarrow_R \mathcal{A}_1(dp)$, wherein st is a state and pk_S a sender public key.

2) $\mathcal{A}_2$ executes with inputs st and pk_S and is given access to a FSO. It outputs $(sk_R, pk_R, C^*, m', nr) \leftarrow_R \mathcal{A}_2^{\mathcal{O}_{\mathsf{Sc}}(\cdot,\cdot)}(st, pk_S)$.

3) $\mathcal{A}$ wins the game if: (a) C^* is valid, $i.\ e.\ \perp \neq m \leftarrow \mathsf{Usc}(sk_R, pk_S, C^*)$, and (b) $m \neq m'$ and $1 = d \leftarrow \mathsf{PV}(C^*, m', nr, pk_S, pk_R)$.

We denote by $\mathsf{Adv}^{\mathsf{snr}}_{\mathcal{A},\mathcal{SC}}(1^k)$ the probability that $\mathcal{A}$ wins the game.

Definition 11. *A signcryption scheme $\mathcal{SC}$ is said to achieve $(t, q_{\mathsf{Sc}}, \varepsilon)$ computational soundness of non-repudiation if for all adversary $\mathcal{A}$ playing Game 4, if $\mathcal{A}$ runs in time t and issues q_{Sc} signcryption queries then $\mathsf{Adv}^{\mathsf{snr}}_{\mathcal{A},\mathcal{SC}}(1^k) \leqslant \varepsilon$.*

Unforgeability of Non-repudiation (NR) Evidence. Contrary to Malone–Lee [17], Fan et al. [11] consider unforgeability of non-repudiation evidence. However, their definition seems too restrictive. Indeed, they consider the capability of both the sender and receiver of a signcrypted text to generate a non-repudiation evidence as a security weakness. As a motivating example, they consider a malicious patient who receives a signcrypted medical report from his doctor, generates a non-repudiation evidence, and exposes the signcryted text together with the NR evidence. The patient can then claim that the doctor has exposed his report. In such a situation a judge cannot decide who, among the patient and the doctor, exposed the report.

As for us, non-repudiation ensures that a message sender (the doctor in the example) cannot deny that the message in the signcryted text (the medical record) is from him. The question considered in the example is *not* about the non-repudiation of the signcrypted message (the report), but about the non-repudiation of the (non-repudiation) evidence. Moreover in many settings, a non-repudiation evidence may be used both for *credit* (the ability of the sender to later claim being the sender of the message) and *responsibility* (the ability of the receiver to hold the sender accountable for the message contents) [9, Chap. 3]. It seems then important that NR evidences can be generated by both the sender (at signcrypted text generation) and the receiver of a signcrypted text.

Game 5. Unforgeability of non–repudiation evidence

$\mathcal{A}$ is an attacker against $\mathcal{SC}$, dp is the domain parameter.

1) The challenger computes $(sk_S, pk_S) \leftarrow_R \mathsf{Gen}_S(dp); (sk_R, pk_R) \leftarrow_R \mathsf{Gen}_R(dp);$

2) $\mathcal{A}$ runs with inputs pk_S and pk_R, and is given access to the oracles $\mathcal{O}_{\mathsf{Sc}}(\cdot,\cdot), \mathcal{O}_{\mathsf{Usc}}(\cdot,\cdot)$, and $\mathcal{O}_{\mathsf{N}}(\cdot,\cdot)$ as in step 5 of Game 2. It outputs $(C^*, m^*, nr^*) \leftarrow_R \mathcal{A}^{\mathcal{O}_{\mathsf{Sc}}(\cdot,\cdot), \mathcal{O}_{\mathsf{Usc}}(\cdot,\cdot), \mathcal{O}_{\mathsf{N}}(\cdot,\cdot)}(pk_S, pk_R)$.

3) $\mathcal{A}$ wins the game if: (a) C^* was generated through $\mathcal{O}_{\mathsf{Sc}}(\cdot,\cdot)$ and (b) $1 = d \leftarrow \mathsf{PV}(C^*, m^*, nr^*, pk_S, pk_R)$, and nr^* was not generated by the oracle $\mathcal{O}_{\mathsf{N}}(\cdot,\cdot)$ on a query on (pk_S, C^*).

We denote by $\mathsf{Adv}^{\mathsf{unr}}_{\mathcal{A},\mathcal{SC}}(1^k)$ the probability that $\mathcal{A}$ wins the game.

Definition 12. *A SCNINR is said to achieve* $(t, q_{Sc}, q_{Usc}, q_N, \varepsilon)$ *unforgeability of non-repudiation evidence if for all adversary $\mathcal{A}$ playing Game 5, if $\mathcal{A}$ runs in time t and issues respectively q_{Sc}, q_{Usc}, and q_N queries to the signcryption, unsigncryption, and non-repudiation evidence generation oracles then $\mathsf{Adv}_{\mathcal{A},\mathcal{SC}}^{unr}(1^k) \leqslant \varepsilon$.*

3   New Identification and Signature Schemes

A domain parameter is given by $dp = (N, G, R, e, k)$ *wherein*

- $N = pq$ is an RSA modulus, $p = 2p' + 1$ and $q = 2q' + 1$ being safe primes.
- e is a $(k+1)$ bit prime. To improve the scheme's efficiency, it can be chosen to be a sparse prime. It is used as an RSA public exponent.
- R is a generator of $\mathbb{J}_N^+$, and $G = R^{\underline{e}}$.
- k is a security parameter, $n(k) = |N|$ is chosen such that the best known algorithm for factoring N runs in time $\approx 2^k$.

For *domain parameter generation*, if there is a party which is trusted by all the users, he can generate the domain parameter. Alternatively, an perhaps *preferably*, the domain parameter may be generated by a set of parties such that each user of the scheme trusts at least one of them. In this case, the parties generating the domain parameter may perform as follows:

(1) They run the distributed shared RSA modulus generation following the protocol given in [1], to get product of two safe primes N, while each party has a share of the primes.
(2) They choose a $(k+1)$ bit prime e and $R \leftarrow_R \mathbb{J}_N^+$, and compute $G = R^{\underline{e}}$ (R is a generator of $\mathbb{J}_N^+$, with all but negligible probability).
(3) The domain parameter is $dp = (N, G, R, e, k)$.

Description of the Scheme. Let $dp = (N, G, R, e, k)$ be a domain parameter, and $l = \lceil N/4 \rceil$. We derive the scheme $\mathcal{I}_{SSN} = (\mathsf{Gen}, \mathsf{P}, \mathsf{V}, \mathsf{ChSet})$ wherein Gen, $\mathsf{P} = (\mathsf{P}_1, \mathsf{P}_2)$, and V are as described hereunder; we denote $[2^k - 1]$ by ChSet.

> $\underline{\mathsf{Gen}(dp)}$: $a \leftarrow_R [l]$; $(sk, pk) \leftarrow (R^{\underline{a}}, G^{\underline{a}})$; Return (sk, pk).
> $\underline{\mathsf{P}_1(sk)}$: $x \leftarrow_R [l]$; $(X, st) \leftarrow (G^{\underline{x}}, R^{\underline{x}})$; Return (X, st).
> $\underline{\mathsf{P}_2(sk, X, c, st)}$: $Y \leftarrow st$; $s \leftarrow Y \circ sk^{\underline{c}}$; Return s.
> $\underline{\mathsf{V}(pk, X, c, s)}$: If $s^{\underline{e}} = X \circ pk^{\underline{c}}$ then Return 1, Else return 0.

For all $(sk, pk) \in \{\mathsf{Gen}(dp)\}$, if (X, c, s) is a transcript generated through P then $1 = \mathsf{V}(pk, X, c, s)$, as $s^{\underline{e}} = (R^{\underline{x+ca}})^{\underline{e}} = (R^{\underline{e}})^{\underline{x+ca}} = G^{\underline{x+ca}} = G^{\underline{x}} \circ (G^{\underline{a}})^{\underline{c}} = X \circ pk^{\underline{c}}$.

Uniqueness and Min Entropy. As the function $\mathsf{Exp}_e : \mathbb{J}_N^+ \to \mathbb{J}_N^+$ which maps Y to $Y^{\underline{e}}$ is bijective, for all $X, pk \in \mathbb{J}_N^+$, all $c \in \mathsf{ChSet}$, there is one and only one $s \in \mathbb{J}_N^+$ such that $s^{\underline{e}} = X \circ pk^{\underline{c}}$. Let δ_0 denote $\max(1/p', 1/q')$. If $x_1 \leftarrow_R [|\mathbb{J}_N^+|]$ and $x_2 \leftarrow_R [l]$ the statistical distance between x_1 and x_2 is $\Delta(x_1, x_2) \leqslant \frac{N/4 - \phi(N)/4}{N/4} \leqslant \delta_0$. So, if $X_1 \leftarrow G^{\underline{x_1}}$ and $X_2 \leftarrow G^{\underline{x_2}}$, then $\Delta(X_1, X_2) \leqslant \delta_0$. Then, if X is generated through $\mathsf{P}_1(\cdot)$, the statistical distance between the distribution of X and the uniform distribution over $\mathbb{J}_N^+$ is not greater than δ_0. And then for all $X_0 \in \mathbb{J}_N^+$, if X is generated through $\mathsf{P}_1(\cdot)$, $|\Pr(X = X_0) - 1/\|\mathbb{J}_N^+\|| \leqslant \delta_0$; the identification scheme has $\alpha \approx -\log_2(\delta_0)$ bits of min-entropy.

Special Soundness. If (X, c, s) and (X, c', s') are two accepting transcripts with respect to a public key pk such that $c \neq c'$ then $s \circ s'^{\underline{-1}} = sk^{\underline{c-c'}}$, and then $\left(s \circ s'^{\underline{-1}}\right)^e = pk^{\underline{c-c'}}$. Now, as $c, c' \in \mathsf{ChSet} = [2^k - 1]$, and $e > 2^k$ is prime, it follows that $\gcd(e, c - c') = 1$. Let $\alpha, \beta \in \mathbb{Z}$ be such that $e\alpha + (c - c')\beta = 1$ and $sk^* = pk^{\underline{\alpha}} \circ \left(s \circ s'^{\underline{-1}}\right)^{\underline{\beta}}$, then $(sk^*)^{\underline{e}} = \left(pk^{\underline{\alpha}} \circ \left(s \circ s'^{\underline{-1}}\right)^{\underline{\beta}}\right)^e = pk^{\underline{e\alpha}} \circ \left(s \circ s'^{\underline{-1}}\right)^{\underline{e\beta}} = pk^{\underline{e\alpha + (c - c')\beta}} = pk$.

Honest Verifier Zero Knowledge. For all public key $pk \in \mathbb{J}_N^+$, the following simulator yields transcripts with the same distribution as real transcripts.

> $\underline{\mathsf{sim}(pk)}$: $c \leftarrow_{\mathrm{R}} \mathsf{ChSet}$; $z \leftarrow_{\mathrm{R}} [l]$; $s \leftarrow R^{\underline{z}}$; $X \leftarrow s^{\underline{e}} \circ pk^{\underline{-c}}$; Return (X, c, s).

Random Self Reducibility. The Rerand, Tran and Derand algorithms are:

> $\underline{\mathsf{Rerand}(pk)}$: $z \leftarrow_{\mathrm{R}} [l]$; $\tau \leftarrow R^{\underline{z}}$; $pk_1 \leftarrow \tau^{\underline{e}} \circ pk$; Return (τ, pk_1).
> $\underline{\mathsf{Derand}(pk, pk_1, sk_1, \tau)}$: $sk^* \leftarrow sk_1 \circ \tau^{\underline{-1}}$; Return sk^*;
> $\underline{\mathsf{Tran}(pk, pk_1, \tau, (X, c, s_1))}$: $Z \leftarrow \tau^{\underline{-c}}$; $s \leftarrow Z \circ s_1$; Return (X, c, s).

The Rerand algorithm outputs a public key pk_1 which has the same distribution as the keys generated through $\mathsf{Gen}(dp)$. The Derand algorithm provides the static private key corresponding to pk. The Tran algorithm produces a valid transcript with respect to the public key pk.

KR-KOA Security. For $sk, pk \in \mathbb{J}_N^+$, if $sk^{\underline{e}} = pk$ then $(\pm sk)^e = pk$. Then under the RSA assumption over $\mathbb{J}_N^+$, $\mathcal{I}_{SSN}$ is secure against KR-KOA.

Lemma 2. *If the RSA problem is (t, ε)-hard over $\mathbb{J}_N^+$ then the identification scheme $\mathcal{I}_{SSN}$ is (t, ε)-KR-KOA-secure.*

The Signature Scheme. As the identification scheme is commitment recoverable, using the (alternative) Fiat–Shamir transform [12], we derive the signature scheme $\mathcal{S}_{SSN} = (\mathsf{Gen}, \mathsf{Sign}, \mathsf{Vrfy})$ we describe hereunder. $\mathsf{H}_1 : \{0, 1\}^* \to \mathsf{ChSet}$ is a hash function.

> $\underline{\mathsf{Gen}(dp)}$: $a \leftarrow_{\mathrm{R}} [l]$; $(sk, pk) \leftarrow (R^{\underline{a}}, G^{\underline{a}})$; Return (sk, pk).
> $\underline{\mathsf{Sign}(sk, m)}$: $x \leftarrow_{\mathrm{R}} [l]$; $X \leftarrow G^{\underline{x}}$; $h \leftarrow \mathsf{H}_1(X, m)$ $s \leftarrow R^{\underline{x}} \circ sk^{\underline{h}}$; Return (h, s).
> $\underline{\mathsf{Vrfy}(pk, m, \sigma)}$: Parse σ as $(h, s) \in \mathsf{ChSet} \times \mathbb{Z}_N$; $X \leftarrow s^{\underline{e}} \circ pk^{\underline{-h}}$; $h' = \mathsf{H}_1(X, m)$. If $pk, s \in \mathbb{J}_N^+$ and $h = h'$ then Return 1; Else Return 0.

Security and Efficiency of the Signature Scheme. We have the following theorem; its proof follows straightly from the SpS, HVZN, RSR, min-entropy, and KR-KOA security attributes of the identification scheme and Theorem 3.1 from [15].

Theorem 1. *If the RSA problem is (t, ε) hard on (N, e), then the scheme $\mathcal{S}_{SSN}$ is $(t', \varepsilon', U, Q_s, Q_h)$-MU-SUF-CMA secure in the random oracle model, where $\varepsilon'/t' \leqslant 24(Q_h + 1) \cdot \varepsilon/t + Q_s/2^\alpha + 1/2^k$.*

Although efficient, the signature scheme is slightly less efficient than the GQ scheme [13]. A key pair generation requires $\mathsf{Exp}(\mathbb{Z}_N, 2, l)$ operations for our scheme while it requires $\mathsf{Exp}(\mathbb{Z}_N, k)$ operations for the GQ scheme. We stress that, using simultaneous exponentiation techniques [18, Sect. 14.6], $\mathsf{Exp}(\mathbb{Z}_N, 2, l) \approx 1.17 \cdot \mathsf{Exp}(\mathbb{Z}_N, l)$. A $\mathcal{S}_{SSN}$ signature generation can be performed in $1.17 \cdot \mathsf{Exp}(\mathbb{Z}_N, l) + \mathsf{Exp}(\mathbb{Z}_N, k)$ operations, while it requires $2 \cdot \mathsf{Exp}(\mathbb{Z}_N, k)$ operations for the GQ scheme. In both schemes, only $\mathsf{Exp}(\mathbb{Z}_N, k)$ operations need to be performed online, all the other operations can be performed offline. A signature verification requires $2 \cdot \mathsf{Jcb}(N) + \mathsf{Exp}(\mathbb{Z}_N, 2, k)$ operations for $\mathcal{S}_{SSN}$ and $\mathsf{Exp}(\mathbb{Z}_N, 2, k)$ operations for the GQ scheme.

4   The Signcryption Scheme

From the $\mathcal{S}_{SSN}$ scheme, which has the advantage of being defined over a group wherein the strong DH assumption is known to hold under the factoring assumption [14], we derive $\mathcal{SC}_{SSN} = (\mathsf{Setup}, \mathsf{Gen}_S, \mathsf{Gen}_R, \mathsf{Sc}, \mathsf{Usc}, \mathsf{N}, \mathsf{PV})$. The Setup algorithm generates a domain parameter dp' as in Sect. 3, together with an encryption scheme $\mathcal{E}$ and two hash functions $\mathsf{H}_1 : \{0,1\}^* \to \mathsf{ChSet}$ and $\mathsf{H}_2 : \{0,1\}^* \to \mathbf{K}$. We consider $dp = (dp', \mathsf{H}_1, \mathsf{H}_2, \mathcal{E})$ as an implicit parameter.

$\underline{\mathsf{Gen}_S(dp)}$: $a \leftarrow_{\mathrm{R}} [l]$; $(sk_S, pk_S) \leftarrow (R^{\underline{a}}, G^{\underline{a}})$; Return (sk_S, pk_S);

$\underline{\mathsf{Gen}_R(dp)}$: $b \leftarrow_{\mathrm{R}} [l]$; $(sk_R, pk_R) \leftarrow (b, G^{\underline{b}})$; Return (sk_R, pk_R);

$\underline{\mathsf{Sc}(sk_S, pk_R, m)}$: $x_1, x_2 \leftarrow_{\mathrm{R}} [l]$; $X_1 \leftarrow G^{\underline{x_1}}$; $Z_1 \leftarrow pk_R^{\underline{x_1}}$; $X_2 \leftarrow G^{\underline{x_2}}$; $Z_2 \leftarrow pk_R^{\underline{x_2}}$;
   $\tau_1 \leftarrow \mathsf{H}_2(X_1, X_2, Z_1, Z_2, pk_S, pk_R)$; $\tau_2 \leftarrow \mathsf{H}_2(X_2, X_1, Z_2, Z_1, pk_S, pk_R)$;
   $h \leftarrow \mathsf{H}_1(X_1, X_2, m, \tau_1)$; $c \leftarrow \mathsf{E}(\tau_2, m)$; $s \leftarrow R^{\underline{x_1}} \circ sk_S^{\underline{h}}$; Return (h, X_2, s, c);

$\underline{\mathsf{Usc}(sk_R, pk_S, C)}$: Parse C as (h, X_2, s, c). If $X_2, pk_S \notin \mathbb{J}_N^+$ then Return $\bot$;
   $X_1 \leftarrow s^{\underline{e}} \circ pk_S^{\underline{-h}}$; $Z_1 \leftarrow X_1^{\underline{sk_R}}$; $Z_2 \leftarrow X_2^{\underline{sk_R}}$; $\tau_1 \leftarrow \mathsf{H}_2(X_1, X_2, Z_1, Z_2, pk_S, pk_R)$; $\tau_2 \leftarrow \mathsf{H}_2(X_2, X_1, Z_2, Z_1, pk_S, pk_R)$; $m \leftarrow \mathsf{D}(\tau_2, c)$;
   If $h = h' \leftarrow \mathsf{H}_1(X_1, X_2, m, \tau_1)$ then Return m; Else return $\bot$;

$\underline{\mathsf{N}(sk_R, pk_S, C)}$: Parse C as (h, X_2, s, c). If $X_2, pk_S \notin \mathbb{J}_N^+$ then Return $\bot$;
   $X_1 \qquad\qquad \leftarrow \qquad\quad s^{\underline{e}} \quad \circ \quad pk_S^{\underline{-h}}; \qquad Z_1 \qquad\qquad \leftarrow \qquad\quad X_1^{\underline{sk_R}};$
   $Z_2 \leftarrow X_2^{\underline{sk_R}}$; $\tau_1 \leftarrow \mathsf{H}_2(X_1, X_2, Z_1, Z_2, pk_S, pk_R)$; $\tau_2 \leftarrow \mathsf{H}_2(X_2, X_1, Z_2, Z_1, pk_S, pk_R)$; $m \leftarrow \mathsf{D}(\tau_2, c)$;
   If $h = h' \leftarrow \mathsf{H}_1(X_1, X_2, m, \tau_1)$ then Return (τ_1, τ_2); Else return $\bot$;

$\underline{\mathsf{PV}(C, m, nr, pk_S, pk_R)}$: Parse C as (h, X_2, s, c) and nr as (τ_1, τ_2); $m' \leftarrow \mathsf{D}(\tau_2, c)$;
   If $m' \neq m$ then Return 0; $X_1 \leftarrow s^{\underline{e}} \circ pk_S^{\underline{-h}}$;
   If $h = h' \leftarrow_{\mathrm{R}} \mathsf{H}_1(X_1, X_2, m, \tau_1)$ then Return 1; Else return 0;

For the consistency of the scheme, one can observe that for all $dp \in \{\mathsf{Setup}(1^k)\}$, all $m \in \mathcal{M}$, all $(sk_S, pk_S) \in \{\mathsf{Gen}_S(dp)\}$, and all $(sk_R, pk_R) \in \{\mathsf{Gen}_R(dp)\}$, $m = \mathsf{Usc}(sk_R, pk_S, \mathsf{Sc}(sk_S, pk_R, m))$. Moreover, if $nr \leftarrow \mathsf{N}(sk_R, pk_S, \mathsf{Sc}(sk_S, pk_R, m))$ then $1 = d \leftarrow \mathsf{PV}(C, m, nr, pk_S, pk_R)$.

Efficiency of the Scheme. Since Malone–Lee's scheme [17] is defined over any Diffie–Hellman group, and Fan et al.'s [11] design makes use of bilinear pairings, it is rather difficult to compare the efficiency of these schemes with our (we use an RSA instance), without considering concrete instances. Nonetheless, our design is a practical and efficient one; it uses the RSA primitive, which remains probably the most widely deployed public key primitive [16]. A sender key pair generation requires $\mathsf{Exp}(\mathbb{Z}_n, 2, l)$ operations (the exponentiations use the same exponent); a receiver key pair generation requires $\mathsf{Exp}(\mathbb{Z}_n, l)$ operations. A signcryption generation requires $\mathsf{Exp}(\mathbb{Z}_n, 6, l)$ operations (we neglect the cost of the three digest operations together with the symmetric encryption). Five of the six exponentiations can be performed off-line. Moreover, three of the five off-line exponentiations share the same exponent, and the remaining two exponentiations have also the same exponent. An unsigncryption or a non-repudiation evidence generation requires four exponentiations; we recall that e can be chosen to be a sparse prime so that exponentiations involving e can be performed using few multiplications. A public verification requires $\mathsf{Exp}(\mathbb{Z}_n, 2, l)$ operations. Assuming that $|c| = |m|$, the communication overhead compared to a signature is one group element.

4.1   Confidentiality of the $\mathcal{SC}_{SSN}$ Signcryption Scheme

We need the following result, its proof is given in the full version of this paper.

Theorem 2. *If X_1, r, s be mutually independent random variables, such r and s are uniformly distributed over $[N/4]$. Let X_2 be defined by $X_2 \leftarrow G^{\underline{s}} \circ X_1^{\frac{-r}{1}}$, and suppose that Y, Z_1, and Z_2 are random variables taking values in $\mathbb{J}_N^+$, and are defined as some functions of X_1 and X_2, then: (a) the statistical distance between X_2 and the uniform distribution over $\mathbb{J}_N^+$ is not greater than $2\delta_0$;(b) If $X_1 = G^{\underline{x_1}}$ and $X_2 = G^{\underline{x_2}}$, then the probability that the truth value of*

$$Z_1^r Z_2 = G^{\underline{s}} \tag{1}$$

does not agree with

$$Z_1 = Y^{\underline{x_1}} \text{ and } Z_2 = Y^{\underline{x_2}} \tag{2}$$

is at most $5\delta_0$; and if (2) holds then so does (1).

Theorem 3. *Under the RO model, if the factorization of N is $(t(k), \varepsilon_{\mathsf{fac}}(k))$-hard and the encryption scheme $\mathcal{E}$ is $(t(k), \varepsilon_{\mathsf{ss}}(k))$-semantically secure, then $\mathcal{SC}_{SSN}$ is $(t(k), q_{\mathsf{Sc}}, q_{\mathsf{Usc}}, q_{\mathsf{N}}, \varepsilon'(k))$-secure in the SKI-MU insider confidentiality in the FSO/FUO-IND-CCA2 sense, wherein*

$$\varepsilon'(k) = \varepsilon_{\mathsf{ss}}(k) + \varepsilon_{\mathsf{fac}}(k) + (1 + 1/2 \cdot q_{\mathsf{Sc}}(q_{\mathsf{Sc}} - 1)) (p'q')^{-2}|\mathbf{K}|^{-1} + (5q_{\mathsf{Sc}} + 2)\delta_0.$$

Proof. We call the steps (1) and (2), (3) and (4), and (5) and (6) of Game 2 the pre-challenge, challenge, and post-challenge phases respectively. We provide a simulator which answers to $\mathcal{A}$'s queries in all phases. The Initialization procedure is executed at the beginning of the game. When the variable abort is set to 1, the whole simulation fails. If the simulation does not fail, the Finalization procedure is executed at the end of the game. The oracle $\mathrm{DDH}_{Y_0}(\cdot, \cdot)$ takes $U, V \in \mathbb{J}_N^+$ as inputs and outputs 1 if $\mathrm{CDH}(Y_0, U) = V$ and 0 otherwise. For a list L and an element X, $\mathsf{Apd}(L, X)$ adds X to L.

Simulation for the SKI MU insider confidentiality game
Input: $dp = (N, G, R, e, k)$, $\mathcal{E} = (\mathsf{E}, \mathsf{D}, \mathbf{K}, \mathbf{M}, \mathbf{C})$, and $X_0, Y_0 \leftarrow_{\mathrm{R}} \mathbb{J}_N^+$.
External Oracles: $\mathrm{DDH}_{Y_0}(\cdot, \cdot)$;
1 <u>Initialization:</u> $pk_R \leftarrow Y_0$; $\mathcal{S}_{\mathsf{H}_1} \leftarrow ()$; $\mathcal{S}_{\mathsf{k}} \leftarrow ()$; $\mathcal{S}_{\mathsf{k\&r}} \leftarrow ()$; $\mathcal{S}_{\mathsf{H}_2} \leftarrow ()$; abort $\leftarrow 0$;

PRE–CHALLENGE PHASE

2 $\mathcal{O}_{\mathsf{H}_1}(s)$:
3 **if** $\exists h : (s, h) \in \mathcal{S}_{\mathsf{H}_1}$ **then** return h; **else** $h \leftarrow_{\mathrm{R}} \mathsf{ChSet}$; $\mathsf{Apd}(\mathcal{S}_{\mathsf{H}_1}, (s, h))$; return h;
4 $\mathcal{O}_{\mathsf{H}_2}(s)$:
5 **if** $\exists \tau : (s, \tau) \in \mathcal{S}_{\mathsf{H}_2}$ **then** return τ;
6 **else if** s has format $(X_1, X_2, Z_1, Z_2, pk, pk' = pk_R) \in \left(\mathbb{J}_N^+\right)^6$ **then**
7   **if** $\exists \tau : ((X_1, X_2, pk, pk_R), \tau) \in \mathcal{S}_{\mathsf{k}}$ **then**
8   **if** $\mathrm{DDH}_{Y_0}(X_1, Z_1) = \mathrm{DDH}_{Y_0}(X_2, Z_2) = 1$ **then** $\mathsf{Apd}(\mathcal{S}_{\mathsf{H}_2}, (s, \tau))$; return τ;
9 **else** $\tau \leftarrow_{\mathrm{R}} \mathsf{ChSet}$; $\mathsf{Apd}(s_{\mathsf{H}_2}, (s, \tau))$; return τ;

10 $\mathcal{O}_{\mathsf{Usc}}(pk, C)$: $\mathcal{O}_{\mathsf{N}}(pk, C)$:
11 **if** $pk \notin \mathbb{J}_N^+$ **then** return $\bot$;
12 Parse C as $(h, X_2, s, c) \in \mathsf{ChSet} \times \mathbb{J}_N^+ \times \mathbb{J}_N^+ \times \mathbf{C}$;   ▶ $\bot$ *is returned if the parsing fails*
13 $X_1 \leftarrow s^{\underline{e}} \circ pk^{\underline{-h}}$;
14 **if** $\exists Z_1, Z_2 \in \mathbb{J}_N^+, \tau \in \mathbf{K} : ((X_1, X_2, Z_1, Z_2, pk, pk_R), \tau) \in \mathcal{S}_{\mathsf{H}_2}$ and $\mathrm{DDH}_{Y_0}(X_1, Z_1) = \mathrm{DDH}_{Y_0}(X_2, Z_2) = 1$ **then**
      $\tau_1 \leftarrow \tau$;   ▶ $\mathsf{H}_2(X_1, X_2, Z_1, Z_2, pk, pk_R)$ *was issued*
15 **else if** $\exists \tau : ((X_1, X_2, pk, pk_R), \tau) \in \mathcal{S}_{\mathsf{k}}$ **then**
16     $\tau_1 \leftarrow \tau$;   ▶ $\mathsf{Usc}(pk, C')$ *or* $\mathsf{N}(pk, C')$ *such that* C' *parses as* (h, X_2, s, c') *was issued*
17 **else** $\tau_1 \leftarrow_{\mathrm{R}} \mathbf{K}$; $\mathsf{Apd}(\mathcal{S}_{\mathsf{k}}, ((X_1, X_2, pk, pk_R), \tau_1))$;
18 **if** $\exists Z_2, Z_1 \in \mathbb{J}_N^+, \tau \in \mathbf{K} : ((X_2, X_1, Z_2, Z_1, pk, pk_R), \tau) \in \mathcal{S}_{\mathsf{H}_2}$ and $\mathrm{DDH}_{Y_0}(X_1, Z_1) = \mathrm{DDH}_{Y_0}(X_2, Z_2) = 1$ **then** $\tau_2 \leftarrow \tau$;   ▶ *the same treatment as for* τ_1
19 **else if** $\exists \tau : ((X_2, X_1, pk, pk_R), \tau) \in \mathcal{S}_{\mathsf{k}}$ **then** $\tau_2 \leftarrow \tau$;
20 **else** $\tau_2 \leftarrow_{\mathrm{R}} \mathbf{K}$; $\mathsf{Apd}(\mathcal{S}_{\mathsf{k}}, ((X_2, X_1, pk, pk_R), \tau_2))$;
21 $m \leftarrow \mathsf{D}(\tau_2, c)$; $h' \leftarrow \mathcal{O}_{\mathsf{H}_1}(X_1, X_2, m, \tau_1)$;

22 **if** $h = h'$ **then** $\boxed{\substack{\mathcal{O}_{\mathsf{Usc}} \\ \text{return } m}}$ $\boxed{\substack{\mathcal{O}_{\mathsf{N}} \\ \text{return } (\tau_1, \tau_2)}}$ **else** return $\bot$;

CHALLENGE PHASE

23 $(m_0, m_1, st, pk_S) \leftarrow_{\mathrm{R}} \mathcal{A}_1^{\mathcal{O}_{\mathsf{Usc}}(\cdot, \cdot), \mathcal{O}_{\mathsf{N}}(\cdot, \cdot), \mathcal{O}_{\mathsf{H}_1}(\cdot), \mathcal{O}_{\mathsf{H}_2}(\cdot)}(pk_R)$;
24 $\hat{h} \leftarrow_{\mathrm{R}} \mathsf{ChSet}$; $\hat{z} \leftarrow_{\mathrm{R}} [l]$; $\hat{s} \leftarrow R^{\hat{z}}$; $\hat{X}_1 \leftarrow \hat{s}^{\underline{e}} \circ pk_S^{\underline{-\hat{h}}}$; $\hat{X}_2 \leftarrow X_0$;
25 $b \leftarrow_{\mathrm{R}} \{0, 1\}$; $\hat{\tau}_1 \leftarrow_{\mathrm{R}} \mathbf{K}$; $\hat{\tau}_2 \leftarrow_{\mathrm{R}} \mathbf{K}$; $\hat{c} \leftarrow \mathsf{E}(\hat{\tau}_2, m_b)$;
26 **if** $\exists h', m' : ((\hat{X}_1, \hat{X}_2, m', \hat{\tau}_1), h') \in \mathcal{S}_{\mathsf{H}_1}$ **then** abort $\leftarrow 1$;

27 $\mathsf{Apd}(\mathcal{S}_{\mathsf{H}_1}, ((\hat{X}_1, \hat{X}_2, m_b, \hat{\tau}_1), \hat{h}));\ \mathsf{Apd}(\mathcal{S}_{\mathsf{k}}, ((\hat{X}_1, \hat{X}_2, pk_S, pk_R), \hat{\tau}_1));$

28 $\mathsf{Apd}(\mathcal{S}_{\mathsf{k}}, ((\hat{X}_2, \hat{X}_1, pk_S, pk_R), \hat{\tau}_2));\ C^* \leftarrow (\hat{h}, \hat{X}_2, \hat{s}, \hat{c});$

POST–CHALLENGE PHASE

$\mathcal{A}_2$ is run with input (C^*, st). It has access to the oracles $\mathcal{O}_{\mathsf{Sc}}(\cdot, \cdot), \mathcal{O}_{\mathsf{Usc}}(\cdot, \cdot), \mathcal{O}_{\mathsf{N}}(\cdot, \cdot),$ $\mathcal{O}_{\mathsf{H}_1}(\cdot),$ and $\mathcal{O}_{\mathsf{H}_2}(\cdot)$. Only changes compared to the pre–challenge phase are drawn.

29 $\mathcal{O}_{\mathsf{Sc}}(pk, m)$:

30 $h \leftarrow_{\mathsf{R}} \mathsf{ChSet};\ z \leftarrow_{\mathsf{R}} [l];\ s_1 \leftarrow R^{\underline{z}};\ X_1 \leftarrow s_1^{\underline{e}} \circ pk_S^{\underline{-h}};$

31 $r \leftarrow_{\mathsf{R}} [l];\ s_2 \leftarrow_{\mathsf{R}} [l];\ X_2 \leftarrow G^{\underline{s_2}} \circ X_1^{\underline{-r}};\ \tau_1 \leftarrow_{\mathsf{R}} \mathbf{K};\ \tau_2 \leftarrow_{\mathsf{R}} \mathbf{K};$

32 if $\exists h', m' : ((X_1, X_2, m', \tau_1), h') \in \mathcal{S}_{\mathsf{H}_1}$ then abort $\leftarrow 1;$

33 $\mathsf{Apd}\,(\mathcal{S}_{\mathsf{H}_1}, ((X_1, X_2, m, \tau_1), h));$

34 if $\quad pk \quad = \quad pk_R \quad$ then $\quad \mathsf{Apd}(\mathcal{S}_{\mathsf{k}}, ((X_1, X_2, pk_S, pk_R), \tau_1));$ $\mathsf{Apd}(\mathcal{S}_{\mathsf{k}}, ((X_2, X_1, pk_S, pk_R), \tau_2));$

35 else $\mathsf{Apd}\,(\mathcal{S}_{\mathsf{k\&r}}, ((X_1, X_2, pk_S, pk), (r, s_2, \tau_1, \tau_2)));$

36 $c \leftarrow \mathsf{E}(\tau_2, m);\ C \leftarrow (h, X_2, s_1, c);$ return $C;$

37 $\mathcal{O}_{\mathsf{H}_2}(s)$:

38 if $\exists\, \tau : (s, \tau) \in \mathcal{S}_{\mathsf{H}_2}$ then return $\tau;$

39 else if s has format $(X_1, X_2, Z_1, Z_2, pk, pk_R) \in \left(\mathbb{J}_N^+\right)^6$ then

40   if $\exists \tau : ((X_1, X_2, pk, pk_R), \tau) \in \mathcal{S}_{\mathsf{k}}$ then

41   if $\mathrm{DDH}_{Y_0}(X_1, Z_1) = \mathrm{DDH}_{Y_0}(X_2, Z_2) = 1$ then $\mathsf{Apd}(\mathcal{S}_{\mathsf{H}_2}, (s, k));$ return $\tau;$

42 else if s has format $(X_1, X_2, Z_1, Z_2, pk_S, pk) \in \left(\mathbb{J}_N^+\right)^6$ then

43   if $\exists r, s, \tau_1, \tau_2 : ((X_1, X_2, pk_S, pk), (r, s, \tau_1, \tau_2)) \in \mathcal{S}_{\mathsf{k\&r}}$ then

44   if $Z_1^r \circ Z_2 = pk^{\underline{s}}$ then return $\tau_1;$ ▶ $2DH(X_1, X_2, pk) = (Z_1, Z_2)$ with all but negligible probability.

45   if $\exists r, s, \tau_1, \tau_2 : ((X_2, X_1, pk_S, pk), (r, s, \tau_1, \tau_2)) \in \mathcal{S}_{\mathsf{k\&r}}$ then

46   if $Z_2^r \circ Z_1 = pk^{\underline{s}}$ then return $\tau_2;$

47 else $\tau \leftarrow_{\mathsf{R}} \mathsf{ChSet};\ \mathsf{Apd}(s_{\mathsf{H}_2}, (s, \tau));$ return $\tau;$

48 Finalization:

49 if $\exists \hat{Z}_1, \hat{Z}_2 \in \mathbb{J}_N^+ : (((\hat{X}_1, \hat{X}_2, \hat{Z}_1, \hat{Z}_2, pk_S, pk_R), \hat{\tau}_1) \in \mathcal{S}_{\mathsf{H}_2}$ or $((\hat{X}_2, \hat{X}_1, \hat{Z}_2, \hat{Z}_1, pk_S, pk_R), \hat{\tau}_2) \in \mathcal{S}_{\mathsf{H}_2})$ and $\mathrm{DDH}_{Y_0}(\hat{X}_1, \hat{Z}_1) = \mathrm{DDH}_{Y_0}(\hat{X}_2, \hat{Z}_2) = 1$ then return $\hat{Z}_2;$

50 else return $\perp;$

In the pre-challenge phase, the simulator answers to $\mathcal{O}_{\mathsf{H}_1}(\cdot), \mathcal{O}_{\mathsf{H}_2}(\cdot), \mathcal{O}_{\mathsf{Usc}}(\cdot, \cdot),$ and $\mathcal{O}_{\mathsf{N}}(\cdot, \cdot)$ queries. The lines 10–22 describe both $\mathcal{O}_{\mathsf{Usc}}(\cdot, \cdot)$ and $\mathcal{O}_{\mathsf{N}}(\cdot, \cdot)$. When executing $\mathcal{O}_{\mathsf{Usc}}(\cdot, \cdot)$ (resp. $\mathcal{O}_{\mathsf{N}}(\cdot, \cdot)$), the instruction return (τ_1, τ_2) (resp. return m) at line 22 is omitted. Digest queries are answered using input-output tables. The $\mathcal{O}_{\mathsf{H}_2}(\cdot)$ digest values of strings with format $(X_1, X_2, Z_1, Z_2, pk, pk_R)$ are not only assigned by the $\mathcal{O}_{\mathsf{H}_2}(\cdot)$ oracle, but also through executions of $\mathcal{O}_{\mathsf{Usc}}(\cdot, \cdot)$ and $\mathcal{O}_{\mathsf{N}}(\cdot, \cdot)$; in the latter two cases $Z_1 = \mathrm{CDH}(X_1, pk_R)$ and $Z_2 = \mathrm{CDH}(X_2, pk_R)$ are unknown. So, for consistency, in addition to $\mathcal{S}_{\mathsf{H}_2}$, we use a list $\mathcal{S}_{\mathsf{k}}$ to store the values of $\mathcal{O}_{\mathsf{H}_2}(X_1, X_2, Z_1, Z_2, pk, pk_R)$ which was assigned while Z_1 and Z_2 are unknown (see at lines 14–20). Doing so, the simulator consistently answers to all digest queries with the help of the $\mathrm{DDH}_{Y_0 = pk_R}(\cdot, \cdot)$ oracle (see at lines 6–8).

In the challenge phase, we essentially simulate a signature generation (at line 24), then X_2 is set to X_0 (the simulator takes X_0 and $Y_0 = pk_R$ as input). The secret keys, τ_1 and τ_2 are chosen uniformly at random from $\mathbf{K}$, and savings are performed for $\mathcal{O}_{H_2}(\cdot)$ digests consistency (lines 27–28). In the post-challenge phase, the changes, compared to the pre-challenge phase, are the (re)definitions of the $\mathcal{O}_{Sc}(\cdot,\cdot)$ and $\mathcal{O}_{H_2}(\cdot)$ oracles. When computing $\mathcal{O}_{Sc}(pk, m)$, the simulator ignores both sk_S and the secret key corresponding to pk. For consistency, we simulate a signature generations (see at line 30), choose r and s_2, and generate X_2 (see at line 31) such that: (i) the statistical distance between the distribution of the X_2 we generate in this way and the distribution of X_2 we obtain through a real execution of $Sc(\cdot,\cdot,\cdot)$ is not greater than $2\delta_0 = 2\max(1/p', 1/q')$; (ii) if Z_1 and Z_2 are such that $Z_1^r Z_2 = G^{\underline{s}}$, then $Z_1 = \mathrm{CDH}(X_1, pk)$ and $Z_2 = \mathrm{CDH}(X_2, pk)$ with overwhelming probability (see Theorem 2). Doing so, we have a way to assign values to τ_1 and τ_2, while keeping the outputs of $\mathcal{O}_{H_2}(\cdot)$ consistent (see at lines 31–35 and 43–46). Let bad be the event: "(a) the simulator aborts (see at lines 26 and 32) or (b) in some execution of $\mathcal{O}_{H_2}(\cdot)$, Z_1 and Z_2 are such that $Z_1^r \circ Z_2 = pk^{\underline{s}}$ while $\mathrm{CDH}(X_1, pk) \neq Z_1$ or $\mathrm{CDH}(X_2, pk) \neq Z_2$ (see at lines 43–46)." Then, from Theorem 2

$$\Pr(\mathsf{bad}) \leqslant (p'q')^{-2}|\mathbf{K}|^{-1} + q_{Sc}(q_{Sc} - 1)\left(2(p'q')^2|\mathbf{K}|\right)^{-1} + 5q_{Sc}\delta_0. \qquad (3)$$

Let $\mathsf{Succ}_{\mathcal{A},sim}^{cca2}$ denote the event "$\mathcal{A}$ succeeds in the simulated environment". Under the RO model, if $\neg\mathsf{bad}$ then, $\mathcal{A}$'s views in the real and simulated environments are the same; so, $\Pr(\mathsf{Succ}_{\mathcal{A}}^{cca2} \wedge \neg\mathsf{bad}) = \Pr(\mathsf{Succ}_{\mathcal{A},sim}^{cca2} \wedge \neg\mathsf{bad})$. Then

$$\mathsf{Adv}_{\mathcal{A}}^{cca2}(1^k) = |\Pr(\mathsf{Succ}_{\mathcal{A}}^{cca2}) - 1/2| \leqslant |\Pr(\mathsf{Succ}_{\mathcal{A}}^{cca2} \wedge \neg\mathsf{bad}) - 1/2| + \Pr(\mathsf{bad}). \qquad (4)$$

Let CDHfound be the event the "Finalization procedure outputs $\hat{Z}_2 \neq \perp$". By the definition of CDHfound, $\Pr(\mathsf{Succ}_{\mathcal{A},sim}^{cca2} \wedge \neg\mathsf{bad} \wedge \mathsf{CDHfound}) \leqslant \mathsf{Adv}_{\mathcal{B}_1}^{sCDH}(\mathbb{J}_N^+)$, where $\mathcal{B}_1$ is obtained from $\mathcal{A}$ and the simulator. Using [14, Theorem 2], we obtain

$$\Pr(\mathsf{Succ}_{\mathcal{A},sim}^{cca2} \wedge \neg\mathsf{bad} \wedge \mathsf{CDHfound}) \leqslant \mathsf{Adv}_{\mathcal{B}_1, \mathsf{RSAGen}}^{fac}(k) + 1/p' + 1/q'. \qquad (5)$$

Now, if $\mathsf{Succ}_{\mathcal{A},sim}^{cca2} \wedge \neg\mathsf{bad} \wedge \neg\mathsf{CDHfound}$, then $\mathcal{A}$ is essentially playing a semantic security game against $\mathcal{E}$, so using $\mathcal{A}$ and the simulator we build an adversary $\mathcal{B}_2$ against $\mathcal{E}$ such that

$$|\Pr(\mathsf{Succ}_{\mathcal{A},sim}^{cca2} \wedge \neg\mathsf{bad} \wedge \neg\mathsf{CDHfound}) - 1/2| = \mathsf{Adv}_{\mathcal{B}_2, \mathcal{E}}^{ss}(k). \qquad (6)$$

The result follows from (3)–(6).   □

4.2 Unforgeability of the $\mathcal{SC}_{SSN}$ Scheme

Theorem 4. *Under the RO model, if the RSA problem is $(t(k), \varepsilon_0(k))$-hard over $\mathbb{J}_N^+$, then $\mathcal{SC}_{SSN}$ is $(t, q_{Sc}, \varepsilon')$-MU insider unforgeable in the FSO/FUO-sUF-CMA sense, with $\varepsilon' \leqslant \sqrt{q\varepsilon_0} + (q+1)|\mathsf{ChSet}|^{-1} + q_{Sc}(q_{Sc}-1)\left(2(p'q')^2|\mathbf{K}|\right)^{-1} + 5q_{Sc}\delta_0$, with $q = q_{H_1} + q_{Sc}$ wherein q_{H_1} is an upper bound on the number of $\mathcal{O}_{H_1}(\cdot)$ queries the adversary issues.*

Proof. Let q_{H_1} and q_{Sc} be upper bounds on the number of queries $\mathcal{A}$ issues to the $\mathcal{O}_{\mathsf{H}_1}(\cdot)$ and $\mathcal{O}_{\mathsf{Sc}}(\cdot,\cdot)$ oracles respectively, and $q = q_{\mathsf{H}_1} + q_{\mathsf{Sc}}$. In addition to the domain parameter and $Y_0 \leftarrow_{\mathsf{R}} \mathbb{J}_N^+$, the simulator takes as an additional input $L_{\mathsf{H}_1} = (h_1, \cdots, h_q)$ such that for all i, $h_i \leftarrow_{\mathsf{R}} \mathsf{ChSet}$.

Simulation for the MU insider Unforgeability in the FSO/FUO–sUF–CMA sense

Input: $dp = (N, G, R, e, k)$, $\mathcal{E} = (\mathsf{E}, \mathsf{D}, \mathbf{K}, \mathbf{M}, \mathbf{C})$, $Y_0 \leftarrow_{\mathsf{R}} \mathbb{J}_N^+$, $L_{\mathsf{H}_1} = (h_1, h_2, \cdots, h_q)$.

100 $\underline{\text{Initialization:}}$ $pk_S \leftarrow Y_0$; $\mathcal{S}_{\mathsf{H}_1} \leftarrow ()$; $\mathsf{cnt} \leftarrow 0$; $\mathcal{S}_{\mathsf{k\&r}} \leftarrow ()$; $\mathcal{S}_{\mathsf{H}_2} \leftarrow ()$; abort $\leftarrow 0$;

101 $\mathcal{O}_{\mathsf{H}_1}(s)$:

102 **if** $\exists\, h : (s, h) \in \mathcal{S}_{\mathsf{H}_1}$ **then** return h;

103 **else** $\mathsf{cnt} \leftarrow \mathsf{cnt} + 1$; $h \leftarrow L_{\mathsf{H}_1}[\mathsf{cnt}]$; $\mathsf{Apd}(\mathcal{S}_{\mathsf{H}_1}, (s, h, \mathsf{cnt}))$; return h;

104 $\mathcal{O}_{\mathsf{H}_2}(s)$:

105 **if** $\exists\, \tau : (s, \tau) \in \mathcal{S}_{\mathsf{H}_2}$ **then** return τ

106 **else if** s has format $(X_1, X_2, Z_1, Z_2, pk_S, pk) \in \left(\mathbb{J}_N^+\right)^6$ **then**

107 $\quad$ **if** $\exists r, s, \tau_1, \tau_2 : ((X_1, X_2, pk_S, pk), (r, s, \tau_1, \tau_2)) \in \mathcal{S}_{\mathsf{k\&r}}$ **then**

108 $\quad\quad$ **if** $Z_1^r \circ Z_2 = pk^s$ **then** return τ_1;

109 $\quad$ **if** $\exists r, s, \tau_1, \tau_2 : ((X_2, X_1, pk_S, pk), (r, s, \tau_1, \tau_2)) \in \mathcal{S}_{\mathsf{k\&r}}$ **then**

110 $\quad\quad$ **if** $Z_2^r \circ Z_1 = pk^s$ **then** return τ_2;

111 **else** $\tau \leftarrow_{\mathsf{R}} \mathsf{ChSet}$; $\mathsf{Apd}(s_{\mathsf{H}_2}, (s, \tau))$; return τ;

112 $\mathcal{O}_{\mathsf{Sc}}(pk, m)$:

113 $\mathsf{cnt} \leftarrow \mathsf{cnt} + 1$; $h \leftarrow L_{\mathsf{H}_1}[\mathsf{cnt}]$; $z \leftarrow_{\mathsf{R}} [l]$; $s_1 \leftarrow R^z$; $X_1 \leftarrow s_1^e \circ pk_S^{-h}$;

114 $r \leftarrow_{\mathsf{R}} [l]$; $s_2 \leftarrow_{\mathsf{R}} [l]$; $X_2 \leftarrow G^{s_2} \circ X_1^{-r}$; $\tau_1 \leftarrow_{\mathsf{R}} \mathbf{K}$; $\tau_2 \leftarrow_{\mathsf{R}} \mathbf{K}$;

115 **if** $\exists h', m', j : ((X_1, X_2, m', \tau_1), h', j) \in \mathcal{S}_{\mathsf{H}_1}$ **then** abort $\leftarrow 1$;

116 $\mathsf{Apd}\left(\mathcal{S}_{\mathsf{H}_1}, ((X_1, X_2, m, \tau_1), h, \mathsf{cnt})\right)$; $\mathsf{Apd}\left(\mathcal{S}_{\mathsf{k\&r}}, ((X_1, X_2, pk_S, pk), (r, s_2, \tau_1, \tau_2))\right)$;

117 $c \leftarrow \mathsf{E}(\tau_2, m)$; $C \leftarrow (h, X_2, s_1, c)$; return C;

118 $\underline{\text{Finalization:}}$

119 **if** $\mathcal{A}$ outputs (sk_R, pk_R, C^*) such that $\perp \neq \hat{m} \leftarrow \mathcal{O}_{\mathsf{Usc}}(sk_R, C^*)$ and $\mathcal{O}_{\mathsf{Sign}}(pk_R, \hat{m})$ was never issued **then**

120 $\quad$ Parse C^* as $(\hat{h}, \hat{X}_2, \hat{s}, \hat{c})$;

121 $\quad$ $\hat{X}_1 \leftarrow \hat{s}^e \circ pk_S^{-\hat{h}}$; $\hat{Z}_1 \leftarrow \hat{X}_1^{sk_R}$; $\hat{Z}_2 \leftarrow \hat{X}_2^{sk_R}$; $\hat{\tau}_1 \leftarrow \mathcal{O}_{\mathsf{H}_2}(\hat{X}_1, \hat{X}_2, \hat{Z}_1, \hat{Z}_2, pk_S, pk_R)$;

122 $\quad$ **if** $\exists j_0 : ((\hat{X}_1, \hat{X}_2, \hat{m}, \hat{\tau}_1), \hat{h}, j_0) \in \mathcal{S}_{\mathsf{H}_1}$ **then** return $(j_0, \hat{X}_1, \hat{s})$;

123 return $(0, \epsilon, \epsilon)$;

As in the previous analysis, bad denotes the event: "(a) abort is set to 1 (see at line 115) or (b) in the execution of $\mathcal{O}_{\mathsf{H}_2}(\cdot)$, Z_1 and Z_2 are such that (see at lines 108 and 110) $Z_1^r \circ Z_2 = pk^s$ and $\mathsf{CDH}(X_1, pk) \neq Z_1$ or $\mathsf{CDH}(X_2, pk) \neq Z_2$." Then

$$\Pr(\mathsf{bad}) \leqslant q_{\mathsf{Sc}}(q_{\mathsf{Sc}} - 1)\left(2(p'q')^2|\mathbf{K}|\right)^{-1} + 5q_{\mathsf{Sc}}\delta_0, \tag{7}$$

and then

$$\mathsf{Adv}_{\mathcal{A},SC}^{\mathsf{suf}}(1^k) \leqslant \Pr(\mathsf{Succ}_{\mathcal{A}}^{\mathsf{suf}} \wedge \neg\mathsf{bad}) + q_{\mathsf{Sc}}(q_{\mathsf{Sc}} - 1)\left(2(p'q')^2|\mathbf{K}|\right)^{-1} + 5q_{\mathsf{Sc}}\delta_0. \tag{8}$$

Let fail be the event "the $\underline{\text{Finalization}}$ procedure outputs $(0, \epsilon, \epsilon)$". If the event $\mathsf{Succ}_{\mathcal{A}}^{\mathsf{suf}} \wedge \neg\mathsf{bad} \wedge \mathsf{fail}$ occurs then the oracle $\mathcal{O}_{\mathsf{H}_1}(\cdot)$ was never queried with value $(\hat{X}_1, \hat{X}_2, \hat{m}, \hat{\tau}_1)$. Which means that $\mathcal{A}$ successfully guessed $\mathcal{O}_{\mathsf{H}_1}(\hat{X}_1, \hat{X}_2, \hat{m}, \hat{\tau}_1)$. Under the RO model,

$$\Pr(\mathsf{Succ}_{\mathcal{A}}^{\mathsf{suf}} \wedge \neg\mathsf{bad} \wedge \mathsf{fail}) \leqslant |\mathsf{ChSet}|^{-1}. \tag{9}$$

Using $\mathcal{A}$ and the simulator, we obtain a machine $\mathcal{B}$ which takes $(dp, \mathcal{E}, Y_0, L_{\mathsf{H}_1} = (h_1, \cdots, h_q))$ as input and outputs $(j_0, \hat{X}_1, \hat{s})$ such that $\hat{s}^{\underline{e}} = X_1 Y_0^{\frac{h_{j_0}}{}}$ with probability $\varepsilon_1 = \Pr(\mathsf{Succ}_{\mathcal{A}}^{\mathsf{suf}} \wedge \neg\mathsf{bad} \wedge \neg\mathsf{fail})$. Let F_B be the forking algorithm [7, Sect. 3] associated to $\mathcal{B}$. By the General Forking Lemma [7, Lemma 1], from F_B's output, we have $(h_{j_0}, h'_{j_0}, X_1, \hat{s}, \hat{s}')$ such that $h_{j_0} \neq h'_{j_0}$, $\hat{s}^{\underline{e}} = X_1 Y_0^{\frac{h_{j_0}}{}}$, and $\hat{s}'^{\underline{e}} = X_1 Y_0^{\frac{h'_{j_0}}{}}$ with probability $\varepsilon_0 \geqslant \varepsilon_1(\varepsilon_1/q - 1/|\mathsf{ChSet}|)$. Then, using F_B and Shamir's trick (we use on page 9 when proving that $\mathcal{I}_{SSN}$ provides special soundness), we obtain a machine $\mathcal{B}_2$ which, on input Y_0, outputs X_0 such that $X_0^{\underline{e}} = Y_0$ with probability ε_0. Again, from the General Forking Lemma [7, Lemma 1],

$$\varepsilon_1 \leqslant q|\mathsf{ChSet}|^{-1} + \sqrt{q\varepsilon_0}. \tag{10}$$

The result follows from (8)–(10).

4.3   Soundness of Non-repudiation

Theorem 5. *Under the RO model, $\mathcal{SC}_{SSN}$ achieves $(t, q_{\mathsf{Sc}}, \varepsilon)$-computational soundness of non-repudiation, with $\varepsilon \leqslant 1/2 \cdot q(q-1)|\mathsf{ChSet}|^{-1} + 1/2 \cdot q_{\mathsf{Sc}}(q_{\mathsf{Sc}} - 1)(p'q')^{-2}|\mathbf{K}|^{-1} + 5q_{\mathsf{Sc}}\delta_0$, where $q = q_{\mathsf{H}_1} + q_{\mathsf{Sc}}$, wherein q_{H_1} is an upper bound on the number of $\mathcal{O}_{\mathsf{H}_1}(\cdot)$ queries $\mathcal{A}$ issues.*

Proof. First, we provide a simulation for Game 4. The simulator takes $dp = (N, G, R, e, k)$ and $\mathcal{E} = (\mathsf{E}, \mathsf{D}, \mathbf{K}, \mathbf{M}, \mathbf{C})$ as inputs. The initialization simply sets $\mathcal{S}_{\mathsf{H}_1} \leftarrow ()$; $\mathcal{S}_{\mathsf{k}} \leftarrow ()$; $\mathcal{S}_{\mathsf{k\&r}} \leftarrow ()$; $\mathcal{S}_{\mathsf{H}_2} \leftarrow ()$. The $\mathcal{O}_{\mathsf{H}_1}(\cdot)$ oracle is as described in lines 2–3 in the simulation for the confidentiality game. The $\mathcal{O}_{\mathsf{H}_2}(\cdot)$ and $\mathcal{O}_{\mathsf{Sc}}(\cdot,\cdot)$ oracles are as in lines 104–111 and 112–117 in the simulation for the unforgeability game, except that the lines 113 and 115 are replaced respectively with the lines 200 and 201, hereunder:

200   $h \leftarrow_{\mathsf{R}} \mathsf{ChSet}$;
201   **if** $\exists h', m' : ((X_1, X_2, m', \tau_1), h') \in \mathcal{S}_{\mathsf{H}_1}$ **then** abort $\leftarrow 1$.

Defining bad as in the proof of Theorem 4, the inequality (7) still holds. Then

$$\mathsf{Adv}_{\mathcal{A}, SC}^{\mathsf{snr}}(1^k) \leqslant \Pr(\mathsf{Succ}_{\mathcal{A}}^{\mathsf{snr}} \wedge \neg\mathsf{bad}) + q_{\mathsf{Sc}}(q_{\mathsf{Sc}} - 1)\left(2(p'q')^2 |\mathbf{K}|\right)^{-1} + 5q_{\mathsf{Sc}}\delta_0. \tag{11}$$

If $\mathcal{A}$ succeeds and $\neg\mathsf{bad}$, $\mathcal{A}$ outputs $(sk_R, pk_R, C^*, m', nr)$ such that $m' \neq m \leftarrow \mathsf{Usc}(sk_R, pk_S, C^*)$ and $1 = d \leftarrow \mathsf{PV}(C^*, m', nr, pk_S, pk_R)$. Let $C^* = (\hat{h}, \hat{X}_2, \hat{s}, \hat{c})$, $nr = (\tau_1, \tau_2)$, $\widehat{nr} = (\hat{\tau}_1, \hat{\tau}_2) \leftarrow \mathsf{N}(sk_R, pk_S, C^*)$, and $\hat{X}_1 \leftarrow \hat{s}^{\underline{e}} \circ pk_S^{-\hat{h}}$. As $m \neq m'$ and $1 = d \leftarrow \mathsf{PV}(C^*, m', nr, pk_S, pk_R) = d' \leftarrow \mathsf{PV}(C^*, m, \widehat{nr}, pk_S, pk_R)$. $\mathcal{A}$ have found $(m, \hat{\tau}_1)$ and (m', τ_1) such that $\hat{h} = h_1 \leftarrow \mathcal{O}_{\mathsf{H}_1}(\hat{X}_1, \hat{X}_2, m, \hat{\tau}_1) = h_2 \leftarrow \mathcal{O}_{\mathsf{H}_1}(\hat{X}_1, \hat{X}_2, m', \tau_1)$. Then

$$\Pr(\mathsf{Succ}_{\mathcal{A}}^{\mathsf{snr}} \wedge \neg\mathsf{bad}) \leqslant q(q-1)(2 \cdot |\mathsf{ChSet}|)^{-1}. \tag{12}$$

The Theorem follows from (11) and (12).   □

4.4   Unforgeability of Non-repudiation Evidence

Theorem 6. *Under the RO model, if the factoring problem is* $(t(k), \varepsilon(k))$ *hard, then the* $\mathcal{SC}_{SSN}$ *scheme achieves* $(t, q_{Sc}, q_{Usc}, q_N, \varepsilon')$ *unforgeability of non-repudiation evidence with* $\varepsilon' \leqslant \varepsilon + |\mathbf{K}|^{-1} + q_{Sc}(q_{Sc} - 1)\left(2(p'q')^2\right)^{-1} + (5q_{Sc} + 2)\delta_0$.

Proof. We consider the following simulation.

Simulation for Unforgeability of non–repudiation evidence
Input: $dp = (N, G, R, e, k)$, $\mathcal{E} = (\mathsf{E}, \mathsf{D}, \mathbf{K}, \mathbf{M}, \mathbf{C})$, $X_0, Y_0 \leftarrow_R \mathbb{J}_N^+$, $L_{H_1} = (h_1, h_2, \cdots, h_q)$.
External Oracles: $\mathrm{DDH}_{Y_0}(\cdot, \cdot)$

300 Initialization: $a \leftarrow [l]$; $(sk_S, pk_S) \leftarrow (R^{\underline{a}}, G^{\underline{a}})$; $pk_R \leftarrow Y_0$; $\mathcal{S}_{H_1} \leftarrow ()$; $\mathsf{cnt} \leftarrow 0$;
$\mathcal{S}_k \leftarrow ()$; $\mathcal{S}_{k\&r} \leftarrow ()$; $\mathcal{S}_{H_2} \leftarrow ()$;

301 $\mathcal{O}_{H_1}(s)$: is defined as in the simulation for the confidentiality game, at lines 2–3.

302 $\overline{\mathcal{O}_{H_2}(s)}$:

303 **if** $\exists \tau : (s, \tau) \in \mathcal{S}_{H_2}$ **then** return τ;

304 **else if** s has format $(X_1, X_2, Z_1, Z_2, pk, pk' = pk_R) \in \left(\mathbb{J}_N^+\right)^6$ **then**

305   **if** $pk = pk_S$ and $\exists \tau, x : ((X_1, X_2, Z_1, \epsilon, pk_S, pk_R), \tau, x)) \in \mathcal{S}_{k\&r}$ and
$\mathrm{DDH}_{Y_0}(X_2, Z_2) = 1$ **then** $\mathsf{Apd}(\mathcal{S}_{H_2}, (s, \tau))$; return τ;

306   **if** $pk = pk_S$ and $\exists \tau, x : ((X_1, X_2, \epsilon, Z_2, pk_S, pk_R), \tau, x)) \in \mathcal{S}_{k\&r}$ and
$\mathrm{DDH}_{Y_0}(X_1, Z_1) = 1$ **then** $\mathsf{Apd}(\mathcal{S}_{H_2}, (s, \tau))$; return τ;

307   **if** $\exists \tau : ((X_1, X_2, pk, pk_R), \tau) \in \mathcal{S}_k$ and $\mathrm{DDH}_{Y_0}(X_1, Z_1) = \mathrm{DDH}_{Y_0}(X_2, Z_2) = 1$
then $\mathsf{Apd}(\mathcal{S}_{H_2}, (s, \tau))$; return τ;

308 **else** $\tau \leftarrow_R \mathsf{ChSet}$; $\mathsf{Apd}(s_{H_2}, (s, \tau))$; return τ;

309 $\mathcal{O}_{Sc}(pk, m)$:

310 $x_1 \leftarrow_R [l]$; $X_1 \leftarrow G^{\underline{x_1}}$; $Z_1 = pk_R^{\underline{x_1}}$; $x_2 \leftarrow_R [l]$;

311 **if** $pk \neq pk_R$ **then**

312      $X_2 \leftarrow G^{\underline{x_2}}$; $Z_2 = pk_R^{\underline{x_2}}$;

313      $\tau_1 \leftarrow \mathcal{O}_{H_2}(X_1, X_2, Z_1, Z_2, pk_S, pk)$; $\tau_2 \leftarrow \mathcal{O}_{H_2}(X_2, X_1, Z_2, Z_1, pk_S, pk)$;

314 **else**

315      $X_2 \leftarrow X_0 \circ G^{\underline{x_2}}$; $\tau_1 \leftarrow_R \mathbf{K}$; $\tau_2 \leftarrow_R \mathbf{K}$;   ▶ *The simulator takes* X_0, Y_0 *as inputs*

316      $\mathsf{Apd}(\mathcal{S}_{k\&r}, ((X_1, X_2, Z_1, \epsilon, pk_S, pk_R), \tau_1, x_2))$;   ▶ $pk = pk_R$;

317      $\mathsf{Apd}(\mathcal{S}_{k\&r}, ((X_2, X_1, \epsilon, Z_1, pk_S, pk_R), \tau_2, x_2))$;

318 $h \leftarrow \mathcal{O}_{H_1}(X_1, X_2, m, \tau_1)$; $c \leftarrow \mathsf{E}(\tau_2, m)$; $s \leftarrow R^{\underline{x_1}} \circ sk_S^{\underline{h}}$; return (h, X_2, s, c);

319 $\mathcal{O}_{Usc}(pk, C)$: $\underline{\mathcal{O}_N(pk, C)}$:

320 **if** $pk \notin \mathbb{J}_N^+$ **then** return $\bot$;

321 Parse C as $(h, X_2, s, c) \in \mathsf{ChSet} \times \mathbb{J}_N^+ \times \mathbb{J}_N^+ \times \mathbf{C}$; $X_1 \leftarrow s^{\underline{e}} \circ pk^{\underline{-h}}$;

322 **if** $\exists Z_1, Z_2 \in \mathbb{J}_N^+, \tau \in \mathbf{K} : ((X_1, X_2, Z_1, Z_2, pk, pk_R), \tau) \in \mathcal{S}_{H_2}$ and $\mathrm{DDH}_{Y_0}(X_1, Z_1) = \mathrm{DDH}_{Y_0}(X_2, Z_2) = 1$ **then**
$\tau_1 \leftarrow \tau$;   ▶ $H_2(X_1, X_2, Z_1, Z_2, pk, pk_R)$ *was issued*

323 **else if** $pk = pk_R$ and $\exists \tau, x : ((X_1, X_2, Z_1, \epsilon, pk_S, pk_R), \tau, x) \in \mathcal{S}_{k\&r}$ **then**

324      $\tau_1 \leftarrow \tau$ ▶ $\mathcal{O}_{Sc}(\cdot, \cdot)$ *returned* (h, X_2, s, c') *for some* c'

325 **else if** $\exists \tau : ((X_1, X_2, pk, pk_R), \tau) \in \mathcal{S}_k$ **then**

326      $\tau_1 \leftarrow \tau$;   ▶ $\mathsf{Usc}(pk, C')$ *or* $\mathsf{N}(pk, C')$ *such that* C' *parses as* (h, X_2, s, c') *was issued*

327 **else** $\tau_1 \leftarrow_R \mathbf{K}$; $\mathsf{Apd}(\mathcal{S}_k, ((X_1, X_2, pk, pk_R), \tau_1))$;

328   **if** $\exists\, Z_2, Z_1 \in \mathbb{J}_N^+, \tau \in \mathbf{K} : ((X_2, X_1, Z_2, Z_1, pk, pk_R), \tau) \in \mathcal{S}_{\mathsf{H}_2}$ and $\mathrm{DDH}_{Y_0}(X_1, Z_1) =$
    $\mathrm{DDH}_{Y_0}(X_2, Z_2) = 1$ **then** $\tau_2 \leftarrow \tau;$ ▶ *the same treatment as for* τ_1

329   **else if** $pk = pk_R$ and $\exists\, \tau, x : ((X_2, X_1, \epsilon, Z_2, pk_S, pk_R), \tau, x) \in \mathcal{S}_{\mathsf{k\&r}}$ **then** $\tau_2 \leftarrow \tau$

330   **else if** $\exists\, \tau : ((X_2, X_1, pk, pk_R), \tau) \in \mathcal{S}_{\mathsf{k}}$ **then** $\tau_2 \leftarrow \tau;$

331   **else** $\tau_2 \leftarrow_{\mathsf{R}} \mathbf{K};\ \mathrm{Apd}(\mathcal{S}_{\mathsf{k}}, ((X_2, X_1, pk, pk_R), \tau_2));$

332   $m \leftarrow \mathrm{D}(\tau_2, c);\ h' \leftarrow \underline{\mathcal{O}_{\mathsf{H}_1}}(X_1, X_2, m, \tau_1);$

333   **if** $h = h'$ **then** $\boxed{\text{return } m}^{\;\mathcal{O}_{\mathsf{Usc}}}$ $\boxed{\text{return } (\tau_1, \tau_2)}^{\;\mathcal{O}_{\mathsf{N}}}$ **else** return $\perp;$

334 **Finalization:**

335 **if** $\mathcal{A}$ outputs (C^*, m^*, nr^*) such that C^* was generated through $\mathcal{O}_{\mathsf{Sc}}(\cdot, \cdot)$, $1 = d \leftarrow$
  $\mathrm{PV}(C^*, m^*, nr^*, pk_S, pk_R)$ and nr^* was not generated by the oracle $\mathcal{O}_{\mathsf{N}}(\cdot, \cdot)$ on a
  query on (pk_S, C^*) **then**

336   Parse C^* as $(\hat{h}, \hat{X}_2, \hat{s}, \hat{c})$ and nr^* as $(\hat{\tau}_1, \hat{\tau}_2);$
    $\hat{X}_1 \leftarrow \hat{s}^{\underline{e}} \circ pk_S^{-\hat{h}};$

337   Recover $((\hat{X}_1, \hat{X}_2, \hat{Z}_1, \epsilon, pk_S, pk_R), \hat{\tau}, x)$ from $\mathcal{S}_{\mathsf{k\&r}}$ ▶ *As C^* was output by $\mathcal{O}_{\mathsf{Sc}}(\cdot, \cdot)$*
  there are some $\hat{Z}_1, \hat{\tau}, x : ((\hat{X}_1, \hat{X}_2, \hat{Z}_1, \epsilon, pk_S, pk_R), \hat{\tau}, x)) \in \mathcal{S}_{\mathsf{k\&r}}$ *(see at line 316)*

338   **if** $\exists\, \hat{Z}_1, \hat{Z}_2 \in \mathbb{J}_N^+ : ((\hat{X}_1, \hat{X}_2, \hat{Z}_1, \hat{Z}_2, pk_S, pk_R), \hat{\tau}_1) \in \mathcal{S}_{\mathsf{H}_2}$ and $\mathrm{DDH}_{Y_0}(\hat{X}_2, \hat{Z}_2) = 1$
  then
    $U_0 \leftarrow Z_2 \circ pk_R^{-x};$ return $U_0;$

339 **return** $\epsilon;$

Let bad denote the event "the same couple (X_1, X_2) is generated in two executions of $\mathcal{O}_{\mathsf{Sign}}(\cdot, \cdot)$". Then, under the RO model,

$$\Pr(\mathsf{bad}) \leqslant \frac{1}{2} q_{\mathsf{Sc}} (q_{\mathsf{Sc}} - 1)(p'q')^{-2} + 5 q_{\mathsf{Sc}} \delta_0. \tag{13}$$

Let fail be the event "the Finalization procedure outputs ϵ". If $\mathrm{Succ}_{\mathcal{A}}^{\mathsf{unr}} \wedge \neg\mathsf{bad} \wedge \mathsf{fail}$ occurs, $\mathcal{A}$ never query the $\mathcal{O}_{\mathsf{H}2}$ oracle on $(\hat{X}_1, \hat{X}_2, \mathrm{CDH}(pk_R, \hat{X}_1), \mathrm{CDH}(pk_R, \hat{X}_2), pk_S, pk_R)$; then $\mathcal{A}$ successfully guessed the corresponding digest value. It follows

$$\Pr(\mathrm{Succ}_{\mathcal{A}}^{\mathsf{unr}} \wedge \neg\mathsf{bad} \wedge \mathsf{fail}) \leqslant |\mathbf{K}|^{-1}. \tag{14}$$

If $\mathrm{Succ}_{\mathcal{A}}^{\mathsf{unr}} \wedge \neg\mathsf{bad} \wedge \neg\mathsf{fail}$ occurs, as $\hat{X}_2 = X_0 \circ G^{\underline{x}}$ and $\hat{Z}_2 = \mathrm{CDH}(X_2, pk_R = Y_0)$

$$U_0 = \mathrm{CDH}(X_0, Y_0) = Z_2 \circ pk_R^{-x}. \tag{15}$$

Using $\mathcal{A}$ and the simulator, we have a machine which takes X_0, Y_0 as input and outputs $\mathrm{CDH}(X_0, Y_0)$ with probability $\Pr(\mathrm{Succ}_{\mathcal{A}}^{\mathsf{unr}} \wedge \neg\mathsf{bad} \wedge \neg\mathsf{fail})$. The result follows from (13), (14), and [14, Theorem 2].   □

5   Concluding Remarks

We have proposed a new identification scheme over the group of signed quadratic residues, wherein the strong Diffie–Hellman assumption holds under the factoring assumption. Using the identification scheme, we derived a new signature scheme we have shown to be strongly unforgeable against chosen message attacks, under the RSA assumption and the Random Oracle model. We proposed an efficient signcryption scheme with non-interactive non-repudiation, we have shown to be insider secure, under the RSA assumption and the RO model, in a variant of Fan *et al.*'s security model. The communication overhead of the signcryption scheme, compared to the corresponding signature scheme is one group element.

Compared to Fan *et al.*'s design which uses bilinear maps, our scheme is RSA based and can be easily deployed in most of the existing platforms.

In a forthcoming stage, we will be interested in the conditions under which our design can be generalized to generic Diffie–Hellman groups. We will investigate also signcryption designs with a tight security reduction.

References

1. Algesheimer, J., Camenisch, J., Shoup, V.: Efficient computation modulo a shared secret with application to the generation of shared safe-prime products. In: Yung, M. (ed.) CRYPTO 2002. LNCS, vol. 2442, pp. 417–432. Springer, Heidelberg (2002). https://doi.org/10.1007/3-540-45708-9_27
2. Badertscher, C., Banfi, F., Maurer, U.: A constructive perspective on signcryption security. In: Catalano, D., De Prisco, R. (eds.) SCN 2018. LNCS, vol. 11035, pp. 102–120. Springer, Cham (2018). https://doi.org/10.1007/978-3-319-98113-0_6
3. Baek, J., Steinfeld, R.: Security for signcryption: the multi-user model. In: Dent, A., Zheng, Y. (eds.) Practical Signcryption. ISC, pp. 43–53. Springer, Heidelberg (2010). https://doi.org/10.1007/978-3-540-89411-7_3
4. Baek, J., Steinfeld, R., Zheng, Y.: Formal proofs for the security of signcryption. In: Naccache, D., Paillier, P. (eds.) PKC 2002. LNCS, vol. 2274, pp. 80–98. Springer, Heidelberg (2002). https://doi.org/10.1007/3-540-45664-3_6
5. Baek, J., Steinfeld, R., Zheng, Y.: Formal proofs for the security of signcryption. J. Cryptol. **20**(2), 203–235 (2007)
6. Bao, F., Deng, R.H.: A signcryption scheme with signature directly verifiable by public key. In: Imai, H., Zheng, Y. (eds.) PKC 1998. LNCS, vol. 1431, pp. 55–59. Springer, Heidelberg (1998). https://doi.org/10.1007/BFb0054014
7. Bellare, M., Neven, G.: Multi-signatures in the plain public-key model and a general forking lemma. In: Proceedings of the 13th ACM Conference on Computer and Communications Security, pp. 390–399. ACM (2006)
8. Bellare, M., Rogaway, P.: Random oracle are practical: a paradigm for designing efficient protocols. In: ACM-CCS 1993, pp. 62–73. ACM (1993)
9. Boyd, C., Mathuria, A.: Protocols for Authentication and Key Establishment. Springer Science & Business Media, Heidelberg (2003). https://doi.org/10.1007/978-3-662-09527-0
10. Cash, D., Kiltz, E., Shoup, V.: The twin Diffie-Hellman problem and applications. J. Cryptol. **22**(4), 470–504 (2009)
11. Fan, J., Zheng, Y., Tang, X.: Signcryption with non-interactive non-repudiation without random oracles. In: Gavrilova, M.L., Tan, C.J.K., Moreno, E.D. (eds.) Transactions on Computational Science X. LNCS, vol. 6340, pp. 202–230. Springer, Heidelberg (2010). https://doi.org/10.1007/978-3-642-17499-5_9
12. Fiat, A., Shamir, A.: How to prove yourself: practical solutions to identification and signature problems. In: Odlyzko, A.M. (ed.) CRYPTO 1986. LNCS, vol. 263, pp. 186–194. Springer, Heidelberg (1987). https://doi.org/10.1007/3-540-47721-7_12

13. Guillou, L.C., Quisquater, J.-J.: A practical zero-knowledge protocol fitted to security microprocessor minimizing both transmission and memory. In: Barstow, D., Brauer, W., Brinch Hansen, P., Gries, D., Luckham, D., Moler, C., Pnueli, A., Seegmüller, G., Stoer, J., Wirth, N., Günther, C.G. (eds.) EUROCRYPT 1988. LNCS, vol. 330, pp. 123–128. Springer, Heidelberg (1988). https://doi.org/10.1007/3-540-45961-8_11
14. Hofheinz, D., Kiltz, E.: The group of signed quadratic residues and applications. In: Halevi, S. (ed.) CRYPTO 2009. LNCS, vol. 5677, pp. 637–653. Springer, Heidelberg (2009). https://doi.org/10.1007/978-3-642-03356-8_37
15. Kiltz, E., Masny, D., Pan, J.: Optimal security proofs for signatures from identification schemes. In: Robshaw, M., Katz, J. (eds.) CRYPTO 2016. LNCS, vol. 9815, pp. 33–61. Springer, Heidelberg (2016). https://doi.org/10.1007/978-3-662-53008-5_2
16. Lenstra, A.K., Hughes, J.P., Augier, M., Bos, J.W., Kleinjung, T., Wachter, C.: Public keys. In: Safavi-Naini, R., Canetti, R. (eds.) CRYPTO 2012. LNCS, vol. 7417, pp. 626–642. Springer, Heidelberg (2012). https://doi.org/10.1007/978-3-642-32009-5_37
17. Malone-Lee, J.: Signcryption with non-interactive non-repudiation. Des. Codes Crypt. **37**(1), 81–109 (2005)
18. Menezes, A., van Oorschot, P., Vanstone, S.: Handbook of Applied Cryptography. CRC Press, Boca Raton (1996)
19. Okamoto, T., Pointcheval, D.: The gap-problems: a new class of problems for the security of cryptographic schemes. In: Kim, K. (ed.) PKC 2001. LNCS, vol. 1992, pp. 104–118. Springer, Heidelberg (2001). https://doi.org/10.1007/3-540-44586-2_8
20. Sarr, A.P., Elbaz–Vincent, P.: On the security of the (F)HMQV protocol. In: Pointcheval, D., Nitaj, A., Rachidi, T. (eds.) AFRICACRYPT 2016. LNCS, vol. 9646, pp. 207–224. Springer, Cham (2016). https://doi.org/10.1007/978-3-319-31517-1_11
21. Sarr, A.P., Elbaz-Vincent, P., Bajard, J.-C.: A secure and efficient authenticated Diffie–Hellman protocol. In: Martinelli, F., Preneel, B. (eds.) EuroPKI 2009. LNCS, vol. 6391, pp. 83–98. Springer, Heidelberg (2010). https://doi.org/10.1007/978-3-642-16441-5_6
22. Shin, J.-B., Lee, K., Shim, K.: New DSA-verifiable signcryption schemes. In: Lee, P.J., Lim, C.H. (eds.) ICISC 2002. LNCS, vol. 2587, pp. 35–47. Springer, Heidelberg (2003). https://doi.org/10.1007/3-540-36552-4_3
23. Zheng, Y.: Digital signcryption or how to achieve cost(signature & encryption) ≪ cost(signature) + cost(encryption). In: Kaliski, B.S. (ed.) CRYPTO 1997. LNCS, vol. 1294, pp. 165–179. Springer, Heidelberg (1997). https://doi.org/10.1007/BFb0052234

Security

Analysis of Neural Network Training and Cost Functions Impact on the Accuracy of IDS and SIEM Systems

Said El Hajji[✉], Nabil Moukafih, and Ghizlane Orhanou

Laboratory of Mathematics, Computing and Applications - Information Security, Faculty of Sciences, Mohammed V University in Rabat, BP1014 RP, Rabat, Morocco
elhajji.said@gmail.com, moukafih.nab@gmail.com, orhanou@fsr.ac.ma

Abstract. Nowadays, companies are implementing security tools such as Intrusion Detection Systems (IDS) and Security Information and Event Management systems (SIEM) to deal with sophisticated computer attacks. These attacks evolve each year in terms of sophistication and complexity in order to steal or alter sensitive information. Machine learning techniques are used in order to provide pattern recognition and adaptation to IDS and SIEM systems. In this paper, we have proposed a model based on neural networks and support vector machines to analyze and identify network intrusions. We studied the impact of some important parameters in neural networks on the classification accuracy. We evaluated and compared 37 different feed-forward neural networks according to these parameters and choose the best training algorithm for our model using NSL-KDD dataset. Our results suggest that the choice of the appropriate performance function and training algorithm may be critical to achieve higher classification accuracy.

Keywords: Neural networks · Classification · Intrustion detection · SIEM · SVM

1 Introduction

Nowadays, as attacks against computer networks evolve rapidly in terms of complexity and sophistication, most companies have realized that the improvement of essential security tools such as SIEM (Security Information and Event Management) systems and IDS (Intrusion Detection System) systems are critical to prevent security incidents and detect attacks. The goal is to analyze security information, detect computer attacks or anomalies and make appropriate decisions, all in real time. Unfortunately, this is quite difficult, especially when attackers develop every day new specific attacks with new signatures not recorded in public databases (zero-day attacks) and targeting specific systems and vulnerabilities. This makes it hard for signature-based systems to prevent and detect complex attacks that use customized and sophisticated approaches

© Springer Nature Switzerland AG 2019
C. Carlet et al. (Eds.): C2SI 2019, LNCS 11445, pp. 433–451, 2019.
https://doi.org/10.1007/978-3-030-16458-4_25

in real-time. In this context, the data breach report produced by Verizon showed that 68% of breaches last year took months or longer to discover [1]. This explains why companies like ThyssenKrupp [2], Lockheed Martin [3] and RSA [4] were breached by sophisticated hackers and lost sensitive information, although they probably implement state-of-the-art security systems.

Researchers therefore are trying to provide adaptation, automatization and pattern recognition for these systems. For intrusion detection systems, researchers are more interested in anomaly-based approach IDS than those that use the misuse-based (also called rule-based) approach, because theoretically, it is capable of detecting both known and new unseen attacks. Unlike the rule-based approach that is limited to its knowledge-base and rules to identify recognized and only previously known attacks [5]. As for SIEM systems, the main objective is to reduce the high false positive rate generated by different security elements such as firewalls, anti-virus solutions and even intrusion detection systems (IDSs). Conceptually, SIEM systems collect and combine network activity data, logs, security events, and external threat data into a powerful management dashboard that intelligently correlates, normalizes, and prioritizes security incidents. However, this dependency on the configuration of the multiple sensors deployed over the network, creates a challenge for SIEM to perform advanced analysis and correlation [6]. So, there is an equal effort to enhance these systems by proposing techniques for combining data from disparate sources so that the inferred information and knowledge facilitate the identification of attacks. Most of them explore data fusion [7], data mining [8] and artificial intelligence (AI), specifically pattern recognition [9].

In this paper we propose a model that uses neural networks for intrusion detection. To achieve our goal, we have studied deeply several related works such as [10–17,19] that applied neural network for intrusion detection in both IDS and SIEM systems. And we have found that many researches vary the following parameters to improve the performance and speed for neural networks (IDS or SIEM model):

- The number of selected features/attributes;
- Normalization of data;
- Architecture of NN, specifically the number of nodes in the hidden layer;
- Activation function;
- Learning rate;
- Momentum term.

Since the choice of the training algorithm and the cost function was arbitrary or intuitive in many papers, we propose to study these parameters in this paper in order to study the influence of the training algorithms and cost functions on intrusion detection models that use neural networks. For this goal, we have implemented 37 neural network using many training algorithms and cost functions and tested the performance and accuracy of the neural network on NSL-KDD dataset. Next, we have added a second layer of classification using SVM.

The reminder of this paper is structured as follows: Sect. 2 examines the related work to the application of neural networks in intrusion detection for SIEM and IDS systems. Section 3 examines the background of this paper such IDS, SIEM and Artificial Neural Networks. The next section describes the proposed approach and an overview of our implementation and the results of the studied parameters. We finally we conclude in the Sect. 5.

2   Related Work

Generally, machine learning was applied to solve various challenges in computer security targeting many areas such as vulnerability discovery [10,11], malware analysis [12,13] and intrusion detection [14].

For intrusion detection, the authors in [15] used back propagation neural network classier in Anomaly Network Intrusion Detection System (ANIDS), in which they have studied the most relevant parameters employed to construct such a classifier. According to the authors, these parameters are: the number of selected entities, the number of hidden units and layers, the activation function and the data normalization function. The study was conducted on a KDD dataset and led to two optimal ANIDS. The authors have used only Gradient Descent with Momentum for training with default learning rate and momentum values. Similarly, Sen et al. [16] studied the parameter that determines the number of hidden units and layers to use in a neural network for intrusion based on anomaly detection approach. The authors have implemented many neural networks with different combinations of hidden layers and various neurons in each hidden layer. The authors have also varied the percentages split of the KDD dataset. The main limitation of the work is the accuracy of the set of tests (97%) produced by their best combination, which is not as high as that found by the authors in [17] and in [18].

In this work [19], the authors have used neural network in SIEM systems for identifying suspicious user behavior. The primary purpose was to detect suspicious activity of attackers attempting to hide between legitimate user action and evade detection using valid credentials and standard administrative tools. The authors were interested in two types of architectures (Feed-forward vs. recurrent neural network) and also in the number of epoch that are used during the training period, since a model requires high computational effort for training, if it has been trained with a greater number of epochs. Suarez-Tangil and et al. [20] have used neural networks with genetic programming to improve the correlation engine withing SIEM systems. They have adopted two subsystems: the first uses a neural network that classifies all the events collected by the SIEM system and the second subsystem generates new correlation rules according to the neural network classification. Since the authors were mainly interested in the performance of the correlation engine, they haven't provided much information about the neural network used parameters.

Ryan et al. [21] used a three-layer backpropagation neural network called NNID (Neural Network Intrusion Detector) to identify user behavior on Unix-based systems. The model detects anomalies based on what commands the users use during the day. NNID was 96% accurate in environment with only 10 users. The authors concluded that they needed more data to represent more users and that they should study different architectures because a larger network would increase the complexity and use more resources.

Other researchers in other fields have focused on the performance of neural network learning algorithms and their impact on the accuracy of the trained model. Sharma et al. [22] compared many training algorithms for brain hematoma classification. Each training algorithm was checked for 10, 20 and 30 number of neurons (H) in the NN's hidden layer with one cost function. In this particular study, *trainlm* and *trainscg* performed really well in terms of convergence speed and accuracy. In a similar study, Hesam et al. [23] studied the performance of the same training algorithms to classify heart diseases data, the authors used a similar environment and measures to evaluate each algorithm. The study concluded that Quasi-Newton methods are generally considered more powerful compared to other training algorithms when considering other factors such as training time, memory need and accuracy. The authors also didn't study the impact of the used cost function on the accuracy of the studied model.

Other machine learning techniques were used in intrusion detection. For instance, the authors in used [24] SVM with fuzzy c-means clustering in intrusion detection. The model used a hybrid of active learning SVM and Fuzzy C-Means clustering iteratively trained to create a classifier that predicts attacks in the NSL-KDD dataset. The binary classifier produced a decent classification rate, but no comparison with other work was done. SVMs were also used by Al-Yaseen and et al. [25], the authors proposed a model with multi-level SVMs and modified K-means to build a high performance intrusion detection system. The model used modified K-means to reduce the number of training datasets and to build new training data sets with high-quality instances to train SVMs. The model gave high classification accuracy in one attack category, but worked moderately when predicting other instances such as normal events.

In summary, many authors are interested in identifying the most important parameters for the performance of a neural network used in intrusion detection. The goal is to use these parameters to construct neural network model that is suitable for the task that should be solved and to monitor the accuracy of the model. Most authors have tried to increase the number of hidden layers, change the activation function, etc., but to our knowledge, no work has been done on the impact of the different algorithms and the cost functions on the performance of the neural network. In this paper, we have studied 8 batch training algorithms and 5 cost functions, in which we have built 37 neural network (IDS) and compared their performances.

3   More About IDS, SIEM and Artificial Neural Networks

In this section we will describe some general related terms such as Intrusion Detection System, Security Information and Event Management and Artificial Neural networks.

3.1   Security Systems

(a) Intrusion Detection Systems

According to NIST, Intrusion detection systems (IDSs) are software or hardware systems that automate the process of monitoring the events occurring in a computer system or network, analyzing them for signs of security *intrusions*, defined as attempts to compromise the integrity, confidentiality, availability, or to circumvent the security mechanisms of a computer or network [26].

IDS systems attempt to detect malicious behaviors targeting a network and its resources. They can either detect certain deviations from expected and normal usage behavior, also known as *anomaly-based* intrusion detection, that indicate hostile activities against the protected network, or search for specific recognized patterns, called *signatures*, in their input stream as it is the case in *misuse-based* intrusion detection systems [27].

- Anomaly-based systems start by building a model of the normal behavior of the system (sometimes called profile) and then look for anomalous activities. Any activity that does not conform and correspond to the created system profile is flagged as possible intrusion attempt. In theory, this type of detection is capable of detecting previously unknown attacks, but this also means that these systems are prone to the generation of many false positives.

- Misuse-based systems are equipped with a knowledge base that contains a number of attack signatures. The audit data collected by the IDS is compared with the content of the database and, if a match is found, an alert is generated. Events that do not match any of the attack models are considered part of legitimate activities, which gives the important advantage of producing very few false positives. One main issue concerning misuse detection is how to develop signatures that include all possible attacks to avoid false negatives, and how to develop signatures that do not match non-intrusive activities to avoid false positives, which makes this task difficult and resource intensive task. Second, the stored patterns (knowledge base) need to be continually updated in order to detect new vulnerabilities and attack techniques, which would normally involve human expertise.

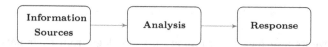

Fig. 1. Process model for intrusion detection

Figure 1 shows the three fundamental functional components in intrusion detection systems:

- Information Sources: It covers event information from different levels of the system, with the most common monitoring of the network, host, and applications. This information is used to determine if an intrusion has occurred.

- Analysis: After collecting events from different information sources, this part is responsible for organizing and making sense of these events. The goal is to decide when these events indicate that intrusions are occurring or have already occurred. The most common analysis approaches are misuse detection and anomaly detection.
- Response: Once an intrusion is detected, the system perform a set of actions that are generally grouped into passive and active measures. Passive measures involve communicating IDS findings to humans, who are then expected to take action based on these reports, while active measures involve automated system intervention.

(b) Security Information and Event Management Systems

SIEM or Security Information and Event Management is a complex set of technologies brought together to provide a holistic view into a technical infrastructure. These technologies combine Security Information Management (SIM) and Security Event Management System (SEM) [28, 29].

SIM essentially provides log management and reporting for security-related events. These are the processes that automate the collection, monitoring, and analysis of security related data from computer logs. SEM covers the tools which provide real-time monitoring for security events, real-time threat analysis, visualization, ticketing, incident response, and security operations. These two technologies work together as illustrated in Fig. 2 in order to provide quicker incident identification, analysis and recovery of security events.

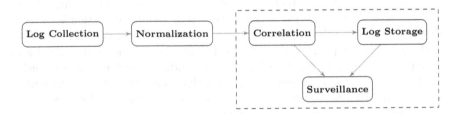

Fig. 2. SIEM's processes

- Collect events and logs by grouping all event logs from their native devices using two fundamental methods: agent-based collection (using dedicated a software) and agentless collection (sending logs remotely).
- Normalization which includes translating computerized jargon to readable data to be processed and displayed often using regular expressions (Regexs).
- Correlation of events and incident response on both internal and external threats.

3.2   Artificial Neural Networks

Artificial Neural Networks are a highly connected networks or "neurons" which exchange messages between each other. They are composed of nodes or **units** (Fig. 3) connected by directed **links**. A link from unit i to unit j serves to propagate the **activation** a_i from i to j. Each link also has a numeric **weight** $w_{i,j}$ associated with it, which determines the strength and sign of the connection [30].

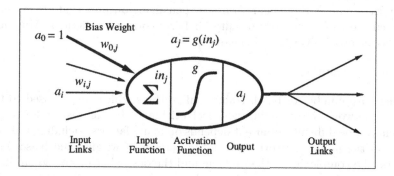

Fig. 3. A simple mathematical model for a neuron.

There are various architectures in Neural Networks. They vary according to the way in which the neurons are connected.

- A **feed-forward network** has connections only in one direction-that is, it forms a directed acyclic graph. Every node receives input from "upstream" nodes and delivers output to "downstream" nodes; there are no loops.
- In a **recurrent network**, we find directed cycles in their connection graph. They can have complicated dynamics and this can make them very difficult to train.

The neural network will be given a dataset (($\mathbf{x}$, $\mathbf{y}$) coordinates), which consists of input (i.e. $\mathbf{x}$) and output data. The output data has the values that we want the neural network to learn to predict. The actual value of the output will be represented by $\mathbf{y}$ and the predicted value will be represented by $\hat{\mathbf{y}}$.

Training the model involves adjusting the weights of the variables for all the different neurons present in the neural network. This is done by minimizing the *Cost Function*.

- Cost Functions

The cost function, as the name suggests is the cost of making a prediction using the neural network. It is a measure of how far off the predicted value, $\hat{y}$, is from the actual or observed value, y. There are many cost functions that are used in practice. In this paper, we will compare the following cost functions:

1. Mean absolute error cost function (mae): It measures network performance as the mean of absolute errors,
2. Mean squared normalized error cost function (mse): This function measures the performance by calculating the mean of squared errors,
3. Sum absolute error cost function (sae): Another cost function that measure the performance of the neural work according to the sum of squared errors,
4. Sum squared error cost function (sse): sse is a network cost function. It measures performance according to the sum of squared errors,
5. Crossentropy cost function (crossentropy): It's a cost function that measure the performance of the neural work by penalizing outputs that are extremely inaccurate with very little penalty for fairly correct predictions. Minimizing cross-entropy leads to good classifiers.

– Training Algorithms

There are number of batch training algorithms which can be used to train a neural network. Determining which algorithm to be the fastest for a given problem can be difficult because it depends on many factors, including the architecture of the neural network such as the number of weights and biases in the network, the complexity of the problem and the desired error and so on. In this problem, we will compare 8 algorithms that can be categorized in three families: Gradient Descent algorithms (traingd, traingdm, trainrp), Conjugate Gradient algorithms (trainscg, traincgf, traincgp), Quasi-Newton algorithms (trainbfg and trainlm) [31].

Gradient Descent Algorithms
Gradient descent is one of the most popular algorithms to perform optimization and by far the most common way to optimize neural networks. It is a way to minimize a cost function $J(\theta)$ parameterized by a model's parameters $\theta \in \mathbb{R}^d$ by updating the parameters in the opposite direction of the gradient of the objective function $\nabla_\theta J(\theta)$ w.r.t. to the parameters.

1. Gradient Descent backpropagation algorithm (traingd) is a gradient descent local search procedure. It measures the output error, calculates the gradient of the error by adjusting the weights and bias values in the direction of the negative gradient of the performance function.
2. Gradient Descent with Momentum (traingdm) algorithm: Sometimes gradient descent has trouble navigating areas where the surface curves much more steeply in one dimension than in another. This often happens around a local optima in which the network gets stuck in to a shallow local minimum. A momentum is a method that helps accelerate GD in the relevant direction by increasing for dimension who gradients point in the same directions and reduces updates for dimensions whose gradients change directions. As a result, the network gains faster convergence and reduced oscillation [32].
3. Resilient backpropagation (trainrp) algorithm takes into account only the sign of the partial derivative over all patterns and eliminates the harmful effects of their magnitudes. These effects come usually from multilayer networks that

use sigmoid transfer functions in the hidden layers. Since the slope of the sigmoid functions approaches zero when the input is large, the gradient can a very small magnitude for such networks using the sigmoid function. As a result, the network will have small changes in the weights and bias, even if the weights and bias are far from their optimal values.

trainrp monitors the changes of the sign of the partial derivative and updates the weights accordingly. For each weight, The update value is decrease by a factor δ^- whenever there was a sign change in partial derivative from the previous iteration and increases by a factor δ^+ whenever the derivative of the performance function with respect to that weight has the same sign for two successive iterations. A complete description of the algorithm is given in [33].

Conjugate Gradient Algorithms

The basic gradient descent algorithm takes steps in the direction of the negative gradient, i.e. the direction in which the performance function decreases most rapidly. This does not necessarily produce the fastest convergence. Conjugate Gradient is simply the method of Conjugate Directions where the search directions are constructed by conjugation of the residual. It improves the steepest descent by avoiding repetitive steps and taking only orthogonal or more specifically A-orthogonal steps [34]. Generally, conjugate gradient algorithms produce faster convergence than basic gradient descent algorithms.

1. Scaled Conjugate Gradient (trainscg): Unlike other conjugate training functions that use a line search technique to approximate the step size. Scaled gradient conjugate gradient is a fully automated algorithm that does not includes no critical user-dependent parameters and doesn't perform a line search at each iteration. Instead, it uses step size scaling mechanism that makes the algorithm faster than any other second order algorithms [35].
2. Conjugate Gradient backpropagation with Fletcher-Reeves Updates (traincgf) is a network function that updates the weights and biases according to the backpropagation gradient convergence with the Fletcher-Reeves update, this update is the ratio of the norm squared of the current gradient to the norm squared of the previous gradient. A detailed analysis of the algorithm can be found in [36].
3. Conjugate Gradient backpropagation with Polak-Riebre Updates (traincgp): This version of was proposed by Polak and Ribière. This version uses the same search direction equation as in traincgf. However, it uses the Polak-Ribiére update to calculate the constant in search direction equation using ratio of the inner product of the previous change in the gradient with the current gradient to the norm squared of the previous gradient [36].

Quasi-Newton Algorithms

The Quasi-Newton algorithms are a class of algorithms also used to either find zeroes or local maxima and minima of functions. They are considered as alternatives to Newton's methods when they're either too time consuming or difficult to compute, especially when it comes to computing the Hessian matrix for feed forward neural networks. Generally, Newton's methods converge faster than conjugate gradient methods but due their complexity, quasi-Newton method are used instead. Strictly speaking, any method that replaces the exact Jacobian or Hessian matrix with an approximation is a quasi-Newton method.

1. BFGS (Broyden-Fletcher-Goldfarb-Shanno) (trainbfg) algorithm: One of the most popular Quasi-Newton methods which estimate the Hessian matrix is BFGS. This algorithm overcomes some of the limitations of plain gradient descent by seeking the second derivative (a stationary point) of the cost function. The gradient should be zero as a necessary condition for optimality. The algorithm has proven to have good performance even for non-smooth optimizations an efficient training function for smaller neural networks. Compared to conjugate gradient methods, it requires more storage and computation, but it converges in fewer iterations.
2. Levenberg-Marquardt backpropagation (trainlm) algorithm: Also known as the damped least-squares method. It's an iterative technique that was designed to work specifically with loss functions which take the form of a sum of squared errors. Although it can't be applied to other loss functions such as the root mean squared error or the cross entropy error, it is considered the fastest training algorithm for networks of moderate size and measured with a sum of squared errors [37].

4 SVM and Neural Network Based Intrusion Detector for IDS and SIEM Systems

In this section we will describe the details of our approach and give our proposed model of our intrusion detector that can be used in IDS and SIEM systems. This section is divided into three main parts:

- The first part describes the proposed model based on neural networks and support vector machines. We also describe the dataset used and the steps taken to prepare the dataset.
- In the second part, we will study the impact of the performance function and training function on the accuracy of neural network-based IDS/SIEM systems.
- In the last part, we add SVMs to our model as a second classification layer to improve accuracy.

4.1 Studied Model

From the above literature review, we find that the existing training algorithms were not evaluated in neural networks for security event classification. Therefore we propose, in this paper, to study some of the most applied training functions in neural networks, and then use best training algorithm in the overall proposed attack recognition system as showed in Fig. 4.

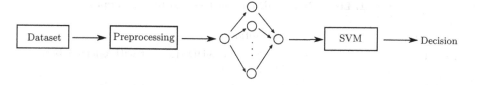

Fig. 4. The new SVM-neural network detection system

The proposed system uses the NSL-KDD (Network Security Layer-Knowledge Discovery Database) dataset as an input. This dataset is a refined version of its predecessor KDD'99 dataset, which is a database that contains TCP/IP connections extracted from the intrusion detection system evaluation data set collected from the DARPA'98 intrusion detection system evaluation program [38].

(a) Dataset
NSL-KDD is a dataset proposed by Tavallaee after criticizing the inherent problems of KDD'99 in 2009 [39]. Because KDD'99 contains many duplicate records, it is likely to be learned by high-frequency attacks when learning algorithms with KDD'99, and it can also affect the evaluation results of test processes. As a result, NSL-KDD comes with the following improvement:

- It does not include redundant and duplicate records in the train and test sets. Thus, the classifiers will not be biased towards more frequent records, and the performance of the learners are not biased by the methods that have better detection rates on the frequent records.
- The number of records in the train and test sets is reasonable, which allows for affordable experiments on the complete set without the need to randomly select a small portion. As a result, the evaluation results of different research studies will be consistent and comparable. More information on the improvements can be found in [39].

NSL-KDD is a collection of downloadable files available to researchers. They are listed in the Table 1.

(b) Data Preprocessing
In each record of the NSL-KDD dataset, there are 41 attributes unfolding different features of the flow and a label assigned to each either as an attack type or as normal. Each feature can have a categorical value such as the protocol used in the connection (**Protocol_type** can have 03 values TCP, UDP or ICMP) or a numeric value like the length of time duration of the connection.

Because Neural networks work best only on numerical data, it requires the conversion of any textual data in the data set to a numerical value, which is the goal of the this phase. Data Preprocessing or "Categorical encoding" refers to the process of assigning numeric values to nonnumeric features/attributes so as to make the processing task much simpler. This can be done using two approaches: one-hot (binary) encoding and integer encoding. While using one-hot encoding

Table 1. List of NSL-KDD dataset files and their description

File name	Description
KDDTrain+.ARFF	The full NSL-KDD train set with binary labels in ARFF format
KDDTrain+.TXT	The full NSL-KDD train set including attack-type labels and difficulty level in CSV format
KDDTrain+_20Perce nt.ARFF	A 20% subset of the KDDTrain+.arff file
KDDTrain+_20Perce nt.TXT	A 20% subset of the KDDTrain+.txt file
KDDTest+.ARFF	The full NSL-KDD test set with binary labels in ARFF format
KDDTest+.TXT	The full NSL-KDD test set including attack-type labels and difficulty level in CSV format
KDDTest-21.ARFF	A subset of the KDDTest+.arff file which does not include records with difficulty level of 21 out of 21
KDDTest-21.TXT	A subset of the KDDTest+.txt file which does not include records with difficulty level of 21 out of 21

certainly takes more space, it also implies an independence assumption among the data. On the other hand, using integers such as 1, 2 and 3 implies some kind of a relationship between them. In this context, since the values of our non-numerical attributes are independent, we used binary coding. For instance, the **Protocol_type** attribute is transformed into 3 binary variables as shown: tcp : $(1, 0, 0)$; udp : $(0, 1, 0)$; icmp : $(0, 0, 1)$.

By using this transformation, each connection record in NSL-KDD will be represented by 122 coordinates instead of 41 according to the above discrete attributes values transformation [40].

(c) Neural Networks and SVMs

Our proposed model consists of two layers of classification: the first layer uses neural networks that take the preprocessed data set as input and classify events as malicious and benign events. The second layer uses support vector machines as a classifier in order to improve accuracy.

To propose our model, we began by studying the impact of training and performance functions on the accuracy of neural networks. Then we added SVMs and compared the performance of two kernels in order to choose the best combination.

4.2   Implementation and Discussion

In this study, our feed-forward neural network was composed of an input layer with 122 inputs, one hidden layers with 25 neurons, and an output with binary classification. We used KDDTrain+.csv and KDDTest+.csv for training and testing respectively. To avoid possible bias in the presentation order of the sample patterns to the ANN, these sample sets were randomized. Sigmoid transfer function is used for the hidden layer. We also used 20% of the training set as a validation set. The algorithm was implemented in Matlab using nntool.

Basic system training parameters are max_epochs = 1000, show = 5, performance goal = 0, time = Inf, min_grad = 1e−010, max_fail = 6 are fixed for each training function (We have also matlab's default parameters for other training algorithms such learning rate = 0.01). The parameters for comparison are execution, no of epoch (E) at the end of training, correct classification (C) percentage for testing set, because the test sets are a good measure of generalization for each respective network. All these parameters are checked for 37 neural networks. The algorithm was tested 10 times in total and the average or more consistent values were added to Table 2.

There are several characteristics that can be deduced from the experiments described. First, the cost function can have significant impact on the performance of the neural network, this is clearly shown in the first algorithm (traingd) Gradient Descent backpropagation, in which by just varying the cost function, the classification precision varies accordingly from 54.82% to 72.56%. The performance of traingd is similar to traingdm. Figure 5 shows the performance of traingd when using mae, mse and crossentropy as cost functions. Here we can see that the algorithm decreases more rapidly when using mean squared normalized error cost function.

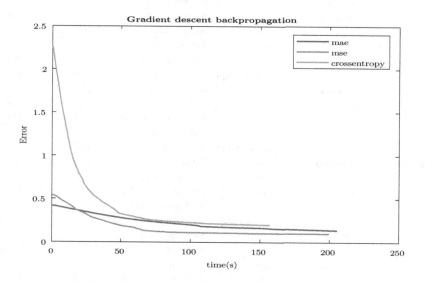

Fig. 5. Gradient descent with mae, mse and crossentropy cost functions

For gradient descent algorithms (traingd, traingdm and trainrp), we see each algorithm converges much faster compared to their execution with other cost functions, but they give worse performance. Figure 6 shows the performance of

Table 2. Comparison of training algorithms with different cost functions

Algorithm	Training function	Cost function	Best validation performance at epoch	Epoch	Classification %	Time
Gradient Descent	traingd	mae	0.21712 at 1000	1000	72.56%	186 s
		mse	0.073076 at 1000	1000	70.6%	190 s
		sae	1617.9656 at 11	17	70.4%	4 s
		sse	7758.32576 at 0	1	54.82%	0 s
		crossentropy	0.200356 at 1000	1000	71.92%	248 s
	traingdm	mae	0.153602 at 1000	1000	74.97%	232 s
		mse	0.11395 at 634	640	73.4%	153 s
		sae	11439.3072 at 3	1	44.1%	3 s
		sse	3254.1949 at 5	8	65.0%	3 s
		crossentropy	0.26043 at 289	295	76.9%	68 s
	trainrp	mae	0.013851 at 116	122	77.7%	27 s
		mse	0.011023 at 150	156	79.2%	40 s
		sae	425.7931 at 95	101	75.2%	23 s
		sse	284.8169 at 128	134	77.8%	34 s
		crossentropy	0.022481 at 98	104	78.8%	25 s
Conjugate Descent	trainscg	mae	0.090774 at 214	221	72.7%	82 s
		mse	0.06374 at 118	129	72.7%	59 s
		sae	1208.1477 at 440	447	70.7%	166 s
		sse	1075.7554 at 268	276	73.7%	109 s
		crossentropy	0.12898 at 999	1000	73.3%	357 s
	traincgp	mae	0.041352 at 261	262	72.8%	259 s
		mse	0.032637 at 43	44	72.1%	57 s
		sae	1942.6034 at 17	18	70.2%	27 s
		sse	1012.5063 at 19	20	71.7%	31 s
		crossentropy	0.20251 at 6	7	72.7%	10 s
	traincgf	mae	0.05335 at 43	44	72.3%	66 s
		mse	0.032927 at 39	40	72.1%	65 s
		sae	1102.785 at 60	61	71.3%	86 s
		sse	1467.7234 at 6	7	73.7%	10 s
		crossentropy	0.15559 at 25	26	72.3%	42 s
Quasi Newton	trainbfg	mae	0.040652 at 254	260	74.6%	29 min
		mse	0.021129 at 127	133	75.8%	13 min
		sae	2141.5896 at 227	233	68%	8 min
		sse	2203.9096 at 188	194	68.2%	8 min
		crossentropy	0.065099 at 159	165	77.4%	17 min
	trainlm	mae	Not supported			
		mse	0.0051341 at 55	61	74.8%	57 min
		sae	Not supported			
		sse	67.1328 at 30	31	79.5%	48 min
		crossentropy	Not supported			

traingd when using absolute errors. The figure shows how traingd tries to find median for the absolute error sae and the mean for sse.

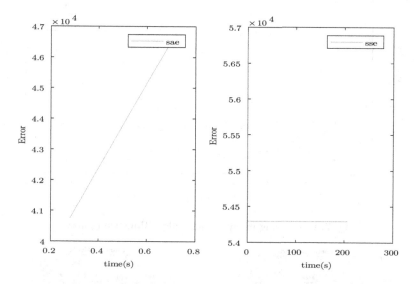

Fig. 6. Gradient descent with sae and sse cost functions

Conjugate gradient algorithms seem to give generally equal performances and do not seem too influenced by the cost function used. However, the algorithms are slightly faster when using the crossentropy cost function as it is the case for traincgp and traincgf.

Quasi Newton algorithm are a lot slower than any other algorithms. Although trainlm offers a high classification accuracy compared to many other training algorithms, training requires a lot of time and resources which is an important issue.

Finally, and by analyzing Fig. 7 which plots gradient descent and conjugate gradient descent algorithms using mse cost function, we can see that trainrp is the fastest algorithm for pattern recognition, since it produced an accuracy of 79.2%, which is already better than the model proposed in [41] that also used neural networks on the same dataset but with more hidden layers. The authors in [42] also used a similar architecture with 2 hidden layers and 25 hidden neurons and achieved a slightly higher 81.2% accuracy using trainlm. But as our comparison indicates, trainlm takes a lot of time and resources to train, this argument was not mentioned in their paper.

4.3   Classifier Based on NN and SVM

After choosing the best training and performance functions for our neural network classifier, we used SVM as the second classifier layer that takes the neuron

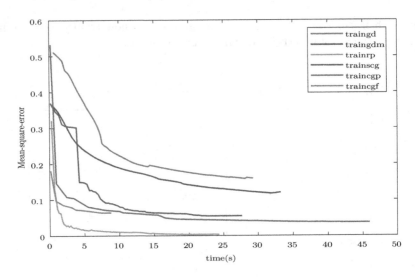

Fig. 7. Comparing many training algorithms using mse

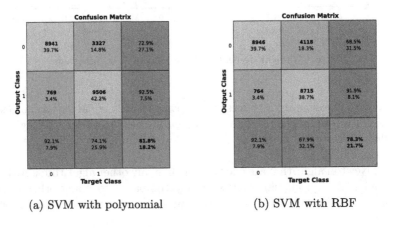

(a) SVM with polynomial   (b) SVM with RBF

Fig. 8. Confusion matrix of the proposed system

network output. The goal of using SVM is to project the output of the neural network to a higher dimension so that the samples of the two classes (predicted and actual value) are separable by a linear plane. This projection if often done using a kernel.

We evaluate a polynomial kernel and a radial basis function (RBF) kernel separately, and the polynomial kernel performed better in the experiments. The optimization parameter of the SVM was set to 1 and the kernel parameter was 1.5. Figure 8 shows the confusion matrix of the whole system.

In this study, we found that the best model uses a neural network with resilient backpropagation as a training function and mean squared normalized error cost function. For the second layer, the study showed an improvement in classification accuracy (81.8%) when using polynomial kernel as opposed to radial basis function (RBF) kernel.

5   Conclusion

The aim of our research is to build an intrusion detection model that can be used in IDS and SIEM systems. We have proposed a two layer classification model. The first model uses neural networks and the second is based on support vector machine.

For neural networks, we highlighted some of the parameters, studied by other researchers, and that can have significant impact on the performance of neural network-based intrusion detectors. Next, we have studied different training algorithms and cost functions in which we have implemented 37 feed-forward neural networks.

Our results show that these parameters are crucial to achieve a high accuracy. For instance, we found that the right cost function can improve the accuracy of traingd algorithm by +17.74%, and for NSL-KDD dataset, the convergence speed and classification accuracy of trainrp is higher than other training functions. The accuracy of trainrp was comparable and sometimes even better than that of other more complex neural networks-based models.

In a future study, we will evaluate the proposed system in a real network. We also want to investigate other architectures and parameters to improve the performance of the proposed system.

References

1. Verizonent: 2018 Data Breach Investigations Report (p. 8) (2018). https://www.verizonenterprise.com
2. Mathews, L.: ThyssenKrupp Attackers Stole Trade Secrets In Massive Hack (2016). http://www.forbes.com/sites/leemathews/2016/12/08/thyssenkrupp-attackers-stole-trade-secrets-in-massive-hack/LeeMathews,Lee. Accessed 12 Oct 2016
3. Schwartz, M.J.: Lockheed Martin Suffers Massive Cyberattack (2011). http://www.darkreading.com/risk-management/lockheed-martin-suffers-massive-cyberattack/d/d-id/1098013. Accessed 2 Mar 2017
4. Markoff, J.: SecurID Company Suffers a Breach of Data Security (2011). http://www.nytimes.com/2011/03/18/technology/18secure.html. Accessed 2 Mar 2017
5. Gogoi, P., Bhattacharyya, D.K., Borah, B., Kalita, J.K.: MLH-IDS: a multi-level hybrid intrusion detection method. Comput. J. **57**(4), 602–623 (2013). https://doi.org/10.1093/comjnl/bxt044
6. Orhanou, G., Lakbabi, A., Moukafih, N., El Hajji, S. (n.d.): Network access control and collaborative security against APT and AET. In: Security and Privacy in Smart Sensor Networks, pp. 201–230. IGI Global. https://doi.org/10.4018/978-1-5225-5736-4.ch010
7. Hall, D.L., Llinas, J.: An introduction to multisensor data fusion. Proc. IEEE **85**(1), 6–23 (1997). https://doi.org/10.1109/5.554205

8. Tan, P.N., Steinbach, M., Kumar, V.: Introduction to Data Mining. Pearson Addison Wesley, Boston (2005)
9. Zhang, C., Jiang, J., Kamel, M.: Intrusion detection using hierarchical neural networks. Pattern Recognit. Lett. **26**(6), 779–791 (2005). https://doi.org/10.1016/j.patrec.2004.09.045
10. Yamaguchi, F., Lindner, F., Rieck, K.: Vulnerability extrapolation: assisted discovery of vulnerabilities using machine learning. In: Proceedings of the 5th USENIX Conference on Offensive Technologies (2011)
11. Livshits, B., Zimmermann, T.: DynaMine. ACM SIGSOFT Softw. Eng. Notes **30**(5), 296 (2005). https://doi.org/10.1145/1095430.1081754
12. Rieck, K., Trinius, P., Willems, C., Holz, T.: Automatic analysis of malware behavior using machine learning. J. Comput. Secur. **19**(4), 639–668 (2011)
13. Kotler, J.Z., Maloof, M.A.: Learning to detect and classify malicious executables in the wild. J. Mach. Learn. Res. **7**, 2721–2744 (2006)
14. Anderson, J.P.: Computer security threat monitoring and surveillance, vol. 17. Technical report, James P. Anderson Company, Fort Washington, Pennsylvania (1980)
15. Chiba, Z., Abghour, N., Moussaid, K., El Omri, A., Rida, M.: A novel architecture combined with optimal parameters for back propagation neural networks applied to anomaly network intrusion detection. Comput. Secur. **75**, 36–58 (2018). https://doi.org/10.1016/j.cose.2018.01.023
16. Sen, R., Chattopadhyay, M., Sen, N.: An efficient approach to develop an intrusion detection system based on multi layer backpropagation neural network algorithm. In: Proceedings of the 2015 ACM SIGMIS Conference on Computers and People Research - SIGMIS-CPR 2015. ACM Press (2015). https://doi.org/10.1145/2751957.2751979
17. Kuang, F., Xu, W., Zhang, S., Wang, Y., Liu, K.: A novel approach of KPCA and SVM for intrusion detection. J. Comput. Inf. Syst. **8**(8), 3237–3244 (2012)
18. Devaraju, S., Ramakrishnan, S.: Performance analysis of intrusion detection system using various neural network classifiers. In: 2011 International Conference on Recent Trends in Information Technology (ICRTIT). IEEE (2011). https://doi.org/10.1109/icrtit.2011.5972289
19. Ussath, M., Jaeger, D., Cheng, F., Meinel, C.: Identifying suspicious user behavior with neural networks. In: 2017 IEEE 4th International Conference on Cyber Security and Cloud Computing (CSCloud). IEEE (2017). https://doi.org/10.1109/cscloud.2017.10
20. Suarez-Tangil, G., Palomar, E., Ribagorda, A., Sanz, I.: Providing SIEM systems with self-adaptation. Inf. Fusion **21**, 145–158 (2015). https://doi.org/10.1016/j.inffus.2013.04.009
21. Rayan, J., Meng-Jang, L., Risto, M.: Intrusion Detection with Neural Networks. AAAI Technical Report WS-97-07 (1997)
22. Sharma, B., Venugopalan, K.: Comparison of neural network training functions for hematoma classification in brain CT images. IOSR J. Comput. Eng. (IOSR-JCE) **16**(1), 31–35 (2014)
23. Hesam, K., Sharareh, R.N., Reza, S.: Comparison of neural network training algorithms for classification of heart diseases. IAES Int. J. Artif. Intell. (IJ-AI) **7**(4), 185–189 (2018)
24. Kumari, V.V., Varma, P.R.K.: A semi-supervised intrusion detection system using active learning SVM and fuzzy c-means clustering. In: 2017 International Conference on I-SMAC (IoT in Social, Mobile, Analytics and Cloud) (I-SMAC). IEEE (2017). https://doi.org/10.1109/i-smac.2017.8058397

Analysis of Neural Network Training and Cost Functions Impact   451

25. Al-Yaseen, W.L., Othman, Z.A., Nazri, M.Z.A.: Intrusion detection system based on modified K-means and multi-level support vector machines. In: Berry, M.W., Mohamed, A.H., Wah, Y.B. (eds.) SCDS 2015. CCIS, vol. 545, pp. 265–274. Springer, Singapore (2015). https://doi.org/10.1007/978-981-287-936-3_25
26. Baceand, R., Mell, P.: NIST Special Publication on Intrusion Detection Systems (2011). www.dtic.mil/dtic/tr/fulltext/u2/a393326.pdf. Accessed Mar 10 2018
27. Intrusion Detection and Correlation: Advances in Information Security. Kluwer Academic Publishers (2005). https://doi.org/10.1007/b101493
28. Moukafih, N., Sabir, S., Lakbabi, A., Orhanou, G.: SIEM selection criteria for an efficient contextual security. In: 2017 International Symposium on Networks, Computers and Communications (ISNCC). IEEE (2017). https://doi.org/10.1109/isncc.2017.8072035
29. Miller, D.: Security Information and Event Management (SIEM) Implementation. McGraw-Hill, New York (2011)
30. Russell, S., Norvig, P., Davis, E.: Artificial Intelligence: A Modern Approach. Prentice Hall, Upper Saddle River (2010)
31. Ali, S., Smith, K.A.: On learning algorithm selection for classification. Appl. Soft Comput. 6(2), 119–138 (2006). https://doi.org/10.1016/j.asoc.2004.12.002
32. Sutton, R.S.: Two problems with backpropagation and other steepest-descent learning procedures for networks. In: Proceedings of the Eighth Annual Conference of the Cognitive Science Society. Erlbaum, Hillsdale, NJ (1986)
33. Riedmiller, M., Braun, H.: A direct adaptive method for faster backpropagation learning: the RPROP algorithm. In: IEEE International Conference on Neural Networks. IEEE (1993) https://doi.org/10.1109/icnn.1993.298623
34. Shewchuk, J.R.: An introduction to the conjugate gradient method without the agonizing pain. School of Computer Science Carnegie Mellon University Pittsburgh, PA 15213 (1994)
35. Møller, M.F.: A scaled conjugate gradient algorithm for fast supervised learning. Neural Netw. 6(4), 525–533 (1993). https://doi.org/10.1016/s0893-6080(05)80056-5
36. Fletcher, R.: Function minimization by conjugate gradients. Comput. J. 7(2), 149–154 (1964). https://doi.org/10.1093/comjnl/7.2.1494
37. Pham, D.T., Sagiroglu, S.: Training multilayered perceptrons for pattern recognition: a comparative study of four training algorithms. Int. J. Mach. Tools Manuf. 41(3), 419–430 (2001). https://doi.org/10.1016/s0890-6955(00)00073-0
38. KDD CUP 99 dataset. http://kdd.ics.uci.edu/databases/kddcup99/kddcup99.html. Accessed 23 Oct 2018
39. NSL-KDD dataset available. https://github.com/defcom17/NSL_KDD. Accessed 23 Oct 2018
40. Tavallaee, M., Bagheri, E., Lu, W., Ghorbani, A.A.: A detailed analysis of the KDD CUP 99 data set. In: 2009 IEEE Symposium on Computational Intelligence for Security and Defense Applications. IEEE (2009). https://doi.org/10.1109/cisda.2009.5356528
41. Ji, H., Kim, D., Shin, D., Shin, D.: A study on comparison of KDD CUP 99 and NSL-KDD using artificial neural network. In: Park, J.J., Loia, V., Yi, G., Sung, Y. (eds.) CUTE/CSA -2017. LNEE, vol. 474, pp. 452–457. Springer, Singapore (2018). https://doi.org/10.1007/978-981-10-7605-3_74
42. Ingre, B., Yadav, A.: Performance analysis of NSL-KDD dataset using ANN. In: 2015 International Conference on Signal Processing and Communication Engineering Systems. IEEE (2015). https://doi.org/10.1109/spaces.2015.7058223

Managing Your Kleptographic
Subscription Plan

George Teşeleanu[1,2(✉)]

[1] Department of Computer Science, "Al.I.Cuza" University of Iaşi,
700506 Iaşi, Romania
george.teseleanu@info.uaic.ro
[2] Advanced Technologies Institute, 10 Dinu Vintilă, Bucharest, Romania
tgeorge@dcti.ro

Abstract. In the classical kleptographic business models, the manufacturer of a device D is paid either in advance or in installments by a malicious entity to backdoor D. Unfortunately, these models have an inherent high risk for the manufacturer. This translates in high costs for clients. To address this issue, we introduce a subscription based business model and tackle some of the technical difficulties that arise.

1 Introduction

Kleptographic attacks have been introduced by Young and Yung [22–26] and are a combination of subliminal channels with public key cryptography. The scope of these attacks is to leak either confidential messages or private keys though a system's outputs without the owner's knowledge. In recent years, this research area has been revitalized and backdooring methodologies can be found for symmetric key primitives [7,8,10], hash functions [5,14], pseudo-random number generators [11,12] or digital signatures [6,21]. Also, a series of countermeasures have been developed [6,15,18,19].

One of the classical business models for kleptographic attacks is the following: a client[1] C pays up front a manufacturer M, whom will later implement a certain backdoor in a tamper proof device[2] and deliver that device to a victim. This model puts the manufacturer at an advantage, because he can charge the customer and not implement the requested backdoor. Since this transaction is illegal, the customer can not file a complain and legally retrieve his money. Thus, this might scare off some of the potential clients.

Another classical model is the following: a client pays the manufacturer half the money up front and the rest after checking the correctness of the backdoor. If the manufacturer does not take certain precautions, then the client is at an advantage. For example, C checks the correctness of the backdoor, but fails to

---

[1] By definition a malicious entity.
[2] In [8] is noted that complex open-source software (*e.g.* OpenSSL) is also vulnerable to these attacks.

C. Carlet et al. (Eds.): C2SI 2019, LNCS 11445, pp. 452–461, 2019.
https://doi.org/10.1007/978-3-030-16458-4_26

pay the second installment. This can be easily avoided if a backdoor deactivation method is put in place by M[3]. A possible deactivation strategy is for M to send D a special input that instructs the device to erase all incriminating evidence. A similar approach is used in [10,14] to trigger backdoors.

Both classical approaches have an inherent risk for the manufacturer: the client can easily prove that M backdoored D either by decrypting all the messages send through that device or by revealing the private keys stored in D. Thus, to make the risk worth while the manufacturer must charge C a high embedding fee. This will certainly scare away certain resource constrained clients (*e.g.* small businesses that do not have the resources of a large corporation). To address this issue, we introduce a subscription based model suitable for the ElGamal encryption algorithm.

Our model draws inspiration from the subscription services offered by companies like Netflix [2], Amazon [3] and HBO [4]. These companies give access to streaming content in exchange for a monthly pay. In our case, a client pays for a backdoor that gives him access to a limited number of private messages. Subsequently, the client has to renew his subscription. This balances the risk and reward factors for the manufacturer[4] and, in consequence, M can lower embedding fees. A risk still remains: no guarantees of output delivery for the clients. But, this is minimum in a subscription based model because the goal of the manufacturer is to keep clients satisfied, so they further renew their subscription[5].

Compared to the classical models, our proposed model has a different issue that needs to be tackled. Clients want access to their services as soon as they pay. But, illegal transactions mostly use cryptocurrencies [9] and the average confirmation time for this type of transactions is large in some cases (*e.g.* for Bitcoin, it takes on average an hour per transaction [1]). Thus, to give the manufacturer sufficient time for deactivating the backdoor[6] if the transaction is not valid, we employ a mechanism similar to time-lock puzzles [17] .

Note that generic kleptographic countermeasures [15,18,19] can protect tamper proof device's users against our proposed mechanisms. Unfortunately, unless users do not explicitly require the implementation of these defences, a manufacturer is not obliged to deploy them. Thus, M is free to implement any kleptographic mechanism.

Structure of the Paper. Notations and definitions are presented in Sect. 2. The core of the paper consists of Sect. 3 and contains a series of kleptographic subscriptions that fit different scenarios. We conclude in Sect. 4.

---

[3] As in the previous model, the transaction is illegal and thus, M can not take legal action against C.

[4] M is exposed only for a limited period of time.

[5] Cheating a client will only bring M a small amount of revenue.

[6] By means of special triggers.

2 Preliminaries

Notations. Throughout the paper, the subset $\{1, \ldots, n\} \in \mathbb{N}$ is denoted by $[1, n]$. The action of selecting a random element x from a sample space X is denoted by $x \xleftarrow{\$} X$, while $x \leftarrow y$ represents the assignment of value y to variable x. The probability of the event E to happen is denoted by $Pr[E]$. To ease description, we use the notation C_k^n to denote binomial coefficients.

2.1 Security Assumptions

Definition 1 (Pseudorandom Function - PRF). *A function $F : \mathbb{G} \times [1, n] \to S$ is a PRF if:*

- *Given a key $K \in \mathbb{G}$ and an input $X \in [1, n]$ there is an efficient algorithm to compute $F_K(X) = F(X, K)$.*
- *Let A be a PPT algorithm with access to an oracle $\mathcal{O}$ that returns 1 if $\mathcal{O} = F_K(\cdot)$. The PRF-advantage of A, defined as*

$$ADV_F^{\mathrm{PRF}}(A) = \left| Pr[A^{F_K(\cdot)} = 1 | K \xleftarrow{\$} \mathbb{G}] - Pr[A^{F(\cdot)} = 1 | F \xleftarrow{\$} \mathcal{F}] \right|$$

must be negligible for any PPT algorithm A, where $\mathcal{F} = \{F : [1, n] \to S\}$.

Definition 2 (Pseudorandom Permutation - PRP). *A PRF $P : \mathbb{G} \times [1, n] \to [1, n]$ is a PRP if P is one-to-one and $\mathcal{F}$ from Definition 1 is changed into $\mathcal{F} = \{F : [1, n] \to [1, n] \mid F \text{ is one-to-one}\}$. The PRP-advantage of A is denoted $ADV_P^{\mathrm{PRP}}(A)$.*

Definition 3 (Decisional Diffie-Hellman - DDH). *Let $\mathbb{G}$ be a cyclic group of order q, g a generator of $\mathbb{G}$. Let A be a PPT algorithm which returns 1 on input (g^x, g^y, g^z) if $g^{xy} = g^z$. We define the advantage*

$$ADV_{\mathbb{G},g}^{\mathrm{DDH}}(A) = |Pr[A(g^x, g^y, g^z) = 1 | x, y \xleftarrow{\$} \mathbb{Z}_q^*, z \leftarrow xy]$$

$$- Pr[A(g^x, g^y, g^z) = 1 | x, y, z \xleftarrow{\$} \mathbb{Z}_q^*]|.$$

If $ADV_{\mathbb{G},g}^{\mathrm{DDH}}(A)$ is negligible for any PPT algorithm A, we say that the Decisional Diffie-Hellman problem is hard in $\mathbb{G}$.

2.2 Public Key Encryption

Definition 4 (Public Key Encryption - PKE). *A Public Key Encryption (PKE) scheme consists of four PPT algorithms: ParamGen, KeyGen, Encrypt and Decrypt. The first one takes as input a security parameter and outputs the system parameters. Using these parameters, the second algorithm generates the public key and the matching secret key. The public key together with the Encrypt algorithm are used to encrypt a message m. Using the secret key, the last algorithm decrypts any ciphertext encrypted using the matching public key.*

Remark 1. For simplicity, public parameters will further be implicit when describing an algorithm.

ElGamal Encryption. The ElGamal encryption scheme was first described in [13] and later generalized in [16]. It can be proven that the generalized ElGamal encryption scheme is secure in the standard model under the DDH assumption [20]. We further describe the generalized version of the scheme and refer to it simply as the ElGamal encryption scheme (EG).

ParamGen(λ): Generate a large prime number q, such that $q \geq 2^\lambda$. Choose a cyclic group $\mathbb{G}$ of order q and let g be a generator of the group. Output the public parameters $pp = (q, g, \mathbb{G})$.

KeyGen(pp): Choose $x \xleftarrow{\$} \mathbb{Z}_q^*$ and compute $y \leftarrow g^x$. Output the public key $pk = y$. The secret key is $sk = x$.

Encryption(m, pk): To encrypt a message $m \in \mathbb{G}$, first generate a random number $k \xleftarrow{\$} \mathbb{Z}_q^*$. Then compute the values $c \leftarrow g^k$ and $d \leftarrow m \cdot y^k$. Output the pair (c, d).

Decryption(c, d, sk): To recover the original message compute $m \leftarrow d \cdot c^{-x}$.

2.3   SETUP Attacks

Definition 5 (Secretly Embedded Trapdoor with Universal Protection - SETUP). *A Secretly Embedded Trapdoor with Universal Protection (SETUP) is an algorithm that can be inserted in a system such that it leaks encrypted confidential messages to an attacker through the system's outputs. Encryption of the messages is performed using an asymmetric encryption scheme. It is assumed that the corresponding decryption function is accessible only to the attacker.*

Definition 6 (SETUP indistinguishability - IND-SETUP). *Let C_0 be a black-box system that uses a secret key sk. Let $\mathcal{AE}$ be the PKE scheme used by a SETUP mechanism as defined above, in Definition 5. We consider C_1 an altered version of C_0 that contains a SETUP mechanism based on $\mathcal{AE}$. Let A be a PPT algorithm which returns 1 if it detects that C_0 is altered. We define the advantage*

$$ADV_{C_0,C_1}^{\text{IND-SETUP}}(A) = |Pr[A^{C_1(\cdot)}(\lambda) = 1] - Pr[A^{C_0(\cdot)}(\lambda) = 1]|.$$

If $ADV_{\mathcal{AE},C_0,C_1}^{\text{IND-SETUP}}(A)$ is negligible for any PPT algorithm A, we say that C_0 and C_1 are polynomially indistinguishable.

All kleptographic subscriptions presented from now on are implemented in a device D. The owner of the device is denoted by V and we assume that he is in possession of his secret key. Note that V thinks that D contains an implementation of the ElGamal scheme as described in Sect. 2.2. When one of the original ElGamal algorithms is not modified by the SETUP attack, the scheme will be omitted when presenting the respective attack.

Throughout the paper, when presenting kleptographic subscriptions, we make use of the following additional algorithms:

- *Device's/Manufacturer's/Customer's KeyGen* − used by the device/manufacturer/customer to generate its/his keys;
- *Token* − used by the customer/manufacturer to extract the access token;
- *Extract* − used by the customer to recover the messages sent by V.

The previously mentioned algorithms are not implemented in D. For simplicity, kleptographic parameters will further be implicit when describing a scheme.

3   Kleptographic Subscriptions

3.1   Free Subscription

The first type of subscription (denoted by FS) is an analog of public television channels. Thus, anyone who is in possession of the transmitted ciphertexts can decrypt them after a certain amount of traffic has been sent. This protocol will form the basis for the mechanisms presented in Sects. 3.2 and 3.3.

Although, this kind of subscription does not bring any revenue, it can still be useful in certain situations. For example, a disgruntled employee can embed it in the source code of certain products before leaving the company. Then, he can anonymously point out that the respective company implemented backdoors in their products. The scope of this scenario is to damage the company's reputation.

Let n be the maximum number of messages that a client needs to wait before recovering all of V's communications. Also, let $F : \mathbb{G} \times \{0,1\}^* \to \mathbb{Z}_q^*$. When searching for the access token, we make use of an auxiliary function *Check* that returns true if the decrypted message is correct. We further present the algorithms for the free subscription SETUP attack.

Device's KeyGen(pp): Choose $x_D \xleftarrow{\$} \mathbb{Z}_q^*$ and $p \xleftarrow{\$} [0,n]$. Output the device's secret key $sk_D = (x_D, p)$.

Encryption Sessions: The possible encryption sessions performed by D are described below. Let $i \neq p$.

Encryption$_i$(m_i, pk, sk_D) : To encrypt a message $m_i \in \mathbb{G}$, first compute $k_i \leftarrow F(g^{x_D}, i)$. Then compute the values $c_i \leftarrow g^{k_i}$ and $d_i \leftarrow m_i \cdot y^{k_i}$. Output the pair (c_i, d_i).

Encryption$_p$(m_p, pk, sk_D): To encrypt a message $m_p \in \mathbb{G}$, compute the values $c_p \leftarrow g^{x_D}$ and $d_p \leftarrow m_p \cdot y^{x_D}$. Output the pair (c_p, d_p). Erase p from D's memory.

Token($c_1, d_1, \ldots, c_n, d_n, pk$): Let $i = 1$. Compute $k_{i+1} \leftarrow F(c_i, i \bmod n + 1)$, $m_{i+1} \leftarrow d_{i+1} \cdot y^{-k_{i+1}}$ and $i \leftarrow i + 1$, until $Check(m_i) = \text{true}$. Output the token p.

The ith Extract(c_i, d_i, p): To recover the ith message compute $k_i \leftarrow F(c_p, i)$ and $m_i \leftarrow d_i \cdot y^{-k_i}$.

Remark 2. It is easy to see that message m_p can only be retrieved by the recipient.

We further state the security margin without proof due to its similarity to the more involved proof of Theorem 2.

Theorem 1. *If F is a* PRF *and* $i \in [1, p-1]$ *then EG and FS are* IND-SETUP. *Formally, let A be an efficient PPT* IND-SETUP *adversary. There exists an efficient algorithm B such that*

$$ADV_{EG, \, FS}^{\text{IND-SETUP}}(A) \leq 2ADV_F^{\text{PRF}}(B).$$

3.2   Paid Subscription

In this subsection, we describe a kleptographic analogue of payed television (denoted by PS). Thus, C pays M for a session's access token, that only M can extract from D. Note that these tokens are unique per session. So, a group of users can pay for only one token and all of them will have access to that session's private messages. Although this can be considered cheating, it is also a reality in other systems (*e.g.* paying for a Netflix account and sharing the credentials with one's friends). We will rectify this problem in the next subsection.

Let t be a security parameter and $P : \mathbb{G} \times [1, n] \rightarrow [1, n]$. After the first message is transmitted the manufacturer will send the clients a set of t positions p_j needed to compute the access token. Note that M has a window of at least $t-1$ messages to receive his payments. If one payment is declined, M can deactivate the backdoor before the t-th message has been issued. A downside of this scheme is that if one of the clients fails to pay for the token, then he deprives all users of their access.

We further state one session of the protocol. After a predetermined number of messages (greater than n) have elapsed, D can generate new keys and start a new session.

Manufacturer's KeyGen(pp): Choose $x_M \xleftarrow{\$} \mathbb{Z}_q^*$ and compute $y_M \leftarrow g^{x_M}$. Output the manufacturer's public key $pk_M = y_M$. The secret key is $sk_M = x_M$. Store pk_M in D's internal memory.

Device's KeyGen(pp): Choose $k_0 \xleftarrow{\$} \mathbb{Z}_q^*$. For each $j \in [1, t]$ compute $p_j \leftarrow P(y_M^{k_0}, j)$ and choose $x_j \xleftarrow{\$} \mathbb{Z}_q^*$. Compute $x_D \leftarrow x_1 + \ldots + x_t$. Store the device's secret key $sk_D = (k_0, p_1, \ldots, p_t, x_1, \ldots, x_t, x_D)$.

Encryption Sessions: The possible encryption sessions performed by D are described below. Let $i \in [0, n]$ and $i \neq p_j$, for each $j \in [1, t]$. The algorithm for $Encryption_i$ are identical to the public subscription and thus are omitted.

$Encryption_0(m_0, pk)$: To encrypt a message $m_0 \in \mathbb{G}$ compute the values $c_0 \leftarrow g^{k_0}$ and $d_0 \leftarrow m_0 \cdot y^{k_0}$. Output the pair (c_0, d_0). Erase k_0 from D's memory.

$Encryption_{p_j}(m_{p_j}, pk, sk_D)$: To encrypt a message $m_{p_j} \in \mathbb{G}$, compute the values $c_{p_j} \leftarrow g^{x_j}$ and $d_{p_j} \leftarrow m_{p_j} \cdot y^{x_j}$. Output the pair (c_{p_j}, d_{p_j}). Erase (p_j, x_j) from D's memory.

$Token(c_0, sk_M)$: For each $j \in [1, t]$ compute $p_j \leftarrow P(c_0^{x_M}, j)$. Output the token $p = (p_1, \cdots, p_t)$.

The ith $Extract(c_i, d_i, p)$: To recover the ith message compute $c_p \leftarrow c_{p_1} \cdot \ldots \cdot c_{p_t}$ and $k_i \leftarrow F(c_p, i)$ and $m_i \leftarrow d_i \cdot y^{-k_i}$.

Remark 3. It is easy to see that messages $m_0, m_{p_1}, \ldots, m_{p_t}$ can not be retrieved by the customers.

Theorem 2. *If* DDH *is hard in* $\mathbb{G}$, P *is a* PRP, F *is a* PRF *and* $(C_n^t)^{-1}$ *is negligible then EG and PS are* IND-SETUP. *Formally, let A be an efficient PPT* IND-SETUP *adversary. There exist three efficient algorithms B_1, B_2 and B_3 such that*

$$ADV_{EG,\,PS}^{\text{IND-SETUP}}(A) \le 2ADV_{\mathbb{G},g}^{\text{DDH}}(B_1) + 2ADV_P^{\text{PRP}}(B_2) + 2ADV_F^{\text{PRF}}(B_3) + (C_n^t)^{-1}.$$

Proof. Let A be an IND-SETUP adversary trying to distinguish between EG and PS. We show that A's advantage is negligible. We construct the proof as a sequence of games in which all the required changes are applied to PS. Let W_i be the event that A wins game i.

Game 0. The first game is identical to the IND-SETUP game[7]. Thus, we have

$$|2Pr[W_0] - 1| = ADV_{EG,PS}^{\text{IND-SETUP}}(A). \tag{1}$$

Game 1. In this game, instead of using $y_M^{k_0}$ as a key to P we use $r_P \xleftarrow{\$} \mathbb{G}$. More precisely, for each $j \in [1, t]$ we compute $p_j \leftarrow P(r_P, j)$. Since this is the only change between *Game 0* and *Game 1*, A will not notice the difference assuming the DDH assumption holds. Formally, this means that there exists an algorithm B_1 such that

$$|Pr[W_0] - Pr[W_1]| = ADV_{\mathbb{G},g}^{\text{DDH}}(B_1). \tag{2}$$

Game 2. Since P is a PRP then we can choose $p_j \xleftarrow{\$} [1, n]$, without A detecting the change. Formally, this means that there exists an algorithm B_2 such that

$$|Pr[W_1] - Pr[W_2]| = ADV_P^{\text{PRP}}(B_2). \tag{3}$$

Game 3. In each $Encryption_{p_j}$ algorithm we make the change $c_{p_j} \leftarrow g^{k_j}$ and $d_{p_j} \leftarrow m_{p_j} y^{k_j}$, where $k_j \xleftarrow{\$} \mathbb{Z}_q^*$. Since k_js and x_js have the same distribution, and the b_js are uniformly distributed in $[1, n]$, then A can only detect the change using a brute-force attack[8]. Formally, we have

$$|Pr[W_2] - Pr[W_3]| = (C_n^t)^{-1}. \tag{4}$$

---

[7] As in Definiton 6.

[8] *i.e.* by trying each t-combination c_{try} of c_is, until on input c_{try} the *Extract* algorithm outputs a message m such that $Check(m) = \texttt{true}$.

Game 4. The last change we make is $k_i \xleftarrow{\$} \mathbb{Z}_q^*$. Adversary A will not notice the difference, since F is a PRF. Formally, this means that there exists an algorithm B_3 such that

$$|Pr[W_3] - Pr[W_4]| = ADV_P^{\text{PRF}}(B_3). \tag{5}$$

The changes made to PS in *Game 1 − Game 4* transformed it into EG. Thus, we have

$$Pr[W_4] = 1/2. \tag{6}$$

Finally, the statement is proven by combining the equalities (1)–(6).   □

3.3   Targeted Subscription

As mentioned in the previous subsection, a coalition of clients can pay for only one token[9]. To avoid this problem we bind a specific session to a certain client. We could not find a method that allows multiple bindings per session. We further present the proposed solution for binding users and sessions (denoted by TS).

Customer's KeyGen(pp): Choose $x_C \xleftarrow{\$} \mathbb{Z}_q^*$ and compute $y_C \leftarrow g^{x_C}$. Output the customer's public key $pk_C = y_C$. The secret key is $sk_C = x_C$. Store pk_C in D's internal memory.

Encryption Sessions: The possible encryption sessions performed by D are described below. Let $i \in [0, n]$ and $i \neq p_j$, for each $j \in [1, t]$. The algorithms for *Encryption$_0$* and *Encryption$_{p_j}$* are identical to the paid subscription and thus are omitted.

Encryption$_i(m_i, pk, pk_C, sk_D)$: To encrypt a message $m_i \in \mathbb{G}$, first compute $k_i \leftarrow F(y_C^{x_D}, i)$. Then compute the values $c_i \leftarrow g^{k_i}$ and $d_i \leftarrow m_i \cdot y^{k_i}$. Output the pair (c_i, d_i).

The ith Extract(c_i, d_i, p): To recover the ith message compute $c_p \leftarrow c_{p_1} \cdot \ldots \cdot c_{p_t}$ and $k_i \leftarrow F(c_p^{x_C}, i)$ and $m_i \leftarrow d_i \cdot y^{-k_i}$.

Theorem 2 assures us that the client has negligible probability of reading V's messages without M's help. We further prove a similar result for any PPT IND-SETUP adversaries.

Theorem 3. *If DDH is hard in* $\mathbb{G}$, P *is a PRP and* F *is a PRF then EG and TS are IND-SETUP. Formally, let* A *be an efficient PPT IND-SETUP adversary. There exist three efficient algorithms* B_1, B_2 *and* B_3 *such that*

$$ADV_{EG,\ TS}^{\text{IND-SETUP}}(A) \leq 4ADV_{\mathbb{G},g}^{\text{DDH}}(B_1) + 2ADV_P^{\text{PRP}}(B_2) + 2ADV_F^{\text{PRF}}(B_3).$$

---

[9] Further used by the whole group to access messages.

Proof. Game 0 – Game 2 and *Game 4* are identical to the games presented in the proof of Theorem 2 and thus, are omitted. Since only the customer is in position of x_C, we can not use the strategy presented in Theorem 2, *Game 3*. Thus, we present a modified version of *Game 3*.

Game 3'. In this game, we replace $y_C^{x_D}$ by $r_F \xleftarrow{\$} \mathbb{Z}_q^*$. Due to the fact that DDH is hard in $\mathbb{G}$, A will not notice the change. Formally, this means that there exists an algorithm B_1' such that

$$|Pr[W_2] - Pr[W_{3'}]| = ADV_{\mathbb{G},g}^{\text{DDH}}(B_1'). \qquad (7)$$

Finally, the statement is proven by combining the equalities (1)–(3) and (5)–(7). □

4 Conclusions

In this paper we introduced the concept of subscription based kleptographic services and tackled the technical challenges associated with this model. The pay-as-you-go approach leads to better costs for the clients and minimizes exposure risks for the manufacturer.

Open Problems. A couple of interesting open problems are the extension of subscription based services to digital signatures and the implementation of multi-targeted subscriptions for one session.

References

1. Bitcoin: Average Confirmation Time. https://www.blockchain.com/charts/avg-confirmation-time
2. Frequently Asked Questions About Netflix Billing. https://help.netflix.com/en/node/41049?ui_action=kb-article-popular-categories
3. How to Manage Your Prime Video Channel Subscriptions. https://www.amazon.com/gp/help/customer/display.html?nodeId=201975160
4. How to Order HBO: Subscriptios & Pricing Options. https://www.hbo.com/ways-to-get
5. Albertini, A., Aumasson, J.-P., Eichlseder, M., Mendel, F., Schläffer, M.: Malicious hashing: eve's variant of SHA-1. In: Joux, A., Youssef, A. (eds.) SAC 2014. LNCS, vol. 8781, pp. 1–19. Springer, Cham (2014). https://doi.org/10.1007/978-3-319-13051-4_1
6. Ateniese, G., Magri, B., Venturi, D.: Subversion-resilient signature schemes. In: ACM-CCS 2015, pp. 364–375. ACM (2015)
7. Bellare, M., Jaeger, J., Kane, D.: Mass-Surveillance without the state: strongly undetectable algorithm-substitution attacks. In: ACM-CCS 2015, pp. 1431–1440. ACM (2015)
8. Bellare, M., Paterson, K.G., Rogaway, P.: Security of symmetric encryption against mass surveillance. In: Garay, J.A., Gennaro, R. (eds.) CRYPTO 2014. LNCS, vol. 8616, pp. 1–19. Springer, Heidelberg (2014). https://doi.org/10.1007/978-3-662-44371-2_1

9. Christin, N.: Traveling the silk road: a measurement analysis of a large anonymous online marketplace. In: WWW 2013, pp. 213–224. ACM (2013)
10. Degabriele, J.P., Farshim, P., Poettering, B.: A more cautious approach to security against mass surveillance. In: Leander, G. (ed.) FSE 2015. LNCS, vol. 9054, pp. 579–598. Springer, Heidelberg (2015). https://doi.org/10.1007/978-3-662-48116-5_28
11. Degabriele, J.P., Paterson, K.G., Schuldt, J.C.N., Woodage, J.: Backdoors in pseudorandom number generators: possibility and impossibility results. In: Robshaw, M., Katz, J. (eds.) CRYPTO 2016. LNCS, vol. 9814, pp. 403–432. Springer, Heidelberg (2016). https://doi.org/10.1007/978-3-662-53018-4_15
12. Dodis, Y., Ganesh, C., Golovnev, A., Juels, A., Ristenpart, T.: A formal treatment of backdoored pseudorandom generators. In: Oswald, E., Fischlin, M. (eds.) EUROCRYPT 2015. LNCS, vol. 9056, pp. 101–126. Springer, Heidelberg (2015). https://doi.org/10.1007/978-3-662-46800-5_5
13. ElGamal, T.: A public key cryptosystem and a signature scheme based on discrete logarithms. IEEE Trans. Inf. Theory **31**(4), 469–472 (1985)
14. Fischlin, M., Janson, C., Mazaheri, S.: Backdoored Hash Functions: Immunizing HMAC and HKDF. IACR Cryptology ePrint Archive 2018/362 (2018)
15. Hanzlik, L., Kluczniak, K., Kutyłowski, M.: Controlled randomness – a defense against backdoors in cryptographic devices. In: Phan, R.C.-W., Yung, M. (eds.) Mycrypt 2016. LNCS, vol. 10311, pp. 215–232. Springer, Cham (2017). https://doi.org/10.1007/978-3-319-61273-7_11
16. Menezes, A.J., Van Oorschot, P.C., Vanstone, S.A.: Handbook of Applied Cryptography. CRC Press, London (1996)
17. Rivest, R.L., Shamir, A., Wagner, D.A.: Time-lock Puzzles and Timed-release Crypto. Technical report (1996)
18. Russell, A., Tang, Q., Yung, M., Zhou, H.-S.: Cliptography: clipping the power of kleptographic attacks. In: Cheon, J.H., Takagi, T. (eds.) ASIACRYPT 2016. LNCS, vol. 10032, pp. 34–64. Springer, Heidelberg (2016). https://doi.org/10.1007/978-3-662-53890-6_2
19. Russell, A., Tang, Q., Yung, M., Zhou, H.S.: Generic semantic security against a kleptographic adversary. In: ACM-CCS 2017, pp. 907–922. ACM (2017)
20. Shoup, V.: Sequences of Games: A Tool for Taming Complexity in Security Proofs. IACR Cryptology ePrint Archive 2004/332 (2004)
21. Teşeleanu, G.: Unifying kleptographic attacks. In: Gruschka, N. (ed.) NordSec 2018. LNCS, vol. 11252, pp. 73–87. Springer, Cham (2018). https://doi.org/10.1007/978-3-030-03638-6_5
22. Young, A., Yung, M.: The dark side of "black-box" cryptography or: should we trust capstone? In: Koblitz, N. (ed.) CRYPTO 1996. LNCS, vol. 1109, pp. 89–103. Springer, Heidelberg (1996). https://doi.org/10.1007/3-540-68697-5_8
23. Young, A., Yung, M.: Kleptography: using cryptography against cryptography. In: Fumy, W. (ed.) EUROCRYPT 1997. LNCS, vol. 1233, pp. 62–74. Springer, Heidelberg (1997). https://doi.org/10.1007/3-540-69053-0_6
24. Young, A., Yung, M.: The prevalence of kleptographic attacks on discrete-log based cryptosystems. In: Kaliski, B.S. (ed.) CRYPTO 1997. LNCS, vol. 1294, pp. 264–276. Springer, Heidelberg (1997). https://doi.org/10.1007/BFb0052241
25. Young, A., Yung, M.: Malicious Cryptography: Exposing Cryptovirology. John Wiley & Sons, Hoboken (2004)
26. Young, A., Yung, M.: Malicious cryptography: kleptographic aspects. In: Menezes, A. (ed.) CT-RSA 2005. LNCS, vol. 3376, pp. 7–18. Springer, Heidelberg (2005). https://doi.org/10.1007/978-3-540-30574-3_2

Model Checking Speculation-Dependent Security Properties: Abstracting and Reducing Processor Models for Sound and Complete Verification

Gianpiero Cabodi, Paolo Camurati, Fabrizio Finocchiaro, and Danilo Vendraminetto[✉]

Dip. di Automatica e Informatica, Politecnico di Torino, Turin, Italy
danilo.vendraminetto@polito.it

Abstract. Though modern microprocessors embed several hardware security mechanisms, aimed at guaranteeing confidentiality and integrity of sensible data, recently disclosed attacks such as Spectre and Meltdown witness weaknesses with potentially great impact on CPU security. Both vulnerabilities exploit speculative execution of modern high-performance micro-architectures, allowing the attacker to observe data leaked via a memory side channel, during speculated and mispredicted instructions.

In this paper we present a methodology to formally verify, by means of a model checker, speculative vulnerabilities, such as the class of Spectre/Meltdown attacks, in microprocessors based on speculative execution. In detail, we discuss the problem of formally verifying confidentiality violations, since we deem it will help preventing new vulnerabilities of the same typology.

We describe our methodology on a pipelined CPU inspired by the DLX RISC processor architecture. Due to scalability issues, and following related approaches in formal verification of correctness, our approach simplifies the model under verification by proper abstraction and reduction steps. The approach is based on flushing the pipeline, abstracting data and most of the speculative execution logic, keeping a subset of control data, plus speculated data state and tainting logic. Illegal propagation (data leakage) is encoded in terms of taint propagation, from a protected/invalid memory address to the address bus on a subsequent memory read, affecting the cache.

We introduce the theoretical flow, relying on known theoretical results combined and exploited to prove soundness and completeness. Finally, using a state-of-the-art model checking tool, we present preliminary data on formal verification based on Bounded Model Checking, that to support our claims and highlight the feasibility of the approach.

Keywords: Model checking · Secure CPU architecture ·
Speculative execution · Taint propagation ·
Abstraction and reduction · Pipeline flushing · Confidentiality ·
Reorder buffer · Spectre · Meltdown

© Springer Nature Switzerland AG 2019
C. Carlet et al. (Eds.): C2SI 2019, LNCS 11445, pp. 462–479, 2019.
https://doi.org/10.1007/978-3-030-16458-4_27

1   Introduction

In information security, confidentiality and integrity represent a major class of security requirements, whereas side channel attacks are a relevant and increasing family of security threats. Confidentiality refers to the property that information is not made available or disclosed to unauthorized individuals, entities, or processes [2], while integrity means maintaining and assuring the accuracy and completeness of data over their entire life-cycle [4].

Side-channel attacks are a class of security breaches attracting increasing interest from mid-nineties: they include any attack based on information gained from the implementation of a device, rather than from weaknesses in the implemented algorithm itself (e.g. software bugs and buffer overflows).

Software running on modern microprocessors utterly depends on hardware security mechanisms in maintaining confidentiality and integrity of certain memory regions such as those used by kernels or hypervisors. Although several side channel attacks have been found in literature, that bypass fundamental hardware-enforced security mechanisms, none of them had the same impact as Spectre [20] and Meltdown [21] did.

Those attacks identify and exploit viable hybrid vulnerabilities related to certain internal processor features in conjunction with state-of-the-art cache-based side channel attacks. Both vulnerabilities involve processors speculatively executing instructions past access check and allowing the attacker to observe the results via a side channel. Rather than exploiting an incorrect implementation of the Instruction Set Architecture (ISA), these attacks leverage the undocumented implementation-specific speculative behaviour of high-performance microarchitectures (MA) to affect the extra-architectural state of the machine (e.g. caches).

Authors in [20,21] developed proof of concepts that were used in breaching the security of hardware protected areas. The huge extent and breaking consequences of such attacks is not entirely understood even now. The attack mechanisms have been explored and possible defences have already been presented and deployed, though the software-based ones in conjunction with operating systems, have a non negligible impact on system performance. There is still a strong need for long term comprehensive best practices to help addressing this problem in order to avoid similar vulnerabilities in next generations of microprocessors.

As widely known in the scientific community, the design phase is the most critical one, where most of the bugs are born. It is also worth noting that although Meltdown and Spectre were the result of specific designs ignoring the impact of speculative execution on security, the rapid rise in processor complexity over time, a key to achieving higher performance, probably made these types of flaws inevitable or at least neglected. When speculation and out of order instructions first saw the light, processors were at least 20x slower than they are now. Speed increased disproportionally once chips reached the capability to contain more transistors. However, the number of potential states in a logic circuit is exponential in the number of instructions of the ISA.

Because of an underestimated vision of keeping security and performance as separate design goals, design architects neglect some potentially dangerous states in their processors. Microarchitects have to deal with complexity and abstraction. The flaw began because of a wrong abstraction. Computer architecture decouples implementation (actual machine) and specification (abstract machine). The fracture between the architectural state (e.g. registers, memory data, pipeline, interrupts) and extra-architectural state (e.g. cache, branch predictor, physical register mapping) is the root cause.

Security should become a major design constraint, if not the leading aspect to any modern IT development. At least, the software development community has already recognized this, and it is now clear that computer architectures must have a holistic view on performance and security. However, this requires revisiting decades of hardware development patterns. This is very important because the Spectre/Meltdown class of attacks are caused by a deep discrepancy between MA and ISA [22]. While the processor is completely (up to verification) correct - hence adherent to the ISA, the actual MA is in a potentially dangerous state, which could be exploited by well known techniques (side channel attacks family [14, 19, 33]) to retrieve confidential information.

Our contribution is a methodology for abstracting and verifying security properties in a pipelined processor model. This model, inspired by the DLX RISC processor architecture presented by Hennessy and Patterson [28], has features like pipelining and speculative (out-of-order) execution.

Our work is intended to address speculation based attacks such as Spectre and Meltdown, which exploit side channels in order to extract useful data (from an attacker's perspective) out of the CPU microarchitecture. The proposed approach is based on model checking alongside taint propagation mechanism.

We pre-process the microprocessor model, by applying property preserving transformations, before feeding it to a Model Checker. The transformations are directly inspired to the state-of-the-art in pipelined processor verification, as well as information flow tracking:

- data abstraction with taint encoding;
- refinement/reduction of pipeline and out-of-order states.

In this work we present the feasibility of our approach: being preliminary, transformations are performed manually on a case study, though our goal will be to put in place an automated approach to model transformation and verification.

The main contribution of this paper is a discussion on the problem of formally verifying confidentiality violations in microprocessors based on speculative execution.

The paper is organized as follows. In Sect. 2 we provide some background notions used in the rest of the paper, Sect. 3 describes the architecture of processor model we used for our activity, while Sect. 5 describes the verification steps on our processor model. Finally, Sect. 6 presents experimental results to show the feasibility of our approach, and Sect. 7 concludes the paper, with some hints of future activities.

2 Preliminaries and Background

We assume the reader to be familiar with basic concepts of formal verification and model checking. We address systems modelled by labelled state transition structures and represented implicitly by Boolean formulas.

From our standpoint, a system M is a triplet $M = (S, S_0, T)$, where S is a finite set of states, $S_0 \subseteq S$ is the set of initial states, and $T \subseteq S \times S$ is a total transition relation. Given a system M, we assume that p is a safety property to be verified over M. In the following, p will correspond to the taint reaching the memory (address bus) of our microprocessor model.

2.1 Spectre and Meltdown Attacks

Speculative (or out-of-order) execution allows microarchitectures to speculatively run computations based on future results of unknown operands or predicted branches. Instructions remain uncommitted in the reorder buffer (ROB) while the missing data dependency is still present. When the dependency is solved, then only the properly predicted instructions will be committed into memory, cancelling those whose prediction was incorrect.

Today, speculative execution is widely deployed in high-performance CPU designs because it allows parallel computations in hardware that substantially improve performance.

Speculative execution is intended to be largely invisible to the architectural state: mispredicted instructions are cancelled, preventing their architectural outcomes (register write-backs, memory stores, etc.) from being exposed. Even if an exception occurs, the pipeline is flushed and no architectural changes that occurred after the excepting instruction are made visible.

This is the main reason for the Spectre and Meltdown attacks, as a memory exception is handled just after the instruction generating it is committed, instead of when it was speculatively executed. The primary exception to this is through timing: where speculation is substantially accurate, performance improves, reducing the time it takes to perform operations that would otherwise be more expensive.

This timing side channel is measurable through a variety of techniques, and allows software to detect when speculation is being effective. Side effects of speculation are especially visible in its impact on caches, which will be filled with memory on the basis not just of architectural execution, but also of speculative execution. Timing side channels therefore allow information to flow in two directions:

1. instruction execution can guide future predictions, impacting the behaviour of future speculation;
2. a committed instruction can observe cache timing information in order to infer prior speculated behaviour.

Though the presence of timing side channels in the microarchitecture has long been understood, only with Spectre and Meltdown the profound implications of those two speculative situations combined together became clear. With these category of attacks, timing side channels allow malicious unprivileged code to extract the memory contents of the kernel or another target process by manipulating instruction speculation and triggering a cache-timing side channel back to the attacker.

2.2 Formal Verification of Microprocessors with Out-of-order Execution

Formal verification of pipelined microprocessors first, and processors with speculative execution then, have represented a huge challenge for formal verification, mostly for scalability reasons. Due to the enormous amount of states in the actual (extra-architectural) machine, model checking is not directly applicable to a real processor model.

All practical formal verification approaches share a couple of common ideas:

- reducing (refining) the model (and the verified behaviour) by just considering a properly timed subset of possible execution traces;
- adopting some form of abstraction on data, based on the assumption that arithmetic and logic functionalities are verified separately.

Burch et al. [6] first described a technique for verifying the control logic of pipelined microprocessors. The technique automatically compares a pipelined implementation to an architectural description using flushing and uninterpreted functions along with a decision procedure. In this work, correctness of the two implementations means that the implemented (simplified) model respects all its specifications, in terms of symbolic function descriptions.

Abstraction based on uninterpreted functions compared to lambda expressions is used in [5], where an efficient decision procedure implementation for the CLU logic is provided. Theorem proving for microprocessor verification was explored by Hunt et al. [16,17].

A broader notion of correctness was proposed by Manolios in [23] and [24], in which it implies that the ISA (Instruction Set Architecture) and MA (Micro-Architecture) machines have the same observable infinite paths. Manolios et al. later extended their previous work in [25–27], where they provide support for liveness properties and overcome the deadlock issue Burch's work suffered for.

There have also been approaches based on the use of automatic engines that aim at decomposing correctness proofs into smaller manageable pieces. For example, the authors of [29] verify an out-of-order execution unit using incremental flushing. Their approach needs an implementation of an intermediate machine, where scheduling logic is abstracted, which is then related to the ISA. Manolios et al. in [26], on the other hand, deal with any refinement map, they have a general theory with a complete rule for relating any number of intermediate machines and they guarantee that all safety and liveness properties are preserved.

Jhala and McMillan [18] relate processor models to their instruction set architecture models using compositional model checking. They apply this approach to verify an abstract microprocessor model with branch prediction, speculative execution and out-of-order execution.

2.3 Verifying Cybersecurity by Tainting

An active and effective strategy to encode cybersecurity problems is Information Flow Tracking, that enables expressing and verifying properties on data flowing between given source/destination pairs. Notable recent works targeting the hardware/software boundary, are [30,31].

Starting from the notion of taint, as a possible attack, or of a confidential information to be leaked, specifying correct/undesirable behaviours entails expressing taint-propagation properties [7,8,30]. Secure Path Verification [15] has recently been proposed as a valuable industrial alternative to (more standard) model checking approaches.

Essentially, a path property explicitly allows the user to specify source, destination, path, as well as environmental constraints for taint-propagation analysis. The novelty of the approach lies in the fact that the model checker engine provides a specific internal support for taint propagation.

Due to the nature of taint propagation, it perfectly fits our context in which we want to prove the confidentiality of the microprocessor architecture, while we omit to verify also the integrity of the same model, leaving this activity to future works as we deem the first to be more closely related to the class of speculative attacks as Spectre/Meltdown.

3   Processor Model

In order to describe our verification methodology, let us now introduce a case study, based on a pipelined machine with speculative execution, inspired by the DLX architecture [28], which was originally presented as an academic architecture to teach the basic concepts used in MIPS2000 and other RISC processors of that generation.

Starting from this academic RISC processor model, we implemented pipelining and speculative (out-of-order) execution, adding reorder buffer and reservation stations.

The high level organization, shown in Fig. 1, includes a seven stage pipeline whose stages are IF1, IF2 (2-cycle fetch), ID (decode), EX (execution), M1, M2 (2-cycle memory access) and WB (write back).

The fetch stages are virtually capable of providing a never-ending supply of instructions. Instructions pass through the front-end pipeline before being dispatched into the reorder buffer. The widths of the fetch, pipeline, dispatch, retire, and maximum issue stages are all abstracted away.

The branch misprediction logic controls the commit or abort of a given instruction. In case of an abort, the fetching of useful instructions is stopped, and the pipeline is flushed. Similarly, in case of instruction cache miss, instruction fetching is stopped and it resumes only after the instructions can be fetched from the cache, or memory. The caches and the memory system are just represented here as a generic memory block, as modelling and verifying the interactions of the processor pipeline, caches and memory system is out of scope: the processor outputs the PC (program counter) and, after a non-deterministic delay, receives the instruction from the memory location addressed by the PC.

After instructions are decoded, they are dispatched to the appropriate functional unit. All functional units are considered to be fully pipelined and are capable of accepting a new instruction on every cycle. Though in reality different instruction types have different execution times, we take here a simplified view and treat all instructions as having the same execution time.

The reorder buffer and the reservation stations form the hardware support for Tomasulo's algorithm [32]. Tomasulo's algorithm allows executing instructions out-of-order, in data-flow order, rather than in sequential order. This can increase the throughput of the unit, by avoiding pipeline stalls.

In the reservation station, instructions are queued up before being issued to an execution unit. An instruction is ready for issue when all the following conditions occur:

1. its inputs are available;
2. its destination register is available;
3. an execution unit is available to execute it.

The reorder buffer is a register file maintained as a first-in-first-out queue. Each entry in the reorder buffer is made up of a tag, the destination register number, the result and a valid bit. The reorder buffer preserves the program order and it supports register renaming. The reorder buffer updates the architectural registers with the computed results from the rename registers and removes entries associated with executed instructions from its register file in program order.

The model features also ALU exceptions, misprediction exceptions and memory exceptions. If an exception occurs, the pipeline is flushed and no architectural changes that occurred after the excepting instruction are made visible. This is the behaviour exploited by Spectre/Meltdown category of attacks.

4   Attack Description

We focus on the well known Meltdown and Spectre attacks, that are depicted, respectively, in [21] and in [20]. The core idea is that side-effects of out-of-order execution can modify the microarchitectural state to leak information. The adversary targets a secret value that is kept somewhere in physical memory. Note that the register contents are also stored in memory upon context switches.

Meltdown enables leaking secrets by bypassing the privileged-mode isolation, giving an attacker full read access to the entire kernel space including any physical memory mapped.

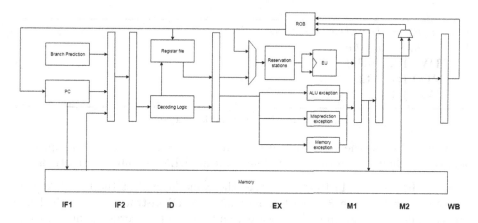

Fig. 1. The pipelined processor model.

Spectre attacks, on the other hand, pursue an orthogonal approach, which tricks speculative executed instructions into leaking information that the victim process is authorized to access.

Despite the differences, the building blocks of both attacks are the same. The first building block is to make the CPU execute one or more instructions that would never occur in the executed path. Using the same naming convention of Meltdown, we call such an instruction, which is executed out of order, leaving measurable side effects, a *transient instruction*.

Furthermore, we call any sequence of instructions containing at least one transient instruction a *transient instruction sequence*. In order to leverage transient instructions for an attack, the transient instruction sequence must use a secret value that an attacker wants to leak.

The second building block of Meltdown is to transfer the microarchitectural side effect of the transient instruction sequence to an architectural state to further process the leaked secret.

Meltdown consists of 3 steps:

Step 1 The content of an attacker-chosen memory location, which is inaccessible to the attacker, is loaded into a register.

Step 2 A transient instruction accesses a cache line based on the secret content of the register.

Step 3 The attacker uses a covert channel to determine the accessed cache line and hence the secret stored at the chosen memory location.

```
1   ; R1 = invalid address
2   ; R3 = probe array
3   LW   R2,  0(R1)
4   ADD R1,  R2,  R3
5   LW   R1,  0(R1)
```

Listing 1. Attack instruction sequence.

Listing 1 shows the basic implementation of the transient instruction sequence and the sending part of the covert channel, using DLX assembly instructions.

Step 1. In line 3 of Listing 1, we load the value located at the target kernel address, stored in the R1 register, into R2. The LW instruction is fetched by the core, decoded into μOPs[1], allocated, and sent to the reorder buffer. There, architectural registers (e.g., R1, R2 and R3 in Listing 1) are mapped to underlying physical registers enabling out-of-order execution.

Trying to use the pipeline as much as possible, subsequent instructions (lines 4–5) are already decoded and allocated as μOPs as well. The μOPs are further sent to the reservation stations holding the μOPs while they wait to be executed by the corresponding execution unit.

The execution of a μOP can be delayed if execution units are already used to their corresponding capacity or operand values have not been calculated yet. When the kernel address is loaded in line 3, it is likely that the CPU has already issued the subsequent instructions as part of the out-or-order execution, and that their corresponding μOPs wait in the reservation station for the content of the kernel address to arrive.

As soon as the fetched data is observed on the common data bus, the μOPs can begin their execution. When the μOPs finish their execution, they retire in-order, and, thus, their results are committed to the architectural state.

During the retirement, any interrupts and exception that occurred during the execution of the instruction are handled. Thus, if the LW instruction that loads the kernel address is retired, the exception is registered and the pipeline is flushed to eliminate all results of subsequent instructions which were executed out of order. However, there is a race condition between raising this exception and our attack step 2 which we describe below.

Step 2. The instruction sequence from step 1 which is executed out of order has to be chosen in a way that it becomes a transient instruction sequence. If this transient instruction sequence is executed before the LW instruction is retired (i.e., it raises the exception), and the transient instruction sequence performed computations based on the secret, it can be used to transmit the secret to the attacker.

We allocate a probe array in memory and ensure that no part of this array is cached. To transmit the secret, the transient instruction sequence contains an

---

[1] Although this is true in general, in our case there is no generation of micro-operations, that is every instruction is one μOP.

indirect memory access to an address which is calculated based on the secret (inaccessible) value.

In the original attack the secret value is multiplied by the page size to prevent the hardware prefetcher from loading adjacent memory locations into the cache. We skip this multiplication to make our attack as generic as possible. Instead, we add secret to the base address of the probe array, forming the target address of the covert channel. This address is read to cache the corresponding cache line. Consequently, our transient instruction sequence affects the cache state based on the secret value that was read in step 1.

Step 3. In step 3, the attacker recovers the secret value (step 1) by leveraging a microarchitectural side-channel attack (i.e., the receiving end of a microarchitectural covert channel) that transfers the cache state (step 2) back into an architectural state.

As mentioned before, Meltdown and Spectre rely on some state-of-the-art cache side-channel attacks. Their details are out of scope in this work.

5 Proof/Verification

The approach we propose is based on model transformations oriented to scalability. We have two kinds of transformations:

- data abstraction: register values, as well as their handling within reservation stations, execution units and reorder buffer, are properly abstracted, and they are augmented/replaced, by tainting information and evaluation/propagation circuitry;
- model reduction: speculation and parallel execution logic are reduced, following the *pipeline flushing* and reduction by *refinement map* approaches typical of state-of-the-art processor verification.

The model we verify is a processor in which no RAM memory is explicitly considered, and confidential data is implicitly associated to a given *protected/invalid* memory address. No explicit program is provided, so an arbitrary sequence of instructions is verified.

Though this is obviously a pessimistic view, it is in line with state-of-the-art processor verification approaches, and it guarantees the completeness of our approach in covering all possible software behaviours.

In the following, we describe the main ideas of the two transformations. Though we do not provide a formal proof of correctness, we provide the basic intuitions that support their applicability.

5.1 Data Abstraction and Tainting

The general idea supporting any abstraction based verification approach is that data (and consequently model behaviour) can be over-approximated provided verification is sound, i.e. an abstract counterexample always implies a concrete one.

In our case, this means that given a register file value V_i (the content of register R_i), V_i is replaced by an abstract value V_i^+, without affecting security properties. A typical strategy used for data abstraction is bit width reduction, which means drastically reducing the range of data values. With respect to standard formal verification of correctness, we have additional room for abstraction, as *processor functionality* (e.g. data evaluation within the ALU) can be *considered correct* (already verified).

As we model confidentiality properties in terms of taints, we basically augment V_i^+ by coupling it with T_i, a taint value, and we also extend the data computing logic with taint propagation logic. Taint values are just stored and propagated through memory and data transfer components.

The ALU is the sole unit able to block/propagate a given taint and/or combine multiple taints. So whenever the arithmetic/logic operation $V_K = OP(V_i, V_j)$ is computed in the original processor model, we replace it by $V_K^+ = OP(V_i^+, V_j^+)$ and $T_k = OP^T(V_i^+, T_i, V_j^+, T_j)$, with the requirement that the transformation is sound. It is worth noticing that data evaluation is independent from taints, whereas taint propagation obviously involves data values.

The degree of over-approximation (abstraction) in taint propagation could be tuned between two extreme cases:

- full data dependence: data values are fully involved in taint computation; whenever computing T_k, actual operand data values are considered; for instance, a bitwise OR operation with and all 1 V_i^+, or a multiplication with $V_i^+ = 0$, could mask (block) a taint on the other operand (T_j);
- full abstraction from data values: for instance, taint propagation through a binary ALU operation propagates a taint on any of the operand terms ($T_k = OP^T(T_i, T_j) = T_i \vee T_j$).

The choice done obviously impacts on the soundness of the overall approach (see Sect. 5.3 for a more detailed comment on this issue).

Without loss of generality/correctness, we also abstracted branch misprediction logic, and replaced it by a non deterministic choice.

As we are targeting memory related data leakages, we focus our effort on taint propagation through memory access logic, whereas we consider arithmetic/logic manipulation as pass-through circuitry for taints.

A taint is thus injected at the memory data input, whenever a protected/invalid address is used:

$$M_{Din} = protected(M_{Addr}) \; ? \; TAINT : NOTAINT;$$

The taint is propagated through the abstract reservation stations, arithmetic/logic execution units and reorder buffer. The only circuitry enabled to clear a taint is related to branch misprediction (instruction not committed and aborted).

The target we observe is the memory address. In terms of information flow, the property we observe is the presence of a taint in memory address logic

($M_{Addr} == TAINT$). A sequence of instructions typical of Spectre and/or Meltdown would clearly:

- inject a taint, due to an invalid/protected memory access within a mispredicted instruction;
- propagate the taint as a data (waiting for commitment) into the (abstract) reorder buffer;
- use the tainted data when computing the address of a subsequent (mispredicted) memory read: the taint thus reaches the target.

The process is described in Fig. 2, that shows the path followed by the taint. Notice how the taint is generated during the memory read when an invalid address is into the address bus.

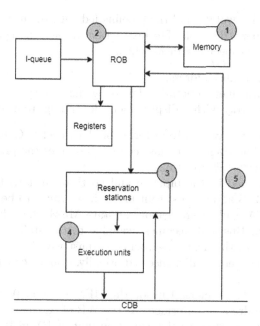

Fig. 2. Taint propagation from source to sink in our abstracted model.

As the pipeline goes on, the taint propagates to the reorder buffer, where it is fed to reservation stations as new instructions come in. The taint enters reservations stations because of its bond with the corresponding data, fetched as operands of newly arrived instructions. Once the operands are available, the taint is in one of the execution units, then on Common Data Bus and eventually again into the reorder buffer.

Table 1. Pipeline evolution of the proposed attack

Clock ↓	IF	ID	EX	MEM	WB	Taint status
1	A					
2	B	A				
3	C	B	A			
4		B/C	S	A		Taint source
5		C	B	S	A	Taint in ROB
6			C	S	B	S	Taint in EX
7			C	S	B	Taint sink / property asserted
8				C	S	
9					C	

A	**LW**	$R2, 0(R1)$
B	**ADD**	$R1, R2, R3$
C	**LW**	$R1, 0(R1)$

Table 1 shows the evolution of the pipeline fed with the instruction sequence provided in the upper right table. The instructions implement a generic simplified version of Meltdown/Spectre attacks which:

(A) reads from an invalid address;
(B) performs an arithmetic operation involving the secret;
(C) reads from an array with a displacement depending from secret.

Time is represented vertically in terms of clock cycles. Columns IF to WB represent the pipeline stages. The last column describes the propagation of the taint. Cells filled with "S" are stalls.

Instructions are fed in the pipeline and go through it without stalls until clock 3. At clock 4, B and C must wait for their operands to be ready so a stall is inserted. When A reads from memory at stage MEM, the value is placed into the Common Data Bus and becomes available to the stalled instructions. At clock 5, B goes on to the next stage, while C must wait for its operands to be prepared by B, thus a new stall is inserted. Finally, from clock 7 to 9 the pipeline proceeds without stalls.

The taint source is at clock 4 inside the MEM stage of A, when the access from the invalid address is performed. At the WB of A, the taint propagates to the ROB. The taint goes on to the execution unit at EX of B and in the next clock is sensed by the taint sink because arrived into the Common Data Bus.

5.2   Model Reduction: Refinement

The processor model is further simplified following standard approaches to formal verification of pipelines and/or speculation units [6,18,26].

In short, our model has already been simplified by turning data into taints. We now simplify all intermediate states related to complex control of parallel executions, by properly reducing/refining the behaviour.

Pipeline flushing as well as refinement maps can be applied, with strategies that still guarantee verification completeness, while strongly simplifying the model under verification.

A detailed description of the refinement strategy is clearly out of our scope in this work, as any reduction/refinement is applicable, provided that it guarantees completeness. For our case study, we did not feel the need to apply any compositional simplification [18], as the model was already highly simplified by tainting based abstraction. So we applied the following simplifications:

- pipeline flushing: an instruction is completed, up to the reorder buffer, before initiating the next one;
- reorder buffer is simplified to a FIFO queue, that basically just implements a delay between instruction execution and availability of its result to the register file; the FIFO strategy keeps the original instruction order, thus guaranteeing data dependency;
- reservation station removal: this is a direct consequence of pipeline flushing and reorder buffer reduction to FIFO;
- unification of execution units: no parallelism is now required on data, so we just need a single instance of each execution unit.

Due to the previously listed simplifications, the full original behaviour, based on pipelining and out-of-order execution is drastically reduced to a fully sequenced execution, with FIFO-based delay between instruction execution and result data availability.

The reduction guarantees completeness, i.e. it doesn't remove taint propagating sets of instructions, under two conditions:

- straight sequences of instructions include mispredicted instructions, that mimic concrete sequences produced in the out-of-order real processor; this is guaranteed by non-deterministically tagging any instruction as mispredicted (done in the abstraction phase, as already noticed in Sect. 5.1;
- the delay of the FIFO queue replacing the reorder buffer encompasses the time required by source to sink illegal taint propagations; we guarantee this by carefully choosing FIFO size and non-deterministically controlling FIFO "get" operations (moving data from reorder buffer back to the register file).

5.3   Correctness of the Approach

The correctness of our approach is directly related to the soundness and completeness of the model transformations performed. We now briefly characterize them in terms of correctness.

Taint Encoding and Manipulation. Strictly speaking, our taint encoding and manipulation steps are unsound as it they involve abstraction.

We allow abstract execution traces that propagate the taint, whereas no information leakage would characterize the actual model. This is clearly due to the chosen taint propagation strategy: our abstraction does not consider that a taint could be masked/blocked due to real data (e.g. logic AND with a 0, arithmetic multiplication by 0, etc.). To this respect, we had two possible choices:

- adopt a finer grained taint abstraction strategy, refining out (based on a more accurate taint propagation model) all false abstract counterexamples;
- work with an high taint abstraction level, thus accepting false abstract counterexamples. To this respect, let us notice that such counterexamples could be post-processed, and transformed to actual counterexamples, by just exploiting them partially (e.g. by removing data and keeping control bits), as constraints for a further BMC run on the concrete model.

In our view the latter strategy is largely consistent with the overall goal of finding confidentiality bugs and removing them. The approach is complete as it just over-approximates the real behaviour.

Model Abstraction and Reduction. As previously stated, we based our model abstraction and refinement steps on existing formal verification approaches [6, 26], that have been proved sound and complete.

The sole critical issue with our approach is to correctly handle taint encoding and manipulation throughout the abstraction end refinement steps. To this respect our approach is correct, based on the observation that a taint (modulo the previous observation on soundness) is essentially an augmented data, whose propagation is verified under the form of a safety property (safety properties are supported in [6, 26]).

6   Experimental Results

The proposed approach has been tested on the case study of Sect. 3. The processor was described as a Verilog model, translated to AIGER format [3] and verified by both Bounded Model Checking and Unbounded Model Checking (interpolation based) algorithms with PdTRAV [13], a state-of-the-art academic tool: specific emphasis was put on model reductions/transformations [9, 12], handling of multiple properties [11] and interpolants-based engines [1, 10].

In particular, taints were represented as binary data, branch prediction/misprediction logic was fully abstracted and replaced by a random binary choice. Execution units were replaced by taint propagation *pass through* logic.

The confidentiality property was encoded by taint not reaching the address output of the microprocessor.

As well known from [18], the original processor model (including data path, speculation logic and Tomasulo's module) would be hard to verify: the model had more than 120 K gates and more than 3 K latches. The model after tainting, abstraction and reduction, was encoded as an AIGER file of 2724 and gates and 106 latches. We could verify it by Bounded Model Checking, finding a counterexample of 9 clock steps in less than 1 s.

The counterexample showed data leakage through a sequence of instructions starting with an invalid memory access (injecting the taint), followed by an address computation (propagating the taint) and a memory read with tainted address. The counterexample is an abstract/reduced version of the one described in Table 1.

The security bug was removed (and verified my model checking, again in less that 1 s) by patching the model as follows: an instruction with invalid memory access prevents speculated instructions with data dependencies.

7 Conclusions and Future Work

In this work we present a formal verification methodology to identify confidentiality violations in modern CPU architectures based on speculative execution.

The methodology we propose follows some of the state-of-the-art ideas in the fields of formal verification and information-flow-tracking, namely, model abstraction/refinement, and taint injection/propagation. Though our work is preliminary, our experimental results show its applicability.

Future works will follow the direction of automating the currently manually driven abstraction/reduction of the model under analysis. Our final goal will be an (at least partially) automated rewriting procedure.

References

1. Cabodi, G., Palena, M., Pasini, P.: Interpolation with guided refinement: revisiting incrementality in SAT-based unbounded model checking. In: Formal Methods in Computer-Aided Design (FMCAD), pp. 43–50. IEEE (2014)
2. Beckers, K., Heisel, M., Hatebur, D.: Pattern and Security Requirements. Springer, Cham (2015). https://doi.org/10.1007/978-3-319-16664-3
3. Biere, A., Heljanko, K., Wieringa, S.: Aiger 1.9 and beyond. http://fmv.jku.at/hwmcc11/beyond1.pdf (2011)
4. Boritz, J.E.: Is practitioners' views on core concepts of information integrity. Int. J. Acc. Inf. Syst. 6(4), 260–279 (2005)
5. Bryant, R.E., Lahiri, S.K., Seshia, S.A.: Modeling and verifying systems using a logic of counter arithmetic with lambda expressions and uninterpreted functions. In: Brinksma, E., Larsen, K.G. (eds.) CAV 2002. LNCS, vol. 2404, pp. 78–92. Springer, Heidelberg (2002). https://doi.org/10.1007/3-540-45657-0_7
6. Burch, J.R., Dill, D.L.: Automatic verification of pipelined microprocessor control. In: Dill, D.L. (ed.) CAV 1994. LNCS, vol. 818, pp. 68–80. Springer, Heidelberg (1994). https://doi.org/10.1007/3-540-58179-0_44
7. Cabodi, G., Camurati, P., Finocchiaro, S., Loiacono, C., Savarese, F., Vendraminetto, D.: Secure embedded architectures: taint properties verification. In: 2016 International Conference on Development and Application Systems (DAS), pp. 150–157. IEEE (2016)
8. Cabodi, G., Camurati, P., Finocchiaro, S.F., Savarese, F., Vendraminetto, D.: Embedded systems secure path verification at the hardware/software interface. IEEE Des. Test 34(5), 38–46 (2017)

9. Cabodi, G., Camurati, P., Garcia, L., Murciano, M., Nocco, S., Quer, S.: Speeding up model checking by exploiting explicit and hidden verification constraints. In: Design, Automation and Test in Europe, DATE 2009, Nice, France, 20–24 April 2009, pp. 1686–1691. IEEE (2009)

10. Cabodi, G., Loiacono, C., Vendraminetto, D.: Optimization techniques for craig interpolant compaction in unbounded model checking. In: Proceedings of DATE, pp. 1417–1422. Grenoble, France (Mar 2013)

11. Cabodi, G., Nocco, S.: Optimized model checking of multiple properties. In: Design, Automation and Test in Europe, DATE 2011, Grenoble, France, March 14-18, 2011. pp. 543–546. IEEE (2011)

12. Cabodi, G., Nocco, S., Quer, S.: Strengthening model checking techniques with inductive invariants. IEEE Trans. CAD Integr. Circuits Syst. **28**(1), 154–158 (2009)

13. Cabodi, G., Nocco, S., Quer, S.: Benchmarking a model checker for algorithmic improvements and tuning for performance. Form. Methods Syst. Des. **39**(2), 205–227 (2011)

14. Fan, J., Guo, X., De Mulder, E., Schaumont, P., Preneel, B., Verbauwhede, I.: State-of-the-art of secure ECC implementations: a survey on known side-channel attacks and countermeasures. In: 2010 IEEE International Symposium on Hardware-Oriented Security and Trust (HOST), pp. 76–87. IEEE (2010)

15. Hanna, Z.: Jasper case study on formally verifying secure on-chip datapaths (2013). http://www.deepchip.com/items/0524-03.html

16. Hunt, W.A.: Microprocessor design verification. J. Autom. Reason. **5**(4), 429–460 (1989)

17. Hunt, W.A. (ed.): FM8501: A Verified Microprocessor. LNCS, vol. 795. Springer, Heidelberg (1994). https://doi.org/10.1007/3-540-57960-5

18. Jhala, R., McMillan, K.L.: Microarchitecture verification by compositional model checking. In: Berry, G., Comon, H., Finkel, A. (eds.) CAV 2001. LNCS, vol. 2102, pp. 396–410. Springer, Heidelberg (2001). https://doi.org/10.1007/3-540-44585-4_40

19. Joy Persial, G., Prabhu, M., Shanmugalakshmi, R.: Side channel attack-survey. Int. J. Adv. Sci. Res. Rev. **1**(4), 54–57 (2011)

20. Kocher, P., et al.: Spectre attacks: exploiting speculative execution. arXiv preprint arXiv:1801.01203 (2018)

21. Lipp, M., et al.: Meltdown. arXiv preprint arXiv:1801.01207 (2018)

22. Lowe-Power, J., Akella, V., Farrens, M.K., King, S.T., Nitta, C.J.: A case for exposing extra-architectural state in the ISA: position paper. In: Proceedings of the 7th International Workshop on Hardware and Architectural Support for Security and Privacy, p. 8. ACM (2018)

23. Manolios, P.: Correctness of pipelined machines. In: Hunt, W.A., Johnson, S.D. (eds.) FMCAD 2000. LNCS, vol. 1954, pp. 181–198. Springer, Heidelberg (2000). https://doi.org/10.1007/3-540-40922-X_11

24. Manolios, P.: Mechanical verification of reactive systems. Ph.D. thesis, The University of Texas at Austin, Department of Computer Sciences, Austin, TX (2001)

25. Manolios, P., Srinivasan, S.K.: Automatic verification of safety and liveness for xscale-like processor models using web refinements. In: Design, Automation and Test in Europe Conference and Exhibition, 2004, Proceedings, vol. 1, pp. 168–173. IEEE (2004)

26. Manolios, P., Srinivasan, S.K.: A complete compositional reasoning framework for the efficient verification of pipelined machines. In: IEEE/ACM International Conference on Computer-Aided Design, 2005, ICCAD-2005, pp. 863–870. IEEE (2005)

27. Manolios, P., Srinivasan, S.K.: Verification of executable pipelined machines with bit-level interfaces. In: Proceedings of the 2005 IEEE/ACM International Conference on Computer-Aided Design. IEEE Computer Society (2005)
28. Patterson, D.A., Hennessy, J.L., Goldberg, D.: Computer Architecture: A Quantitative Approach, vol. 2. Morgan Kaufmann, San Mateo (1990)
29. Skakkebæk, J.U., Jones, R.B., Dill, D.L.: Formal verification of out-of-order execution using incremental flushing. In: Hu, A.J., Vardi, M.Y. (eds.) CAV 1998. LNCS, vol. 1427, pp. 98–109. Springer, Heidelberg (1998). https://doi.org/10.1007/BFb0028737
30. Subramanyan, P., Arora, D.: Formal verification of taint-propagation security properties in a commercial SOC design. In: Proceedings of the Conference on Design, Automation & Test in Europe, p. 313. European Design and Automation Association (2014)
31. Subramanyan, P., Malik, S., Khattri, H., Maiti, A., Fung, J.: Verifying information flow properties of firmware using symbolic execution. In: Design, Automation & Test in Europe Conference & Exhibition (DATE), 2016, pp. 337–342. IEEE (2016)
32. Tomasulo, R.M.: An efficient algorithm for exploiting multiple arithmetic units. IBM J. Res. Dev. 11(1), 25–33 (1967)
33. Zhou, Y., Feng, D.: Side-channel attacks: ten years after its publication and the impacts on cryptographic module security testing. IACR Cryptol. ePrint Arch. 2005, 388 (2005)

Author Index

Printed in the United States
By Bookmasters